SHAPING THE FU
AND ADOLESCI
HEALTH

SHAPING THE FUTURE OF CHILD AND ADOLESCENT MENTAL HEALTH

Towards Technological Advances and Service Innovations

Edited by

MATTHEW HODES

*Division of Psychiatry, Imperial College London, London, United Kingdom;
Central and North West London NHS Foundation Trust, London,
United Kingdom*

PETRUS J. DE VRIES

*Division of Child and Adolescent Psychiatry, University of Cape Town, Cape Town,
South Africa*

IACAPAP

International Association for Child and
Adolescent Psychiatry and Allied Professions

ACADEMIC PRESS

An imprint of Elsevier

ELSEVIER

Academic Press is an imprint of Elsevier
125 London Wall, London EC2Y 5AS, United Kingdom
525 B Street, Suite 1650, San Diego, CA 92101, United States
50 Hampshire Street, 5th Floor, Cambridge, MA 02139, United States
The Boulevard, Langford Lane, Kidlington, Oxford OX5 1GB, United Kingdom

Notices
Knowledge and best practice in this field are constantly changing. As new research and
experience broaden our understanding, changes in research methods, professional
practices, or medical treatment may become necessary.

Practitioners and researchers must always rely on their own experience and knowledge
in evaluating and using any information, methods, compounds, or experiments
described herein. In using such information or methods they should be mindful of
their own safety and the safety of others, including parties for whom they have a
professional responsibility.

To the fullest extent of the law, neither the Publisher nor the authors, contributors, or
editors, assume any liability for any injury and/or damage to persons or property as a
matter of products liability, negligence or otherwise, or from any use or operation of
any methods, products, instructions, or ideas contained in the material herein.

ISBN: 978-0-323-91709-4

For information on all Academic Press publications visit our website at
https://www.elsevier.com/books-and-journals

Publisher: Nikki P. Levy
Acquisitions Editor: Joslyn T. Chaiprasert-Paguio
Editorial Project Manager: Timothy J. Bennett
Production Project Manager: Kiruthika Govindaraju
Cover Designer: Miles Hitchen

Typeset by TNQ Technologies

Working together
to grow libraries in
developing countries

www.elsevier.com • www.bookaid.org

Contents

I

Children and adolescents in the digital age

1. Looking beyond the adverse effects of digital technologies on adolescents: the case for resilience and mindfulness

F. Hugo Theron, David A. Rosenstein and Dean McCoubrey

2. Cyberbullying in young people

Ana Pascual-Sanchez and Dasha Nicholls

II

Innovations to improve our understanding of Child and Adolescent Mental Health

3. Clinical applications of big data to child and adolescent mental health care
Alice Wickersham and Johnny Downs

4. Machine learning and child and adolescent mental health services: challenges and opportunities
Paul A. Tiffin and Lewis W. Paton

III

Innovative approaches to helping young people in adversity

5. The COVID-19 pandemic and child and adolescent mental health—what has been learned and lessons for the future
Tamsin Newlove-Delgado, Frances Mathews, Lauren Cross,
Eva Wooding and Tamsin Ford

6. Trauma-related psychopathology in children and adolescents: recent developments and future directions
Stephanie J. Lewis and Andrea Danese

IV

Treatments for the future

V

Innovations in treatment delivery and training

10. Innovations in scaling up interventions in low- and middle-income countries: parent-focused interventions in the perinatal period and promotion of child development

Ahmed Waqas and Atif Rahman

11. Technology-enhanced learning and training for child and adolescent mental health professionals

Anthea A. Stylianakis, David J. Hawes and Valsamma Eapen

VI

Shaping the future of Child and Adolescent Mental Health in the Eastern Mediterranean Region

12. Child and adolescent mental health research in the Eastern Mediterranean Region—now and in the future

Fadi T. Maalouf, Riwa Haidar and Fatima Mansour

13. Child and adolescent psychiatry training in the Arab Gulf region

Ammar Albanna, Khalid Bazaid, Bibi AlAmiri, Hanan Derby, Hassan Mirza,
Finza Latif, Ahmed Malalla Al-Ansari and Yasser Ad-Dab'bagh

Contributors

Yasser Ad-Dab'bagh   Mental Health Department, King Fahad Specialist Hospital-Dammam; Ministry of Health, Scientific Council for Training in Psychiatry at the SCFHS, Riyadh, Saudi Arabia

Madison Aitken   Cundill Centre for Child and Youth Depression, Centre for Addiction and Mental Health Department of Psychiatry, University of Toronto, Toronto, ON, Canada

Ahmed Malalla Al-Ansari   Department of Psychiatry College of Medicine and Medical Sciences, Arabian Gulf University, Manama, Kingdom of Bahrain

Bibi AlAmiri   Almanara for Child and Adolescent Mental Health, Kuwait Center for Mental Health, Shuwaikh Industrial, Kuwait

Ammar Albanna   Center of Excellence, Mohamed Bin Rashid University of Medicine and Health Sciences; Emirates Society of Child and Adolescent Mental Health, Dubai, UAE

Khalid Bazaid   Youth Psychiatry Program, Royal Ottawa Mental Health Centre; Scientific Council for Training in Psychiatry at the Saudi Commission for Health Specialties (SCFHS), Canadian Academy of Child and Adolescent Psychiatry Education Committee, Undergraduate Education Program, Department of Psychiatry, University of Ottawa, Ottawa, ON, Canada

Lauren Cross   University of Cambridge, Department of Psychiatry, Cambridge, United Kingdom

Andrea Danese   Department of Child and Adolescent Psychiatry, and Social, Genetic and Developmental Psychiatry Centre, Institute of Psychiatry, Psychology and Neuroscience, King's College London, London, United Kingdom; National and Specialist CAMHS Clinic for Trauma, Anxiety, and Depression, South London and Maudsley NHS Foundation Trust, London, United Kingdom

Petrus J. de Vries   Division of Child and Adolescent Psychiatry, University of Cape Town, Cape Town, South Africa

Hanan Derby   Fellowship in Child and Adolescent Psychiatry, Al Jalila Children's Specialty Hospital, Mohamed Bin Rashid University of Medicine and Health Sciences, Dubai, UAE

Johnny Downs   CAMHS Digital Lab, Department of Child and Adolescent Psychiatry, Institute of Psychiatry, Psychology and Neuroscience, King's College, London, United Kingdom

Chelsea M. Durber   University of Alberta, Edmonton, AB, Canada

Valsamma Eapen   The University of New South Wales, School of Clinical Medicine, Faculty of Medicine and Health, Sydney, NSW, Australia; University of New South Wales, 2031 & Academic Unit of Child Psychiatry SWSLHD, L1 MHC Liverpool Hospital, Sydney, NSW, Australia

Tamsin Ford   University of Cambridge, Department of Psychiatry, Cambridge, United Kingdom

Ian M. Goodyer   Department of Psychiatry, University of Cambridge, Cambridge, England

Riwa Haidar   Department of Psychiatry, American University of Beirut, Beirut, Lebanon

David J. Hawes   The University of Sydney, School of Psychology, Faculty of Science, Sydney, NSW, Australia

Matthew Hodes   Division of Psychiatry, Imperial College London, London, United Kingdom; Central and North West London NHS Foundation Trust, London, United Kingdom

F. Hugo Theron   De Mist Private Practice, Cape Town, South Africa

Nathalie JJF. Janssen   Department of Psychiatry, Maastricht University Medical Center +, Maastricht, the Netherlands

Finza Latif   Department of Psychiatry, Sidra Medicine and Research Center, Weill Cornell-Qatar, Doha, Qatar

Stephanie J. Lewis   Department of Child and Adolescent Psychiatry, Institute of Psychiatry, Psychology and Neuroscience, King's College London, London, United Kingdom; South London and Maudsley NHS Foundation Trust, London, United Kingdom

Fadi T. Maalouf   Department of Psychiatry, American University of Beirut, Beirut, Lebanon

Fatima Mansour   Department of Psychiatry, American University of Beirut, Beirut, Lebanon

Frances Mathews   University of Exeter Medical School, Exeter, United Kingdom

Dean McCoubrey   My Social Life, Cape Town, South Africa

Hassan Mirza   Adult ADHD Service, Department of Behavioural Medicine, Sultan Qaboos University Hospital, Psychiatry Residency Program, Oman Medical Specialty Board, Muscat, Sultanate of Oman

Tamsin Newlove-Delgado   University of Exeter Medical School, Exeter, United Kingdom

Dasha Nicholls   Division of Psychiatry, Imperial College London, London, United Kingdom

Ana Pascual-Sanchez   Division of Psychiatry, Imperial College London, London, United Kingdom

Lewis W. Paton   Health Professions Education Unit, Hull York Medical School, Heslington, United Kingdom

Atif Rahman   Department of Primary Care & Mental Health, Institute of Population Health, University of Liverpool, Liverpool, United Kingdom

David A. Rosenstein   Division of Child and Adolescent Psychiatry, University of Cape Town, South Africa

Husam HKZ. Salamah   Department of Psychiatry, Maastricht University Medical Center +, Maastricht, the Netherlands

Jan NM. Schieveld   Department of Psychiatry, Maastricht University Medical Center +, Maastricht, the Netherlands; Mutsaers Academy, Mutsaers Founding Pediatric Mental Health & Youth Care, Venlo, the Netherlands

Paul Stallard   Child and Family Mental Health, Department for Health, University of Bath, Bath, United Kingdom

Jacqueline JHM. Strik   Department of Psychiatry, Maastricht University Medical Center +, Maastricht, the Netherlands; Mutsaers Academy, Mutsaers Founding Pediatric Mental Health & Youth Care, Venlo, the Netherlands

Anthea A. Stylianakis   The University of New South Wales, School of Clinical Medicine, Faculty of Medicine and Health, Sydney, NSW, Australia; University of New South Wales, 2031 & Academic Unit of Child Psychiatry SWSLHD, L1 MHC Liverpool Hospital, Sydney, NSW, Australia

Paul A. Tiffin   Department of Health Sciences, University of York and Health Professions Education Unit, Hull York Medical School, Heslington, United Kingdom

Kim AM. Tijssen   Department of Psychiatry, Maastricht University Medical Center +, Maastricht, the Netherlands

Ahmed Waqas   Department of Primary Care & Mental Health, Institute of Population Health, University of Liverpool, Liverpool, United Kingdom

Alice Wickersham   CAMHS Digital Lab, Department of Child and Adolescent Psychiatry, Institute of Psychiatry, Psychology and Neuroscience, King's College, London, United Kingdom

Eva Wooding   University of Exeter Medical School, Exeter, United Kingdom

Preface

Matthew Hodes [a,b], *Petrus J. de Vries* [c]

[a] Division of Psychiatry, Imperial College London, London, United Kingdom

[b] Central and North West London NHS Foundation Trust, London, United Kingdom

[c] Division of Child and Adolescent Psychiatry, University of Cape Town, Cape Town, South Africa

The International Association for Child and Adolescent Psychiatry and Allied Professions (IACAPAP) has a tradition of organizing a biennial congress, regular study groups, and ongoing support for the training and development of child and adolescent mental health professionals across the globe. The 2020 SARS-CoV-2 (COVID-19) pandemic affected how these activities could be provided and significant adjustments had to be made to how IACAPAP functions. The 2020 congress (originally scheduled as an in-person meeting in Singapore) was changed to become an online event. We were delighted that the Monograph prepared for that event (Hodes, Gau, & de Vries, 2020) was published as planned and is now available as an open-access book (see https://iacapap.org/resources/monographs.html). The 25th congress scheduled to take place in December 2022 in Dubai is expected to return to a traditional in-person meeting with potential for hybrid or remote access. Over the past 2 years, we have been preparing this Monograph for release in time for the IACAPAP 2022 congress in Dubai.

The choice of Dubai as the venue for the 2022 IACAPAP Congress is highly significant. It is the first time the congress has taken place in an Arabian Gulf country. Over recent decades, Dubai has grown spectacularly fast with an extraordinarily high level of technological, service, and cultural innovation. It is now known as the "City of the future" and even includes the "Dubai Museum of the Future," which was opened in February 2022. Against this background, the congress theme is very appropriate: Child and Adolescent Mental Health: Shaping the Future! As in previous years, the congress theme was the inspiration for the contents of this Monograph, which stands both to reinforce the congress themes and as a scholarly book in its own right. The Monograph was written and compiled for a global target readership of child and adolescent mental health practitioners, researchers, and policy-makers.

There are three overarching themes of this book. Firstly, the impact of the Internet and computer technology on the well-being of children and adolescents, including computerized therapies, and their fundamental role in advancing knowledge in the field. Secondly, the expansion of knowledge regarding psychiatric disorders and their treatment for children and adolescents, exemplified by chapters on the effect of COVID-19, advances in PTSD, and a chapter on precision therapeutics. Thirdly, a theme on child and adolescent mental health in the Eastern Mediterranean Region, focusing on research and training.

We are very grateful for the continuing support of Elsevier, who have supported a publication policy that allows for open-access publication via the IACAPAP website 12 months after Monographs have been published. The site already provides links to three books in the series (see https:// iacapap.org/resources/monographs.html). By mid-2023, this Monograph will therefore also be available open access to readers. This form of "hybrid" publication has contributed to the IACAPAP mission of disseminating timely, robust, and evidence-based information that address globally important topics, as well as regionally and culturally diverse perspectives on child and adolescent mental health (CAMH).

The COVID-19 pandemic has given many of us the feeling that time has become faster, and with it, more rapid changes seem to occur. The pandemic has also brought forward many changes in training and dissemination, including greater use of the Internet and remote methods, and has challenged the need for in-person conferences. This questioning has been reinforced by a coincidental increase in our awareness of the need for a less ecologically destructive attitude to travel and conference attendance.

All these changes have also impacted the thinking of the IACAPAP Bureau and Executive Committee, IACAPAP finances, as well as congress budgets, which provided funding for the IACAPAP Monograph Series. In addition, there have been significant changes in the publishing environments with increasing pressures on university academics to publish in high-impact, peer-reviewed journals indexed in the main databases, e.g., PubMed to make publications rapidly accessible. These pressures have increasingly acted as a disincentive for many academics, particularly earlier in their career, to contribute to chapters in books. Against this background, the future of the IACAPAP Monograph has been much discussed and is in doubt at the time of writing this preface. Currently, there are no finalized plans to publish a Monograph to accompany the scheduled 2024 IACAPAP congress in Rio de Janeiro, Brazil. IACAPAP will continue to evolve and review its publication strategy, including the future of the Monograph, to ensure that new knowledge and evidence of relevance to the lives of infants, children, and adolescents with mental health problems around the globe can be disseminated in acceptable, accessible, and affordable ways to all who may benefit from it.

Acknowledgements

We would like to thank Drs Ammar Albanna and Hesham Hamoda, and the IACAPAP Dubai Congress Local Organising Committee for support for this Monograph.

Reference

Hodes, M., Gau, S.-F. S., & de Vries, P. J. (Eds.). (2020). *Starting at the beginning: Laying the foundation for lifelong mental health*. London: Academic Press.

Introduction

Matthew Hodes [a, b], Petrus J. de Vries [c]

[a] Division of Psychiatry, Imperial College London, London,
United Kingdom
[b] Central and North West London NHS Foundation Trust, London, United
Kingdom
[c] Division of Child and Adolescent Psychiatry, University of Cape Town,
Cape Town, South Africa

1. Children and adolescents in the digital world

One of the most dramatic global changes in the past few decades has been the massive increase in availability of computers and hand-held electronic devices. Much of the use is linked to the Internet, which has spread to all countries, and, in addition to its known high penetration in many Asian countries, is becoming increasingly available in low- and middle-income countries (LMICs) around the globe, including in Africa (see Kumm, Viljoen & de Vries, 2022 and https://www.statista.com/statistics/1176668/internet-penetration-rate-in-africa-by-region/ accessed 16th April 2022). This has changed the world for children and adolescents who are growing up as "digital natives" with exposure to these technologies since early childhood. Digital technologies are now part of everyday communication, entertainment, education, and academic life. For this reason, the first section of the book begins with discussions of two aspects of this enormous change for children and adolescents.

The opening chapter by Theron and colleagues assesses whether the digital environment in which children and adolescent now grow up can make positive contributions to their development. The authors' starting point is that many of the negative aspects of the digital world such as narrowing of the range of activities and negative effects on physical and mental well-being have been well described. The topic of gaming disorder for example, now recognized in ICD-11 (World Health Organization, 2019), was addressed in the 2020 Monograph (King & Delfabbro, 2020). Theron and colleagues instead embed the use of digital technologies into Bronfenbrenner's socioecological model as an inevitable contextual factor in the lives of young people. They include discussion of the developmental neurobiology focusing on the mesolimbic system and nucleus accumbens for understanding the propensity of adolescents for high levels of engagement in the digital world. Within this framework, they make the case that mindfulness may protect against overuse and also that digital systems may contribute to the growth of mindfulness and thus resilience.

In contrast to the positive first chapter, Chapter 2 by Pascual-Sanchez and Nicholls focuses on cyberbullying, as a specific example of harm that may arise from participation in the digital world. As discussed by the authors, cyberbullying is not a very precisely defined term but may be taken to refer to repeated aggressive acts using digital media. Interestingly, some children do not recognize that they are being bullied in this way, but research data suggest that it occurs among a significant minority of children, some of whom become cybervictims and cyberbullies. The authors discuss why cyberbullying might arise and present some of the mental health effects. The chapter concludes with an accessible and practical account of assessment and interventions to deal with cyberbullying.

2. Digital innovations to improve our understanding of child and adolescent mental health

The enormous increase in availability of relatively cheap and powerful computers that can manage large amounts of data has created important opportunities for mental health research and innovation. This section addresses some of these advances. The chapter by Wickersham and Downs (Chapter 3) provides an insightful account of how large and linked data sets often held by different agencies have the potential to reveal new findings about child and adolescent mental health (CAMH) and service utilization. The authors outline the substantial methodological challenges in data linkage. They illustrate the strengths and challenges using the electronic medical records developed at the South London and Maudsley NHS Foundation Trust associated with the Institute of Psychiatry Psychology and Neuroscience at Kings College London. The final sections of the chapter place the work in global perspectives and address future directions.

Chapter 4, by Tiffin and Lewis, addresses the related topic of machine learning. Developments in computer science have enabled machines to learn and alter their problem-solving according to new inputs. The authors describe how these advances can potentially be applied in CAMH for tasks such as diagnosis, prediction of rare events, and the analysis of large data sets in genomics and related fields. Some principles of machine learning are described as well as the various mechanisms and models for carrying out the tasks.

3. Innovative approaches to children and adolescents in adversity

The challenges to global health, including CAMH arising from the COVID-19 pandemic, were acknowledged early on in the COVID-19 pandemic in the 2020 Monograph (Hodes, Gau, & de Vries, 2020a). However, at that time, there were no systematic data on the subject. We are therefore pleased to include here a masterful overview of the topic by Newlove-Delgado and colleagues (Chapter 5) that includes key studies from the rapidly increasing body of research. They discuss the massive effects of the COVID-19 pandemic on family life, on educational provision with school closures, and on sporting and social activities, all of which represent risk factors for psychological distress. A surprising number of cross-sectional and cohort studies have been carried out investigating community populations as well as clinical samples in various countries around the globe. The interesting findings suggest that, although for many children and adolescents their mental health deteriorated with lower mood and increased anxiety, there was a subgroup who reported improvement, probably related to not having to attend school and with greater family contact. The authors discuss the impact of the pandemic on CAMH service access and key aspects of service delivery including the increased use of remote consultation. The authors acknowledge that the chapter had been shaped by the availability of research reports, much of which came from high-income countries, even though it is well known that the majority of children and adolescents live in low- and middle-income countries (LMICs).

The 2022 congress takes place in Dubai situated in the Easter Mediterranean Region (which includes the region loosely referred to as the "Middle East"). This part of the world has seen a tragically high level of organized violence and war. Some of the consequences of war were described in the 2018 Monograph (e.g., the migration of Syrian and other refugees to central Europe in 2015–2016, Fegert, Sukale, & Brown, 2018). However, it felt important to address again the theme of trauma. We had not foreseen the war and violence in Ukraine at the time of developing this Monograph, but a chapter on PTSD seems particularly poignant today. Lewis and Danese (Chapter 6) provide an account of contemporary developments in the PTSD field. They describe the changes to the classification of PTSD in ICD-11, including discussion of the new diagnosis of "complex PTSD." The authors suggest that the construct of complex PTSD needs further research to establish its validity within the child and adolescent age group. Their own insightful and carefully conducted studies using longitudinal data reveal the range of outcomes following trauma exposure. The chapter discusses the potential mechanisms for these outcomes. The final sections address key aspects of treatment and prevention. Some of the themes are amplified in the chapter by Maalouf and colleagues on research in the Eastern Mediterranean Region (Chapter 12), which also addresses the psychological consequences of organized violence and war on children and adolescents.

4. Treatments for the future

There is a general hope for significant changes in treatments for mental health disorders in the coming decades. A significant proportion of this hope is based on potential discoveries in neuroscience and in our understanding of disease mechanisms that may enable the creation of specific drug treatments. Existing neurological and psychiatric disorders and existing behavioral phenotypes may be broken down into specific subtypes or subgroups that will aid the development of therapeutics. A good example of this approach is provided by Schieveld and colleagues (Chapter 7) who describe forms of autoimmune encephalitis that may present with a wide range of psychiatric phenomena, often followed by neurological symptoms. Autoimmune encephalitis itself is a broad diagnostic category that arises when central nervous system antibodies are produced to neuronal cell surface, synaptic proteins, or ion channels. The emphasis in the chapter is on anti-NMDAR encephalitis, the most prevalent type, which may be misdiagnosed as schizophrenia. The authors provide a detailed account of the characteristics of this disorder and diagnostic challenges. The range of interventions and contribution of the psychiatric team to multidisciplinary management is described, alongside practical information about drug regimens to treat some of the challenging behavioral problems, including confusion and aggression.

Another innovation that is generating increasing attention is "precision psychiatry" in which interventions are tailored to the most likely positive response, rather than relying on a "one size fits all" approach (Kambeitz-Ilankovic, Koutsouleris, & Upthegrove, 2022). In Chapter 8, Aitken and colleagues consider precision therapeutics in relation to adolescent depression. The need for such innovation is clear from their introduction where they explain that 40% of adolescents do not respond adequately to depression treatment and that those who do respond show a higher relapse rate than seen in adults. The authors describe a number of approaches to this problem including machine learning (see also Tiffin and Lewis, Chapter 4). The authors then discuss the relevance of findings from the IMPACT trial, a large randomized controlled trial of psychological therapies for adolescent depression, including the heterogeneity of treatment response. The authors discuss at the biological level the importance of variations in the function in the hypothalamic pituitary axis and cortisol. Precision therapeutics appears a promising approach that could have major implications for treatment delivery for adolescent depression and most likely commonly associated problems.

Some of the ideas from earlier chapters such as the potential for digital interventions and the need to recognize patient preference and timely access to evidence-based psychological treatments underpin Chapter 9 by Stallard on computerized cognitive behavioral therapy (cCBT) for children and adolescents with depression and anxiety. He provides a succinct account of developments in the field. CBT, being a structured manualized intervention, potentially lends itself well to computerized delivery. The large gap between those who could benefit from CBT and the relatively low capacity of trained therapists to deliver it suggest that cCBT might have real potential to reduce this treatment gap, especially in LMICs. The chapter reviews the main cCBT programs currently available, and the evidence base for their effectiveness. This is an area of great potential, but Stallard reminds us that further work is needed to consider many aspects of implementation including their place in treatment pathways, the place of therapist-supported cCBT, and evaluation, especially in LMIC contexts.

Linking to the need for special considerations in LMICs, Chapter 10 focuses on scaling up of interventions during the perinatal period in LMICs, and on the potential impact on child development. It skillfully interweaves the evidence from randomized controlled trials and describes the potential elements of intervention effectiveness. Waqas and Rahman describe approaches such as task shifting/task sharing that involves nonspecialist providers to deliver treatments. The authors also consider the impact of technological developments such as big data (see Wickersham and Downs, Chapter 3) and digital technologies to support treatment delivery. In global terms, the approaches as outlined in the chapter may have profound impact, given the huge scale of need, and the potential impact on child development.

It is accepted now that technology can be used extensively for teaching and training in child and adolescent mental health. Implementation of these innovations has been accelerated as a result of the COVID-19 pandemic. Stylianakis and colleagues (Chapter 11) recognize this and provide examples of the way in which technology-enhanced learning (TEL) can reach professionals, including in LMICs and remote locations. They describe the processes for developing TEL and propose an approach to evaluate the impact of TEL in future.

5. Shaping the future of child and adolescent mental health in the Eastern Mediterranean Region

The final section addresses developments in CAMH in the Eastern Mediterranean Region. Maalouf and colleagues provide a synthesis (Chapter 12) of many key aspects of research in the region. They start by describing the significant socioeconomic and demographic diversity of countries in the region, ranging from politically stable high-income countries such as the United Arab Emirates, to low-income countries such as Afghanistan and Somalia, which have been severely affected by political instability and war. The authors summarize the main findings from studies of prevalence of psychiatric disorders and pay particular attention to studies of children and adolescents exposed to war and organized violence. They also describe the (smaller number of) intervention studies. Given the high population of the region, there is a relatively lack of research activity, and potential reasons for this, as well as possible ways to ameliorate this challenge, are presented.

One of the reasons for the low research activity in the Gulf region is the shortage of trained child and adolescent mental health practitioners. This is the focus of the final chapter (Chapter 13) that outlines training in child and adolescent psychiatry in the Gulf countries. Albanna and his co-authors (all based in the Gulf region) describe the specialist training in child and adolescent psychiatry from their national perspective. In the context of rapid socioeconomic development and a relatively low child and adolescent mental health workforce, the authors describe impressive initiatives underway to establish their own training programs and networking initiatives.

6. Concluding note

The authors describe major changes in the lives of children and adolescents brought about by the growth and reach of the digital sphere. The changes may have not only potential harmful effects but also major potential for promoting child and adolescent mental health by contributing to the growth of knowledge and improved systems for delivery of interventions. New technologies have already had and will continue to have an impact on teaching and training. In the light of these changes, IACAPAP will continue to evolve and review its publication strategy, including the future of the Monograph, to ensure that new knowledge and evidence of relevance to the lives of infants, children, and adolescents with mental health problems around the globe can be disseminated in acceptable, accessible, and affordable ways to all who may benefit from it.

Matthew Hodes and Petrus J. de Vries
May 2022

References

Fegert, J. M., Sukale, T., & Brown, R. C. (2018). Mental health service provision for child and adolescent refugees: European perspectives. In M. Hodes, S.-F. S. Gau, & P. J. de Vries

(Eds.), *Understanding uniqueness and diversity in child and adolescent mental health* (pp. 195—222). London: Academic Press.

Hodes, M., Gau, S.-F. S., & de Vries, P. J. (2020a). Introduction. In M. Hodes, S.-F. S. Gau, & P. J. de Vries (Eds.), *Starting at the beginning. Laying the foundation for lifelong mental health* (pp. xxi—xxvi). London Academic Press.

Starting at the Beginning. In Hodes, M., Gau, S.-F. S., & de Vries, P. J. (Eds.), *Laying the foundation for lifelong mental health*, (2020). London Academic Press.

Kambeitz-Ilankovic, L., Koutsouleris, N., & Upthegrove, R. (2022). The potential of precision psychiatry: What is in reach? *British Journal of Psychiatry, 220*(4), 175—178. https://doi.org/10.1192/bjp.2022.23

King, D. L., & Delfabbro, P. H. (2020). Gaming disorder in young people. In M. Hodes, S.-F. S. Gau, & P. J. de Vries (Eds.), *Starting at the beginning. Laying th eFoundatoin for lifelong mental health* (pp. 159—187). London: Academic Press.

Kumm, A. J., Viljoen, M., & de Vries, P. J. (2022). The digital divide in technologies for autism: feasibility considerations for low- and middle-income countries. *Journal of Autism and Developmental Disorders, 52*, 2300—2313.

World Health Organization. (2019). *International statistical classification of diseases and related health problems.* Retrieved from https://icd.who.int/.

PART I

Children and adolescents in the digital age

1

Looking beyond the adverse effects of digital technologies on adolescents: the case for resilience and mindfulness

F. Hugo Theron[1], David A. Rosenstein[2], and Dean McCoubrey[3]

[1] De Mist Private Practice, Cape Town, South Africa; [2] Division of Child and Adolescent Psychiatry, University of Cape Town, South Africa; [3] My Social Life, Cape Town, South Africa

1. Introduction—a society saturated with information and communication technologies

In 1964, Marshall McLuhan published his opus magnus, *Understanding Media*, a scholarly "prophecy" (Carr, 2010) that imagined a world where the "process of knowing will be collectively ... extended to the whole of human society" (McLuhan, 1964, p. 3). McLuhan's future was neither utopic nor dystopic; it was a future that acknowledged and celebrated the transformative power of new communication technologies, but also forewarned against that exact same power and the risk of being oblivious to it. McLuhan's envisaged tomorrow has become our present day, and his cautionary prophetic words are now our daily reality.

It is the reality of a society saturated with digital technologies (Telecommunication Development Sector, 2014; Viner et al., 2019), including computers, mobile phones, radios, television, the Internet, and social media applications and platforms (e.g., Facebook, WhatsApp, Instagram, Snapchat, and Twitter) (Chatfield, 2012; Schiliro & Choo, 2017; Weber & Kauffman, 2011). In 2014, the year that the World Wide Web turned 25 (Berners-Lee, 2000), close to 80% of all human beings were

3

already connected to the Internet (Rosen, 2012). The presence of digital technology is all-pervasive in high-income countries (HIC) and rapidly increasing in low- and middle-income countries (LMICs) (Mihajlov & Vejmelka, 2017). The use of social media has grown swiftly, with the possibility of being constantly connected to the Internet. It is a phenomenon that is not just changing the societal landscape at large but also affecting the most ordinary aspects of individuals' everyday lives (Odgers & Jensen, 2020; Turkle, 2011). For most people, engaging with digital technology is often the first and last action in their daily routine (Rosen, 2012; Twenge et al., 2019), and in numerous studies (e.g., Rodriguez-Garcia & Moreno-Guerrero, 2019), participants reported themselves unable to comprehend not having a mobile phone, with many adults struggling to put down their devices (Mihajlov & Vejmelka, 2017; Nelson & Pieper, 2020).

Throughout history, humans have been concerned about possible adverse effects of new technologies, especially on developing young people (Johnson, 2006). Socrates, for example, warned against taking up writing (because it would erode the memory) (Mills, 2014). The ubiquitous presence of digital technology is a fact of life for the present generation of children and adolescents (often referred to as "digital natives"—a generation born into a world where digital technology has always existed) (Palfrey & Gasser, 2008; Wang et al., 2019), and worldwide, digital technology use has become the preferred activity for the majority of them (Strasburger et al., 2013; Wallace, 2014; Weinstein, 2018; Øverby et al., 2013).

Young children (0–8 years) from across the globe have ever-increasing access to digital technology (Paudel et al., 2017), and several publications highlight both the risks and the resilience-building opportunities inherent to digital technology exposure (Mantilla & Edwards, 2019; Sohn et al., 2019). In a world where it is estimated that one in three Internet users is a child (with the number even higher in LMICs) (Livingstone et al., 2015), many professional interest groups (e.g., American Paediatric Association, Global Kids Online, Canadian Paediatric Society, and Early Childhood Australia) have published guidelines and reports on technology use in early childhood (Stoilova et al., 2021; Straker et al., 2018).

Notwithstanding the concerns and opportunities associated with the early childhood exposure to digital technology, the preponderance of empirical focus has been on both young and older adolescent use (Dienlin & Johannes, 2020; Odgers & Jensen, 2020; Odgers et al., 2020; Orben, 2020). Adolescents from most HIC spend almost a third of their waking hours engaging with digital technology (Calvert & Wartella, 2014), with international data indicating almost 100% Internet penetration among adolescents in HIC (Telecommunication Development Sector, 2014). Most adolescents in the United Kingdom, Canada, and the United States spend more than 50% of their waking time using digital technology

(Rideout, 2015; Sigman, 2012). According to a 2018 US survey, 45% of adolescents who participated indicated that they are almost constantly online (Cataldo et al., 2021). Banaji et al. (2017) highlighted the challenges of accessing correct data relating to digital technology use by adolescents in LMICs. From the available statistical information on adolescent digital technology use, it can be seen that LMICs are lagging slightly in terms of access and use (Blignaut & Els, 2010; Mihajlov & Vejmelka, 2017), but that improved mobile technology is driving an ever-increasing number of adolescent digital technology users (Ye & Yang, 2020). More than half of all adolescents use a social media site at least daily, with almost a quarter accessing sites 10 times or more per day (O'Keeffe & Clarke-Pearson, 2011; Prinstein et al., 2020). During the COVID-19 pandemic, there have been even larger spikes in the use of digital technology by adolescents (Montag & Elhai, 2020).

Developmental processes (both physical and psychological) make adolescents especially susceptible to the impact of this rapidly changing societal landscape that is driven by the rate of technological progress and the almost universal uptake of these technologies (Ahn, 2011; Bailin et al., 2014; Davis et al., 2020; Dwyer et al., 2020; Gilmore & Meersand, 2014).

A central question is then what the effects of this ever-increasing digital technology use are on adolescents who are challenged with developmental demands, juxtaposed to dwindling communal support (Park et al., 2012). Understanding the effects of digital technology on the development of adolescents has become even more pertinent as young people seek more social interaction online and where classrooms have had to move online due to social distancing and mitigation procedures in place due to the COVID-19 pandemic. A nuanced look at the effects of digital technology use, considering both benefits and adverse outcomes, is therefore necessary.

2. The effects of digital technology on adolescents—the call for balanced research

Research on the effects of digital technology use on adolescents and their development is substantial (Odgers et al., 2020; Shapiro & Margolin, 2014), although the majority of published studies focuses on the possible negative consequences of digital technology use for developing adolescents (e.g., Hoge et al., 2017; Holtz & Appel, 2011; Hong et al., 2013; Kaess et al., 2014). Empirical studies have examined the adverse effects of adolescent digital technology use on developmental areas ranging from physical health including sleep (Choi et al., 2009; Hardy et al., 2010; Mei et al., 2018), relationships (Amichai-Hamburger & Hayat, 2011), and psychoemotional well-being (Huang, 2010; Mao et al., 2021), to academic functioning (Weinstein et al., 2014), and eventual long-term outcomes for communities at large (Karlsen et al., 2013).

There is, however, an emerging research discourse on possible positive effects of digital technology use for adolescents. Ahiauzu and Odili (2012) argued eloquently in support of research that is more balanced in studying the effect of digital technology on adolescent development—a "middle ground" approach, where technology and its use is neither judged to be intrinsically detrimental nor beneficial, but where effects are associated with the specifics of digital technology use (e.g., amount of use) (Belanger et al., 2011; Prinstein et al., 2020). There are many possible positive outcomes of social media use, but problematic use can lead to negative biological, cognitive, psychological, and social outcomes. For instance, certain social media platforms can encourage risky alcohol consumption among adolescents, but, conversely, they can also facilitate online-based interventions (Cataldo et al., 2021). Similarly, social media sites can negatively impact on self-harming tendencies, but they can also be the first base of support (Cataldo et al., 2021).

Odgers (2018) argued that the majority of research fails to account for the nuances of the type of device, the type of platform, the extent of exposure and time online, the personal interests or curiosity of the child, their home structure, previous trauma, and other factors. The resulting effects are broad and hard to categorize. It is important to distinguish between various social media platforms, as each of them has unique characteristics. Text, video, and pictures, through various forms of social media, impact differentially upon adolescents' development, and problematic use of each may manifest in different psychological problems (Cataldo et al., 2021). These psychological issues, which affect the entire developmental spectrum from early to late adolescence, include depression, anxiety, and eating disorders. They also include the exacerbation of and contribution toward neurodevelopmental disorders such as autism spectrum disorder (ASD) and attention deficit hyperactivity disorder (ADHD) (Cataldo et al., 2021).

The bioecological model is a theoretical model that explains the complex interplay between adolescents and their environment and may give us a better understanding of the ways in which digital technology use and overuse can affect adolescents.

3. The bioecological model—a framework to explain the interaction between adolescent and their (techno-) environment

The bioecological model of Bronfenbrenner (2005) provides a potential theoretical framework to understand the important interplay between an individual and their environment. Johnson and Puplampu's (2008) addition of a technosubsystem to Bronfenbrenner's model acknowledges the growing importance of digital technology in the daily functioning of individuals.

The bioecological model encompasses a lifespan approach to development and is theoretically applicable to childhood, adolescence, and adulthood (Sigelman & Rider, 2014). The model highlights the importance of bidirectional effects between developing individuals and their surrounding environments (Bronfenbrenner & Morris, 2006). It consists of five interconnected systems of which the first, the *microsystem*, is contextually closest to the individual and encompasses interpersonal relationships and direct exchanges with the immediate surroundings (e.g., school, friends, family members). The second system, the *mesosystem*, defines reciprocity between different entities associated with the microsystem (e.g., a good relationship between an adolescent boy's father and his sport coach). The third system, the *exosystem*, does not directly impact on individuals but is characterized by aspects of structures within the microsystem (e.g., parental job loss resulting in financial difficulties). The fourth system, the *macrosystem*, is the outermost layer of the bioecological model and integrates social beliefs or cultural ideologies that often shape an individual's environment. The macrosystem also includes the value attached to digital technology (Lanigan, 2009). Lastly, the *chronosystem*, explains how time is an important component in the way that people, their environments, and ultimately their interactions will change over time. The different effects of digital technology use on the same group of adolescents at different times during adolescence are therefore important to consider.

As shown in Fig. 1.1, the technosubsystem is an extension of the microsystem and explains the interaction between the adolescent and digital technology (e.g., playing games on the computer), as well as interaction with the adolescent's microsystem mediated by digital technology (e.g., communicating to peers on social media platforms) (Johnson, 2010a). An example relating to the mesosystem would be parents'/caregivers' monitoring of school attendance or school marks by logging onto the school's website, or teacher and parents/caregivers communicating via email about the adolescent's classroom behavior. Socioeconomic realities of parents/caregivers often dictate the technological realities present in the home environment, i.e., mesosystem (e.g., if the parent/caregiver is a computer programmer and generates enough income, the child might have an excellent computer with a fast Internet connection, or the latest and best smartphone). Macrosystem relevance for the technosubsystem can be conceptualized in terms of the cultural value attached to digital technology use (e.g., as an enhancer of education). The older an adolescent is, the more autonomy he or she is allowed, also with regard to Internet use (i.e., chronosystem). Excessive digital technology

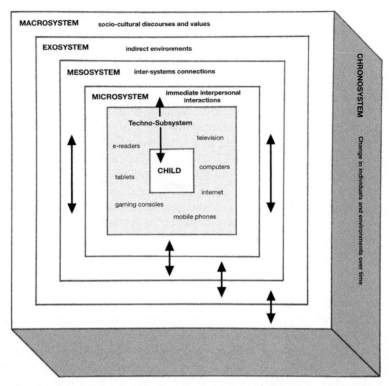

FIGURE 1.1   The ecological technosubsystem. *Based on Johnson, G. M., & Puplampu, P. (2008). A conceptual framework for understanding the effect of the internet on child development: The ecological techno-subsystem.* Canadian Journal of Learning and Technology, 34(1), 19–28.

use will affect all of the adolescent's interactional systems as defined by Bronfenbrenner's model (for example, excessive Internet online gaming will lead to less time to invest in reciprocal interaction between an individual and his or her peers and family members, adversely influencing the microsystem) (Johnson, 2010b).

Bronfenbrenner's (2005) model thus explains how the complex interactions between personal attributes and environmental circumstances, mediated by internal mechanisms of the adolescent himself or herself, will dictate how well adolescents manage and adapt to their environment (Luthar et al., 2000). With the addition of the technosubsystem, the model provides a theoretical framework within which the impact of adolescent digital technology use within a specific context can be studied (Blignaut & Els, 2010). One aspect, seated within the adolescent, that determines the interactions with the various systems in the model, including the technosubsystem, is personal resilience.

4. Digital technology use and resilience in adolescents—lessening negative consequences and encouraging positive outcomes

The effect of digital technology use on adolescents' sense of mastery and intrapersonal strengths is best understood in terms of its importance against the larger theoretical and empirical backdrop of resilience and adolescent development. Resilience-related empirical work focuses on how to lessen the negative consequences of digital technology use and even encourage positive outcomes (Friedman & Chase-Lansdale, 2003). Resilience is defined as "the ability to demonstrate successful development and adaptation within contexts of risk" (Rutter & Taylor, 2003, p. 264) or "a product of complex interactions of personal attributes and environmental circumstances, mediated by internal mechanisms" (Prince-Embury & Saklofske, 2013, p. 3), which becomes "a dynamic process encompassing *positive adaptation* within the context of significant adversity" (Luthar et al., 2000, p. 543).

Self-efficacy is the belief that one can optimally handle life's challenges (Zheng et al., 2009). Successful adolescent development is characterized by the establishment of personal identity, which is tied to a healthy development of self-efficacy (Arnett, 2014; Erikson, 1968) and the exploration of the self in relation to others (Louw & Louw, 2007) by utilizing ever-increasing complex cognitive abilities (Keating, 2012; Piaget, 1964). The prototypical self-knowledge developed in early childhood directs later internalized schemas of human interaction in middle childhood and eventually forms the complex appraisal systems used to interpret environmental and relational cues in adolescence (Friedman & Chase-Lansdale, 2003). Social relationships are especially significant in adolescent development (Blakemore, 2012), and social relatedness is vitally important for adolescents (Padilla-Walker et al., 2014) who interpret social support to be specific in nature and context (Anderson et al., 2004). This, in turn, shapes expectations for future support that are internalized (Lakey & Orehek, 2011) and that impact on the psychological well-being of individuals (Lynch, 2012). Successful, developmentally appropriate assimilation of coping skills is therefore an internally and environmentally driven process, of which interpersonal skills leading to a sense of relatedness and social support are paramount (Barber & Schluterman, 2008; Shapka, 2018; Van den Berg et al., 2013).

Sense of mastery, perception of self-efficacy, optimism, and adaptability are important for developing resilience (Prince-Embury & Saklofske, 2013). Early research emphasizes the importance of curiosity as catalyst for environmental exploration (White, 1959)—an interaction that is intrinsically rewarding, teaches the child the joys of active agency in cause and effect dynamics, and most importantly is the source of problem-solving skills (Sroufe, 1996). White (1959), and subsequent researchers (Masten et al., 2006) suggest that a sense of mastery, self-efficacy, and competence is derived from and "grows" in relation to this interaction with the environment. Adolescents' self-efficacy beliefs also impact on their academic motivation and success (Bandura, 1993; Liu & Cheng, 2018), and a sense of mastery can prevent or ameliorate emotional and behavioral problems through better adaptation to stressful contexts (Brownlee et al., 2013). A sense of mastery grows as adolescents begin to control and influence greater parts of their lives, which in turn (in optimal contexts) improves self-esteem (Erol & Orth, 2011).

Judi et al. (2013) emphasize the empowering ability of digital technologies. Adolescents' drive toward autonomy is enhanced by owning a mobile phone (Blair & Fletcher, 2011) or having access to (unregulated) information via the Internet (Campbell, 2006). Initial face-to-face social anxieties are often negated by digital technology communication (Bonetti et al., 2010), and it provides substantial social support for adolescents in need (Colasante et al., 2020; Valkenburg & Peter, 2011). Even relationships that started solely via digital technology communication often led to face-to-face contact (Schiffrin et al., 2010). Digital technology use can bring about adolescents' sense of mastery and intrapersonal strengths (Brown, 2014; Shank & Cotten, 2014). It enhances their desire for identity exploration and experimentation (Amichai-Hamburger & Hayat, 2011) and enables them to gain greater autonomy (Duran et al., 2011), as well as access to information and digital technology skills (including problem-solving skills) (Binkley et al., 2012). In the process, intrapersonal skills are strengthened, and a sense of mastery over the environment is established (Shank & Cotten, 2014). Digital technology use offers adolescents opportunities to develop empowering self-efficacy beliefs when adult limit-setting is present (Brown, 2014). Strong self-efficacy motivates perseverance and enhances learning, ultimately leading to achievement, especially in academic settings (Liu & Cheng, 2018; Luszczynska et al., 2005). Peer-to-peer relationships are important for teenagers, and the solidifying of face-to-face friendships via digital technology creates feelings of satisfaction and connectedness in adolescent girls (Schofield-Clark, 2005; Weinstein, 2018) and thereby strengthens self-efficacy beliefs (Brown, 2014). Self-esteem rests on two pillars: belief that one can control one's environment and acceptance from others (Valkenburg & Peter, 2011). Digital technology use provides adolescents with both. The more often digital technology communication is used, the more (mostly positive) feedback is generated, which in turn leads to higher self-esteem (Valkenburg & Peter, 2009; Weinstein, 2018). Conversely, adolescents who receive negative feedback experience diminished self-esteem (Shapiro & Margolin, 2014; Weinstein, 2018). Research indicates a positive relationship between digital technology use and sense of mastery, self-esteem, and self-efficacy (Shank & Cotten, 2014; Valkenburg & Peter, 2011), but these studies do not include excessive digital technology use (Kaess et al., 2014; Moreno et al., 2013). Results from studies on adolescent digital technology overuse clearly indicate excessive use may negatively influence these same outcomes (Ghassemzadeh et al., 2008; Odgers, 2018; Yu & Shek, 2013).

The effect of digital technology use on adolescents' intrapersonal strengths and sense of mastery is often reported as either being all harmful or all beneficial (Suoranta, 2003). All the aforementioned positive effects of digital technology usage can also be supplanted by pernicious consequences, depending on factors separated from or associated with digital technology use (Weinstein et al., 2014). Some researchers highlight how digital technology use tends to isolate adolescents (Schiffrin et al., 2010), may result in deterioration of in-person interaction (Misra et al., 2014), and cause a more permeable geographical sense of belonging (Crisp, 2010; Palfrey & Gasser, 2008).

4.1 Mechanisms for the effects of digital technology on adolescents

The nature of the effect of digital technology use on adolescents can be explained by three hypotheses. The *augmentation or stimulation hypothesis* (Valkenburg & Peter, 2006) reasons that the use of one medium enhances engagement with other mediums (Huang, 2010) (e.g., digital technology—mediated communication enhances eye-to-eye communication in established relationships (Allen et al., 2014)). The *displacement hypothesis* (Valkenburg & Peter, 2006) argues that excessive digital technology usage prevents engagement in other developmentally important activities (Endestad et al., 2011). The *threshold effect theory* (Endestad et al., 2011) stipulates a critical time limit for digital technology use, after which negative effects occur (Belanger et al., 2011). There is currently no consensus as to the number of hours that would define this critical time threshold (Belanger et al., 2011), and definitions of excessive use range from 2 h per day (Meerkerk et al., 2009) to 6 or more hours per day (Hawi, 2012; Tonioni et al., 2012). Odgers et al. (2020) argue the case for future studies that investigate the complexities and nuances of digital harm (Vuorre et al., 2021) to move beyond simple screen time metrics and other conceptualizations of screen time, and focus on the more relevant *nature* of online interaction (e.g., the type and features of online activities and consumed content), rather than merely the amount of time spent engaging with it (Tang et al., 2021).

Gross et al. (2002) view adolescents' online communication as an extension of their off-line relationships and see digital technology as just another communication tool. In that sense, the outcomes of digital technology use are related to variables associated with the individual rather than the medium of communication (Lai et al., 2013). Amount of time spent on digital technology use has also proven to be an important predictor of relational impact, with higher usage leading to increased negative effects (Belanger et al., 2011; Tonioni et al., 2012).

4.2 Overuse of digital technology

Research has shown digital technology overuse to impact negatively on the physical health of adolescents (Bailin et al., 2014), for example, sleeping patterns (Chassiakos et al., 2016; Choi et al., 2009; Mei et al., 2018). More frequent use is associated with less adequate sleep (Shimoga et al., 2019). Diet is also affected by overuse of digital technology (Jackson et al., 2011) in the sense that it is associated with obesity (Chassiakos et al., 2016). Evidence also suggests that social media overuse is related to lower levels of vigorous physical activity in girls, but much less so in boys (Buda et al., 2020). It has also been observed that girls with problematic social media usage have more negative health perceptions than boys (Buda et al., 2020). Contrary to the higher incidence of digital overuse associated with less physical activity in adolescents, some research has shown that regular social media use was associated with higher likelihoods of daily vigorous exercise (Shimoga et al., 2019).

There are also correlations between overuse and mood disorders and anxiety disorders (Cataldo et al., 2021; Shapira et al., 2000), academic functional decline (Skoric et al., 2009), externalizing behavior problems (Holtz & Appel, 2011), and suboptimal social/peer interaction (Valkenburg & Peter, 2009). The more adolescents share their lives online, the greater their risk are of feeling the constant urge to check their profiles for updates and feedback, possibly triggering addictive behaviors and exacerbating anxiety symptoms (Cataldo et al., 2021). Adolescents with disrupted family environments, who struggle with learning problems, social isolation, low self-esteem, and impulsivity, are more vulnerable to negative effects of digital technology overuse (Ma et al., 2011). A feeling of loneliness is also a predictor of social media overuse (Kross et al., 2013).

More than 6 hours of digital technology use per day profoundly affects adolescents' resilience (Li et al., 2010), specifically their intrapersonal strengths and sense of mastery. Overuse negatively affects self-esteem (Wallace, 2014), with moderate users displaying higher self-esteem than excessive users (Ghassemzadeh et al., 2008). Weinstein et al. (2014) also found that adolescents with low self-esteem and self-efficacy experience a greater need for control, often leading to excessive digital technology use. Low self-esteem poses a risk factor for negative affect when adolescents compare their lives with that of others on social media (Niu et al., 2018; Odgers, 2018). According to Vannucci and Ohannessian (2019), excessive social media use is associated with depressive symptoms and low offline social support from others. Problematic digital technology use is also related to low problem-solving skills (Yu & Shek, 2013). Moderate digital technology use is associated with emotionally warm parenting and healthy parent—adolescent communication, while parental rejection or overprotection is associated with excessive use (Yao et al., 2014). Over time, parents/caregivers of excessive digital technology using adolescents often "give up," thus exacerbating the problem (Van Den Eijnden et al., 2010). Research has also shown that stricter rule-setting without bettering the parent/caregiver—adolescent relationship does not decrease excessive digital technology use (Van den Eijnden et al., 2010). Younger adolescents are more significantly affected by excessive digital technology use than older adolescents (Koo & Kwon, 2014). Older excessive users perceive and experience themselves and their lives as more negative than moderate users (Yan et al., 2014). Excessive digital technology use might decrease over time because of (1) a decrease in the novelty factor, (2) psychophysiological maturing, leading to better self-control and increased self-efficacy, and (3) more social and academic distractions (Yu & Shek, 2013). The amount of digital technology use and its relationship with intrapersonal variables is most probably bidirectional in nature (Koo & Kwon, 2014; Wallace, 2014). For instance, social media engagement can be very luring for adolescents with social anxiety issues, as information is shared in a more controlled fashion (Cataldo et al., 2021). This can, however, lead to problematic social media usage.

The type of engagement with digital technology also seems to play a role in the effects on the adolescent. For instance, passive social media use (browsing other users' photos or news feeds) is bidirectionally linked to depression (Cataldo et al., 2021)—passive social media use exacerbates depressive symptoms, while depressive symptoms tend to increase passive social media use.

We have now considered various possible effects of digital technology use and misuse on adolescent psychology, and along with it the role that personal resilience plays, but what effects do digital technology use have on brain development from a neurodevelopmental perspective?

5. Neurodevelopmental effects of digital technology use—the need for a multipronged approach

The effects of digital technology on the maturational trajectories of brain regions involved in social interactions remain unclear and are contentious (Crone & Konijn, 2018). There is still a paucity of research examining the effects of digital technology on brain development in children and adolescents; however, there are an increasing number of studies beginning to address these gaps. Many of the difficulties with examining the effects of digital technology on brain development are the pace and rapidity at which new technologies emerge and the length of time it takes research to investigate these changes in technology and their associated impacts. Examining a single digital technology or subset and then generalizing these processes across all types of digital technology would be incorrect. We therefore suggest that a multipronged approach would be necessary when examining or exploring the effects of digital technology on adolescent brain development.

In a review of the neural development of adolescence and associated media usage, Crone and Konijn (2018) indicated how neuroscience may provide a deeper understanding of the developmental sensitivities related to adolescents' media and digital technology use. They concluded that adolescents are highly sensitive to both acceptance and rejection through social media and that their heightened emotional sensitivity and protracted development of reflective processing and cognitive control may make them specifically reactive to emotion-arousing media (Crone & Konijn, 2018).

Cataldo et al. (2021), in their review, examined the usage of social media and the development of psychiatric disorders in late childhood and adolescence. The authors' review examined two neurodevelopmental disorders: autism spectrum disorder and ADHD. The neuro-developmental condition ADHD can be defined by either persistent inattention, hyperactivity, and/or impulsivity. These cognitive traits have been correlated with greater overuse of digital technology (Gul at al., 2018), greater propensities for addictive or compulsive usage relating to digital technology (Settanni et al., 2018), and problematic usage and poorer capacity to change and stop these problematic behaviors relating to digital technology (Choi, 2019) compared with adolescents without ADHD.

Although social media interfere with offline interaction by reducing the investment of time and resources in them while offering a more im-mediate alternative to satisfy social needs, they can also simplify the engagement in social contacts. This feature might be suitable, for instance, for youths with autism spectrum disorders, as they can have difficulties in decoding complex social information (Gwynette et al., 2017; van Schalkwyk et al., 2017). Smartphone-based technologies to assist autism spectrum adolescents can be feasible in both HIC and LMIC (Kumm et al., 2021).

The brain has regions that react to stimuli that are exciting or rewarding, and regions that help planning and impulse control, with both systems working together to help learning. As children and adolescents develop, their brains change and the balance between the reward regions and control regions also changes. These brain changes accompany the behavioral processes of exploration, risk taking, and learning from peers. During these periods of calibration, children and adolescents also find it hard to regulate their behaviors, and this is more evident when among peers. Digital technology can enhance learning by tapping into the balance between rewards and control. However, there are many types of digital technology that may lead to an imbalance in this process and promote unhealthy social interactions and decrease the young person's ability to modulate their impulses online (Magis-Weinberg & Berger, 2020). Research has, for example, indicated dopamine reward pathways in the brain (associated with an increased sense of pleasure that can lead to addiction behavior) to be actively involved in the use of most digital technologies (Han et al., 2011).

The nucleus accumbens (NA) is part of the mesolimbic system, which is dopamine rich, and is involved in reward-based learning (Berridge & Kringelbach, 2013), and in the motivation of goal-oriented behavior (Ikemoto & Panksepp, 1999). It has been implicated in behaviors related to the use of social media, like sharing information (Tamir & Mitchell, 2012) and receiving positive feedback (Davey et al., 2010; Sherman et al., 2016). Sherman et al. (2016) found the NA region to exhibit a robust response when participants received positive feedback on their own posts (i.e., when they viewed their own photos that had accumulated many likes), and also when viewing popular posts from peers. These preliminary results can begin to shed insight into why individuals devote so much time to maintaining social media portfolios, as these platforms provide a constant arena for self-disclosure to wide audiences.

Having considered the neurodevelopmental effects of digital technology use, it is also important to acknowledge differences between sexes in terms of both patterns of use and outcomes.

6. Sex differences in digital technology use and the effects thereof—a culturally shaped phenomenon?

Adolescence brings major life changes, related to biology, psychosocial status, and larger environmental contexts (e.g., moving from primary school to secondary school) (Gilmore & Meersand, 2014). The evolving psychosocial status of adolescents is comprehensive and far-reaching, while also equivocal—they are migrating away from the dependent and controlled environment of childhood but are not yet afforded the autonomy of adulthood (Pettit et al., 2001). Societal norms toward adolescent girls and boys are often different, with gender-biased parenting practices (Varner & Mandara, 2013). Young adolescent girls are often afforded less autonomy than their male counterparts, while expectations of responsibility for them are higher than for boys (Varner & Mandara, 2013). These sex differences, and their significance for successful environmental adjustment, and ultimately for adolescent resilience development, are well documented (Oberle et al., 2010; Werner, 2013).

Culturally shaped values and discourses can specifically impact on the way adolescent girls and boys engage with digital technology, with a larger digital divide between adolescent boys and girls found in LIMC (Tyers-Chowdhury & Binder, 2021). A UNICEF report highlighted that the greatest disparities were in South Asian countries, as well as sub-Saharan Africa, specifically as it pertains to mobile technology access and digital technology usage skills (Johnson, 2021; UNICEF, 2017), with adolescent boys having greater access to digital technology and (because of their increased exposure) higher digital literacy than their female peers (Masanet et al., 2021). This is especially important for the future of adolescent girls in countries where the digital divide is sizable, because increased digital technology adoption is vital for future employment participation (Tyers-Chowdhury & Binder, 2021). Tyers and Banyan Global (2020) call attention to specific factors such as inequitable access to education and specific social norms (e.g., male gatekeepers control access to digital technology to protect female family or community members from the "immorality" or danger associated with Internet and/or digital exposure). All effort should continue to be made to address these factors (Jayachandran, 2015).

Notwithstanding these sociocultural forces, research has shown a decrease in sex-specific differences in adolescent digital technology use in several HIC and LMIC (Drabowicz, 2014; Jayachardran, 2015), emulating a larger societal shift in sex identities and roles (Williams et al., 2009). The differences that do remain point to female digital technology use often linked to information seeking and communication (Chen & Tzeng, 2010), while male digital technology use focuses primarily on entertainment (Lai & Gwung, 2013). Both adolescent girls and adolescent boys spend less time with digital technology as they grow older (Yu & Shek, 2013), while younger adolescent males are more likely to use digital technology excessively, possibly because females report stricter monitoring by their parents than males (Rosen et al., 2008).

Yurdagül et al. (2019) found that problematic Instagram usage in boys was linked to general anxiety, while in girls there was an association with body image dissatisfaction. In general, girls who engage in problematic social media usage seem more prone to developing a negative body image—a risk compounded by misleading social media content (Cataldo et al., 2021). One study conducted in the Netherlands found that a positive mother–adolescent relationship can be a protecting factor against the negative outcomes of social media usage on body image (De Vries et al., 2019).

Adolescents of both sexes may benefit from mindfulness practices to negate the possible adverse outcomes of digital technology overuse and misuse.

7. Mindfulness—a protective factor against problematic digital technology use

Various recent studies show that mindfulness practices and dispositional mindfulness can effectively reduce negative emotional reactions resulting from and/or aggravating psychiatric problems and exposure to stressors among children and adolescents (Clear et al., 2020; Marusak et al., 2018; Perry-Parrish et al., 2016), although some researchers warn that excitement about mindfulness in younger populations may outpace the evidence in favor thereof (Saunders & Kober, 2020). In addition, mindfulness has also been observed to improve resilience in children and adolescents (Arpaci & Gundogan, 2020).

Cásedas et al. (2019) found evidence in support of the enhancing effects of mindfulness meditation on executive control in adults. A study assessing difficulties with executive functioning and mindfulness in children found, similarly, that improvements in executive functions such as response inhibition, working memory, and task shifting were significantly associated with mindfulness practice (Geronimi et al., 2020). Other studies concluded that mindfulness-based interventions can improve self-regulation in adolescents (Felver et al., 2014; Lyons & DeLange, 2016). Marusak et al. (2018) presented novel evidence that, over time, mindfulness in youth is related to functional neural dynamics and interactions between neurocognitive networks.

Although there is still a paucity of evidence demonstrating that mindfulness apps may assist children in improving their mental health (Nunes Castro & Limpo 2020), it seems that mindfulness practices may have an ameliorating effect with regard to problematic digital technology use. One study demonstrated that trait mindfulness moderated the effects of feeling left out on social media—participants with higher levels of mindfulness reported lower levels of psychological distress, negative affect, hostility, and antisocial tendency after receiving little attention on social media (Poon & Jiang, 2020). Another study investigated the moderating role of mindfulness in the relationship between early maladaptive schemas and smartphone addiction and found that as mindfulness increases, the number of schemas related to smartphone addiction decreases (Arpaci, 2019). Similarly, results from multiple regression analyses by Yang et al. (2019) indicate that the associations between mobile phone addiction and both anxiety and depression were moderated by mindfulness. In this study, 470 adolescent students participated and completed a questionnaire comprising measures of childhood emotional abuse, cyberbullying, trait emotional intelligence, and mindfulness. Path analysis showed that trait mindfulness, but not trait emotional intelligence, was a partial mediator between childhood emotional abuse and cyberbullying among the total sample of male and female adolescents. These effects were statistically significant and were indicative of effects confirming other research findings, which have demonstrated the effects of mindfulness-based interventions in reducing aggression and problematic online behaviors that often cooccur with cyberbullying (Yang et al., 2019). Furthermore, findings from another study indicate that mindfulness-based intervention programs for adolescents who have been emotionally abused in childhood may reduce their engagement in cyberbullying (Emirtekin et al., 2019). Yang et al. (2019) examined 1258 adolescents—high school students—measuring their mobile phone addiction, anxiety, depression, and mindfulness. Results from multiple regression analyses indicated that the relationships between mobile phone addiction and both anxiety and depression were moderated by mindfulness. Both anxiety and depression were more severe in adolescents with lower levels of mindfulness.

Increased use of digital technology may relate to decreases in trait mindfulness, where an individual is more likely to use problematic emotion-focused coping strategies (Sriwilai & Charoensukmongkol, 2015). Roberts (2018) notes various considerations in her paper "Mindfulness in the social media age." Firstly, children need to understand the meaning of their digital footprint. This means many social media posts remain online, accumulate, and can be considered permanent. Their immediate social media posts all have potential future consequences for them. Secondly, children and teenagers need to learn how to be more discriminatory of information they read, watch, or experience online. Much of it may not be true and could be intentionally misleading or false. Finally, parents/caregivers need to model digital life skills to their children. They must take time to know and understand why children seek out digital technology as forms of social communication and bonding. Then they must also engage openly with them and demonstrate an understanding as well as model behaviors that demonstrate healthy patterns of use of digital technology.

While mindfulness can thus be a protective factor against problematic digital technology use, digital technology can also be used to enhance mindfulness.

8. Achieving mindfulness through digital technology

Donovan et al. (2016) suggest that a mobile app may be a practical way to widely distribute a mindfulness program among adolescents. One study showed a brief mindfulness app intervention to reduce rumination, worry, and anxiety in adolescents (Hilt & Swords, 2021). In a review of mindfulness-based apps for children, Nunes et al. (2020) found that while such apps are becoming increasingly popular, there is room for improvement in their quality. Recent research suggests that wearable neurofeedback devices may improve mindfulness practices (Balconi et al., 2019). The authors observed decreased stress and anxiety measures, decreased mental fatigue, and increased vigor in participants who made use of technology-mediated mindfulness practices.

It can be demonstrated that mindfulness interventions delivered through online platforms can boost resilience (Joyce et al., 2018). Mindfulness as a means of boosting resilience has been observed to negatively predict Internet addiction (Arslan & Coşkun, 2021). Reducing social isolation and building healthy connection, as well as developing effective and healthy intrapersonal coping strategies, are key components of adaptability to stress and factors of resilience (Arslan & Coşkun, 2021; Poon & Jiang, 2020; Sriwilai & Charoensukmongkol, 2015). Mindfulness practice may have potent effects in reducing feelings of isolation and being left out online (Poon & Jiang, 2020) as well as mediating the role of rumination as a problematic cognitive process contributing to poor stress management and coping (Hong et al., 2021, pp. 282−287).

It may be important to note that, of the many advances in technology, virtual reality (VR) may still be set to be the new reality in which many children and adolescents engage with digital technology (Perry & Singh, 2016). As VR is becoming increasingly accessible and potentially more appealing to adolescents, there is some evidence to suggest that VR as a means of mindfulness delivery may be as effective as cellphone-based or other digital media−based mindfulness applications (Seabrook et al., 2020; Wren et al., 2021). Besides the possible uses of VR as a delivery medium for mindfulness, there are numerous other applications of VR technology, such as indicated by Chavez et al. (2020) who used VR to assess adolescents' experiences of being homeless and Farič et al. (2019) who examined VR as a means of increasing physical activity of youth to improve mental and physical health and well-being. VR may be a means of boosting resilience in youth, through mindfulness applications delivered through VR, yet we know very little of the (long term) mental health and social effects that VR may have on children and adolescents.

9. Conclusion

In his 1985 book, *Amusing ourselves to death,* Neil Postman juxtaposes the futurist doctrines of Dystopian novelists Aldous Huxley and George Orwell (Postman, 1985). He points out that Orwell feared information deprivation, while Huxley's concern was an overload of information leading to passivity and egotism. Orwell envisaged a future where people would be controlled by pain, while Huxley felt that society would be controlled by an obsessive urge for pleasure. In today's digital technology—saturated society, neither Huxley nor Orwell might have been right—a concern echoed by a plethora of published research (e.g., Judi et al., 2013; O'Keeffe & Clarke-Pearson, 2011). While excessive and problematic digital technology use has been shown to have dire consequences, resilience enhancement is associated with moderate digital technology use (Li et al., 2010). The mediating effect of mindfulness practices on digital technology overuse/misuse and the potential of digital technology to increase mindfulness seems to be promising, although further research in this regard is necessary.

References

Ahiauzu, L. U., & Odili, S. O. (2012). The Influence of information and communication technologies (ICTs) on parents/adolescents relationship. *Mediterranean Journal of Social Sciences, 3*(13), 127–136. https://doi.org/10.5901/mjss.2012.v3n13p127

Ahn, J. (2011). The effect of social network sites on adolescents' social and academic development: Current theories and controversies. *Journal of the American Society for Information Science and Technology, 62*(8), 1435–1445. https://doi.org/10.1002/asi.21540

Allen, K. A., Ryan, T., Gray, D. L., McInerney, D. M., & Waters, L. (2014). Social media use and social connectedness in adolescents: The positives and the potential pitfalls. *The Australian Educational and Developmental Psychologist, 31*(1), 18–31. https://doi.org/10.1017/edp.2014.2

Amichai-Hamburger, Y., & Hayat, Z. (2011). The impact of the internet on the social lives of users: A representative sample from 13 countries. *Computers in Human Behavior, 27*(1), 585–589.

Anderson, A. R., Christenson, S. L., Sinclair, M. F., & Lehr, C. A. (2004). Check & connect: The importance of relationships for promoting engagement with school. *Journal of School Psychology, 42*(2), 95–113.

Arnett, J. J. (2014). Chapter 4: Identity development from adolescence to emerging adulthood: What we know and (especially) don't know. In K. C. McLean, & M. Syed (Eds.), *The Oxford Handbook of identity development* (pp. 53–64). Oxford, UK: Oxford University Press.

Arpaci, I. (2019). Relationships between early maladaptive schemas and smartphone addiction: The moderating role of mindfulness. *International Journal of Mental Health and Addiction.* https://doi.org/10.1007/s11469-019-00186-y

Arpaci, I., & Gundogan, S. (2020). Mediating role of psychological resilience in the relationship between mindfulness and nomophobia. *British Journal of Guidance & Counselling.* https://doi.org/10.1080/03069885.2020.1856330

Arslan, G., & Coşkun, M. (2021). Social exclusion, self-forgiveness, mindfulness, and internet addiction in college students: A moderated mediation approach. *International Journal of Mental Health and Addiction*, 1–15. https://doi.org/10.1007/s11469-021-00506-1

Bailin, A., Milanaik, R., & Adesman, A. (2014). Health implication of new age technologies for adolescents: A review of the research. *Current Opinion in Pediatrics, 26*(5), 605–619. https://doi.org/10.1097/MOP.0000000000000140

Balconi, M., Fronda, G., & Crivelli, D. (2019). Effects of technology-mediated mindfulness practice on stress: Psychophysiological and self-report measures. *Stress, 22*(2), 200–209. https://doi.org/10.1080/10253890.2018.1531845

Banaji, S., Livinstone, S., Nandi, A., & Stoilova, M. (2017). Instrumentalising the digital: Findings from a rapid evidence review of development interventions to support adolescents' engagement with ICTs in low and middle income countries. *Development in Practice.* https://doi.org/10.1080/09614524.2018.1438366. ISSN 0961-4524.

Bandura, A. (1993). Perceived self-efficacy in cognitive development and functioning. *Educational Psychologist, 28*(2), 117–148.

Barber, B. K., & Schluterman, J. M. (2008). Connectedness in the lives of children and adolescents: A call for greater conceptual clarity. *Journal of Adolescent Health, 43*(3), 209–216.

Belanger, R. E., Akre, C., Berchtold, A., & Michaud, P. A. (2011). A u-shaped association between intensity of internet use and adolescent health. *Pediatrics, 127*(2), e330–e335.

Berners-Lee, T. (2000). *Weaving the Web*. New York, NY: Harper Collins.

Berridge, K., & Kringelbach, M. (2013). Neuroscience of affect: Brain mechanisms of pleasure and displeasure. *Current Opinion in Neurobiology, 23*(3), 294–303. https://doi.org/10.1016/j.conb.2013.01.017

Binkley, M., Erstad, O., Herman, J., Raizen, S., Ripley, M., Miller-Ricci, M., & Rumble, M. (2012). Defining twenty-first century skills. In P. Griffin, B. McGaw, & E. Care (Eds.), *Assessment and teaching of 21st century skills* (pp. 17–66). Dordrecht: Springer.

Blair, B. L., & Fletcher, A. C. (2011). "The only 13-year-old on Planet Earth without a cell phone": Meanings of cell phones in early adolescents' everyday lives. *Journal of Adolescent Research, 26*(2), 155–177.

Blakemore, S. J. (2012). Development of the social brain in adolescence. *Journal of the Royal Society of Medicine, 105*(3), 111–116.

Blignaut, S., & Els, C. (2010). Towards a research framework for ICT use in developing contexts. *Journal of Systemics, Cybernetics & Informatics, 8*(1), 25–33.

Bonetti, L., Campbell, M. A., & Gilmore, L. (2010). The relationship of loneliness and social anxiety with children's and adolescents' online communication. *Cyberpsychology, Behavior, and Social Networking, 13*(3), 279–285.

Bronfenbrenner, U. (2005). *Making human beings human: Bioecological perspectives of human development*. Thousand Oaks, CA: Sage.

Bronfenbrenner, U., & Morris, P. A. (2006). The bio-ecological model of human development. In W. Damon, & R. M. Lerner (Eds.), *Handbook of child psychology: Vol: 1. Theoretical models of human development* (pp. 793–828). Hoboken, NJ: Wiley.

Brown, T. M. (2014). "I just want to work hard": Self-efficacy and the social contexts in adolescents' ICT use. *Youth and Society, 46*(6), 853–874. https://doi.org/10.1177/0044118X12455026

Brownlee, K., Rawana, J., Franks, J., Harper, J., Bajwa, J., O'Brien, E., & Clarkson, A. (2013). A systematic review of strengths and resilience outcome literature relevant to children and adolescents. *Child and Adolescent Social Work Journal, 30*(5), 435–459. https://doi.org/10.1007/s10560-013-0301-9

Buda, G., Lukoševičiūtė, J., Šalčiūnaitė, L., & Šmigelskas, K. (2020). Possible effects of social media use on adolescent health behaviors and perceptions. *Psychological Reports, 124*(3), 1031–1048. https://doi.org/10.1177/0033294120922481

Calvert, S. L., & Wartella, E. A. (2014). Children and electronic media. In E. T. Gershoff, R. S. Mistry, & D. A. Crosby (Eds.), *Societal contexts of child development: Pathways of influence and implications for practice and policy* (pp. 175–187). New York, NY: Oxford University Press.

Campbell, R. (2006). Teenage girls and cellular phones: Discourses of independence, safety and "rebellion". *Journal of Youth Studies, 9*(2), 195–212.

Carr, N. (2010). *The shallows: What the internet is doing to our brains.* New York, NY: W.W. Norton & Company.

Cásedas, L., Pirruccio, V., Vadillo, M. A., & Lupiáñez, J. (2019). Does mindfulness meditation training enhance executive control? A systematic review and meta-analysis of randomized controlled trials in adults. *Mindfulness, 11*, 411–424. https://doi.org/10.1007/s12671-019-01279-4

Cataldo, I., Lepri, B., Neoh, M. J. Y., & Esposito, G. (2021). Social media usage and development of psychiatric disorders in childhood and adolescence: A review. *Frontiers in Psychiatry, 11*, 508595. https://doi.org/10.3389/fpsyt.2020.508595

Chassiakos, Y. L. R., Radesky, J., Christakis, D., Moreno, M. A., Cross, C., & Council on Communications and Media. (2016). Children and adolescents and digital media. *The Official Journal of the Academy of Pediatrics, 138*(5), e20162593. https://doi.org/10.1542/peds.2016-2593

Chatfield, T. (2012). *How to thrive in the digital age.* London, UK: Macmillan.

Chavez, L. J., Kelleher, K., Slesnick, N., Holowacz, E., Luthy, E., Moore, L., & Ford, J. (2020). Virtual reality meditation among youth experiencing homelessness: Pilot randomized controlled trial of feasibility. *JMIR Mental Health, 7*(9), e18244. https://doi.org/10.2196/18244

Chen, S. Y., & Tzeng, J. Y. (2010). College female and male heavy internet users' profiles of practices and their academic grades and psychosocial adjustment. *Cyberpsychology, Behavior, and Social Networking, 13*(3), 257–262.

Choi, B. Y., Huh, S., Kim, D. J., Suh, S. W., Lee, S. K., & Potenza, M. N. (2019). Transitions in problematic internet use: A one-year longitudinal study of boys. *Psychiatry Investigation, 16*, 433–442. https://doi.org/10.30773/pi.2019.04.02.1

Choi, K., Son, H., Park, M., Han, J., Kim, K., Lee, B., & Gwak, H. (2009). Internet overuse and excessive daytime sleepiness in adolescents. *Psychiatry and Clinical Neurosciences, 63*(4), 455–462. https://doi.org/10.1111/j.1440-1819.2009.01925.x

Clear, S. J., Zimmer-Gembeck, M. J., Duffy, A. L., & Barber, B. L. (2020). Internalizing symptoms and loneliness: Direct effects of mindfulness and protection against the negative effects of peer victimization and exclusion. *International Journal of Behavioral Development, 44*(1), 51–61. https://doi.org/10.1177/0165025419876358

Colasante, T., Lin, L., De France, K., & Hollenstein, T. (2020). *Any time and place? Digital emotional support for digital natives.* American Psychologist. Advance online publication. https://doi.org/10.1037/amp0000708

Crisp, B. R. (2010). Belonging, connectedness and social exclusion. *Journal of Social Inclusion, 1*(2), 123–132.

Crone, E. A., & Konijn, E. A. (2018). Media use and brain development during adolescence. *Nature Communications, 9*, 588. https://doi.org/10.1038/s41467-018-03126-x

Davey, C., et al. (2010). Being liked activates primary reward and midline self-related brain regions. *Human Brain Mapping, 31*(4), 660–668. https://doi.org/10.1002/hbm.20895

Davis, K., Charmaraman, L., & Weinstein, E. (2020). Introduction to special issue: Adolescent and emerging adult development in an age of social media. *Journal of Adolescent Research, 35*(1), 3–15. https://doi.org/10.1177/0743558419886392

Dienlin, T., & Johannes, N. (2020). The impact of digital technology use on adolescent wellbeing. *Dialogues in Clinical Neuroscience, 22*(2), 135–142. https://doi.org/10.31887/DCNS.2020.22.2/tdienlin

Donovan, E., Rodgers, R. F., Cousineau, T. M., McGowan, K. M., Luk, S., Yates, K., & Franko, D. L. (2016). Brief report: Feasibility of a mindfulness and self-compassion based mobile intervention for adolescents. *Journal of Adolescence, 53*, 217–221. https://doi.org/10.1016/j.adolescence.2016.09.009

Drabowicz, T. (2014). Gender and digital usage inequality among adolescents: A comparative study of 39 countries. *Computers and Education, 74*, 98–111.

Duran, R. L., Kelly, L., & Rotaru, T. (2011). Mobile phones in romantic relationships and the dialectic of autonomy versus connection. *Communication Quarterly, 59*(1), 19–36.

Dwyer, D. S., Kreier, R., & Sanmartin, M. X. (2020). Technology use: Too much of a good thing? *Atlantic Economic Journal, 48*, 475–489. https://doi.org/10.1007/s11293-020-09683-1

Emirtekin, E., Balta, S., Kircaburun, K., & Griffiths, M. D. (2019). Childhood emotional abuse and cyberbullying perpetration among adolescents: The mediating role of trait mindfulness. *International Journal of Mental Health and Addiction, 18*, 1548–1559. https://doi.org/10.1007/s11469-019-0055-5

Endestad, T., Heim, J., Kaare, B., Torgersen, L., & Brandtzæg, P. B. (2011). Media user types among young children and social displacement. *Nordicom Review, 32*(1), 17–30.

Erikson, E. H. (1968). *Identity, youth and crisis*. New York, NY: W.W. Norton.

Erol, R. Y., & Orth, U. (2011). Self-esteem development from age 14 to 30 years: A longitudinal study. *Journal of Personality and Social Psychology, 101*(3), 607–619. https://doi.org/10.1037/a0024299

Farič, N., Yorke, E., Varnes, L., Newby, K., Potts, H. W., Smith, L., Hon, A., Steptoe, A., & Fisher, A. (2019). Younger adolescents' perceptions of physical activity, exergaming, and virtual reality: Qualitative intervention development study. *JMIR Serious Games, 7*(2), e11960. https://doi.org/10.2196/11960

Felver, J. C., Tipsord, J. M., Morris, M. J., Racer, K. H., & Dishion, T. J. (2014). The effects of mindfulness-based intervention on children's attention regulation. *Journal of Attention Disorders*, 1–10. https://doi.org/10.1177/1087054714548032

Friedman, R., & Chase-Lansdale, P. L. (2003). Chronic adversities. In M. Rutter, & E. Taylor (Eds.), *Child and adolescent psychiatry* (4th ed., pp. 261–276). Malden, Massachusetts: Blackwell Science.

Geronimi, E. M. C., Arellano, B., & Woodruff-Borden, J. (2020). Relating mindfulness and executive function in children. *Clinical Child Psychology and Psychiatry, 25*(2), 435–445. https://doi.org/10.1177/1359104519833737

Ghassemzadeh, L., Shahraray, M., & Moradi, A. (2008). Prevalence of Internet addiction and comparison of Internet addicts and non-addicts in Iranian high schools. *CyberPsychology & Behavior, 11*(6), 731–733.

Gilmore, K., & Meersand, P. (2014). Normal child and adolescent development. In R. E. Hales, S. C. Yudofsky, & L. W. Roberts (Eds.), *The American psychiatric publishing textbook of psychiatry* (6th ed., pp. 139–174). Arlington, VA: American Psychiatric Publishing, Inc.

Gross, E. F., Juvonen, J., & Gable, S. L. (2002). Internet use and well-being in adolescence. *Journal of Social Issues, 58*(1), 75–98.

Gul, H., Yurumez Solmaz, E., Gul, A., & Onder, O. (2018). Facebook overuse and addiction among Turkish adolescents: Are ADHD and ADHD-related problems risk factors? *Psychiatry and Clinical Psychopharmacology, 28*, 80–90. https://doi.org/10.1080/24750573.2017.1383706

Gwynette, M. F., Morriss, D., Warren, N., Truelove, J., Warthen, J., Ross, C. P., Mood, G., Snook, C. A., & Borckardt, J. (2017). Social skills training for adolescents with autism spectrum disorder using facebook (project rex connect): A survey study. *JMIR Mental Health, 4*, e4. https://doi.org/10.2196/mental.6605

Han, D. H., Bolo, N., Daniels, M. A., Arenella, L., Lyoo, I. K., & Renshaw, P. F. (2011). Brain activity and desire for internet video game play. *Comprehensive Psychiatry, 52*, 88—95.

Hardy, L. L., Denney-Wilson, E., Thrift, A. P., Okely, A. D., & Baur, L. A. (2010). Screen time and metabolic risk factors among adolescents. *Archives of Pediatrics and Adolescent Medicine, 164*(7), 643—649.

Hawi, N. S. (2012). Internet addiction among adolescent in Lebanon. *Computers in Human Behavior, 28*, 1044—1053. https://doi.org/10.1016/j.chb. 2012.01.007

Hilt, L. M., & Swords, C. M. (2021). Acceptability and preliminary effects of a mindfulness mobile application for ruminative adolescents. *Behavior Therapy.* https://doi.org/10.1016/j.beth.2021.03.004

Hoge, E., Bickham, D., & Cantor, J. (2017). Digital media, anxiety, and depression in children. *Pediatrics, 140*(s2), S76. https://doi.org/10.1542/peds.2016-1758G

Holtz, P., & Appel, M. (2011). Internet use and video gaming predict problem behavior in early adolescence. *Journal of Adolescence, 34*, 49—58.

Hong, W., Liu, R. D., Ding, Y., Fu, X., Zhen, R., & Sheng. (2021). *Cyberpsychology, behavior, and social networking.* https://doi.org/10.1089/cyber.2020.0387

Hong, S. B., Zalesky, A., Cocchi, L., Fornito, A., Choi, E. J., Kim, H. H., ... Yi, S. H. (2013). Decreased functional brain connectivity in adolescents with internet addiction. *PloS One, 8*(2), e57831. https://doi.org/10.1371/journal.pone. 0057831

Huang, C. (2010). Internet use and psychological well-being: A meta-analysis. *Cyberpsychology, Behavior, and Social Networking, 13*(3), 241—249.

Ikemoto, S., & Panksepp, J. (1999). The role of nucleus accumbens dopamine in motivated behavior: A unifying interpretation with special reference to reward-seeking. *Brain Research. Brain Research Reviews, 31*(1), 6—41.

Jackson, L. A., von Eye, A., Fitzgerald, H. E., Witt, E. A., & Zhao, Y. (2011). Internet use, video-game playing and cell phone use as predictors of children's body mass index (BMI), body weight, academic performance, and social and overall self-esteem. *Computers in Human Behavior, 27*, 599—604.

Jayachandran, S. (2015). The roots of gender inequality in developing countries. *Annual Review of Economics, 7*, 63—88. https://doi.org/10.1146/annurev-economics-080614-115404

Johnson, G. M. (2006). Internet use and cognitive development: A theoretical framework. *E-learning, 4*, 565—573.

Johnson, G. M. (2010a). Internet use and child development: The techno-microsystem. *Australian Journal of Educational & Developmental Psychology, 10*, 32—43.

Johnson, G. M. (2010b). Internet use and child development: Validation of the ecological techno-subsystem. *Educational Technology & Society, 13*(1), 176—185.

Johnson, A. (2021). *Human rights and the gender digital divide in Africa's COVID-19 era.* GC Human Rights Preparedness. https://gchumanrights.org/preparedness/article-on/human-rights-and-the-gender-digital-divide-in-africas-covid-19-era.html.

Johnson, G. M., & Puplampu, P. (2008). A conceptual framework for understanding the effect of the internet on child development: The ecological techno-subsystem. *Canadian Journal of Learning and Technology, 34*(1), 19—28.

Joyce, S., Shand, F., Bryant, R. A., Lal, T. J., & Harvey, S. B. (2018). Mindfulness-based resilience training in the workplace: Pilot study of the internet-based Resilience@Work (RAW) mindfulness program. *Journal of Medical Internet Research, 20*(9). https://doi.org/10.2196/10326

Judi, H. M., Ashaari, N., Zin, N. A. M., & Yusof, Z. M. (2013). Framework of ICT impact on adolescent. *Procedia Technology, 11*, 1034—1040.

Kaess, M., Durkee, T., Brunner, R., Carli, V., Parzer, P., Wasserman, C., ... Wasserman, D. (2014). Pathological internet use among European adolescents: Psychopathology and self-destructive behaviours. *European Child and Adolescent Psychiatry, 23*(1), 1093—1102. https://doi.org/10.1007/s00787-014-0562-7

Karlsen, J. E., Gual, A., & Anderson, P. (2013). Foresighting addiction and lifestyles in Europe 2030+. *European Journal of Futures Research, 1*(1), 1–10.

Keating, D. P. (2012). Cognitive and brain development in adolescence. *Enfance, 3,* 267–279. https://doi.org/10.4074/S0013754512003035

Koo, H. J., & Kwon, J. H. (2014). Risk and protective factors of internet addiction: A meta-analysis of empirical studies in Korea. *Yonsei Medical Journal, 55*(6), 1691–1711.

Kross, E., Verduyn, P., Demiralp, E., Park, J., Lee, D. S., Lin, N., Shablack, H., Jonides, J., & Ybarra, O. (2013). Facebook use predicts declines in subjective well-being in young adults. *PLoS ONE, 8,* e69841. https://doi.org/10.1371/journal.pone.0069841

Kumm, A. J., Viljoen, M., & de Vries, P. J. (2021). The digital divide in technologies for autism: Feasibility considerations for low- and middle-income countries. *Journal of Autism and Developmental Disorders.* https://doi.org/10.1007/s10803-021-05084-8

Lai, C.-H., & Gwung, H.-L. (2013). The effect of gender and internet usage on physical and cyber interpersonal relationships. *Computers and Education, 69,* 303–309.

Lai, C. H., Lin, C. Y., Chen, C. H., Gwung, H. L., & Li, C. H. (2013). Can internet usage positively or negatively affect interpersonal relationship?. In *Advances in intelligent systems and applications: Volume 1* (pp. 373–382). Berlin: Springer.

Lakey, B., & Orehek, E. (2011). Relational regulation theory: A new approach to explain the link between perceived social support and mental health. *Psychological Review, 118*(3), 482.

Lanigan, J. D. (2009). A sociotechnological model for family research and intervention: How information and communication technologies affect family life. *Journal of Marriage & Family Review, 45,* 587–609. https://doi.org/10.1080/01494920903224194

Li, X., Shi, M., Wang, Z., Shi, K., Yang, R., & Yang, C. (August 2010). Resilience as a predictor of internet addiction: The mediation effects of perceived class climate and alienation. In *Web society (SWS), 2010 IEEE 2nd symposium on* (pp. 66–70). IEEE. https://doi.org/10.1109/SWS.2010.5607478

Liu, L., & Cheng, L. (2018). The relationship between self-efficacy and achievement motivation in adolescents: A moderated mediating model of self-identity and hope. *Psychology and Behavioral Sciences, 7*(3), 69–76. https://doi.org/10.11648/j.pbs.20180703.15

Livingstone, S., Carr, J., & Byrne, J. (2015). *One in three: Internet governance and children's rights. Report no. 2016-01, January 2016.* Florence, Italy: UNICEF Office of Research—Innocenti.

Louw, D., & Louw, A. (2007). *Child and adolescent development. Bloemfontein.* South Africa: Psychology Publications.

Luszczynska, A., Gutierrez-Dona, B., & Schwarzer, R. (2005). General self-efficacy in various domains of human functioning: Evidence from five countries. *International Journal of Psychology, 40*(2), 80–89.

Luthar, S. S., Cicchetti, D., & Becker, B. (2000). The construct of resilience: A critical evaluation and guidelines for future work. *Child Development, 71*(3), 543–562.

Lynch, J. G. (2012). *Perceived stress and the buffering hypothesis of perceived social support on Facebook.* Los Angeles, CA: Antioch University (Unpublished doctoral dissertation).

Lyons, K. E., & DeLange, J. (2016). Mindfulness matters in the classroom: The effects of mindfulness training on brain development and behavior in children and adolescents. In K. A. Schonert-Reichl, & R. W. Roeser (Eds.), *Mindfulness in behavioral health. Handbook of mindfulness in education: Integrating theory and research into practice* (pp. 271–283). Springer-Verlag Publishing. https://doi.org/10.1007/978-1-4939-3506-2_17

Magis-Weinberg, L., & Berger, E. (2020). Mind games: Technology and the developing teenage brain. *Frontiers for Young Minds, 8,* 76. https://doi.org/10.3389/frym.2020.00076

Ma, H. K., Li, S. C., & Pow, J. W. C. (2011). The relation of internet use to prosocial and anti-social behavior in Chinese adolescents. *Cyberpsychology, Behavior, and Social Networking, 14*(3), 123–130.

Mantilla, A., & Edwards, S. (2019). Digital technology use by and with young children: A systematic review for the statement on young children and digital technologies. *Australasian Journal of Early Childhood, 44*(2), 182−195. https://doi.org/10.1177/1836939119832744

Mao, J., Xie, J., & Wang, J. (2021). A review of researches on the intervention of problematic social media use (PSMU) by adolescent. *Advances in Social Science, Education and Humanities Research, 551*, 100−103.

Marusak, H. A., Elrahal, F., Peters, C. A., Kundu, P., Lombardo, M. V., Calhoun, V. D., Goldberg, E. K., Cohen, C., Taub, J. W., & Rabinak, C. A. (2018). Mindfulness and dynamic functional neural connectivity in children and adolescents. *Behavioral Brain Research, 336*, 211−218. https://doi.org/10.1016/j.bbr.2017.09.010

Masanet, M. J., Pires, F., & Gomez-Puertas, L. (2021). The risks of the gender digital divide among teenagers. *El Profesional de la Informacion, 30*(1), 1−15.

Masten, A. S., Burt, K. B., & Coatsworth, J. D. (2006). Competence and psychopathology in development. In D. Cicchetti, & D. Cohen (Eds.), *Handbook of developmental psychopathology* (2nd ed.,, *3* pp. 696−738). New York, NY: Wiley.

McLuhan, M. (1964). *Understanding media: The extensions of man*. London, UK: Routledge.

Meerkerk, G. J., Van den Eijnden, R. J., Vermulst, A. A., & Garretsen, H. F. (2009). The compulsive internet use scale (CIUS): Some psychometric properties. *CyberPsychology & Behavior, 12*(1), 1−6.

Mei, X., Zhou, Q., Li, X., Jing, P., Wang, X., & Hu, Z. (2018). Sleep problems in excessive technology use among adolescent: A systemic review and meta-analysis. *Sleep Science and Practice, 2*(10), 1−10. https://doi.org/10.1186/s41606-018-0028-9

Mihajlov, M., & Vejmelka, L. (2017). Internet addiction: A review of the first twenty years. *Psychiatria Danubina, 29*(3), 260−272. https://doi.org/10.24869/psyd.2017.260

Mills, K. L. (2014). Effects of internet use on the adolescent brain: Despite popular claims, experimental evidence remains scarce. *Trends in Cognitive Sciences, 18*(8), 385−387.

Misra, S., Cheng, L., Genevie, J., & Yuan, M. (2014). The iPhone effect: The quality of in-person social interactions in the presence of mobile devices. *Environment and Behavior*, 1−24. https://doi.org/10.1177/0013916514539755

Montag, C., & Elhai, J. D. (2020). Discussing digital technology overuse in children and adolescents during the COVID-19 pandemic and beyond: On the importance of considering affective neuroscience theory. *Addictive Behaviors Reports, 12*, 1−4. https://doi.org/10.1016/j.abrep.2020.100313

Moreno, M. A., Jelenchick, L. A., & Christakis, D. A. (2013). Problematic internet use among older adolescents: A conceptual framework. *Computers in Human Behavior, 29*, 1879−1887.

Nelson, J. J., & Pieper, C. M. (2020). Who's an iAddict? A sociodemographic exploration of device addiction among American adults. *Social Science Quarterly, 101*(5), 2071−2084. https://doi.org/10.1111/ssqu.12833

Niu, G. F., Luo, Y. J., Sun, X. J., Zhou, Z. K., Yu, F., Yang, S. L., & Zhao, L. (2018). Qzone use and depression among Chinese adolescents: A moderated mediation model. *Journal of Affective Disorders, 231*, 58−62. https://doi.org/10.1016/j.jad.2018.01.013

Nunes, A., Castro, S. L., & Limpo, T. (2020). A review of mindfulness-based apps for children. *Mindfulness, 11*, 2089−2101. https://doi.org/10.1007/s12671-020-01410-w

O'Keeffe, G. S., & Clarke-Pearson, K. (2011). The impact of social media on children, adolescents, and families. *Pediatrics, 127*(4), 800−804.

Oberle, E., Schonert-Reichl, K. A., & Thomson, K. C. (2010). Understanding the link between social and emotional well-being and peer relations in early adolescence: Gender-specific predictors of peer acceptance. *Journal of Youth and Adolescence, 39*(11), 1330−1342.

Odgers, C. L. (2018). Smartphones are bad for some adolescents, not all. *Nature, 554*(7693), 432−434. https://doi.org/10.1038/d41586-018-02109-8

Odgers, C. L., & Jensen, M. R. (2020). Annual research review: Adolescent mental health in the digital age: Facts, fears, and future directions. *Journal of Child Psychology and Psychiatry, 61*(3), 336–348. https://doi.org/10.1111/jcpp.13190

Odgers, C. L., Schueller, S. M., & Ito, M. (2020). Screen time, social media use, and adolescent development. *Annual Review of Developmental Psychology, 2*, 485–502. https://doi.org/10.1146/annurev-devpsych-121318-084815

Orben, A. (2020). Teenagers, screens and social media: A narrative review of reviews and key studies. *Social Psychiatry and Psychiatric Epidemiology, 55*, 407–414. https://doi.org/10.1007/s00127-019-01825-4

Øverby, N. C., Klepp, K. I., & Bere, E. (2013). Changes in screen time activity in Norwegian children from 2001 to 2008: Two cross sectional studies. *BMC Public Health, 13*(1), 80.

Padilla-Walker, L. M., Fraser, A. M., Black, B. B., & Bean, R. A. (2014). Associations between friendship, sympathy, and prosocial behavior toward friends. *Journal of Research on Adolescence*. https://doi.org/10.1111/jora.12108

Palfrey, J., & Gasser, U. (2008). *Born digital: Understanding the first generation of digital natives*. New York, NY: Basic Books.

Park, A., Clery, E., Curtice, J., Phillips, M., & Utting, D. (Eds.). (2012). *British social attitudes*. London: Sage Publications.

Paudel, S., Jancey, J., Subedi, N., & Leavy, J. (2017). Correlates of mobile screen media use among children aged 0–8: A systematic review. *British Medical Journal Open, 7*, e014585. https://doi.org/10.1136/bmjopen-2016-014585

Perry-Parrish, C., Copeland-Linder, N., Webb, L., Shields, A. H., & Sibinga, E. M. S. (2016). Improving self-regulation in adolescents: Current evidence for the role of mindfulness-based cognitive therapy. *Adolescent Health, Medicine and Therapeutics, 7*, 101–108.

Perry, B., & Singh, S. (2016). A virtual reality: Technology's impact on youth mental health. *Indian Journal of Social Psychiatry, 32*. https://doi.org/10.4103/0971-9962.193190

Pettit, G. S., Laird, R. D., Dodge, K. A., Bates, J. E., & Criss, M. M. (2001). Antecedents and behavior-problem outcomes of parental monitoring and psychological control in early adolescence. *Child Development, 72*, 583–598. https://doi.org/10.1111/1467- 8624.00298

Piaget, J. (1964). Part I: Cognitive development in children: Piaget development and learning. *Journal of Research in Science Teaching, 2*(3), 176–186.

Poon, K.-T., & Jiang, Y. (2020). Getting less likes on social media: Mindfulness ameliorates the detrimental effects of feeling left out online. *Mindfulness, 11*, 1038–1048. https://doi.org/10.1007/s12671-020-01313-w

Postman, N. (1985). *Amusing ourselves to death: Public discourse in the age of show business*. London, UK: Penguin Books.

Prince-Embury, S., & Saklofske, D. H. (Eds.). (2013). *Resilience in children, adolescents, and adults: Translating research into practice*. New York, NY: Springer.

Prinstein, M. J., Nesi, J., & Telzer, E. H. (2020). Commentary: An updated agenda for the study of digital media use and adolescent development—future directions following Odgers & Jensen (2020). *Journal of Child Psychology and Psychiatry, 61*(3), 349–352. https://doi.org/10.1111/jcpp.13190

Rideout, V. (2015). *The common sense census: Media use by tweens and teens*. Los Angeles, CA: Common Sense Media.

Roberts, F. C. (2018). Mindfulness in the social media age. *Proceedings (Baylor University. Medical Center), 31*(2), 250–252. https://doi.org/10.1080/08998280.2018.1441474

Rodriguez-Garcia, A.-M., & Moreno-Guerrero, A.-J. (2019). Nomophobia: An individual's growing fear of being without a smartphone—a systematic literature review. *International Journal of Environmental Research and Public Health, 17*, 580–598. https://doi.org/10.3390/ijerph17020580

Rosen, L. D. (2012). *iDisorder: understanding our obsession with technology and overcoming is hold on us*. New York, NY: Palgrave MacMillan.

Rosen, L. D., Cheever, N. A., & Carrier, L. M. (2008). The association of parenting style and child age with parental limit setting and adolescent MySpace behavior. *Journal of Applied Developmental Psychology, 29*(6), 459–471.

Rutter, M., & Taylor, E. (2003). *Child and adolescent psychiatry* (4th ed.). Malden, MA: Blackwell Science.

Saunders, D., & Kober, H. (2020). Mindfulness-based intervention development for children and adolescents. *Mindfulness, 11,* 1868–1883. https://doi.org/10.1007/s12671-020-01360-3

Schiffrin, H., Edelman, A., Falkenstern, M., & Stewart, C. (2010). The associations among computer-mediated communication, relationships, and well-being. *Cyberpsychology, Behavior, and Social Networking, 13*(3), 299–306.

Schiliro, F., & Choo, K. K.-R. (2017). Chapter 5: The role of mobile devices in enhancing the policing system to improve efficiency and effectiveness: A practitioner's perspective. In M. H. Au, & K.-K. R. Choo (Eds.), *Mobile security and privacy* (pp. 85–99). Rockland, MA: Syngress Publishing.

Schofield-Clark, L. (2005). The constant contact generation: Exploring teen friendship networks online. In S. R. Mazzarella (Ed.), *Girl wide web: Girls, the internet and the negotiation of identity* (pp. 203–221). New York, NY: Peter Lang.

Seabrook, E., Kelly, R., Foley, F., Theiler, S., Thomas, N., Wadley, G., & Nedeljkovic, M. (2020). Understanding how virtual reality can support mindfulness practice: Mixed methods study. *Journal of Medical Internet Research, 22*(3), e16106. https://doi.org/10.2196/16106

Settanni, M., Marengo, D., Fabris, M. A., & Longobardi, C. (2018). The interplay between ADHD symptoms and time perspective in addictive social media use: A study on adolescent facebook users. *Children and Youth Services Review, 89,* 165–170. https://doi.org/10.1016/j.childyouth.2018.04.031

Shank, D. B., & Cotten, S. R. (2014). Does technology empower urban youth? The relationship of technology use to self-efficacy. *Computers & Education, 70,* 184–193. https://doi.org/10.1016/j.compedu.2013.08.018

Shapira, N. A., Goldsmith, T. D., Keck, P. E., Khosla, U. M., & McElroy, S. L. (2000). Psychiatric features of individuals with problematic internet use. *Journal of Affective Disorders, 57*(1–3), 267–272.

Shapiro, L. A. S., & Margolin, G. (2014). Growing up wired: Social networking sites and adolescent psychosocial development. *Clinical Child and Family Psychology Review, 17*(1), 1–18.

Shapka, J. D. (2018). Adolescent technology engagement: It is more complicated than a lack of self-control. *Human Behavior and Emerging Technologies, 1*(2), 103–110. https://doi.org/10.1002/hbe2.144

Sherman, L. E., Payton, A. A., Hernandez, L. M., Greenfield, P. M., & Dapretto, M. (2016). The power of the like in adolescence: Effects of peer influence on neural and behavioral responses to social media. *Psychological Science, 27*(7), 1027–1035. https://doi.org/10.1177/0956797616645673

Shimoga, S. V., Erlyana, E., & Rebello, V. (2019). Associations of social media use with physical activity and sleep adequacy among adolescents: Cross-sectional survey. *Journal of Medical Internet Research, 21*(6), e14290.

Sigelman, C. K., & Rider, E. A. (2014). *Life-span human development.* Belmont, CA: Cengage Learning.

Sigman, A. (2012). Time for view on screen time. *Archive of Disease in Childhood, 97*(11), 935–942.

Skoric, M. M., Teo, L. L. C., & Neo, R. L. (2009). Children and video games: Addiction, engagement, and scholastic achievement. *Cyberpsychology and Behavior, 12*(5), 567–572.

Sohn, S. Y., Rees, P., Wildridge, B., Kalk, N. J., & Carter, B. (2019). Prevalence of problematic smartphone usage and associated mental health outcomes amongst children and young people: A systematic review, meta-analysis and GRADE of the evidence. *BMC Psychiatry, 19*, 356–365. https://doi.org/10.1186/s12888-019-2350-x

Sriwilai, K., & Charoensukmongkol, P. (2015). Face it, don't facebook it: Impacts of social media addiction on mindfulness, coping strategies and the consequence on emotional exhaustion: Social media addiction, mindfulness and coping. *Stress and Health: Journal of the International Society for the Investigation of Stress, 32.* https://doi.org/10.1002/smi.2637

Sroufe, L. A. (1996). *Emotional development: The organization of emotional life in the early years.* New York, NY: Cambridge University Press.

Stoilova, M., Livingstone, S., & Khazbak, R. (2021). *Investigating risks and opportunities for children in a digital world: A rapid review of the evidence on children's internet use and outcomes, Innocenti Discussion Papers no. 2021-01.* Florence: UNICEF Office of Research - Innocenti.

Straker, L., Zabatiero, J., Danby, S., Thorpe, K., & Edwards, S. (2018). Conflicting guidelines on young children's screen time and use of digital technology create policy and practice dilemmas. *Journal of Pediatrics, 202*, 300–303. https://doi.org/10.1016/jpeds.2018.07.019

Strasburger, V. C., Hogan, M. J., Mulligan, D. A., Ameenuddin, N., Christakis, D. A., Cross, C., & Swanson, W. S. L. (2013). Children, adolescents, and the media. *Pediatrics, 132*(5), 958–961.

Suoranta, J. (2003). The world divided in two: Digital divide, information and communication technologies, and the "Youth Question". *Journal for Critical Education Policy Studies, 1*(2), 1–31.

Tamir, D., & Mitchell, J. (2012). Disclosing information about the self is intrinsically rewarding. *PNAS, 109*(21), 8038–8043. https://doi.org/10.1073/pnas.1202129109

Tang, S., Werner-Seidler, A., Torok, M., & Mackinnon, A. J. (2021). The relationship between screen time and mental health in young people: A systematic review of longitudinal studies. *Clinical Psychology Review, 86*, 1–15. https://doi.org/10.1016/j.cpr.2021.102021

Telecommunication Development Sector (ITU-D). (2014). Secretariat of Telecommunication Development Bureau (BDT), United Nations (UN). *The World in 2014: ICT Facts and Figures.* https://www.itu.int/en/ITU-D/Statistics/Documents/facts/ICTFactsFigures2014-e.pdf

Tonioni, F., D'Alessandris, L., Lai, C., Martinelli, D., Corvino, S., Vasale, M., ... Bria, P. (2012). Internet addiction: Hours spent online, behaviors and psychological symptoms. *General Hospital Psychiatry, 34*(1), 80–87.

Turkle, S. (2011). *Alone together: Why we expect more from technology and less from each other.* New York, NY: Basic Books.

Twenge, J. M., Martin, G. N., & Spitzberg, B. H. (2019). Trends in U.S. adolescents' media use, 1976-2016: The rise of digital media, decline of TV, and the (near) demise of print. *Psychology of Popular Media Culture, 8*(4), 329–345. https://doi.org/10.1037/ppm0000203

Tyers-Chowdhury, A., & Binder, G. (2021). What we know about the gender digital divide for girls: A literature review. *UNICEF Gender and Innovation, Evidence Briefs—Insights into the Gender Digital Divide for Girls.*

Tyers, A., & Global, B. (2020). *USAID Gender digital divide desk review report.* Available at: https://www.marketlinks.org/weege-wiki/gdd-desk-review-report.

United Nations Children's Fund (UNICEF). (2017). *The state of the world's children 2017: Children in a digital world.* New York: UNICEF.

Valkenburg, P. M., & Peter, J. (2009). Social consequences of the internet for adolescents: A decade of research. *Current Directions in Psychological Science, 18*(1), 1–5.

Valkenburg, P. M., & Peter, J. (2011). Online communication among adolescents: An integrated model of its attraction, opportunities, and risks. *Journal of Adolescent Health, 48*(2), 121–127.

Valkenburg, P. M., Peter, J., & Schouten, A. P. (2006). Friend networking sites and their relationship to adolescents' well-being and social self-esteem. *Cyberpsychology and Behavior, 9*, 584–590.

Van Den Eijnden, R. J., Spijkerman, R., Vermulst, A. A., van Rooij, T. J., & Engels, R. C. (2010). Compulsive internet use among adolescents: Bidirectional parent–child relationships. *Journal of Abnormal Child Psychology, 38*(1), 77–89.

Van Schalkwyk, G. I., Marin, C. E., Ortiz, M., Rolison, M., Qayyum, Z., McPartland, J. C., Lebowitz, E. R., Volkmar, F. R., & Silverman, W. K. (2017). Social media use, friendship quality, and the moderating role of anxiety in adolescents with autism spectrum disorder. *Journal of Autism and Developmental Disorders, 47*, 2805–2813. https://doi.org/10.1007/s10803-017-3201-6

Van den Berg, H. S., George, A. A., Du Plessis, E. D., Botha, A., Basson, N., De Villiers, M., & Makola, S. (2013). The pivotal role of social support in the well-being of adolescents. In M. P. Wissing (Ed.), *Well-being research in South Africa* (pp. 315–339). Amsterdam, Netherlands: Springer.

Vannucci, A., & Ohannessian, C. M. (2019). Social media use subgroups differentially predict psychosocial well-being during early adolescence. *Journal of Youth and Adolescence, 48*, 1469–1493. https://doi.org/10.1007/s10964-019-01060-9

Varner, F., & Mandara, J. (2013). Differential parenting of African American adolescents as an explanation for gender disparities in achievement. *Journal of Research on Adolescence, 24*(4), 667–680. https://doi.org/10.1111/jora.12063

Viner, R. M., Gireesh, A., Stiglic, N., Hudson, L. D., Goddings, A.-L., Ward, J. L., & Nicholls, D. E. (2019). Roles of cyberbullying, sleep, and physical activity in mediating the effects of social media use on mental health and wellbeing among young people in England: A secondary analysis of longitudinal data. *Lancet Child and Adolescent Health, 3*, 685–696. https://doi.org/10.1016/S2352-4642(19)30186-5

de Vries, D. A., Vossen, H. G. M., & van der Kolk-van der Boom, P. (2019). Social media and body dissatisfaction: Investigating the attenuating role of positive parent-adolescent relationships. *Journal of Youth and Adolescence, 48*, 527–536. https://doi.org/10.1007/s10964-018-0956-9

Vuorre, M., Orben, A., & Przybylski, A. K. (2021). There is no evidence that associations between adolescents' digital technology engagement and mental health problems have increased. *Clinical Psychological Science*, 1–13. https://doi.org/10.1177/21677026 21994549

Wallace, P. (2014). Internet addiction disorder and youth. *EMBO Reports, 15*(1), 12–16. https://doi.org/10.1002/embr.201238222

Wang, H.-Y., Sigerson, L., & Cheng, C. (2019). Digital nativity and information technology addiction: Age cohort versus individual difference approaches. *Computers in Human Behavior, 90*, 1–9. https://doi.org/10.1016/j.chb.2018.08.031

Weber, D. M., & Kauffman, R. J. (2011). What drives global ICT adoption? Analysis and research directions. *Electronic Commerce Research and Applications, 10*(6), 683–701.

Weinstein, E. (2018). The social media see-saw: Positive and negative influences on adolescents' affective well-being. *New Media & Society, 20*(10), 3597–3623. https://doi.org/10.1177/1461444818755634

Weinstein, A., Feder, L. C., Rosenberg, K. P., & Dannon, P. (2014). Internet addiction disorder: Overview and controversies. *Behavioral Addictions*, 99–117. https://doi.org/10.1016/B978-0-12-407724-9.00005-7

Werner, E. E. (2013). What can we learn about resilience from large-scale longitudinal studies? In S. Goldstein, & R. B. Brooks (Eds.), *Handbook of resilience in children* (pp. 87–109). New York, NY: Springer.

White, R. W. (1959). Motivation reconsidered: The concept of competence. *Psychological Review, 66*, 297–333.

Williams, D., Consalvo, M., Caplan, S., & Yee, N. (2009). Looking for gender: Gender roles and behaviors among online gamers. *Journal of Communication, 59*(4), 700–725.

Wren, A. A., Neiman, N., Caruso, T. J., Rodriguez, S., Taylor, K., Madill, M., Rives, H., & Nguyen, L. (2021). Mindfulness-based virtual reality intervention for children and young adults with inflammatory bowel disease: A pilot feasibility and acceptability study. *Children, 8*, 368. https://doi.org/10.3390/children8050368

Yang, X., Zhou, Z., Liu, Q., & Fan, C. (2019). Mobile phone addiction and adolescents' anxiety and depression: The moderating role of mindfulness. *Journal of Child and Family Studies, 28*, 822–830. https://doi.org/10.1007/s10826-018-01323-2

Yan, W., Li, Y., & Sui, N. (2014). The relationship between recent stressful life events, personality traits, perceived family functioning and internet addiction among college students. *Stress and Health, 30*(1), 3–11.

Yao, M. Z., He, J., Ko, D. M., & Pang, K. (2014). The influence of personality, parental behaviors, and self-esteem on internet addiction: A study of Chinese college students. *Cyberpsychology, Behavior and Social Networking, 17*(2), 104–110. https://doi.org/10.1089/cyber.2012.0710

Ye, L., & Yang, H. (2020). From digital divide to social inclusion: A tale of mobile platform empowerment in rural areas. *Sustainability, 12*, 2424–2439. https://doi.org/10.3390/su12062424

Yurdagül, C., Kircaburun, K., Emirtekin, E., Wang, P., & Griffiths, M. D. (2019). Psychopathological consequences related to problematic instagram use among adolescents: The mediating role of body image dissatisfaction and moderating role of gender. *International Journal of Mental Health and Addiction*, 1–13. https://doi.org/10.1007/s11469-019-00071-8

Yu, L., & Shek, D. T. L. (2013). Internet addiction in Hong Kong adolescents: A three-year longitudinal study. *Journal of Pediatric and Adolescent Gynecology, 26*(3), S10–S17. https://doi.org/10.1016/j.jpag.2013.03.010

Zheng, R., McAlack, M., Wilmes, B., Kohler-Evans, P., & Williamson, J. (2009). Effects of multimedia on cognitive load, self-efficacy, and multiple rule-based problem solving. *British Journal of Educational Technology, 40*(5), 790–803. https://doi.org/10.1111/j.1467-8535.2008.00859.x

Cyberbullying in young people

Ana Pascual-Sanchez, and Dasha Nicholls

Division of Psychiatry, Imperial College London, London, United Kingdom

1. What is cyberbullying?

With the rapid proliferation of new technologies, young people have embraced a broad range of Internet-based means of communication (Ólafsson et al., 2014). It is estimated that more than 90% of adolescents in the United States use the Internet for social networking, while its impact on psychological distress has received more interest in recent years (Viner et al., 2019). Low- and middle-income countries (LMICs) have also seen an increase in technology use in the past few years (Quaglio et al., 2016), although literature related to technology and cyberbullying in these countries is scarce. However, despite having benefits (Reid Chassiakos et al., 2016), attention has also been drawn to their potential for use in interpersonal aggression. Children and young people may be vulnerable to online harms, e.g., distressing material, sexual exploitation, or cyberbullying (Royal College of Psychiatrists, 2020), and those who spent longer periods of time online could be more likely to be affected by cyberbullying (Frith, 2017). Current generations of young people are "digital natives," with wide access to Internet devices and access to social media. Since technology allows information to spread quickly and reach a much wider audience than in person communication, this could increase the risk of being exposed to online aggression or to perform it.

There is no clear definition of cyberbullying. Some authors define it as "an aggressive, intentional act carried out by a group or individual, using electronic forms of contact, repeatedly and over time against a victim who cannot easily defend himself or herself" (Smith et al., 2008). From young people's perspective, a recent report (Office for National Statistics, 2020) showed that half of the children who experienced online bullying behavior reported that they would not describe their experiences as bullying, 29% described the behaviors experienced as bullying, and 19% did not know. Several explanations are possible, from not considering the incident as significant/not recognizing them as bullying to not wanting to admit that they had been bullied. Furthermore, previous studies have highlighted that the nature of cyberbullying, with the absence of face-to-face interaction, contributes to the perception of an ambiguous intention (Dennehy et al., 2020).

A systematic review that explored young people's conceptualizations of the nature of cyberbullying (Dennehy et al., 2020) found that young people perceived that victims are targeted because of physical and social characteristics such as appearance, sexuality, personality, friends (or lack of) and popularity, and that this boosts the perpetrator's self-esteem. The omnipresent nature of technology, which makes it more repetitive and difficult to escape from, facilitates cyberbullying and is a key difference from face-to-face bullying.

The identity of the perpetrator(s) has been estimated to be unknown in one-fifth of the cases (Smith et al., 2008). It has been suggested that the anonymity and non—face-to-face nature of the interactions provided by online means to perpetrators may constitute a new platform for bullying to occur (Mateu et al., 2020). Anonymity has also been identified as a barrier for the ability of cybervictims to tell parents or teachers, as they may think that there is no way to prove that the perpetrator carried out the acts (e.g., excuses such as someone hacked the account of the perpetrator).

Cyberbullying can be performed through different types of Internet devices, such as mobile phones or computers, from text messages or e-mails to instant messages or social media. In this context, it has been proposed that cyberbullying poses specific risks, since it can occur both day and night, across home, school, and community contexts, is very fast, audio—visual, anonymous, repetitive, reaches a wide audience, may be less visible to adults, and victims may find it difficult to remove themselves from it and for perpetrators to desist (Ferrara et al., 2018; Slonje & Smith, 2008). Cyberbullying may therefore have particular potency as a mental health stressor.

1.1 Types of cyberbullying and cyberbullying roles

Cyberbullying involvement has been traditionally split into different roles: victims, known as "cybervictims," and perpetrators, known as "cyberbullies." However, as with other forms of abuse, cyber victimization represents the strongest predictor of becoming a perpetrator (Livazović & Ham, 2019). There is therefore also a category in which people have both roles (victims and perpetrators), known as "cyberbully victims." As noted, cybervictims can be victims only or both victims and bullies, and the same pattern applies to cyberbullies. In this chapter, we use the term cybervictims to refer to cybervictims only, and cyberbullies to refer to cyberbullies only, unless we have specified that cyberbully victims are included. "Noninvolved" young people would be those who are not affected by this kind of aggression, either as victims or as perpetrators. Among the noninvolved, the role of "online bystanders" has also been identified (Ranney et al., 2020), which could be more widely defined as those who witness aggression through online means (group chat, social media, etc.). The way in which bystanders respond to cyberbullying has a huge impact on cyberbullying: they could reinforce the perpetrator (e.g., having fun, making the aggression viral), they could blame the victim (e.g., for not defending her/himself), they could confront the perpetrator, and/or they could try to help the victim (Myers & Cowie, 2019). Furthermore, they can also be afraid of being a victim themselves, or even not recognize the cyberaggression as actual cyberbullying (Kraft, 2011). These roles can overlap, for example, a cybervictim could not only also be a cyberbully (cyberbully victim), but also a cybervictim in one context could be an online bystander in others, or an online bystander could be a cyberbully in other circumstances, having learned the behavior from that other situation. It is estimated that one in three cybervictims could be cyberbully victims, whereas around two out of three cyberbullies could be cyberbully victims, or at least have been a cybervictim before being a cyberbully (Mateu et al., 2020) (Fig. 2.1). The prevalence of the online bystanders is difficult to estimate as most of them would remain anonymous. Future research could shed more light on their prevalence and role.

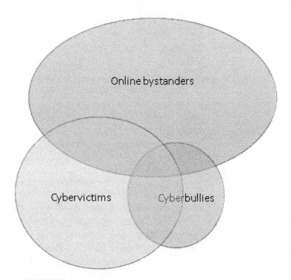

FIGURE 2.1 Overlap between cyberbullying roles.

Cyberbullying can be performed in many forms, from direct forms of aggression to other more indirect cyberbullying methods. To name a few examples, cyberbullies can harass via insults or threats, spread rumors, overt trickery (gaining victim's trust and distributing secrets), or exclude an individual from activities (Peebles, 2014). A recent report (Office for National Statistics, 2020) has found that name calling or insulting or being sent nasty messages is the most frequent experience reported for children and adolescents aged 10–15, followed by being excluded from a group/ activity, rumors being spread or nasty comments posted online or threats (Fig. 2.2). Half of those who have experienced cyberbullying reported being subject to two or more types of cyberbullying behaviors.

Interestingly, most of the attacks seem to be carried out privately (Fig. 2.3) or in group messaging, but not that frequently through online means that could be accessed by anyone. A systematic review including low-, middle-, and high-income countries found that verbal violence was the most commonly reported behavior in both perpetration and victimization rates and that fewer studies reported the prevalence data for visual violence and group violence (Zhu et al., 2014), which is in line with these findings. This poses specific risks as the likelihood of others helping

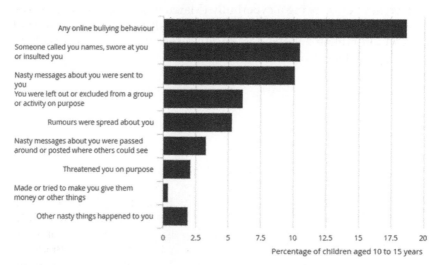

FIGURE 2.2   Proportion of children 10–15 years old who reported cyberbullying experiences in the past 12 months, by type of bullying behavior ($n = 764{,}000$ children). *Source: Office for National Statistics – Crime Survey for England and Wales; Office for National Statistics. (2020).* Online bullying in England and Wales: Year ending March 2020. Estimates of the prevalence and nature of online bullying among children using data from the 10- to 15-year-olds' Crime Survey for England and Wales (CSEW). *Retrieved from https://www. ons.gov.uk/peoplepopulationandcommunity/crimeandjustice/bulletins/onlinebullyinginenglandand wales/yearendingmarch2020. Contains public sector information licensed under the Open Government Licence v3.0.*

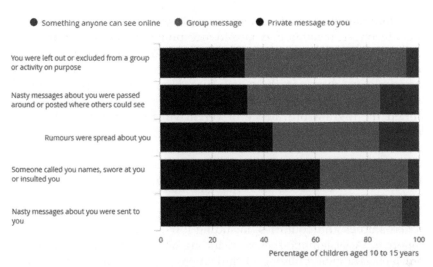

FIGURE 2.3 Proportion of privacy levels of the attacks received by children 10–15 years old by type of bullying behavior ($n = 764{,}000$ children). *Source: Office for National Statistics — Crime Survey for England and Wales; Office for National Statistics. (2020). Online bullying in England and Wales: Year ending March 2020. Estimates of the prevalence and nature of online bullying among children using data from the 10- to 15-year-olds' Crime Survey for England and Wales (CSEW). Retrieved from https://www.ons.gov.uk/peoplepopulationandcommunity/ crimeandjustice/bulletins/onlinebullyinginenglandandwales/yearendingmarch2020. Contains public sector information licensed under the Open Government Licence v3.0.*

decreases if the victim (or "online bystanders") does not report the aggression.

1.2 Overlap between cyberbullying and traditional bullying

There is ongoing debate about the overlap between traditional bullying (i.e., face-to-face bullying, which includes physical, verbal, and relational bullying) and cyberbullying (Olweus, 2012). Cyberbullying and traditional bullying correlated in several studies (Englander et al., 2017). Increasing evidence indicates that many of those who are cyberbullied are also traditionally bullied (Gradinger et al., 2009; Waasdorp & Bradshaw, 2015). However, cyberbullying can provide a platform to some perpetrators who do not bully in traditional ways, as they may take advantage of online anonymity (Wolke, 2017). Other studies showed that half of the cybervictims are also victims of traditional bullying (Mateu et al., 2020). For both cyberbullying and traditional bullying, school-related features may be relevant (Cassidy et al., 2012). In fact, 70% children and adolescent cybervictims reported that the aggressor was from their own school (Office for National Statistics, 2020). Recent literature also suggested that cyberbullying is part of a continuum of peer violence, which would include physical fights and face-to-face bullying (Ranney et al., 2020). Given the paucity of research on specific methods used for cyberbullying in LMICs, it is difficult to draw conclusions about how and whether cyberbullying differs in these countries. However, a systematic review including several countries across the world showed that Malaysia reported the highest prevalence of verbal violence in cyberbullying followed by China (Zhu et al., 2021).

2. Epidemiology

The prevalence rate of cyberbullying among adolescents varies widely across studies and countries, including low-, middle-, and high-income countries. A systematic review including 63 studies concluded that the prevalence of cyberbullying victimization ranged from 13.99% to 57.5% and of cyberbullying perpetration ranged from 6.0% to 46.3% (Zhu et al., 2021), although data on LMICs were lacking. Despite this wide range, recent data seem to suggest that almost one in five children reported having experienced at least one type of cyberbullying behavior in the previous 12 months (Office for National Statistics, 2020).

2.1 Age

Whereas traditional bullying (e.g., face-to-face bullying) is more common in younger children, cyberbullying is more common in adolescents. It seems to be more common among 13- to 15-year-olds than 11-year-olds (Arnarsson et al., 2020) and also more common in adolescents than in young adults (Kim et al., 2018). The rapid development of digital technologies and earlier access to them could potentially change this pattern. Furthermore, being younger than the aggressor increases the risk of being a cybervictim (Cappadocia et al., 2013). Longitudinal continuity has also been proposed regarding the cyberbullying role, so it would be easier to be a cybervictim in adolescence if the young person was a cybervictim earlier in life, and a similar pattern would apply to cyberbullies (Myers & Cowie, 2019).

2.2 Gender

Gender differences in rates of cyberbullying involvement are inconclusive, with some indicating girls are more likely to report being cyberbullied (Arnarsson et al., 2020; Strohacker et al., 2019) and some indicating boys are more likely to be victimized (Sharma et al., 2017), and a number of studies showing no sex differences (Office for National Statistics, 2020). In terms of cyberaggression, boys seem to be more likely to cyberbully than girls (Sharma et al., 2017; Wang et al., 2019).

2.3 Socioeconomic status and ethnicity

A large study based on the Global School—based Student Health Survey of 317,869 secondary school children across all World Health Organization (WHO) regions suggests that cybervictims were more likely to live in a below-average socioeconomic household. Furthermore, the prevalence of bullying seems to be lower in high-income countries than in LMICs (Biswas et al., 2020), although more research is needed. However, in another large study that included 25,142 European youth aged 9—16 years, it was suggested that cyberbullies may be more likely to come from a higher socioeconomic background (Goerzig & Machackova, 2015). This could be explained by a higher access to technology: the higher the access to Internet devices, the higher the risk to be involved in this kind of aggression. Findings on socioeconomic risk are therefore mixed.

In terms of ethnicity, cyberbullying perpetration seems to be associated with being from a nonwhite background in the United States, but the same is not true for cybervictimization (Wang et al., 2009). However, another study from the United States concluded that children from nonwhite ethnicity experience lower levels of cybervictimization than their white peers (Edwards et al., 2016), and a recent UK report suggested that Asian children were significantly less likely to have experienced any online bullying behavior than white children, black children, or children from mixed ethnic groups (Office for National Statistics, 2020). Yet another study in the United States suggested that white students were more likely to be either cybervictims or cyberbullies than Hispanic secondary students, but that no differences were found when compared with African Americans (Kupczynski et al., 2013). Other authors concluded that ethnicity does not seem to be significantly associated with involvement in cyberbullying (Guo, 2016). Results are therefore inconclusive.

In addition, there might be some cultural differences when understanding cyberbullying. For example, in a study comparing Chinese and Canadian students, Chinese young people were more prone to report cyberbullying to adults (either as cybervictims or as bystanders) than their Canadian counterparts and perceived adults as helpful in stopping aggression (Qing, 2008). A similar pattern was found in another study comparing the United States and Japan, where it was found that cyberbullying was more likely in cultures that promote independence such as Western countries (Barlett et al., 2013).

Spriggs et al. (2007) reported that traditional bully and traditional bully victims of black ethnicity reported poorer classmate relations, which might be relevant. In a study including 1288 young people in the United Kingdom, we found an association between cyberbullying and ethnicity, but this association was no longer significant when adjusted for socioeconomic status (Pascual-Sanchez et al., 2021). This could mean that it is not ethnicity itself what makes a difference, but that socioeconomic status may act as a moderator of these differences.

In summary, the links between socioeconomic deprivation, school factors, ethnicity, culture, and cyberbullying experiences deserve further exploration in longitudinal studies. Early detection of school and peer difficulties should be encouraged to protect adolescents from developing behavioral problems, and the role of socioeconomic factors and racism should be considered as part of approaches to antibullying interventions.

2.4 Chronic conditions, disabilities, and preexisting mental health problems

The prevalence of cyberbullying is significantly higher in children with a long-term illness or disability than those without (Kowalski & Toth, 2018; Office for National Statistics, 2020). For example, students with intellectual disabilities attending special education classes have been found to be more likely to be cybervictims and cyberbully victims (Heiman & Olenik-Shemesh, 2015). People with long-term physical conditions (e.g., asthma, diabetes, epilepsy, or intestinal diseases) are also more likely to be cybervictims than their peers, and those with other conditions such as obesity, hearing impairments, or visual impairments (Pinquart, 2017) are at higher risk of being targeted for them (Alhaboby et al., 2019). Illness-specific teasing was the most frequent way in which they were cyberbullied, but they were also more likely to be cyberbully victims (Pinquart, 2017). Furthermore, those with preexisting mental health problems (e.g., depression) are also more likely to be cyberbullied than their peers (Kwan et al., 2020; Marín-Cortés et al., 2019).

3. Risk and protective factors

A broad understanding of risk and protective factors is key for prevention, early detection, and intervention. Several variables have been identified as risk factors for cyberbullying, in both victim and perpetrator roles. These include a range of individual and contextual factors (see Table 2.1).

TABLE 2.1   Risk and protective factors for cyberbullying in young people.

	Cybervictims	Cyberbullies
Risk factors	Internalizing problems Long-term conditions or disabilities Lack of social skills	Antisocial behaviors Alcohol and drug abuse Negative school climate Negative peer influence Lack of conflict resolution skills Exposure to violence Being a male Have been a cybervictim Lower school attainment
	Both cybervictims and cyberbullies	
Risk factors	Externalizing problems Internet use Low self-esteem Authoritarian parenting	
Protective factors	Social support Positive neighborhood Parental affection and communication Promotion of autonomy	

3.1 Individual factors

Externalizing problems and antisocial behaviors are risk factors for being a cyberbully, whereas externalizing or internalizing problems and antisocial personality predict being a cybervictim (Guo, 2016). Alcohol and drug abuse are associated with being a cyberbully (Gaete et al., 2017), whereas being younger (lower-grade level) increases the risk of being a cybervictim (Cappadocia et al., 2013). As already noted, cybervictimization seems to be a strong predictor for cyberbullying perpetration (Livazović & Ham, 2019).

Low self-esteem seems to be associated with cyberbullying, either as a victim or as a perpetrator (Lei et al., 2020). Lack of empathy, assertiveness, conflict resolution skills, and communicative and relational skills could predict cyberaggression, whereas lack of social skills has predicted cybervictimization (Rodríguez-Hidalgo et al., 2020). Impulsivity and callous-unemotionality traits are associated with cyberbullies who also bully others in a traditional way (face-to-face), but not with those who only cyberbullied (Pascual-Sanchez et al., 2021).

Other individual factors such as higher Internet use and use of social media have been both associated with higher risk of cybervictimization and of cyberbullying others (Marín-Cortés et al., 2019; Smith et al., 2008), whereas lower school attainment and academic achievement predict being a cyberbully (Livazović & Ham, 2019).

3.2 Contextual factors

The context in which children and adolescents live is relevant to their behaviors, at a developmental stage where they learn what is right or wrong, how relationships work, and how to communicate with others. Exposure to violence is highly relevant, as it increases the risk of being a cyberbully. However, living in a positive neighborhood (e.g., sense of community, less conflicts) appears to be a protective factor for cyberbullying, either as a victim or as a perpetrator (Leemis et al., 2019), and social support in general has been highlighted as a protective factor (Marín-Cortés et al., 2019). Support from bystanders could act as a protective factor for the negative consequences of cyberbullying on cybervictims (Kwan et al., 2020). Negative peer influence and negative school climate increase the risk of being a cyberbully but have relatively low effect for being a cybervictim (Guo, 2016). Lower-quality family life predicts both cybervictimization and cyberaggression (Livazović & Ham, 2019).

Parents have an important role in modeling behaviors and supervising child development, and parenting styles and parenting practices have been studied as potential protective and risk factors. Authoritarian parenting is a risk factor for cyberbullying, for being both a victim or a bully, especially for male cyberbullies (Charalampous et al., 2018; Zurcher et al., 2018). The use of punitive practices by parents, with higher use of physical and psychological violence to deal with conflicts, could explain the higher risk of cyberaggression. Children exposed in this way may normalize violence and also find it difficult to report cyberbullying if they are victims, as they may feel that their parents are insensitive to their own problems (Charalampous et al., 2018).

Affection (also described as parental warmth), communication and promotion of autonomy, features of positive parenting, and parental involvement appear to act as protective factors for cyberbullying involvement (as victim or perpetrator) (Gómez-Ortiz et al., 2018). These variables, as part of a wider idea of positive parenting (Fig. 2.1), could be one of the most important protective factors for cyberbullying in any role. Positive parenting aims to promote a secure attachment, including helping children to develop autonomy through exploration, positive emotions, communication, and praising (Kyriazos & Stalikas, 2018). In fact, positive parenting, assessed as a parenting practice dimension with validated measures, has shown to be a protective factor against cyberbullying involvement, either as a cybervictim or as a cyberbully, whereas

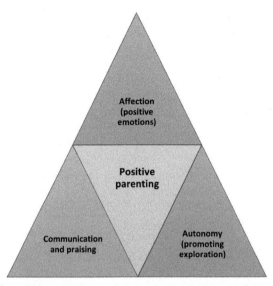

FIGURE 2.4 Positive parenting components involved as protective factors of cyberbullying.

poor monitoring and inconsistent discipline have been associated with higher risk of being a cyberbully (Pascual-Sanchez et al., 2021). Furthermore, family contact and communication has been proposed as a moderator of the relationship between cyberbullying and mental health problems (Elgar et al., 2014). Family communication and strong relationships with parents have been highlighted as one of the most important variables that could protect for involvement in cyberbullying (Marín-Cortés et al., 2019) (Fig. 2.4).

4. The impact of cyberbullying on mental health

Adolescence is a particularly vulnerable period for the impact of cyberbullying on mental health (Kim et al., 2018). In a large adolescent cohort study in the United Kingdom, the association between frequent social media use and mental health and well-being, especially in girls, was mediated by cyberbullying (Viner et al., 2019). A study analyzing adolescent perspectives on the relationship between social media and mental health found that they considered that it may be a platform for cyberbullying and that the use of social media can be addictive (O'Reilly et al., 2018).

Life satisfaction is lower in young people who are cybervictims compared with those who are not, even when adjusting for age, gender, and family structure (Arnarsson et al., 2020). Furthermore, some authors have suggested the existence of a vicious circle between previous psychosocial problems and cyberbullying in which psychosocial problems increase the risk of cyberbullying, which in turn exacerbates psychosocial problems (Kwan et al., 2020).

Cybervictims are more likely to report poor mental health, impairment in daily functioning for mental health problems, academic difficulties, and alcohol or drug use (Khine et al., 2020; Kim et al., 2018). Since irritability is a key symptom of depression in young people, it is important to highlight that anger has been described as one of the most common responses in cybervictims (Nixon, 2014). Cybervictims are more likely to report the presence of emotional symptoms, especially anxiety and depression (Fahy et al., 2016), which tend to be higher with higher levels of cyberbullying (Nixon, 2014).

In general, cybervictims tend to suffer more from internalizing symptoms, whereas cyberbullies tend to show more externalizing symptoms. Cyberbully victims are more likely to show a combination of internalizing and externalizing symptoms that have been demonstrated for cyberbully victims, with more severe psychopathological profiles (Nixon, 2014). A summary of the most common mental health consequences of cyberbullying is provided in Table 2.2.

Gender differences have also been identified, although studies are inconclusive. Among cybervictims, girls were much more likely to have experienced depressive symptoms and suicidal ideation than boys, whereas boys tended to spend more time online and were more likely to report drug use. However, while suicidal attempts were higher in girls, greater suicidal planning (which was associated with higher risk of committing suicide) in the context of distress from cyberbullying was higher among boys. Nevertheless, this association seems to be mediated by depressive symptoms, a reminder of how important it is to address them to reduce risk (Strohacker et al., 2019). Other studies suggested that

TABLE 2.2   Most common mental health problems in cybervictims and cyberbullies

Cybervictims (more internalizing)	Cyberbullies (more externalizing)
Anxiety	Hyperactivity
Depression	Behavioral problems
Somatization	Somatization
Self-harm and suicidal behaviors	Posttraumatic stress symptoms
Posttraumatic stress symptoms	Alcohol and drug abuse
Alcohol and drug abuse	

male cyberbully victims experience more emotional and somatic symptoms than females (Kowalski & Limber, 2013).

Cybervictims present to primary care with higher nonspecific health complaints more frequently, but this is also true for cyberbullies (Alhaboby et al., 2019; Sourander et al., 2010). It is important to highlight that somatization may be a sign of emotional distress, especially in children who do not yet have the skills to verbalize their emotional distress (Karkhanis & Winsler, 2016).

Emergency visits for mental health reasons (e.g., self-harm) are much more frequent in cybervictims than those who attend the emergency room for other reasons (Hellstrand et al., 2020). Furthermore, one study analyzing adolescent psychiatric inpatients found that 20% reported having been victimized by cyberbullying and having higher scores in posttraumatic stress symptoms (Saltz et al., 2020).

Posttraumatic stress symptoms were mostly associated with cybervictims in the existing literature (Ranney et al., 2016), but recent data showed that they may be common also in cyberbullies, although less intense Mateu et al. (2020). This could be explained by the increased risk for cybervictims of becoming bullies (Livazović & Ham, 2019).

Hyperactivity, conduct problems, delinquent behaviors, alcohol and drug abuse, low prosocial behavior, and somatic symptoms have been associated with being a cyberbully (Nixon, 2014; Sourander et al., 2010), although the casual link between cyberbullying and these type of symptoms is not clear. A systematic review found that self-harm and suicidal risk is increased for cybervictims, and the risk of suicidal behaviors is also increased in cyberbullies, although to a lesser extent (John et al., 2018).

It has been suggested that the anonymity of cyberbullying behaviors might impose a greater feeling of helplessness for the victims (Myers & Cowie, 2019). Furthermore, cyberbullying methods also matter. Cyberbullying via video has been found to be more distressing for victims than via text messages or instant messages (Smith et al., 2008), resulting in higher levels of negative affect (Pieschl et al., 2013).

5. Assessment and intervention

5.1 Assessment

The first step is recognizing cyberbullying as a problem (Waseem & Nickerson, 2020). Typical assumptions such as "these are children's issues" or assuming that unless teachers or parents have seen it, it has not happened, may reduce recognition.

In both clinical settings and research studies, it is common to address this by asking if young people have "experienced any cyberbullying through the Internet, mobile phone use, or other source" (e.g., Viner et al., 2019). For example, a systematic review identified that several studies asked a question from the Youth Risk Behavior Survey: "During the past 12 months, have you ever been electronically bullied (include being bullied through email, chat rooms, instant messaging, websites, or texting)?" (John et al., 2018). The language used when addressing cyberbullying is important, as it has implications in children and adolescents. For example, it has been suggested that the term "cyberbullying" itself is rejected by some young people for the stigma associated with the term, as well as its association with mental health issues (Ranney et al., 2020). Considering this when asking for online experiences deserves consideration.

In a systematic review analyzing cyberbullying assessment instruments, Berne et al. (2013) found that half of the instruments used the actual concept of cyberbullying. There has also been significant heterogeneity in assessment instruments, which may contribute to the lack of consensus in the conceptualization and prevalence of cyberbullying. In fact, some authors have stated that this lack of consensus is the most important methodological limitation when investigating cyberbullying (Tokunaga, 2010). No single instrument has been widely recommended or used, despite efforts to validate several measures in the literature. It is thus unusual to find the same instrument being used across studies (Lucas-Molina et al., 2016), making comparison of findings difficult. A summary of these instruments could be found in Berne et al. (2013) and Lucas-Molina et al. (2016).

Assessment of cyberbullying involves not only exploring whether the children or adolescent is suffering or perpetrating cyberbullying but also addressing whether they are involved in other types of bullying or subject to other forms of abuse, whether they have any mental health symptoms, medical unexplained symptoms, family and social problems, or impairment in school functioning (e.g., school performance). Proposed areas to explore when doing a thorough assessment of children and adolescent involvement (or suspected involvement) in cyberbullying are provided in Table 2.3.

5.2 Intervention

It is important to identify bullying interactions at an early stage to prevent severe consequences such as mental health issues or impairment in functioning (e.g., social relationships, school attainment). Prevention should be the first line when addressing bullying, rather than to wait until cyberbullying is clearly a problem.

TABLE 2.3 Assessment of cyberbullying: areas to explore.

Areas to explore	Specific domains
Cyberbullying involvement	Role: cybervictim, cyberbully, both (cyberbully victim) Involvement in traditional bullying (face-to-face) Frequency Internet use, social media use Methods used for being cyberbullied/cyberbully Degree of anonymity (aggressor)
Mental health	Screening for emotional or behavioral symptoms History of mental health problems Particular attention to self-harm or suicidal ideation, alcohol/drug use Other, such as medical unexplained symptoms
School functioning	School performance School attainment Social interactions (e.g., friends)
Family and social environment	Family environment Parenting practices (e.g., positive parenting, parental monitoring) Social support

Some suggestions regarding working with beliefs in the class (e.g., addressing beliefs such as thinking that calling somebody nasty names is not aggression) or reducing the time spent online could help to reduce the risk of cyberbullying (Nixon, 2014). Cyberbullying prevention should be promoted through educational programs in schools, so that students can recognize the behaviors in themselves or in their peers. Students should be aware of what cyberbullying is and how it may occur, the dangers of cyberbullying, the role of technology and how electronic messages can be traced, and the role of bystanders on reporting cyberbullying, among others (Diamanduros et al., 2008). Cunningham et al. (2015) stated that five key areas need to be considered when addressing cyberbullying with students: (1) emphasize the impact of cyberbullying on victims; (2) change cyberbullying prevention attitudes; (3) teach anticyberbullying strategies; (4) enable anonymous online reporting; and (5) combine prevention with consequences that are contingent to specific behaviors (e.g., reinforcing positive behaviors, removing privileges for aggressive behaviors).

However, when cyberbullying is already taking place, intervention is needed. It is important to understand individual needs and the context in which they arise to tailor appropriate interventions. First of all, a risk assessment should be conducted to determine the degree and the type of violence in place and the mental health impact on the cybervictim, with the emphasis on providing safety in the first place. Once this is ensured, other interventions can be introduced.

There is increased interest in suggesting interventions directed toward self-esteem and specific problem behaviors (Nixon, 2014). As poor social skills predict being either a cybervictim or a cyberbully, social skills training could be a potential preventative and therapeutic intervention, as well as problem-solving interventions, due to higher difficulties in conflict resolution skills in cyberbullies (Rodríguez-Hidalgo et al., 2020). In a systematic review of cyberbullying interventions (Hutson et al., 2018), programs that included social skills training, empathy training, or coping skills training showed significant reductions in both cyberaggression and cybervictimization. Regarding other interventions such as changing attitudes regarding cyberbullying, results are inconclusive, with less than half of the studies analyzed being successful in reducing either cyberaggression or cybervictimization (Hutson et al., 2018). A summary of interventions is provided in Table 2.4.

Bystander support could be a protective factor for the negative consequences of cyberbullying for cybervictims (Kwan et al., 2020) and therefore a potential target for prevention and intervention strategies if safe pathways can be established for them to report cyberbullying events and provide help to cybervictims. Other studies suggest that parenting interventions may be helpful. Parent interventions have been associated with a reduction of aggression and victimization in face-to-face bullying (Ttofi & Farrington, 2011). Parent education and having an adult to talk to have been proven as effective elements in interventions aimed to reduce cyberbullying (Hutson et al., 2018). Since parenting styles and practices seem to be either protective or risk factors for cyberbullying, more

TABLE 2.4   Summary of interventions for cyberbullying.

Interventions	
Individual	Social skills training Empathy training Coping skills Problem-solving
Family	Parent education Parenting programs—positive parenting
School	Emphasize the impact of cyberbullying on victims Teach anticyberbullying strategies Enable anonymous online reporting Define and apply consequences for cyberbullies Support from bystanders

research is needed to develop parenting evidence-based interventions that are useful for reducing cyberbullying rates and their consequences.

There is a strong need to develop antibullying programs in schools, to promote research in evidence-based interventions that will ensure that programs contain elements that have been proved to be effective in addressing cyberbullying (Ttofi & Farrington, 2011). Bonell et al. (2018) designed a whole-school intervention, engaging students in school decision-making and providing social and emotional skills education, with good results in reducing bullying victimization (either cyberbullying or traditional bullying) compared with schools continuing their standard practice. Antibullying school policies need to be tailored to the specific needs and culture of secondary schools or college students. Some countries, such as Australia, the United Kingdom, and the United States, have made it a legal requirement to have antibullying policies that address all forms of bullying (Chalmers et al., 2016). Attempts to implement antibullying policies have also been studied in LMICs such as Romania, Malaysia, or South Africa (Nye et al., 2018). However, policies aimed at reducing cyberbullying might require very different approaches from those aimed at reducing traditional bullying. In fact, it is important that policies indicate that not only is cyberbullying a prohibited behavior at school, but also that online aggression directed to other students could cause emotional harm that might in turn have potential consequences in the school environment (Diamanduros et al., 2008). Clear procedures for reporting, investigating, and intervening should be clarified in antibullying policies.

6. Summary

In a world in which technology is widely used, cyberbullying is a great problem among young people. Although there is no consensus regarding its definition, characteristics such as aggression and power imbalance using electronic means have been highlighted. However, a consensus for the definition of cyberbullying has not been reached, and no specific tools to measure it in a comprehensive way have been agreed, which poses a limitation to compiling and comparing research findings. Involved roles include being either a cybervictim, cyberbully, or both. Bystanders could also play a relevant role as witnesses to cyberaggression. Cyberbullying can be performed in many forms, from direct forms of aggression (e.g., insults, threats) to other more emotional harms (e.g., excluding the victim from activities).

Cyberbullying is more common in older adolescents, and boys are more likely to be cyberbullies than girls. Furthermore, those with long-term conditions or preexisting mental health problems are more likely to be cyberbullied than their peers.

Social support and positive parenting have been identified as protective factors against being involved in cyberbullying, irrespective of the role, whereas those experiencing internalizing symptoms, long-term conditions, or low self-esteem are more likely to be cybervictims, and those with externalizing symptoms, negative peer influence, lack of conflict resolution skills, or exposure to violence are more likely to be cyberbullies.

Cyberbullying also involves potential risks for mental health in those who are involved, as either cybervictims, cyberbullies, or both. In general, cybervictims tend to suffer more internalizing symptoms, self-harm, and suicidal behaviors, whereas cyberbullies tend to show more externalizing symptoms; cyberbully victims may suffer a mixed of internalizing and externalizing symptoms. Both cyberbullies and cybervictims show high levels of posttraumatic stress disorder symptoms.

A thorough assessment is needed when cyberbullying is suspected, including involvement role if applicable, frequency, methods, and Internet use. However, it is also necessary to address if there are any mental health symptoms, medical unexplained symptoms, family and social problems, or impairment in school functioning. Prevention is key in cyberbullying, where school and families play an important role. Special attention should be given to vulnerable groups (e.g., young people with mental health problems, or physical long-term conditions) at both home and school to protect them from potential risk, either from suffering cybervictimization or to both being cybervictims and cyberbullies. However, if cyberbullying is already in place, intervention is needed. Programs that include social skills training, empathy training, or coping skills have proved to reduce cyberaggression and cybervictimization, and parenting interventions seem also to be effective. Finally, it is important that antibullying policies are in place, including prevention attitudes, clear consequences, and methods of reporting cyberaggression.

7. Future directions

Future research should explore cyberbullying in LMICs, as most of the studies are from high-income countries. Furthermore, most of the research is focused on cybervictims and cyberbullies; bystanders should receive more attention due to their potential role as moderators in cyberbullying.

A wider consensus on cyberbullying definition and assessment is needed, which will also help to do a proper formulation of each case to tailor interventions. The range of interventions for individuals, families, and schools needs further research to inform evidence-based treatments.

Acknowledgments

APS has been supported by an Advanced Clinical Research Fellowship in Child and Adolescent Clinical Psychology from the Alicia Koplowitz Foundation, Spain.

References

Alhaboby, Z. A., Barnes, J., Evans, H., & Short, E. (2019). Cyber-victimization of people with chronic conditions and disabilities: A systematic review of scope and impact. *Trauma Violence Abuse, 20*(3), 398−415. https://doi.org/10.1177/1524838017717743

Arnarsson, A., Nygren, J., Nyholm, M., Torsheim, T., Augustine, L., Bjereld, Y., ... Bendtsen, P. (2020). Cyberbullying and traditional bullying among Nordic adolescents and their impact on life satisfaction. *Scandinavian Journal of Public Health, 48*(5), 502−510. https://doi.org/10.1177/1403494818887411

Barlett, C., Gentile, D., Anderson, C., Suzuki, K., Sakamoto, A., & Katsura, R. (2013). Cross-cultural differences in cyberbullying behavior: A short-term longitudinal study. *Journal of Cross-Cultural Psychology, 45*, 300−313. https://doi.org/10.1177/0022022113504622

Berne, S., Frisén, A., Schultze-Krumbholz, A., Scheithauer, H., Naruskov, K., Luik, P., ... Zukauskiene, R. (2013). Cyberbullying assessment instruments: A systematic review. *Aggression and Violent Behavior, 18*(2), 320−334. https://doi.org/10.1016/j.avb.2012.11.022

Biswas, T., Scott, J., Munir, K., Thomas, H., Huda, M. M., Hasan, M. M., ... Mamun, A. (2020). Global variation in the prevalence of bullying victimisation amongst adolescents: Role of peer and parental supports. *EClinicalMedicine, 20*, 100276. https://doi.org/10.1016/j.eclinm.2020.100276

Bonell, C., Allen, E., Warren, E., McGowan, J., Bevilacqua, L., Jamal, F., ... Viner, R. (2018). Effects of the learning together intervention on bullying and aggression in English secondary schools (INCLUSIVE): A cluster randomised controlled trial. *The Lancet, 392*. https://doi.org/10.1016/S0140-6736(18)31782-3

Cappadocia, M. C., Craig, W. M., & Pepler, D. (2013). Cyberbullying: Prevalence, stability, and risk factors during adolescence. *Canadian Journal of School Psychology, 28*(2), 171−192. https://doi.org/10.1177/0829573513491212

Cassidy, W., Brown, K., & Jackson, M. (2012). 'Under the radar': Educators and cyberbullying in schools. *School Psychology International, 33*, 520−532. https://doi.org/10.1177/0143034312445245

Chalmers, C., Campbell, M. A., Spears, B. A., Butler, D., Cross, D., Slee, P., & Kift, S. (2016). School policies on bullying and cyberbullying: Perspectives across three Australian states. *Educational Research, 58*(1), 91−109. https://doi.org/10.1080/00131881.2015.1129114

Charalampous, K., Demetriou, C., Tricha, L., Ioannou, M., Georgiou, S., Nikiforou, M., & Stavrinides, P. (2018). The effect of parental style on bullying and cyber bullying behaviors and the mediating role of peer attachment relationships: A longitudinal study. *J Adolesc, 64*, 109−123. https://doi.org/10.1016/j.adolescence.2018.02.003

Cunningham, C. E., Chen, Y., Vaillancourt, T., Rimas, H., Deal, K., Cunningham, L. J., & Ratcliffe, J. (2015). Modeling the anti-cyberbullying preferences of university students: Adaptive choice-based conjoint analysis. *Aggressive Behavior, 41*(4), 369−385. https://doi.org/10.1002/ab.21560

Dennehy, R., Meaney, S., Walsh, K., Sinnott, C., Cronin, M., & Arensman, E. (2020). Young people's conceptualizations of the nature of cyberbullying: A systematic review and synthesis of qualitative research. *Aggression and Violent Behavior, 51*, 101379. https://doi.org/10.1016/j.avb.2020.101379

Diamanduros, T., Downs, E., & Jenkins, S. (2008). The role of school psychologists in the assessment, prevention, and intervention of cyberbullying. *Psychology in the Schools, 45*, 693–704. https://doi.org/10.1002/pits.20335

Edwards, L., Edwards, A., & Fisher, C. (2016). Cyberbullying, race/ethnicity and mental health outcomes: A review of the literature. *Media and Communication, 4*, 71. https://doi.org/10.17645/mac.v4i3.525

Elgar, F. J., Napoletano, A., Saul, G., Dirks, M. A., Craig, W., Poteat, V. P., … Koenig, B. W. (2014). Cyberbullying victimization and mental health in adolescents and the moderating role of family dinners. *JAMA Pediatr, 168*(11), 1015–1022. https://doi.org/10.1001/jamapediatrics.2014.1223

Englander, E., Donnerstein, E., Kowalski, R., Lin, C. A., & Parti, K. (2017). Defining cyberbullying. *Pediatrics, 140*(Suppl. 2), S148–s151. https://doi.org/10.1542/peds.2016-1758U

Fahy, A. E., Stansfeld, S. A., Smuk, M., Smith, N. R., Cummins, S., & Clark, C. (2016). Longitudinal associations between cyberbullying involvement and adolescent mental health. *J Adolesc Health, 59*(5), 502–509. https://doi.org/10.1016/j.jadohealth.2016.06.006

Ferrara, P., Ianniello, F., Villani, A., & Corsello, G. (2018). Cyberbullying a modern form of bullying: Let's talk about this health and social problem. *Italian Journal of Pediatrics, 44*(1). https://doi.org/10.1186/s13052-018-0446-4, 14.

Frith, E. (2017). *Social media and children's mental health: A review of the evidence* [Online]. Retrieved from https://epi.org.uk/publications-and-research/social-media-childrens-mental-health-review-evidence/ Accessed 6 November 2020.

Gaete, J., Tornero, B., Valenzuela, D., Rojas-Barahona, C. A., Salmivalli, C., Valenzuela, E., & Araya, R. (2017). Substance use among adolescents involved in bullying: A cross-sectional multilevel study. *Frontiers in Psychology, 8*, 1056. https://doi.org/10.3389/fpsyg.2017.01056

Goerzig, A., & Machackova, H. (2015). Cyberbullying from a socio-ecological perspective: A contemporary synthesis of findings from EU Kids online. *Media@LSE Working Paper Series, 36*.

Gómez-Ortiz, O., Romera, E. M., Ortega-Ruiz, R., & Del Rey, R. (2018). Parenting practices as risk or preventive factors for adolescent involvement in cyberbullying: Contribution of children and parent gender. *International Journal of Environmental Research and Public Health, 15*(12). https://doi.org/10.3390/ijerph15122664

Gradinger, P., Strohmeier, D., & Spiel, C. (2009). Traditional bullying and cyberbullying: Identification of risk groups for adjustment problems. *Zeitschrift für Psychologie/Journal of Psychology, 217*(4), 205–213. https://doi.org/10.1027/0044-3409.217.4.205

Guo, S. (2016). A meta-analysis of the predictors of cyberbullying perpetration and victimization. *Psychology in the Schools, 53*, 432–453. https://doi.org/10.1002/pits.21914

Heiman, T., & Olenik-Shemesh, D. (2015). Cyberbullying experience and gender differences among adolescents in different educational settings. *Journal of Learning Disabilities, 48*(2), 146–155. https://doi.org/10.1177/0022219413492855

Hellstrand, K., Rogers, S. C., DiVietro, S., Clough, M., & Sturm, J. (2020). Prevalence of cyberbullying in patients presenting to the Pediatric Emergency Department. *Pediatric Emergency Care.* https://doi.org/10.1097/pec.0000000000002243

Hutson, E., Kelly, S., & Militello, L. K. (2018). Systematic review of cyberbullying interventions for youth and parents with implications for evidence-based practice. *Worldviews on Evidence-Based Nursing, 15*(1), 72–79. https://doi.org/10.1111/wvn.12257

John, A., Glendenning, A. C., Marchant, A., Montgomery, P., Stewart, A., Wood, S., ... Hawton, K. (2018). Self-harm, suicidal behaviours, and cyberbullying in children and young people: Systematic review. *Journal of Medical Internet Research, 20*(4), e129. https://doi.org/10.2196/jmir.9044

Karkhanis, D., & Winsler, A. (2016). Somatization in children and adolescents: Practical implications. *Journal of Indian Association for Child and Adolescent Mental Health, 12*, 79–115.

Khine, A. T., Saw, Y. M., Htut, Z. Y., Khaing, C. T., Soe, H. Z., Swe, K. K., ... Hamajima, N. (2020). Assessing risk factors and impact of cyberbullying victimization among university students in Myanmar: A cross-sectional study. *PLoS One, 15*(1), e0227051. https://doi.org/10.1371/journal.pone.0227051

Kim, S., Boyle, M. H., & Georgiades, K. (2018). Cyberbullying victimization and its association with health across the life course: A Canadian population study. *Canadian Journal of Public Health, 108*(5–6), e468–e474. https://doi.org/10.17269/cjph.108.6175

Kowalski, R. M., & Limber, S. P. (2013). Psychological, physical, and academic correlates of cyberbullying and traditional bullying. *Journal of Adolescent Health, 53*(1 Suppl. l), S13–S20. https://doi.org/10.1016/j.jadohealth.2012.09.018

Kowalski, R. M., & Toth, A. (2018). Cyberbullying among youth with and without disabilities. *Journal of Child & Adolescent Trauma, 11*(1), 7–15. https://doi.org/10.1007/s40653-017-0139-y

Kraft, E. (2011). *Online bystanders: Are they the key to preventing cyberbullying*. Retrieved from: https://www.researchgate.net/publication/237726378_Online_Bystanders_Are_They_the_Key_to_Preventing_Cyberbullying. Accesed on November 30 2020.

Kupczynski, L., Mundy, M.-A., & Green, M. E. (2013). *The prevalence of cyberbullying among ethnic groups of high school students.*

Kwan, I., Dickson, K., Richardson, M., MacDowall, W., Burchett, H., Stansfield, C., ... Thomas, J. (2020). Cyberbullying and children and young people's mental health: A systematic map of systematic reviews. *Cyberpsychology, Behavior, and Social Networking, 23*(2), 72–82. https://doi.org/10.1089/cyber.2019.0370

Kyriazos, T., & Stalikas, A. (2018). Positive parenting or positive psychology parenting? Towards a conceptual framework of positive psychology parenting. *Psychology, 9*, 1761–1788. https://doi.org/10.4236/psych.2018.97104

Leemis, R. W., Espelage, D. L., Basile, K. C., Mercer Kollar, L. M., & Davis, J. P. (2019). Traditional and cyber bullying and sexual harassment: A longitudinal assessment of risk and protective factors. *Aggressive Behavior, 45*(2), 181–192. https://doi.org/10.1002/ab.21808

Lei, H., Mao, W., Cheong, C. M., Wen, Y., Cui, Y., & Cai, Z. (2020). The relationship between self-esteem and cyberbullying: A meta-analysis of children and youth students. *Current Psychology, 39*(3), 830–842. https://doi.org/10.1007/s12144-019-00407-6

Livazović, G., & Ham, E. (2019). Cyberbullying and emotional distress in adolescents: The importance of family, peers and school. *Heliyon, 5*(6), e01992. https://doi.org/10.1016/j.heliyon.2019.e01992

Lucas-Molina, B., Pérez-Albéniz, A., & Giménez-Dasí, M. (2016). The assessment of cyberbullying: The present situation and future challenge. *Papeles del Psicologo, 37*(1), 27–35.

Marín-Cortés, A., Hoyos De Los Ríos, O., & Pérez, A. (2019). Factores de riesgo y factores protectores relacionados con el ciberbullying entre adolescentes: Una revisión sistemática. *Papeles del Psicologo, 40*, 109–124. https://doi.org/10.23923/pap.psicol2019.2899

Mateu, A., Pascual-Sánchez, A., Martinez-Herves, M., Hickey, N., Nicholls, D., & Kramer, T. (2020). Cyberbullying and post-traumatic stress symptoms in UK adolescents. *Archives of Disease in Childhood, 105*(10), 951–956. https://doi.org/10.1136/archdischild-2019-318716

Myers, C., & Cowie, H. (2019). Cyberbullying across the lifespan of education: Issues and interventions from school to university. *International Journal of Environmental Research and Public Health, 16*, 1217. https://doi.org/10.3390/ijerph16071217

Nixon, C. L. (2014). Current perspectives: The impact of cyberbullying on adolescent health. *Adolescent Health, Medicine and Therapeutics, 5*, 143−158. https://doi.org/10.2147/AHMT.S36456

Nye, E., Bowes, L., & Sivaraman, B. (2018). School-based anti-bullying interventions for adolescents in low- and middle-income countries: A systematic review. *Aggression and Violent Behavior, 45*, 154−162.

O'Reilly, M., Dogra, N., Whiteman, N., Hughes, J., Eruyar, S., & Reilly, P. (2018). Is social media bad for mental health and wellbeing? Exploring the perspectives of adolescents. *Clinical Child Psychology and Psychiatry, 23*(4), 601−613. https://doi.org/10.1177/1359104518775154

Office for National Statistics. (2020). *Online bullying in England and Wales: Year ending March 2020. Estimates of the prevalence and nature of online bullying among children using data from the 10- to 15-year-olds' Crime Survey for England and Wales (CSEW).* Retrieved from https://www.ons.gov.uk/peoplepopulationandcommunity/crimeandjustice/bulletins/onlinebullyinginenglandandwales/yearendingmarch2020.

Ólafsson, K., Livingstone, S., & Haddon, L. (2014). *Children's use of online technologies in Europe: A review of the European evidence base* (revised edition).

Olweus, D. (2012). Cyberbullying: An overrated phenomenon? *European Journal of Developmental Psychology, 9*(5), 520−538. https://doi.org/10.1080/17405629.2012.682358

Pascual-Sanchez, A., Hickey, N., Mateu, A., Martinez-Herves, M., Kramer, T., & Nicholls, D. (2021). Personality traits and self-esteem in traditional bullying and cyberbullying. *Personality and Individual Differences, 177*, 110809. https://doi.org/10.1016/j.paid.2021.110809

Peebles, E. (2014). Cyberbullying: Hiding behind the screen. *Paediatrics & Child Health, 19*(10), 527−528. https://doi.org/10.1093/pch/19.10.527

Pieschl, S., Porsch, T., Kahl, T., & Klockenbusch, R. (2013). Relevant dimensions of cyberbullying — results from two experimental studies. *Journal of Applied Developmental Psychology, 34*, 241−252. https://doi.org/10.1016/j.appdev.2013.04.002

Pinquart, M. (2017). Systematic review: Bullying involvement of children with and without chronic physical illness and/or physical/sensory disability-a meta-analytic comparison with healthy/nondisabled peers. *Journal of Pediatric Psychology, 42*(3), 245−259. https://doi.org/10.1093/jpepsy/jsw081

Qing, L. (2008). A cross-cultural comparison of adolescents' experience related to cyberbullying. *Educational Research, 50*(3), 223−234. https://doi.org/10.1080/00131880802309333

Quaglio, G., Dario, C., Karapiperis, T., delponte, L., Mccormack, S., Tomson, G., Micheletti, G., Bonnardot, L., Putoto, G., & Zanaboni, P. (2016). Information and communications technologies in low and middle-income countries: Survey results on economic development and health (Part I). *Health Policy and Technology.* https://doi.org/10.1016/j.hlpt.2016.07.003

Ranney, M. L., Patena, J. V., Nugent, N., Spirito, A., Boyer, E., Zatzick, D., & Cunningham, R. (2016). PTSD, cyberbullying and peer violence: Prevalence and correlates among adolescent emergency department patients. *General Hospital Psychiatry, 39*, 32−38. https://doi.org/10.1016/j.genhosppsych.2015.12.002

Ranney, M. L., Pittman, S. K., Riese, A., Koehler, C., Ybarra, M. L., Cunningham, R. M., ... Rosen, R. K. (2020). What counts?: A qualitative study of adolescents' lived experience with online victimization and cyberbullying. *Academic Pediatrics, 20*(4), 485−492. https://doi.org/10.1016/j.acap.2019.11.001

Reid Chassiakos, Y., Radesky, J., Christakis, D., Moreno, M. A., & Cross, C. (2016). Children and adolescents and digital media. *Pediatrics, 138*(5), e20162593. https://doi.org/10.1542/peds.2016-2593

Rodríguez-Hidalgo, A. J., Mero, O., Solera, E., Herrera-López, M., & Calmaestra, J. (2020). Prevalence and psychosocial predictors of cyberaggression and cybervictimization in adolescents: A Spain-Ecuador transcultural study on cyberbullying. *PLoS One, 15*(11), e0241288. https://doi.org/10.1371/journal.pone.0241288

Royal College of Psychiatrists. (2020). *Technology use and the mental health of children and young people*. Retrieved from https://www.rcpsych.ac.uk/docs/default-source/improving-care/better-mh-policy/college-reports/college-report-cr225.pdf Accessed 17 November 2020.

Saltz, S. B., Rozon, M., Pogge, D. L., & Harvey, P. D. (2020). Cyberbullying and its relationship to current symptoms and history of early life trauma: A study of adolescents in an acute inpatient psychiatric unit. *The Journal of Clinical Psychiatry, 81*(1). https://doi.org/10.4088/JCP.18m12170

Sharma, D., Kishore, J., Sharma, N., & Duggal, M. (2017). Aggression in schools: Cyberbullying and gender issues. *Asian Journal of Psychiatry, 29*, 142–145. https://doi.org/10.1016/j.ajp.2017.05.018

Slonje, R., & Smith, P. K. (2008). Cyberbullying: Another main type of bullying? *Scandinavian Journal of Psychology, 49*(2), 147–154. https://doi.org/10.1111/j.1467-9450.2007.00611.x

Smith, P. K., Mahdavi, J., Carvalho, M., Fisher, S., Russell, S., & Tippett, N. (2008). Cyberbullying: Its nature and impact in secondary school pupils. *Journal of Child Psychology and Psychiatry, 49*(4), 376–385. https://doi.org/10.1111/j.1469-7610.2007.01846.x

Sourander, A., Brunstein Klomek, A., Ikonen, M., Lindroos, J., Luntamo, T., Koskelainen, M., … Helenius, H. (2010). Psychosocial risk factors associated with cyberbullying among adolescents: A population-based study. *Archives of General Psychiatry, 67*(7), 720–728. https://doi.org/10.1001/archgenpsychiatry.2010.79

Spriggs, A. L., Iannotti, R. J., Nansel, T. R., & Haynie, D. L. (2007). Adolescent bullying involvement and perceived family, peer and school relations: Commonalities and differences across race/ethnicity. *Journal of Adolescent Health, 41*(3), 283–293. https://doi.org/10.1016/j.jadohealth.2007.04.009

Strohacker, E., Wright, L. E., & Watts, S. J. (2019). Gender, bullying victimization, depressive symptoms, and suicidality. *International Journal of Offender Therapy and Comparative Criminology.* https://doi.org/10.1177/0306624x19895964

Tokunaga, R. S. (2010). Following you home from school: A critical review and synthesis of research on cyberbullying victimization. *Computers in Human Behavior, 26*(3), 277–287. https://doi.org/10.1016/j.chb.2009.11.014

Ttofi, M. M., & Farrington, D. P. (2011). Effectiveness of school-based programs to reduce bullying: A systematic and meta-analytic review. *Journal of Experimental Criminology, 7*(1), 27–56. https://doi.org/10.1007/s11292-010-9109-1

Viner, R. M., Gireesh, A., Stiglic, N., Hudson, L. D., Goddings, A. L., Ward, J. L., & Nicholls, D. E. (2019). Roles of cyberbullying, sleep, and physical activity in mediating the effects of social media use on mental health and wellbeing among young people in England: A secondary analysis of longitudinal data. *The Lancet Child & Adolescent Health, 3*(10), 685–696. https://doi.org/10.1016/s2352-4642(19)30186-5

Waasdorp, T. E., & Bradshaw, C. P. (2015). The overlap between cyberbullying and traditional bullying. *Journal of Adolescent Health, 56*(5), 483–488. https://doi.org/10.1016/j.jadohealth.2014.12.002

Wang, J., Iannotti, R. J., & Nansel, T. R. (2009). School bullying among adolescents in the United States: Physical, verbal, relational, and cyber. *Journal of Adolescent Health, 45*(4), 368–375. https://doi.org/10.1016/j.jadohealth.2009.03.021

Wang, P., Wang, X., & Lei, L. (2019). Gender differences between student-student relationship and cyberbullying perpetration: An evolutionary perspective. *Journal of Interpersonal Violence, 886260519865970.* https://doi.org/10.1177/0886260519865970

Waseem, M., & Nickerson, A. B. (2020). Bullying. In StatPearls. *Treasure Island.* (FL: StatPearls Publishing.

Wolke, D. (2017). Cyberbullying: How big a deal is it? *Lancet Child and Adolescent Health, 1*(1), 2–3. https://doi.org/10.1016/s2352-4642(17)30020-2

Zhu, C., Huang, S., Evans, R., & Zhang, W. (2021). cyberbullying among adolescents and children: A comprehensive review of the global situation, risk factors, and preventive measures. *Front Public Health, 11*(9), 634909. https://doi.org/10.3389/fpubh.2021.634909

Zurcher, J. D., Holmgren, H. G., Coyne, S. M., Barlett, C. P., & Yang, C. (2018). Parenting and cyberbullying across adolescence. *Cyberpsychology, Behavior, and Social Networking, 21*(5), 294–303. https://doi.org/10.1089/cyber.2017.0586

PART II

Innovations to improve our understanding of Child and Adolescent Mental Health

3

Clinical applications of big data to child and adolescent mental health care

Alice Wickersham, and Johnny Downs

CAMHS Digital Lab, Department of Child and Adolescent Psychiatry, Institute of Psychiatry, Psychology and Neuroscience, King's College, London, United Kingdom

1. What are big data?

There is no rigorous definition for big data, but at its simplest, big data refers to any electronic data that are too large and complex to be feasibly stored or processed by traditional computers or software (Raghupathi & Raghupathi, 2014). Big data are often defined using the "three Vs": volume, variety, and velocity (Ford et al., 2020). Volume refers to the size of the data, where it is not uncommon for terabytes or petabytes to be available for analyses. Variety refers to the different types of data format (structured fields, free text, images, video, etc.) and multiple contributing sources. Velocity indicates the dynamic nature of data, where the volume and types of data held change, evolve, and update. Veracity has also been suggested as a fourth "V", highlighting some big data's credibility and accuracy (Raghupathi & Raghupathi, 2014), although data quality is not guaranteed (Davis et al., 2016). Data scientific technologies and tools are often needed to interpret these complex structures, often using automated processes and algorithms.

2. Why do we need big data for child and adolescent mental health research?

Improving the prevention and treatment of child and adolescent mental health disorders remains one of the greatest health challenges of the 21st century. The overall cost of mental health disorders to the global economy through poor health and lost productivity exceeds US$ 1 trillion each year (The Lancet Global, 2020). As the majority of these mental health disorders have their origins in childhood and adolescence (Kessler et al., 2005), there is a strong economic case for investing in better detection and treatment in childhood. Also, the immediate individual and societal costs of child- and adolescent-onset mental health disorders are high—their global prevalence is estimated at 13.4% (Polanczyk et al., 2015), and they are a leading cause of global burden of disease in young-age groups (Vos et al., 2020).

The impacts of these disorders are wide ranging and often long term; they are associated with lower levels of school attendance and educational attainment (Finning et al., 2019; Wickersham, Sugg, et al., 2021), physical health problems (Keenan-Miller et al., 2007), adult unemployment (Clayborne et al., 2019), and offending behavior (Fergusson et al., 2005).

Therefore, this area presents a major research priority, with ongoing calls for research which develops an understanding of risk factors and effective prevention and treatment for child and adolescent mental health disorders (National Institute for Health Research Maudsley Biomedical Research Centre, 2020).

Traditionally, studies rely on primary data collections and surveys to carry out this kind of research. However, these approaches have various drawbacks. Experimental trials such as randomized control trials (RCTs) are one such approach, conventionally conducted to provide evidence in support of treatments and identify potentially causal and modifiable risk factors for mental health disorders. RCTs are often viewed as "gold standard" sources of causal evidence, but increasingly this reputation is being called into question (Deaton & Cartwright, 2018). Experimental trials require huge resources if they are aiming to detect effects on rare outcomes, such as childhood suicide attempts, or outcomes that occur several years after the intervention (Black, 1996). Relative to adult studies, experimental trials in children operate under greater ethical scrutiny and heightened risk concerns from parents (Caldwell et al., 2004), which can lead to rarefied populations being recruited with subsequent limitations on generalizability (Rothwell, 2005).

With limits on the applicability of experimental designs, researchers also rely on well-designed observational or quasi-experimental methods to understand risk and protective factors for mental illness. Since the 1960s, epidemiological approaches have been applied to child psycho-pathology and, in high-income countries, often encompass large-scale cross-sectional surveys and prospective cohorts, which integrate biolog-ical measures and multi-informant behavioral assessments to understand etiological mechanisms (Verhulst & Tiemeier, 2015). However, these too have their limitations.

Nationally representative cross-sectional surveys for child and adolescent mental health disorders are expensive to conduct and occur infrequently. Taking England as an example, many of the national "Mental Health of Children and Young People" survey waves have taken place either 3 or 14 years apart (Vizard et al., 2020). Cross-sectional data quickly become out of date, with environmental factors such as neigh-borhood deprivation, technological advances, schools, and social policy constantly changing, which in turn can change patterns of mental health need and detection. In isolation, these surveys may also provide an un-reliable picture of prevalence and risk factors, both through selection bias against mentally unwell populations (Knudsen et al., 2010), and the ef-fects of averaging data over large and diverse populations, so that the findings may not be relevant or informative for local or vulnerable groups (Hatch et al., 2012). There are also growing concerns that responders to surveys are becoming an increasingly unusual group—response rates are associated with sociodemographic characteristics, and can be especially low in younger-age groups (Helakorpi et al., 2015). In England, response rates for the national Mental Health of Children and Young People Sur-veys have fallen from 76% in 2004 to 52% in 2017 and 45% in 2020 (Green et al., 2005; NHS Digital, 2020; Vizard et al., 2018).

Prospective cohort studies not only have made an extensive contri-bution to child and adolescent mental health research as well, but also have important limitations. They are very expensive to set up and run. For example, the National Children's Study in the United States was canceled after a lengthy pilot phase due to concerns over its feasibility and the considerable costs involved (McCarthy, 2014). As with cross-sectional surveys, prospective cohort studies can also face challenges of being out of date, following up individuals born many decades previously, and may therefore not be representative of today's children and adolescents.

Population-based cohort samples are unlikely to capture many in-dividuals effected by rare mental health events, such as exposure to antipsychotic treatment in mid-childhood or development of an early-onset psychotic disorder, reducing their statistical power to analyze these exposures and outcomes (Okkels et al., 2013; Rani et al., 2008). Cohort studies can also be impacted by nonparticipation at certain time points, or even complete loss to follow-up—this can introduce bias, as nonparticipation is in turn associated with sociodemographic and clinical characteristics (Kho et al., 2009; Wolke et al., 2009).

In light of these issues, conventional epidemiological approaches may not be sufficient to estimate reliably and accurately the population need for child and adolescent mental health services, the extent to which these needs are being met, and the risk factors contributing to these needs. Big data offer an opportunity to overcome some of these challenges.

3. Current applications of big data in child and adolescent mental health research

3.1 Routinely collected health data

Electronic health records are a key source of administrative child and adolescent mental health data. In England, health data are routinely collected by the National Health Service (NHS) and can be accessed for research. An example of this is the Clinical Record Interactive Search (CRIS) hosted by South London and Maudsley NHS Foundation Trust (SLaM). SLaM provides secondary mental healthcare services, including Child and Adolescent Mental Healthcare Services (CAMHS), to a catchment of four south London boroughs: Croydon, Lambeth, Lewisham, and Southwark. Clinical records for SLaM services have been fully electronic since 2006, and in 2008, the SLaM Biomedical Research Centre Case Register was set up to derive data directly from these electronic health records by making them available for research through the CRIS application (Stewart et al., 2009). CRIS extracts data from the electronic health records and removes personal identifiers, so that the resulting pseudonymized data can be safely accessed by researchers with minimal risk of deidentification (Fernandes et al., 2013). Because CRIS updates regularly, it is a dynamic data resource and ideal for conducting longitudinal work, which tracks patients at the individual level over time.

Multiple child and adolescent mental health research projects have drawn on the CRIS data resource. These have shed light on ethnic inequalities in CAMHS referral pathways (Chui et al., 2020), high prevalence of revised or supplementary diagnoses being made more than 30 days after a first diagnosis (O'Connor et al., 2020), psychiatric comorbidities predicting antipsychotic use among children with autism (Downs et al., 2016), mental health consequences of child trafficking (Ottisova et al., 2018), and negative symptoms as a predictor of early-onset psychosis treatment failure (Downs, Dean, et al., 2019).

Data available for extraction in CRIS include both structured data (where clinicians select from a range of preset options) and unstructured data (consisting of free-text, such as clinical notes or correspondence). Clinicians sometimes favor free-text notes over more structured, preset fields. Free text gives clinicians the flexibility to write more nuanced notes, which supports the complexity of clinical practice (Rosenbloom et al., 2011). However, these unstructured and complex data are difficult to incorporate into research. To support this, unstructured data can be further processed using natural language processing (NLP) to discern the meaning or semantic content of text, and using prespecified algorithms, to generate structured data on entities of interest for analysis (CRIS Archive, 2021). NLP applications can be rule based, which relies on generating a protocol of how a combination of text-based terms may be combined with logic rules for a particular entity to be positively or negatively identified, or be based on machine learning techniques, which use pattern recognition methods. Applications following either approach can then be validated in terms of their precision and sensitivity by comparing their output to a gold standard output, often created by a manual review of the same text.

NLP provides considerable advantages compared with performing key word searches in health data. For example, an NLP application has been developed and validated which can be used to successfully identify suicidal adolescents from clinical notes (Vellupillai et al., 2019). In contrast, key word searches on the term *suicide* will provide every mention of the term in the health record and will not provide context: key word searches will not discriminate whether *suicide* references a patient's history, their current mental state, or simply a routine clinical screen. Manual review is required to clarify meaning for every instance where *suicide* is identified, which is labor intensive and makes this approach difficult to use in any large-scale analysis.

CRIS is being reproduced across other mental healthcare systems in England, many of them covering child and adolescent mental health services. The CRIS model permits health researchers to develop and validate a range of manual and automated methods for data extraction and analysis (CRIS Network, n.d.). This opens opportunities for clinical researchers to integrate data across multiple care systems and develop samples of sufficient size to identify potential risk factors for mental illness onset or treatment response. These federated approaches may be particularly beneficial for rare disorder or rare treatment studies.

3.2 Administrative data linkages

To further contextualize routinely collected mental health data, data linkage can be undertaken with other administrative health, social, and education records. Data linkage refers to the process of merging two or more data sources, where each pair of records being merged pertains to the same entity (such as an individual person) (Jutte et al., 2011). This provides researchers with an opportunity to take a more holistic view by investigating mental health risk factors and outcomes from different disciplines. It also allows researchers an opportunity to validate variables and minimize missing data by triangulating variables common to both data sources (Mars et al., 2016; Mathur et al., 2013).

Data linkages are, however, challenging to undertake, because the relationships between records in each data source are not known for certain, and there may be no unique identifier common to both data sources. This necessitates using personal identifiers such as names, birth dates, and addresses to match records. Broadly, there are two classes of data linkage methods, which make use of personal identifiers to match records from multiple data sources: deterministic and probabilistic (Harron, Dibben, et al., 2017). Deterministic linkages are rule based, with records classified as links or nonlinks depending on whether certain criteria are met. This process can be strict (e.g., the surname SMITH must match exactly, and the birth date May 29, 1994 must match exactly), or "fuzzy" (e.g., a partial identifier based on the first two letters of the surname and the birth month must match exactly, SM05 using the previous example). Conversely, probabilistic linkages use personal identifiers to produce match weights for each pair of records, indicating the probability that they are a true match. If a match weight reaches a chosen threshold, then the records are linked. Deterministic methods can be faster and easier to undertake, but probabilistic methods can be more accurate when using lower-quality data (Zhu et al., 2015).

In both classes of linkage method, there remains the possibility of linkage error. Linkage error is failing to match records which refer to the same individual (missed match, or false negative, an indicator of linkage sensitivity), or matching records that are not in fact referring to the same individual (false match, or false positive, an indicator of linkage specificity) (Harron, Doidge, et al., 2017). Linkage rules are often designed to minimize error, sometimes prioritizing high specificity or high sensitivity depending on the purpose of the linkage.

Linkage errors can introduce bias if they are systematically associated with particular characteristics (Bohensky et al., 2010). For example, if patients from a certain age group are less likely to engage with healthcare services, then that healthcare service may have fewer opportunities to collect data from those patients. With less data to use as identifiers in the linkage process, those age groups may in turn be less likely to successfully link with another data source (missed matches), resulting in a linked sample which is biased due to underrepresentation of that age group. Where the existence of these biases is known and measurable, they can be quantified and further investigated when conducting research using the linked data, for example, by generating weights and conducting sensitivity analyses (Harron, Doidge, et al., 2017).

In Wales, the Secure Anonymised Information Linkage (SAIL) Databank is an example service that stores and links anonymized administrative data for health research (Jones et al., 2017). Administrative data that can be linked for research using this service include family justice, education, careers, social care, and primary and secondary health data. For example, linkage between primary care, hospital admission, and education records in the SAIL Databank has produced research showing increased risk of depression and self-harm among children and adolescents with declining educational attainment (Rahman et al., 2018), and increased risk of respiratory disease, epilepsy, and diabetes among children prescribed antipsychotics (Brophy et al., 2018).

Similar data linkages have also been developed in England. SLaM CRIS has been linked to hospital admission, census, education, family court, welfare, and pensions data (Maudsley Biomedical Research Centre, n.d.). As an example, Box 3.1 describes the linkage process between SLaM CRIS and the Department for Education's National Pupil Database (NPD) in greater detail. The NPD is an administrative data resource collected and curated by the Department for Education (Department for Education, 2013), containing pupil- and school-level data for all pupils in England's state nurseries, primary, secondary, and special schools. As well as making a wider range of variables available for analysis, this sort of linkage also provides reference to a local area's nonclinical population—this is important context, as it is difficult to assess how well services are meeting the local needs if only using clinical data. The CRIS-NPD data linkage has led to research showing associations between mental health disorders and school absence (Downs, Ford, et al., 2019), and between child and adolescent depression and educational attainment outcomes (Wickersham et al., 2020; Wickersham, Ford, et al., 2021).

Other administrative data linkages are also being undertaken elsewhere in England. For example, the Education and Child Health Insights from Linked Data (ECHILD) project has linked data from Hospital Episode Statistics and the NPD and will be able to conduct further research on the associations between child and adolescent health, education, and social care (University College London, n.d.).

3.3 Blended survey and administrative data approaches

In addition to linking multiple administrative data sets, there is also scope for linking surveys and longitudinal cohort studies to routinely collected administrative data. Such blended approaches combine the benefits of more traditional survey-based methods and big data. Multiple longitudinal cohort studies have undergone linkage with administrative data sources to enrich their data, including the United Kingdom's Avon

---

BOX 3.1

Case study of an administrative data linkage between child and adolescent mental health and education records.

The South London and Maudsley Biomedical Research Centre hosts an administrative data linkage between Clinical Record Interactive Search (CRIS) and the National Pupil Database (NPD) (Downs, Ford, et al., 2019; Downs, Gilbert, et al., 2017).

To undertake the CRIS-NPD data linkage, approvals were sought from data owners and a data flow process established to satisfy governance requirements of both the National Health Service and the Department for Education (DfE). The legal basis for data processing under General Data Protection Regulation was "public benefit," such that individual-level consent from patients and caregivers was not sought. This approach was supported by consultation with several clinical, patient, and caregiver stakeholder groups.

Once approvals were in place, SLaM referrals eligible to be linked to the NPD were identified via CRIS. Referrals to SLaM were eligible for linkage to the NPD if they took place between 2007 and 2013 for children and adolescents aged from 4 to 18 years. Personal identifiers on which to conduct the linkage were then extracted for these referrals, including date of birth, forename, surname, and postcode. With many CRIS cases having multiple addresses on record, and also being likely to have multiple addresses in the NPD, a set of rules were developed to identify a postcode most likely to match with the NPD. The resulting extract was checked and cleaned, for example, removing impossible and incomplete values, and only keeping referrals who had their fourth birthday before September 1, 2012 to fit with the UK school calendar.

The resulting $n = 35,509$ cases could all theoretically appear as pupils in the NPD if they attended an English state-maintained school or sat a nationally standardized exam. Their personal identifiers were sent via secure file transfer from the SLaM Confidential Data Linkage Service (CDLS) to the DfE Data and Statistics Department, where data linkage with the NPD was undertaken. Data linkage followed a fuzzy deterministic matching process, seeking matches in the following stages:

1. Full match on any combination of names, date of birth, and postcode
2. Full match on date of birth, postcode, plus fuzzy match on names
3. Full match on names and date of birth, plus partial character match on postcode
4. Full match on names and postcode, plus "near" date of birth match

---

BOX 3.1 *(cont'd)*

Case study of an administrative data linkage between child and adolescent mental health and education records.

Matches made based on stages 2–4 were manually checked. The resulting data set contained linked CRIS-NPD cases and unlinked NPD-only controls who were residents of the SLaM catchment area. This data set was returned to the SLaM CDLS and was made available to approved researchers.

Linkage rates and biases were investigated, with successful matching to NPD school absence data as the outcome, because school absence is systematically recorded for all pupils in the NPD and is also of clinical interest (Finning et al., 2019). In total, $n = 29,278$ CAMHS cases were successfully linked to NPD absence data, a match rate of 82.5%. Individuals were less likely to successfully link to the NPD if they were aged 16–18 years at first referral to mental health services (as compared with aged <7 years), if their ethnicity was Asian/Asian British, Black British/African, or "other ethnic group" (as compared with White/White British), if they resided in neighborhoods from the second or third national quartiles of deprivation (as compared with the first, most deprived quartile), or if they did not have a SLaM-recorded postcode likely to coincide with the school census before age 16 years. Individuals were more likely to successfully link if they were aged 7–11 years at first referral to mental health services (as compared with aged <7 years), and if they had any ICD-10 disorder. However, in a subsequent analysis of risk factors for persistent school absence, adjusting for these linkage biases using inverse probability weights did not materially change the strength or direction of any results.

Longitudinal Study of Parents and Children (Audrey et al., 2016), Next Steps (Thornby et al., 2018), and the 1970 British Cohort Study (Centre for Longitudinal Studies).

Survey and cohort studies can also benefit from linkage to electronic health records. For example, a three-way data linkage between CRIS, the NPD, and surveys from a program called Targeted Mental Health in Schools was recently conducted to demonstrate associations between child-reported mental health symptoms, quality of life, and referral onward to CAMHS (Yoon et al., 2021). The SAIL Databank also incorporates data from the Millennium Cohort Study, an ongoing cohort study based in the United Kingdom, which follows up a group of participants born in

2000–02 (Connelly & Platt, 2014). Linking the Millennium Cohort Study to electronic health records has been used to show that children with borderline conduct problem scores on the parent-reported Strengths and Difficulties Questionnaire are at increased risk of injury-related hospital admissions or accident and emergency attendances (Bandyopadhyay et al., 2020).

4. Areas for future development

Other complex big data can be adapted for use in child and adolescent mental health research. These are currently areas of ongoing development. For example, accelerometer and actigraphy data can be gathered from mobile phones or wearables to understand physical activity patterns (Wickersham, Carr, et al., 2021) and can be used to detect abnormal movement patterns in children and adolescents with mental health disorders such as attention deficit hyperactivity disorder (Young et al., 2014). These data could aid clinical decision-making in these groups.

Video, audio, and speech data also show promise in this regard. Machine learning approaches combining acoustic feature and automatically transcribed spoken content from five minutes of speech show promise in recognising parental Expressed Emotion, an important family environment indicator and predictor of later childhood psychopathology (Mirheidari et al., 2022). Additionally, recent feasibility work shows promise for automated and intelligible machine learning analysis of video data (primarily comprising mothers interacting with their babies) to assist healthcare professional decision-making in Mother and Baby Units (Boman et al., 2020). The hope for these projects, and many similar, is that big data methodologies may eventually be integrated into health records to enhance the evaluation of clinical interventions and service provision.

5. Ethics and governance

Many jurisdictions across the world have created governance systems which permit data collected from public services, including health services, to be analyzed without explicit consent from individual patients. Big data analyses using electronic health records for clinical research in child and adolescent populations provoke a number of ethical considerations (Piasecki et al., 2021). Broadly, we can combine these considerations into a single question: does the proposed public benefit of the research—including data collection, analysis, outputs, and dissemination—create sufficient public benefit to outweigh the risks to individuals' and families' privacy and autonomy?

Anonymization or deidentification has been generally accepted as a method to reduce individuals'—or if under 16 years of age their caregivers'—ownership and control of their data. However, electronic health records are personalized accounts of an individual's engagement with the health sector, and anonymization does not completely deindividualize the link between a patient and their data. For example, it does not fully resolve an individual's right to hold a religious or moral objection to the purpose of a study, nor entirely mitigate the possibility of a breach of privacy (Carter et al., 2015).

To guide researchers on how to balance public benefit against the potential costs to personal autonomy and privacy, a best practice for mental health data science checklist was recently developed in consultation with stakeholders and people with lived experience of mental health problems (Kirkham et al., 2020). This checklist was developed in the United Kingdom, but may be informative for other countries. A key message is that patients need to be made aware that their data are being used for research purposes. Wherever possible, research should also include patient and public involvement to ensure that the patient perspective is incorporated (Sacristán et al., 2016). Otherwise, patients could feel ignored or misled, which undermines public trust in research and in the healthcare system.

In child and adolescent research, various different models of data sharing and linkage have been developed in response to concerns around confidentiality (Mansfield et al., 2020). These include sharing personal data without explicit consent from individual "data subjects," sharing personal data with participant and parental consent, or conducting linkage using deidentified data so that personal identifiers are not shared. Each of these models has drawbacks: for instance, using opt-in consenting processes can result in more linkage biases compared to opt-out (Downs, Setakis, et al., 2017). However, opt-out processes often require legal and ethical approvals that take considerable time and scrutiny. In the United Kingdom and Europe, sharing personal identifiers between organizations to conduct data linkages without consent requires a "lawful basis" under the General Data Protection Regulation, and many countries have developed a specific legal and governance gateway. In England, health researchers require approval from the Health Research Authority and Confidentiality Advisory Group (CAG), which has ongoing oversight over the linked data.

The risk of individual disclosure and loss of privacy remain even when personal identifiers are removed and only a pseudonymized linked data set is available. With increasingly varied and sensitive information now available for individual record linkages, risk of reidentification through triangulation of information increases.

Using big data for mental health research therefore necessitates strict data access regulations, technical security, and governance procedures. There is a trade-off, however. While protecting patient data is of paramount importance, additional governance often creates long delays, such that mental health service provision is not always evidenced by up-to-date clinical data. There are ethical concerns about risks of underusing data, and because of delays, data linkages and analyses are currently not delivering sufficient patient benefit (Ford et al., 2021).

Attitudes among the general public are generally favorable toward contributing electronic health records to research (Piasecki et al., 2021) and toward data sharing for research purposes (Kalkman et al., 2019). But this is counterbalanced by a lack of trust that large organizations will always use individual data responsibly, and uncertainty over whether the consenting systems currently in place are appropriate given the sensitivity of health data (Shaw, 2014). Hopefully insightful and clinically useful research arising from these data can further strengthen public confidence in these methods.

6. A global perspective

This chapter has primarily focused on examples of big data and data linkage from England and the United Kingdom. However, these methods are also being widely adopted elsewhere. Scandinavian countries have led the way in whole population data repositories which can be easily linked. Whereas many models of data linkage in other countries rely on using personal identifiers to infer that two records probably refer to the same person, Scandinavian countries have unique personal identity numbers for each of their residents which match across registries (Public Health Research Data Forum, 2015). Maintaining and managing access to these registries is resource-intensive, but a clear advantage of this approach is that a wide variety of data can be easily obtained for large samples, without too much concern over biases introduced by linkage error. For example, a recent Danish study of adolescent mental health data linked to school performance data was able to leverage a sample of over 500,000 individuals (Dalsgaard et al., 2020).

Some countries have developed their use of administrative records to the point where these are now routinely substituted for the more traditional ways of generating data resources for health, social, and economic research. In Finland, instead of primary data collection via a census survey delivered to households, 30 different registers and administrative files are linked to provide census data (Statistics Finland, n.d.).

Outside of Scandinavia, very few other countries are able to conduct administrative data linkages routinely. Hence, administrative data linkages in many other countries are in their infancy. Nonetheless, the International Population Data Linkage Network has members from 35 different countries (International Population Data Linkage Network, n.d.), indicating the growing interest in these methods worldwide.

Western Australia also has a long history of population-based data linkage, such as the Western Australian Maternal and Child Health Research Database, which linked various records including births, deaths, and birth defects (Smith & Flack, 2021). A recent systematic review identified a number of studies in Australia which used population-based administrative data and longitudinal data in child protection settings to conduct mental health research, particularly using data from the Queensland Department of Families, Youth and Community Care (Chikwava et al., 2021). A few examples of other high-income countries using administrative data for mental health research in this age group include the United States (Bains et al. 2017), Canada (Reid et al., 2015), and France (Revet et al., 2018).

Administrative data research is also growing in low- to middle-income countries (LMICs). For example, in Brazil, national mortality data have successfully been leveraged to investigate suicide rates for various age groups, including adolescents (McDonald et al., 2021). Electronic health record systems are also increasingly being adopted in LMICs and have been used for public health research in several Asian LMICs (Dornan et al., 2019). However, establishing the required infrastructures is not straightforward: a systematic review conducted to inform electronic health record implementation in South Africa highlighted that high costs and a lack of local expertise, political support, relevant legislation, and technical equipment could all pose challenges (Katurura & Cilliers, 2018). Nonetheless, a design model was recently proposed to do this affordably in developing countries such as sub-Saharan Africa (Adetoyi & Raji, 2020), and data linkages using medical records have been conducted successfully in sub-Saharan and South Africa (Public Health Research Data Forum, 2015).

7. Strengths and limitations of using big data in child and adolescent mental health research

In many high-income countries, every school age child has a comprehensive digital record, which captures nearly every encounter they have with health, social, and education services. Clinical data, in particular, are widely collected in many countries (increasingly electronically), and it is imperative that they be used to benefit recipients of mental healthcare through meaningful research.

Administrative data are rich, characterizing the diverse interactions healthcare staff, social workers, police, and teachers have with young people living in their community. These data can be ideal for conducting epidemiological analyses with high statistical power, and for modeling dynamic changes over time. Compared with traditional cohort studies, administrative data can also cover whole populations, be less costly, and be less likely to suffer from methodological limitations such as nonresponse and attrition biases.

A challenge in analyzing administrative data is that they have not been collected for research purposes. Methodological considerations important to traditional cohort studies (such as sample representativeness, data completeness, measure reliability and validity, and clear metadata documentation) are often not priorities in the creation of administrative datasets (Connelly et al., 2016). This limitation highlights that researchers only have access to variables which have operational value (i.e., pertinent to clinical or administrative practice) rather than those which are most relevant to the risk factor or health outcome under investigation. This compromises the "veracity" or quality of these data, which can be problematic (Munk-Jørgensen et al., 2014). For example, administrative and diagnostic error can arise when assigning diagnoses in routine health data (Davis et al., 2016), and the recording of routine outcome measures is often inconsistent and biased (Morris et al., 2021).

The burden is therefore on the users of administrative data to understand and remain mindful of who collects the data, for what purpose, and how this might impact on research analyses and findings. For example, researchers using administrative data can determine the extent of misclassification and whether it is systematic, by undertaking a validation exercise with a subset of patients (Holowka et al., 2014). In SLaM, there is also ongoing work to improve the process for families and children accessing CAMHS to report outcome measures (Morris et al., 2021).

Findings from administrative datasets can occasionally contradict findings from other big data sources or from survey methods. One example of this comes from the Autism and Developmental Disabilities Monitoring (ADDM) Network in the United States of America. The ADDM uses health records and special education records to estimate prevalence rates of autism spectrum disorder (Maenner et al., 2020). ADDM autism prevalence estimates have been much higher than estimates arising from other administrative datasets (Nevison et al., 2018), but lower than estimates from the nationally representative National Health Interview Survey (Xu et al., 2018). With each approach having different data collection techniques, limitations, and biases, it can be difficult to know how to reconcile such different findings.

Nonetheless, the advent of big data approaches to mental health research presents a powerful resource for researchers who wish to study clinical issues "in vivo" (Stewart & Davis, 2016). Linking data across very large-scale administrative databases can also be beneficial for epidemiological studies, providing whole population coverage and therefore highly generalizable results.

8. Conclusion

Big data are a rich but complex source of information for child and adolescent mental health research. At present, routinely collected health data and administrative data linkages are being successfully leveraged to better understand risk factors and treatment for mental health disorders in this age group. There is also promise for incorporating other novel big data sources into this research, such as video, audio, and actigraphy data. Big data overcome known issues with more traditional epidemiological approaches but also introduce their own challenges and biases that researchers need to monitor and mitigate.

References

Adetoyi, O. E., & Raji, O. A. (2020). Electronic health record design for inclusion in sub-Saharan Africa medical record informatics. *Scientific African, 7*, e00304. https://doi.org/10.1016/j.sciaf.2020.e00304

Audrey, S., Brown, L., Campbell, R., Boyd, A., & Macleod, J. (2016). Young people's views about consenting to data linkage: Findings from the PEARL qualitative study. *BMC Medical Research Methodology, 16*(1), 34. https://doi.org/10.1186/s12874-016-0132-4

Bains, R. M., Cusson, R., White-Frese, J., & Walsh, S. (2017). Utilization of mental health services in school-based health centers. *Journal of School Health, 87*(8), 584–592.

Bandyopadhyay, A., Tingay, K., Akbari, A., Griffiths, L., Bedford, H., Cortina-Borja, M., … Brophy, S. (2020). Behavioural difficulties in early childhood and risk of adolescent injury. *Archives of Disease in Childhood, 105*(3), 282. https://doi.org/10.1136/archdischild-2019-317271

Black, N. (1996). Why we need observational studies to evaluate the effectiveness of health care. *BMJ, 312*(7040), 1215–1218.

Bohensky, M. A., Jolley, D., Sundararajan, V., Evans, S., Pilcher, D. V., Scott, I., & Brand, C. A. (2010). Data linkage: A powerful research tool with potential problems. *BMC Health Services Research, 10*(1), 1–7. https://doi.org/10.1186/1472-6963-10-346

Boman, M., Downs, J., Karali, A., & Pawlby, S. (2020). Toward learning machines at a mother and baby unit. *Frontiers in Psychology, 11*, 567310.

Brophy, S., Kennedy, J., Fernandez-Gutierrez, F., John, A., Potter, R., Linehan, C., & Kerr, M. (2018). Characteristics of children prescribed antipsychotics: Analysis of routinely collected data. *Journal of Child and Adolescent Psychopharmacology, 28*(3), 180–191. https://doi.org/10.1089/cap.2017.0003

Caldwell, P. H., Murphy, S. B., Butow, P. N., & Craig, J. C. (2004). Clinical trials in children. *The Lancet, 364*(9436), 803–811.

Carter, P., Laurie, G. T., & Dixon-Woods, M. (2015). The social licence for research: Why care.-data ran into trouble. *Journal of Medical Ethics, 41*(5), 404—409. https://doi.org/10.1136/medethics-2014-102374

Centre for Longitudinal Studies. (n.d.). 1970 British cohort study. Retrieved from https://cls.ucl.ac.uk/cls-studies/1970-british-cohort-study/

Chikwava, F., Cordier, R., Ferrante, A., O'Donnell, M., Speyer, R., & Parsons, L. (2021). Research using population-based administration data integrated with longitudinal data in child protection settings: A systematic review. *PLoS One, 16*(3), e0249088. https://doi.org/10.1371/journal.pone.0249088

Chui, Z., Gazard, B., MacCrimmon, S., Harwood, H., Downs, J., Bakolis, I., … Hatch, S. L. (2020). Inequalities in referral pathways for young people accessing secondary mental health services in south east London. *Eur Child Adolesc Psychiatry.* https://doi.org/10.1007/s00787-020-01603-7

Clayborne, Z. M., Varin, M., & Colman, I. (2019). Systematic review and meta-analysis: Adolescent depression and long-term psychosocial outcomes. *Journal of the American Academy of Child & Adolescent Psychiatry, 58*(1), 72—79. https://doi.org/10.1016/j.jaac.2018.07.896

Connelly, R., & Platt, L. (2014). Cohort profile: UK Millennium cohort study (MCS). *International Journal of Epidemiology, 43*(6), 1719—1725. https://doi.org/10.1093/ije/dyu001

Connelly, R., Playford, C. J., Gayle, V., & Dibben, C. (2016). The role of administrative data in the big data revolution in social science research. *Social Science Research, 59*, 1—12. https://doi.org/10.1016/j.ssresearch.2016.04.015

CRIS Archive. (2021). *CRIS natural language processing applications library* (p. v1.5). Retrieved from https://www.maudsleybrc.nihr.ac.uk/facilities/clinical-record-interactive-search-cris/cris-natural-language-processing/.

CRIS Network. (n.d.). Members. Retrieved from https://crisnetwork.co/members

Dalsgaard, S., McGrath, J., Østergaard, S. D., Wray, N. R., Pedersen, C. B., Mortensen, P. B., & Petersen, L. (2020). Association of mental disorder in childhood and adolescence with subsequent educational achievement. *JAMA Psychiatry, 77*(8), 797—805. https://doi.org/10.1001/jamapsychiatry.2020.0217

Davis, K. A., Sudlow, C. L., & Hotopf, M. (2016). Can mental health diagnoses in administrative data be used for research? A systematic review of the accuracy of routinely collected diagnoses. *BMC Psychiatry, 16*, 263. https://doi.org/10.1186/s12888-016-0963-x

Deaton, A., & Cartwright, N. (2018). Understanding and misunderstanding randomized controlled trials. *Social Science & Medicine, 210*, 2—21. https://doi.org/10.1016/j.socscimed.2017.12.005

Department for Education. (2013). *National pupil database.* Retrieved from https://www.gov.uk/government/collections/national-pupil-database.

Dornan, L., Pinyopornpanish, K., Jiraporncharoen, W., Hashmi, A., Dejkriengkraikul, N., & Angkurawaranon, C. (2019). Utilisation of electronic health records for public health in Asia: A review of success factors and potential challenges. *BioMed Research International, 2019*, Article 7341841. https://doi.org/10.1155/2019/7341841

Downs, J., Dean, H., Lechler, S., Sears, N., Patel, R., Shetty, H., … Pina-Camacho, L. (2019). Negative symptoms in early-onset psychosis and their association with antipsychotic treatment failure. *Schizophrenia Bulletin, 45*(1), 69—79. https://doi.org/10.1093/schbul/sbx197

Downs, J., Ford, T., Stewart, R., Epstein, S., Shetty, H., Little, R., … Mostafa, T. (2019). An approach to linking education, social care and electronic health records for children and young people in South London: A linkage study of child and adolescent mental health service data. *BMJ Open, 9*(1), e024355. https://doi.org/10.1136/bmjopen-2018-024355

Downs, J., Gilbert, R., Hayes, R. D., Hotopf, M., & Ford, T. (2017). Linking health and education data to plan and evaluate services for children. *Archives of Disease in Childhood, 102*(7), 599–602. https://doi.org/10.1136/archdischild-2016-311656

Downs, J., Hotopf, M., Ford, T., Simonoff, E., Jackson, R. G., Shetty, H., ... Hayes, R. D. (2016). Clinical predictors of antipsychotic use in children and adolescents with autism spectrum disorders: A historical open cohort study using electronic health records. *Eur Child Adolesc Psychiatry, 25*(6), 649–658. https://doi.org/10.1007/s00787-015-0780-7

Downs, J., Setakis, E., Mostafa, T., Hayes, R., Hotopf, M., Ford, T., & Gilbert, R. (2017). Linking strategies and biases when matching cohorts to the National Pupil Database. *International Journal of Population Data Science, 1*(1), 348. https://doi.org/10.23889/ijpds.v1i1.369

Fergusson, D. M., John Horwood, L., & Ridder, E. M. (2005). Show me the child at seven: The consequences of conduct problems in childhood for psychosocial functioning in adulthood. *Journal of Child Psychology and Psychiatry, 46*(8), 837–849.

Fernandes, A. C., Cloete, D., Broadbent, M. T. M., Hayes, R. D., Chang, C.-K., Jackson, R. G., ... Callard, F. (2013). Development and evaluation of a de-identification procedure for a case register sourced from mental health electronic records. *BMC Medical Informatics and Decision Making, 13*, 71. https://doi.org/10.1186/1472-6947-13-71

Finning, K., Ukoumunne, O. C., Ford, T., Danielsson-Waters, E., Shaw, L., Romero De Jager, I., ... Moore, D. A. (2019). The association between child and adolescent depression and poor attendance at school: A systematic review and meta-analysis. *Journal of Affective Disorders, 245*, 928–938. https://doi.org/10.1016/j.jad.2018.11.055

Ford, T., Mansfield, K. L., Markham, S., McManus, S., John, A., O'Reilly, D., ... Shenow, S. (2021). The challenges and opportunities of mental health data sharing in the UK. *The Lancet Digital Health, 3*(6), e333–e336. https://doi.org/10.1016/S2589-7500(21)00078-9

Ford, T., Stewart, R., & Downs, J. (2020). Surveillance, case registers, and big data. In J. Das-Munshi, T. Ford, M. Hotopf, M. Prince, & R. Stewart (Eds.), *Practical psychiatric epidemiology* (Second edition ed., pp. 219–236). Oxford, United Kingdom: Oxford University Press.

Green, H., McGinnity, A., Meltzer, H., Ford, T., & Goodman, R. (2005). *Mental health of children and young people in Great Britain, 2004*. United States of America. Retrieved from New York https://digital.nhs.uk/data-and-information/publications/statistical/mental-health-of-children-and-young-people-in-england/mental-health-of-children-and-young-people-in-great-britain-2004.

Harron, K., Dibben, C., Boyd, J., Hjern, A., Azimaee, M., Barreto, M. L., & Goldstein, H. (2017). Challenges in administrative data linkage for research. *Big Data & Society, 4*(2), 1–12. https://doi.org/10.1177/2053951717745678

Harron, K. L., Doidge, J. C., Knight, H. E., Gilbert, R. E., Goldstein, H., Cromwell, D. A., & van der Meulen, J. H. (2017). A guide to evaluating linkage quality for the analysis of linked data. *International Journal of Epidemiology, 46*(5), 1699–1710. https://doi.org/10.1093/ije/dyx177

Hatch, S. L., Woodhead, C., Frissa, S., Fear, N. T., Verdecchia, M., Stewart, R., ... McManus, S. (2012). Importance of thinking locally for mental health: Data from cross-sectional surveys representing South East London and England. *PLoS One, 7*(12), e48012.

Helakorpi, S., Mäkelä, P., Holstila, A., Uutela, A., & Vartiainen, E. (2015). Can the accuracy of health behaviour surveys be improved by non-response follow-ups? *European Journal of Public Health, 25*(3), 487–490. https://doi.org/10.1093/eurpub/cku199

Holowka, D. W., Marx, B. P., Gates, M. A., Litman, H. J., Ranganathan, G., Rosen, R. C., & Keane, T. M. (2014). PTSD diagnostic validity in Veterans Affairs electronic records of Iraq and Afghanistan veterans. *Journal of Consulting and Clinical Psychology, 82*(4), 569.

International Population Data Linkage Network. (n.d.). The Network. Retrieved from https://www.ipdln.org/network

Jones, K. H., Ford, D. V., & Lyons, R. A. (2017). *The SAIL Databank: 10 years of spearheading data privacy and research utility, 2007–2017*. https://doi.org/10.23889/sail-databank.1001101. Retrieved from.

Jutte, D. P., Roos, L. L., & Brownell, M. D. (2011). Administrative record linkage as a tool for public health research. *Annual Review of Public Health, 32*, 91–108. https://doi.org/10.1146/annurev-publhealth-031210-100700

Kalkman, S., van Delden, J., Banerjee, A., Tyl, B., Mostert, M., & van Thiel, G. (2019). Patients' and public views and attitudes towards the sharing of health data for research: A narrative review of the empirical evidence. *Journal of Medical Ethics*. https://doi.org/10.1136/medethics-2019-105651

Katurura, M. C., & Cilliers, L. (2018). Electronic health record system in the public health care sector of South Africa: A systematic literature review. *African Journal of Primary Health Care & Family Medicine, 10*, 1–8. Retrieved from http://www.scielo.org.za/scielo.php?script=sci_arttext&pid=S2071-29362018000100081&nrm=iso.

Keenan-Miller, D., Hammen, C. L., & Brennan, P. A. (2007). Health outcomes related to early adolescent depression. *Journal of Adolescent Health, 41*(3), 256–262. https://doi.org/10.1016/j.jadohealth.2007.03.015

Kessler, R. C., Berglund, P., Demler, O., Jin, R., Merikangas, K. R., & Walters, E. E. (2005). Lifetime prevalence and age-of-onset distributions of DSM-IV disorders in the National Comorbidity Survey Replication. *Archives of General Psychiatry, 62*(6), 593–602.

Kho, M. E., Duffett, M., Willison, D. J., Cook, D. J., & Brouwers, M. C. (2009). Written informed consent and selection bias in observational studies using medical records: Systematic review. *BMJ, 338*, b866.

Kirkham, E. J., Iveson, M., Beange, I., Crompton, C. J., Mcintosh, A., & Fletcher-Watson, S. (2020). *A stakeholder-derived, best practice checklist for mental health data science in the UK*. Retrieved from University of Edinburgh.

Knapp, M., Ardino, V., Brimblecombe, N., Evans-Lacko, S., Iemmi, V., King, D., … Crane, S. (2016). *Youth mental health: New economic evidence*. London: London School of Economics and Political Science.

Knudsen, A. K., Hotopf, M., Skogen, J. C., Øverland, S., & Mykletun, A. (2010). The health status of nonparticipants in a population-based health study: The Hordaland health study. *American Journal of Epidemiology, 172*(11), 1306–1314. https://doi.org/10.1093/aje/kwq257

Maenner, M. J., Shaw, K. A., & Baio, J. (2020). Prevalence of autism spectrum disorder among children aged 8 years—autism and developmental disabilities monitoring network, 11 sites, United States, 2016. *MMWR Surveillance Summaries, 69*(4), 1.

Mansfield, K. L., Gallacher, J. E., Mourby, M., & Fazel, M. (2020). Five models for child and adolescent data linkage in the UK: A review of existing and proposed methods. *Evidence-based Mental Health, 23*, 39–44. https://doi.org/10.1136/ebmental-2019-300140

Mars, B., Cornish, R., Heron, J., Boyd, A., Crane, C., Hawton, K., … Gunnell, D. (2016). Using data linkage to investigate inconsistent reporting of self-harm and questionnaire non-response. *Arch Suicide Res, 20*(2), 113–141. https://doi.org/10.1080/13811118.2015.1033121

Mathur, R., Bhaskaran, K., Chaturvedi, N., Leon, D. A., vanStaa, T., Grundy, E., & Smeeth, L. (2013). Completeness and usability of ethnicity data in UK-based primary care and hospital databases. *Journal of Public Health, 36*(4), 684–692. https://doi.org/10.1093/pubmed/fdt116

Maudsley Biomedical Research Centre. (n.d.). CRIS linked databases. Retrieved from https://www.maudsleybrc.nihr.ac.uk/facilities/clinical-record-interactive-search-cris/cris-data-linkages/

McCarthy, M. (2014). US cancels plan to study 100 000 children from "womb" to age 21. *BMJ: British Medical Journal, 349*, g7775. https://doi.org/10.1136/bmj.g7775

McDonald, K., Machado, D. B., Castro-de-Araujo, L. F. S., Kiss, L., Palfreyman, A., Barreto, M. L., ... Lewis, G. (2021). Trends in method-specific suicide in Brazil from 2000 to 2017. *Social Psychiatry and Psychiatric Epidemiology, 56*(10), 1779–1790. https://doi.org/10.1007/s00127-021-02060-6

Mirheidari, B., Bittar, A., Cummins, N., Downs, J., Fisher, H. L., & Christensen, H. (2022). *Automatic detection of expressed emotion from five-minute speech samples: Challenges and opportunities.* Interspeech (in press) https://arxiv.org/abs/2203.17242.

Morris, A. C., Ibrahim, Z., Heslin, M., Moghraby, O. S., Stringaris, A., Grant, I. M., Zalewski, L., Pritchard, M., Stewart, R., Hotopf, M., Pickles, A., Dobson, R. J. B., Simonoff, E., & Downs, J. (2022). Assessing the feasibility of a web-based outcome measurement system in child and adolescent mental health services — myHealthE a randomised controlled feasibility pilot study. *Child and Adolescent Mental Health.* https://doi.org/10.1111/camh.12571

Morris, A. C., Macdonald, A., Moghraby, O., Stringaris, A., Hayes, R. D., Simonoff, E., ... Downs, J. M. (2021). Sociodemographic factors associated with routine outcome monitoring: A historical cohort study of 28,382 young people accessing child and adolescent mental health services. *Child and Adolescent Mental Health, 26*(1), 56–64. https://doi.org/10.1111/camh.12396

Munk-Jørgensen, P., Okkels, N., Golberg, D., Ruggeri, M., & Thornicroft, G. (2014). Fifty years' development and future perspectives of psychiatric register research. *Acta Psychiatrica Scandinavica, 130*(2), 87–98.

National Institute for Health Research Maudsley Biomedical Research Centre. (2020). *NIHR announces mental health research goals for next decade.* Retrieved from https://maudsleybrc.nihr.ac.uk/posts/2020/october/nihr-announces-mental-health-research-goals-for-next-decade/.

Nevison, C., Blaxill, M., & Zahorodny, W. (2018). California autism prevalence trends from 1931 to 2014 and comparison to national ASD data from IDEA and ADDM. *Journal of Autism and Developmental Disorders, 48*(12), 4103–4117. https://doi.org/10.1007/s10803-018-3670-2

NHS Digital. (2020). Mental health of children and young people in England, 2020. *Wave 1 follow up to the 2017 survey survey design and methods report.* Retrieved from https://digital.nhs.uk/data-and-information/publications/statistical/mental-health-of-children-and-young-people-in-england/2020-wave-1-follow-up.

O'Connor, C., Downs, J., Shetty, H., & McNicholas, F. (2020). Diagnostic trajectories in child and adolescent mental health services: Exploring the prevalence and patterns of diagnostic adjustments in an electronic mental health case register. *European Child & Adolescent Psychiatry, 29*(8), 1111–1123. https://doi.org/10.1007/s00787-019-01428-z

Okkels, N., Vernal, D., Jensen, S. O. W., McGrath, J. J., & Nielsen, R. (2013). Changes in the diagnosed incidence of early onset schizophrenia over four decades. *Acta Psychiatrica Scandinavica, 127*(1), 62–68.

Ottisova, L., Smith, P., Shetty, H., Stahl, D., Downs, J., & Oram, S. (2018). Psychological consequences of child trafficking: An historical cohort study of trafficked children in contact with secondary mental health services. *PLoS One, 13*(3), e0192321.

Piasecki, J., Walkiewicz-Żarek, E., Figas-Skrzypulec, J., Kordecka, A., & Dranseika, V. (2021). Ethical issues in biomedical research using electronic health records: A systematic review. *Medicine, Health Care and Philosophy, 24*(4), 633–658. https://doi.org/10.1007/s11019-021-10031-6

Polanczyk, G. V., Salum, G. A., Sugaya, L. S., Caye, A., & Rohde, L. A. (2015). Annual research review: A meta-analysis of the worldwide prevalence of mental disorders in children and adolescents. *Journal of Child Psychology and Psychiatry, 56*(3), 345–365. https://doi.org/10.1111/jcpp.12381

Public Health Research Data Forum. (2015). *Enabling data linkage to maximise the value of public health research data: Full report.* Retrieved from London, United Kingdom. https://wellcomecollection.org/works/zymnf3ka.

Raghupathi, W., & Raghupathi, V. (2014). Big data analytics in healthcare: Promise and potential. *Health Information Science and Systems, 2,* 3. https://doi.org/10.1186/2047-2501-2-3

Rahman, M. A., Todd, C., John, A., Tan, J., Kerr, M., Potter, R., … Brophy, S. (2018). School achievement as a predictor of depression and self-harm in adolescence: linked education and health record study. *The British Journal of Psychiatry, 212*(4), 215–221. https://doi.org/10.1192/bjp.2017.69

Rani, F., Murray, M. L., Byrne, P. J., & Wong, I. C. (2008). Epidemiologic features of antipsychotic prescribing to children and adolescents in primary care in the United Kingdom. *Pediatrics, 121*(5), 1002–1009.

Reid, G., Stewart, S. L., Zaric, G. S., Carter, J. R., Neufeld, R. W., Tobon, J. I., … Vingilis, E. R. (2015). Defining episodes of care in children's mental health using administrative data. *Administration and Policy in Mental Health and Mental Health Services Research, 42*(6), 737–747.

Revet, A., Montastruc, F., Raynaud, J.-P., Baricault, B., Montastruc, J.-L., & Lapeyre-Mestre, M. (2018). Trends and patterns of antidepressant use in French children and adolescents from 2009 to 2016: A population-based study in the French health insurance database. *Journal of Clinical Psychopharmacology, 38*(4), 327–335. https://doi.org/10.1097/jcp.0000000000000891

Rosenbloom, S. T., Denny, J. C., Xu, H., Lorenzi, N., Stead, W. W., & Johnson, K. B. (2011). Data from clinical notes: A perspective on the tension between structure and flexible documentation. *Journal of the American Medical Informatics Association, 18*(2), 181–186. https://doi.org/10.1136/jamia.2010.007237

Rothwell, P. M. (2005). External validity of randomised controlled trials:"to whom do the results of this trial apply?". *The Lancet, 365*(9453), 82–93.

Sacristán, J. A., Aguarón, A., Avendaño-Solá, C., Garrido, P., Carrión, J., Gutiérrez, A., … Flores, A. (2016). Patient involvement in clinical research: Why, when, and how. *Patient Preference and Adherence, 10,* 631–640. https://doi.org/10.2147/PPA.S104259

Shaw, D. (2014). Care. data, consent, and confidentiality. *The Lancet, 383*(9924), 1205.

Smith, M., & Flack, F. (2021). Data linkage in Australia: The first 50 years. *International Journal of Environmental Research and Public Health, 18*(21), 11339. Retrieved from https://www.mdpi.com/1660-4601/18/21/11339.

Statistics Finland. (n.d.). Population census 2010. Retrieved from https://www.stat.fi/tup/vl2010/index_en.html

Stewart, R., & Davis, K. (2016). 'Big data' in mental health research: Current status and emerging possibilities. *Social Psychiatry and Psychiatric Epidemiology, 51*(8), 1055–1072. https://doi.org/10.1007/s00127-016-1266-8

Stewart, R., Soremekun, M., Perera, G., Broadbent, M., Callard, F., Denis, M., … Lovestone, S. (2009). The South London and Maudsley NHS Foundation Trust Biomedical Research Centre (SLAM BRC) case register: Development and descriptive data. *BMC Psychiatry, 9,* 51. https://doi.org/10.1186/1471-244X-9-51

The Lancet Global, H. (2020). Mental health matters. *The Lancet Global Health, 8*(11), e1352. https://doi.org/10.1016/S2214-109X(20)30432-0

Thornby, M., Calderwood, L., Kotecha, M., Beninger, K., & Gaia, A. (2018). Collecting multiple data linkage consents in a mixed-mode survey: Evidence from a large-scale longitudinal study in the UK. *Survey Methods: Insights from the Field,* 1–14.

University College London. (n.d.). Welcome to the ECHILD project website. Retrieved from https://www.ucl.ac.uk/child-health/research/population-policy-and-practice-research-and-teaching-department/cenb-clinical-20

Velupillai, S., Epstein, S., Bittar, A., Stephenson, T., Dutta, R., & Downs, J. (2019). Identifying suicidal adolescents from mental health records using natural language processing. *Studies in Health Technology and Informatics, 264*, 413–417. https://doi.org/10.3233/shti190254

Verhulst, F. C., & Tiemeier, H. (2015). Epidemiology of child psychopathology: Major milestones. *European Child & Adolescent Psychiatry, 24*(6), 607–617. https://doi.org/10.1007/s00787-015-0681-9

Vizard, T., Sadler, K., Ford, T., Merad, S., Brodie, E., Forbes, N., ... McManus, S. (2018). Mental health of children and young people in England, 2017. In *Survey design and methods report*. Retrieved from https://digital.nhs.uk/data-and-information/publications/statistical/mental-health-of-children-and-young-people-in-england/2017/2017.

Vizard, T., Sadler, K., Ford, T., Newlove-Delgado, T., McManus, S., Marcheselli, F., ... Cartwright, C. (2020). *Mental health of children and young people in England, 2020* (Retrieved from).

Vos, T., Lim, S. S., Abbafati, C., Abbas, K. M., Abbasi, M., Abbasifard, M., ... Murray, C. J. L. (2020). Global burden of 369 diseases and injuries in 204 countries and territories, 1990–2019: A systematic analysis for the Global Burden of Disease Study 2019. *The Lancet, 396*(10258), 1204–1222. https://doi.org/10.1016/S0140-6736(20)30925-9

Wickersham, A., Carr, E., Hunt, R., Davis, J. P., Hotopf, M., Fear, N. T., ... Leightley, D. (2021). Changes in physical activity among United Kingdom university students following the implementation of coronavirus lockdown measures. *International Journal of Environmental Research and Public Health, 18*(6), 2792.

Wickersham, A., Dickson, H., Jones, R., Pritchard, M., Stewart, R., Ford, T., & Downs, J. (2020). Educational attainment trajectories among children and adolescents with depression, and the role of sociodemographic characteristics: Longitudinal data-linkage study. *The British Journal of Psychiatry, 218*(3), 151–157. https://doi.org/10.1192/bjp.2020.160

Wickersham, A., Ford, T., Stewart, R., & Downs, J. (2021). Estimating the impact of child and early adolescent depression on subsequent educational attainment: Secondary analysis of an existing data linkage. *Epidemiology and Psychiatric Sciences, 30*, e76. https://doi.org/10.1017/S2045796021000603

Wickersham, A., Sugg, H., Epstein, S., Stewart, R., Ford, T., & Downs, J. (2021). The association between child and adolescent depression and later educational attainment: A systematic review and meta-analysis. *Journal of the American Academy of Child & Adolescent Psychiatry, 60*(1), 105–118.

Wolke, D., Waylen, A., Samara, M., Steer, C., Goodman, R., Ford, T., & Lamberts, K. (2009). Selective drop-out in longitudinal studies and non-biased prediction of behaviour disorders. *The British Journal of Psychiatry, 195*(3), 249–256.

World Health Organization. (2014). *Health for the world's adolescents: A second chance in the second decade: Summary*. Retrieved from https://apps.who.int/iris/handle/10665/112750.

Xu, G., Strathearn, L., Liu, B., & Bao, W. (2018). Prevalence of autism spectrum disorder among US children and adolescents, 2014–2016. *JAMA, 319*(1), 81–82. https://doi.org/10.1001/jama.2017.17812

Yoon, Y., Deighton, J., Wickersham, A., Edbrooke-Childs, J., Osborn, D., Viding, E., & Downs, J. (2021). The role of mental health symptomology and quality of life in predicting referrals to special child and adolescent mental health services. *BMC Psychiatry, 21*(1), 366. https://doi.org/10.1186/s12888-021-03364-2

Young, Z., Craven, M. P., Groom, M., & Crowe, J. (2014). *Snappy app: A mobile continuous performance test with physical activity measurement for assessing attention Deficit hyperactivity disorder*. Paper presented at the International Conference on Human-Computer Interaction.

Zhu, Y., Matsuyama, Y., Ohashi, Y., & Setoguchi, S. (2015). When to conduct probabilistic linkage vs. deterministic linkage? A simulation study. *Journal of Biomedical Informatics, 56*, 80–86. https://doi.org/10.1016/j.jbi.2015.05.012

4

Machine learning and child and adolescent mental health services: challenges and opportunities

Paul A. Tiffin[1], and Lewis W. Paton[2]

[1] Department of Health Sciences, University of York and Health Professions
Education Unit, Hull York Medical School, Heslington, United Kingdom;
[2] Health Professions Education Unit, Hull York Medical School, Heslington,
United Kingdom

1. What is machine learning?

Enter the machine learning world, and one can be faced with a dizzying array of technical terms: "artificial intelligence," "deep learning," "supervised," "unsupervised," and so on. So, what is machine learning, and why is it attracting so much attention?

At its core, as the name suggests, machine learning is a technique that allows a machine to learn from data to carry out, or automate, a particular task. This task is often the prediction of a particular outcome. To do this, it links predictor variables (or "features") to these outcomes via algorithms (rules and mathematical functions). At times, the machine learns with help from examples ("supervised learning"), and at other times, it learns without help ("unsupervised"). Algorithms now influence many everyday decisions. These can be the next online video you will view or whether a prisoner is paroled. Machine learning is often the basis of artificial intelligence (AI). AI itself has a number of definitions but can be thought of as an attempt to emulate, and automate, human decision-making processes (Copeland, 2020).

Predicting outcomes of interest from data using mathematics is not new—statistical modeling has been established for decades. So why is

81

machine learning of such interest? Well, it harnesses the power of computers to create algorithms of such complexity that they are frequently unfathomable to their human developers. These complex models often provide predictive powers beyond those offered by traditional statistics. That is, the machine can learn things from data that humans previously could not. However, this complexity often comes at a price, which is discussed later.

There have been a number of studies highlighting the potential of machine learning to improve the delivery of healthcare. In this context machine learning has mainly been used to automate, or semiautomate, diagnosis or suggested management. There have been a number of well-publicized "proof of concepts," some of which will be discussed in this chapter. However, examples of automated systems likely to deliver actual patient benefit in the immediate future remain sparse, especially in the field of mental health. The possible reasons for this are outlined later.

Like many new technologies, machine learning and the wider field of AI tend to polarize opinion. On one hand, proponents of such automated prediction, as in the time of the industrial revolution, claim that these approaches will free mankind from the drudgery of everyday tasks, ushering in a utopia of leisureliness (Vyas, 2021). Conversely, critics suggest that machine intelligence is heralding the end of human civilization (Cellan-Jones, 2014). Neither view is likely correct. Rather, as with all innovations, it is a matter of machine learning finding its optimal place within the delivery of mental healthcare (Tiffin & Paton, 2018).

To consider what this might mean in child and adolescent mental health services (CAMHS), we present in Table 4.1 our general framework for deciding whether machine learning is likely to result in improved efficiency or effectiveness for a given problem or task. This framework categorizes, into four domains, the conditions usually required for machine learning to add value over existing processes. These form the tetrad of *right task, right data, right method/s,* and *right context.* While the first three of these areas are relatively self-explanatory, what we mean by "right context" may require some preliminary explanation. We will discuss the "human—computer interaction" (HCI)—how people engage with, and respond to, predictions made by a machine.

There is a growing body of literature relating to the potential of machine learning to be applied to issues relating to mental health and psychological well-being in general (Shatte et al., 2019). However, there is relatively little published work relating specifically to how services that serve a younger population can be enhanced by predictive technologies. Therefore, this chapter inevitably must at times speculate and draw inferences from studies in more general mental health settings. We turn to, first, the fundamental issue of what jobs, or tasks, one might want a machine to do in CAMHS.

TABLE 4.1   The four domains to consider when selecting an area likely to benefit from machine learning approaches.

Domain	General considerations	Examples of CAMHS-specific issues
Right task	• Will completing the task positively influence patient care? • How effective are the current predictive approaches used for the task? • What are the costs associated with the existing approaches? • How common is the outcome of interest?	• Is the developmental or mental health issue or behavior amenable to intervention, if identified or predicted? • Is the process of assessment and diagnosis one that would normally consume much clinician time?
Right data	• Are there sufficient data to train and validate a machine model? • How representative are the data of the final, general population of interest? • Are the data of sufficient quality to build a model?	• What is the quality of routinely collected outcome and demographic data in CAMHS? • If the aim is to diagnose a relatively uncommon disorder or outcome (e.g., psychosis in under 18s), are there sufficient data to build an accurate model? • What is the prevalence of the target condition or outcome in the population of interest? This will determine the potential usefulness of any predictive process.
Right methods	• Are the methods well suited to the nature of the data? • If the data are structured, would classical statistical methods be more appropriate than machine learning? • Is recalibration of the predicted probabilities required? • Is the method likely to give rise to some level of interpretability? • How computationally intensive is the approach?	• Does the threshold for flagging risk/caseness need to be altered? For example, to minimize "false negatives" (e.g., for suicide risk assessment). If so, is recalibration of the predicted probabilities needed? • If a young person is flagged as "high risk" for an adverse outcome by a system, how easy is it to understand why? Can it be explained to the young person or family easily?

Continued

TABLE 4.1   The four domains to consider when selecting an area likely to benefit from machine learning approaches.—cont'd

Domain	General considerations	Examples of CAMHS-specific issues
	• How replicable (stable) are the results? • How generalisable are the predictions from the model likely to be across population samples and time?	
Right context	• How likely is it that humans will respond to automated decision support suggestions? • Are the results, and other feedback, reported in a clear and impactful way? • Is the "wrapper" for the automated or interactive system appealing and engaging to humans? • Does the system have features that positively reinforce continued human engagement and use?	• Does the young person understand any automated feedback? • Will the feedback positively influence the young person, clinician or family, in terms of decisions or behaviors? • If the system (e.g., computerized therapy) requires regular and long-term engagement, is the design appealing to young people? Are there features that reinforce (reward) regular, appropriate, use of the system over time? For example, "gamification" features such as progress charts and leaderboards.

2. Finding the right task for machine learning

For machine learning to add value to healthcare, we must ask it to perform a task that is either directly, or indirectly, clinically useful. That is, the additional information provided by the machine must influence the assessment and management of a patient, increasing the overall likelihood of a positive outcome.

At first glance, this seems like a self-evident statement. However, history is littered with examples of diagnostic tests and disorder screening programs that, on a population level at least, may have done little good and potentially even some harm (Hofmann & Welch, 2017). Perhaps the most common reason for this is that, even if a condition is detected with a reasonable level of precision, the subsequent intervention offered makes little difference to overall prognosis. Ideally, machine-derived predictions should provide stakeholders—clinicians, young people, and their families—with novel information. Indeed, one pragmatic definition of "information" is knowledge that is relatively surprising (Cole et al., 2021). For example, if one is told that the Pope is a practising Catholic, that is of little surprise to anyone. However, if you found out that he was a talented goalkeeper in soccer (this was true of Pope John Paul II), then that would be novel and surprising information! Box 4.1 provides an illustrative example of some of the considerations that may be important in relation to the choice of task.

BOX 4.1

Some considerations regarding the choice of task for a machine.

Walsh et al. (2018) used machine learning on routinely collected clinical data to attempt to predict nonfatal suicide attempts in adolescents.

Firstly, it is important to ask whether this task was generally of clinical use? Acts of intentional self-harm in adolescents are clearly something to be avoided if possible, and are themselves associated with a substantially increased risk of completed suicide or misadventure. However, if a clinician knows a particular young person is at elevated risk of imminent self-harm, is there something that can be done to reduce this hazard? In this sense, the evidence for effective interventions for reducing self-harm in adolescents is limited, with, for example, mixed results for approaches such as dialectical behavior therapy (Freeman et al., 2016). There may, however, be immediate steps that could be employed, such as increased supervision and monitoring. In this particular study, the machine was evaluated in relation to a number of tasks. It was asked to identify those who attempted suicide (as established in case notes) and distinguish them from those with other forms of self-injury, those adolescents with depressive symptoms (but no suicide attempts) and those young people who were undergoing general hospital medical care. These tasks clearly have different degrees of usefulness depending on the clinical context. Perhaps unsurprisingly, the machine performed best when attempting to discriminate between general hospital patients and those with a subsequent suicide attempt. This task might be less useful though, than, say, identifying high self-harm risk in a depressed patient.

2.1 What tasks would clinicians find useful? Findings from a Delphi study

When considering which tasks performed by a machine may add most value in clinical care, one stakeholder is the clinicians themselves. To explore this, and whether there was consensus among clinicians as to which machine learning tasks would most enhance their practice, we conducted a Delphi study (Jones & Hunter, 1995). Following invitations to existing networks of psychiatrists, including academic child psychiatrists, an expert panel consisting of 15 individuals was formed. This panel consisted of clinicians across a range of mental health disciplines (both adult and CAMHS, inpatient and outpatient), experience (ranging from 2 years to more than 30), and all working in high-income countries. A variety of potential tasks were presented to the panel, who were asked to rate the usefulness of the tasks on a five-point Likert scale from *"not at all"* to *"extremely"* useful, over and above current clinical practice. The tasks primarily related to diagnosing and prognosing young people, but also included logistical tasks. We evaluated the median usefulness and degree of consensus among the panel for each task after the third round. Consensus was defined as > 75% of participants agreeing. A summary of the results, previously unpublished, is shown in Table 4.2.

As can be seen, consensus was reached in a number of areas. Firstly, supporting specific diagnoses would at best be only "moderately useful." As one participant said *"skilled clinicians can diagnose most things well."* Other issues raised were that *"many of these conditions exist on a continuum"* and that *"to diagnose any of [them] well, you have to diagnose all of them."* This is a common issue in predicting outcomes in mental health, particularly in contrast to physical health. Thus, defining the "ground truth"—the unambiguous, "hard" outcome that the machine must learn to predict—is often challenging in a CAMHS context.

In contrast, the panel reached consensus that "predicting medication side effects" would be "very useful." Administrative tasks, such as rota planning, outcome monitoring, and improving patient clinic attendance, were generally rated "very useful" with consensus. Indeed, such systems aiming to improve clinic attendance, for example, already exist (Nelson et al., 2019), although they would not necessarily require machine learning.

On average, the panel rated automated feedback of treatment response to both clinicians and patients as "very useful." Consensus was not strictly reached with this statement, although more than 75% of respondents thought it would be "very" or "extremely" useful. More common conditions—such as anxiety and depression—were rated as more useful in this context than other conditions, such as conduct disorders and psychosis. This may be due to the commonness of the conditions, or their perceived treatment responsiveness. In this context, automated systems have been shown to have potential for improving outcomes in adult psychological therapy services via "feedback-informed treatment." Symptom trajectories for subgroups of patients are estimated. The therapist is then alerted if the patient does not appear to be reporting the expected improvements during treatment. A trial reported

TABLE 4.2   Results from the Delphi exercise.

Task	Median usefulness	Consensus?
General personalized treatment tasks		
Predicting medication side effects	Very	Yes
Predicting medication response	Very	No
Predicting significant adverse events (e.g., serious self-harm)	Moderately	Yes
Suggesting optimal psychotherapy modality	Moderately	Yes
Supporting diagnosis	Moderately	No
Triaging to interventions or care pathways	Moderately	No
Predicting nonengagement or dropout from any treatment	Moderately	No
Logistical tasks		
Improving clinic attendance	Very	Yes
Rota planning	Very	Yes
Supporting outcome monitoring	Very	Yes
Automatically updating involved professionals	Very	No
Drafting clinical reports	Moderately	No
Condition specific diagnoses		
Anxiety	Moderately	Yes
Attention deficit hyperactivity disorder	Moderately	No
Autism spectrum disorder	Moderately	Yes
Bipolar affective disorder	Moderately	Yes
Depression	Moderately	Yes
Learning disabilities	Moderately	Yes
Obsessive compulsive disorder	Moderately	Yes
Psychosis	Moderately	Yes
Emerging personality disorder	Slightly	Yes
Post-traumatic stress disorder	Slightly	Yes
Condition-specific treatment response		
Anxiety	Very	No
Attention deficit hyperactivity disorder	Very	No

Continued

TABLE 4.2   Results from the Delphi exercise.—cont'd

Task	Median usefulness	Consensus?
Bipolar affective disorder	Very	No
Depression	Very	No
Obsessive compulsive disorder	Very	No
Post-traumatic stress disorder	Very	No
Attachment disorders	Moderately	Yes
Autism spectrum disorders	Moderately	Yes
Conduct disorders	Moderately	Yes
Emerging personality disorder	Moderately	Yes
Psychosis	Moderately	Yes

significantly superior improvements in participants randomized to the feedback intervention (Delgadillo et al., 2018). Although this study employed traditional statistical prediction approaches, machine learning could offer advantages, particularly as more routine data become available.

A scoping review highlighted that addressing public health issues might be one area that machine learning could support (Shatte et al., 2019). In relation to youth mental health, one could speculate on the kind of population-level tasks that might be useful. For example, an algorithm could be developed to flag schools where the students might be especially vulnerable to a stressful, national (or international) event, such as the impact of the coronavirus pandemic. This may help target mental health interventions at the school or community level with a greater degree of accuracy than currently possible.

2.2 Predicting rare events in child and adolescent mental health services

Many of the predictions we would like to make in CAMHS are in relation to rare events, such as suicide. However, predicting uncommon events is difficult for machines, as well as humans. Technical tricks (such as "oversampling" rare cases so the machine "sees" more of these uncommon outcomes) can help the machine learn how to predict the outcome (Fernández et al., 2018). However, it is worth considering the implications of predicting rare outcomes in practice, even with a reasonable level of accuracy. All algorithms make mistakes and misclassify individuals. The percentage of those flagged as "at risk" by the machine who were true positive cases (i.e., those who did go on to self-harm) is known as the positive predictive value (PPV). In contrast, the percentage of those flagged not at risk who actually were not at risk is the negative predictive value (NPV). Even if these values appear reasonably high for a particular algorithm in a particular setting, the predictive model practice may not actually be clinically useful if the outcome of interest is rare. An illustrative example of this is shown in Box 4.2.

2.3 "Omics"

One clear area of research where the benefits of machine learning have been realized is in the field sometimes summarized as "omics"

BOX 4.2

The clinical implications of predicting rare events.

Suppose the positive predictive value (PPV) for a suicide risk assessment system for discriminating between general medical patients and those at risk of a significant suicide attempt was 0.87 (as reported in the Walsh study (Walsh et al., 2018)). That is, 87% of positive predictions were associated with adolescents actually at risk. The negative predictive value (NPV) was not reported in the Walsh study, so let us assume it was 0.95. What would this mean in absolute numbers for general hospital seeing around a hundred adolescent patients a day?

Assume, for illustrative purposes, that on average, 1% of patients carry out a significant act of self-harm in the following 7 days. If the algorithm was run on the case records of 1000 patients, out of truly at-risk young people, roughly nine would be correctly identified as at risk. However, of the remaining 990 low-risk patients, only around 940 would be correctly deemed low risk. This means roughly 60 patients, in total, would have to be further assessed for suicidality, of which nine would be actually at high risk. This further assessment may not be feasible, depending on the resources required, as well as any unwanted effects, such as distress to the patients. Furthermore, if clinicians are constantly receiving a stream of "false alerts," they may start to disregard the feedback. Thus, it is important when evaluating machine learning algorithms to look beyond the raw performance metrics and consider what these might mean in terms of absolute numbers and unintended consequences for a health service.

(Reel et al., 2021). This includes genomics, epigenomics, proteomics, microbiomics, and metabolomics. The tasks in this context are to identify patterns of association between often vast numbers of variables. The "brute force" aspects of machine learning are particularly advantageous with these large data sets. Computers can run for many hours, days, or months, exhaustively evaluating possible combinations of potential associations in the complex and vast data often found in "omics" (Oh et al., 2020). The information gained from such analyses could give rise to a huge range of personalized treatments in mental health (Eyre et al., 2016). The benefits of such biological data mining in routine CAMHS practice are probably some way off, as these data are not yet routinely available. Indeed, even if a promising potential task is identified, it relies on the availability of suitable data to train the predictive algorithm. This is now discussed in the next section.

3. Finding the right data for machine learning

Even the most sophisticated of machine learning approaches are of little use without sufficient quality and quantity of data. This is exemplified by the old adage: "garbage in garbage out …" (Kilkenny & Robinson, 2018). The learning process may exaggerate biases, or amplify noise, within data in some cases, leading to poor predictions. Thus, the search for the right data on which to develop machine learning applications has become a major challenge in the field. As the saying goes, "data is [are] the new oil."

3.1 Structured data

There are many aspects to "good" data. Two of the most common considerations are its accuracy and completeness. There have been attempts to standardize the symptom and outcome measures used in practice, such as the CAMHS Outcome Research Consortium in the United Kingdom (Fleming et al., 2016). Such data are known as "structured" (already numeric or otherwise machine readable). However, achieving a high rate of quality and coverage of routine structured outcome measures is extremely challenging. Firstly, busy clinicians working in relatively underresourced services may struggle to find the time to complete and enter data relating to symptoms and functioning routinely. Secondly, in research settings, there are usually resources to support and maintain the reliability and validity of psychological measures. This can include intensive and repeated training for instrument raters, as well as other quality assurance steps such as evaluating interrater reliability in a subsample of ratings. These are often unavailable in routine clinical practice.

However, the drive to standardize assessment is likely to give rise to greater quantities, and overall a higher quality, of structured data. The development of linked data sets across service providers, such as the Clinical Record Interactive Search system (see Box 4.3), may also drive increases in data quality and quantity. Data quantity is also an important consideration, as machine learning is relatively "data hungry"—large quantities of data are often needed. This is partly due to the way in which machine learning models are trained and their performance tested, often requiring portions of data to be held back (see Section 4).

3.2 Unstructured data

In contrast to structured data, "unstructured" data, such as free text, images, or audio recordings, are not readily machine readable. Mental health services generate considerable quantities of unstructured data, usually from free text in medical records. Indeed, it has been suggested that psychiatry services produce more data than other specialities; something that may have not gone unnoticed by large technology firms ("Big Tech") such as Google (Eyre et al., 2016). To date, other sources of unstructured data (e.g., neuroimaging data) are not always available outside of research settings. Speech samples may also provide unstructured data for machine learning—based tasks, with promising results (see Box 4.4).

BOX 4.3
___

The Clinical Record Interactive Search system.

The Clinical Record Interactive Search (CRIS) (NIHR Maudsley Biomedical Research Centre, 2021) is a system in the United Kingdom, which allows both structured and unstructured (i.e., free-text) data from mental health records to be analyzed at scale. The data can be dei-dentified and also linked to a variety of data sources, including those from education and social care. Due to the size of routinely arising data sets such as CRIS, they provide an opportunity to apply machine learning approaches to address important clinical questions. For example, whether the presence of a comorbid autism spectrum disorder is associated with treatment resistance in early-onset psychosis (Downs et al., 2017, see Wickersham and Downs, chapter 3, this volume).

BOX 4.4

Examples of the use of Natural Language Processing.

One study applied natural language processing (NLP) to the text from 30 suicidal and 30 nonsuicidal adolescents. It was able to differentiate the two groups of teenagers with an accuracy of 90% (Pestian et al., 2016). The features of the speech samples that helped the system differentiate the two groups included word count, but also pause length, prosody, vowel spacing, and other voice characteristics (Scherer et al., 2013).

NLP has also been used to predict onset of psychosis at 2.5-year follow-up in 34 adolescents and young adults (14–27 years of age) deemed at "clinically high risk" (Bedi et al., 2015). The system was evaluated as predicting the outcome (transition to psychosis, which occurred in five participants) with 100% accuracy.

However, given the relatively small number of participants, these performances would have to be replicated in separate, large sample populations, before strong inferences are drawn. As highlighted earlier, machine learning is well suited to exploiting the vast swathes of data within the various "omics" fields, although such data are not often yet routinely available in practice. However, routine genetic testing is likely to become increasingly commonplace in mental health services in the near future (Curtis et al., 2019). In the future, information from such biological sources could also be combined with other routinely available data, such as demographics and symptom scores, to enhance the accuracy of predictions.

3.3 Digital health platforms

The increasing implementation of digital health platforms may exponentially increase the availability of data in the near future. This includes "mHealth" approaches (see Box 4.5). Globally, and particularly in high-income countries, mobile technology is extremely common—in the United Kingdom, 96% of young people aged 16–24 years own a smartphone (Statista, 2020). In contrast, at the time of writing, wearable technology (electronic devices worn by the user which can record, analyze, and transmit data) usage rates are somewhat lower (18%) though increasing (Ofcom, 2020). Such high rates of technology ownership and use raise the possibility of using mHealth approaches to identify and

---

BOX 4.5

MHealth.

MHealth is defined by the World Health Organization as the "use of mobile and wireless technologies to support the achievement of health objectives" (World Health Organization, 2011).

Examples include mobile device applications (apps) designed to support well-being and mental health that may also capture regular self-ratings of mood (Widnall et al., 2020). "Fitbit" wristbands can also be used to capture continuous kinaesthetic (movement) data.

---

prevent deteriorating mental health in young people. There are well-documented difficulties in accessing timely and effective youth mental health assessment and treatment. For example, in England, only 1 in 4 under 18s with a mental health problem accessed specialist care in the preceding year (NHS Digital, 2018). The use of data from mobile devices, combined with machine learning—based predictions to generate feedback and facilitate self-help, could be one, scalable, solution to more children and adolescents accessing support.

Once suitable data have been acquired, then, to maximize the information gained, the most appropriate machine learning approaches should be applied. This is now addressed in the following section.

4. Choosing the right methods

There are a wide variety of mathematical approaches used to link predictors ("features") and outcomes of interest. Some of these share their basic underpinnings with classical statistical modeling techniques, such as regression, or can be considered extensions or special cases of these. Some methods are highly complex combinations of multiple methodologies. Furthermore, the "no free lunch theorem" postulates that one specific technique does not necessarily have the advantage over any others for a particular data set (Wolpert & Macready, 1997). How then do we choose the most appropriate method to use?

4.1 Supervised versus unsupervised learning

The choice of algorithm to use partly depends on the data and task. Machine learning methods can be broadly categorized into two principal types of learning: "supervised" and "unsupervised." Supervised learning is where a machine is shown a series of labeled examples, and the system links the features to the target outcome. In contrast, in "unsupervised" learning, a system attempts to cluster or categorize variables in the absence of labeled training data. Box 4.6 discusses some everyday examples of these two distinct types of learning.

As a consequence of the "no free lunch" theorem, it is common to try a range of methods to evaluate which has the best predictive performance for a particular data set. Moreover, a frequently used strategy to improve predictive performance in a task is to combine varying methods and summarize the predictions from these using some kind of averaging or voting approach. This is known as "ensembling" (Dietterich, 2000).

Despite the "no free lunch theorem," in actual practice, the most popular, and often most effective, approaches to predictive modeling with small- to medium-sized structured data sets (several hundred to thousand observations) are based on ensembles of "boosted trees." Simple hierarchical-based classification models have been used for hundreds of years. Many of us may recall, as schoolchildren, using a classification tree to identify the plant that a leaf may have come from. Trees can also be used to predict continuous outcomes, in which case they are "regression trees." Tree-based approaches tend to be good at capturing complex nonlinear relationships between variables. Single trees are easy to implement and are actually interpretable. Moreover, they may be sufficiently uncomplicated to lend themselves to paper- and pencil-based flow algorithms that can be used as clinical decision support tools in settings

---

BOX 4.6

Supervised and unsupervised machine learning.

One example of *supervised learning* would be the automatic conversion of the handwritten characters of the postcode written on an envelope into numbers and letters. The machine may learn how to perform this task by being shown thousands of examples of handwritten characters, which are also annotated by a human with the correct number or letter attached (hence, "supervised").

Unsupervised learning, in contrast, has been used for some time by retailers for "basket analysis"; that is, supermarkets are keen to know how buying habits in customers might be grouped. Such insights are of obvious value when arranging the layout of your store or targeting clients for vouchers or special offers.

---

such as accident and emergency units. Computers build trees by creating rules that sequentially split data to create groups of observations. These groups are as similar within group as possible, while each group is as distinct as possible. One example of the application of decision trees in mental health research is described in Box 4.7.

However, an individual tree can be "biased"—it might not have accurately captured the relationship between the features and the outcome of interest. A solution to this is to "grow" a "forest." Random forests contain many trees (often thousands), each grown using a different randomly selected subset of features from the training data. An individual tree may be more or less biased, but summarizing the results (e.g., via a vote, or an average) decreases the overall risk of bias but increases the spread of results. Thus, forests decrease the risk of bias but increase the variance of the results. "Boosting" often improves prediction further. In this case, trees are sequentially grown, but at each iteration, the machine uses the new tree to model those observations not modeled by the previous tree (the "residuals"). That is, the machine increasingly focuses on difficult to predict observations. See, for example, Chen & Guestrin (2016) or Prokhorenkova et al. (2017) for further detail on two common boosted tree approaches.

BOX 4.7

An example of the use of decision trees.

Mann et al. (2008) used a categorical decision tree to classify (among other outcomes) those with recent suicide attempts from those with no attempts in a general population sample.

Decision trees contain *nodes*, which represent the features of the data set from which we wish to predict the outcome of interest. The simplest tree generated in Mann et al. contains only one "node," which split individuals into attempters and nonattempters based on their Scale for Suicide Ideation (SSI) score (<17.5 were classified as nonattempters, ≥17.5 as attempters). These final states (attempter or nonattempter) are known as *leaves*.

Another tree introduced one further node, based on whether someone was diagnosed with borderline personality disorder (BPD), with a *branch* connecting the two nodes. For those with a low SSI score, they were split further into those with BPD (recent attempters) and those without BPD (nonattempters). For those with a high SSI score, no branch connected SSI score with BPD status. That is, they were not further split on BPD status and were all classified as recent attempters.

Naturally, there are many other machine learning algorithms, including support vector machines (Cortes & Vapnik, 1995), naïve Bayes (Chauhan, 2018), and neural networks (explained later) (Bishop, 1995). Support vector machines attempt to locate a line or surface ("hyperplane") that most accurately separates two or more classes of observation. These lines or surfaces are known as "support vectors." If the data are not easily separable via straight lines or "flat" surfaces (i.e., "linearly separable"), a "kernel trick" can be used to transform the data. This aims to make the transformed data more linearly separable. Naïve Bayes classifiers are based on probability theory. They use Bayes theorem (Bayes, 1763) to predict the probability of a particular (categorical) outcome for a particular combination of features, given what is observed in the training data. The "naïve" refers to the assumption that all features are independent of each other. While this is often implausible, it substantially reduces the computational power required and still frequently produces predictions that are accurate enough to be of practical use. These algorithms can also be combined in ensembles of multiple approaches to a single prediction task. However, in general, boosted ensembles of trees often appear to outperform other methods with structured (numeric) data. This is evidenced by their popularity in machine learning competitions, most famously "Kaggle" (Kaggle Forum, 2016). However, this is not always the case. In a comparison across a range of methods for predicting mental health problems in adolescents, random forests, support vector machines, boosted ensemble of trees, a neural network, and logistic regression all performed broadly similarly (Tate et al., 2020). Indeed, machine learning does not always offer a clear advantage over more traditional statistical techniques such as logistic regression on structured data. For example, a metaanalysis observed no statistically significant difference when predicting readmission to hospital in systems that used machine learning over those that did not (Mahmoudi et al., 2020).

Despite the popularity and effectiveness of boosted tree ensembles for machine learning, it is deep learning and neural networks that have probably gathered the most publicity in recent years. Neural networks attempt to mimic neuronal connections in the brain, as the name suggests. In deep learning, "neurones" with inputs and outputs are organized into layers. These can be arranged to perform a similar function to the visual cortex in mammals. The upper layers of neurons organize features into larger meaningful sets, and this information is passed to the deeper layers, which then produce the final prediction. For example, deep neural networks have been developed to phenotype youth depression from medical records (Geraci et al., 2017) and to screen for autism in a data set containing both adults and children (Shahamiri & Thabtah, 2020).

In terms of unsupervised learning, there may be situations where clustering or characterizing groups of patients may be useful in identifying patterns of symptoms. A range of algorithms exist for this purpose, the most commonly used ones involving evaluating the clustering of observations, such as "k-means," according to the (hypothetical) distances between each data point, or a central cluster focus ("centroid") (Celebi & Aydin, 2016). An alternative approach, which emerged from traditional statistics, but is sometimes considered a form of unsupervised learning, is "latent class analysis". This seeks to explain the correlation between a number of observed variables ("indicators") by identifying different underlying groups of individuals ("latent classes"). The method has been effective in identifying different trajectories of enuresis in children (Croudace et al., 2003). The use of such clustering algorithms may thus have implications for how we might diagnose or prognosticate in a CAMHS setting.

4.2 Common problems in machine learning

One of the perennial problems of machine learning is that they are often too successful in linking predictors and outcomes. Machines can frequently create models that fit the data they are trained on perfectly, but subsequently have little generalisability to other previously unseen data sets. This issue is known as "overfitting" (Ying, 2019). Numerous approaches have been developed to address this issue. One common approach is to split the available data into a "training" data set and a "test" ("validation") data set. As the names suggest, the model learns how to link the features to the outcome in the training data set, and its performance is then assessed on the previously unseen test data. Other technical approaches also exist. One is the use of "regularization" functions, which act as a metaphorical "hand brake" when machine learning algorithms are being trained. Another is "cross-fold validation"—a well-established technique in statistics also used in machine learning for repeatedly evaluating algorithm performance in relatively small portions (folds) of data that have not been used to train the algorithm (Stone, 1974).

Despite the name "artificial intelligence," human toddlers have more ability to reason, causally, about why events occur than even than the most sophisticated AI systems (Pearl & Mackenzie, 2018). Developing systems that can causally reason could theoretically reduce overfitting and enhance the prediction accuracy (Richens et al., 2020). It has been suggested that "hybrid" approaches, which combine mechanistic (causal) and data-driven models, might be most useful in healthcare (Doyle et al., 2013). Indeed, a proof of concept of this approach suggested some promise. A model of treatment response in ADHD, derived from the literature, was combined with data from a CAMHS clinic. The resulting machine learning model predicted treatment response better than conventional methods for some, though not all, outcomes (Wong et al., 2017).

Finally, machine learning studies have been frequently criticized, for both lack of transparency in their reporting of methods and also issues relating to reproducibility (Collins & Moons, 2019; Vollmer et al., 2020). When developing machine learning algorithms, there are many steps where randomness can be introduced. For example, how missing values are handled, or the particular subsets of data on which the models were trained and validated on. For this reason, we suggest that many models are iteratively built and their average performance is evaluated. Research employing machine learning should adhere to the same reporting standards as those in other fields though few do (Yusuf et al., 2020). At the time of writing, a specific machine learning reporting standard was not available, although this is likely to change in the near future (Collins & Moons, 2019). The ability of researchers to report the development of machine learning systems in a transparent and reproducible way will be pivotal in influencing the extent to which people have confidence in the usefulness and fairness of the system. Achieving this will have a positive effect on the way people engage and respond to the technology. It is to this issue of human computer interaction (HCI) we now turn.

5. Finding the right context

Ultimately, how people respond to automated systems will determine the overall effectiveness of a system in achieving the desired outcomes, as much as the accuracy of any predictions it makes. Fundamentally, will patients and clinicians accept decisions made by a machine?

5.1 The human—computer interaction

This study area is known as "human—computer interaction" (Dix et al., 2003). Automated systems for supporting clinical decision-making have been in use for some time (Roshanov et al., 2013). Paradoxically, as healthcare becomes more automated, the human qualities of practitioners, rather than clinical skills, will become more important. That is, they will be required to effectively communicate the feedback from machines and support adherence to these recommendations. However, it has been reported that effect sizes observed in trials involving computerized clinical decision support systems tended to be small to moderate (Kwan et al., 2020). These modest effects can probably be explained by the fact that automated management suggestions are frequently overridden by clinicians. Separately, it has been reported that those decision support systems where suggestions were more likely to be acted upon were those where a clinician had to provide a reason for overriding the tool. Similarly, suggestions were more likely to be acted on when the results were shared with both patient and clinician (Roshanov et al., 2013). Such design features should be taken into consideration when embedding automated systems in clinical settings. In some respects, feedback from decision support systems can be considered, in this context, as a three-way conversation between the clinician, the computer, and patient. In CAMHS, the situation may be further complicated by the potential role of caregivers and other agencies involved in the care of a young person.

A systematic review of the Human Computer Interaction (HCI) literature relating to machine learning in mental health identified 54 relevant papers (Thieme et al., 2020). Only one paper identified was specific to under-18 year olds and reported an approach that enabled a robot to appear more "socially aware" when playfully interacting with a child, via mimicking human distance regulation (Feil-Seifer & Matarić, 2012). The possibility of the machine improving relations between the human clinician and patient was raised. This included a study where a machine analyzed audio recordings of therapy sessions to improve communication between clinicians and service users via automatically feeding back on motivational interviewing style (Hirsch et al., 2018). Various HCI design features, relevant to the application of this technology to young people, were also highlighted. These included the importance of timely, but unobtrusive access to patient generated data. This could be via access to social media or information generated from sensors in, for example, wearable technologies. This highlights the confidence that mental health service users would need to have in technology providers and how they treat sensitive data.

Machine learning systems should not be seen as impacting adversely on either clinical or patient autonomy. Given the tragic history of some of the coercive practises in mental health, this would seem to be a particularly sensitive area (Szasz, 1997). The issue of "nonmaleficence" was also mentioned in several papers identified within the review (Nobles et al., 2018; Salekin et al., 2018; Zakaria et al., 2019), referring to the potential for automation to have negative, unintended, and at times, unforeseen consequences. In a CAMHS setting, it is easy to see how misclassifying a young person as having a developmental or mental health disorder could negatively impact on the individual and their family. There are many accounts of algorithms, aiming to improve the efficiency of both public and private sector service, having adverse consequences for both individuals and communities (O'Neil, 2008). Indeed, some scientists have described algorithms as being "infected with biases" (McDonald, 2019).

5.2 Interpretability and ethical issues

Machine learning algorithms are sometimes referred to as "black box" models; one knows what goes in and what comes out, but it is a mystery what goes on inside the "box" (Bathaee, 2017). This lack of "interpretability" is a crucial barrier to the implementation of such systems in practice, both ethically and legally (Goodman & Flaxman, 2017). Legally, patients often have a "right to explanation" of why decisions have been made. This has led to a drive toward "explainable AI" (Arrieta et al., 2020). This interpretability can occur at two levels (Linardatos et al., 2020). It can be "global"—understanding how a machine learning model generally derives its predictions, or "local"—understanding, to some extent, why the machine made a particular prediction on a specific observation (e.g., patient). Ethically, being able to explain outputs would increase the confidence of end-users in the systems, as well as allow discussions of the decisions.

Another ethical issue that has arisen is the question of when an algorithm becomes a "medical device" (Ordish, 2019). If classified as such, predictive technologies would be subject to a range of regulation and requirements for evidence of safety, efficacy, and effectiveness prior to implementation. At present, many systems are marketed as "lifestyle" or "well-being" aids, or as support for health providers in assessing and managing patients. Existing definitions of medical devices are not well suited to algorithm development and have been subject to judicial review. Although not clear-cut, the main distinction, currently, seems to be that if software is specifically intended by the manufacturer to be used for one or more medical purposes, and presumably therefore impacts on diagnosis and/or treatment in its own right, then it may be classed as a medical device. Software used for general, or supportive purposes, even in a medical setting, might not be deemed to fulfill these criteria (Ordish, 2019). However, this situation is likely to be under review for some time.

5.3 Gamification

Young people are often caricatured, somewhat unhelpfully, as inattentive and easily bored. This is unfair on a number of levels. Firstly, the attention span of humans generally appears to have decreased, at least in relation to some situations and tasks, perhaps due to the uptake of mobile technology (Subramanian, 2018). It has been speculated that, in an online world constantly vying for one's attention, switching tasks is a natural, and logical, cognitive adaptation (Rushkoff, 2020). Nevertheless, adolescents are, by nature, generally more novelty seeking than adults (Kelley et al., 2004). This has implications for the design of human—computer interfaces. There have been attempts to "gamify" interactive therapy packages aimed at young people (see Box 4.8, see Stallard chapter 9, this volume). However, videogame creation is now a multibillion-dollar global business (Statista, 2021). Thus, the software quality that

BOX 4.8

SPARX and gamification.

One of the oldest and best-known gamified digital interventions is "SPARX" (SPARX, 2009), a computerized cognitive behavioral therapy (CBT) package implemented as a three-dimensional fantasy game. A randomized control trial of SPARX used for depression demonstrated its noninferiority compared with treatment as usual (face-to-face counseling) (Merry et al., 2012). SPARX might not be considered to have an AI component to it, but it serves as an important example of how gamified digital interventions may impact on functionality.

individuals are now accustomed to experiencing will be challenging to emulate by those designing therapeutic game systems.

One intriguing area that has been a strong focus for exploring HCIs is "chatbots." Indeed, the 2013 movie, "Her," dramatized a fictional situation where a man falls in love with an AI-based system. Chatbots are surprisingly old, the original one being ELIZA, developed in the 1960s (Weizenbaum, 1966). Although apparently created to demonstrate the superficiality of most human conversation, Weizenbaum, who developed the system, was surprised at how many people related to ELIZA as though it was a conscious, sentient being (Weizenbaum, 1976). More recently, efforts have been made to develop therapeutic chatbots, something that would seem a priority given the often limited access to effective psychological therapies (Timimi, 2015), with reasonable results (Box 4.9). Adherence levels to online CBT packages are sometimes relatively low. Simulating human interaction is considered one way of making

BOX 4.9

Woebot: An example of a therapy chatbot.

A randomized trial of one chatbot ("Woebot") versus information provision only has been conducted for 18–28 year olds affected by depression (Fitzpatrick et al., 2017). Those allocated to Woebot reported lower levels of depressive symptoms at outcome compared with those who were given information only, though anxiety levels did not differ significantly between the groups.

computerized therapy more engaging (Fitzpatrick et al., 2017). Certainly, as chatbots advance, they may offer hope of increasing access to such "synthetic" therapists.

6. The potential use of machine learning in low- and middle-income countries

When considering the potential global impact of machine learning to CAMHS, we must consider the broader context in which the technology might be applied. Internationally, there is a mental health workforce shortage. However, this situation is more pronounced in low- and middle-income countries (LMICs); in high-income countries, there are over 60 mental health workers per 100,000 population, including 5.5 child psychiatrists. In contrast, in low-income countries, there are only 1.4 mental health workers, and 0.003 child psychiatrists per 100,000 (World Health Organization, 2021, see Waqas and Rahman, chapter 10 and Maalouf et al, chapter 12, this volume). Differentials in mental health expenditure per capita are also pronounced, ranging from 46.5 US$ per capita in Europe to 0.1 US$ per capita in Southeast Asia (World Health Organization, 2021). These constrained resources have contributed to the low levels of diagnosis and treatment in lower-income countries for mental health conditions (Patel et al., 2008). As such, the potential benefits of machine learning—based mental healthcare, as discussed throughout this chapter, may be particularly valuable in less well-resourced settings. One can easily see the potential benefits of mobile phone—based tools which can diagnose, and even treat, mental health conditions, with little or no input from mental health professionals, where such clinicians are rare.

However, there are two key issues relevant to LMICs that may be a barrier to realizing these benefits. Firstly, historically the vast majority of mental health research globally has been carried out in higher-income countries (Saxena et al., 2006). This trend has continued, with the majority of studies relating to machine learning and CAMHS being carried out in this context. Considering the "black box" nature of many of these algorithms (as discussed earlier), it would be unwise to assume that the findings of studies carried out in higher-income countries would directly apply to LMICs, considering differences in demographics, healthcare settings, and disorder prevalence. More research is thus urgently needed in LMICs. Of course, clinical usefulness is also context specific. While the Delphi exercise presented earlier (Section 2.1) highlighted areas of potential use to clinicians, it only contained experts working in high-income countries. If a similar exercise was repeated with clinicians working in LMICs, we may observe that what was deemed useful in a higher-income country may not be perceived as so in other contexts.

Secondly, many of the potential applications of machine learning discussed in this chapter may require access to high-quality data, mHealth devices, or Internet access. The availability of many of these may be limited in some LMICs. This has been described as the "digital divide" (The World Bank, 2016). For example, there is a gap in smartphone ownership between higher-income countries and LMICs, although this gap is closing (Silver, 2019). Other technologies, such as wearables, remain rare in lower-income countries. This digital divide raises questions as to the feasibility of currently implementing many of the methods discussed in this chapter.

Therefore, paradoxically, due to the digital divide, while machine learning–based mental healthcare may be the most beneficial in LMICs, it may be hardest to implement in such contexts. While the digital divide may close over time, work must be done to ensure that machine learning–based systems are built with feasibility in LMICs in mind. For example, it has been reported that systems built on data from smartphones are highly feasible in LMICs for the development of technologies for autism spectrum disorders (Kumm et al., 2021). This raises the prospect that, for example, interactive chatbots on smartphones (see Section 5.3) which offer gains (or even comparable outcomes) with treatment as usual in high-income countries may have a particular large benefit in LMICs where mental health resources, both financial and workforce, are scarce.

7. Conclusion

Machine learning has the potential to enhance the efficiency and effectiveness of CAMHS, especially if the increasing quantities of routinely arising data and "digital footprints" are leveraged. Increasing the effectiveness and reach of psychological therapies may be a particularly promising area, especially when machine learning is combined with digital technologies. The potential value of machine learning to automate some aspects of CAMHS in LMICs may be particularly high, given the relatively scarcity of available resources.

However, if these benefits are to be realized, it is important to consider the nature of the task being asked of the machine, the quality and quantity of the data available, the methods being applied, as well as how the final system is implemented and "wrapped" for human consumption. Further research is required specifically in LMICs, and work needs to done to understand the impact of the digital divide on the potential of machine learning in this context. Moreover, a certain amount of skepticism about the value of machine learning approaches in CAMHS should be maintained at times, in the absence of robust evaluations demonstrating actual patient benefit. Such caution should be countered by the increased transparency and standards of reporting of machine learning–based studies, as well as the further development of "interpretable AI." Finally, after implementation and initial evaluation, surveillance for any unintended adverse consequences for young people and their families should continue.

References

Arrieta, A. B., Díaz-Rodríguez, N., Del Ser, J., Bennetot, A., Tabik, S., Barbado, A., Garcia, S., Gil-Lopez, S., Molina, D., Benjamins, R., Chatila, R., & Herrera, F. (2020). Explainable Artificial Intelligence (XAI): Concepts, taxonomies, opportunities and challenges toward responsible AI. *Information Fusion, 58*, 82–115.

Bathaee, Y. (2017). The artificial intelligence black box and the failure of intent and causation. *Harvard Journal of Law & Technology, 31*(2), 889–938.

Bayes, T. (1763). An essay towards solving the problem in the doctrine of chances. By the late Rev. Mr. Bayes, F. R. S. communicated by Mr. Price, in a letter to John Canton, A. M. F. R. S. *Philisophical Transactions of the Royal Society, 53*, 370–418.

Bedi, G., Carrillo, F., Cecchi, G. A., Slezak, D. F., Sigman, M., Mota, N. B., Ribeiro, S., Javitt, D. C., Copelli, M., & Corcoran, C. M. (2015). Automated analysis of free speech predicts psychosis onset in high-risk youths. *NPJ Schizophrenia, 1*(1), 1–7.

Bishop, C. M. (1995). *Neural networks for pattern recognition.* Oxford University Press.

Celebi, M. E., & Aydin, K. (2016). *Unsupervised learning algorithms.* Springer.

Cellan-Jones, R. (2014). Stephen Hawking warns artificial intelligence could end mankind. BBC News. https://www.bbc.co.uk/news/technology-30290540. Accessed 14.07.21.

Chauhan, G. (2018). All about Naive Bayes. https://towardsdatascience.com/all-about-naive-bayes-8e13cef044cf. Accessed 14.07.21.

Chen, T., & Guestrin, C. (2016). Xgboost: A scalable tree boosting system. In *Proceedings of the 22nd ACM SIGKDD international conference on knowledge discovery and data mining.*

Cole, S. R., Edwards, J. K., & Greenland, S. (2021). Surprise. *American Journal of Epidemiology, 190*(2), 191–193.

Collins, G. S., & Moons, K. G. M. (2019). Reporting of artificial intelligence prediction models. *The Lancet, 393*(10181), 1577–1579.

Copeland, B. (2020). Encyclopedia Britannica: Artificial intelligence. https://www.britannica.com/technology/artificial-intelligence. Accessed 13.07.21.

Cortes, C., & Vapnik, V. (1995). Support-vector networks. *Machine Learning, 20*(3), 273–297.

Croudace, T. J., Jarvelin, M.-R., Wadsworth, M. E., & Jones, P. B. (2003). Developmental typology of trajectories to nighttime bladder control: Epidemiologic application of longitudinal latent class analysis. *American Journal of Epidemiology, 157*(9), 834–842.

Curtis, D., Adlington, K., & Bhui, K. S. (2019). Pursuing parity: Genetic tests for psychiatric conditions in the UK National Health Service. *The British Journal of Psychiatry, 214*(5), 248–250.

Delgadillo, J., de Jong, K., Lucock, M., Lutz, W., Rubel, J., Gilbody, S., Ali, S., Aguirre, E., Appleton, M., Nevin, J., O'Hayon, H., Patel, U., Sainty, A., Spencer, P., & McMillan, D. (2018). Feedback-informed treatment versus usual psychological treatment for depression and anxiety: A multisite, open-label, cluster randomised controlled trial. *The Lancet Psychiatry, 5*(7), 564–572.

Dietterich, T. G. (2000). *Ensemble methods in machine learning.* International workshop on multiple classifier systems.

Dix, A., Dix, A. J., Finlay, J., Abowd, G. D., & Beale, R. (2003). *Human-computer interaction.* Pearson Education.

Downs, J. M., Lechler, S., Dean, H., Sears, N., Patel, R., Shetty, H., Simonoff, E., Hotopf, M., Ford, T. J., Diaz-Caneja, C. M., Arango, C., MacCabe, J. H., Hayes, R. D., & Pina-Camacho, L. (2017). The association between comorbid autism spectrum disorders and antipsychotic treatment failure in early-onset psychosis: A historical cohort study using electronic health records. *Journal of Clinical Psychiatry, 78*(9), e1233—e1241. https://doi.org/10.4088/JCP.16m11422

Doyle, O., Tsaneva-Atanasova, K., Harte, J., Tiffin, P., Tino, P., & Díaz-Zuccarini, V. (2013). Bridging paradigms: Hybrid mechanistic-discriminative predictive models. *IEEE Transactions on Bio-Medical Engineering, 60.*

Eyre, H. A., Singh, A. B., & Reynolds, C., III (2016). Tech giants enter mental health. *World Psychiatry, 15*(1), 21—22.

Feil-Seifer, D., & Matarić, M. J. (2012). Distance-based computational models for facilitating robot interaction with children. *Journal of Human-Robot Interaction, 1*(1), 55—77.

Fernández, A., Garcia, S., Herrera, F., & Chawla, N. V. (2018). SMOTE for learning from imbalanced data: Progress and challenges, marking the 15-year anniversary. *Journal of Artificial Intelligence Research, 61*, 863—905.

Fitzpatrick, K. K., Darcy, A., & Vierhile, M. (2017). Delivering cognitive behavior therapy to young adults with symptoms of depression and anxiety using a fully automated conversational agent (Woebot): A randomized controlled trial. *JMIR Mental Health, 4*(2), e19.

Fleming, I., Jones, M., Bradley, J., & Wolpert, M. (2016). Learning from a learning collaboration: The CORC approach to combining research, evaluation and practice in child mental health. *Administration and Policy in Mental Health and Mental Health Services Research, 43*(3), 297—301.

Kaggle Forum. (2016). Ranking of Kaggle algorithms by competitions won. https://www.kaggle.com/general/25913. Accessed 29.04.21.

Freeman, K. R., James, S., Klein, K. P., Mayo, D., & Montgomery, S. (2016). Outpatient dialectical behavior therapy for adolescents engaged in deliberate self-harm: Conceptual and methodological considerations. *Child & Adolescent Social Work Journal, 33*(2), 123—135.

Geraci, J., Wilansky, P., de Luca, V., Roy, A., Kennedy, J. L., & Strauss, J. (2017). Applying deep neural networks to unstructured text notes in electronic medical records for phenotyping youth depression. *Evidence-based Mental Health, 20*(3), 83—87.

Goodman, B., & Flaxman, S. (2017). European Union regulations on algorithmic decision-making and a "right to explanation". *AI Magazine, 38*(3), 50—57.

Hirsch, T., Soma, C., Merced, K., Kuo, P., Dembe, A., Caperton, D. D., Atkins, D. C., & Imel, Z. E. (2018). It's hard to argue with a computer": Investigating psychotherapists' attitudes towards automated evaluation. In *Proceedings of the 2018 designing interactive systems conference, Hong Kong, China.*

Hofmann, B., & Welch, H. G. (2017). New diagnostic tests: More harm than good. *BMJ, 358.*

Jones, J., & Hunter, D. (1995). Qualitative research: Consensus methods for medical and health services research. *BMJ, 311*(7001), 376—380.

Kelley, A. E., Schochet, T., & Landry, C. F. (2004). Risk taking and novelty seeking in adolescence: Introduction to part I. *Annals of the New York Academy of Sciences, 1021*, 27—32.

Kilkenny, M. F., & Robinson, K. M. (2018). Data quality:"Garbage in—garbage out". *Health Information Management Journal, 47*(3), 103—105.

Kumm, A. J., Viljoen, M., & de Vries, P. J. (2021). The digital divide in technologies for autism: Feasibility considerations for low-and middle-income countries. *Journal of Autism and Developmental Disorders*, 1—14.

Kwan, J. L., Lo, L., Ferguson, J., Goldberg, H., Diaz-Martinez, J. P., Tomlinson, G., Grimshaw, J. M., & Shojania, K. G. (2020). Computerised clinical decision support systems and absolute improvements in care: meta-analysis of controlled clinical trials. *BMJ, 370.*

Linardatos, P., Papastefanopoulos, V., & Kotsiantis, S. (2020). Explainable AI: A review of machine learning interpretability methods. *Entropy, 23*(1), 18.

Mahmoudi, E., Kamdar, N., Kim, N., Gonzales, G., Singh, K., & Waljee, A. K. (2020). Use of electronic medical records in development and validation of risk prediction models of hospital readmission: Systematic review. *BMJ, 369.*

Mann, J. J., Ellis, S. P., Waternaux, C. M., Liu, X., Oquendo, M. A., Malone, K. M., Brodsky, B. S., Haas, G. L., & Currier, D. (2008). Classification trees distinguish suicide attempters in major psychiatric disorders: A model of clinical decision making. *Journal of Clinical Psychiatry, 69*(1), 23.

McDonald, H. (2019). AI expert calls for end to UK use of 'racially biased' algorithms. The Guardian. https://www.theguardian.com/technology/2019/dec/12/ai-end-uk-use-racially-biased-algorithms-noel-sharkey. Accessed 29.04.21.

Merry, S. N., Stasiak, K., Shepherd, M., Frampton, C., Fleming, T., & Lucassen, M. F. (2012). The effectiveness of SPARX, a computerised self help intervention for adolescents seeking help for depression: Randomised controlled non-inferiority trial. *BMJ, 344.*

Nelson, A., Herron, D., Rees, G., & Nachev, P. (2019). Predicting scheduled hospital attendance with artificial intelligence. *NPJ Digital Medicine, 2*(1), 26.

NHS Digital. (2018). *Mental health of children and young people in England, 2017.* https://digital.nhs.uk/data-and-information/publications/statistical/mental-health-of-children-and-young-people-in-england/2017/2017. Accessed 12.07.21.

NIHR Maudsley Biomedical Research Centre. (2021). Clinical record interactive search (CRIS). https://www.maudsleybrc.nihr.ac.uk/facilities/clinical-record-interactive-search-cris/> Accessed 14.07.21.

Nobles, A. L., Glenn, J. J., Kowsari, K., Teachman, B. A., & Barnes, L. E. (2018). Identification of imminent suicide risk among young adults using text messages. In *Proceedings of the 2018 CHI conference on human factors in computing systems.*

O'Neil, C. (2008). *Weapons of math destruction: How big data increases inequality and threatens democracy.* Penguin Books.

Ofcom Online Nation: 2020 report. (2020). http://www.ofcom.org.uk/__data/assets/pdf_file/0027/196407/online-nation-2020-report.pdf. Accessed 29.04.21.

Oh, M., Park, S., Kim, S., & Chae, H. (2020). Machine learning-based analysis of multi-omics data on the cloud for investigating gene regulations. *Briefings in Bioinformatics, 22*(1), 66–76.

Ordish, J. (2019). *Algorithms as medical devices.* PHG Foundation.

Patel, V., Flisher, A. J., Nikapota, A., & Malhotra, S. (2008). Promoting child and adolescent mental health in low and middle income countries. *Journal of Child Psychology and Psychiatry, 49*(3), 313–334.

Pearl, J., & Mackenzie, D. (2018). *The book of why: The new science of cause and affect.* Allen Lane.

Pestian, J. P., Grupp-Phelan, J., Bretonnel Cohen, K., Meyers, G., Richey, L. A., Matykiewicz, P., & Sorter, M. T. (2016). A controlled trial using natural language processing to examine the language of suicidal adolescents in the emergency department. *Suicide & Life Threatening Behavior, 46*(2), 154–159.

Prokhorenkova, L., Gusev, G., Vorobev, A., Dorogush, A. V., & Gulin, A. (2017). *CatBoost: Unbiased boosting with categorical features. arXiv preprint arXiv:1706.09516.*

Reel, P. S., Reel, S., Pearson, E., Trucco, E., & Jefferson, E. (2021). Using machine learning approaches for multi-omics data analysis: A review. *Biotechnology Advances, 49,* 107739.

Richens, J. G., Lee, C. M., & Johri, S. (2020). Improving the accuracy of medical diagnosis with causal machine learning. *Nature Communications, 11*(1), 1–9.

Roshanov, P. S., Fernandes, N., Wilczynski, J. M., Hemens, B. J., You, J. J., Handler, S. M., Nieuwlaat, R., Souza, N. M., Beyene, J., Van Spall, H. G. C., Garg, A. X., &

Haynes, R. B. (2013). Features of effective computerised clinical decision support systems: meta-regression of 162 randomised trials. *BMJ*, 346.

Rushkoff, D. (2020). *Team human*. https://www.teamhuman.fm/. Accessed 14.07.21.

Salekin, A., Eberle, J. W., Glenn, J. J., Teachman, B. A., & Stankovic, J. A. (2018). A weakly supervised learning framework for detecting social anxiety and depression. *Proceedings of the ACM on Interactive, Mobile, Wearable and Ubiquitous Technologies, 2*(2), 1–26.

Saxena, S., Paraje, G., Sharan, P., Karam, G., & Sadana, R. (2006). The 10/90 divide in mental health research: Trends over a 10-year period. *The British Journal of Psychiatry, 188*(1), 81–82.

Scherer, S., Pestian, J., & Morency, L. (2013). Investigating the speech characteristics of suicidal adolescents. In *IEEE international conference on acoustics, speech and signal processing*, 2013.

Shahamiri, S. R., & Thabtah, F. (2020). Autism AI: A new autism screening system based on artificial intelligence. *Cognitive Computation, 12*(4), 766–777.

Shatte, A. B. R., Hutchinson, D. M., & Teague, S. J. (2019). Machine learning in mental health: A scoping review of methods and applications. *Psychological Medicine, 49*(9), 1426–1448.

Silver, L. (2019). *Smartphone ownership is growing rapidly around the world, but not always equally.* https://www.pewresearch.org/global/2019/02/05/smartphone-ownership-is-growing-rapidly-around-the-world-but-not-always-equally/. Accessed 14.07.21.

SPARX. (2009). *S: Take control.* https://www.sparx.org.nz/home. Accessed 14.07.21.

Statista. (2020). *Do you personally use a smartphone? By age.* https://www.statista.com/statistics/300402/smartphone-usage-in-the-uk-by-age/. Accessed 29.04.21.

Statista. (2021). *Video game industry - statistics & facts.* https://www.statista.com/topics/868/video-games/#:~:text=Video%20games%20are%20a%20billion,over%2077%20billion%20U.S.%20dollars. Accessed 14.07.21.

Stone, M. (1974). Cross-validatory choice and assessment of statistical predictions. *Journal of the Royal Statistical Society: Series B (Methodological), 36*(2), 111–133.

Subramanian, K. R. (2018). Myth and mystery of shrinking attention span. *International Journal of Trend in Research and Development, 5*(1).

Szasz, T. (1997). The case against psychiatric coercion. *The Independent Review, 1*(4), 485–498.

Tate, A. E., McCabe, R. C., Larsson, H., Lundström, S., Lichtenstein, P., & Kuja-Halkola, R. (2020). Predicting mental health problems in adolescence using machine learning techniques. *PLoS One, 15*(4), e0230389.

Thieme, A., Belgrave, D., & Doherty, G. (2020). Machine learning in mental health: A systematic review of the HCI literature to support the development of effective and implementable ML systems. *ACM Transactions on Computer-Human Interaction (TOCHI), 27*(5), 1–53.

Tiffin, P. A., & Paton, L. W. (2018). Rise of the machines? Machine learning approaches and mental health: Opportunities and challenges. *The British Journal of Psychiatry, 213*(3), 509–510.

Timimi, S. (2015). Children and young people's improving access to psychological therapies: Inspiring innovation or more of the same? *BJPsych Bulletin, 39*(2), 57–60. https://doi.org/10.1192/pb.bp.114.047118

Vollmer, S., Mateen, B. A., Bohner, G., Király, F. J., Ghani, R., Jonsson, P., Cumbers, S., Jonas, A., McAllister, K. S. L., Myles, P., Grainger, D., Birse, M., Branson, R., Moons, K. G. M., Collins, G. S., Ioannidis, J. P. A., Holmes, C., & Hemingway, H. (2020). Machine learning and artificial intelligence research for patient benefit: 20 critical questions on transparency, replicability, ethics, and effectiveness. *BMJ*, 368.

Vyas, K. (2021). *7 benefits of AI that will help humanity, not harm it.* https://interestingengineering.com/7-ways-ai-will-help-humanity-not-harm-it. Accessed 07.07.21.

Walsh, C. G., Ribeiro, J. D., & Franklin, J. C. (2018). Predicting suicide attempts in adolescents with longitudinal clinical data and machine learning. *Journal of Child Psychology and Psychiatry, 59*(12), 1261–1270.

Weizenbaum, J. (1966). ELIZA—a computer program for the study of natural language communication between man and machine. *Communications of the ACM, 9*(1), 36—45.

Weizenbaum, J. (1976). *Computer power and human reason: From judgment to calculation.* W. H. Freeman & Co.

Widnall, E., Grant, C. E., Wang, T., Cross, L., Velupillai, S., Roberts, A., Stewart, R., Simonoff, E., & Downs, J. (2020). User perspectives of mood-monitoring apps available to young people: Qualitative content analysis. *JMIR mHealth and uHealth, 8*(10). e18140-e18140.

Wolpert, D. H., & Macready, W. G. (1997). No free lunch theorems for optimization. *IEEE Transactions on Evolutionary Computation, 1*(1), 67—82.

Wong, H. K., Tiffin, P. A., Chappell, M. J., Nichols, T. E., Welsh, P. R., Doyle, O. M., ... Tino, P. (2017). Personalized medication response prediction for attention-deficit hyperactivity disorder: Learning in the model space vs. learning in the data space. *Frontiers in Physiology, 8*, 199.

World Bank, The (2016). *Digital dividends.*

World Health Organisation. mHealth. New horizons for health through mobile technologies. Global Observatory for eHealth Series — Volume 3. (2011). https://www.who.int/goe/publications/goe_mhealth_web.pdf. Accessed 29.04.21.

World Health Organization. (2021). *Mental health atlas 2020.* Geneva: World Health Organization.

Ying, X. (2019). An overview of overfitting and its solutions. *Journal of Physics: Conference Series, 1168*(2).

Yusuf, M., Atal, I., Li, J., Smith, P., Ravaud, P., Fergie, M., Callaghan, M., & Selfe, J. (2020). Reporting quality of studies using machine learning models for medical diagnosis: A systematic review. *BMJ Open, 10*(3), e034568.

Zakaria, C., Balan, R., & Lee, Y. (2019). StressMon: Scalable detection of perceived stress and depression using passive sensing of changes in work routines and group interactions. *Proceedings of the ACM on Human-Computer Interaction, 3*(CSCW), 1—29.

PART III

Innovative approaches to helping young people in adversity

The COVID-19 pandemic and child and adolescent mental health—what has been learned and lessons for the future

Tamsin Newlove-Delgado[1], Frances Mathews[1], Lauren Cross[2], Eva Wooding[1], and Tamsin Ford[2]

[1] University of Exeter Medical School, Exeter, United Kingdom; [2] University of Cambridge, Department of Psychiatry, Cambridge, United Kingdom

1. Introduction

COVID-19 (officially known as severe acute respiratory syndrome coronavirus 2 [SARS-CoV-2]) was declared a pandemic by the World Health Organization on March 11, 2020 (Hu et al., 2021). While children and young people are at lower risk of severe illness and death, this group as a whole have arguably been among those most affected by the COVID-19 societal response. For example, figures from UNESCO suggest that between March and May 2020, up to 1.5 billion children worldwide were out of school as part of restrictions and lockdowns to control the spread (COVID-19 Education Response, 2020). Restrictions brought about many other changes and disruptions to the daily lives of children, young people, and their families including disruption to health services, restrictions on socializing, and cancellation or curtailment of cocurricular activities, trips, and milestone celebrations. These represent circumstances well beyond "normal" childhood experience. In this chapter, we draw on the available evidence to discuss what is known about the impacts of the pandemic on the mental health of children and young people at the time of writing. The chapter offers an overview of a spectrum of topics, from the effects of acute COVID-19 illness on children and young people, to the impact on at-risk groups, and access to mental health services and education during the pandemic. With such a varied global context and body of literature concerning child mental health and COVID-19, this chapter is unable to present an exhaustive review. We direct interested readers to the Living Systematic Review of Mental Health in Covid (https://www.depressd.ca/covid-19-mental-health), which at the time of writing in early March 2022 had screened 83,731 titles and abstracts, but included only 170 studies as sufficiently robust. Only 11 of these included children or young people under the age of 18 years. While a brief review of global evidence is included, the chapter primarily presents examples from a UK, US, and European context, where there has been greater research activity. This is a fast-moving field, and the effects of COVID-19 are likely to be felt long into the future.

2. The impact of acute illness with COVID-19

Rates of hospital admission for COVID-19-related illness are markedly lower in children and young people, compared with adults, with those admitted more likely to be from a minority ethnic background or to have complex comorbidities (Kim et al., 2020; Swann et al., 2020).

In children and young people, COVID-19 infection has been linked with Multisystem Inflammatory Syndrome in Children (MIS-C) and Pediatric Multisystem Inflammatory Syndrome (PIMS-TS). These are both terms used to describe inflammatory processes, which can affect various systems, including the nervous system. Reports have shown a strong geographical and temporal association between COVID-19 infection rates and PIMS-TS cases. Taken together with evidence of infection in many patients, the current consensus is that PIMS-TS is COVID-19 related (Flood et al., 2020). The Centers for Disease Control (CDC) and World Health Organization (WHO) definitions of MIS-C necessitate positive SARS-CoV-2 serology, antigen or PCR, or recent known SARS-CoV-2 exposure to diagnose (Centres for Disease Control and Prevention, 2020; World Health Organisation, 2020). The CDC criteria stipulate that exposure must have been within 4 weeks prior to symptom onset, but there is no such requirement for the WHO criteria.

However, such complications related to COVID-19 infection in children and young people appear extremely rare. Recently, the UK's Royal College of Pediatrics and Child Health (RCPCH) has suggested that PIMS-TS affects less than 0.5% of children who have (or who have had) COVID-19 (Royal College of Paediatrics and Child Health, 2021). Much of the evidence therefore comes from in-process surveillance studies or individual case studies.

Lindan et al. (2021) collated case reports of abnormalities identified on neuroimaging children presenting with COVID-19. Postinfectious immune-mediated acute disseminated encephalomyelitis-like changes of the brain, myelitis, and neural enhancement were reported (Lindan et al., 2021). Neurocognitive symptoms reported in children have mostly included mild symptoms such as headaches and loss of taste and smell (DeBiasi et al., 2020). More severe neurological complications such as encephalitis, seizures, and cerebrovascular infarctions have been reported in pediatric case studies, but appear much rarer than in the adult population (Feldstein et al., 2020; Kim et al., 2020).

The longer-term neuropsychiatric sequelae of PIMS-TS and MISC-C are as yet unknown, but surveillance and follow-up studies are currently under way across the globe. Finally, children and young people who have been severely unwell with COVID-19 or inflammatory complications may suffer other mental health impacts relating to this experience. Both adults and children admitted to intensive care units are at higher risk of a range of outcomes including anxiety, depression, and posttraumatic stress disorder (PTSD) (Hatch et al., 2018; Rady et al., 2020; Taquet et al., 2021). While thankfully this will affect very few children and young people on a population level given the low prevalence of admissions, it highlights the importance of postadmission monitoring and support for children and young people admitted with COVID-19, and their families.

3. Long-COVID: an emerging problem

There is increasing concern about the persistence of significant symptoms even after mild or asymptomatic SARS-COV-2 A infection among children as well as adults, although the literature is patchy and confused by a lack of consensus about the diagnosis. Over 200 symptoms have been associated with long COVID (Amin-Chowdhury & Ladhani, 2021; Davis et al., 2021). A recent systematic review including 23,141 children and young people from 12 countries reported in 22 papers reported only small increases in cognitive difficulties, headache, loss of smell, sore throat, and sore eyes in those following confirmed SARS-COV-2 infection compared with those who tested negative (Behnood et al., 2021).

Both those who were symptomatic or asymptomatic at time of test and those with or without laboratory confirmation of infection have reported symptoms of long COVID, while symptoms may begin at or after acute infection, and may be persistent or intermittent in nature (Amin-Chowdhury & Ladhani, 2021; Lopez-Leon et al., 2021). The CLoCk study is following a UK cohort of test-positive ($n = 3065$) and age-, sex-, and geographically matched test-negative children and adolescents ($n = 3802$) (Stephenson et al., 2022) At 3 months, 30.3% of test positives and 16.2% of test negatives reported three or more symptoms, while tiredness and headache were common in both groups, but more frequent in the test positives. Latent class analysis identified two classes, characterized by either "few" or "multiple" symptoms. This latter class was more frequent among test positives, including more females, older teenagers, and those with worse pretest health.

Given how common infection for children and young people has become, issues related to long COVID will clearly continue to emerge. A UK national survey of 313,216 people asked about symptoms persisting for more than 4 weeks after the first suspected coronavirus infection that were not explained by something else and reported a prevalence of 0.14% for 2–11 years, 0.50% for 12–16 years, and 1.51% for 17–24 years (Office for National Statistics, 2021). While most children and young people suffer mild symptoms if symptomatic at all, and most recover promptly, the absolute numbers struggling in the longer term may be substantial and warrant careful monitoring.

4. Impact on child and adolescent mental health: population level

The impact of COVID-19 and of associated restrictions quickly emerged as a key concern during the pandemic, with children and young people identified as a particularly vulnerable group (Holmes et al., 2020; Pierce, Hope, et al., 2020). At the time of writing this chapter, the long-term impacts are yet to be felt and measured. However, it appears that the pandemic has been associated with an overall deterioration in mental health in children and young people at a population level, but with evidence of unequal impacts on different groups. This section presents some selected findings to illustrate these impacts; a fuller overview of the global research on child mental health and COVID-19 is given in the Global Impacts section later in this chapter.

Although the volume of studies published on the impact of COVID-19 on children's mental health has greatly expanded, the living systematic review of studies led by the DEPRESSD project to date has found only a limited number of high-quality studies focusing on children with both pre- and within-pandemic data (Sun et al., 2021). One of these is the Mental Health of Children and Young People in England (MHCYP) survey series, which follows up a carefully constructed, nationally representative probability sample from 2017 (Vizard et al., 2020). The study demonstrated an increase in the proportion of 5- to 16-year-olds with a probable mental health condition from 10.8% in 2017 (prepandemic) to 16.0% in July 2020 (shortly after the first lockdown in England). This increase was seen across the included age range and for boys and girls. A further follow-up wave in February and March 2021 found that this increase was maintained, with 17.4% of 6- to 16-year-olds having a probable mental health condition in 2021 (Newlove-Delgado, Williams, et al., 2021; Newlove-Delgado, McManus, et al. 2021). Similarly, an international collaboration of 12 longitudinal studies from the United States (10 studies), Peru (1), and the Netherlands (1) with pre- and post-COVID-19 data suggested a moderate increase in symptoms of depression among adolescent populations following the COVID-19 pandemic (Baradense et al., 2021), with those living in lockdown restrictions at the point of follow-up faring worse. Similarly, a longitudinal study of a convenience sample (CoSPACE) reported that mental health as reported by parents and young people on the Strengths and Difficulties Questionnaire (SDQ) fluctuated in line with lockdown restrictions (Waite et al., 2021). A limited number of systematic reviews and metaanalyses published to date support this overall picture of elevated symptoms of depression and anxiety in particular, compared with prepandemic (for example, Racine et al., 2021).

However, the population-level figures mask the diverse range of experiences of children and young people during COVID-19. The evidence is clear that the impact of the pandemic has not been universally felt. Studies during the early part of pandemic suggested that some children and young people experienced improvement in well-being and mental health. For example, Widnall et al. (2020) found that an improvement in emotional symptoms was reported among those feeling less connected to their school, suggesting that certain children may have benefitted from time away from the school environment (see further discussion under Education below). The Mental Health of Children and Young People in England (MHCYP) survey also asked young people how the restrictions during the first lockdown had affected their lives. Just under half of 11- to 16-year-olds felt that lockdown had made their life worse (42.8%); however, approximately a quarter (26.6%) felt lockdown had made their lives a little or a lot better (Vizard et al., 2020). More recently, the OxWell Student Survey, a repeated cross-sectional survey of over 17,000 school students in England, found a self-reported improvement in well-being in over a third of their sample (Soneson et al., 2022).

Various factors are likely to play a role in these differential impacts, including relationships with school, family circumstances, social connectedness, socioeconomic circumstances, and pre-existing conditions, to name only a few. Many factors are likely to cluster together and reinforce each other, leading to the potential for vicious and virtuous (Calvano et al., 2021; Gadermann et al., 2021; Shum et al., 2021). For some, experiences have been characterized by a positive cycle of more time spent as a family, engagement in enjoyable pastimes, and a reduction in stress and increase in well-being. Conversely, others have experienced cycles of increased stress and increasingly pressured relationships creating layers of disadvantage and vulnerability, particularly among families experiencing poor mental health, substance misuse, or domestic violence. A deterioration in parental mental health and an increase in stressors for parents emerged during the early part of the COVID-19 pandemic (Pierce et al., 2021). However, Canadian study by Gadermann et al. (2021) found that parents reported increases in both negative and positive interactions with their children due to the COVID-19 pandemic, with many noting an increase in feelings of closeness, as well as in parent−child conflict.

Children living at risk of abuse and neglect are another group of particular concern. Health and educational services are the most frequent agencies to identify vulnerable children. Reduced in-person contacts during the pandemic have correspondingly reduced opportunities to detect children at risk. Identifying children and young people in need is complex, and problematic from a distance or online. In England, reports suggest children's social care referrals fell by one-fifth during the first national lockdown (Local Government Association, 2020), whereas systemic review by Viner et al. (2021) on the impacts of school closures found that child protection referrals fell by up to a third, with a halving of the expected number of referrals originating from a school setting. While the specific mental health impacts of this unidentified risk have not been quantified, the effects are likely to be felt in the future.

5. Children and young people with existing mental health conditions

Children and young people with existing conditions may have been affected in different ways by the restrictions imposed on their lives and by changing levels of restrictions in particular (Adegboye et al., 2021). A large cross-sectional Canadian study compared changes in mental health in children and young people with and without preexisting psychiatric diagnoses (Cost et al., 2021). The authors reported that while both populations experienced deteriorating mental health during the first wave of COVID-19, this was more marked among those with a preexisting diagnosis. Children and adolescents with autism spectrum disorder (ASD) diagnoses were reported to have the greatest deterioration in measures of depression, irritability, attention, and hyperactivity. This was hypothesized to be due to changes in school-based and other therapeutic services, and disruption to routine (Cost et al., 2021). Overall, research suggests that those with neurodevelopmental disorders, including ASD and attention deficit hyperactivity disorder (ADHD), may have experienced more difficulties during lockdowns (Bobo et al., 2020; Colizzi et al., 2020; Melegari et al., 2021; Nonweiler et al., 2020; O'Sullivan et al., 2021; Pearcey, Shum, Waite, Patalay, & Creswell, 2020; Pearcey, Shum, Waite, & Creswell, 2020; Vizard et al., 2020). Restriction levels due to COVID-19 were found to have a direct negative social impact on children and young people's well-being and were associated with reports of boredom and little enjoyment or interest (Melegari et al., 2021; O'Sullivan et al., 2021). Young people with ADHD reported fewer routines and increased difficulties in remote learning compared with those without the condition (Becker et al., 2020), and those with ASD reported increased problems associated with the changes in routine (O'Sullivan et al., 2021).

A number of studies examined the impact of the pandemic on children and young people with special educational needs and disabilities (SEND). The findings suggested that the effects on this group may have evolved over time; research early in the pandemic suggests an initial reduction in emotional difficulties in some children (Pearcey, Shum, Waite, Patalay, & Creswell, 2020; Pearcey, Shum, Waite, & Creswell, 2020; Shum et al., 2021). However, overall, a sustained and higher level of difficulties was reported, with parents describing feelings of loss, worry, and changes in their child's mood and behavior (Asbury et al., 2020; Tso et al., 2020; Waite et al., 2021). The United Kingdom's Office for Standards in Education (Ofsted)'s COVID-19 Series (2020) briefing on SEND provision reported that children with SEND had additional barriers to face-to-face school attendance in comparison with their peers owing to worries about the pandemic, existing medical needs requiring them to shield and problems accessing transport. More parents/carers of children with SEND compared with those without reported that they could not meet the needs of both their child and their work (Shum et al., 2021). Levels of support were also affected. In the 2021 Mental Health of Children and Young People in England survey, almost half of parents of 6- to 16-year-olds with SEND reported a reduction in the support their child received for special educational needs due to the coronavirus pandemic (Newlove-Delgado, Williams, et al., 2021; Newlove-Delgado, McManus, et al. 2021).

There has been little research into the impact of the pandemic on those with less common disorders. Increased presentations of children, adolescents, and emerging adults with eating disorders have been reported across the world, particularly but not exclusively in higher-income countries, and experts estimate that these potentially life-threatening disorders may have up to four times the previously estimated prevalence (Zipfel et al., 2022). Others have reported a sudden and substantial increase in the presentation of the sudden onset of explosive and complex functional tic-like movements, particularly among teenage girls, some with a history or vulnerability to tics (Buts et al., 2022; Heyman et al., 2021). Some have undiagnosed neurodevelopmental difficulties, and anxiety often seems to be the precipitating factor. However, a study from Italy of parent-reported impact of COVID-19 on children and young people known to have Tourette syndrome (TS) highlighted the variance of TS symptoms (Conte et al., 2020). While two-thirds reported worsening symptoms, the remained reported either improvement, variation without directional impact, or no change in symptoms. This disparity was attributed to the child or young person's level of social anxiety.

6. Global perspectives on the mental health impact of COVID-19

The wide variation in the scale and timing of the pandemic and the restrictions imposed across countries create multiple different contexts for children and young people's mental health and well-being. For example, New Zealand has consistently experienced very few restrictive periods, whereas children and young people in Spanish provinces spent weeks unable to leave the confines of their home (Pizarro-Ruiz & Ordóñez-Camblor, 2021; Robert, 2020). This section presents some of the key findings and narratives from a global perspective.

A number of cross-sectional and national population-level children and young people's mental health surveys have taken place in response to the pandemic. Some of these were new, whereas others constituted follow-ups to previous national surveys (e.g., England's Mental Health of Children and Young People surveys (Vizard et al., 2020)), allowing exploration of change over time. The volume of research has grown to such an extent that it is impossible to summarize all the cross-sectional and cohort studies now published on COVID-19 across the globe; those reported in Table 5.1 therefore include examples of cross-sectional survey studies available in the English language from a scoping search of peer-reviewed literature conducted in March and April 2021, and updated in October 2021. Included papers were cross-sectional or longitudinal studies that collected data during the pandemic and that included outcomes on child and adolescent mental health and well-being. Commonly used measures included measures of emotional and behavioral symptoms, including the SDQ General Anxiety Disorder scale (GAD), and Patient/General Health Questionnaire (PHQ/GHQ) (see Table 5.1) (Goldberg & Hillier, 1979; Goodman, 2001; Spitzer et al., 2006).

Overall, national population surveys from the United Kingdom, Germany, Japan, Canada, China, Switzerland, Norway, and the United States

TABLE 5.1   Selected international studies of COVID-19 and children and young people's mental health.

Continent Country	Reference	No., participants, age, data collection, and measures	Findings
Oceania			
Australia	*De Young et al. (2021)	$n = 776$, parents of children aged 1–5 years, online survey, PROMIS-Early Childhood, Depression Anxiety Stress Scale (DASS-21)	Significant increase in MH difficulties for children who experienced second lockdown between surveys 1 and 2: Up to 12% experienced "very high" levels of MH difficulties and 21%–47% had scores in the "high" range compared with a normative sample; 77.3% of children reported being most affected by not seeing friends and family.
Europe			
Italy	Amerio et al. (2020)	$n = 8177$ students >18 years, online survey, GHQ-9, GAD-7, ISI-7, BIS-11, 12-HS	Poor housing associated with increased risk of depressive symptoms during lockdown; participants reporting worsened working performance from home were over four times more likely to also report depression.
Italy	Spinelli et al. (2020)	$n = 854$, parents of 2- to 14-year-olds, online survey, 15-PSI, 7-DASS, parent SDQ	Perception of the difficulty of quarantine is a crucial factor that underlies both parents' and children's well-being; parents who reported more difficulties in dealing with quarantine showed more stress and children had a higher level of problems.
Italy	Di Giorgio et al. (2020)	$n = 245$, mothers of 2- to 5-year-olds; online	Reported general worsening of sleep quality and distortion of time

Continued

TABLE 5.1   Selected international studies of COVID-19 and children and young people's mental health.—cont'd

Continent Country	Reference	No., participants, age, data collection, and measures	Findings
		survey, PSQI, STQ, BRIEF-P, parent SDQ, DERS	experience in both mothers and children, as well as increasing emotional symptoms and self-regulation difficulties in children.
Italy and Spain	Orgilés et al. (2020)	$n = 1143$, parents of children aged 3–18 years, online survey	85.7% perceived changes in their children's emotional state and behaviors during the quarantine; most frequent symptoms were difficulty concentrating (76.6%), boredom (52%), irritability (39%), restlessness (38.8%), nervousness (38%), feelings of loneliness (31.3%), uneasiness (30.4%), and worries (30.1%); Spanish parents reported more symptoms than Italians.
Spain	Ezpeleta et al. (2020)	$n = 226$, parents of CYP, (Mage: 13.9; SD: 0.28), online survey, Parent SDQ	Conduct, peer, prosocial, and total problems scores increased after lockdown; worse adolescents' mental health during COVID-19 lockdown was associated with unhealthy activities, worsening of the relationships with others, and dysfunctional parenting style.
Germany	Ravens-Sieberer et al. (2021)	$n = 1586$ families with 7- to 17-year-old children and adolescents, online survey, KIDSCREEN-10, parent SDQ, SCARED, CES-DC	Two-thirds of the children and adolescents reported being highly burdened by the COVID-19 pandemic. They experienced significantly lower HRQoL (40.2% vs. 15.3%), more mental health problems (17.8% vs. 9.9%), and

TABLE 5.1 Selected international studies of COVID-19 and children and young
people's mental health.—cont'd

Continent Country	Reference	No., participants, age, data collection, and measures	Findings
			higher anxiety levels (24.1% vs. 14.9%) than before the pandemic; children with low socioeconomic status, migrant background, and limited living space were affected significantly more.
Greece	*Magklara et al. (2020)	N = 1232 parents of CYP <18 years; online questionnaire based on the tools used by "The CoRonavIruS Health Impact Survey" (CRISIS)	Approximately one-third (35.1%) of parents reported that the psychological health of their children was considerably affected; the most significant concern was social isolation; unemployment, increased family conflicts, no opportunity for tele work, and a deteriorating psychological health of the parent, as well as children's previous history of physical health conditions were all significantly associated with adverse mental health impact.
Switzerland	Mohler-Kuo et al. (2021)	n = 1627 aged 19–24 years; n = 1146 aged 12–17 years; S-YESMH questionnaire; GAD-7; PHQ-9; ASRS-v1; K-SADS; SCAS-C; PHQ-2; RSQ	One-fifth of the young adults met the criteria for at least one of the mental health problems (attention deficit hyperactivity disorder [ADHD], depression, generalized anxiety disorder), while one-third of children/ adolescents screened positive for at least one of the mental health problems (ADHD, oppositional defiant disorder,

Continued

TABLE 5.1 Selected international studies of COVID-19 and children and young people's mental health.—cont'd

Continent Country	Reference	No., participants, age, data collection, and measures	Findings
			depression, anxiety). 30.1% of children and 21.3% of young adults met the criteria for problematic internet use.
Norway	Hafstad et al. (2021)	$n = 3572$ aged 13—16 years; online survey; HSCL-1; UCLA	Anxiety and depressive symptoms increased slightly in Norwegian youths between 2019 and 2020, but this change seemed to be driven by increase in age rather than pandemic-related measures. Symptom levels were unevenly distributed across demographic groups both before and during the pandemic outbreak, indicating that health disparities persist for adolescents in risk groups during a pandemic. Health inequities related to living conditions need to be addressed in future action plans
United Kingdom	Vizard et al. (2020); Newlove-Delgado Williams, et al. (2021); Newlove-Delgado, McManus, et al. (2021)	2020: $n = 3570$, CYP aged 5—22 years, online survey, parent SDQ, young person SDQ 2021: $n = 3667$, CYP aged 6—23 years	One in six (16.0%) 5- to 16-year-olds were identified as having a probable mental disorder; an increase from one in nine in the previous survey in 2017. 58.9% of 5- to 22-year-olds with a probable mental disorder reported having sleep problems; about six in ten (62.6%) aged 5—16 years with a probable mental disorder had regular support from their school or college; (16.3%); CYP with a probable mental disorder were more likely to say that

TABLE 5.1   Selected international studies of COVID-19 and children and young people's mental health.—cont'd

Continent Country	Reference	No., participants, age, data collection, and measures	Findings
			lockdown had made their life worse (54.1% of 11- to 16-year-olds, and 59.0% of 17- to 22-year-olds). Follow-up in 2021 indicated the increase between 2017 and 2020 had been maintained, with 17.4% of 6- to 16-year-olds having a probable mental disorder.
United Kingdom	Shum et al. (2021)	$n = 8386$, parents of CYP aged 4–16 years, online survey, parent and young person SDQ	Children and young people's behavioral, emotional, and restless/attentional difficulties increased again from January 2021 to February 2021. For emotional difficulties, these have surpassed the level reported in the first lockdown (March–June 2020); parent/carer anxiety, stress, and depression have increased since November 2020 and have surpassed the level reported in the first lockdown.
Asia			
India	Saurabh et al. (2020)	$n = 121$ quarantined and $n = 131$ nonquarantined CYP and parents, interview	Quarantined children and adolescents experienced greater psychological distress than nonquarantined children and adolescents ($P < .001$). Worry (68.59%), helplessness (66.11%), and fear (61.98%) were the most common feelings experienced under quarantine.

Continued

TABLE 5.1 Selected international studies of COVID-19 and children and young people's mental health.—cont'd

Continent Country	Reference	No., participants, age, data collection, and measures	Findings
Bangladesh	Islam et al. (2020)	$n = 476$ university students (17–20 $n = 115$, 21–24 $n = 319$), online survey, PHQ-9, GAD-7	Students reported heightened depression and anxiety; around 15% of the students reportedly had moderately severe depression, whereas 18.1% were severely suffering from anxiety.
China	Guo et al. (2020)	$n = 6196$, 11- to 18-year-olds, online survey, PCL-5, SAS	The largest variance in posttraumatic stress symptoms (PTSS) and anxiety problems was explained by adverse childhood experiences, with more prepandemic maltreatment experiences predicting more PTSS and more anxiety; participants who had adverse childhood experiences and had experienced exposure to COVID-19 showed elevated PTSS.
China	Zhou et al. (2020)	$n = 8079$, 12- to 18-year-olds, online survey, PHQ-9, GAD-7	Prevalence of depressive symptoms, anxiety symptoms, and a combination of depressive and anxiety symptoms was 43.7%, 37.4%, and 31.3%, respectively, among Chinese high school students during the COVID-19 outbreak.
Japan	Horiuchi et al. (2020)	$n = 1200$, parents of CYP aged 3–14 years, online survey, KPDS-6, author-developed questionnaire	289 (24.1%) had moderate and 352 (29.3%) severe mental distress. Child health issues increased among caregivers with moderate mental distress and severe mental distress compared with caregivers with no mental distress; the

TABLE 5.1   Selected international studies of COVID-19 and children and young people's mental health.—cont'd

Continent Country	Reference	No., participants, age, data collection, and measures	Findings
			number of caregivers with mental distress was more than double that reported during the 2016 national survey.
Japan	*Hangai et al. (2020)	$n = 2591$, CYP aged 7–17 years, $n = 6116$ parents/ guardians of CYP aged 0–17 years, online survey, KINDL^R, KPDS-6	Nearly half of parents/ guardians refrained from seeking medical care for the child's symptoms during the pandemic; Nine in ten parents/guardians of school-aged children reported their child had at least one acute stress symptom in the past month, such as irritable or aggressive behavior, sleep disorder, and poor concentration; average mental health subscale scores from KINDL-R questionnaire on quality of life were lower than the previous national average for all grades.
Indonesia	Wiguna et al. (2020)	$n = 113$, YP aged 11–17 years, online survey; SDQ	14.2% "at risk" on total difficulties scale; 38.1% "at-risk" on peer relationship problems subscale, 15% "at risk" on conduct problems subscale, and 10.6% "at risk" on emotional problems subscale. The number of adolescents that reported poor well-being increased during the COVID-19 pandemic.
Iran	Rajabi (2020)	$n = 1600$, parents/carers of CYP aged 4–18 years, online	Child's well-being was the most frequent source of stress for Iranian parents, followed by their child's

Continued

TABLE 5.1   Selected international studies of COVID-19 and children and young people's mental health.—cont'd

Continent Country	Reference	No., participants, age, data collection, and measures	Findings
		survey, parent SDQ (completed and not reported)	future. Over two-thirds of parents reported that their children were spending "nothing" or less than 30 min of energetic physical activity per day, inside or outside the house. SDQ results were not reported.
North America			
United States	Margolius et al. (2020)	$n = 3300$, 13- 19-year-olds, online survey	30% of young people said they have more often been feeling unhappy or depressed, and nearly as many said they were much more concerned than usual about having their basic needs met. More than one-quarter of students (29%) said they did not feel connected at all to school adults. A similar percentage did not feel connected to classmates or to their school community.
Canada	Gadermann et al., 2021	$n = 3000$, parents with children <18 years currently living at home ($n = 618$), online survey; informed survey questions	44.3% of parents with children <18 years living at home reported worse mental health as a result of the COVID-19 pandemic compared with 35.6% of respondents without children <18 living at home; 24.8% of parents reported their children's mental health had worsened since the pandemic.

TABLE 5.1 Selected international studies of COVID-19 and children and young people's mental health.—cont'd

Continent Country	Reference	No., participants, age, data collection, and measures	Findings
South America			
Brazil	Garcia de Avila et al. (2020)	$n = 289$, CYP 6–12 years, online survey, CAQ 4–12, NRS 0–10	Based on CAQ ≥9, the prevalence of anxiety was 19.4% ($n = 56$). This was higher among children with parents with essential jobs or where parents could not socially distance.
Africa			
Egypt	Alamrawy et al. (2021)	$n = 447$ Egyptian participants aged 14–24 years, online survey, GAD-7, PHQ-9, ISI	80.5%, 74.0%, and 73.8% of the participants had different grades of depression, anxiety, and insomnia symptoms. 37.4% gained weight; adolescents (aged 14–19 years) had significantly higher scores of depression and anxiety. Those with a history of physical illness had significantly higher scores of anxiety and insomnia. Bodyweight and dietary changes were significantly associated with depression, anxiety, and insomnia.

15-PSI, 15 items Parent/Child Dysfunctional interaction domain of the Parenting-Stress Index Short Form; *ASRS-v1*, Adult ADHD Self-Report Scale Screener; *BIS-11*, Barratt Impulsiveness Scale—11; *BRIEF-P*, Behavior Rating Inventory of Executive Functions (preschool version); *CAQ 4–12*, Children's Anxiety Questionnaire scores 4–12; *CES-DC*, Center for Epidemiological Studies Depression Scale; *CYP*, children and young people; *DERS*, difficulties in emotion regulation; *GAD-7*, 7-item Generalized Anxiety Disorder scale; *GAD-7*, generalized anxiety disorder-7; *GHQ-9*, 9-item general health questionnaire; *HSCL-10*, Hopkins Symptom Checklist-10; *ISI-7*, 7-item Insomnia Severity Index; *ISI*, Insomnia Severity Index; *KPDS-6*, Kessler Psychological Distress Scale-6; *K-SADS*, Kiddie Schedule for Affective Disorders and Schizophrenia; *NRS 0–10*, Numerical Rating Scale scores 0–10; *PHQ-2*, Patient Health Questionnaire-2; *PHQ-9*, Patient Health Questionnaire-9; *PSQI*, Pittsburgh Sleep Quality Index; *RSQ*, Responses to Stress Questionnaire; *SAS*, Zung Self-rated Anxiety Scale; *12-HS*, Short Form 12-item Health Survey; *7-DASS*, Stress subscale of the Depression Anxiety Stress Scale—Short form; *SDQ*, Strength and Difficulties Questionnaire; *STQ*, Subjective Time Questionnaire; *SCARED*, Screen for Child Anxiety Related Disorders; *SCAS-C*, Spence Children's Anxiety Scale for Children; UCLA Loneliness Scale Short Form PCL-5 = self-report PTSD checklist for DSM-5; * Early findings/survey not complete/not peer reviewed.

reported increased behavioral or emotional problems experienced by children and young people compared with prepandemic or, in Australia, in comparison with populations in different states that did not experience a second lockdown (De Young et al., 2021; Gadermann et al., 2021; Hafstad et al., 2021; Hangai et al., 2020; Horiuchi et al., 2020; Margolius et al., 2020; Mohler-Kuo et al., 2021; Ravens-Sieberer et al., 2021; Vizard et al., 2020; Zhou et al., 2020). Surveys from Brazil, Egypt, and Iran reported greater increases in symptoms of depression and anxiety experienced by adolescents, those who had parents with "essential" jobs and found negative impacts of reduced physical activity as a result of implemented lockdown restrictions (Alamrawy et al., 2021; Garcia de Avila et al., 2020; Rajabi, 2020). In general, surveys from across the globe commonly reported a more marked impact on the mental health of children and young people from lower socioeconomic backgrounds compared with those from more affluent backgrounds (Amerio et al., 2020; Hafstad et al., 2021; Islam et al., 2020; Ravens-Sieberer et al., 2021; Saurabh et al., 2020; Vizard et al., 2020). A number of European studies found deprivation impacted the quality of the home environment for children and young people, which more negatively impacted mental health (Amerio et al., 2020; Hafstad et al., 2021; Ravens-Sieberer et al., 2021; Spinelli et al., 2020). Social disconnection due to social distancing restrictions and closure of learning environments (i.e., school/college/university) and reduced connectedness to peers were also widely reported findings (Ezpeleta et al., 2020; Islam et al., 2020; Magklara et al., 2020; Margolius et al., 2020; Mohler-Kuo et al., 2021; Orgilés et al., 2020; Rajabi, 2020; Wiguna et al., 2020; Zhou et al., 2020).

The quality of the evidence base globally on the impact of COVID-19 on child mental health is highly variable, and it is important to note some common limitations, which should be considered when interpreting and applying the findings. Firstly, very few surveys used probability samples, meaning that the participants were unlikely to be representative of their populations (Pierce, Hope, et al., 2020). Many studies report on convenience samples, which tend to skew toward more affluent demographic despite persistent attempts to encourage broader participation (e.g., Waite et al., 2021). Weighting data toward the population structure will not address potential bias if responses vary by characteristics associated with nonresponse. The survey mode is also likely to have affected who was able to respond, particularly in lower-income countries as online methods will have excluded a significant proportion of the most disadvantaged children and young people who would not have data to spare even if they had access to a device. While the majority of studies used validated and reliable common measures, such as the SDQ, others used more bespoke questions, asked about self-reported perceptions of changes in mental health, or developed new measures intended to capture COVID-19 impact. Many studies reviewed, even those including adolescents, also relied on parent report instead of including the young person, although in internalizing disorders in older adolescents, self-report is likely to be more valuable (Kuhn et al., 2017). Importantly, some studies failed to report on all the included measures (e.g., Rajabi et al., 2020 used the SDQ but did not report on the findings). The timing of the studies and their follow-ups (if present) in relation to lockdowns or waves of COVID-19 also varied, which makes the comparison of responses harder to interpret. Some studies asked participants about their perception of changes in their mental health and well-being since the pandemic instead of comparing with previous survey data. Not all had recent prepandemic data available, limiting the inferences that could be drawn with regard to temporal causality.

7. Mental health—related help seeking and service access during COVID-19

7.1 Referrals and service contacts

Data from the early part of the pandemic in many countries suggested a sharp drop in the number of children and young people accessing a range of health services for mental health concerns. A framework synthesis from March to April 2020 of experiences across 28 countries reported an overall theme of lack of access to mental health services and resources across all age groups (Rains et al., 2020). In England, referrals to Child and Adolescent Mental Health Services (CAMHS) dropped by 47% in April and May 2020, compared with the previous year (Mind, 2020). Analysis of primary care data in the United Kingdom reported a trend of decreasing primary care—coded self-harm, depression, anxiety, and antidepressant prescribing in 10- to 17-year-olds in March and April, followed by an increase over time, reaching expected rates again by autumn 2020 (Carr et al., 2021). The same study found a disproportionate effect on people from deprived communities, who experienced the largest decreases in primary care—recorded mental illness and self-harm, as well as referrals to mental health services.

Similar patterns have been reported globally. A survey of heads of academic child and adolescent psychiatry services from 20 European countries asked for participants' subjective judgments on the impacts on service delivery (Revet et al., 2021). The findings of the initial survey wave, between April and May 2020, suggested that there had been closure or reduction of services including outpatient and daycare units. In line with findings from the United Kingdom and United States, a reduction in referrals and patient load was also reported. Analysis of mental health—related emergency department (ED) attendances in the United States from March 2020 onward also found a pronounced drop in the number of visits over the first months of the pandemic (Leeb et al., 2020). However, over time, the number increased, and notably, the proportion of all pediatric ED attendances that were mental health—related also increased, by 24% in 5- to 11-year-olds and by 31% in 12- to 17-year-olds. The United Kingdom data also suggest that child and adolescent eating disorder services have seen increased demand over the course of the past year, with urgent and routine referrals almost doubling combined with a smaller but still substantial increase in routine referrals (NHS England, 2021). The 2021 Mental Health of Children and Young People in England follow-up reported a substantial increase in children aged 11—16 years with eating problems (from 5% to 8% among boys, 8% to 18% among girls) and young people aged 17—19 years (30%—41% among boys, 61%—74% among girls) from 2017. We await the completion of the diagnostic assessment used at baseline in those screening positive, but these initial data suggest that the increased presentations reflect a true increase in population prevalence of eating disorders among children and young people. This is troubling, given the potential to persist, and the accompanying morbidity and mortality.

8. Help seeking and experience of services

From the perspectives of children and young people, the COVID-19 pandemic appears to have affected both help-seeking behaviors, and their experience of receiving help when sought. The Mental Health of Children and Young People in England survey collected data from a population sample of children, young people, and parents between July and August 2020, asking about help seeking for mental health concerns during the pandemic (Vizard et al., 2020). Almost half (44.6%) of 17- to 22-year-olds with a probable mental disorder decided not to seek help for a mental health, or a mental and physical health concern due to the COVID-19 pandemic. The survey does not explore the reasons why, but there have been wider concerns that messaging around health service capacity, fears around infection, and, in some countries, "Stay at Home" messaging have influenced intention to ask for support. This may lie behind the initial drop in referrals reported.

The impact of COVID-19 on children, parents, and young people's experiences of mental health services has not yet been widely reported but appears to be mixed. For example, in the English MHCYP, one in ten young people with a probable disorder reported not getting the help they sought in the early part of the pandemic (Vizard et al., 2020). This being said, high levels of unmet needs have been the norm for some time in many child mental health systems across the world—as highlighted in the Europe by the Milestone study (Signorini et al., 2017). Mode of delivery, however, has been a major change. Globally, child and adolescent mental healthcare in developed countries, in common with other services, shifted much assessment and treatment online. In general, initial evaluations of online delivery during COVID-19 report that many young people have viewed this positively. Nicholas et al. (2021) found that young people were significantly more likely to rate telehealth as having a positive impact on service quality than clinicians. Reports from CAMHS practitioners from the East of England indicate that most were coping with remote assessment and intervention, but that the experience varied by team and concern remained about safeguarding and confidentiality in some cases (Bhardwaj et al., 2021). Some teams reported increased engagement and attendance at appointments, which suggests benefits for remote working that may persist beyond the pandemic. The authors argue for a need to coproduce guidelines for best practice and to ensure that practitioners are adequately trained. There are also concerns over how digital delivery may exacerbate inequalities, stemming from both lack of reliable Internet access and a lack of privacy to use devices within the home (Office for National Statistics, 2019). In the Mental Health of Children and Young People in England surveys, those with a probable mental disorder were less likely to have reliable Internet at home than those without a disorder, and overall more than one in ten did not have access to this resource (Vizard et al., 2020).

There have been calls for the COVID-19 pandemic to stimulate the restructuring of mental health services for children and young people. Raballo and colleagues (2020) note that traditional CAMHS have been set up for a smaller group of children with more stable conditions, rather than being responsive to fluctuations between subthreshold symptoms and syndromal states, which may particularly follow societal changes such as the COVID-19 response. They argue that this is the opportunity to expand services, which will be able to respond at lower thresholds, as well as to capitalize on digital delivery to support help seeking.

9. Education and mental health during COVID-19

Schools increasingly play a central role in both identification of and intervention for mental health difficulties in children and young people. However, protective policies deployed to curb the spread of COVID-19 mandated the restriction of face-to-face education as well as the physical closure of schools in some form for most countries across the globe. While there is a public health precedent for utilizing school closures within a pandemic context (Jackson et al., 2014), in some more extreme cases, students did not physically attend school for the majority of the academic year in 2020—21 (Covid 19 Education Response, 2020). Consequently, disruption and disregulation of educational provision has had a profound impact on children and young people. This impact extends beyond anticipated challenges associated with school absence and academic attainment (Hancock et al., 2017), with early evidence highlighting effects on mental health and well-being of students. A systematic review exploring the impacts of school closures identified 27 studies suggesting an association with emotional, behavioral, and restlessness/inattention problems (Viner et al., 2021). 18%—60% of children and young people scored above risk thresholds for distress in included studies, particularly anxiety and depressive symptoms. Two studies reported nonsignificant rises in suicide rates.

Variability in provision of care and learning from home environments are important factors in understanding the impact of school closures in reaction to COVID-19 on the mental health of children and young people, including for individuals with SEND (Shepherd & Hancock et al., 2020). In the Mental Health of Children and Young People in England surveys, those with a probable mental disorder were more likely to report a lack of support from their school than those unlikely to have a disorder (Vizard et al., 2020). In addition, many were unable to access online learning due to resource factors including lack of technology, poorly connected Wi-Fi and/or a lack of a quiet space to focus on learning. Indeed, there was more marked deterioration and slower recovery among children aged 10—15 years from the Understanding Society study without access to a computer (but not poor Wi-Fi connection) during 2020 and 2021 than their better connected peers (Metherell et al., preprint). This is not surprising given the prominence of anxieties about keeping up at school both before and during the pandemic (Widnall et al., 2020), and struggling to access remote schooling may cause young people further anxiety about falling behind. Changes in the nature and level of educational support provided are also particularly likely to affect children and young people with SEND. It is therefore feared that these changes in education provision will further amplify existing inequalities and disproportionately harm children and families who are already the most disadvantaged (Buonsenso et al., 2020).

However, the impacts of school closure do not appear to be universally negative with a minority reporting little impact, or even improvements to mental health and well-being (e.g., Asbury et al., 2020). In particular, school closures and the associated move to online learning provided a welcome respite for those who found school a stressful environment prior to the pandemic, for reasons including academic and social pressures or anxieties, or for those experiencing bullying. A longitudinal study exploring the impact of school closures on the mental health of children and young people highlighted a decrease in depressive symptoms following school closure in Shanghai (Xiang et al., 2020). This unexpected finding led the authors to hypothesize that the reduction of academic pressure associated with standardized exams may have been a key factor resulting in increases to well-being. Similarly, Widnall et al. (2020) found that those who were struggling with their mental health prior to the pandemic experienced reduced anxiety and depression and improved well-being while attending school in person was not possible.

10. Looking to the future

COVID-19 is arguably a *syndemic* rather than pandemic, a term applied to an illness where social and biological factors interact to amplify the impact on certain parts of the population (Mendenhall, 2020). Previous research suggests that adverse childhood experience, particularly abuse, neglect, or bullying, as well as poverty and income inequality are important influences in the prevalence of mental health conditions (Collishaw, 2015; Patel et al., 2018). As we have described before, the pandemic, resulting restrictions, and anticipated economic crises are likely to increase the number of children exposed to these adversities, and thus to increase their vulnerability to poor mental health as well as other adverse outcomes that may further undermine their well-being (Bryant et al., 2020; Holmes et al., 2020). All agencies that relate to children, young people, and families should be executing and planning their response in terms of policy, commission, practice, and research.

Many predicted a significant impact of COVID-19 on population mental health, and children and young people were highlighted as one of the particularly vulnerable subgroups (Holmes et al., 2020). We therefore need to promote mental health, prevent the deterioration of mental health among vulnerable groups, and provide prompt effective intervention for those who are currently struggling to mitigate the impact on a generation's life chances. Many reports have highlighted the importance of incorporating mental health into government COVID-19 policy (Di Giorgio et al., 2020; Ezpeleta et al., 2020; Garcia de Avila et al., 2020; Spinelli et al., 2020; Zhou et al., 2020), as well as the need for additional financial support for families during and following the pandemic (Gadermann et al., 2021; Islam et al., 2020; Ravens-Sieberer et al., 2021; Saurabh et al., 2020). Interesting multidisciplinary work from Scotland proposed the use of closed-care family support bubbles for vulnerable families to relieve the pressure on those with economic insecurity, parental mental ill health or substance misuse, or risk of domestic violence should further school closures be required (Petri -Romao et al., 2020).

For interventions to be effective, they must be informed by robust evidence. Understanding nuanced risk, unmet need, and *where* and *how* support would be most effective is essential. Ongoing tracking of mental health of the whole population with robust methodology and ensuring adequate representation of vulnerable groups is needed (Holmes et al., 2020). The current data suggest that teenage girls and young women, those facing socioeconomic insecurity, and parents with young children, particularly during periods of lockdown are currently the most vulnerable groups (Pierce, Hope, et al., 2020). More data are required to understand the experiences of children with preexisting mental health conditions, although among working age adults, this group is at risk of consistently poor mental health (Pierce., 2021), as well as children with special educational needs or disability (Newlove-Delgado, Williams, et al., 2021; Newlove-Delgado, McManus, et al. 2021).

We should also focus on increasing the availability and sustainability of prevention and intervention programs for children, young people, and parents, as well as better integration of such programs in everyday school and working life (Di Giorgio et al., 2020; De Young et al., 2021; Gadermann et al., 2021; Garcia de Avila et al., 2020; Guo et al., 2020; Horiuchi et al., 2020; Margolius et al., 2020; Orgilés et al., 2020; Ravens-Sieberer et al., 2021; Wiguna et al., 2020). Schools are a setting in which prevention and mental health promotion could be offered as part of a whole school approach (Fazel et al., 2014a, 2014b). School climate or culture, relationships between pupils and with staff as well as general ethos, which are potentially tractable predictors of the variance in pupil mental health in schools, offer targets for prevention and the promotion of mental health and resilience (Ford et al., 2021; Moore et al., 2019). Evidence suggests that behavioral management strategies that emphasize the encouragement of desired behaviors with praise, rewards, and celebrations, backed up with clear expectations reduce classroom disruption but also improve mental health particularly among those who are struggling (Nye et al., 2019). Teaching knowledge and skills that protect mental health, such as keeping active, sleeping well, conflict resolution, and emotional literacy, should be available to all pupils as a core component of personal social, health, and economic education. Bullying is arguably our most tractable public mental health risk factor, and many effective whole school programs are available that should be implemented at scale (Ford et al., 2014).

Prompt access to information and support is required for those who are struggling or vulnerable. Given the association of admission to intensive care with subsequent mental health conditions, rehabilitation for children and young people after discharge should include monitoring of mental health for posttraumatic stress disorder or depression (Davydow et al., 2010). The literature on what has been termed long COVID, or post-COVID-19, syndrome in children and young people has been rapidly expanding, yet evaluation of longer-term physical and mental health sequelae of infection is complicated by the lack of baseline mental health data in many studies, in addition to problems with unbalanced samples, recall bias, and a diminishing pool of never-infected children (Molteni et al., 2022). Well-designed and funded longitudinal studies and collaboration within and between countries remain essential in terms of sharing findings about etiology and response to intervention.

However, one clear implication of research to date is the close relationship between physical and mental health, particularly in relation to long COVID-19. As reported before, the CLoCk study in England reported that those with multiple symptoms at 3 months were more likely to have poorer physical and mental health before COVID-19 and that even among test negatives, those with multiple physical symptoms at 3 months after the test had poorer initial physical and mental health (Stephenson et al., 2022). Similarly, the sudden surge in presentations of eating disorders and functional complex tic-like disorders highlights the need for well-integrated responses to longer-term symptoms following COVID-19 infection, involving multidisciplinary teams that can assess and adapt to the heterogenous needs and experiences of children and improve well-being (Heyman et al., 2021; Molteni et al., 2022; NHS England, 2021). Pediatric child and adolescent psychiatry liaison services have much to offer here but may lack capacity to respond.

The anticipated increase in the prevalence of mental health conditions is likely to include increased demand on services, which makes it even more essential to target interventions appropriately to the level of need (Hood, 2020; Wolpert et al., 2019). A stepped care approach may help to manage numbers should services become overwhelmed with referrals as rapid response and return to function is important to reduce the developmental price of long-term illness (Van Straten et al., 2015). Given the lack of empirical evidence of low-intensity services, particularly for this age group, services should monitor outcomes carefully to optimize care (Van Straten et al., 2015). Additionally, upskilling of staff who spend time informally supporting young people's mental health, such as teaching assistants and pastoral workers in schools or specialist nurses in acute hospitals, offers opportunities for earlier intervention and allows CAMHS to focus on those with the more severe and entrenched difficulties (Shafran et al., 2021). There are also many unanswered research questions regarding the balance of face-to-face and digital services provided in mental health services during lockdowns. We need to understand where remote working is both safe and effective, and for which groups of young people, as well as to co-develop guidelines for best practice. Coproduction of guidelines for best practice, particularly in relation to confidentiality and safeguarding, should be developed (Bhardwaj et al., 2021). Any restructure or redesign of services needs to be carefully considered and supported by evidence, taking into account the need for flexibility, responsiveness, accessibility and to avoid exacerbating existing inequalities.

Practitioners, commissioners, and policy leaders involved in the planning of education, social care, and health services for children need to mitigate the impact of COVID-19 on health, social, and education inequalities. We also need to ensure that we learn from 2020 and ensure that children's needs are included in policy decisions during the next crisis, in contrast to our consummate failure to do so this time. The National Institute for Health Research in the United Kingdom recently published research targets for the next decade; the first of these is that research should halve the number of children with persistent mental health conditions by 2030 (Wykes et al., 2021). We are off to a bad start and have a great deal of work to do to realize this goal.

References

Adegboye, D., Williams, F., Collishaw, S., Shelton, K., Langley, K., Hobson, C., Burley, D., & van Goozen, S. (2021). Understanding why the COVID-19 pandemic-related lockdown increases mental health difficulties in vulnerable young children. *JCPP Advances, 1,* e12005. https://doi.org/10.1111/jcv2.12005

Alamrawy, R. G., Fadl, N., & Khaled, A. (2021). Psychiatric morbidity and dietary habits during COVID-19 pandemic: A cross-sectional study among Egyptian youth (14—24 years). *Middle East Current Psychiatry, 28,* 6. https://doi.org/10.1186/s43045-021-00085-w

Amerio, A., Brambilla, A., Morganti, A., Aguglia, A., Bianchi, D., Santi, F., Costantini, L., Odone, A., Costanza, A., Signorelli, C., Serafini, G., Amore, M., & Capolongo, S. (2020). Covid-19 lockdown: Housing built environment's effects on mental health. *International Journal of Environmental Research and Public Health.* https://doi.org/10.3390/ijerph17165973

Amin-Chowdhury, Z., & Ladhani, S. N. (2021). Causation or confounding: why controls are critical for characterizing long COVID. *Nature Medicine, 27,* 1129—1130. https://doi.org/10.1038/s41591-021-01402-w

Asbury, K., Fox, L., Deniz, E., Code, A., & Toseeb, U. (2020). How is COVID-19 affecting the mental health of children with special educational needs and disabilities and their families? *Journal of Autism and Developmental Disorders.* https://doi.org/10.1007/s10803-020-04577-2

Barendse, M., Flannery, J. E., Cavanagh, C., Aristizabal, M., Becker, S. P., Berger, E., … Pfeifer, J. H. (2021). *Longitudinal change in adolescent depression and anxiety symptoms from before to during the COVID-19 pandemic: A collaborative of 12 samples from 3 countries.* https://doi.org/10.31234/osf.io/hn7us

Becker, S. P., Breaux, R., Cusick, C. N., Dvorsky, M. R., Marsh, N. P., Sciberras, E., & Langberg, J. M. (2020). Remote learning during COVID-19: Examining school practices, service continuation, and difficulties for adolescents with and without attention-deficit/hyperactivity disorder. *Journal of Adolescent Health.* https://doi.org/10.1016/j.jadohealth.2020.09.002

Behnood, S. A., Shafran, R., Bennett, S. D., et al. (2021). Persistent symptoms following SARS-CoV-2 infection amongst children and young people: A meta-analysis of controlled and uncontrolled studies. *Journal of Infection.* https://doi.org/10.1016/j.jinf.2021.11.011 [published Online First: 20211120].

Bhardwaj, A., Moore, A., Cardinal, R., Bradley, C., Cross, L., & Ford, T. (2021). Survey of CAMHS clinicians about their experience of remote consultation: Brief report. *BJPsych Open, 7*(1), E34. https://doi.org/10.1192/bjo.2020.160

Bobo, E., Lin, L., Acquaviva, E., Caci, H., Franc, N., Gamon, L., Picot, M. C., Pupier, F., Speranza, M., Falissard, B., & Purper-Ouakil, D. (2020). How do children and adolescents with Attention Deficit Hyperactivity Disorder (ADHD) experience lockdown during the COVID-19 outbreak? *Encephale.* https://doi.org/10.1016/j.encep.2020.05.011

Bryant, D. J., Oo, M., & Damian, A. J. (2020). The rise of adverse childhood experiences during the COVID-19 pandemic. *Psychological Trauma: Theory, Research, Practice, and Policy, 12*(S1), S193−S194. https://doi.org/10.1037/tra0000711

Buonsenso, D., Roland, D., De Rose, C., Vásquez-Hoyos, P., Ramly, B., Chakakala-Chaziya, J. N., Munro, A., & González-Dambrauskas, S. (2020). Schools closures during the COVID-19 pandemic: A catastrophic global situation. *The Pediatric Infectious Disease Journal, 40*(4), e146−e150.

Buts, S., Duncan, M., Owen, T., et al. (2022). Paediatric tic-like presentations during the COVID-19 pandemic. *Archives of Disease in Childhood, 107*, e17.

Calvano, C., Engelke, L., Di Bella, J., et al. (2021). Families in the COVID-19 pandemic: parental stress, parent mental health and the occurrence of adverse childhood experiences—results of a representative survey in Germany. *European Child & Adolescent Psychiatry.* https://doi.org/10.1007/s00787-021-01739-0

Carr, M. J., Steeg, S., Webb, R. T., Kapur, N., Chew-Graham, C. A., Abel, K. M., Hope, H., Pierce, M., & Ashcroft, D. M. (2021). Effects of the COVID-19 pandemic on primary care-recorded mental illness and self-harm episodes in the UK: A population-based cohort study. *The Lancet Public Health, 6*(2), e124−e135.

Centres for Disease Control and Prevention. (2020). *Information for Healthcare Providers about Multisystem Inflammatory Syndrome in Children (MIS-C).* https://www.cdc.gov/mis-c/hcp/index.html.

Colizzi, M., Sironi, E., Antonini, F., Ciceri, M. L., Bovo, C., & Zoccante, L. (2020). Psychosocial and behavioral impact of COVID-19 in autism spectrum disorder: An online parent survey. *Brain Sciences.* https://doi.org/10.3390/brainsci10060341

Collishaw, S. (2015). Annual research review: Secular trends in child and adolescent mental health. *Journal of Child Psychology and Psychiatry, 56*(3), 370−393.

Conte, G., Baglioni, V., Valente, F., Chiarotti, F., & Cardona, F. (2020). Adverse mental health impact of the COVID-19 lockdown in individuals with Tourette syndrome in Italy: An online survey. *Frontiers in Psychiatry, 11*, 583744. https://doi.org/10.3389/fpsyt.2020.583744

Cost, K. T., Crosbie, J., Anagnostou, E., et al. (2021). Mostly worse, occasionally better: impact of COVID-19 pandemic on the mental health of Canadian children and adolescents. *European Child & Adolescent Psychiatry.* https://doi.org/10.1007/s00787-021-01744-3

COVID-19 Education Response. (2020). UNESCO. https://en.unesco.org/covid19/educationresponse/globalcoalition. Accessed January 15, 2021.

COVID-19 Series (2020). Briefing on special educational needs and disabilities provision, November 2020. Ofsted. England. Retrieved from: www.gov.uk/government/organisations/ofsted.

Davis, H. E., Assaf, G. S., McCorkell, L., Wei, H., Low, R. J., Re'em, Y., Redfield, S., Austin, J. P., & Akrami, A. (2021). Characterizing long COVID in an international cohort: 7 months of symptoms and their impact. *EClinicalMedicine*, 101019. https://doi.org/10.1016/j.eclinm.2021.101019

Davydow, D. S., Richardson, L. P., Zatzick, D. F., & Katon, W. J. (2010). Psychiatric morbidity in pediatric critical illness survivors: A comprehensive review of the literature. *Archives of Pediatrics & Adolescent Medicine, 164*(4), 377−385. https://doi.org/10.1001/archpediatrics.2010.10

III. Innovative approaches to helping young people in adversity

De Young, A., Paterson, R., March, S., Hoehn, E., Alisic, Cobham, V., Donovan, C., Middeldorp, C., Gash, T., & Vasileva, M. (2021). *COVID-19 unmasked young children report 2: Impact of the second wave in Australia on the mental health of young children and parents.* Brisbane: Queensland Centre for Perinatal and Infant Mental Health, Children's Health Queensland Hospital and Health Service.

DeBiasi, R. L., Song, X., Delaney, M., Bell, M., Smith, K., Pershad, J., Ansusinha, E., Hahn, A., Hamdy, R., Harik, N., Hanisch, B., Jantausch, B., Koay, A., Steinhorn, R., Newman, K., & Wessel, D. (2020). Severe coronavirus disease-2019 in children and young adults in the Washington, DC, metropolitan region. *The Journal of Pediatrics, 223*, 199–203. https://doi.org/10.1016/j.jpeds.2020.05.007

Di Giorgio, E., Di Riso, D., Mioni, G., & Cellini, N. (2020). The interplay between mothers' and children behavioral and psychological factors during COVID-19: An Italian study. *European Child and Adolescent Psychiatry.* https://doi.org/10.1007/s00787-020-01631-3

Ezpeleta, L., Navarro, J. B., de la Osa, N., Trepat, E., & Penelo, E. (2020). Life conditions during COVID-19 lockdown and mental health in Spanish adolescents. *International Journal of Environmental Research and Public Health.* https://doi.org/10.3390/ijerph17197327

Fazel, M., Hoagwood, K., Stephan, S., & Ford, T. (2014). Mental health interventions in schools in high-income countries. *The Lancet Psychiatry, 1*(5), 377–387.

Fazel, M., Patel, V., Thomas, S., & Tol, W. (2014). Mental health interventions in schools in low-income and middle-income countries. *Lancet Psychiatry, 1*(5), 388–398. https://doi.org/10.1016/S2215-0366(14)70357-8. Epub 2014 Oct 7. PMID: 26361001.

Feldstein, L. R., Rose, E. B., Horwitz, S. M., Collins, J. P., Newhams, M. M., Son, M. B. F., Newburger, J. W., Kleinman, L. C., Heidemann, S. M., Martin, A. A., Singh, A. R., Li, S., Tarquinio, K. M., Jaggi, P., Oster, M. E., Zackai, S. P., Gillen, J., Ratner, A.,. J., Walsh, R. F., ... Randolph, A. G. (2020). Overcoming COVID-19 Investigators; CDC COVID-19 response team. Multisystem inflammatory syndrome in U.S. Children and adolescents. *New England Journal of Medicine, 383*(4), 334–346. https://doi.org/10.1056/NEJMoa2021680. Epub 2020 Jun 29. PMID: 32598831; PMCID: PMC7346765.

Flood, J.,S., Shingleton, J., Bennett, E., Walker, B., Amin-Chowdhury, Z., Oligbu, G., Avis, J., Lynn, R., Davis, P., Bharucha, T., Pain, C. E., Jyothish, D., Whittaker, E., Dwarakanathan, B., Wood, R., Williams, C., Swann, O., Semple, M. G., Ramsay, M. E., ... Ladhani, S. N. (2020). Paediatric multisystem inflammatory syndrome temporally associated with SARS-CoV-2 (PIMS-TS): Prospective, National Surveillance, UK and Ireland. *The Lancet Regional Health-Europe, 3*, 100075. Available at: SSRN: https://ssrn.com/abstract=3771324 or https://doi.org/10.2139/ssrn.3771324.

Ford, T., Degli Esposti, M., Crane, C., Taylor, L., Montero-Marín, J., Blakemore, S. J., Bowes, L., Byford, S., Dalgleish, T., Greenberg, M. T., Nuthall, E., Phillips, A., Raja, A., Ukoumunne, O. C., Viner, R. M., Williams, J. M. G., Allwood, M., Aukland, L., Casey, T.,, , ... MYRIAD Team, Kuyken, W. (2021). The role of schools in early adolescents' mental health: Findings from the MYRIAD study. *Journal of the American Academy of Child and Adolescent Psychiatry, S0890–8567*(21), 00143–X. https://doi.org/10.1016/j.jaac.2021.02.016. Epub ahead of print. PMID: 33677037.

Ford, T., Mitrofan, O., & Wolpert, M. (2014). Life course: Children and young people's mental health. Treatment, recovery and rehabilitation. In *The annual report of the chief medical officer 2013. Public mental health priorities; investing in the evidence* (pp. 99–114). London: TSO.

Gadermann, A. C., Thomson, K. C., Richardson, C. G., et al. (2021). Examining the impacts of the COVID-19 pandemic on family mental health in Canada: Findings from a national cross-sectional study. *BMJ Open, 11*, e042871. https://doi.org/10.1136/bmjopen-2020-042871

Garcia de Avila, M. A., Hamamoto Filho, P. T., Jacob, F., Alcantara, L., Berghammer, M., Jenholt-Nolbris, M., Olaya-Contreras, P., & Nilsson, S. (2020). Children's anxiety and factors related to the COVID-19 pandemic: An exploratory study using the children's anxiety questionnaire and the numerical rating scale. *International Journal of Environmental Research and Public Health, 17*(16), 5757. https://doi.org/10.3390/ijerph17165757

Goldberg, D. P., & Hillier, V. F. (1979). A scaled version of the general health questionnaire. *Psychological Medicine, 9*(1), 139–145.

Goodman, R. (2001). Psychometric properties of the strengths and difficulties questionnaire. *Journal of the American Academy of Child and Adolescent Psychiatry, 40*(11), 1337–1345.

Guo, J., Fu, M., Liu, D., Zhang, B., Wang, X., & van IJzendoorn, M. H. (2020). Is the psychological impact of exposure to COVID-19 stronger in adolescents with pre-pandemic maltreatment experiences? A survey of rural Chinese adolescents. *Child Abuse and Neglect.* https://doi.org/10.1016/j.chiabu.2020.104667

Hafstad, G., Saetren, S., Wentzel-Larsen, T., & Augusti, E.-M. (2021). Adolescents' symptoms of anxiety and depression before and during the Covid-19 outbreak – a prospective population-based study of teenagers in Norway. *The Lancet Regional Health – Europe, 5*, 100093. https://doi.org/10.1016/j.lanepe.2021.100093

Hancock, K. J., Lawrence, D., Shepherd, C. C. J., Mitrou, F., & Zubrick, S. R. (2017). Associations between school absence and academic achievement: Do socioeconomics matter? *British Educational Research Journal, 43*(3), 415–440.

Hangai, M., Piedvache, A., Sawada, N., and Okubo, Y., Sampei, M., Yamaoka, Y., Tanaka, K., Hosozawa, M., Morisaki, N., & Igarashi, T. (2020). Findings from the first national online survey of children's well-being during the COVID-19 pandemic in Japan (CORONA-CODOMO survey). [Pre-print]. Available at: SSRN: https://ssrn.com/abstract=3701551 or https://doi.org/10.2139/ssrn.3701551.

Hatch, R., Young, D., Barber, V., et al. (2018). Anxiety, depression and post traumatic stress disorder after critical illness: A UK-wide prospective cohort study. *Critical Care, 22*, 310. https://doi.org/10.1186/s13054-018-2223-6

Heyman, I., Liang, H., & Hedderly, T. (2021). COVID-19 related increase in childhood tics and tic-like attacks. *Archives of Disease in Childhood, 106*, 420–421.

Holmes, E. A., O'Connor, R. C., Perry, V. H., Tracey, I., Wessely, S., Arseneault, L., Ballard, C., Christensen, H., Silver, R. C., Everall, I., Ford, T., John, A., Kbir, T., King, K., Madan, I., Michie, S., Przybylski, A., Shafran, R., Sweeney, A., … Bullmore, E. (2020). Multidisciplinary research priorities for the COVID-19 pandemic: A call for action for mental health science. *The Lancet Psychiatry, 7*(6), 547–560. https://doi.org/10.1016/S2215-0366(20)30168-1

Hood, A. (2020). Estimating the impacts of COVID-19 on mental health services in England: Summary of results and methods. *The strategy unit.* https://www.strategyunitwm.nhs.uk/sites/default/files/2020-11/Modelling%20Covid-19%20%20MH%20services%20in%20England_20201109_v2.pdf.

Horiuchi, S., Shinohara, R., Otawa, S., Akiyama, Y., Ooka, T., Kojima, R., Yokomichi, H., Miyake, K., & Yamagata, Z. (2020). Caregivers' mental distress and child health during the COVID-19 outbreak in Japan. *PLoS One.* https://doi.org/10.1371/journal.pone.0243702

Hu, B., Guo, H., Zhou, P., & Shi, Z. L. (2021). Characteristics of SARS-CoV-2 and COVID-19. *Nature Reviews Microbiology*, (3), 141–154. https://doi.org/10.1038/s41579-020-00459-7. Epub 2020 Oct 6. PMID: 33024307; PMCID: PMC7537588.

Islam, M. A., Barna, S. D., Raihan, H., Khan, M. N. A., & Hossain, M. T. (2020). Depression and anxiety among university students during the COVID-19 pandemic in Bangladesh: A web-based cross-sectional survey. *PLoS One, 15*(8), e0238162. https://doi.org/10.1371/journal.pone.0238162

Jackson, C., Mangtani, P., Hawker, J., Olowokure, B., & Vynnycky, E. (2014). The effects of school closures on influenza outbreaks and pandemics: Systematic review of simulation studies. *PLoS One, 9*(5), e97297. https://doi.org/10.1371/journal.pone.0097297. PMID: 24830407; PMCID: PMC4022492.

Kim, L., Whitaker, M., O'Halloran, A., Kambhampati, A., Chai, S. J., Reingold, A., Armistead, I., Kawasaki, B., Meek, J., Yousey-Hindes, K., Anderson, E. J., Openo, K. P., Weigel, A., Ryan, P., Monroe, M. L., Fox, K., Kim, S., Lynfield, R., Bye, E., & Shrum Davis, S. (2020). COVID-NET surveillance team (2020). Hospitalization rates and characteristics of children aged <18 Years hospitalized with laboratory-confirmed COVID-19 - COVID-NET, 14 states. MMWR. *Morbidity and Mortality Weekly Report, 69*(32), 1081−1088. https://doi.org/10.15585/mmwr.mm6932e3

Kuhn, C., Aebi, M., Jakobsen, H., et al. (2017). Effective mental health screening in adolescents: Should we collect data from youth, parents or both? *Child Psychiatry & Human Development, 48,* 385−392. https://doi.org/10.1007/s10578-016-0665-0

Leeb, R. T., Bitsko, R. H., Radhakrishnan, L., Martinez, P., Njai, R., & Holland, K. M. (2020). Mental health-related emergency department visits among children aged <18 Years during the COVID-19 pandemic - United States, January 1−October 17, 2020. *Morbidity and Mortality Weekly Report (MMWR), 69*(45), 1675−1680.

Lindan, C. E., Mankad, K., Ram, D., Kociolek, L. K., Silvera, V. M., Boddaert, N., Stivaros, S. M., Palasis, S; ASPNR PECOBIG Collaborator Group. (2021). Neuroimaging manifestations in children with SARS-CoV-2 infection: a multinational, multicentre collaborative study. *Lancet Child Adolesc Health. 3,* 167−177. https://doi.org/10.1016/S2352-4642(20)30362-X. PMID: 33338439; PMCID: PMC7744016.CopyDownload .nbib

Local Government Association (2020). Retrieved from: COVID-19 series - briefing on children's social care providers, October 2020 (publishing.service.gov.uk).

Lopez-Leon, S., Wegman-Ostrosky, T., Perelman, C., Sepulveda, R., Rebolledo, P. A., Cuapio, A. & Villapol, S. (2021). More than 50 long-term effects of COVID-19: a systematic review and meta-analysis. *Sci Rep* **11,** 16144 (2021). https://doi.org/10.1038/s41598-021-95565-8

Magklara, K., Lazaratou, H., Barbouni, A., Poulas, K., & Farsalinos, K. (2020). *Impact of COVID-19 pandemic and lockdown measures on mental health of children and adolescents in Greece.* https://doi.org/10.1101/2020.10.18.20214643 [Pre-print].

Margolius, M., Doyle Lynch, A., Pufall Jones, E., & Hynes, M. (2020). *The state of young people during COVID-19: Findings from a nationally representative survey of high school youth.* Americas Promise Alliance.

Markham, S., Levis, B., Azar, M., Thombs-Vite, I., Neupane, D., Santo, T. D., Tasleem, A., Yao, A., Agic, B., & Thombs, B. D. (2021). Comparison of mental health symptoms prior to and during COVID-19: Evidence from a living systematic review and meta-analysis. *medRxiv.* https://doi.org/10.1101/2021.05.10.21256920, 2005.2010.21256920.

Melegari, M. G., Giallonardo, M., Sacco, R., Marcucci, L., Orecchio, S., & Bruni, O. (2021). Identifying the impact of the confinement of Covid-19 on emotional-mood and behavioural dimensions in children and adolescents with attention deficit hyperactivity disorder (ADHD). *Psychiatry Research, 296,* 113692. https://doi.org/10.1016/j.psychres.2020.113692

Mendenhall, E. (2020). The COVID-19 syndemic is not global: Context matters. *The Lancet.* https://doi.org/10.1016/S0140-6736(20)32222-4. Retrieved from.

Metherell, T., Ghai, S., McCormick, E. M., Ford, T. J., & Orben, A. (2021). Digital exclusion predicts worse mental health among adolescents during COVID-19. *medRxiv, 11*(25), 21266853. https://doi.org/10.1101/2021.11.25.21266853

Mind. (2020). *A review of mental health services for children and young people (2020).* https://www.mind.org.uk/media/6865/briefing-on-cyp-mhs-2020-final.pdf.

Mohler-Kuo, M., Dzemaili, S., Foster, S., Werlen, L., & Walitza, S. (2021). Stress and mental health among children/adolescents, their parents, and young adults during the first COVID-19 lockdown in Switzerland. *International Journal of Environmental Research and Public Health, 18*(9), 4668. https://doi.org/10.3390/ijerph18094668. MDPI AG. Retrieved from.

Molteni, E., Absoud, M., & Duncan, E. L. (2022). Assessing the impact of the pandemic in children and adolescents: SARS-CoV-2 infection and beyond. *The Lancet Child & Adolescent Health.* https://doi.org/10.1016/S2352-4642(22)00035-9

Moore, D., Benham-Clarke, S., Kenchington, R., Boyle, C., Ford, T., Hayes, R., & Rogers, M. (2019). *Improving behaviour in schools: Guidance report: Improving behaviour in schools: Guidance report*. Education Endowment Foundation.

Newlove-Delgado, T., McManus, S., Sadler, K., Thandi, S., Vizard, T., Cartwright, C., & Ford, T. (2021). Mental health of children and young people group. Child mental health in England before and during the COVID-19 lockdown. *Lancet Psychiatry, 8*(5), 353–354. https://doi.org/10.1016/S2215-0366(20)30570-8. Epub 2021 Jan 11. PMID: 33444548.

Newlove-Delgado, T., Williams, T., Robertson, K., McManus, S., Sadler, K., Vizard, T., Cartwright, C., Mathews, F., Norman, S., Marcheselli, F., & Ford, T. (2021). *Mental health of children and young people in England* (Vol 2021). Leeds: NHS Digital.

NHS. Children and young people with an eating disorder waiting times. https://www.england.nhs.uk/statistics/statistical-work-areas/cypedwaiting-times. Accessed March 16, 2021.

NHS England (2021). Admissions analysis by age group April 2021. *National Health Service England*. Retrieved from: https://www.england.nhs.uk/statistics/statistical-work-areas/Covid-19-hospital-activity/.

Nicholas, J., Bell, I. H., Thompson, A., Valentine, L., Simsir, P., Sheppard, H., & Adams, S. (2021). Implementation lessons from the transition to telehealth during COVID-19: A survey of clinicians and young people from youth mental health services. *Psychiatry Research, 299*, 113848.

Nonweiler, J., Rattray, F., Baulcomb, J., Happé, F., & Absoud, M. (2020). Prevalence and associated factors of emotional and behavioural difficulties during COVID-19 pandemic in children with neurodevelopmental disorders. *Children*. https://doi.org/10.3390/children7090128

Nye, E., Melendez-Torres, G. J., & Gardner, F. (2019). Mixed methods systematic review on effectiveness and experiences of the Incredible Years Teacher Classroom Management programme. *Review of Education, 7*(3), 631–669.

Office for National Statistics. (2019). Internet access – households and individuals, Great Britain: 2019. Internet access – households and individuals, Great Britain - Office for National Statistics (ons.gov.uk)

Office for National Statistics. (2021). *Prevalence of ongoing symptoms following coronavirus (COVID-19) infection in the UK: 4 June 2021*. https://www.ons.gov.uk/peoplepopulationandcommunity/healthandsocialcare/conditionsanddiseases/bulletins/prevalenceofongoingsymptomsfollowingcoronaviruscovid19infectionintheuk/4june2021.

Orgilés, M., Morales, A., Delvecchio, E., Mazzeschi, C., & Espada, J. P. (2020). Immediate psychological effects of the COVID-19 quarantine in youth from Italy and Spain. *Frontiers in Psychology*. https://doi.org/10.3389/fpsyg.2020.579038

O'Sullivan, K., Clark, S., McGrane, A., Rock, N., Burke, L., Boyle, N., Joksimovic, N., & Marshall, K. A. (2021). Qualitative study of child and adolescent mental health during the COVID-19 pandemic in Ireland. *International Journal of Environmental Research and Public Health, 18*, 1062. https://doi.org/10.3390/ijerph18031062

Patel, V., Saxena, S., Lund, C., Thornicroft, G., Baingana, F., Bolton, P., Chisholm, D., Collins, P. Y., Cooper, J. L., Eaton, J., Herrman, H., Herzallah, M. M., Huang, Y., Jordans, M. J. D., Kleinman, A., Medina-Mora, M. E., Morgan, E., Naiz, U., Omigbodun, O., … UnUtzer, J. (2018). The Lancet Commission on global mental health and sustainable development. *The Lancet, 392*(10157), 1553–1598.

Pearcey, S., Shum, A., Waite, P., & Creswell, C. (2020). Parents/carers report on their own and their children's concerns about children attending school (Report 3). Retrieved from: http://cospaceoxford.org/findings/cospace-report-3/.

Pearcey, S., Shum, A., Waite, P., Patalay, P., & Creswell, C. (2020). Changes in children and young people's emotional and behavioural difficulties through lockdown. (Report 4). Retrieved from: http://cospaceoxford.org/findings/4th-update/.

III. Innovative approaches to helping young people in adversity

Petri-Romao, P., Bali, E., Enright, J., O'Neill, I., Dyas, R., English, O., Butcher, J., & Minnis, H. Safe model for school return during the COVID-19 pandemic. Accessed 2/6/2021: https://www.gla.ac.uk/media/Media_736441_smxx.pdf.

Pierce, M., Hope, H., Ford, T., Hatch, S., Hotopf, M., John, A., Kontopantellis, E., Webb, R., Wessely, S., McManus, S., & Abel, K. (2020). Mental health before and during the COVID-19 pandemic: A longitudinal probability sample survey of the UK population. *The Lancet Psychiatry, 7*(10), 883−892.

Pierce, M., McManus, S., Hope, H., Hotopf, M., Ford, T., Hatch, S., John, A., Kontopantelis, E., Webb, R. T., Wessely, S., & Abel, K. (2021). Mental health responses to the COVID-19 pandemic: A latent class trajectory analysis using longitudinal UK data. *The Lancet Psychiatry.* https://doi.org/10.1016/S2215-0366(21)00151-6

Pierce, M., McManus, S., Jessop, C., John, A., Hotopf, M., Ford, T., Hatch, S., Wessely, S., & Abel, K. M. (2020). Says who? The significance of sampling in mental health surveys during COVID-19. *The Lancet Psychiatry, 7*(7), 567−568. https://doi.org/10.1016/S2215-0366(20)30237-6

Pizarro-Ruiz, J. P., & Ordóñez-Camblor, N. (2021). Effects of Covid-19 confinement on the mental health of children and adolescents in Spain. *Scientific Reports, 11*, 11713. https://doi.org/10.1038/s41598-021-91299-9

Raballo, A., Poletti, M., Valmaggia, L., & McGorry, P. (2020). Editorial perspective: Rethinking child and adolescent mental health care after COVID-19. Advance online publication. In *The Journal of Child Psychology and Psychiatry.* https://doi.org/10.1111/jcpp.13371

Racine, N., McArthur, B. A., Cooke, J. E., Eirich, R., Zhu, J., & Madigan, S. (2021). Global prevalence of depressive and anxiety symptoms in children and adolescents during COVID-19: A meta-analysis. *JAMA Pediatrics, 175*(11), 1142−1150. https://doi.org/10.1001/jamapediatrics.2021.2482

Rady, H. I., Ismail, O. R., Abdelkader, M. S., & Abdelgalil, A. A. (2020). Increased psychiatric risk in children after pediatric intensive care unit admission. *The Journal of Nervous and Mental Disease, 208*(2), 147−151. https://doi.org/10.1097/nmd.0000000000001123

Rains, S. L., Johnson, S., Barnett, P., Steare, T., Needle, J. J., Carr, S., Lever Taylor, B., Bentivegna, F., Edbrooke-Childs, J., Scott, H. R., Rees, J., Shah, P., Lomani, J., Chipp, B., Barber, N., Dedat, Z., Oram, S., Morant, N., Simpson, A., & COVID-19 Mental Health Policy Research Unit Group. (2020). Early impacts of the COVID-19 pandemic on mental health care and on people with mental health conditions: Framework synthesis of international experiences and responses. *Social Psychiatry and Psychiatric Epidemiology.* https://doi.org/10.1007/s00127-020-01924-7

Revet, A., Hebebrand, J., Anagnostopoulos, D., Kehoe, L. A., COVID-19 Child and Adolescent Psychiatry Consortium, Klauser, P. (2021). ESCAP CovCAP survey of heads of academic departments to assess the perceived initial (April/May 2020) impact of the COVID-19 pandemic on child and adolescent psychiatry services. European Child & Adolescent Psychiatry, 1-10.

Rajabi, M. (2020). Report 02: Parent/carer stress, work and child's needs, reported child activity, communicating with friends and family living outside the household: Results from the first 1600 participants in Iran. Co-Space Iran Study. University of Tehran. http://cospaceoxford.org/findings/results-from-the-first-1600-participants-in-iran/.

Ravens-Sieberer, U., Kaman, A., Erhart, M., et al. (2021). Impact of the COVID-19 pandemic on quality of life and mental health in children and adolescents in Germany. *European Child & Adolescent Psychiatry.* https://doi.org/10.1007/s00787-021-01726-5

Robert, A. (2020). Lessons from New Zealand's COVID-19 outbreak response. In *The Lancet Public Health.* https://doi.org/10.1016/S2468-2667(20)30237-1

Royal College of Paediatrics and Child Health. (2021). PIMS: the COVID-19 linked syndrome affecting children - information for families. Retrieved from: PIMS: the COVID-19 linked syndrome affecting children - information for families | RCPCH

Saurabh, K., & Ranjan, S. (2020). Compliance and psychological impact of quarantine in children and adolescents due to Covid-19 pandemic. *Indian Journal of Pediatrics.* https://doi.org/10.1007/s12098-020-03347-3

Shafran, R., Myles-Hooton, P., Bennett, S., & Öst, L.-G. (2021). The concept and definition of 'low intensity' cognitive behaviour therapy. *Behaviour Research and Therapy, 138*, 103803. https://doi.org/10.1016/j.brat.2021.103803

Shepherd, J., & Hancock, C. (2020). *Education and Covid-19: Perspectives from parent carers of children with SEND.* University of Sussex. Retrieved from https://www.acorns-sussex.org.uk/wp-content/uploads/2020/09/Education-and-Covid-19-Perspectives-from-parent-ca rers-of-children-with-SEND_3.9.2020.pdf.

Shum, A., Skripkauskaite, S., Pearcey, S., Waite, P., & Creswell, C. (2021). Update on children's & parents/carers' mental health; Changes in parents/carers' ability to balance childcare and work: March 2020 to February 2021. (Report 9). Retrieved from: http://cospaceoxford.org/findings/changes-in-parents-carers-ability-to-balance-childcare-and-work-march-2020-to-february-2021/.

Signorini, G., Singh, S. P., Boricevic-Marsanic, V., Dieleman, G., Dodig-Ćurković, K., Franic, T., Gerritsen, S. E., Griffin, J., Maras, A., McNicholas, F., O'Hara, L., Purper-Quakil, D., Paul, M., Santosh, P., Schulze, U., Street, C., Tremmery, S., Tuomainen, H., ... de Girolamo, G. (2017). Architecture and functioning of child and adolescent mental health services: A 28-country survey in Europe. *The Lancet, 4*(9), 715−724.

Soneson, E., Puntis, S., Chapman, N., et al. (2022). Happier during lockdown: A descriptive analysis of self-reported wellbeing in 17,000 UK school students during covid-19 lockdown. *European Journal of Child and Adolescent Psychiatry.* https://doi.org/10.1007/s00787-021-01934-z

Spinelli, M., Lionetti, F., Pastore, M., & Fasolo, M. (2020). Parents' stress and children's psychological problems in families facing the COVID-19 outbreak in Italy. *Frontiers in Psychology.* https://doi.org/10.3389/fpsyg.2020.01713

Spitzer, R. L., Kroenke, K., Williams, J. B., & Löwe, B. (2006). A brief measure for assessing generalized anxiety disorder: The GAD-7. *Archives of Internal Medicine, 166*(10), 1092−1097. https://doi.org/10.1001/archinte.166.10.1092. PMID: 16717171.

Stephenson, T., Pinto Pereira, S. M., Shafran, R., de Stavola, B. L., Rojas, N., McOwat, K., Simmons, R., Zavala, M., O'Mahoney, L., Chalder, T., Crawley, E., Ford, T. J., Harnden, A., Heyman, I., Swann, O., Whittaker, E., Stephenson, T., Shafran, R., Buszewicz, M., & Ladhani, S. N. (2022). Physical and mental health 3 months after SARS-CoV-2 infection (long COVID) among adolescents in England (CLoCk): A national matched cohort study. *The Lancet Child & Adolescent Health.* https://doi.org/10.1016/S2352-4642(22)00022-0

Sun, Y., Wu, Y., Bonardi, O., Krishnan, A., He, C., Boruff, J. T., ... Thombs, B. D. (2021). Comparison of mental health symptoms prior to and during COVID-19: Evidence from a living systematic review and meta-analysis. medRxiv 2021. https://doi.org/10.1101/2021.05.10.21256920

Swann, O. V., Holden, K. A., Turtle, L., Pollock, L., Fairfield, C. J., Drake, T. M., et al. (2020). Clinical characteristics of children and young people admitted to hospital with Covid-19 in United Kingdom: Prospective multicentre observational cohort study. *British Medical Journal, 370*, m3249. https://doi.org/10.1136/bmj.m3249

Taquet, M., Geddes, J. R., Husain, M., Luciano, S., & Harrison, P. J. (2021). 6-month neurological and psychiatric outcomes in 236379 survivors of COVID-19: A retrospective cohort study using electronic health records. *Lancet Psychiatry, 8*, 416−427. https://doi.org/10.1016/S2215-0366(21)00084-5

III. Innovative approaches to helping young people in adversity

Thombs, B. D., Bonardi, O., Rice, D. B., Boruff, J. T., Azar, M., He, C., Markham, S., Sun, Y., Wu, Y., Krishnan, A., Thombs-Vite, I., & Benedetti, A. (2020). Curating evidence on mental health during COVID-19: A living systematic review. *Journal of Psychosomatic Research, 133,* 110113. https://doi.org/10.1016/j.jpsychores.2020.110113

Tso, W. W. Y., Wong, R. S., Tung, K. T. S., Rao, N., Fu, K. W., Yam, J. C. S., Chua, G. T., Chen, E. Y. H., Lee, T. M. C., Chan, S. K. W., Wong, W. H. S., Xiong, X., Chui, C. S., Li, X., Wong, K., Leung, C., Tsang, S. K. M., Chan, G. C. F., Tam, P. K. H., … Lp, P. (2020). Vulnerability and resilience in children during the COVID-19 pandemic. *European Child & Adolescent Psychiatry, 17,* 1—16. https://doi.org/10.1007/s00787-020-01680-8. Epub ahead of print. PMID: 33205284; PMCID: PMC7671186.

Van Straten, A., Hill, J., Richards, D., & Cuijpers, P. (2015). Stepped care treatment delivery for depression: A systematic review and meta-analysis. *Psychological Medicine, 45*(2), 231—246. https://doi.org/10.1017/S0033291714000701

Viner, R., Russell, S., Saulle, R., Croker, H., Stansfeld, C., Packer, J., Nicholls, D., Goddings, A.-L., Bonell, C., Hudson, L., Hope, S., Schwalbe, N., Morgan, A., & Minozzi, S. (2021). *Impacts of school closures on physical and mental health of children and young people: A systematic review.* https://doi.org/10.1101/2021.02.10.21251526 [Pre-print].

Vizard, T., Sadler, K., Ford, T., et al. (2020). Mental health of children and young people in England: Wave 1 follow-up to the 2017 survey. *Health and Social Care Information Centre.* https://files.digital.nhs.uk/CB/C41981/mhcyp_2020_rep.pdf.

Waite, P., Pearcey, S., Shum, A., Raw, J. A. L., Patalay, P., & Creswell, C. (2021). How did the mental health symptoms of children and adolescents change over early lockdown during the COVID-19 pandemic in the UK? *JCPP Advances, 1,* e12009. https://doi.org/10.1111/jcv2.12009

Widnall, E., Winstone, L., Mars, B., Haworth, C.M.A., & Kidger, J. (2020). Young people's mental health during the Covid-19 pandemic: Initial findings from a secondary school survey study in south west England. Retrieved from: https://sphr.nihr.ac.uk/wp-content/uploads/2020/08/Young-Peoples-Mental-Health-during-the-COVID-19-Pandemic-Report.pdf.

Wiguna, T., Anindyajati, G., Kaligis, F., Ismail, R. I., Minayati, K., Hanafi, E., Murtani, B. J., Wigantara, N. A., Putra, A. A., & Pradana, K. (2020). Brief research report on adolescent mental well-being and school closures during the COVID-19 pandemic in Indonesia. *Frontiers in Psychiatry, 11,* 1157. https://doi.org/10.3389/fpsyt.2020.598756

Wolpert, M., Harris, R., Hodges, S., Fuggle, P., James, R., Wiener, A., & Munk, S. (2019). *THRIVE Framework for system change.* London: CAMHS Press.

World Health Organisation. (2020). *Multisystem inflammatory syndrome in children and adolescents with COVID-19. Clinical Care.* WHO/2019-nCoV/Sci_Brief/Multisystem_Syndrome_Children/2020.1.

Wykes, T., Bell, A., Carr, S., Coldham, T., Gilbody, S., Hotopf, M., Johnson, S., Kabir, T., Pinfold, V., Sweeney, A., Jones, P. B., & Creswell, C. (2021). Shared goals for mental health research: What, why and when for the 2020s. *Journal of Mental Health.* https://doi.org/10.1080/09638237.2021.1898552

Xiang, M., Yamamoto, S., & Mizoue, T. (2020). Depressive symptoms in students during school closure due to COVID-19 in Shanghai. *Psychiatry and Clinical Neuroscience, 74*(12), 664—666.

Zhou, S. J., Zhang, L. G., Wang, L. L., Guo, Z. C., Wang, J. Q., Chen, J. C., Liu, M., Chen, X., & Chen, J. X. (2020). Prevalence and socio-demographic correlates of psychological health problems in Chinese adolescents during the outbreak of COVID-19. *European Child and Adolescent Psychiatry.* https://doi.org/10.1007/s00787-020-01541-4

Zipfel, S., Schmidt, U., & Giel, K. E. (2022). The hidden burden of eating disorders during the COVID-19 pandemic. *Lancet Psychiatry, 9*(1), 9—11. https://doi.org/10.1016/S2215-0366(21)00435-1. PMID: 34921799; PMCID: PMC8673860.

6

Trauma-related psychopathology in children and adolescents: recent developments and future directions

Stephanie J. Lewis[1,2], and Andrea Danese[1,3,4]

[1] Department of Child and Adolescent Psychiatry, Institute of Psychiatry, Psychology and Neuroscience, King's College London, London, United Kingdom; [2] South London and Maudsley NHS Foundation Trust, London, United Kingdom; [3] Social, Genetic and Developmental Psychiatry Centre, Institute of Psychiatry, Psychology and Neuroscience, King's College London, London, United Kingdom; [4] National and Specialist CAMHS Clinic for Trauma, Anxiety, and Depression, South London and Maudsley NHS Foundation Trust, London, United Kingdom

1. Introduction to trauma-related psychopathology in children and adolescents

Trauma exposure—defined as an event that involves actual or threatened death, serious injury, or sexual violation (American Psychiatric Association, 2013)—is a key risk factor for psychopathology. Not only are trauma-exposed individuals more likely to develop mental illness, but they are also more likely to have severe, recurrent, and treatment-resistant psychopathology, compared with their unexposed peers (Agnew-Blais & Danese, 2016; Lewis et al., 2019; Nanni et al., 2012; Schaefer et al., 2018).

Trauma-related psychopathology may be particularly problematic in children and adolescents for two reasons. Firstly, young people experience high rates of trauma, possibly higher than other age groups (Breslau et al., 1998, 2004). Epidemiological studies have found that 21%—85% of participants report trauma exposure by late adolescence, with estimates varying according to the sampling frame and the assessment method used (Breslau et al., 2004, 2006; Copeland et al., 2007; Giaconia et al., 1995; Landolt et al., 2013; Lewis et al., 2019; McLaughlin et al., 2013; Orozco et al., 2008; Perkonigg et al., 2000; Seedat et al., 2004). Secondly, young people may be particularly vulnerable to the adverse effects of trauma. They are undergoing important neurobiological, emotional, and social development, so they may not yet have the skills needed to manage the impact of trauma, and their development may be disrupted by trauma (Blakemore & Mills, 2014; Lee et al., 2014). Therefore, addressing trauma-related psychopathology should be a key priority in child and adolescent mental healthcare. Here, we highlight recent developments in this field and discuss implications for clinical practice and future research.

2. Presentations of trauma-related psychopathology in children and adolescents

Immediately following trauma exposure, most children and adolescents experience some psychological symptoms, such as preoccupation with the event, emotional difficulties, or behavioral disturbances (Meiser-Stedman et al., 2007). For many, these symptoms resolve within days to weeks and do not cause substantial problems. However, a proportion experience longer-lasting distressing symptoms that interfere with their daily lives, indicating the onset of a mental health disorder. Recent developments have influenced how we conceptualize this significant trauma-related psychopathology.

2.1 Posttraumatic stress disorder in adolescents

The most commonly studied trauma-related disorder is posttraumatic stress disorder (PTSD). Somewhat different approaches to defining PTSD were taken in the *Diagnostic and Statistical Manual of Mental Disorders, fifth edition* (*DSM-5*; American Psychiatric Association, 2013) and the *International Classification of Diseases, eleventh revision* (*ICD-11*; World Health Organization, 2018). On the one hand, the *DSM-5* aimed to capture the full scope of clinically significant PTSD presentations, including fear-based, dysphoric/anhedonic, and externalizing phenotypes (Friedman, 2013; Friedman et al., 2011). *DSM-5* PTSD includes 20 symptom items organized in four criteria: intrusions such as distressing memories, flashbacks, or dreams about the trauma; avoidance of thoughts, feelings, or external reminders of the trauma; negative alterations in cognitions and mood after the trauma; and alterations in arousal and reactivity after the trauma (Table 6.1). On the other hand, the *ICD-11* defined PTSD more narrowly, in an attempt to simplify the

TABLE 6.1 PTSD diagnostic criteria.

Criteria and items	DSM-5 PTSD	ICD-11 PTSD	DSM-5 PTSD in young children	ICD-11 complex PTSD
Trauma exposure	✔	✔	✔	✔
Intrusion/reexperiencing symptoms				
Intrusive distressing sensory memories of the trauma	✔		✔	
Nightmares related to the trauma	✔	✔	✔	✔
Flashbacks of the trauma (with some loss of awareness)	✔	✔	✔	✔
Psychological distress when exposed to reminders	✔		✔	
Physiological reactions to reminders	✔		✔	
Number of items needed to meet criterion	1	1	1	1
Avoidance symptoms				
Persistent avoidance of trauma memories and thoughts	✔	✔	✔	✔
Persistent avoidance of external reminders	✔	✔	✔	✔
Number of items needed to meet criterion	1	1		1
Negative alterations in cognitions and mood symptoms				
Dissociative amnesia of the trauma	✔			
Persistent negative expectations	✔			
Persistent blame of self or others about the trauma	✔			
Persistent negative emotional state	✔		✔	

Continued

TABLE 6.1   PTSD diagnostic criteria.—cont'd

Criteria and items	DSM-5 PTSD	ICD-11 PTSD	DSM-5 PTSD in young children	ICD-11 complex PTSD
Diminished interest or participation in activities	✔		✔	
Feeling of detachment or estrangement	✔		✔	
Persistent inability to experience positive emotions	✔		✔	
Number of items needed to meet criterion	2			
Number of avoidance or cognitions/mood symptom items needed to meet criterion			1	
Arousal/sense of threat symptoms				
Irritable behavior or angry outbursts	✔		✔	
Reckless or self-destructive behavior	✔			
Hypervigilance	✔	✔	✔	✔
Exaggerated startle response	✔	✔	✔	✔
Concentration problems	✔		✔	
Sleep disturbance	✔		✔	
Number of items needed to meet criterion	2	1	2	1
Affect dysregulation				✔
Negative self-concept				✔
Relationship difficulties				✔
Duration of symptoms	>1 month	Several weeks	>1 month	Several weeks
Impact				
Symptoms cause significant distress	✔		✔	
Symptoms cause functional impairment	✔	✔	✔	✔

TABLE 6.1   PTSD diagnostic criteria.—cont'd

Criteria and items	*DSM-5* PTSD	*ICD-11* PTSD	*DSM-5* PTSD in young children	*ICD-11* complex PTSD
Number of items needed to meet criterion	1	1	1	1

The table shows diagnostic criteria from the *Diagnostic and Statistical Manual of Mental Disorders, fifth edition (DSM-5)* for PTSD and PTSD in young children (American Psychiatric Association. (2013). *Diagnostic and statistical manual of mental disorders* (5th ed.). American Psychiatric Association; Friedman, (2013). Finalizing PTSD in DSM-5: Getting here from there and where to go next. *Journal of Traumatic Stress, 26* (5), 548—556. https://doi.org/10.1002/jts.21840). The table also shows diagnostic criteria from the *International Classification of Diseases, eleventh revision (ICD-11)* for PTSD (Brewin, C. R., Cloitre, M., Hyland, P., Shevlin, M., Maercker, A., Bryant, R. A.,Humayun, A., Jones, L. M., Kagee, A., Rousseau, C., Somasundaram, D., Suzuki, Y., Wessely, S., van Ommeren, M., & Reed, G. M. (2017). A review of current evidence regarding the ICD-11 proposals for diagnosing PTSD and complex PTSD. *Clinical Psychology Review, 58* , 1—15. https://doi.org/10.1016/j.cpr.2017.09.001; World Health Organization. (2018). *International classification of diseases, 11th revision.* World Health Organization. icd.who.int/en). Criteria (bold text, left column) or items (standard text, left column) included in each diagnosis are indicated with ticks. The number of items needed to meet criteria therefore applies to the relevant ticked items only. All included criteria are required for a diagnosis.

diagnosis (Brewin et al., 2017; Maercker et al., 2013). *ICD-11* PTSD includes only six symptoms in three criteria: reexperiencing, avoidance, and sense of threat (Table 6.1). Unlike *DSM-5*, *ICD-11* PTSD does not include symptoms that might overlap with other disorders. For example, it does not include a "negative alterations in cognitions and mood" criterion, or the hyperarousal symptoms of sleep disturbance and concentration problems, which might also be seen in depression or generalized anxiety disorder. Both *DSM-5* and *ICD-11* PTSD include criteria for trauma exposure, symptom duration (one month in *DSM-5* and several weeks in *ICD-11*), and significant functional impairment (or significant distress in *DSM-5*). Despite these diverging definitions of PTSD, which were largely developed based on the adult literature, research shows that PTSD according to both *DSM-5* and *ICD-11* has important validity and utility for trauma-exposed adolescents.

To investigate the prevalence and clinical features of PTSD in young people, we conducted the most comprehensive epidemiological study of PTSD to date. We studied *DSM-5* PTSD in young people in the Environmental Risk (E-Risk) Longitudinal Twin Study, a population-representative sample of over 2000 British young people (Lewis et al., 2019). We found that 7.8% of participants had experienced PTSD by age 18 years and 4.4% had PTSD in the past year. Within trauma-exposed young people, 25.0% had PTSD by age 18 years, and 14.0% had PTSD in the past year. Young people exposed to direct interpersonal traumas, such as violence and abuse, were seven times more likely to have had PTSD than those exposed to other types of trauma, including accidents and illness. Young people with PTSD often experienced cooccurring mental health disorders. For example, of those with PTSD in the past year, 58% also had depression, 32% had generalized anxiety disorder, and 28% had conduct disorder during that year. Furthermore, those with PTSD had a high risk of harm and functional impairment. For example, of those with PTSD by age 18, 49% had self-harmed, 20% had attempted suicide in adolescence, and 27% were not in education, employment, or training (NEET) at age 18. Our study, therefore, reveals the significant mental health burden of PTSD in young people and highlights the need for comprehensive clinical care to identify and address PTSD and cooccurring problems in trauma-exposed young people.

Our findings are consistent with and extend the previous epidemiological research on adolescent PTSD undertaken in Europe and the United States (Breslau et al., 2004, 2006; Copeland et al., 2007; Giaconia et al., 1995; Kilpatrick & Saunders, 1997; Landolt et al., 2013; McLaughlin et al., 2013; Perkonigg et al., 2000). In recent years, an increasing amount of research has investigated rates of PTSD symptoms in young people in low- and middle-income countries (LMICs). These studies have taken place in three main contexts. Firstly, some studies have focused on young people exposed to war and organized violence, who may have experienced displacement within their own country or beyond its borders and become asylum seekers or refugees (see Maalouf et al, chapter 12, this volume). The majority of these studies have relied on self-report questionnaires and have found high rates of PTSD symptoms but with wide confidence intervals indicating uncertain estimates (Attanayake et al., 2009; Betancourt et al., 2013; Charlson et al., 2019). Nevertheless, these elevated rates are consistent with a review of young refugees that included only interview-based studies, carried out in middle-income and high-income countries with young people from mainly low-income countries, which found a current PTSD prevalence of 22.71% (95% confidence interval: 12.79% −32.64%) (Blackmore et al., 2020). The second setting for research on PTSD in young people from LMIC has been societies with high levels of endemic domestic-, community-, or gang-related violence, as occurs in parts of South and Central America and South Africa. The accumulation of violence exposures with other risk factors such as substance misuse, family conflict and losses, and other adversities, is associated with high rates of PTSD symptoms in young people from these regions (Foster & Brooks-Gunn, 2015; Stupar et al., 2021). The third context for research on PTSD in young people from LMIC has been the aftermath of natural disasters, such as earthquakes and floods, which can have devastating impacts on affected regions that lack resources to prepare for and manage these events. During disasters in these areas, young people may experience or witness serious injury or death, destruction of homes and property, and displacement. A recent review has estimated a rate of current PTSD symptoms of about 20% after earthquakes or floods (Rezayat et al., 2020). Overall, these studies in LMIC often have methodological limitations such as use of self-report questionnaire measures and cross-sectional designs. Further research is therefore needed to improve our understanding of the epidemiology of PTSD in young people in LMICs.

Studies comparing *DSM-5* and *ICD-11* PTSD in young people have mostly found no significant differences in PTSD prevalence and comorbidity rates, and both classification systems have identified young people with clinically important difficulties. However, some of these studies have also found only modest agreement between *DSM-5* and *ICD-11* PTSD, indicating that they may identify somewhat different groups of individuals (Bruckmann et al., 2020; Danzi & La Greca, 2016; Elliott et al., 2021; Hafstad et al., 2017; Sachser et al., 2018). This inconsistency presents challenges for researchers and clinicians. Diagnosis according to one of these classification systems is usually required for study inclusion and access to clinical services, but will likely miss individuals with clinically significant difficulties who would have been uniquely identified by the other classification system. These findings therefore support considering both diagnostic systems and intervening to help young people with either *DSM-5* or *ICD-11* PTSD criteria or clinically important PTSD symptoms, as is generally advocated in PTSD guidelines (Jensen et al., 2020; National Institute for Health and Care Excellence, 2018a). In future, optimizing and reconciling these differing definitions of PTSD would ensure more consistent identification of young people with clinically important PTSD.

2.2 Posttraumatic stress disorder in young children

Although the adult-based PTSD definitions may be appropriate for adolescents, research suggests that young children may require adjusted criteria (Scheeringa et al., 2011). Preschool-aged children have not yet developed the abstract cognitive abilities and language skills needed to recognize and report their internal experiences, so it is very difficult to assess introspective symptoms in this age group. Michael Scheeringa et al. (2011) therefore recommended that PTSD diagnostic criteria for young children should be anchored on observable behavioral manifestations of these symptoms. For example, the symptoms of diminished interest in significant activities may manifest as constricted play, and feelings of detachment or estrangement from others may manifest as social withdrawal. Additionally, they recommended a lower threshold for avoidance, cognition, and mood symptoms. This proposed alternative algorithm (PTSD-AA) formed the basis of the *DSM-5* subtype of PTSD for young children (aged 6 years or younger), which requires the presence of only one symptom item from the two criteria of avoidance, and negative alterations in cognitions and mood (Table 6.1) (Friedman, 2013; Scheeringa et al., 2011). In contrast, the *ICD-11* did not include separate criteria for young children.

These PTSD-AA criteria were recently investigated in a general population sample for the first time (Hitchcock et al., 2021). This sample included over 3000 5- to 6-year-old British children. The researchers also studied a sample of 137 5- to 6-year-old British looked-after-children. PTSD-AA criteria led to higher current prevalence estimates in the general population sample (0.4%) and in looked-after-children (14%), compared with *DSM-IV* PTSD criteria (0% and 1.2%, respectively). Importantly, PTSD-AA criteria led to improved identification of up to four times as many young children who had functional impairment due to their PTSD symptoms. PTSD-AA was additionally studied in school-aged children and also identified children in this age group who experienced functional impairment, suggesting that the diagnosis may have clinical utility in children up to 8 years old and potentially beyond. These findings are consistent with previous research in clinical and convenience samples (Scheeringa et al., 2011) and highlight the importance of recognizing the influence of developmental stage on PTSD presentations.

2.3 Complex posttraumatic stress disorder

To capture the broad psychopathology experienced by some trauma-exposed people, a new disorder of complex PTSD (CPTSD) has been included in the *ICD-11*. For this disorder to be diagnosed, all three core PTSD symptom criteria must be present as well as three additional symptom criteria collectively called "disturbances in self-organization" (DSO); specifically, sustained and pervasive affect dysregulation, negative self-concept, and difficulties with relationships (Table 6.1) (Brewin et al., 2017; Maercker et al., 2013). Research suggests that CPTSD is associated with "complex trauma" exposure—namely, traumatic experiences that involve multiple interpersonal assaults during childhood or adolescence, for example, repeated maltreatment—but CPTSD can occur in people exposed to other types of trauma. The concept of CPTSD was originally proposed by Judith Herman and was operationalized and tested in *DSM-IV* field trials, with a wider range of additional complex symptoms termed "disorders of extreme stress, not otherwise specified" (DESNOS) (Herman, 1992; van der Kolk et al., 2005). The *DSM-IV* Work Group and subsequently the *DSM-5* Work Group both decided there was insufficient evidence to add CPTSD or DESNOS as a new independent diagnosis. Instead, DESNOS symptoms were listed as possible associated features of PTSD (Friedman, 2013; Friedman et al., 2011; Resick, Bovin, et al., 2012; Resick, Wolf, et al., 2012). The *ICD-11* Working Group took a different view and argued that defining CPTSD as a disorder separate and distinct from PTSD would promote equal attention on DSO and PTSD symptoms in research and clinical practice, leading to progress in the field (Brewin et al., 2017).

Most CPTSD research to date has involved adults, with only a small number of studies focusing on young people. Therefore, the validity and utility of this new diagnosis in children and adolescents is unclear. Emerging research using methods such as latent class analysis has identified different groups of young people with symptoms that might reflect PTSD and CPTSD (Haselgruber et al., 2020; Li et al., 2021; Perkonigg et al., 2016; Sachser et al., 2017; Villalta et al., 2020). While some researchers interpret these findings as support for distinct constructs of PTSD and CPTSD (Brewin et al., 2017; Cloitre et al., 2020; Herman, 2012), others argue against this conclusion because the groups might not have clear boundaries and may differ only by symptom severity rather than type of psychopathology (Achterhof et al., 2019). To shed light on whether this distinction is clinically meaningful, further research is needed to investigate if CPTSD versus PTSD has different etiology, course of illness, or treatment response, and ultimately whether its use can improve clinical care for trauma-exposed young people.

2.4 Broad trauma-related psychopathology

Although PTSD is often the focus of trauma research, trauma-exposed young people are also at increased risk of other types of psychopathology (Copeland et al., 2007; Giaconia et al., 1995; Perkonigg et al., 2000). In the E-Risk Study, we found that trauma-exposed young people were significantly more likely than their unexposed peers to experience a wide range of mental health disorders (Fig. 6.1). Several of these disorders, including depression, conduct disorder, and alcohol dependence (with past-year prevalence of 29.2%, 22.9%, and 15.9%, respectively), were more common in trauma-exposed participants than PTSD (with past-year prevalence of 14.0%). Our findings clearly demonstrate that trauma-related psychopathology in young people extends well beyond PTSD, highlighting the need to assess for varied and potentially broad presentations in clinical practice and research (Lewis et al., 2019).

Observations of cooccurring and broad psychopathology have led to recent research efforts to investigate the structure and boundaries of psychopathology. This work indicates that traditional distinct categorical disorders may be less parsimonious descriptions than transdiagnostic continuous dimensions (Caspi & Moffitt, 2018). Research using factor analytic modeling suggests that a single dimension may exist, reflecting liability to all disorders, comorbidity, severity, and persistence of psychopathology, termed "p." Importantly, research has found that maltreatment might be a risk factor for "p" rather than more specific forms of psychopathology (Caspi et al., 2014; Schaefer et al., 2018). This possibility of a single "p" factor would fit with the observations that

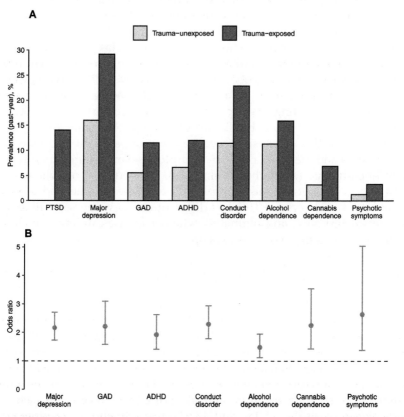

FIGURE 6.1 **Mental health disorders in trauma-exposed and unexposed young people.** Panel A shows the prevalence of mental health disorders in trauma-unexposed and trauma-exposed E-Risk Study participants at age 18 years. Panel B shows odds ratios with 95% confidence intervals (bars) for associations between trauma exposure and mental health disorders in E-Risk Study participants at age 18 years, based on univariable (unadjusted) models. The dashed horizontal line is a line of no difference. *ADHD* attention deficit hyperactivity disorder; *GAD* generalized anxiety disorder; *PTSD* posttraumatic stress disorder. *Adapted from Lewis, S. J., Arseneault, L., Caspi, A., Fisher, H. L., Matthews, T., Moffitt, T. E., Odgers, C. L., Stahl, D., Teng, J. Y., & Danese, A. (2019). The epidemiology of trauma and posttraumatic stress disorder in a representative cohort of young people in England and Wales. The Lancet Psychiatry, 6(3), 247–256. https://doi.org/10.1016/S2215-0366(19)30031-8.*

trauma confers an increased risk across varied disorders and is associated with comorbidity, and that the distinction between PTSD and CPTSD seems unclear. However, "p" is a relatively new concept and requires further research to better understand whether and how it can be operationalized and applied to helpfully inform clinical assessment and interventions.

3. Underlying mechanisms of trauma-related psychopathology in children and adolescents

Research that investigates the mechanisms through which trauma exposure is linked with psychopathology has the potential to reveal targets for interventions to prevent and treat trauma-related psychopathology. Recent developments have informed our understanding of these mechanisms.

3.1 Dominant hypothesis of toxic brain injury

The dominant biological hypothesis proposes that childhood trauma might cause brain injury by strongly or repeatedly activating the stress response giving rise to high levels of neurotoxic mediators. The hypothesis suggests that if traumas occur during sensitive periods when the brain is developing, these mediators might disrupt development and permanently damage the brain. The hypothesis posits that damage would be detectable through cognitive deficits and would be responsible for psychopathology (Danese & McEwen, 2012; Lupien et al., 2009; Sapolsky, 1996).

The strongest evidence to support this hypothesis has come from experiments with animals. In such studies, random assignment to either experimental or control conditions minimizes systematic differences between groups with respect to preexisting vulnerabilities. Additionally, precise manipulation of these conditions ensures consistent differences between groups with respect to the exposure. It is therefore possible to infer that the experimental condition caused outcomes in those exposed versus controls. By taking advantage of these design features, studies have found that, for example, early life stress can cause progressive learning and memory dysfunction in rats (Brunson et al., 2005). However, these findings may not translate to humans for several reasons, including brain development differences across species, greater individual differences in humans than laboratory animals, or compensatory interventions in humans (e.g., schooling or child protection services) (Clancy et al., 2007; Danese, 2020; Danese et al., 2017; van der Worp et al., 2010).

It is not possible to implement randomized precisely manipulated experiments that involve inflicting trauma in humans for obvious ethical reasons, and instead, we must make use of observational data. Cross-sectional studies have consistently found that childhood maltreatment is associated with impaired cognitive function, including lower IQ, poorer executive function, and impaired memory (Hart & Rubia, 2012; Malarbi et al., 2017). Although these cross-sectional findings might be consistent with the dominant causal hypothesis described before, they might alternatively reflect noncausal mechanisms. Because in these observational studies children had not been randomly assigned to trauma exposure, it is likely that those exposed were systematically different with respect to preexisting vulnerabilities, compared with unexposed participants. These preexisting vulnerabilities might lead to both trauma exposure and cognitive deficits, resulting in associations between trauma and cognition despite the lack of causal relationships, termed confounding. Alternatively, preexisting vulnerabilities might include cognitive deficits themselves, which could increase risk for trauma exposure and remain stable over time explaining later group differences in cognitive function, termed reverse causation (Danese, 2020; Danese et al., 2017).

To investigate the role of preexisting vulnerabilities in trauma-related cognitive deficits, observational studies require important design features, such as longitudinal assessments with repeated measures or genetically informed methods. To study this topic, we took advantage of these features in the E-Risk Study. Consistent with previous research, participants who had been exposed to multiple interpersonal traumas (e.g., repeated maltreatment)—termed "complex trauma"—had lower IQ and poorer executive function at age 18, compared with their trauma-unexposed peers (Fig. 6.2, light bars). However, we found that these associations were largely accounted for by preexisting vulnerabilities (Fig. 6.2, dark bars). The preexisting vulnerabilities we considered were IQ, psychopathology, family history of mental illness, family socioeconomic disadvantage, and female sex, measured at age 5 years. Correspondingly, within twin pairs who grew up in the same family environment and shared genetic material, complex trauma was not associated with cognitive deficits. This finding suggests that family environment and genetic factors likely explain the associations observed at the individual level (Lewis et al., 2021).

Our research provides convincing evidence against the dominant hypothesis that childhood trauma causes overt brain damage reflected in cognitive deficits and instead suggests that preexisting vulnerabilities explain cognitive impairments. We therefore caution against simplistic causal interpretations of associations between trauma exposure and all aspects of presentations, in both clinical case formulation and research interpretation. Instead, cognitive deficits would be better conceptualized

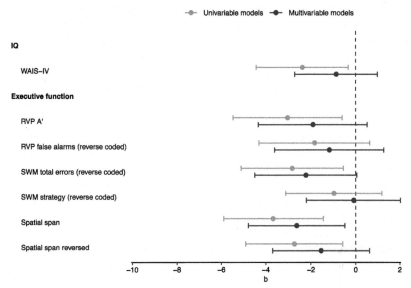

FIGURE 6.2   Associations between complex trauma exposure and cognitive function in young people. The plot shows linear regression coefficients (b) with 95% confidence intervals (bars) for associations between complex trauma exposure versus no trauma exposure and cognitive function in E-Risk Study participants at age 18 years. Light bars indicate results from univariable (unadjusted) models. Dark bars indicate results from multivariable models adjusted for preexisting variabilities (IQ at age 5 years, internalizing symptoms at age 5 years, externalizing symptoms at age 5 years, proportion of family members with a history of mental illness, lower family socioeconomic status at age 5 years, and female sex). Scores were scaled to a mean of 100 and standard deviation of 15 in the total sample. Scores were reverse-coded for some tests (if lower scores = better cognitive functioning), so that for all measures of cognition lower scores = poorer functioning. Dashed vertical lines are lines of no difference. *RVP* rapid visual information processing; *SWM* spatial working memory; *WAIS-IV* Wechsler adult intelligence scale, fourth edition. *Adapted from Lewis, S. J., Koenen, K. C., Ambler, A., Arseneault, L., Caspi, A., Fisher, H. L., Moffitt, T. E., & Danese, A. (2021). Unravelling the contribution of complex trauma to psychopathology and cognitive deficits: A cohort study. The British Journal of Psychiatry, 219(2), 448–455. https://doi.org/10.1192/bjp.2021.57.*

as risk factors for trauma exposure and potential complicating features during assessment and treatment. Addressing cognitive deficits might therefore enhance strategies to prevent trauma exposure and improve assessment and treatment approaches for trauma-exposed young people (Danese, 2020; Danese et al., 2017; Lewis et al., 2021).

3.2 Investigations of causality

It is, however, possible that trauma might have more subtle biological effects, which do not give rise to cognitive deficits, but are causally linked to psychopathology. Proposed biological pathways include alterations in specific aspects of brain function including threat and reward processing (McCrory et al., 2017), changes in endocrine function including in the hypothalamic—pituitary—adrenal axis (Koss & Gunnar, 2018), differences in immune function (Danese & Lewis, 2017), and epigenetic processes that alter gene expression (Parade et al., 2021). Additionally, psychological responses to trauma might have a causal role in the development of psychopathology. Potential psychological pathways involve maladaptive cognitions and coping strategies (Ehlers & Clark, 2000; Meiser-Stedman, 2002), described in the following section (3.3 Psychological processes). Furthermore, social factors could also be causally linked to trauma-related psychopathology. Social pathways might include poor family functioning and limited social support, which have been found to be associated with PTSD risk in children and adolescents (Trickey et al., 2012).

To consider whether confounding can exclude the possibility of trauma causing psychopathology, we investigated the role of preexisting vulnerabilities in trauma-related psychopathology in the E-Risk Study. We found that complex trauma-exposed participants had more severe psychopathology and were more likely to experience a range of disorders at age 18 years, compared with their trauma-unexposed peers (Fig. 6.3, light bars). Importantly, these associations were not accounted for by preexisting vulnerabilities (Fig. 6.3, dark bars). Correspondingly, within twin pairs, complex trauma was associated with more severe psychopathology (Lewis et al., 2021). These findings are consistent with some previous victimization research (Arseneault et al., 2006, 2011; Brown et al., 2014; Kendler et al., 2000; Nelson et al., 2002; Schaefer et al., 2018; Silberg et al., 2016; Singham et al., 2017). However, other victimization studies have found conflicting results (Baldwin et al., 2019; Berenz et al., 2013; Bornovalova et al., 2013; Dinwiddie et al., 2000; Shakoor et al., 2015; Young-Wolff et al., 2011), with some finding that links between maltreatment and neurodevelopmental disorders might be explained by preexisting vulnerabilities (Capusan et al., 2016; Dinkler et al., 2017; Stern et al., 2018).

To provide further insights into the likelihood of confounding or causal links between trauma exposure and psychopathology, recent research has capitalized on molecular genetic techniques. A small number of studies have investigated whether genetic vulnerability to psychopathology, measured as polygenic risk scores (PRS), is linked with trauma exposure. PRSs are calculated based on each individual's genetic data by summing their single nucleotide polymorphisms (SNPs) known to be associated with the phenotype of interest (e.g., depression), weighted according to effect sizes obtained in a genome-wide association study. As such, PRSs provide an individual measure of genetic risk for particular mental health disorders. Research has found that PRSs for various types of psychopathology were associated with exposure to a range of potentially traumatic

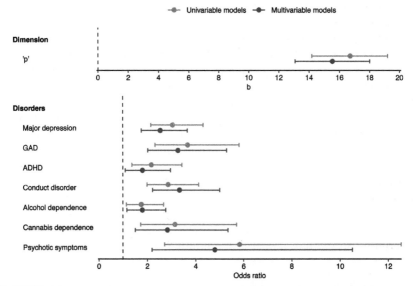

FIGURE 6.3 **Associations between complex trauma exposure and psychopathology in young people.** The plot shows linear regression coefficients (b) and odds ratios with 95% confidence intervals (bars) for associations between complex trauma exposure versus no trauma exposure and psychopathology in E-Risk Study participants at age 18 years. Light bars indicate results from univariable (unadjusted) models. Dark bars indicate results from multivariable models adjusted for preexisting variabilities (IQ at age 5 years, internalizing symptoms at age 5 years, externalizing symptoms at age 5 years, proportion of family members with a history of mental illness, and lower family socioeconomic status at age 5 years). General psychopathology dimension "p" scores were scaled to a mean of 100 and standard deviation of 15 in the total sample. Dashed lines are lines of no difference. *ADHD* attention deficit hyperactivity disorder; *GAD*, generalized anxiety disorder. *Adapted from Lewis, S. J., Koenen, K. C., Ambler, A., Arseneault, L., Caspi, A., Fisher, H. L., Moffitt, T. E., & Danese, A. (2021). Unravelling the contribution of complex trauma to psychopathology and cognitive deficits: A cohort study. The British Journal of Psychiatry, 219(2), 448–455. https://doi.org/10.1192/bjp.2021.57.*

events, specifically maltreatment, bullying, and other forms of adversity, reported retrospectively or prospectively by a range of informants (Bolhuis et al., 2021; Pergola et al., 2019; Ratanatharathorn et al., 2021; Sallis et al., 2020; Schoeler et al., 2019). This genetic risk may therefore contribute to both trauma exposure and psychopathology, giving rise to genetic confounding. Additionally, a recent large genome-wide association study of childhood maltreatment applied Mendelian randomization (MR) to inform causal inference. MR uses genetic variants associated with an exposure as unconfounded proxies for that exposure to investigate its effect on potential outcomes such as psychopathology (Davey Smith & Hemani, 2014). These early MR findings suggested a potential bidirectional causal role of childhood maltreatment on mental health disorders (Warrier et al., 2021).

Although this research cannot yet provide clear answers regarding the direction of effects and specific pathways, taken together these findings suggest that preexisting vulnerabilities likely contribute to trauma exposure and related psychopathology, and there may also be bidirectional causal links between trauma and psychopathology. It seems likely that these mechanisms vary by trauma type—for instance, some preexisting vulnerabilities (e.g., genetic risk for mental illness) may increase risk for certain trauma exposures (e.g., maltreatment) more than others (e.g., natural disasters)—which could partly explain heterogeneity of psychopathology by trauma type (Lewis et al., 2021). In future, longitudinal and family-based designs, as well as large genotyped and phenotyped samples, combined with novel computational tools and statistical innovations, will continue to reveal new insights and strengthen causal inference (Pingault et al., 2018; Polimanti & Wendt, 2021).

3.3 Psychological processes

Perhaps the best evidence for pathways involved in maintaining trauma-related psychopathology implicates psychological processes. A widely used psychological conceptualization is Ehlers and Clark's cognitive model of PTSD, which proposes that PTSD is maintained by several cognitive processes including negative appraisals of the event, self, and future, such as "it was my fault," "I'm going mad," and "my life will never be the same again"; the presence of a poorly elaborated, fragmented, and sensory-based memory of the trauma; and maladaptive cognitive and behavioral avoidance, which prevents change in negative appraisals and memory disturbances (Ehlers & Clark, 2000; Meiser-Stedman, 2002).

In line with this theory, longitudinal research indicates that these cognitive processes, particularly cognitive appraisals, predict subsequent PTSD symptoms in trauma-exposed children and adolescents and may also contribute to additional complex symptoms (Hiller et al., 2021; Meiser-Stedman et al., 2019). These processes are targeted by PTSD therapies that use cognitive and behavioral techniques. Importantly, research reveals that altering these psychological processes in this treatment mediates improvement of PTSD symptoms in young people, and perhaps also depression symptoms (Jensen et al., 2018; McLean et al., 2015; Meiser-Stedman et al., 2017; Pfeiffer et al., 2017). These studies demonstrate the importance of identifying and addressing underlying mechanisms to effectively treat trauma-related psychopathology.

4. Interventions for trauma-related psychopathology in children and adolescents

The ultimate benefit of understanding trauma-related psychopathology and underlying mechanisms is to inform the development and evaluation of interventions that either treat symptoms or prevent difficulties developing. Recent research has investigated the effectiveness of such interventions and highlighted healthcare gaps.

4.1 Treatment

Most interventions developed to treat trauma-related psychopathology in young people have aimed to address PTSD. The strongest evidence for clinical and cost-effectiveness has been found for individual psychological therapies that use cognitive and behavioral techniques, mentioned before, including trauma-focused cognitive behavioral therapy (TF-CBT) (Cohen et al., 2004), cognitive therapy for PTSD (Smith et al., 2007), prolonged exposure (Foa et al., 2013), and narrative exposure therapy (Ruf et al., 2010). These therapies have several components in common, such as psychoeducation about PTSD and the treatment rationale; coping skills training to help manage emotions; gradual exposure to trauma memories and reminders to help build a coherent narrative and address avoidance; and cognitive restructuring to adjust misappraisals and develop an updated meaning that is integrated into the trauma memory. Multiple randomized-controlled trials have found that these therapies are effective at improving PTSD in children and adolescents, as well as reducing cooccurring depressive, anxious, and behavioral symptoms. These trials were conducted in young people exposed to a wide range of traumas, across development, and in diverse cultures. Based on this evidence, these therapies are the recommended first-line treatment for children and adolescents with PTSD. Another therapy that aims to address PTSD is eye movement desensitization and reprocessing (EMDR), for which there is limited but growing evidence of effectiveness for treating PTSD in young people (Gillies et al., 2012; Gutermann et al., 2016; Jensen et al., 2020; Lewis & Danese, 2020; Mavranezouli, Megnin-Viggars, Daly, et al., 2020; Mavranezouli, Megnin-Viggars, Trickey, et al., 2020; Morina et al., 2016; National Institute for Health and Care Excellence, 2018c; Smith et al., 2019; Thomas et al., 2020). No pharmacological interventions have been found to be effective for treating PTSD in children and adolescents, but medication can be effective for comorbid disorders such as depression or anxiety (Cohen et al., 2010; Danese, 2021; Jensen et al., 2020; Lewis & Danese, 2020; National Institute for Health and Care Excellence, 2018e).

Evidence for treatment of CPTSD in children and adolescents is limited to one post hoc analysis of a TF-CBT trial. This study found that participants with CPTSD who completed treatment had significantly reduced PTSD symptoms and complex symptoms posttreatment compared with pretreatment. Notably, there was no significant difference in PTSD symptoms change between participants with CPTSD and those with PTSD among treatment completers, but participants with CPTSD had more PTSD symptoms at the start and end of treatment than those with PTSD (Sachser et al., 2017). It is therefore unclear whether CPTSD patients might benefit from a higher treatment dose (e.g., more sessions) or a different treatment model. Based on expert opinion, however, some guidelines recommend building in extra time when treating CPTSD (National Institute for Health and Care Excellence, 2018a).

4.2 Prevention

There has been interest in the potential for interventions delivered soon after trauma exposure to prevent the development of psychopathology. Universal single-session debriefing has not been found to be beneficial and is not recommended (Stallard et al., 2006; Zehnder et al., 2010). However, early psychological interventions, particularly CBT-based approaches, have shown some promise in reducing PTSD symptoms and preventing PTSD onset in trauma-exposed young people (Gillies et al., 2016; National Institute for Health and Care Excellence, 2018b). Additionally, some studies in low resource humanitarian settings suggest that psychosocial interventions may reduce PTSD symptoms (Purgato et al., 2018). However, further evidence is needed before firm recommendations can be made.

Preventing trauma exposure itself has also been considered, mainly focusing on maltreatment. Studies of parenting or home visiting programs have found only modest effectiveness in reducing or preventing maltreatment (van IJzendoorn et al., 2020). It should be noted that no studies have investigated the effects of improving families' socioeconomic resources, the lack of which is a key risk factor for maltreatment.

4.3 Healthcare gaps

Evidence-based interventions can only be provided for young people who access health services and see a mental health specialist. However, in the E-Risk Study, we found that only a minority of trauma-exposed young people had done so. About one in ten trauma-exposed participants and one in four of those with PTSD had seen a mental health professional in the past year (Fig. 6.4) (Lewis et al., 2019). In lower-income countries

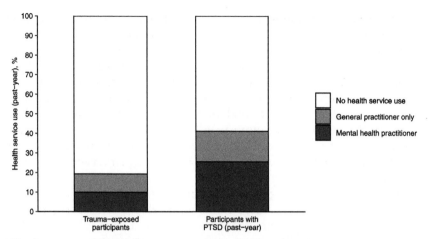

FIGURE 6.4 **Health service use in trauma-exposed young people and those with PTSD.** The plot shows rates of health service use for mental health problems in age-18 E-Risk Study participants who had been exposed to trauma in their lifetime and those who met criteria for PTSD in the past year. Mental health practitioner = psychiatrist, psychologist, psychotherapist, or counselor. *Adapted from Lewis, S. J., Arseneault, L., Caspi, A., Fisher, H. L., Matthews, T., Moffitt, T. E., Odgers, C. L., Stahl, D., Teng, J. Y., & Danese, A. (2019). The epidemiology of trauma and post-traumatic stress disorder in a representative cohort of young people in England and Wales. The Lancet Psychiatry, 6(3), 247–256. https://doi.org/10.1016/S2215-0366(19)30031-8.*

where resources are more scarce, health service use is likely to be even rarer (Koenen et al., 2017). These findings are concerning because, although natural recovery occurs in some cases, a substantial proportion of young people with PTSD do not recover without treatment (Hiller et al., 2016). Therefore, our results indicate that trauma-exposed young people have high unmet mental health needs (Danese et al., 2020; Lewis & Danese, 2020). Barriers to healthcare use are likely to include factors that prevent young people and their families from seeking help (e.g., avoidance, stigma, and limited mental health knowledge), as well as factors within health services that hinder access to required care (e.g., limited resources and training) (Radez et al., 2021).

Overcoming barriers to healthcare use might be facilitated by identifying young people most likely to have psychopathology, through screening or use of prediction models, and prioritizing their care (Danese et al., 2020; Lewis & Danese, 2020). Prediction models combine information about a person's risk factors to estimate their risk of an outcome such as psychopathology. The models are developed using modern statistical and machine learning methods to maximize accuracy of risk prediction in individuals previously "unseen" by the model. In the E-Risk Study, we used these methods to develop a model, which predicts the risk of PTSD in trauma-exposed young people based on psychosocial data, and we used internal validation to assess its prediction performance. We found that this risk calculator had adequate accuracy, with a 74% probability that a young person who developed PTSD had a higher risk score than a trauma-exposed young person who did not (AUC = 0.74). These findings provide initial proof-of-principle evidence that assessment of risk factors might be used to make individualized predictions of trauma-related psychopathology risk in young people. Development of such models, and subsequent validation in external samples, could provide clinically useful tools to identify young people most in need of interventions (Lewis et al., 2019).

To reduce healthcare gaps, further research is also needed to better understand barriers to healthcare, and to develop and evaluate methods of overcoming these barriers (Danese et al., 2020; Lewis & Danese, 2020). Importantly, reducing healthcare gaps will require innovative approaches as well as increased resources to improve clinical capacity and training. These approaches might utilize digital technology, for example, for computerized therapy, which has shown some promise in adults with PTSD (National Institute for Health and Care Excellence, 2018d). Because untreated trauma-related psychopathology has high individual and societal costs (Kessler, 2000; Lewis et al., 2019), there is a strong ethical and economic case to invest in improving healthcare for affected young people.

5. Conclusions about recent developments and future directions to address trauma-related psychopathology in children and adolescents

Recent research has provided important insights into trauma-related psychopathology experienced by young people, underlying mechanisms, and interventions for these difficulties. We now understand that trauma-related psychopathology is broad and challenges traditional diagnostic boundaries. The mechanisms underlying this psychopathology are varied and likely bidirectional, involving multiple biological, psychological, and social pathways. Current interventions, especially those that target psychological mechanisms, can effectively treat PTSD in young people. However, there are still many unknowns and substantial room to improve mental healthcare for trauma-exposed young people, who currently have high unmet mental health needs.

To build on recent progress, we need to better understand broad trauma-related psychopathology and how to describe, assess, and treat these presentations using transdiagnostic approaches. Additionally, we need to continue to improve mechanistic understanding and strengthen causal inference by capitalizing on informative study designs, large rich data sets, and sophisticated analytical methods. Finally, and perhaps most importantly, we need to increase healthcare access, perhaps utilizing prediction, digital technology, and other innovations, so that more affected young people can receive beneficial care.

Funding

SJL has been supported by a UK Medical Research Council Clinical Research Training Fellowship, and is now funded by South London and Maudsley NHS Foundation Trust. AD is funded by the National Institute for Health Research Biomedical Research Centre at South London and Maudsley National Health Service Foundation Trust and King's College London, and by grant MR/P005918/1 from the UK Medical Research Council.

References

Achterhof, R., Huntjens, R. J. C., Meewisse, M.-L., & Kiers, H. A. L. (2019). Assessing the application of latent class and latent profile analysis for evaluating the construct validity of complex posttraumatic stress disorder: Cautions and limitations. *European Journal of Psychotraumatology, 10*(1), 1698223. https://doi.org/10.1080/20008198.2019.1698223

Agnew-Blais, J., & Danese, A. (2016). Childhood maltreatment and unfavourable clinical outcomes in bipolar disorder: A systematic review and meta-analysis. *The Lancet Psychiatry, 3*(4), 342–349. https://doi.org/10.1016/S2215-0366(15)00544-1

American Psychiatric Association. (2013). *Diagnostic and statistical manual of mental disorders* (5th ed.). American Psychiatric Association.

Arseneault, L., Walsh, E., Trzesniewski, K., Newcombe, R., Caspi, A., & Moffitt, T. E. (2006). Bullying victimization uniquely contributes to adjustment problems in young children: A nationally representative cohort study. *Pediatrics, 118*(1), 130–138. https://doi.org/10.1542/peds.2005-2388

Attanayake, V., McKay, R., Joffres, M., Singh, S., Burkle, F., & Mills, E. (2009). Prevalence of mental disorders among children exposed to war: A systematic review of 7,920 children. *Medicine, Conflict and Survival, 25*(1), 4–19. https://doi.org/10.1080/13623690802568913

Arseneault, L., Cannon, M., Fisher, H. L., Polanczyk, G., Moffitt, T. E., & Caspi, A. (2011). Childhood trauma and children's emerging psychotic symptoms: A genetically sensitive longitudinal cohort study. *American Journal of Psychiatry, 168*(1), 65–72. https://doi.org/10.1176/appi.ajp.2010.10040567

Baldwin, J. R., Arseneault, L., Caspi, A., Moffitt, T. E., Fisher, H. L., Odgers, C. L., Ambler, A., Houts, R. M., Matthews, T., Ougrin, D., Richmond-Rakerd, L. S., Takizawa, R., & Danese, A. (2019). Adolescent victimization and self-injurious thoughts and behaviors: A genetically sensitive cohort study. *Journal of the American Academy of Child & Adolescent Psychiatry, 58*(5), 506–513. https://doi.org/10.1016/j.jaac.2018.07.903

Berenz, E. C., Amstadter, A. B., Aggen, S. H., Knudsen, G. P., Reichborn-Kjennerud, T., Gardner, C. O., & Kendler, K. S. (2013). Childhood trauma and personality disorder criterion counts: A co-twin control analysis. *Journal of Abnormal Psychology, 122*(4), 1070–1076. https://doi.org/10.1037/a0034238

Betancourt, T. S., Borisova, I., Williams, T. P., Meyers-Ohki, S. E., Rubin-Smith, J. E., Annan, J., & Kohrt, B. A. (2013). Research Review: Psychosocial adjustment and mental health in former child soldiers - a systematic review of the literature and recommendations for future research. *Journal of Child Psychology and Psychiatry, 54*(1), 17–36. https://doi.org/10.1111/j.1469-7610.2012.02620.x

Blackmore, R., Gray, K. M., Boyle, J. A., Fazel, M., Ranasinha, S., Fitzgerald, G., Misso, M., & Gibson-Helm, M. (2020). Systematic review and meta-analysis: The prevalence of mental illness in child and adolescent refugees and asylum seekers. *Journal of the American Academy of Child & Adolescent Psychiatry, 59*(6), 705–714. https://doi.org/10.1016/j.jaac.2019.11.011

Blakemore, S.-J., & Mills, K. L. (2014). Is adolescence a sensitive period for sociocultural processing? *Annual Review of Psychology, 65*(1), 187–207. https://doi.org/10.1146/annurev-psych-010213-115202

Bolhuis, K., Steenkamp, L. R., Blanken, L. M. E., Neumann, A., Jansen, P. R., Hillegers, M. H. J., Cecil, C. A. M., Tiemeier, H., & Kushner, S. A. (2021). *Schizophrenia polygenic risk is associated with child mental health problems through early childhood adversity: Evidence for a gene–environment correlation.* European Child & Adolescent Psychiatry. https://doi.org/10.1007/s00787-021-01727-4

Bornovalova, M. A., Huibregtse, B. M., Hicks, B. M., Keyes, M., McGue, M., & Iacono, W. (2013). Tests of a direct effect of childhood abuse on adult borderline personality disorder traits: A longitudinal discordant twin design. *Journal of Abnormal Psychology, 122*(1), 180–194. https://doi.org/10.1037/a0028328

Breslau, N., Kessler, R. C., Chilcoat, H. D., Schultz, L. R., Davis, G. C., & Andreski, P. (1998). Trauma and posttraumatic stress disorder in the community: The 1996 Detroit Area Survey of Trauma. *Archives of General Psychiatry, 55*(7), 626–632. https://doi.org/10.1001/archpsyc.55.7.626

Breslau, N., Wilcox, H. C., Storr, C. L., Lucia, V. C., & Anthony, J. C. (2004). Trauma exposure and posttraumatic stress disorder: A study of youths in urban America. *Journal of Urban Health: Bulletin of the New York Academy of Medicine, 81*(4), 530–544. https://doi.org/10.1093/jurban/jth138

Breslau, N., Lucia, V. C., & Alvarado, G. F. (2006). Intelligence and other predisposing factors in exposure to trauma and posttraumatic stress disorder: A follow-up study at age 17 years. *Archives of General Psychiatry, 63*(11), 1238. https://doi.org/10.1001/archpsyc.63.11.1238

Brewin, C. R., Cloitre, M., Hyland, P., Shevlin, M., Maercker, A., Bryant, R. A., Humayun, A., Jones, L. M., Kagee, A., Rousseau, C., Somasundaram, D., Suzuki, Y., Wessely, S., van Ommeren, M., & Reed, G. M. (2017). A review of current evidence regarding the ICD-11 proposals for diagnosing PTSD and complex PTSD. *Clinical Psychology Review, 58*, 1–15. https://doi.org/10.1016/j.cpr.2017.09.001

Brown, R. C., Berenz, E. C., Aggen, S. H., Gardner, C. O., Knudsen, G. P., Reichborn-Kjennerud, T., Kendler, K. S., & Amstadter, A. B. (2014). Trauma exposure and Axis I psychopathology: A co-twin control analysis in Norwegian young adults. *Psychological Trauma: Theory, Research, Practice, and Policy, 6*(6), 652–660. https://doi.org/10.1037/a0034326

Bruckmann, P., Haselgruber, A., Sölva, K., & Lueger-Schuster, B. (2020). Comparing rates of ICD-11 and DSM-5 posttraumatic stress disorder in Austrian children and adolescents in foster care: Prevalence, comorbidity and predictors. *European Journal of Psychotraumatology, 11*(1), 1767988. https://doi.org/10.1080/20008198.2020.1767988

Brunson, K. L., Kramár, E., Lin, B., Chen, Y., Colgin, L. L., Yanagihara, T. K., Lynch, G., & Baram, T. Z. (2005). Mechanisms of late-onset cognitive decline after early-life stress. *Journal of Neuroscience, 25*(41), 9328–9338. https://doi.org/10.1523/JNEUROSCI.2281-05.2005

Capusan, A. J., Kuja-Halkola, R., Bendtsen, P., Viding, E., McCrory, E., Marteinsdottir, I., & Larsson, H. (2016). Childhood maltreatment and attention deficit hyperactivity disorder symptoms in adults: A large twin study. *Psychological Medicine, 46*(12), 2637–2646. https://doi.org/10.1017/S0033291716001021

Caspi, A., Houts, R. M., Belsky, D. W., Goldman-Mellor, S. J., Harrington, H., Israel, S., Meier, M. H., Ramrakha, S., Shalev, I., Poulton, R., & Moffitt, T. E. (2014). The p factor:

One general psychopathology factor in the structure of psychiatric disorders? *Clinical Psychological Science, 2*(2), 119−137. https://doi.org/10.1177/2167702613497473

Caspi, A., & Moffitt, T. E. (2018). All for one and one for all: Mental disorders in one dimension. *American Journal of Psychiatry, 175*(9), 831−844. https://doi.org/10.1176/appi.ajp.2018.17121383

Charlson, F., van Ommeren, M., Flaxman, A., Cornett, J., Whiteford, H., & Saxena, S. (2019). New WHO prevalence estimates of mental disorders in conflict settings: A systematic review and meta-analysis. *The Lancet, 394*(10194), 240−248. https://doi.org/10.1016/S0140-6736(19)30934-1

Clancy, B., Finlay, B. L., Darlington, R. B., & Anand, K. J. S. (2007). Extrapolating brain development from experimental species to humans. *NeuroToxicology, 28*(5), 931−937. https://doi.org/10.1016/j.neuro.2007.01.014

Cloitre, M., Brewin, C. R., Bisson, J. I., Hyland, P., Karatzias, T., Lueger-Schuster, B., Maercker, A., Roberts, N. P., & Shevlin, M. (2020). Evidence for the coherence and integrity of the complex PTSD (CPTSD) diagnosis: Response to Achterhof et al., (2019) and Ford (2020). *European Journal of Psychotraumatology, 11*(1), 1739873. https://doi.org/10.1080/20008198.2020.1739873

Cohen, J. A., Bukstein, O., Walter, H., Benson, S. R., Chrisman, A., Farchione, T. R., Hamilton, J., Keable, H., Kinlan, J., Schoettle, U., Siegel, M., Stock, S., Medicus, J., & AACAP Work Group On Quality Issues. (2010). Practice parameter for the assessment and treatment of children and adolescents with posttraumatic stress disorder. *Journal of the American Academy of Child and Adolescent Psychiatry, 49*(4), 414−430. https://doi.org/10.1016/j.jaac.2009.12.020

Cohen, J. A., Deblinger, E., Mannarino, A. P., & Steer, R. A. (2004). A multisite, randomized controlled trial for children with sexual abuse−related PTSD symptoms. *Journal of the American Academy of Child & Adolescent Psychiatry, 43*(4), 393−402. https://doi.org/10.1097/00004583-200404000-00005

Copeland, W. E., Keeler, G., Angold, A., & Costello, E. J. (2007). Traumatic events and posttraumatic stress in childhood. *Archives of General Psychiatry, 64*(5), 577. https://doi.org/10.1001/archpsyc.64.5.577

Danese, A. (2020). Annual Research Review: Rethinking childhood trauma-new research directions for measurement, study design and analytical strategies. *Journal of Child Psychology and Psychiatry, 61*(3), 236−250. https://doi.org/10.1111/jcpp.13160

Danese, A. (2021). Post-traumatic stress disorder in children and adolescents. In D. M. Taylor, T. R. Barnes, & A. H. Young (Eds.), *The Maudsley prescribing guidelines in psychiatry* (14th ed.). Wiley Blackwell.

Danese, A., & Lewis, S. J. (2017). Psychoneuroimmunology of early-life stress: The hidden wounds of childhood trauma? *Neuropsychopharmacology, 42*(1), 99−114. https://doi.org/10.1038/npp.2016.198

Danese, A., & McEwen, B. S. (2012). Adverse childhood experiences, allostasis, allostatic load, and age-related disease. *Physiology & Behavior, 106*(1), 29−39. https://doi.org/10.1016/j.physbeh.2011.08.019

Danese, A., Moffitt, T. E., Arseneault, L., Bleiberg, B. A., Dinardo, P. B., Gandelman, S. B., Houts, R., Ambler, A., Fisher, H. L., Poulton, R., & Caspi, A. (2017). The origins of cognitive deficits in victimized children: Implications for neuroscientists and clinicians. *American Journal of Psychiatry, 174*(4), 349−361. https://doi.org/10.1176/appi.ajp.2016.16030333

Danese, A., McLaughlin, K. A., Samara, M., & Stover, C. S. (2020). Psychopathology in children exposed to trauma: Detection and intervention needed to reduce downstream burden. *BMJ*, m3073. https://doi.org/10.1136/bmj.m3073

Danzi, B. A., & La Greca, A. M. (2016). DSM-IV, DSM-5, and ICD-11: Identifying children with posttraumatic stress disorder after disasters. *Journal of Child Psychology and Psychiatry, 57*(12), 1444−1452. https://doi.org/10.1111/jcpp.12631

Davey Smith, G., & Hemani, G. (2014). Mendelian randomization: Genetic anchors for causal inference in epidemiological studies. *Human Molecular Genetics, 23*(R1), R89−R98. https://doi.org/10.1093/hmg/ddu328

III. Innovative approaches to helping young people in adversity

Dinkler, L., Lundström, S., Gajwani, R., Lichtenstein, P., Gillberg, C., & Minnis, H. (2017). Maltreatment-associated neurodevelopmental disorders: A co-twin control analysis. *Journal of Child Psychology and Psychiatry, 58*(6), 691−701. https://doi.org/10.1111/jcpp.12682

Dinwiddie, S., Heath, A. C., Dunne, M. P., Bucholz, K. K., Madden, P. A. F., Slutske, W. S., Bierut, L. J., Statham, D. B., & Martin, N. G. (2000). Early sexual abuse and lifetime psychopathology: A co-twin−control study. *Psychological Medicine, 30*(1), 41−52. https://doi.org/10.1017/S0033291799001373

Ehlers, A., & Clark, D. M. (2000). A cognitive model of posttraumatic stress disorder. *Behaviour Research and Therapy, 38*(4), 319−345. https://doi.org/10.1016/S0005-7967(99)00123-0

Elliott, R., McKinnon, A., Dixon, C., Boyle, A., Murphy, F., Dahm, T., Travers-Hill, E., Mul, C., Archibald, S., Smith, P., Dalgleish, T., Meiser-Stedman, R., & Hitchcock, C. (2021). Prevalence and predictive value of ICD-11 post-traumatic stress disorder and Complex PTSD diagnoses in children and adolescents exposed to a single-event trauma. *Journal of Child Psychology and Psychiatry, 62*(3), 270−276. https://doi.org/10.1111/jcpp.13240

Foa, E. B., McLean, C. P., Capaldi, S., & Rosenfield, D. (2013). Prolonged exposure vs supportive counseling for sexual abuse−related PTSD in adolescent girls: A randomized clinical trial. *JAMA, 310*(24), 2650. https://doi.org/10.1001/jama.2013.282829

Foster, H., & Brooks-Gunn, J. (2015). Children's exposure to community and war violence and mental health in four African countries. *Social Science & Medicine, 146*, 292−299. https://doi.org/10.1016/j.socscimed.2015.10.020

Friedman, M. J. (2013). Finalizing PTSD in DSM-5: Getting here from there and where to go next. *Journal of Traumatic Stress, 26*(5), 548−556. https://doi.org/10.1002/jts.21840

Friedman, M. J., Resick, P. A., Bryant, R. A., & Brewin, C. R. (2011). Considering PTSD for DSM-5. *Depression and Anxiety, 28*(9), 750−769. https://doi.org/10.1002/da.20767

Giaconia, R. M., Reinherz, H. Z., Silverman, A. B., Pakiz, B., Frost, A. K., & Cohen, E. (1995). Traumas and posttraumatic stress disorder in a community population of older adolescents. *Journal of the American Academy of Child & Adolescent Psychiatry, 34*(10), 1369−1380. https://doi.org/10.1097/00004583-199510000-00023

Gillies, D., Taylor, F., Gray, C., O'Brien, L., & D'Abrew, N. (2012). Psychological therapies for the treatment of post-traumatic stress disorder in children and adolescents. *Cochrane Database of Systematic Reviews*. https://doi.org/10.1002/14651858.CD006726.pub2

Gillies, D., Maiocchi, L., Bhandari, A. P., Taylor, F., Gray, C., & O'Brien, L. (2016). Psychological therapies for children and adolescents exposed to trauma. *Cochrane Database of Systematic Reviews*. https://doi.org/10.1002/14651858.CD012371

Gutermann, J., Schreiber, F., Matulis, S., Schwartzkopff, L., Deppe, J., & Steil, R. (2016). Psychological treatments for symptoms of posttraumatic stress disorder in children, adolescents, and young adults: A meta-analysis. *Clinical Child and Family Psychology Review, 19*(2), 77−93. https://doi.org/10.1007/s10567-016-0202-5

Hafstad, G. S., Thoresen, S., Wentzel-Larsen, T., Maercker, A., & Dyb, G. (2017). PTSD or not PTSD? Comparing the proposed ICD-11 and the DSM-5 PTSD criteria among young survivors of the 2011 Norway attacks and their parents. *Psychological Medicine, 47*(7), 1283−1291. https://doi.org/10.1017/S0033291716002968

Hart, H., & Rubia, K. (2012). Neuroimaging of child abuse: A critical review. *Frontiers in Human Neuroscience, 6*. https://doi.org/10.3389/fnhum.2012.00052

Haselgruber, A., Sölva, K., & Lueger-Schuster, B. (2020). Validation of ICD-11 PTSD and complex PTSD in foster children using the International Trauma Questionnaire. *Acta Psychiatrica Scandinavica, 141*(1), 60−73. https://doi.org/10.1111/acps.13100

Herman, J. L. (1992). Complex PTSD: A syndrome in survivors of prolonged and repeated trauma. *Journal of Traumatic Stress, 5*(3), 377−391. https://doi.org/10.1002/jts.2490050305

Herman, J. L. (2012). CPTSD is a distinct entity: Comment on Resick et al. (2012). *Journal of Traumatic Stress, 25*(3), 256−257. https://doi.org/10.1002/jts.21697

Hiller, R. M., Meiser-Stedman, R., Fearon, P., Lobo, S., McKinnon, A., Fraser, A., & Halligan, S. L. (2016). Research Review: Changes in the prevalence and symptom severity of child post-traumatic stress disorder in the year following trauma - a meta-analytic study. *Journal of Child Psychology and Psychiatry, 57*(8), 884–898. https://doi.org/10.1111/jcpp.12566

Hiller, R. M., Meiser-Stedman, R., Elliott, E., Banting, R., & Halligan, S. L. (2021). A longitudinal study of cognitive predictors of (complex) post-traumatic stress in young people in out-of-home care. *Journal of Child Psychology and Psychiatry, 62*(1), 48–57. https://doi.org/10.1111/jcpp.13232

Hitchcock, C., Goodall, B., Sharples, O., Meiser-Stedman, R., Watson, P., Ford, T., & Dalgleish, T. (2021). Population prevalence of the posttraumatic stress disorder subtype for young children in nationwide surveys of the British general population and of children-in-care. *Journal of the American Academy of Child & Adolescent Psychiatry.* https://doi.org/10.1016/j.jaac.2020.12.036. S0890856721001398.

van IJzendoorn, M. H., Bakermans-Kranenburg, M. J., Coughlan, B., & Reijman, S. (2020). Annual Research Review: Umbrella synthesis of meta-analyses on child maltreatment antecedents and interventions: Differential susceptibility perspective on risk and resilience. *Journal of Child Psychology and Psychiatry, 61*(3), 272–290. https://doi.org/10.1111/jcpp.13147

Jensen, T. K., Holt, T., Mørup Ormhaug, S., Fjermestad, K. W., & Wentzel-Larsen, T. (2018). Change in post-traumatic cognitions mediates treatment effects for traumatized youth—a randomized controlled trial. *Journal of Counseling Psychology, 65*(2), 166–177. https://doi.org/10.1037/cou0000258

Jensen, T. K., Cohen, J., Jaycox, L., & Rosner, R. (2020). Treatment of PTSD and complex PTSD. In D. Forbes, J. I. Bisson, C. M. Monson, & L. Berliner (Eds.), *Effective treatments for PTSD: Practice guidelines from the international society for traumatic stress studies* (3rd ed.). Guilford Press.

Kendler, K. S., Bulik, C. M., Silberg, J., Hettema, J. M., Myers, J., & Prescott, C. A. (2000). Childhood sexual abuse and adult psychiatric and substance use disorders in women: An epidemiological and cotwin control analysis. *Archives of General Psychiatry, 57*(10), 953. https://doi.org/10.1001/archpsyc.57.10.953

Kessler, R. C. (2000). Posttraumatic stress disorder: The burden to the individual and to society. *The Journal of Clinical Psychiatry, 61*(Suppl. 5), 4–12.

Kilpatrick, D. G., & Saunders, B. E. (1997). *Prevalence and consequences of child victimization: Results from the national survey of adolescents.* National Crime Victims Research and Treatment Center.

Koenen, K. C., Ratanatharathorn, A., Ng, L., McLaughlin, K. A., Bromet, E. J., Stein, D. J., Karam, E. G., Meron Ruscio, A., Benjet, C., Scott, K., Atwoli, L., Petukhova, M., Lim, C. C. W., Aguilar-Gaxiola, S., Al-Hamzawi, A., Alonso, J., Bunting, B., Ciutan, M., de Girolamo, G., ... Kessler, R. C. (2017). Posttraumatic stress disorder in the World Mental Health Surveys. *Psychological Medicine, 47*(13), 2260–2274. https://doi.org/10.1017/S0033291717000708

van der Kolk, B. A., Roth, S., Pelcovitz, D., Sunday, S., & Spinazzola, J. (2005). Disorders of extreme stress: The empirical foundation of a complex adaptation to trauma. *Journal of Traumatic Stress, 18*(5), 389–399. https://doi.org/10.1002/jts.20047

Koss, K. J., & Gunnar, M. R. (2018). Annual Research Review: Early adversity, the hypothalamic—pituitary—adrenocortical axis, and child psychopathology. *Journal of Child Psychology and Psychiatry, 59*(4), 327–346. https://doi.org/10.1111/jcpp.12784

Landolt, M. A., Schnyder, U., Maier, T., Schoenbucher, V., & Mohler-Kuo, M. (2013). Trauma exposure and posttraumatic stress disorder in adolescents: A national survey in Switzerland. *Journal of Traumatic Stress, 26*(2), 209–216. https://doi.org/10.1002/jts.21794

Lee, F. S., Heimer, H., Giedd, J. N., Lein, E. S., estan, N., Weinberger, D. R., & Casey, B. J. (2014). Adolescent mental health—opportunity and obligation. *Science, 346*(6209), 547—549. https://doi.org/10.1126/science.1260497

Lewis, S. J., Arseneault, L., Caspi, A., Fisher, H. L., Matthews, T., Moffitt, T. E., Odgers, C. L., Stahl, D., Teng, J. Y., & Danese, A. (2019). The epidemiology of trauma and post-traumatic stress disorder in a representative cohort of young people in England and Wales. *The Lancet Psychiatry, 6*(3), 247—256. https://doi.org/10.1016/S2215-0366(19)30031-8

Lewis, S. J., & Danese, A. (2020). Trauma-related mental illness in children and adolescents. In E. Taylor, F. C. Verhulst, J. Wong, K. Yoshida, & A. Nikapota (Eds.), *Mental health and illness of children and adolescents* (pp. 1—17). Springer Singapore. https://doi.org/10.1007/978-981-10-0753-8_64-1

Lewis, S. J., Koenen, K. C., Ambler, A., Arseneault, L., Caspi, A., Fisher, H. L., Moffitt, T. E., & Danese, A. (2021). Unravelling the contribution of complex trauma to psychopathology and cognitive deficits: A cohort study. *The British Journal of Psychiatry, 219*(2), 448—455. https://doi.org/10.1192/bjp.2021.57

Li, J., Wang, W., Hu, W., Yuan, Z., Zhou, R., Zhang, W., & Qu, Z. (2021). Validation of posttraumatic stress disorder (PTSD) and complex PTSD in Chinese children as per the ICD-11 proposals using the International trauma questionnaire. *European Journal of Psychotraumatology, 12*(1), 1888525. https://doi.org/10.1080/20008198.2021.1888525

Lupien, S. J., McEwen, B. S., Gunnar, M. R., & Heim, C. (2009). Effects of stress throughout the lifespan on the brain, behaviour and cognition. *Nature Reviews Neuroscience, 10*(6), 434—445. https://doi.org/10.1038/nrn2639

Maercker, A., Brewin, C. R., Bryant, R. A., Cloitre, M., van Ommeren, M., Jones, L. M., Humayan, A., Kagee, A., Llosa, A. E., Rousseau, C., Somasundaram, D. J., Souza, R., Suzuki, Y., Weissbecker, I., Wessely, S. C., First, M. B., & Reed, G. M. (2013). Diagnosis and classification of disorders specifically associated with stress: Proposals for ICD-11. *World Psychiatry, 12*(3), 198—206. https://doi.org/10.1002/wps.20057

Malarbi, S., Abu-Rayya, H. M., Muscara, F., & Stargatt, R. (2017). Neuropsychological functioning of childhood trauma and post-traumatic stress disorder: A meta-analysis. *Neuroscience & Biobehavioral Reviews, 72*, 68—86. https://doi.org/10.1016/j.neubiorev.2016.11.004

Mavranezouli, I., Megnin-Viggars, O., Daly, C., Dias, S., Stockton, S., Meiser-Stedman, R., Trickey, D., & Pilling, S. (2020). Research review: Psychological and psychosocial treatments for children and young people with post-traumatic stress disorder: A network meta-analysis. *Journal of Child Psychology and Psychiatry, 61*(1), 18—29. https://doi.org/10.1111/jcpp.13094

Mavranezouli, I., Megnin-Viggars, O., Trickey, D., Meiser-Stedman, R., Daly, C., Dias, S., Stockton, S., & Pilling, S. (2020). Cost-effectiveness of psychological interventions for children and young people with post-traumatic stress disorder. *Journal of Child Psychology and Psychiatry, 61*(6), 699—710. https://doi.org/10.1111/jcpp.13142

McCrory, E. J., Gerin, M. I., & Viding, E. (2017). Annual research review: Childhood maltreatment, latent vulnerability and the shift to preventative psychiatry - the contribution of functional brain imaging. *Journal of Child Psychology and Psychiatry, 58*(4), 338—357. https://doi.org/10.1111/jcpp.12713

McLaughlin, K. A., Koenen, K. C., Hill, E. D., Petukhova, M., Sampson, N. A., Zaslavsky, A. M., & Kessler, R. C. (2013). Trauma exposure and posttraumatic stress disorder in a national sample of adolescents. *Journal of the American Academy of Child & Adolescent Psychiatry, 52*(8), 815—830. https://doi.org/10.1016/j.jaac.2013.05.011. e14.

McLean, C. P., Yeh, R., Rosenfield, D., & Foa, E. B. (2015). Changes in negative cognitions mediate PTSD symptom reductions during client-centered therapy and prolonged exposure for adolescents. *Behaviour Research and Therapy, 68*, 64—69. https://doi.org/10.1016/j.brat.2015.03.008

Meiser-Stedman, R. (2002). Towards a cognitive-behavioral model of PTSD in children and adolescents. *Clinical Child and Family Psychology Review, 5*(4), 217–232. https://doi.org/10.1023/a:1020982122107

Meiser-Stedman, R., Smith, P., Glucksman, E., Yule, W., & Dalgleish, T. (2007). Parent and child agreement for acute stress disorder, post-traumatic stress disorder and other psychopathology in a prospective study of children and adolescents exposed to single-event trauma. *Journal of Abnormal Child Psychology, 35*(2), 191–201. https://doi.org/10.1007/s10802-006-9068-1

Meiser-Stedman, R., Smith, P., McKinnon, A., Dixon, C., Trickey, D., Ehlers, A., Clark, D. M., Boyle, A., Watson, P., Goodyer, I., & Dalgleish, T. (2017). Cognitive therapy as an early treatment for post-traumatic stress disorder in children and adolescents: A randomized controlled trial addressing preliminary efficacy and mechanisms of action. *Journal of Child Psychology and Psychiatry, 58*(5), 623–633. https://doi.org/10.1111/jcpp.12673

Meiser-Stedman, R., McKinnon, A., Dixon, C., Boyle, A., Smith, P., & Dalgleish, T. (2019). A core role for cognitive processes in the acute onset and maintenance of post-traumatic stress in children and adolescents. *Journal of Child Psychology and Psychiatry, 60*(8), 875–884. https://doi.org/10.1111/jcpp.13054

Morina, N., Koerssen, R., & Pollet, T. V. (2016). Interventions for children and adolescents with posttraumatic stress disorder: A meta-analysis of comparative outcome studies. *Clinical Psychology Review, 47*, 41–54. https://doi.org/10.1016/j.cpr.2016.05.006

Nanni, V., Uher, R., & Danese, A. (2012). Childhood maltreatment predicts unfavorable course of illness and treatment outcome in depression: A meta-analysis. *American Journal of Psychiatry, 169*(2), 141–151. https://doi.org/10.1176/appi.ajp.2011.11020335

National Institute for Health and Care Excellence. (2018a). *Post-traumatic stress disorder.* www.nice.org.uk/guidance/ng116.

National Institute for Health and Care Excellence. (2018b). *Post-traumatic stress disorder: [A] Evidence reviews for psychological, psychosocial and other non-pharmacological interventions for the prevention of PTSD in children.* https://www.nice.org.uk/guidance/ng116/evidence/evidence-review-a-psychological-psychosocial-and-other-nonpharmacological-interventions-for-the-prevention-of-ptsd-in-children-pdf-6602621005.

National Institute for Health and Care Excellence. (2018c). *Post-traumatic stress disorder: [B] evidence reviews for psychological, psychosocial and other non-pharmacological interventions for the treatment of PTSD in children and young people.* https://www.nice.org.uk/guidance/ng116/evidence/evidence-review-b-psychological-psychosocial-and-other-nonpharmacological-interventions-for-the-treatment-of-ptsd-in-children-and-young-people-pdf-6602621006.

National Institute for Health and Care Excellence. (2018d). *Post-traumatic stress disorder: [D] Evidence reviews for psychological, psychosocial and other non-pharmacological interventions for the treatment of PTSD in adults.* https://www.nice.org.uk/guidance/ng116/evidence/evidence-review-d-psychological-psychosocial-and-other-nonpharmacological-interventions-for-the-treatment-of-ptsd-in-adults-pdf-6602621008.

National Institute for Health and Care Excellence. (2018e). *Post-traumatic stress disorder: [E] Evidence reviews for pharmacological interventions for the prevention and treatment of PTSD in children.* https://www.nice.org.uk/guidance/ng116/evidence/evidence-review-b-psychological-psychosocial-and-other-nonpharmacological-interventions-for-the-treatment-of-ptsd-in-children-and-young-people-pdf-6602621006.

Nelson, E. C., Heath, A. C., Madden, P. A. F., Cooper, M. L., Dinwiddie, S. H., Bucholz, K. K., Glowinski, A., McLaughlin, T., Dunne, M. P., Statham, D. J., & Martin, N. G. (2002). Association between self-reported childhood sexual abuse and adverse psychosocial outcomes: Results from a twin study. *Archives of General Psychiatry, 59*(2), 139. https://doi.org/10.1001/archpsyc.59.2.139

Orozco, R., Borges, G., Benjet, C., Medina-Mora, M. E., & López-Carrillo, L. (2008). Traumatic life events and posttraumatic stress disorder among Mexican adolescents: Results from a survey. *Salud Pública de México, 50*. https://doi.org/10.1590/S0036-36342008000700006

Parade, S. H., Huffhines, L., Daniels, T. E., Stroud, L. R., Nugent, N. R., & Tyrka, A. R. (2021). A systematic review of childhood maltreatment and DNA methylation: Candidate gene and epigenome-wide approaches. *Translational Psychiatry, 11*(1), 134. https://doi.org/10.1038/s41398-021-01207-y

Pergola, G., Papalino, M., Gelao, B., Sportelli, L., Vollerbergh, W., Grattagliano, I., & Bertolino, A. (2019). Evocative gene-environment correlation between genetic risk for schizophrenia and bullying victimization. *World Psychiatry, 18*(3), 366−367. https://doi.org/10.1002/wps.20685

Perkonigg, A., Kessler, R. C., Storz, S., & Wittchen, H.-U. (2000). Traumatic events and post-traumatic stress disorder in the community: Prevalence, risk factors and comorbidity. *Acta Psychiatrica Scandinavica, 101*(1), 46−59. https://doi.org/10.1034/j.1600-0447.2000.101001046.x

Perkonigg, A., Höfler, M., Cloitre, M., Wittchen, H.-U., Trautmann, S., & Maercker, A. (2016). Evidence for two different ICD-11 posttraumatic stress disorders in a community sample of adolescents and young adults. *European Archives of Psychiatry and Clinical Neuroscience, 266*(4), 317−328. https://doi.org/10.1007/s00406-015-0639-4

Pfeiffer, E., Sachser, C., de Haan, A., Tutus, D., & Goldbeck, L. (2017). Dysfunctional posttraumatic cognitions as a mediator of symptom reduction in trauma-focused cognitive behavioral therapy with children and adolescents: Results of a randomized controlled trial. *Behaviour Research and Therapy, 97*, 178−182. https://doi.org/10.1016/j.brat.2017.08.001

Pingault, J.-B., O'Reilly, P. F., Schoeler, T., Ploubidis, G. B., Rijsdijk, F., & Dudbridge, F. (2018). Using genetic data to strengthen causal inference in observational research. *Nature Reviews Genetics, 19*(9), 566−580. https://doi.org/10.1038/s41576-018-0020-3

Polimanti, R., & Wendt, F. R. (2021). Posttraumatic stress disorder: From gene discovery to disease biology. *Psychological Medicine, 1−11*. https://doi.org/10.1017/S0033291721000210

Purgato, M., Gross, A. L., Betancourt, T., Bolton, P., Bonetto, C., Gastaldon, C., Gordon, J., O'Callaghan, P., Papola, D., Peltonen, K., Punamaki, R.-L., Richards, J., Staples, J. K., Unterhitzenberger, J., van Ommeren, M., de Jong, J., Jordans, M. J. D., Tol, W. A., & Barbui, C. (2018). Focused psychosocial interventions for children in low-resource humanitarian settings: A systematic review and individual participant data meta-analysis. *The Lancet Global Health, 6*(4), e390−e400. https://doi.org/10.1016/S2214-109X(18)30046-9

Radez, J., Reardon, T., Creswell, C., Lawrence, P. J., Evdoka-Burton, G., & Waite, P. (2021). Why do children and adolescents (not) seek and access professional help for their mental health problems? A systematic review of quantitative and qualitative studies. *European Child & Adolescent Psychiatry, 30*(2), 183−211. https://doi.org/10.1007/s00787-019-01469-4

Ratanatharathorn, A., Koenen, K. C., Chibnik, L. B., Weisskopf, M. G., Rich-Edwards, J. W., & Roberts, A. L. (2021). Polygenic risk for autism, attention-deficit hyperactivity disorder, schizophrenia, major depressive disorder, and neuroticism is associated with the experience of childhood abuse. *Molecular Psychiatry*. https://doi.org/10.1038/s41380-020-00996-w

Resick, P. A., Bovin, M. J., Calloway, A. L., Dick, A. M., King, M. W., Mitchell, K. S., Suvak, M. K., Wells, S. Y., Stirman, S. W., & Wolf, E. J. (2012). A critical evaluation of the complex PTSD literature: Implications for DSM-5. *Journal of Traumatic Stress, 25*(3), 241−251. https://doi.org/10.1002/jts.21699

Resick, P. A., Wolf, E. J., Stirman, S. W., Wells, S. Y., Suvak, M. K., Mitchell, K. S., King, M. W., & Bovin, M. J. (2012). Advocacy through science: Reply to comments on Resick et al. (2012). *Journal of Traumatic Stress, 25*(3), 260−263. https://doi.org/10.1002/jts.21702

Rezayat, A., Sahebdel, S., Jafari, S., Kabirian, A., Rahnejat, A., Farahani, R., Mosaed, R., & Nour, M. (2020). Evaluating the prevalence of PTSD among children and adolescents after earthquakes and floods: A systematic review and meta-analysis. *Psychiatric Quarterly, 91,* 1265–1290. https://doi.org/10.1007/s11126-020-09840-4

Ruf, M., Schauer, M., Neuner, F., Catani, C., Schauer, E., & Elbert, T. (2010). Narrative exposure therapy for 7- to 16-year-olds: A randomized controlled trial with traumatized refugee children. *Journal of Traumatic Stress, 23*(4), 437–445. https://doi.org/10.1002/jts.20548

Sachser, C., Berliner, L., Holt, T., Jensen, T., Jungbluth, N., Risch, E., Rosner, R., & Goldbeck, L. (2018). Comparing the dimensional structure and diagnostic algorithms between DSM-5 and ICD-11 PTSD in children and adolescents. *European Child & Adolescent Psychiatry, 27*(2), 181–190. https://doi.org/10.1007/s00787-017-1032-9

Sachser, C., Keller, F., & Goldbeck, L. (2017). Complex PTSD as proposed for ICD-11: Validation of a new disorder in children and adolescents and their response to trauma-focused cognitive behavioral therapy. *Journal of Child Psychology and Psychiatry, 58*(2), 160–168. https://doi.org/10.1111/jcpp.12640

Sallis, H. M., Croft, J., Havdahl, A., Jones, H. J., Dunn, E. C., Davey Smith, G., Zammit, S., & Munafò, M. R. (2020). Genetic liability to schizophrenia is associated with exposure to traumatic events in childhood. *Psychological Medicine,* 1–8. https://doi.org/10.1017/S0033291720000537

Sapolsky, R. M. (1996). Why stress is bad for your brain. *Science, 273*(5276), 749–750. https://doi.org/10.1126/science.273.5276.749

Schaefer, J. D., Moffitt, T. E., Arseneault, L., Danese, A., Fisher, H. L., Houts, R., Sheridan, M. A., Wertz, J., & Caspi, A. (2018). Adolescent victimization and early-adult psychopathology: Approaching causal inference using a longitudinal twin study to rule out noncausal explanations. *Clinical Psychological Science, 6*(3), 352–371. https://doi.org/10.1177/2167702617741381

Scheeringa, M. S., Zeanah, C. H., & Cohen, J. A. (2011). PTSD in children and adolescents: Toward an empirically based algorithm. *Depression and Anxiety, 28*(9), 770–782. https://doi.org/10.1002/da.20736

Schoeler, T., Choi, S. W., Dudbridge, F., Baldwin, J., Duncan, L., Cecil, C. M., Walton, E., Viding, E., McCrory, E. J., & Pingault, J.-B. (2019). Multi–polygenic score approach to identifying individual vulnerabilities associated with the risk of exposure to bullying. *JAMA Psychiatry, 76*(7), 730. https://doi.org/10.1001/jamapsychiatry.2019.0310

Seedat, S., Nyamai, C., Njenga, F., Vythilingum, B., & Stein, D. J. (2004). Trauma exposure and post-traumatic stress symptoms in urban African schools: Survey in Cape Town and Nairobi. *British Journal of Psychiatry, 184*(2), 169–175. https://doi.org/10.1192/bjp.184.2.169

Shakoor, S., McGuire, P., Cardno, A. G., Freeman, D., Plomin, R., & Ronald, A. (2015). A shared genetic propensity underlies experiences of bullying victimization in late childhood and self-rated paranoid thinking in adolescence. *Schizophrenia Bulletin, 41*(3), 754–763. https://doi.org/10.1093/schbul/sbu142

Silberg, J. L., Copeland, W., Linker, J., Moore, A. A., Roberson-Nay, R., & York, T. P. (2016). Psychiatric outcomes of bullying victimization: A study of discordant monozygotic twins. *Psychological Medicine, 46*(9), 1875–1883. https://doi.org/10.1017/S0033291716000362

Singham, T., Viding, E., Schoeler, T., Arseneault, L., Ronald, A., Cecil, C. M., McCrory, E. J., Rijsdijk, F., & Pingault, J.-B. (2017). Concurrent and longitudinal contribution of exposure to bullying in childhood to mental health: The role of vulnerability and resilience. *JAMA Psychiatry, 74*(11), 1112. https://doi.org/10.1001/jamapsychiatry.2017.2678

Smith, P., Yule, W., Perrin, S., Tranah, T., Dalgleish, T., & Clark, D. M. (2007). Cognitive-behavioral therapy for PTSD in children and adolescents: A preliminary randomized controlled trial. *Journal of the American Academy of Child & Adolescent Psychiatry, 46*(8), 1051–1061. https://doi.org/10.1097/CHI.0b013e318067e288

III. Innovative approaches to helping young people in adversity

Smith, P., Dalgleish, T., & Meiser-Stedman, R. (2019). Practitioner review: Posttraumatic stress disorder and its treatment in children and adolescents. *Journal of Child Psychology and Psychiatry, 60*(5), 500—515. https://doi.org/10.1111/jcpp.12983

Stallard, P., Velleman, R., Salter, E., Howse, I., Yule, W., & Taylor, G. (2006). A randomised controlled trial to determine the effectiveness of an early psychological intervention with children involved in road traffic accidents. *Journal of Child Psychology and Psychiatry, 47*(2), 127—134. https://doi.org/10.1111/j.1469-7610.2005.01459.x

Stern, A., Agnew-Blais, J., Danese, A., Fisher, H. L., Jaffee, S. R., Matthews, T., Polanczyk, G. V., & Arseneault, L. (2018). Associations between abuse/neglect and ADHD from childhood to young adulthood: A prospective nationally-representative twin study. *Child Abuse & Neglect, 81*, 274—285. https://doi.org/10.1016/j.chiabu.2018.04.025

Stupar, D., Stevanovic, D., Vostanis, P., Atilola, O., Moreira, P., Dodig-Curkovic, K., Franic, T., Doric, A., Davidovic, N., Avicenna, M., Multazam, I. N., Nussbaum, L., Thabet, A. A., Ubalde, D., Petrov, P., Deljkovic, A., Monteiro, A. L., Ribas, A., Jovanovic, M., ... Knez, R. (2021). Posttraumatic stress disorder symptoms among trauma-exposed adolescents from low- and middle-income countries. *Child and Adolescent Psychiatry and Mental Health, 15*(1), 26. https://doi.org/10.1186/s13034-021-00378-2

Thomas, F. C., Puente-Duran, S., Mutschler, C., & Monson, C. M. (2020). Trauma-focused cognitive behavioral therapy for children and youth in low and middle-income countries: A systematic review. *Child and Adolescent Mental Health*, 12435. https://doi.org/10.1111/camh.12435

Trickey, D., Siddaway, A. P., Meiser-Stedman, R., Serpell, L., & Field, A. P. (2012). A meta-analysis of risk factors for post-traumatic stress disorder in children and adolescents. *Clinical Psychology Review, 32*(2), 122—138. https://doi.org/10.1016/j.cpr.2011.12.001

Villalta, L., Khadr, S., Chua, K.-C., Kramer, T., Clarke, V., Viner, R. M., Stringaris, A., & Smith, P. (2020). Complex post-traumatic stress symptoms in female adolescents: The role of emotion dysregulation in impairment and trauma exposure after an acute sexual assault. *European Journal of Psychotraumatology, 11*(1), 1710400. https://doi.org/10.1080/20008198.2019.1710400

Warrier, V., Kwong, A. S. F., Luo, M., Dalvie, S., Croft, J., Sallis, H. M., Baldwin, J., Munafò, M. R., Nievergelt, C. M., Grant, A. J., Burgess, S., Moore, T. M., Barzilay, R., McIntosh, A., van IJzendoorn, M. H., & Cecil, C. A. M. (2021). Gene—environment correlations and causal effects of childhood maltreatment on physical and mental health: A genetically informed approach. *The Lancet Psychiatry, 8*, 373—386. https://doi.org/10.1016/S2215-0366(20)30569-1

World Health Organization. (2018). International classification of diseases, 11th revision. *World Health Organization.* https://icd.who.int/en

van der Worp, H. B., Howells, D. W., Sena, E. S., Porritt, M. J., Rewell, S., O'Collins, V., & Macleod, M. R. (2010). Can animal models of disease reliably inform human studies? *PLoS Medicine, 7*(3), e1000245. https://doi.org/10.1371/journal.pmed.1000245

Young-Wolff, K. C., Kendler, K. S., Ericson, M. L., & Prescott, C. A. (2011). Accounting for the association between childhood maltreatment and alcohol-use disorders in males: A twin study. *Psychological Medicine, 41*(1), 59—70. https://doi.org/10.1017/S0033291710000425

Zehnder, D., Meuli, M., & Landolt, M. A. (2010). Effectiveness of a single-session early psychological intervention for children after road traffic accidents: A randomised controlled trial. *Child and Adolescent Psychiatry and Mental Health, 4*(1), 7. https://doi.org/10.1186/1753-2000-4-7

PART IV

Treatments for the future

The inflamed brain: implications of autoimmune encephalitis for child- and adolescent neuropsychiatry—a multidisciplinary approach

Jan NM. Schieveld[1,2], Husam HKZ. Salamah[1], Nathalie JJF. Janssen[1], Kim AM. Tijssen[1], and Jacqueline JHM. Strik[1,2]

[1] Department of Psychiatry, Maastricht University Medical Center +, Maastricht, the Netherlands; [2] Mutsaers Academy, Mutsaers Founding Pediatric Mental Health & Youth Care, Venlo, the Netherlands

To share is to multiply

1. The inflamed brain—autoimmune encephalitis

Encephalitis is defined as an inflammation of the brain. Inflammation stems from the Latin verb inflammare meaning "being on fire." The neuropsychiatric symptoms and severity can be variable with symptoms including headache, fever, confusion, neck stiffness, and vomiting. Complications may include seizures, dystonia's, hallucinations and delusions, executive functioning problems, expressive language difficulties/formal thought disorders, memory problems, and problems with hearing. Incidence varies between studies but is generally between 3.5 and 7.4 per 100,000 patient-years, with incidence tending to be higher in the pediatric population compared with adults. Although both sexes are affected, most studies have shown a slight predominance in males (Granerod, 2007).

Encephalitis can be classified in a number of ways according to the clinical presentation and/or cause. Infection is the most common cause identified, with viruses (for example, herpes simplex virus, HSV) being the most important known etiological agents. Many other causes of encephalitis have been identified including (1) acute para infectious or postvaccination encephalitis, such as acute disseminated encephalomyelitis (ADEM), (2) bacterial infections such as meningococcal and mycobacterium tuberculosis, (3) parasites such as malaria or toxoplasmosis, and (4) autoimmune diseases, such as SLE (systemic lupus erythematosus). To date, infection of the CNS is considered to be the major cause of encephalitis, and more than 100 different pathogens have been recognized as causative agents (Xhao et al., 2019).

Given the wide spectrum of encephalitis based on etiology alone, the focus of this chapter will be on autoimmune encephalitis of the brain, which is increasingly recognized in the pediatric population (Scheer & John, 2016). This subset of autoimmune encephalitis is a broad diagnostic category, resulting from the production of antibodies within the central nervous system of the brain against neuronal cell surface, synaptic proteins, or ion channels (Dalmau & Graus, 2018). Autoimmune encephalitis is a serious condition that can rapidly develop over time with core symptoms resembling infectious encephalitis and with neurological and/ or psychiatric manifestations without fever or cerebrospinal fluid (CSF) pleiocytosis (Graus et al., 2016). Of note, the new and often acute onset of symptoms restricted to the psychiatric domain (e.g., catatonia and refractory agitation) as an expression of autoimmune encephalitis is often overlooked (Creten et al., 2011). A famous contemporary example is the case of Susannah Cahalan, whose encephalitis was initially mistaken for "madness" as she recounted in her New York Times bestseller book "*Brain on Fire: My Month of Madness*" (Cahalan, 2012). Patients of any age may initially present to psychiatrists who may not have the necessary knowledge to suspect the diagnosis of an autoimmune encephalitis and or to treat appropriately, thereby increasing the risk of delay by doctors and so worsening of symptoms and subsequent (irreversible) damage to the brain (Barbagallo et al., 2017; Esseveld et al., 2013; Mooneyham et al., 2018). And so, it is important to improve awareness and recognition of autoimmune encephalitis at an early stage to make early treatment possible and to improve prognosis (Schieveld, van de Riet, et al., 2019; Schieveld, Strik, et al. 2019). The fact that autoimmune encephalitis involves a broad and complex spectrum of differential diagnoses and often severe neurologic and/or psychiatric and or even critical care symptomatology (see the following) highlights the importance of a multidisciplinary approach often preferably in a tertiary university hospital.

After describing the clinical presentation of the major subtypes of autoimmune encephalitis, the emphasis will be on the most prevalent of these, anti-NMDAR encephalitis, which also has an important resemblance to and potential for misdiagnosis with schizophrenia. We present the (1) current developments in the diagnostic process, (2) the various treatments used and their efficacy, and (3) outcomes of NMDAR encephalitis. We present a critical discussion and conclude with recommendations for clinical practice.

2. Clinical syndromes of autoimmune encephalitis

Autoimmune encephalitis is an umbrella term for a subgroup of antibody-mediated encephalitides that are associated with antibodies against neuronal cell surface proteins, receptors, or ion channels. This autoimmune process may be triggered by an infection, vaccine, or occult neoplasm (Barbagallo et al., 2017; Mooneyham et al., 2018). The condition is a relatively new category of immune-mediated diseases (Kelley et al., 2017). Noteworthy in this context is the historic hallmark paper of Stauder (1934) in which he discussed patients with catatonic agitation and or inhibition and symptomatology of frequent high fevers, severe agitation, and a lethal course. Everybody was puzzled by this disorder, which was sometimes also called "pernicious psychosis." Now, Anno 2022, based on our current knowledge, these cases were in hindsight most probably of organic origin such as (autoimmune) encephalitis.

A prospective, population-based study in adults found that the prevalence and incidence of autoimmune disorder is comparable with infectious encephalitis, and its detection is increasing over time (Dubey et al., 2018). Primary clinical features may include a broad change in behavior, psychosis, seizures, memory and cognitive deficits, abnormal movements (such as dystonia or catatonia), a reduced level of consciousness, and autonomic dysfunction (dysautonomia). The condition occurs in persons of all ages, although some types predominantly affect children and young adults. In adults, autoimmune encephalitis is more prevalent in females. However, an association with malignancy is less probable in children and more common in adults.

In the next section, the pathophysiology, epidemiology, and clinical presentation of the most common subtypes are presented.

2.1 Anti-N-methyl-D-aspartate receptor encephalitis

2.1.1 Pathophysiology and epidemiology

A breakthrough in the field of brain inflammation has been the discovery of a relationship between the presentation of acute psychiatric symptoms, seizures, and other neuropsychiatric symptoms on the one hand (e.g., memory deficits and decreased levels of consciousness), and the presence of antibodies in the CSF due to an ovarian teratoma (OT) on the other (Vitaliani et al., 2005). Subsequently, this clinical presentation was identified as anti-N-methyl–aspartate receptor (NMDAR) encephalitis. The identified antibodies had extracellular targets, namely the extracellular part of the NMDAR, which can have a direct pathogenic effect (Dalmau et al., 2007). As stated earlier, anti-NMDAR encephalitis is the most common extracellular antibody-mediated disorder. The prevalence of anti-NMDAR encephalitis exceeds that of any individual viral cause of encephalitis in young persons, but the exact incidence remains unknown (Ford et al., 2019).

2.1.2 Clinical presentation

In general, major neurologic features of anti-NMDAR encephalitis are fever, confusion, epilepsy, and dystonia, whereas major neuropsychiatric features are catatonic features/stereotypical movements, psychosis, hyperactive/excited delirium, sometimes with an agitated psychomotor hyperactivity that does not respond to any treatment (i.e., refractory agitation accompanied by severe cognitive sequelae, such as executive functioning problems (Schieveld, van de Riet, et al., 2019; Schieveld, Strik, et al. 2019)). The clinical presentation typically starts with a prodromal phase, including headaches, fever or hyperthermia, nausea, vomiting, gastrointestinal symptoms, or upper respiratory tract symptoms, suggesting a nonspecific viral infection (Barbagallo et al., 2017). Particularly in children and adolescents, initial symptoms can also be accompanied by movement disorders such as dystonia, choreoathetoid movements and orofacial, limb, or trunk dyskinesias (Barbagallo et al., 2017; Bigi et al., 2015). There is usually not one single symptom or predictable symptom cluster that is pathognomonic for NMDAR encephalitis (Barbagallo et al., 2017; Schumacher et al., 2016), and most patients develop more than one neuropsychiatric symptom. The clinical presentation can be one of delirium and/or mimic a first psychotic episode with clouded consciousness and/or schizophrenia. The presentation of anti-NMDAR encephalitis in children and adolescents is largely comparable with that in adults. However, the severity is reflected in the finding that children and adolescents regularly have to be admitted to pediatric intensive care unit (PICU) as a result of their neuropsychiatric critical illness (Riet van de et al., 2013; Schumacher et al., 2016).

2.2 Limbic autoimmune encephalitis

Limbic autoimmune encephalitis (LE) is a rare type of autoimmune encephalitis associated with inflammation in the structures of the limbic system. It is notorious because of its relation with oncological disorders, and therefore, it must be considered as a paraneoplastic syndrome. Main features associated with LE are memory loss, seizures, and psychiatric symptoms. Refractory seizures may be a prominent marker of the condition. Several antineuronal antibodies have been associated with the diagnosis of LE (Mooneyham et al., 2018). In the current section, we will briefly mention two different variants: anti–voltage-gated potassium channel (VGKC) encephalitis and antiglutamic acid decarboxylase encephalitis (anti-GAD).

2.2.1 Anti–voltage-gated potassium channel encephalitis

This subtype of limbic encephalitis antibodies targets the voltage-gated potassium channels (anti-VGKC) in the limbic area. The condition was first referred to as "potassium channel antibody-associated encephalopathy." It mainly occurs in adult males, although it has also been described in postpartum females and in children (Mooneyham et al., 2018). In adults, the clinical picture is more clearly defined than in children and often presents with short-term memory loss, cognitive changes, and seizures. In children, limited reports show varied clinical manifestations. Most presentations are characterized by subacute memory and cognitive decline, refractory seizures or status epilepticus, and psychiatric symptoms. Presenting symptoms may also include movement disorders, dysarthria, and developmental regression (Brenton & Goodkin, 2016).

2.2.2 Antiglutamic acid decarboxylase encephalitis

This subtype of limbic encephalitis is characterized with antibodies against glutamic acid decarboxylase (GAD). Although rarely described, anti-GAD encephalitis can ultimately lead to severe and potentially fatal autonomic disturbances. In children, anti-GAD encephalitis often expressed as focal seizures (often arising from the temporal lobe) together with short-term memory loss and cognitive decline given the involvement of the hippocampus. This can lead to progressive neurodevelopmental deficits (American Psychiatric Association, 2013, p. 31). A broad spectrum of psychiatric symptoms can also occur (Barbagallo et al., 2017; Mooneyham et al., 2018).

2.3 Basal ganglia encephalitis (encephalitis lethargica/von Economo's disease)

The condition of encephalitis lethargica (EL), nowadays referred to as basal ganglia encephalitis or dopamine-2 receptor (D2R) encephalitis, was first described by Constantin von Economo in 1917, von Economo linked EL to the 1918 influenza pandemic. 12 of 17 children (Brenton & Goodkin,

2016; Dale et al., 2017) with dopamine-2 receptor (D2R) antibodies had a movement disorder, characterized by Parkinsonism, dystonia, and chorea. Psychiatric symptoms including emotional lability, attention deficit, and psychosis were seen in 9 of the 12 children. Oculogyric crises, ocular flutter, ataxia, sleep disturbance, lethargy, drowsiness, mutism, brainstem dysfunction, and seizures were observed less frequently. In a recent review by Barbagallo et al. (2017), psychiatric symptoms occurred together with dystonia, lethargy, and abnormal movements. The late Oliver Sacks wrote his famous "Awakenings (Sachs, 1973)" about this disorder, and it also has been adapted and released as a movie (1990).

2.4 Hashimoto encephalitis

Hashimoto encephalitis (HE) is associated with autoimmune thyroiditis. The condition is characterized by acute encephalopathy and elevated antithyroid antibodies. It is rare in the pediatric population, with only about 60 cases described to date (Armangue et al., 2012; Lee et al., 2018.) Therefore, its prevalence is still unknown (Lee et al., 2018). Clinical features are not specific and can include stroke-like symptoms, but myoclonus and disorientation are often noticed. Other symptoms are transient aphasia, tremor, sleep, seizures, ataxia, and hallucinations (Mooneyham et al., 2018).

3. Review of diagnosis, treatment and outcomes of anti-NMDAR encephalitis

3.1 Diagnosis of anti-NMDAR encephalitis

When children present with an acute to subacute onset of new neurologic and/or psychiatric symptoms/first-onset psychosis, healthcare professionals should also consider autoimmune encephalitis and start a systematic, multidisciplinary workup accordingly. Infectious causes must be ruled out first, together with other etiologies (metabolic, genetic, and other syndromes). Creating the differential diagnosis for a patient presenting with an acute first-onset psychosis can be very challenging. In this respect, the history of the patient including the collateral history from the parent(s) is of the upmost importance in finding the pieces of the puzzle of the diagnostic process. In adolescents or young adults, the differential diagnosis of suspected autoimmune encephalitis may include a primary psychiatric disorder, drug abuse, adverse effects of antipsychotic medications, a sudden onset of a type of epilepsy, or a neurological movement disorder. If any of these diagnoses are part of the differential diagnosis, autoimmune encephalitis should be seriously considered as well. In this process, a multidisciplinary collaboration between pediatric neurology, pediatrics, and child neuropsychiatry is imperative. Although consensus regarding a single diagnostic battery for autoimmune encephalitis has not yet been established, there are some important diagnostic issues to consider.

Firstly, the mental state examination (MSE) can guide us as—intermittent—clouding of consciousness (which is highly unusual in pure psychiatric disorders), attentional problems, and/or formal thought disorders, frequently presenting as (hyperactive) delirium, may be important clues suggestive of an underlying somatic cause (Schieveld, van de Riet, et al., 2019; Schieveld, Strik, et al. 2019; Schieveld & Strik 2018, 2021). "I WATCH DEATH" is the Michael G. Wise famous acronym- in which letters and nouns have been cleverly ordered regarding delirium in which any letter covers all of the most important underlying somatic differential diagnoses (see Fig. 7.1). For example, the "I" represents any Infection, or Inflammation such as autoimmune encephalitis, and the "W" represents Withdrawal of, e.g., alcohol or medication such as opioids and so on (Wise, 2002). This acronym is also brilliant because (1) the two most important differential diagnoses appear at the beginning and (2) it warns the medical team "Your patient may be dying!" In addition, delirium is indeed "acute brain failure in man" and associated with many negative outcomes such as a higher mortality.

Secondly, there is a list of laboratory and imaging investigations (Table 7.1) that may be considered. The literature reports that the MRI shows hyperintensities of the medial temporal lobes, hippocampi, corpus callosum, and/or cerebral/cerebellar cortex (Abe et al., 2016; Agarwal et al.,

I	Infectious	Infections
W	Withdrawal	Withdrawal of psychotropic medication and drugs, such as painkillers/benzodiazepines/anaesthetics/alcohol
A	Acute Metabolic	Acute metabolic diseases such as liver- or kidney dysfunction, electrolyte disturbance, alkalosis, acidosis
T	Trauma	Traumas such as neurotrauma, operations
C	CNS Pathology	Diseases of the central nervous system, such as a tumor or a stroke
H	Hypoxia	Hypoxia such as cardiogenic or hypovolemic shock
D	Deficiencies	Deficiencies such as Vitamin B12 deficiency
E	Endocrinopathies	Endocrine diseases such as hypo- or hyperglycaemia
A	Acute Vascular	Acute vascular diseases such as vasculitis
T	Toxic or drugs	Toxicity such poisoning or overdoses with medication or drugs
H	Heavy metals	Heavy metals such as lead or mercury

*Wise et al, 2002

FIGURE 7.1   Acronym I WATCH DEATH*.

TABLE 7.1 Diagnostic pathways in anti-NMDAR encephalitis.

Laboratories	EEG	Brain imaging
CSF (*abnormal in 80%–85%*) - Anti-NMDAR antibody testing o Production can be stimulated by an underlying tumor - Lymphocytic pleocytosis - CSF protein elevation - IgG oligoclonal bands - PCR: bacterial/viral cultures - Glucoses (normal 100%) - Serum should be tested for specific autoimmune biomarkers Serum - Anti-NMDAR antibody testing (45%–100%) - Serum should be tested for specific autoimmune biomarkers - ESR	Abnormal (70%–90%) - Generalized, focal, or diffuse slowing - Disorganized slowing - Back slowing (100%) - Extreme delta brush pattern (30%) - Epileptiform activity (35%–50%) - Electrographic seizures (29%–60%)	MRI abnormal (15%–50%) - Hyperintensities on T2-weighted sequences or FLAIR images can be found in every anatomical structure of the brain - Thalamic signal alteration - Focal and/or global atrophy - Leptomeningeal and cortical contrast enhancement - Diffuse atrophy - Normal MRI at onset and atrophy by 6 months CT of the head without intravenous contrast PET SPECT Note: There is no classic pattern for Anti-NMDAR encephalitis

Abbreviations: CT, computerized tomography; CSF, cerebrospinal fluid; ESR, erythrocyte sedimentation rate; FLAIR, fluid-attenuated inversion recovery; IgG, immunoglobulin G; PCR, polymerase chain reaction; PET, positron emission tomography; SPECT, Single Photon Emission Computed Tomography.

2020). In some cases, hyperintensities were even found in the spinal cord and medulla oblongata (Agarwal et al., 2020). Furthermore, small frontal or frontoparietal white matter lesions together with more extensive white matter cortical lesions, hippocampal, and thalamic alterations as well as focal and/or global atrophy could be detected (Bartels et al., 2020). In up to 30% of female patients, screening was positive for the presence of a tumor (Armangue et al., 2013; Brenton et al., 2016).

Thirdly, new/acute onset of psychosis in combination with neurological symptoms such as epilepsy and/or involuntary (asymmetric) movements is very alarming. An early/timely EEG—if feasible—can be very helpful in clarifying the true nature of the psychotic episode. After all a "pure" psychiatric psychosis should result in a normal EEG, and disturbances are therefore highly indicative of an underlying neuropsychiatric/somatic condition. In anti-NMDAR encephalitis, generalized frontotemporal slowing or disorganized activity was in some cases reflected in the EEG as (extreme) delta brush (Abe et al., 2016; Bartels et al., 2020). Also, EEG was found to be abnormal in up to 95%–100% of the children (Qu et al., 2020; Sartori et al., 2015; Tong et al., 2020), and seizures were reported in up to 38% of the patients (Haberlandt et al., 2017; Kim et al., 2014).

Finally, the only gold standard regarding the diagnosis is the combination of specific lab and CSF findings. CSF was found to be abnormal in up to 80% of children with anti-NMDAR encephalitis under the age of 18 (Abe et al., 2016). NMDAR antibodies have been found in up to 100% of cases, together with lymphocytic pleocytosis (70% of the cases) and elevated CSF protein (up to 27%) (Armangue et al., 2013; Chakrabarty et al., 2014; Sakpichaisakul et al., 2018; Sartori et al., 2015).

However, it is noteworthy that although these tools are very powerful, they do not provide an iron-clad diagnosis as both false positives and false negatives can occur. Potential biomarkers could be affected by many different clinical or patient variables—such as disease activity, therapeutic intervention, or the presence of comorbidities. There exists also the question of the clinical validity of the detected biomarker: if it is indeed a true measure of the clinical process, it is intended to reflect (Tektonidou & Ward, 2011). MRI and or CT scan imaging can also be very helpful in providing further confirmation. So the final diagnosis may be made in function of the whole clinical presentation and collateral history of the patient and family, combined with the clinical wisdom and experience of the multidisciplinary medical team.

3.2 Serum-negative encephalitis

Children presenting with autoimmune encephalitis syndrome are a diagnostic challenge because although criteria and guidelines for the clinical diagnosis of autoimmune encephalitis in adults have recently been developed, there are no consensus definitions for pediatric-specific seronegative autoimmune encephalitis (Graus, 2016). Appropriate auto-antibody testing done along with exclusion of infectious causes confirms specific diagnoses (Dalea 2017; Lee, 2021). Detection of autoantibodies for diagnosing autoimmune encephalitis is, however, not perfect for several reasons: (1) false negatives due to low titers, (2) delay between antibody titer assessment and start clinical features, (3) possibility of unknown antibodies, and (4) not always accessible and expensive (Lee, 2021).

There are many children with suspected autoimmune encephalitis, who are serum negative and have normal routine CSF testing, and who would fail to fulfill current criteria (Lee, 2021). Clinical characteristics of patients diagnosed with autoimmune encephalitis were indeed mostly similar regardless of their serological status, with favorable treatment outcomes after initiating immunomodulatory agents. For example, Hacohen et al. (2013) reported that clinical features (seizure predominance) and treatment outcomes of pediatric seronegative and seropositive autoimmune encephalitis patients were similar at presentation.

A first consensus definition for "seronegative but suspected autoimmune encephalitis" was generated by Graus et al. (2016); however, a revised definition may be required for children (Fig. 7.2). Although the detection of autoantibodies is a confirmatory diagnostic test, a substantial part of all clinically proven autoimmune encephalitis series is antibody negative. Therefore, a strong clinical suspicion is essential for the diagnosis. And although increased levels of serum C-reactive protein (CRP) or erythrocyte sedimentation rate (ESR) are more common in systemic inflammation, also in autoimmune encephalitis, it is reported to be increased (Lokhorst, 2019)! And as this CRP laboratory test is not expensive (about 5 Euro's for the test itself) and almost globally available, it is worthwhile to test in first-onset psychosis.

3.3 Treatment of anti-NMDAR encephalitis

3.3.1 In general

Despite the substantial gain in scientific knowledge about the disease over the past decade, studies to date still primarily focus upon, if present, tumor management and immunotherapy. Thus, in the first stage of treatment corticosteroids, monoclonal antibodies (like rituximab) and/or plasmapheresis are administered (de Bruijn et al., 2018). The possibility of more effective alternative treatments still needs to be explored. Where anti-NMDAR encephalitis was once regarded as a condition primarily affecting adult women and frequently associated with ovarian tumors, it is increasingly recognized in the *absence* of tumors, and occurring in the pediatric population as well.

3.3.1.1 The multidisciplinary approach to autoimmune encephalitis

Critical care management is often necessary in patients with autoimmune encephalitis due to severe problems across domains of pediatrics/ internal medicine (the support of vital organs that are endangered especially the brain, lungs, and heart), neurology, and psychiatry. So many children with anti-NMDAR encephalitis end up in a PICU (Riet van de et al., 2013; Schumacher et al., 2016). In this case, long-term mechanic ventilation and sedation are often required. Persistent dysautonomia, seizures, hyperthermia, and fluctuations in mental status can be difficult

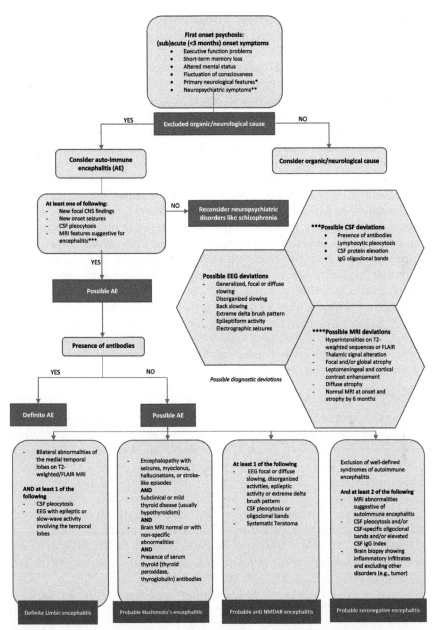

FIGURE 7.2   Algorithm from first-onset psychosis to autoimmune encephalitis.
* Primary neurological features: seizures, abnormal involuntary movements, asymmetric EPS side effect.
** Neuropsychiatric symptoms including headache, fever, confusion, neck stiffness, vomiting, hallucinations, and delusions.
*** If no other tests are available, then consider to check for increased levels of serum CRP (C reactive protein) or ESR (erythrocyte sedimentation rate).
*** See "possible MRI deviations" for MRI features suggestive for encephalitis.

IV. Treatments for the future

to manage. Furthermore, airway management is complicated because of severe movement disorders or delirium resulting in dislocation and malfunction of devices.

In general, intensive and long-term treatment is necessary, which may include a pharmacologically induced coma with *midazolam, propofol,* and/ or *remifentanil or dexmedetomidine.* Prolonged status epilepticus, despite deep sedation, might require a barbiturate (*pentothal*)-induced coma. While patients can remain in this induced coma for quite a while, the neurological overall outcome still can be good and brain imaging will often reveal only little or reversible abnormalities. However, the psychiatric and frequently even more subtle neuropsychological outcomes frequently are less favorable (Mooneyham et al., 2018).

Treatment of anti-NMDAR encephalitis is thus (1) first targeted toward the causal antibodies; this often happens by means of immunotherapy; (2) occasionally, this has to be combined with a specific targeted oncological approach such as in the case of a limbic encephalitis in the context of a paraneoplastic syndrome; (3) management is defined as the whole set of other multidisciplinary supporting interventions especially in the possible context of a clinical decline toward critical illness (failure of the major organ systems), thus leading to an admission to a PICU. This should always be combined with (4) neuropsychiatric behavioral interventions regarding the patient, and (5) the support and empowerment of the family (see Section 3.3.1.2).

3.3.1.2 The ABCDEF bundle

As stated earlier, a substantial number of patients with anti-NMDAR/ autoimmune encephalitis become severely or even critically ill in which case intensive treatment in an ICU setting is needed. Although patients often survive because of the improvements in critical care, cognitive impairment, disabilities in activities of daily living (ADLs) and mental health impairment can persist after hospitalization. This wide range of disabilities are referred to by the umbrella term "post—intensive care syndrome," which is a variation of acquired, nontraumatic brain injury (Marra et al., 2018). And the paper by Esseveld et al. (2013), in open access, presents a visual/pictorial insight into neuropsychiatric and neuropsychological processing and recovery after NMDAR encephalitis.

As these impairments can pose a serious burden on both the patients as well as their families, the "ICU Liberation Collaborative" evolved to optimize recovery and prognosis (Ely, 2017). This Collaborative is a quality improvement initiative that has been implemented across 76 ICUs in the United States (US) designed to strategically engage the ABCDEF bundle by means of team- and evidence-based care to improve recovery and to prevent symptoms of post—intensive care syndrome. The ABCDEF bundle represents a progressively evidence-based coordinated guide for all (para-)

medical disciplines and nursing teams to coordinate care needed for optimizing ICU patient recovery and outcomes. The ABCDEF bundle includes the organization of (1) the Assessment, prevention, and management of pain; (2) both spontaneous awakening and spontaneous Breathing; (3) multidisciplinary Brain rounds; (4) well-considered Choice of analgesia and sedation; (5) the assessment, prevention, and management of Delirium; (6) the assessment and management of Early mobility and Exercise; and (7) Family empowerment and engagement (Fig. 7.3).

The bundle focuses on the patients as well as their families and tries to minimalize the "iatrogenic" harm that is, unfortunately, frequently unavoidable and inherent to critical illness and its multidisciplinary treatment. Fortunately, it has been proven that the implementation of this guide decreases mortality as well as length of ICU stay, e.g., in delirium (Barnes-Daly et al., 2017). The strongest aspect of the initiative's philosophy is its holistic approach. It shifts the focus from monitors to human connection and thereby helps to preserve self-worth and self-confidence, which are imperative components of the recovery process (Ely, 2017).

3.3.2 Specific neuropsychiatric symptomatology

3.3.2.1 Psychopharmacology

Besides immunotherapy and multidisciplinary supporting interventions as described before, symptomatic treatment of neuropsychiatric symptoms is needed. For this purpose, a substantial number of patients need psychiatric medication, including antipsychotics and/or benzodiazepines. However, in this specific scenario, antipsychotics and especially haloperidol are not recommended (but please see at 3.3.2.2), because they could possibly provoke or exacerbate motor symptoms (Schumacher et al., 2016). Moreover, these patients may already present with motor disturbances such as dystonia and/or chorea or are hypersensitive to the extrapyramidal side effects (EPS) of antipsychotics. Unfortunately, many psychotropic drugs, not only antipsychotics, can cause EPS as well. Benzodiazepines are increasingly known to be avoided, and

A	Assessment	Assess, Prevent, and Manage Pain
B	Both	Both Spontaneous Awakening Trials and Spontaneous Breathing Trials
C	Choice	Choice of analgesia and sedation
D	Delirium	Delirium: Assess, Prevent, and Manage
E	Early	Early mobility and Exercise
F	Family	Family engagement and empowerment.

* Marra et al. CCM, 2017.

FIGURE 7.3   Acronym ABCDEF bundle*.

are even becoming notorious, for causing or worsening agitation (Schieveld, van de Riet, et al., 2019; Schieveld, Strik, et al. 2019; Schumacher et al., 2016).

3.3.2.2 The hyperactive delirium issue

The main neuropsychiatric symptoms that can manifest are problems in attention, executive functioning, and/or formal thought disorders combined with an agitation, or a less frequent inhibition, syndrome. Therefore, the clinical picture must be considered as a serious case of hyperactive delirium/excited delirium driven by an autoimmune encephalitis. The clinical picture is often further complicated by psychotic features: hallucinations and or delusions (see also Tables 7.2 and 7.3). The treatment of neuropsychiatric symptoms is an important step of the treatment procedure as it can take weeks up to months until a good clinical response is achieved, and sometimes very severe (refractory) agitation has leveled off, which can be potentially harmful, not only for

TABLE 7.2   Other additional diagnostic cues and considerations.

Other diagnostic cues

- Diagnostic criteria of Graus et al. (90%) (use with caution in children younger than 5 years old)
  1. Rapid onset (<3 months) of at least four out of six major groups of clinical symptoms ((1) abnormal (psychiatric) behavior or cognitive dysfunction; (2) speech dysfunction; (3) seizures; (4) movement disorders, dyskinesias, or rigidity/abnormal postures; (5) decreased level of consciousness; and (6) autonomic dysfunction or central hypoventilation)
  2. Presence of at least one of the laboratory study results ((1) abnormal EEG or (2) CSF with pleocytosis or oligoclonal bands)
  3. Exclusion of other disorders
- Cellucci classification criteria (fulfill all 4 criteria for definite antiantibody positive encephalitis)
  1. Neurologic and psychiatric symptoms, alone or in combination, develop over 3 months
  2. ≥2 clinical features of neurologic dysfunction
  3. CSF or serum positive for well-characterized autoantibodies
     - If CSF is negative, but serum is positive: ≥1 paraclinical feature of neuroinflammation also required
  4. Exclusion of alternative etiologies for presentation and neuroinflammation
- Tumor screening
  ○ MRI abdomen and pelvis for ovarian teratoma (10%–30%)
  ○ CT/PET-scan chest, abdomen and pelvis for identifying most tumors
  ○ Abdominal or testicular ultrasound

Note: VEEG: may be beneficial in diagnosing seizures PET-FDG: frontotemporal hypermetabolism and occipitoparietal hypometabolism

Abbreviations: PET-FDG, *positron emission tomography–fluorodeoxyglucose;* (V)EEG, *(video) electroencephalograph.*

TABLE 7.3   Prognosis in anti-NMDAR encephalitis in children <18 years.

Outcomes	Residual symptoms
Relapses (2%–25%)	**Neurocognitive**
Recovery	- Language dysfunction
- Full recovery (29%–85%)	- Word finding difficulties
- Mild sequelae (3%–50%)	- Memory problems (persistent
Mortality 0%–10%	(fragmented or complete)
	amnesia).[a]
	Neurological
	Seizures/epilepsy
	Motor/movement symptoms:
	- Mild dyskinesia
	- Motor retardation
	- Exhibited ataxia
	- Abnormal movements and lack
	of communication skills
	Psychiatric
	- Behavioral problems
	- Sleep disorder
	- Irritability and anger outbursts
	- Attention and concentration
	deficits
	- Impulsiveness
	- Anxiety
	- Indecisiveness

[a]*As part of executive functioning problems (EFPs): problems with attention, memory, planning and organization, learning and feedback, and inhibition.*

the patient but for the staff and family as well. Although hyperactive delirium is routinely treated with first- and second-generation antipsychotic medications, treatment is complicated in case of comorbid catatonic agitation and or dystonic symptoms, as these medications are known to potentially exacerbate catatonia inhibition. In contrast, catatonic agitation or inhibition is treated effectively with benzodiazepines; however, this in turn may also exacerbate agitation or delirium. The treatment may be further complicated by the presence of autonomic instability in autoimmune encephalitis (Mooneyham et al., 2018).

3.3.2.3 Antipsychotics

Up to 5 years ago, evaluations of the effectiveness of *haloperidol* in children and adolescents diagnosed with autoimmune encephalitis were mainly limited to case reports. However, in recent studies, larger groups of children with anti-NMDAR encephalitis with sleep disturbances and involuntary movements were treated with haloperidol (Florance-Ryan &

Dalmau, 2010; Qu et al., 2020). Noteworthy, in most studies to date, *haloperidol* was reported to have little to no significant clinical effect (Barbagallo et al., 2017). However, it is important to note in this respect that in these studies there was no mention of the symptom-specific effect of haloperidol (Basheer et al., 2017) Clinically, this is a highly relevant observation given the fact that *haloperidol* is expected to have a symptom-dependent effect, e.g., on hallucinations and or delusions and on agitation levels but not on pure movement disturbances. Thus, the actual effect could have been masked in these studies and warrants further investigation on symptom level. Note, also side effects were described in a substantial number of the patients, but their nature was not specified on medication level or even on type of psychotropic drug.

Risperidone is more often studied in children with autoimmune encephalitis than haloperidol. The main neuropsychiatric symptoms for which it was prescribed in these studies were agitation, insomnia, aggression, and psychiatric symptoms (not otherwise specified; NOS) (Alvarez et al., 2020; Nagappa et al., 2016). With respect to the psychiatric symptoms, findings on the effectiveness of *risperidone* were inconsistent. In addition, no improvements (nor deterioration) on agitation, aggression, or insomnia were reported. The main side effect was suspected neuroleptic malignant syndrome (NMS), which has perhaps been found in the minority of the patients.

Olanzapine was only prescribed in a few studies in children with anti-NMDAR and other autoimmune encephalitis (Lee et al., 2018; Nagappa et al., 2016; Tong et al., 2020). In these studies, symptoms of abnormal behavior and mental symptoms (without further specification), as well as aggression, irritability, hallucinations, disorientations, and anterograde amnesia, were described.

Quetiapine was prescribed in several papers (Agarwal et al., 2020; Mooneyham et al., 2018; Nagappa et al., 2016) in children with anti-NMDAR encephalitis. The main symptoms were sleep disturbances, extreme and refractory agitation, "catatonic symptoms," mood dysregulation, and psychotic and behavioral symptoms.

3.3.2.4 Benzodiazepines

The specific benzodiazepines used in patients with anti-NMDAR encephalitis and other autoimmune encephalitis were *lorazepam, midazolam, diazepam, zolpidem, temazepam, and clonazepam* (Agarwal et al., 2020; Barbagallo et al., 2017; Lin et al., 2020; Mooneyham et al., 2018; Nagappa et al., 2016; Qu et al., 2020; Schumacher et al., 2016). In general, benzodiazepines were given in case of sleep disturbances, abnormal behavior, and disturbances in cognition and agitation, particularly if presented with comorbid catatonia. A preference for *lorazepam* was observed in cases of severe agitation, delirium, and catatonia. When presented with seizures, the use of benzodiazepines such as *midazolam* and *diazepam* were reported as well. In some reports, *diazepam* was given to treat psychiatric symptoms and insomnia as a result of delirium and agitation (Mooneyham et al., 2018). Schumacher et al. (2016) mentioned that benzodiazepines could worsen delirium in critically ill patients given the anticholinergic effects and the possible occurrence of a paradoxical effect, thereby worsening agitation and or by disturbance of the chloride homeostasis (Schieveld et al., 2018).

3.3.2.5 Antidepressants

Antidepressants such as SSRIs, SNRIs, and tricyclic antidepressants were prescribed mainly for residual symptoms such as anxiety and features of obsessive–compulsive disorder (OCD), panic, irritability, and depression (Bigi et al., 2015). In one study of children with anti-NMDAR encephalitis, even *lithium* and *gabapentin* were given for mood regulation (Agarwal et al., 2020). Finally, in case of sleep disturbances, *trazodone* and *clonidine* were used (Agarwal et al., 2020; Alvarez et al., 2020).

3.3.2.6 Antiepilepsy medications

Regardless of the type of autoimmune encephalitis, the condition is frequently associated with epilepsy and other seizure disorders. Treatment with antiepileptics is indicated in these cases, but only when given in combination with immunotherapy to treat the underlying cause (Agarwal et al., 2020; Alvarez et al., 2020; Barbagallo et al., 2017; Bigi et al., 2015; Chavez-Castillo et al., 2020; Lin et al., 2020). In the past decade, antiepileptics such as *carbamazepine, oxcarbazepine, and valproic acid* were especially prescribed for seizures and symptoms of movement disorder, mood disturbances, psychiatric symptoms, agitation, and depression, all with inconsistent effects (Agarwal et al., 2020; Barbagallo et al., 2017; Chaves-Castillo et al., 2020; Lin et al., 2020; Mooneyham et al., 2018). Finally, it is worth to mention that the majority of recovered patients require no maintenance treatment with antiepileptics.

To conclude, there are still important questions concerning the (side) effects of NDMAR pharmacological treatments that remain to be answered. Currently, there are no guidelines yet to describe preferred treatment options and strategies.

3.3.3 *Other treatment options*

3.3.3.1 Electroconvulsive therapy

Electroconvulsive therapy (ECT) as a nonpharmacological treatment is known as a reasonably successful treatment option for neuropsychiatric symptoms in anti-NMDAR encephalitis, especially for refractory agitation and/or catatonia (Agarwal et al., 2020; Lin et al., 2020). The mechanism of action of ECT, however, remains largely unclear. In animal models, ECT has been shown to upregulate NMDA receptors. This may, in part, explain the efficacy of this treatment option in anti-NMDAR encephalitis (Braakman et al., 2010). Even though the cases describing ECT in autoimmune encephalitis in children are limited, none of them describe adverse effects. As a result, it seems to be a safe option to consider. However, given the lack of larger high-quality studies, controversy still surrounding its application, the risk of additional long-term cognitive problems and high chances of relapse ECT, still needs to be carefully considered as a treatment option.

3.4 Outcomes of anti-NMDAR encephalitis

Most patients with anti-NMDAR encephalitis tend to have a favorable neurological outcome with full recovery in up to 85% of the children with autoimmune encephalitis (Abe et al., 2016; Brenton et al., 2016; Gastaldi et al., 2018; Pruetarat et al., 2019; Sakpichaisakul et al., 2018; Wright & Wood, 2020). Nevertheless, this is not always accompanied by a favorable psychiatric and neuropsychological prognosis. Prominent disturbances can last up to 2 years after the onset of the event. Mortality is estimated to be less than 10% (Armangue et al., 2013; Singer, 2017; Wang et al., 2017).

A substantial proportion of patients who recovered from anti-NMDAR encephalitis still had persistent cognitive deficits (Ho et al., 2018; Jones et al., 2013). These deficits are mainly found in the domains of attention, executive functioning, and behavior. In addition, symptoms of mild mental problems, dyskinesia, language dysfunction, sleep disorder, motor- and mental retardation are reported (Ho et al., 2018).

Relapse can occur in up to 25% of the cases of anti-NMDAR encephalitis, with an onset from weeks to years after the initial episode (Brenton et al., 2016; Dale et al., 2017; Gastaldi et al., 2018; Jones et al., 2013; Sai et al., 2018; Sartori et al., 2015; Wang et al., 2017; Wright et al., 2017). These relapses most often occur in patients who were previously untreated or partially treated, especially in the presence of a causative tumor that has not yet been identified and removed (Brenton et al., 2016). Furthermore, CSF and serum titers of antibody levels were significantly higher in patients with a poor prognosis (Abe et al., 2016). In fully treated patients, the risk of relapse was reported to substantially lower and estimated at about 10% within the first 2 years (Pruetarat et al., 2019).

4. Discussion

4.1 Autoimmune encephalitis versus psychiatric disorder: a critical note

It is often difficult to distinguish anti-NMDAR encephalitis from a major primary psychiatric disorder. It can happen that patients who are diagnosed with primary psychosis or schizophrenia in fact suffer from encephalitis. This raises an important question: how to distinguish these two conditions?

Anti-NMDAR encephalitis, like other types of encephalitis, frequently begins, in contrast to onset of psychosis, with nonspecific prodromal symptoms such as fever, headache, upper respiratory symptoms, vomiting, and diarrhea (Abe et al., 2016; Armangue et al., 2013). Following, more psychosis specific, symptoms can develop, such as (severe) agitation with or without catatonia (both agitated and apathetic/inhibited), memory loss, confusion, delirium, emotional disturbances, delusions, hallucinations, and sleep dysregulation. In addition, somatic symptoms as movement disorders and seizures often occur (Abe et al., 2016; Armangue et al., 2013). It is noteworthy that autoimmune encephalitis in children, especially in adolescents, may even start off with the development of psychiatric symptoms (Abe et al., 2016; Dalmau et al., 2011). In this case, the initial presentation can easily be confused with a manic or psychotic episode (e.g., as schizophrenia in young adults) or with drug intoxication. To make matters even more complicated, in young children, the early signs of autoimmune encephalitis can present as subtle and nonspecific behavioral changes such as temper tantrums, hyperactivity, or irritability. Consequently, these signs are unfortunately often ignored or overlooked and not identified as possible red flags, indicative of a serious medical condition. However, the underlying autoimmune encephalitis becomes more apparent with the onset of neurological symptoms, such as seizures, gait abnormalities, verbal reduction, or mutism. Furthermore, tardive dyskinesia can occur, which can be a bit of a puzzle if patients were treated with antipsychotic medications earlier in the course of the disease as tardive dyskinesia can also be a side effect of antipsychotics. In a later stage of the disease, individuals may stop eating and drinking and subsequently will regularly need assistance in most, if not all, activities of daily living as well. At this stage, the expressed behavior should not be considered as symptomatic for a primary eating disorder, like anorexia nervosa, but as a secondary eating disorder.

4.2 Treatment options: a critical discussion regarding the sense and nonsense of using antipsychotics

To date, findings on pharmacological treatment outcomes in brain inflammation have been primarily published as case reports and series. Only a few larger studies have been conducted in cohorts of pediatric departments in hospitals (e.g., Zhang et al., 2019). Taking a closer look at the tables, two central issues stand out: (1) a great diversity in treatment choices for psychiatric symptoms across studies, and (2) in general, a polypharmacological approach was preferred. These findings illustrate the fact that physicians appear to struggle with the treatment, because of the lack of evidence regarding which drugs to use in this illness.

Furthermore, in these studies, the most frequently prescribed psychopharmacological drugs were *antipsychotics*, mainly for severe and/or refractory agitation with or without catatonia, but also for psychosis, personality changes, (involuntary) movements, and delirium. Overall, antipsychotics had little effect on nonpsychotic symptoms. Antipsychotics with sedative qualities such as olanzapine and quetiapine appear to have had the strongest effect, albeit inconsistently. The fact that antipsychotics are not always effective and can have (serious) side effects, can cause hesitation among clinicians in their use, and even lead to discussions in multidisciplinary teams. However, one has to keep in mind that refractory agitation is often more harmful and requires further intervention, in which case the end justifies the means.

Next to antipsychotics the use of benzodiazepines was described. These were merely prescribed in case of sleep disturbances, abnormal behavior, and, again, severe agitation, especially in the combination with catatonia. The observed effects were inconsistent. In the current review, administration of benzodiazepines has been associated with paradoxical effects (e.g., aggravation of agitation) as well. Aggravated agitation is common in general practice in patients with a vulnerable brain, including autoimmune encephalopathy. In some studies, the prescription of benzodiazepines was even proposed to be a risk factor for delirium, in accordance with the literature concerning critically ill children in which the relationship between benzodiazepines and their highly deliriogenic effects is clearly demonstrated (Schumacher et al., 2016; Schieveld, van de Riet, et al., 2019; Schieveld, Strik, et al. 2019). However, in critical illness, the differential diagnosis between paradoxical agitation and hyperactive delirium is hard—if not impossible—to make. Thus, relying on scarce data, although the sedative effect is clearly present in benzodiazepines, the risk of paradoxal agitation and the development of delirium has to be seriously considered and balanced.

4.3 Other situations

For autoimmune encephalitis, treatment tackles the underlying disease process and is combined with symptomatic treatment. This approach results in polypharmacy with its concomitant problems, and caution is required. Treatment procedure will depend on multiple factors such as urgency, convictions, clinical wisdom, and previous clinical experience.

4.3.1 Indications for and procedure for rapid tranquilization

Rapid tranquilization (RT) is sometimes necessary, mainly when faced with severe or catatonic agitation, for example, in children with hyperactive delirium. In this case, the previously described antipsychotic approach in itself does not suffice and has to be combined with the additional administration of either one of the following:

- A benzodiazepine such as lorazepam (keeping in mind that benzodiazepines can increase risk of delirium as mentioned before).
- The use of iv Nozinan (a phenothiazine: levomepromazine = methotrimeprazine) max: 1 mg/kg/iv/ divided over 24 h, but first starting with a loading dosage (Schieveld et al., 2010; van der Zwaan et al., 2012), or droperidol (a butyrophenone: dehydrobenzperidol) max: *0.1 mg/kg/iv over 24 h in total*, also first starting with a loading dosage (Gelder et al., 2009). A black box warning was issued on the latter, but this warning should be seriously questioned, especially when compared with other butyrophenones like haloperidol.

Always keep in mind the need to balance the high necessity/urgency for rapid tranquilization and its benefits (e.g., limiting severe agitation, aggression, pulling out of lines, extubating oneself, climbing or falling out of bed) on the one hand, and the potential dangers of side effects such as torsades des pointes, EPS, or NMS on the other hand.

4.3.2 Last resort options for treatment

- In cases of refractory agitation/excited delirium and or exhaustion and despair of the patient, family, and or medical team, either (deep) sedation and or mechanical ventilation may be finally indicated. This deep sedation can be performed best at an (P)ICU by an intensivist or anesthesiologist and by a standard procedure using opioids and midazolam and/or dexmedetomidine, ketamine, or propofol.

- This can be combined with an ECT procedure sometimes even in blocks (a block consists of at least two ECT administrations on two different days per one week) in case of catatonia and/or an agitated/hyperactive/excited delirium or apathetic state, which does not respond to any other treatment.

5. Limitations

When studying the literature focusing on autoimmune encephalitis, the available data are sometimes very heterogenous in nature, which is due to (1) the substantial number of subtypes, (2) often reported in few case reports, (3) contrasted with larger studies, e.g., regarding NMDAR encephalitis, and (4) an overlap with comorbid disorders. For example, regarding treatment, there are no large pharmacological studies or randomized controlled trials available, nor are there any metaanalyses. Therefore, one must be very careful in the practical application of the presented conclusions based on these data and always let clinical wisdom, experience, urgency, and family consent be the decisive factors.

6. Conclusions

This chapter describes and discusses the main evidence-based and up-to-date child and adolescent neuropsychiatric aspects of a specific and rapidly evolving domain of brain inflammation, namely autoimmune encephalitis. Diagnosing autoimmune encephalitis—especially in children—can be very challenging. This is due to an overlap in psychiatric, neuropsychological, and neurological symptoms combined with severe medical problems regarding autonomic dysregulations, fever, and mechanical ventilation problems. The psychiatric differential diagnosis can be first-onset psychosis/schizophrenia/hyperactive delirium. The underlying somatic differential is given by I WATCH DEATH. Because of this complexity, it is important to consider and to treat all these children as—potentially—being critically ill in a PICU context, and to give them a multidisciplinary specialized treatment preferably in a tertiary university hospital. Given that the involvement of different medical specialties is imperative in the diagnostic and treatment process, multidisciplinary guidelines (ABCDEF bundle) for assessment and treatment of autoimmune encephalitis are vital. More research, especially RCTs, is urgently needed.

Acknowledgments

We kindly acknowledge Shelly Habets, secretary of Prof. Dr. Jacqueline Strik at MUMC + for her support in the layout and completion of this chapter, tables, and figures, and Duo Vertaalburo B.V. Maastricht, the Netherlands, for their final editing of the text.

References

Abe, K. K., Koli, R. L., & Yamamoto, L. G. (2016). Emergency department presentations of anti-N-methyl-D-aspartate receptor encephalitis. *Pediatric Emergency Care, 32*(2), 107–112. https://doi.org/10.1097/pec.0000000000000713. quiz 113-105.

Agarwal, R., & Gupta, V. (2020). Anti-NMDA receptor encephalitis in children. In *StatPearls*. Treasure Island (FL): StatPearls Publishing.

Alvarez, G., Krentzel, A., Vova, J., Blackwell, L., & Howarth, R. (2020). Pharmacologic treatment and early rehabilitation outcomes in pediatric patients with anti-NMDA receptor encephalitis. *Archives of Physical Medicine and Rehabilitation*. https://doi.org/10.1016/j.apmr.2020.09.381

American Psychiatric Association. (2013). *Diagnostic and statistical manual of mental disorders* (5th ed.). Washington, DC: Author.

Armangue, T., Petit-Pedrol, M., & Dalmau, J. (2012). Autoimmune encephalitis in children. *Journal of Child Neurology, 27*(11), 1460–1469. https://doi.org/10.1177/0883073812448838

Armangue, T., Titulaer, M. J., Málaga, I., Bataller, L., Gabilondo, I., Graus, F., & Dalmau, J. (2013). Pediatric anti-N-methyl-D-aspartate receptor encephalitis-clinical analysis and novel findings in a series of 20 patients. *Journal of Pediatrics, 162*(4), 850–856. https://doi.org/10.1016/j.jpeds.2012.10.011. e852.

Barbagallo, M., Vitaliti, G., Pavone, P., Romano, C., Lubrano, R., & Falsaperla, R. (2017). Pediatric autoimmune encephalitis. *Journal of Pediatric Neurosciences, 12*(2), 130–134. https://doi.org/10.4103/jpn.JPN_185_16

Barnes-Daly, M. A., Phillips, G., & Ely, E. W. (2017). Improving hospital survival and reducing brain dysfunction at seven California community hospitals: Implementing PAD guidelines via the ABCDEF bundle in 6,064 patients. *Critical Care Medicine, 45*(2), 171–178. https://doi-org.ezproxy.ub.unimaas.nl/10.1097/CCM.0000000000002149.

Bartels, F., Krohn, S., Nikolaus, M., Johannsen, J., Wickström, R., Schimmel, M., ... Finke, C. (2020). Clinical and magnetic resonance imaging outcome predictors in pediatric anti-N-methyl-D-aspartate receptor encephalitis. *Annals of Neurology, 88*(1), 148–159. https://doi.org/10.1002/ana.25754

Basheer, S., Nagappa, M., Mahadevan, A., Bindu, P. S., Taly, A. B., & Girimaji, S. C. (2017). Neuropsychiatric manifestations of pediatric NMDA receptor autoimmune encephalitis: A case series from a tertiary care center in India. *The Primary Care Companion for CNS Disorders, 19*(4). https://doi.org/10.4088/PCC.17m02110

Bigi, S., Hladio, M., Twilt, M., Dalmau, J., & Benseler, S. M. (2015). The growing spectrum of antibody-associated inflammatory brain diseases in children. *Neurology-Neuroimmunology Neuroinflammation, 2*(3), e92. https://doi.org/10.1212/nxi.0000000000000092

Braakman, H. M., Moers-Hornikx, V. M., Arts, B. M., Hupperts, R. M., & Nicolai, J. (2010). Pearls & oy-sters: Electroconvulsive therapy in anti-NMDA receptor encephalitis. *Neurology, 75*(10), e44–e46. https://doi-org.ezproxy.ub.unimaas.nl/10.1212/WNL.0b013e3181f11dc1.

Brenton, J. N., & Goodkin, H. P. (2016). Antibody-mediated autoimmune encephalitis in childhood. *Pediatric Neurology, 60*, 13–23. https://doi.org/10.1016/j.pediatrneurol.2016.04.004

de Bruijn, M., Aarsen, F. K., van Oosterhout, M. P., van der Knoop, M. M., Catsman-Berrevoets, C. E., Schreurs, M. W. J., … Titulaer, M. J. (2018). Long-term neuropsychological outcome following pediatric anti-NMDAR encephalitis. *Neurology, 90*(22), e1997–e2005. https://doi.org/10.1212/wnl.0000000000005605

Cahalan, S. (2012). *Brain on fire: My month of madness*. Simon & Schuster.

Chakrabarty, B., Tripathi, M., Gulati, S., Yoganathan, S., Pandit, A. K., Sinha, A., & Rathi, B. S. (2014). Pediatric anti-N-methyl-D-aspartate (NMDA) receptor encephalitis: Experience of a tertiary care teaching center from north India. *Journal of Child Neurology, 29*(11), 1453–1459. https://doi.org/10.1177/0883073813494474

Chavez-Castillo, M., Ruiz-Garcia, M., & Herrera-Mora, P. (2020). Characterization and outcomes of epileptic seizures in Mexican pediatric patients with anti-N-methyl-D-aspartate receptor encephalitis. *Cureus, 12*(5), e8211. https://doi.org/10.7759/cureus.8211

Creten, C., van der Zwaan, S., Blankespoor, R. J., Maatkamp, A., Nicolai, J., van Os, J., & Schieveld, J. N. (2011). Late onset autism and anti-NMDA-receptor encephalitis. *Lancet (London, England), 378*(9785), 98. https://doi-org.ezproxy.ub.unimaas.nl/10.1016/S0140-6736(11)60548-5.

Dale, R. C., Gorman, M. P., & Lim, M. (2017). Autoimmune encephalitis in children: Clinical phenomenology, therapeutics, and emerging challenges. *Current Opinion in Neurology, 30*(3), 334–344. https://doi.org/10.1097/wco.0000000000000443

Dalea, R. C., Gormanb, M. P., & Lim, M. (2017). Autoimmune encephalitis in children: Clinical phenomenology, therapeutics, and emerging challenges. *Current Opinion in Neurology, 30*, 334–344.

Dalmau, J., & Graus, F. (2018). Antibody-mediated encephalitis. *The New England Journal of Medicine, 378*(9), 840–851. https://doi-org.ezproxy.ub.unimaas.nl/10.1056/NEJMra1708712.

Dalmau, J., Tüzün, E., Wu, H. Y., Masjuan, J., Rossi, J. E., Voloschin, A., Baehring, J. M., Shimazaki, H., Koide, R., King, D., Mason, W., Sansing, L. H., Dichter, M. A., Rosenfeld, M. R., & Lynch, D. R. (2007). Paraneoplastic anti-N-methyl-D-aspartate receptor encephalitis associated with ovarian teratoma. *Annals of Neurology, 61*(1), 25–36. https://doi-org.ezproxy.ub.unimaas.nl/10.1002/ana.21050.

Dalmau, J., Lancaster, E., Martinez-Hernandez, E., Rosenfeld, M. R., & Balice-Gordon, R. (2011). Clinical experience and laboratory investigations in patients with anti-NMDAR encephalitis. *The Lancet Neurology, 10*(1), 63–74. https://doi-org.ezproxy.ub.unimaas.nl/10.1016/S1474-4422(10)70253-2.

Dubey, D., Pittock, S. J., Kelly, C. R., McKeon, A., Lopez-Chiriboga, A. S., Lennon, V. A., Gadoth, A., Smith, C. Y., Bryant, S. C., Klein, C. J., Aksamit, A. J., Toledano, M., Boeve, B. F., Tillema, J. M., & Flanagan, E. P. (2018). Autoimmune encephalitis epidemiology and a comparison to infectious encephalitis. *Annals of Neurology, 83*(1), 166–177. https://doi-org.ezproxy.ub.unimaas.nl/10.1002/ana.25131.

Ely, E. W. (2017). The ABCDEF bundle: Science and philosophy of how ICU liberation serves patients and families. *Critical Care Medicine, 45*(2), 321–330. https://doi-org.ezproxy.ub.unimaas.nl/10.1097/CCM.0000000000002175.

Esseveld, M. M., van de Riet, E. H., Cuypers, L., & Schieveld, J. N. (2013). Drawings during neuropsychiatric recovery from anti-NMDA receptor encephalitis. *The American Journal of Psychiatry, 170*(1), 21–22. https://doi-org.ezproxy.ub.unimaas.nl/10.1176/appi.ajp.2012.12070965.

Florance-Ryan, N., & Dalmau, J. (2010). Update on anti-N-methyl-D-aspartate receptor encephalitis in children and adolescents. *Current Opinion in Pediatrics, 22*(6), 739–744. https://doi.org/10.1097/MOP.0b013e3283402d2f

Ford, B., McDonald, A., & Srinivasan, S. (2019). Anti-NMDA receptor encephalitis: A case study and illness overview. *Drugs in Context, 8*, 212589. https://doi.org/10.7573/dic.212589

Gastaldi, M., Nosadini, M., Spatola, M., Sartori, S., & Franciotta, D. (2018). N-methyl-D-aspartate receptor encephalitis: Laboratory diagnostics and comparative clinical features in adults and children. *Expert Review of Molecular Diagnostics, 18*(2), 181−193. https://doi.org/10.1080/14737159.2018.1431124

Gelder, M., Andreasen, N., Lopez-Ibor, J., & Geddes, J. (2009). *Oxford medical publications.Oxford textbook of psychiatry* (2nd ed.). Oxford University Press.

Granerod, J., & Crowcroft, N. (2007). The epidemiology of acute encephalitis. *Neuropsychological Rehabilitation, 17,* 406−428. https://doi.org/10.1080/09602010600989620

Graus, F., Titulaer, M. J., Balu, R., Benseler, S., Bien, C. G., Cellucci, T., Cortese, I., Dale, R. C., Gelfand, J. M., Geschwind, M., Glaser, C. A., Honnorat, J., Höftberger, R., Iizuka, T., Irani, S. R., Lancaster, E., Leypoldt, F., Prüss, H., Rae-Grant, A., Reindl, M., … Dalmau, J. (2016). A clinical approach to diagnosis of autoimmune encephalitis. *The Lancet Neurology, 15*(4), 391−404. https://doi-org.ezproxy.ub.unimaas.nl/10.1016/S1474-4422(15)00401-9.

Haberlandt, E., Ensslen, M., Gruber-Sedlmayr, U., Plecko, B., Brunner-Krainz, M., Schimmel, M., … Rostásy, K. (2017). Epileptic phenotypes, electroclinical features and clinical characteristics in 17 children with anti-NMDAR encephalitis. *European Journal of Paediatric Neurology, 21*(3), 457−464. https://doi.org/10.1016/j.ejpn.2016.11.016

Hacohen, Y., Wright, S., Waters, P., Agrawal, S., Carr, L., Cross, H., et al. (2013). Paediatric autoimmune encephalopathies: Clinical features, laboratory investigations and outcomes in patients with or without antibodies to known central nervous system autoantigens. *Journal of Neurology, Neurosurgery & Psychiatry, 84,* 748−755.

Ho, A. C., Chan, S. H., Chan, E., Wong, S. S., Fung, S. T., Cherk, S. W., … Wong, V. C. (2018). Anti-N-methyl-d-aspartate receptor encephalitis in children: Incidence and experience in Hong Kong. *Brain and Development, 40*(6), 473−479. https://doi.org/10.1016/j.braindev.2018.02.005

Jones, K. C., Benseler, S. M., & Moharir, M. (2013). Anti-NMDA receptor encephalitis. *Neuroimaging Clinics of North America, 23*(2), 309−320. https://doi.org/10.1016/j.nic.2012.12.009

Kelley, B. P., Patel, S. C., Marin, H. L., Corrigan, J. J., Mitsias, P. D., & Griffith, B. (2017). Autoimmune encephalitis: Pathophysiology and imaging review of an overlooked diagnosis. *AJNR American Journal of Neuroradiology, 38*(6), 1070−1078. https://doi-org.ezproxy.ub.unimaas.nl/10.3174/ajnr.A5086.

Kim, S. Y., Choi, S. A., Ryu, H. W., Kim, H., Lim, B. C., Hwang, H., … Lee, S. K. (2014). Screening autoimmune anti-neuronal antibodies in pediatric patients with suspected autoimmune encephalitis. *Journal of Epilepsy Research, 4*(2), 55−61. https://doi.org/10.14581/jer.14012

Lee, J., Yu, H. J., & Lee, J. (2018). Hashimoto encephalopathy in pediatric patients: Homogeneity in clinical presentation and heterogeneity in antibody titers. *Brain and Development, 40*(1), 42−48. https://doi.org/10.1016/j.braindev.2017.07.008

Lee, S., Kim, H. D., Lee, J. S., Kang, H.-C., & Kim, S. H. (2021). Clinical features and treatment outcomes of seronegative pediatric autoimmune encephalitis. *Journal of Clinical Neurology, 17*(2), 300−306. https://doi.org/10.3988/jcn.2021.17.2.300

Lin, K. L., & Lin, J. J. (2020). Neurocritical care for Anti-NMDA receptor encephalitis. *Biomedical Journal, 43*(3), 251−258. https://doi.org/10.1016/j.bj.2020.04.002

Lokhorst, M.,H., Erkelens, C., van Laar, P.,J., den Dunnen, W.,F.,A., Titulaer, M.,J., & Bethlehem, C. (2019). The clinical approach to a patient with suspected auto-immune encephalitis. *Netherlands Journal of Critical Care, 27,* 207−211.

Marra, A., Pandharipande, P. P., Girard, T. D., Patel, M. B., Hughes, C. G., Jackson, J. C., Thompson, J. L., Chandrasekhar, R., Ely, E. W., & Brummel, N. E. (2018). Co-occurrence of post-intensive care syndrome problems among 406 survivors of critical illness. *Critical Care Medicine, 46*(9), 1393–1401. https://doi-org.ezproxy.ub.unimaas.nl/10.1097/CCM.0000000000003218.

Mooneyham, G. C., Gallentine, W., & Van Mater, H. (2018). Evaluation and management of autoimmune encephalitis: A clinical overview for the practicing child psychiatrist. *Child and Adolescent Psychiatric Clinics of North America, 27*(1), 37–52. https://doi.org/10.1016/j.chc.2017.08.011

Nagappa, M., Bindu, P. S., Mahadevan, A., Sinha, S., Mathuranath, P. S., & Taly, A. B. (2016). Clinical features, therapeutic response, and follow-up in pediatric anti-N-methyl-D-aspartate receptor encephalitis: Experience from a tertiary care university hospital in India. *Neuropediatrics, 47*(1), 24–32. https://doi.org/10.1055/s-0035-1569464

Pruetarat, N., Netbaramee, W., Pattharathitikul, S., & Veeravigrom, M. (2019). Clinical manifestations, treatment outcomes, and prognostic factors of pediatric anti-NMDAR encephalitis in tertiary care hospitals: A multicenter retrospective/prospective cohort study. *Brain and Development, 41*(5), 436–442. https://doi.org/10.1016/j.braindev.2018.12.009

Qu, X. P., Vidaurre, J., Peng, X. L., Jiang, L., Zhong, M., & Hu, Y. (2020). Seizure characteristics, outcome, and risk of epilepsy in pediatric anti-N-methyl-d-aspartate receptor encephalitis. *Pediatric Neurology, 105*, 35–40. https://doi.org/10.1016/j.pediatrneurol.2019.11.011

Riet van de, E. H. C. W., Esseveld, M. M., Cuypers, L., & Schieveld, J. N. M. (2013). Anti-NMDAR encephalitis: A new, severe and challenging enduring entity. *European Child & Adolescent Psychiatry, 22*(5), 319–323. https://doi.org/10.1007/s00787-012-0351-0. Epub 2012 Dec 19.

Sachs, O. W. (1973). *Awakenings* (xiii, p. 255). London: Duckworth.

Sai, Y., Zhang, X., Feng, M., Tang, J., Liao, H., & Tan, L. (2018). Clinical diagnosis and treatment of pediatric anti-N-methyl-D-aspartate receptor encephalitis: A single center retrospective study. *Experimental and Therapeutic Medicine, 16*(2), 1442–1448. https://doi.org/10.3892/etm.2018.6329

Sakpichaisakul, K., Patibat, L., Wechapinan, T., Sri-Udomkajrorn, S., Apiwattanakul, M., & Suwannachote, S. (2018). Heterogenous treatment for anti-NMDAR encephalitis in children leads to different outcomes 6–12 months after diagnosis. *Journal of Neuroimmunology, 324*, 119–125. https://doi.org/10.1016/j.jneuroim.2018.09.007

Sartori, S., Nosadini, M., Cesaroni, E., Falsaperla, R., Capovilla, G., Beccaria, F., … Suppiej, A. (2015). Paediatric anti-N-methyl-D-aspartate receptor encephalitis: The first Italian multicenter case series. *European Journal of Paediatric Neurology, 19*(4), 453–463. https://doi.org/10.1016/j.ejpn.2015.02.006

Scheer, S., & John, R. M. (2016). Anti-N-methyl-D-aspartate receptor encephalitis in children and adolescents. *Journal of Pediatric Health Care, 30*(4), 347–358. https://doi.org/10.1016/j.pedhc.2015.09.004

Schieveld, J. N., Staal, M., Voogd, L., Fincken, J., Vos, G., & van Os, J. (2010). Refractory agitation as a marker for pediatric delirium in very young infants at a pediatric intensive care unit. *Intensive Care Medicine, 36*(11), 1982–1983. https://doi-org.ezproxy.ub.unimaas.nl/10.1007/s00134-010-1989-z.

Schieveld, J. N. M., & Strik, J. J. M. H. (2018). Hypoactive delirium is more appropriately named as "acute apathy syndrome". *Critical Care Medicine, 46*(10), 1561–1562. https://doi.org/10.1097/CCM.0000000000003334

Schieveld, J. N. M., & Strik, J. J. M. H. (2021). A note on common apathy versus hypoactive delirium in critical illness. *Am American Journal of Respiratory and Critical Care Medicine, 12*. https://doi.org/10.1164/rccm.202011-4108LE (Open Access).

Schieveld, J. N. M., Strik, J. J. M. H., & Bruining, H. (2018). On benzodiazepines, paradoxical agitation, hyperactive delirium, and chloride homeostasis. *Critical Care Medicine, 46*(9), 1558–1559. https://doi.org/10.1097/CCM.0000000000003231

Schieveld, J., Strik, J., van Kraaij, S., & Nicolai, J. (2019). Psychiatric manifestations and psychopharmacology of autoimmune encephalitis: A multidisciplinary approach.

Handbook of Clinical Neurology, 165, 285–307. https://doi-org.ezproxy.ub.unimaas.nl/10.1016/B978-0-444-64012-3.00017-4.

Schieveld, J. N. M., van de Riet, E. H. C. W., & Strik, J. J. M. H. (2019). Between being healthy and becoming comatose: The neuropsychiatric landscape of critical illness with a focus on delirium, DSM-5 and ICD-11. *BMC Psychiatry, 16;19*(1), 222. https://doi.org/10.1186/s12888-019-2201-9

Schumacher, L. T., Mann, A. P., & MacKenzie, J. G. (2016). Agitation management in pediatric males with anti-N-methyl-D-aspartate receptor encephalitis. *Journal of Child and Adolescent Psychopharmacology, 26*(10), 939–943. https://doi.org/10.1089/cap.2016.0102

Singer, H. S. (2017). Autoantibody-associated movement disorders in children: Proven and proposed. *Seminars in Pediatric Neurology, 24*(3), 168–179. https://doi.org/10.1016/j.spen.2017.08.003

Stauder, K. H. (1934). Die tödliche Katatonie. *Archiv f. Psychiatrie, 102*, 614–634. https://doi.org/10.1007/BF01813829

Tektonidou, M. G., & Ward, M. M. (2011). Validation of new biomarkers in systemic autoimmune diseases. *Nature Reviews Rheumatology, 7*(12), 708–717. https://doi-org.ezproxy.ub.unimaas.nl/10.1038/nrrheum.2011.157.

Tong, L. L., Yang, X. F., Zhang, S. Q., Zhang, D. Q., Yang, X. R., Li, B. M., & Sheng, G. M. (2020). Clinical and EEG characteristics analysis of autoimmune encephalitis in children with positive and negative anti-N-methyl- D-aspartate receptor antibodies. *Annals of Palliative Medicine, 9*(5), 2575–2585. https://doi.org/10.21037/apm-19-484

Van der Zwaan, S., Blankespoor, R. J., Wolters, A. M., Creten, C., Leroy, P. L., & Schieveld, J. N. (2012). Additional use of methotrimeprazine for treating refractory agitation in pediatric patients. *Intensive Care Medicine, 38*(1), 175–176. https://doi-org.ezproxy.ub.unimaas.nl/10.1007/s00134-011-2414-y.

Vitaliani, R., Mason, W., Ances, B., Zwerdling, T., Jiang, Z., & Dalmau, J. (2005). Paraneoplastic encephalitis, psychiatric symptoms, and hypoventilation in ovarian teratoma. *Annals of Neurology, 58*(4), 594–604. https://doi-org.ezproxy.ub.unimaas.nl/10.1002/ana.20614.

Wang, Y., Zhang, W., Yin, J., Lu, Q., Yin, F., He, F., & Peng, J. (2017). Anti-N-methyl-d-aspartate receptor encephalitis in children of Central South China: Clinical features, treatment, influencing factors, and outcomes. *Journal of Neuroimmunology, 312*, 59–65. https://doi.org/10.1016/j.jneuroim.2017.09.005

Wise, M. G., Hilty, D. M., Cerda, G. M., & Trzepacz, P. T. (2002). Delirium (confusional states). In M. G. Wise, & J. R. Rundell (Eds.), *Textbook of consultation-liaison psychiatry in the medically ill* (pp. 257–272). Washington: American Psychiatric Publishing.

Wright, S., & Vincent, A. (2017). Pediatric autoimmune epileptic encephalopathies. *Journal of Child Neurology, 32*(4), 418–428. https://doi.org/10.1177/0883073816685505

Wright, S. K., & Wood, A. G. (2020). Neurodevelopmental outcomes in paediatric immune-mediated and autoimmune epileptic encephalopathy. *European Journal of Paediatric Neurology, 24*, 53–57. https://doi.org/10.1016/j.ejpn.2019.12.010

Xhao, J., Wang, C., Xu, X., Zhang, Y., Ren, H., Ren, Z., Gai, L., Zhang, J., & Guan, H. (2019). Coexistence of autoimmune encephalitis and other systemic autoimmune diseases. *Frontiers in Neurology, 31*, 406–428. https://doi.org/10.3389/fneur.2019.01142

Zhang, M., Li, W., Zhou, S., Zhou, Y., Yang, H., Yu, L., … Zhang, L. (2019). Clinical features, treatment, and outcomes among Chinese children with anti-methyl-D-aspartate receptor (Anti-NMDAR) encephalitis. *Frontiers in Neurology, 10*, 596. https://doi.org/10.3389/fneur.2019.00596

IV. Treatments for the future

Precision therapeutics—personalizing psychological therapy for depression in adolescents

Madison Aitken[1], Chelsea M. Durber[2], and Ian M. Goodyer[3]

[1] Cundill Centre for Child and Youth Depression, Centre for Addiction and Mental Health Department of Psychiatry, University of Toronto, Toronto, ON, Canada; [2] University of Alberta, Edmonton, AB, Canada; [3] Department of Psychiatry, University of Cambridge, Cambridge, England

1. Introduction

Depression is the most common mental health disorder in the world and is one of the largest contributors to global disability (Liu et al., 2020). Symptoms of depression often emerge before adulthood, with adolescence reflecting the most common age of onset (Avenevoli et al., 2015). In fact, depression is highly prevalent in adolescents, such that 7.5% have met diagnostic criteria for major depressive disorder within the past year, and 11% at any point in their lives (Avenevoli et al., 2015). Adolescents with depression are at risk for a range of negative outcomes later in life, including reduced school engagement and success, unemployment, and difficulties with peer and romantic relationships (Clayborne et al., 2019). Given the number of young people affected and the lasting negative effects, there is a great need for innovations that can improve outcomes for adolescents with depression. This chapter provides an overview of current efforts to improve psychological therapy outcomes for adolescent depression by selecting therapy approaches most likely to be helpful for a specific individual.

205

2. Psychological therapy for depression

Several psychological therapies for depression have demonstrated effectiveness with adolescents. Numerous treatment guidelines have been developed for adolescent depression (Bennett et al., 2018). We focus on recommendations in the National Institute for Health and Clinical Excellence (NICE) guidelines (NICE, 2019), because they are the most up-to-date of the guidelines for adolescent depression and were determined to be of high quality in a recent systematic review (Bennett et al., 2018).

For adolescents, the first-line psychological therapies for mild depression include digital or online cognitive behavioral therapy (CBT); group therapies, including CBT, interpersonal psychotherapy (IPT), and nondirective supportive therapy (NDST); individual CBT; as well as family therapy (NICE, 2019). For adolescents with moderate to severe depression, individual CBT is recommended as the first-line therapy, based on its ability to reduce symptoms of depression, lead to remission, improve functioning, and reduce suicidal ideation (NICE, 2019). The second-line psychological treatment options for adolescents with moderate to severe depression include IPT for adolescents (IPT-A), family therapy, brief psychosocial intervention (BPI; a goal-oriented therapy that provides psychoeducation about depression and focuses on increasing positive activities), and psychodynamic psychotherapy (NICE, 2019).

Unfortunately, up to 40% of adolescents with depression do not respond adequately to treatment (Goodyer & Wilkinson, 2019; Maalouf et al., 2011), and rates of relapse between 50% and 75% have been reported among those who do respond to treatment (Dunn & Goodyer, 2006). Given that a relatively large proportion of adolescents with depression do not benefit sufficiently from available evidence-based psychological therapies, it is essential to determine which individuals will benefit from what treatment, and why, to improve treatment outcomes.

3. Precision therapeutics

The term "precision medicine" is primarily used within the medical literature, often interchangeably with terms like personalized medicine (Bickman et al., 2016; Gillett et al., 2020). There is a growing focus on applying a precision, or personalized, approach to mental health, sometimes referred to as "precision therapeutics" (Aitken et al., 2020; Slater et al., 2015). Precision therapeutics refers to identifying which intervention will be most effective for an individual and why, and then tailoring psychological therapies to meet the individual's unique needs (Bickman et al., 2016; Ng & Weisz, 2016). The majority of research on precision therapeutics is explanatory, such that researchers have sought to identify the underlying mechanisms that drive behavior and treatment effects (Gillett et al., 2020; Wright & Woods, 2020). Other areas of focus within the precision therapeutics literature include personalizing intervention modalities or sequences and leveraging technology, such as smartphones, to tailor treatment to individual characteristics and changing needs (August & Gewirtz, 2019; Bickman et al., 2016; Gillett et al., 2020).

Precision therapeutics offers especially promising leads in the treatment of adolescent depression given the heterogeneity of clinical presentations and treatment response in this population (Chen et al., 2014; Liu et al., 2006). Rather than being a unitary construct, depression in adolescents is more accurately characterized as consisting of multiple interrelated dimensions, including dysphoric mood, physical symptoms, academic and behavioral problems, anhedonia, and maladaptive cognitions (Chen et al., 2014). Adolescents with depression also have high rates of comorbidity, with anxiety disorders, obsessive compulsive disorder, attention deficit/hyperactivity disorder, and oppositional defiant disorder being especially common additional diagnoses (Avenevoli et al., 2015; March et al., 2005). There is also considerable heterogeneity in how adolescents respond to psychological therapy, with a substantial minority showing an abrupt plateau in symptom reduction following the initial weeks of therapy (Davies et al., 2020), or not experiencing any significant symptom improvement (Scott et al., 2019), whereas other adolescents experience a rapid response to treatment (Renaud et al., 1998). Precision therapeutics starts with the assumption of heterogeneity in psychopathology presentations and treatment response, meaning that it may allow a personalized approach to treatment planning for adolescent depression (Wright & Woods, 2020). In the following, we review current clinical and research approaches to precision therapeutics for adolescent depression and highlight an example from our own research using the general psychopathology factor.

3.1 Testing moderators of treatment outcome

The majority of research on personalizing treatment for adolescent depression has focused on identifying individual characteristics that may moderate or predict treatment outcomes, to optimize treatment selection (Fisher & Bosley, 2015; Wright & Woods, 2020). Researchers have examined many potential moderator and predictor variables, including biomarkers (e.g., genetics, neuroimaging), clinical features (e.g., depression severity), and sociodemographic characteristics (e.g., gender, age) (van Bronswijk et al., 2019). In adults with depression, the strongest predictor of treatment outcomes is baseline depression severity, with greater severity indicating poorer treatment outcomes (American Psychiatric Association, 2010; Huang et al., 2014; Webb et al., 2019). However, many other significant moderators of treatment outcomes for adolescent depression have been identified, including comorbid anxiety or conduct problems, family relationship problems, and the presence of suicidal ideation or self-harm (Brent et al., 1999; Davies et al., 2020; Nilsen et al., 2013; Wilkinson et al., 2011). There is also some evidence that adolescents who are older, who have lower verbal abilities, or who exhibit more conduct problems, are more likely to drop out of treatment for depression than other adolescents (O'Keeffe et al., 2018). That said, no single variable has been found to reliably predict treatment outcomes for depression (Simon & Perlis, 2010), likely because depression is too clinically heterogenous in its presentation and prognosis to be accurately predicted by one variable (Cohen & Derubeis, 2018; van Bronswijk et al., 2019).

3.2 Matching individuals with treatments

The various psychological therapy approaches available for adolescent depression target different factors believed to underlie and/or maintain depressive symptoms. For example, cognitive behavioral approaches target maladaptive thinking patterns and aim to increase adaptive behavior (Sburlati et al., 2014), whereas interpersonal approaches aim to reduce depression by improving current relationships and social functioning (Moreau et al., 1991). A small number of studies have tested the effects of matching adolescents to treatments for depression based on their clinical profiles. For example, Young and colleagues assessed community adolescents' cognitive and interpersonal risks at baseline and then randomly assigned them to a preventive intervention based on CBT or IPT-A principles (Young et al., 2020). They found that adolescents whose assigned intervention matched their risk profile (cognitive vs. interpersonal risks) had fewer depression symptoms across postintervention and follow-up than adolescents mismatched to intervention. While further research is needed in larger samples and in samples of adolescents experiencing clinical levels of depression, these results provide preliminary evidence that a personalized approach to matching adolescents to treatment based on their individual profile may improve treatment outcomes.

3.3 Machine learning approaches

Machine learning is a domain of computer science with its base in computational mathematics and statistics. Machine learning is an iterative process in which a large volume of information is used to develop an algorithm that can be used to make predictions. In psychiatry, machine learning has been used to identify patterns in baseline data that best predict a predetermined outcome such as clinical recovery, defined as no longer meeting clinical criteria for major depression after receiving treatment: this is known as supervised learning because the algorithm uses data to predict a defined outcome (see Tiffin and Paton, chapter 4, this volume). Alternatively, and perhaps more powerfully, the algorithm can identify all patterns in baseline data and use these patterns to predict groups of individuals who subsequently show more or less treatment response over time: this means the algorithm gets no help to learn which individuals had a good or a poor outcome. In effect, unsupervised learning can be used to cluster individuals from a set of variables assessed at baseline whose predictive effects on treatment response and outcomes are not known. A third type of machine learning is referred to as machine reinforcement learning, which is probably the closest to how we as humans learn. In this case, the computer learns continually from its environment by interacting with it. In psychiatry, for example, this method can be applied when measures are repeated over time such as in a randomized controlled trial. For example, adolescents with severe depression at baseline can be hypothesized as less likely to respond to treatment. Reassessment during treatment may reveal a cluster of individuals with more severe depression at baseline who indeed do not appear to respond. This result will reinforce the original prediction and, importantly, improve the algorithm's ability to identify factors that may contribute to poor treatment response. In reinforcement mode, the computer learns how effective baseline severity is as a predictor of outcome as treatment progresses by taking subsequent information into account. This information helps the algorithm to make better clinical decisions about the trajectory of recovery and the likelihood of treatment response. Machine learning is therefore a set of techniques that, by using a range of computational patterning methods, may optimize prediction of an outcome and, importantly, help to make better clinical decisions about what is in the best interest of an individual with depression as treatment proceeds (Aafjes-van Doorn et al., 2021; Tiffin and Paton, chapter 4, this volume).

To date, there are very few machine learning analyses reported from randomized controlled trials of adolescent depression. The techniques have, however, been applied to a number of studies of adults with depression. For example, the Personalized Advantage Index (PAI; DeRubeis et al., 2014) is one widely used approach to treatment response prediction based on machine learning. The PAI method compares the outcomes of two or more treatments based on the inclusion of baseline factors (e.g., severity, family history, mental illness history) and then provides a personalized treatment recommendation. From the analysis, an estimate of the percentage advantage of implementing the indicated treatment compared with the nonindicated treatment can be reported (Huibers et al., 2015; van Bronswijk et al., 2019; Webb et al., 2019). Matching individuals with treatments based on a pattern of background factors and clinical factors may help identify what treatment works best for which individual (Huibers et al., 2015; van Bronswijk et al., 2019). However, replicable estimators of treatment response have not yet been found, and the method, while promising, has not delivered results of sufficient reliability for clinical practice (DeRubeis et al., 2014; van Bronswijk et al., 2019). Only one study has reported results of PAI on adolescent depression, suggesting baseline depression severity, a history of childhood trauma, and positive expectations of treatment may predict value for CBT with medication compared with medication alone (Foster et al., 2019).

3.4 SMART designs

Sequential Multiple Assignment Randomized Trial (SMART) methods involve randomly assigning participants to various treatment conditions at several points during the course of a trial. Individuals can also be assigned to the same condition more than once, depending on the design (Collins et al., 2007). SMART designs provide information on ways to optimize the timing and sequencing of intervention components (Collins et al., 2007) and can inform decisions about when to change treatment approaches if individuals are not responding (Gunlicks-Stoessel et al., 2016).

Despite their usefulness for informing treatment decisions, uptake of SMART designs in psychological therapy research has been slow and only a handful of studies have applied this method in trials targeting adolescent depression. As an example, Gunlicks-Stoessel and colleagues used a SMART design to test early versus late decision points for augmentations to weekly IPT-A for adolescents with depression (Gunlicks-Stoessel et al., 2019). Participants were randomized to a decision point at 4 weeks (early) or 8 weeks (late). At their assigned decision point, those who had not shown a sufficient response (20% symptom reduction) in weekly IPT-A were randomized either to the addition of fluoxetine or to more frequent IPT-A. They found that adolescents in the early decision-point arm had fewer depression symptoms at posttreatment than adolescents in the late decision-point arm, providing some of the first evidence supporting early review of response and modifications to the treatment plan for adolescents not showing a sufficient response to treatment. The benefits of the early decision point were only detected for adolescents randomized to augmentation by more frequent IPT-A, suggesting that it may be especially important to modify psychological therapy plans sooner than later when adolescents are not responding to standard treatment

(Gunlicks-Stoessel et al., 2019). With further research and applications to a broader range of evidence-based treatments, it is likely that SMART will provide more information that clinicians can use to personalize treatment decisions for adolescent depression.

3.5 Measurement-based care

Measurement-based care involves the systematic measurement of individual outcomes over time and the use of this information to inform treatment decisions (Scott & Lewis, 2015). An additional feature of measurement-based care is its inclusion of the individual in a collaborative decision-making process, based on the information gathered and their personal priorities (Connors et al., 2021). By collecting information on symptom and/or functioning change over time, clinicians may be better equipped to determine what modifications are needed and when during the course of an intervention for a specific individual (Morris et al., 2012). For example, it is recommended in the current guidelines for the treatment of adolescent depression that there be a multidisciplinary review of the treatment plan, with consideration of adding to or changing the psychological therapy if a young person has not experienced a reduction in symptoms after 4—6 psychotherapy sessions (NICE, 2019).

Across primarily adult samples with a range of presenting concerns, metaanalytic effect sizes for measurement-based care are moderate to large (0.49—0.70; Connors et al., 2021). However, a recent review of the literature testing the effects of measurement-based care with adolescents reported inconsistent outcomes across studies and concluded that evidence is not sufficient at present to determine whether measurement-based care improves adolescents' treatment outcomes (Bergman et al., 2018). Fortunately, several trials are currently underway that will provide additional information to inform the use of measurement-based care for adolescents with depression and other emotional—behavioral disorders (Bergman et al., 2018).

3.6 The general psychopathology factor as a treatment outcome

While there is little doubt that personalized models hold great promise for improving outcomes for adolescent depression, progress in identifying individual characteristics that consistently predict treatment outcomes, and could therefore be used to guide treatment decisions, has been slow. An alternative approach to personalizsing interventions may, somewhat paradoxically, be derived by changing our level of analysis and separating out broad and specific effects of psychological therapy on psychopathology (Haltigan, 2019).

The general psychopathology ("p") factor is derived using bifactor modeling and captures shared variance in symptoms across the spectrum of psychopathology (see Fig. 8.1; Caspi et al., 2014; Caspi & Moffitt, 2018; Haltigan et al., 2018). This general psychopathology factor appears to reflect an overall liability to psychopathology and has been described as an indicator of relevant transdiagnostic processes, such as emotion dysregulation, negative emotionality, and maladaptive or distorted thoughts (Carver et al., 2017; Caspi & Moffitt, 2018). An increasing body of evidence supports the validity of the general psychopathology factor. For example, higher general psychopathology factor scores are associated with increased suicidal ideation and/or behavior (Haltigan et al., 2018) and delinquency (Waldman et al., 2016) and are predictive of negative outcomes across development, including increased rates of psychiatric diagnosis and psychotropic medication use, poor academic achievement, and criminal convictions (Pettersson et al., 2018).

In addition to the general psychopathology factor, bifactor modeling also generates specific psychopathology factors, representing narrower aspects of psychopathology once shared variance has been accounted for by the general psychopathology factor (Caspi et al., 2014). Thus, these specific factors represent relatively pure constructs. In studies of child and adolescent psychopathology, these often include internalizing, externalizing, and thought problems (Caspi et al., 2014; Laceulle et al., 2015; Patalay et al., 2015), although different sets of specific factors have been derived, depending on the measures being used (Brodbeck et al., 2014; Constantinou et al., 2019; St Clair et al., 2017). For example, in Fig. 8.1, the specific psychopathology factors identified include melancholic features,

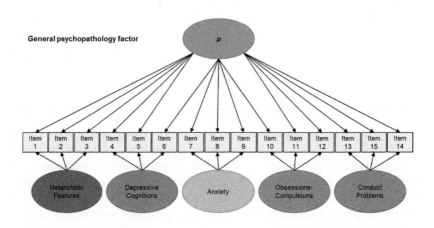

FIGURE 8.1   Bifactor model of psychopathology.

depressive cognitions, anxiety, obsessions/compulsions, and conduct problems (Aitken et al., 2020). While some caution is warranted given the generally lower reliability of the specific factors compared with the general psychopathology factor (Aitken et al., 2020; Haltigan et al., 2018), there is also evidence that these specific factors are meaningful and predictive of important outcomes, such as sleep, risky sexual behavior, and self-esteem (Sunderland et al., 2020).

A small number of studies have used the general psychopathology factor, along with specific psychopathology or personality factors, as outcomes to evaluate the effects of various therapies (Constantinou et al., 2019; Wade et al., 2018). These studies, conducted in adolescents participating in psychological therapy for conduct problems (Constantinou et al., 2019) and in institutionalized children placed in foster care (Wade et al., 2018), have consistently demonstrated that psychological therapy interventions have broad effects on psychopathology.

4. The general psychopathology factor and response to psychological therapy in the IMPACT trial

How, then, might the general psychopathology factor increase our understanding of precision therapeutics for adolescent depression? We summarize the results of our own analysis of the effects of three psychological therapies targeting adolescent depression on general and specific psychopathology factors and discuss their implications for precision therapeutics.

The Improving Mood with Psychoanalytic and Cognitive Therapies (IMPACT) trial was a pragmatic randomized superiority effectiveness trial for adolescent depression conducted at multiple National Health Service (NHS) Child and Adolescent Mental Health Services sites in the United Kingdom (Goodyer et al., 2011, 2017a, 2017b). Adolescents aged 11−17 years ($N = 465$) with a primary diagnosis of major depressive disorder were randomly assigned to one of three psychological therapies: (1) CBT, (2) short-term psychoanalytic psychotherapy (STPP), or (3) brief psychosocial intervention (BPI; Cregeen et al., 2017; Goodyer et al., 2017b). The primary goal of the trial was to compare the effects of the established psychological therapies (CBT and STPP) with BPI, an active control condition developed to be similar to routine care in the community. As this was a pragmatic trial, adolescents were prescribed medication as usual by their physician, and 30% of adolescents were prescribed a selective serotonin reuptake inhibitor (SSRI) during the trial.

The main outcome paper from the IMPACT trial used linear mixed effects models to compare the effects of the three treatment approaches on total depression, anxiety, obsessions/compulsions, and antisocial behaviors. CBT, STPP, and BPI were associated with similar decreases in depression symptoms from pre- to posttreatment (36 weeks) and one-year follow-up (Goodyer et al., 2017b). Anxiety, obsessions/compulsions, and antisocial behaviors were significantly lower posttreatment in the established therapies (CBT and STPP) than in BPI, although these differences were nonsignificant at one-year follow-up (Goodyer et al., 2017b). Inspired by the seemingly broad treatment effects in the IMPACT trial, we used bifactor modeling to extract a general psychopathology factor, along with five specific factors (melancholic features, depressive cognitions, anxiety, obsessions/compulsions, and conduct problems), based on adolescent self-report ratings. We then examined change in the general and specific psychopathology factors across treatment and follow-up in the whole sample and in each treatment condition.

We found that participating in psychological therapy was primarily associated with decreases in general psychopathology (see Fig. 8.2).

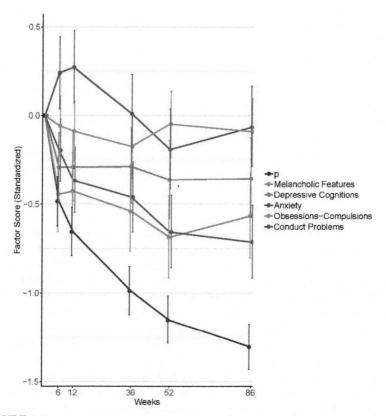

FIGURE 8.2 Change in general and specific psychopathology factors across treatment and follow-up in adolescents in the IMPACT trial.

General factor scores decreased significantly between each time point (6, 12, 36, and 52 weeks from baseline), although no further significant changes were observed between 52 weeks and the final follow-up at 86 weeks (Aitken et al., 2020). Our reanalysis using bifactor modeling suggests that even when treatments are designed to reduce depression specifically, effects are generally broad and are not limited to the disorder being targeted. Broad decreases in psychopathology may be due to improvements in transdiagnostic processes theorized to underlie the general psychopathology factor, including emotion dysregulation, maladaptive cognitions, and negative emotionality (Aitken et al., 2020; Asarnow et al., 2009; Carver et al., 2017; Caspi & Moffitt, 2018).

When we compared the effects of the three types of psychological therapies (CBT, STPP, and BPI) on general psychopathology, we found that the three treatments had comparable effects. These findings are consistent with evidence noting the importance of the "common factors" of psychological therapy (Messer & Wampold, 2006; Wampold, 2015). According to the common factors view, therapeutic approaches share components, including the therapeutic relationship (e.g., therapist empathy, alliance with therapist), an understanding by individuals of their disorder and its treatment, and expectations that therapy may be helpful (Wampold, 2015), which collectively explain a substantial portion of the effects of psychological therapy. Therefore, it is possible that participation in psychological therapy with a skilled clinician has broad effects on psychopathology for adolescent depression and that these broad effects may explain a substantial proportion of treatment outcomes.

When we examined change in the specific factors, we found quite a different pattern than what was reported in the original IMPACT trial analysis (see Fig. 8.2). It is at this level that a more detailed understanding of treatment response for adolescent depression may be gained. First, we found that specific melancholic features and depressive cognitions decreased significantly from baseline to 6 weeks and then remained relatively stable across the remainder of treatment and follow-up. Additionally, specific conduct problems decreased significantly from baseline to 6 weeks and then showed a protracted but significant decrease across treatment and follow-up. We interpret these results as evidence that psychological therapy for adolescent depression seems to exert initial effects on overall psychopathology *and* on specific depression-oriented factors (melancholic, cognitive) and conduct problem factors. Thus, psychological therapy for depression has both broad and specific effects in the initial weeks.

We also found that the specific obsessions/compulsions factor was relatively stable and did not change significantly across treatment, and the specific anxiety factor showed an unexpected pattern, increasing significantly from baseline to 6 weeks and then returning to baseline levels by the end of treatment (36 weeks; see Fig. 8.2). We interpret the lack of improvement in obsessions/compulsions and anxiety as evidence that these specific factors are not amenable to psychological therapy for depression. Instead, improvements in obsessions/compulsions and anxiety during treatment for depression demonstrated in previous analyses (Goodyer et al., 2017b) may be primarily due to decreases in overall psychopathology, rather than disorder-specific improvements. Given that higher specific anxiety and obsessions/compulsions factor scores were associated with significantly lower impairment in our analysis, these residual symptoms may not require additional focused intervention. These results shed new light on how therapy for adolescent depression differentially influences broad and specific aspects of psychopathology across treatment and follow-up.

We also found that the three therapies (CBT, STPP, and BPI) had similar effects on the specific psychopathology factors, with one exception: the specific conduct problems factor decreased significantly more in BPI than in CBT from posttreatment (36 weeks) to follow-up (52 weeks; see Fig. 8.3). Decreases in specific conduct problems in the BPI condition were also maintained at the final 86-week follow-up. These findings were especially noteworthy given that BPI was developed as the control

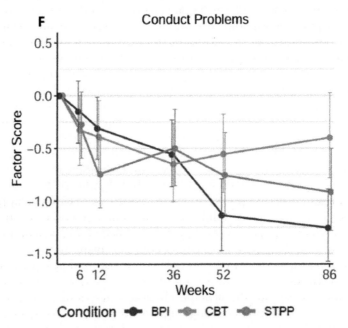

FIGURE 8.3 Change in specific conduct problem factor (derived through bifactor modeling) in three treatment conditions.

condition and was expected to be associated with fewer gains in treatment than the established psychological therapies (CBT and STPP). Instead, our findings suggest that a relatively brief, goal-oriented, supportive approach may be especially helpful for specific conduct problems that may be present alongside depression symptoms.

5. Incorporating individual preferences

The approaches to personalizing intervention for adolescent depression reviewed before have all focused on using research evidence to guide treatment decisions; however, there is increasing recognition of the value of incorporating the preferences of the individual in treatment decisions (Winter & Barber, 2013). Individuals may be more likely to agree to receive a proposed treatment, more engaged during the treatment process, and less likely to discontinue treatment early when the treatment is more acceptable to them (Winter & Barber, 2013). Available treatments for adolescent depression vary in how acceptable they are to adolescents. For example, adolescents perceive individual counseling or psychological therapy as more acceptable treatment options than medication or family therapy for depression (Caporino & Karver, 2012; Jaycox et al., 2006). In addition, there is some evidence that comprehensive, team-based approaches that take into account the adolescent and family's preferences are associated with significantly better adolescent depression outcomes than standard care (Asarnow et al., 2005). However, a study of adults with depression found that those randomly assigned to their preferred treatment were less likely to drop out but had comparable outcomes to those not matched to their preferred treatment (Dunlop et al., 2017). Further research is therefore needed to isolate the unique benefits of individual preferences in terms of treatment outcomes versus retention alone.

6. Issues and prospects

The past five decades have seen a marked improvement in how we recognize and treat depression in adolescents. Utilizing the diagnostic classification systems that have emerged over this time has undoubtedly led to an increase in our understanding of this etiologically and clinically heterogenous mental disorder. We now accept that adolescence is a period when major depression episodes typically first emerge with measurable incidence in the human life course. Understanding how neuromaturation influences the liability for mental illnesses in general, and depressions in particular, over the adolescent age range is a key research theme to help understand causal mechanisms and processes involved in onsets and, we suggest, in therapeutics. Currently, we have a list of candidate risk factors from both genetic and environmental research, but we know little about how such factors operate together at the level of the brain and mind. Precision psychiatry will benefit when we have a better understanding as to whether causal mechanisms contribute to therapeutic decision-making through effects on treatment sensitivities, outcome trajectories, and liabilities for relapse and chronicity.

We have come to recognize that clinical diagnoses, while immensely valuable in the reliable classification of mental illnesses and behavioral syndromes, have low validity for therapeutic precision. We have to consider the critical importance of clinical heterogeneity and its effects on therapeutics. We have outlined how modern multivariate techniques are contributing to efforts to reclassify mental disorders with greater validity than hitherto. These methods should be pursued in both longitudinal cohorts and trials data sets so that we can unravel the value of methodologies revealing mechanisms of therapeutic action.

A further complementary multivariate method is to examine the value inherent in each item rather than start with a construct based theoretically on a cluster of items (Fried & Nesse, 2014, 2015). One such theory proposes that items such as "I feel sad" or "I am worthless" are only of psychopathological value when they are understood in their relationship to each other. Examining the role of selected items with therapeutic mechanisms of action in mind may be a highly effective additional method of determining what treatment works for whom or when treatments work best (Ng & Weisz, 2016). Such approaches may also identify items that are of more or less value for developmental reasons during adolescence than they are at other periods in the life course. Might an interaction between two items be of value in understanding depression with greater precision than a factorial model of many items? For example, examining a set of clinical interview schedules assessing for major depression in over 3000 adolescents with depression has suggested that some symptoms reflected higher levels of depression and were more discriminating than others (Cole et al., 2011). According to item response theory, these results indicate that the assumption that items purporting to measure depression carry equal value for the diagnosis is not true. Indeed, one source of clinical error for therapeutics may be that treatments target symptoms that are in fact low in validity for diagnosis and treatment response. This risk of low item validity in adolescence was demonstrated in the same study of clinical assessment data which, using item response theory, noted that changes in shape and weight are in fact more likely to reflect general changes in physical growth than they are part of a clinical diagnosis of depression (Cole et al., 2011). In other words, asking adolescents about recent changes in shape, weight, diet, and appetite may only be of value knowing their growth maturation and not just their current mental state (Maxwell & Cole, 2009). Thus, focusing treatment on the weight of an adolescent with depression may have no therapeutic effects if they are merely following their expected growth curve. Considerable interest is also now being shown in how the connections between items, rather than their individual differences, may be important to a diagnosis (Schweren et al., 2018; Van Borkulo et al., 2015). There may be important elements of clinical therapeutic validity in the connections between items for both clinical typologies and treatment planning purposes.

6.1 Mental components as a network

In addition to the importance of individual "symptoms" such as "I feel sad," the connectivity between self-reported symptoms can be computationally defined to reveal potential patterns of moods, thoughts, and feeling sensations of differing strengths over time (Borsboom, 2017). Such mental network structures may be complementary and related to hierarchical bifactor models, and both the structures and models may aid in revealing phenotype precision, thereby informing psychological therapy selection. One interesting aspect of networks is the strength of association between items. For example, a sparse network is one that has fewer links (pairwise associations) than the number of components that could be linked. In contrast, a dense network is where every component is linked with every other. The functional consequences for therapeutics are as yet unclear, although knowing expected mental network density in well adolescents would be worthwhile to determine what connections may be abnormal (McElroy et al., 2018). Currently, sparse networks are being noted as potentially indexing a high degree of functionality within their fewer interactions. This observation is accompanied by a growing consensus that denser networks may contain interactions between components that are not truly functional (Cramer et al., 2012, 2016). Thus, high connectivity in adolescents with depression may be an effortful but inefficient recruitment of mental components whose functional contribution to resolving suboptimal information processing may be trivial or even additionally dysfunctional.

One of the common mechanisms inferred from the treatment equivalence in the IMPACT trial may be that overly dense networks are disaggregated in certain respects by treatments. A pilot examination suggested, for example, that local density may exist between poor concentration and increased agitation that is sensitive to psychological therapies, thereby reducing the mental illness (Schweren et al., 2018). Future studies should consider revealing the network characteristics of the connectivity that exists in the current mental state. These future results may implicate the importance of interactions between items, which may differ across items and across results derived from extant item or subscale analyses. Such analyses may reveal the interconnections between symptoms that are more or less treatment sensitive, which could help improve the validity of therapeutic decision-making.

6.2 Therapeutic biomarkers

Therapeutic precision would be greatly enhanced when we have identified biomarkers that predict treatment response. These biomarkers would allow clinicians to add an index not observable through clinical assessment alone. Currently, most studies have looked for biomarkers as indexing causality or natural course of disorder. These are of course essential in their own right, but we should not assume that any such discoveries are of themselves predicting treatment response. Of value to the clinician would be a test that was evidence for prescribing a particular treatment or, equally of value, for not prescribing one. Some such therapeutic markers may well be found in clinical history or presentation. For example, current maternal mental illness may be associated with a need for greater intervention in adolescent offspring experiencing depression (Brent et al., 2015). Peripheral physiological markers may also aid treatment decision-making: for example, a slower response to treatment is associated with higher baseline evening cortisol (within the normal physiological range; Chadha et al., 2021): this effect of elevated evening cortisol on treatment response is shown in Fig. 8.4. Here the reduction in self-reported depression scores is slower in those with evening salivary

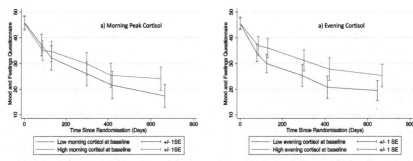

FIGURE 8.4 Growth trajectories of depressive symptoms, with sample split by median cortisol at baseline at morning peak (A) and evening (B). Each point on the graph shows mean depressive symptoms and mean time since randomization for that group at that planned assessment point.

cortisol levels above the median for this sample of adolescents with depression.

Importantly, this corticoid-mediated slower recovery was not associated with self-reported depression scores at baseline so this is not merely an epiphenomenon of more severe illness. Note that there is no such effect for elevated morning cortisol levels, which is associated with programming the hypothalamic—pituitary—adrenal (HPA) axis, and not with mental illness. Elevated evening cortisol levels found on two nights in a row might provide additional information for the clinician that a slower time to recovery might be expected. Other peripheral biomarkers may include proinflammatory indices, but these have yet to be introduced into clinical trials and therapeutics research in adolescents with depression.

Finally, more central markers from both cognitive and imaging neurosciences may likely provide information about individual differences in brain and mental function and whether information from these parameters might act as moderators of treatment response. For example, in the IMPACT study, neural connectivity in the association cortices decreases with a good response to psychological treatment, suggesting that, as with mental networks, there is a more dense neural connectivity during depression that is sensitive to treatment (Chattopadhyay et al., 2017; Villa et al., 2020).

7. Depressed adolescents in the developing world

We need to remember that almost all research to date has taken place in high- and middle-income countries (HMICs) despite the fact that more than 85% of the world's population live in the 153 low- and middle-income countries (LMICs). Furthermore, more than 80% of people who have mental disorders, including substance abuse, are residing in LMICs. Overall, up to 16.6% of the total burden of disease in LMICs is due to mental illnesses. There are many challenges in the provision of mental health services in LMICs including the importance of sociocultural factors in service delivery, training a mental health workforce and embedding mental health funding in healthcare policy (Rathod et al., 2017). Psychotherapeutic interventions are not currently included in mainstream treatments in many LMICs. This can be attributed to two main reasons: lack of resources and inadequate training. Cultural and religious attributes of illness and belief systems also exert considerable influence on help-seeking behavior and may further complicate access to services, implementation of psychological treatments, and therefore outcomes for mental health problems. Many individuals first seek help from complementary practitioners or spiritual or faith healers. Depression is, however, predicted to be a major source of morbidity in LMICs by the middle of this century emphasizing the need for the implementation and evaluation of culturally acceptable psychological interventions. While many of the aforementioned research methods have direct applicability to LMIC services, sociocultural factors are likely important in determining precise treatments that may be acceptable to the populations concerned. This is a key mental health policy issue, as adolescents make up a large proportion (between 20% and 50%) of the total populations in many LMICs. Classical psychological intervention developed in HMICs given to young depressed people may be unacceptable to subsections of the population, as it can clash with cultural and family values and religious beliefs concerning the origins of the mind and the ability to be in charge of and change one's own life course. Interventions that focus formally on external interpersonal relations including environment systems such as schools and neighborhoods may be preferable in such circumstances. Additionally briefer more direct problem-solving and solution-focused strategies that offer both an understanding of the disordered mind and behavior together with a method to return to a state of well-being may be acceptable. From the perspectives of the many LMICs with adolescent populations reporting high mental morbidity, considerably more research into what works for whom is urgently needed.

We contend it is likely that many of the design aspects developed in HMIC-based research discussed in previous sections of this chapter will be applicable in LMICs. To date, however, there have been very few trials of treatment for anxiety and depression in LMICs, and while the preliminary data are suggestive that active interventions are significantly better than control conditions, there remain no clear and confirmatory effects for any particular treatment (Uppendahl et al., 2020). As noted before, focused interventions using external strategies such as social prescribing, behavioral activation, and interpersonal methods are likely to be more acceptable to youth living in LMICs. Selecting the precise types of interventions for depressed young people will need to take a range of sociocultural values into account in future research trials and clinical service developments and consider how to reach many young people who will have little or no access to traditional walk in services in hospitals and community centers.

8. Summary and implications

Adolescent depression is a heterogenous condition with high rates of nonresponse, despite the availability of multiple empirically supported psychological therapy approaches (Eckshtain et al., 2020; Maalouf et al., 2011; NICE, 2019). Efforts to personalize intervention to date have focused on selecting the best fitting treatment at the outset, based on an individual's clinical profile derived through simple screening measures (Young et al., 2020) or an algorithm derived through machine learning (Foster et al., 2019). Other approaches to personalization focus on decisions about when to modify an adolescents' treatment plan, such as measurement-based care and SMART (Gunlicks-Stoessel et al., 2019; Morris et al., 2012), or incorporating the preferences of the adolescent seeking treatment (Asarnow et al., 2005).

Several key messages can be distilled from the studies reviewed before. First, there is evidence that limited response to psychological therapy in the initial phase of treatment for adolescents with depression is an indication that it may be beneficial to update the treatment plan, such as by increasing the intensity of psychological therapy or adding fluoxetine (Gunlicks-Stoessel et al., 2019). Although measurement-based care alone has not yet demonstrated clear benefits for adolescent psychological therapy outcomes (Bergman et al., 2018), it is certainly essential for monitoring treatment response and informing treatment modifications. Second, we are beginning to learn more about the information that may be most useful to base personalization decisions on through machine learning–derived personalized prediction algorithms (van Bronswijk et al., 2019), as well as approaches that more closely resemble clinicians' decision-making processes, such as selecting a treatment approach based on underlying risk factors (Young et al., 2020) or by engaging adolescents in a collaborative process of treatment planning (Asarnow et al., 2005). While these approaches hold great promise, further research is needed to provide guidance clinicians can use in practice, especially for treating adolescent depression. Lastly, a transdiagnostic perspective on psychopathology based on the general psychopathology factor provides additional insights, demonstrating that current psychological therapies for adolescent depression have broad effects on overall psychopathology that continue across treatment and follow-up, as well as specific effects on depression- and conduct-related psychopathology that occur in the initial weeks of therapy. In addition, there is some evidence that a supportive, goal-oriented therapy approach (BPI) may be especially effective at treating specific conduct problems in adolescents with depression.

The field of precision therapeutics as applied to adolescent depression is in its infancy, and much work remains to be done. Particularly promising areas for further research include the development of predictive treatment algorithms, such as the PAI, for adolescents; the use of SMART to test a wider variety of treatment sequences and modifications; the use of the general and specific psychopathology factors as treatment outcomes for additional psychological therapy approaches, including transdiagnostic treatments; and the identification of therapeutically sensitive symptom networks and biomarkers that predict treatment response.

References

Aafjes-van Doorn, K., Kamsteeg, C., Bate, J., & Aafjes, M. (2021). A scoping review of machine learning in psychotherapy research. *Psychotherapy Research, 31*(1), 92—116. https://doi.org/10.1080/10503307.2020.1808729

Aitken, M., Haltigan, J. D., Szatmari, P., Dubicka, B., Fonagy, P., Kelvin, R., Midgley, N., Reynolds, S., Wilkinson, P. O., & Goodyer, I. M. (2020). Toward precision therapeutics: General and specific factors differentiate symptom change in depressed adolescents. *Journal of Child Psychology and Psychiatry and Allied Disciplines, 61*(9), 998—1008. https://doi.org/10.1111/jcpp.13194

Asarnow, J. R., Emslie, G., Clarke, G., Wagner, K. D., Spirito, A., Vitiello, B., Iyengar, S., Shamseddeen, W., Ritz, L., Birmaher, B., Ryan, N., Kennard, B., Mayes, T., DeBar, L., McCracken, J., Strober, M., Suddath, R., Leonard, H., Porta, G., … Brent, D. (2009). Treatment of selective serotonin reuptake inhibitor-resistant depression in adolescents: Predictors and moderators of treatment response. *Journal of the American Academy of Child and Adolescent Psychiatry, 48*(3), 330—339. https://doi.org/10.1097/CHI.0b013e3181977476

Asarnow, J. R., Jaycox, L. H., Duan, N., LaBorde, A. P., Rea, M. M., Murray, P., Anderson, M., Landon, C., Tang, L., & Wells, K. B. (2005). Effectiveness of a quality improvement intervention for adolescent depression in primary care clinics: A randomized controlled trial. *Journal of the American Medical Association, 293*(3), 311—319. https://doi.org/10.1001/jama.293.3.311

August, G. J., & Gewirtz, A. (2019). Moving toward a precision-based, personalized framework for prevention science: Introduction to the special issue. *Prevention Science, 20*(1), 1—9. https://doi.org/10.1007/s11121-018-0955-9

Avenevoli, S., Swendsen, J., He, J., Burstein, M., Merikangas, K., & Activities, E. (2015). Major depression in the national comorbidity survey-adolescent supplement: Prevalence, correlates, and treatment. *Journal of the American Academy of Child & Adolescent Psychiatry, 54*(1), 37—44. https://doi.org/10.1016/j.jaac.2014.10.010

Bennett, K., Courtney, D., Duda, S., Henderson, J., & Szatmari, P. (2018). An appraisal of the trustworthiness of practice guidelines for depression and anxiety in children and youth. *Depression and Anxiety, 35*(6), 530—540. https://doi.org/10.1002/da.22752

Bergman, H., Kornør, H., Nikolakopoulou, A., Hanssen-Bauer, K., Soares-Weiser, K., Tollefsen, T., & Bjørndal, A. (2018). Client feedback in psychological therapy for children and adolescents with mental health problems. *Cochrane Database of Systematic Reviews, 8*, 1—67. https://doi.org/10.1002/14651858.CD011729.pub2.www.cochranelibrary.com

Bickman, L., Lyon, A. R., & Wolpert, M. (2016). Achieving precision mental health through effective assessment, monitoring, and feedback processes: Introduction to the special issue. *Administration and Policy in Mental Health and Mental Health Services Research, 43*(3), 271—276. https://doi.org/10.1007/s10488-016-0718-5

Borsboom, D. (2017). A network theory of mental disorders. *World Psychiatry, 16*(1), 5—13. https://doi.org/10.1002/wps.20375

Brent, D. A., Brunwasser, S. M., Hollon, S. D., Weersing, V. R., Clarke, G. N., Dickerson, J. F., Beardslee, W. R., Gladstone, T. R. G., Porta, G., Lynch, F. L., Iyengar, S., & Garber, J. (2015). Effect of a cognitive-behavioral prevention program on depression 6 years after implementation among at-risk adolescents: A randomized clinical trial. *JAMA Psychiatry, 72*(11), 1110—1118. https://doi.org/10.1001/jamapsychiatry.2015.1559

Brent, D. A., Kolko, D. J., Birmaher, B., Baugher, M., & Bridge, J. (1999). A clinical trial for adolescent depression: Predictors of additional treatment in the acute and follow-up phases of the trial. *Journal of the American Academy of Child and Adolescent Psychiatry, 38*(3), 263—270. https://doi.org/10.1097/00004583-199903000-00012

Brodbeck, J., Goodyer, I. M., Abbott, R. A., Dunn, V. J., St Clair, M. C., Owens, M., Jones, P. B., & Croudace, T. J. (2014). General distress, hopelessness-suicidal ideation and worrying in adolescence: Concurrent and predictive validity of a symptom-level bifactor model for clinical diagnoses. *Journal of Affective Disorders, 152−154*(1), 299−305. https://doi.org/10.1016/j.jad.2013.09.029

van Bronswijk, S. C., DeRubeis, R. J., Lemmens, L. H. J. M., Peeters, F. P. M. L., Keefe, J. R., Cohen, Z. D., & Huibers, M. J. H. (2019). Precision medicine for long-term depression outcomes using the Personalized Advantage Index approach: Cognitive therapy or interpersonal psychotherapy? *Psychological Medicine*, 1−11. https://doi.org/10.1017/s0033291719003192

Caporino, N. E., & Karver, M. S. (2012). The acceptability of treatments for depression to a community sample of adolescent girls. *Journal of Adolescence, 35*(5), 1237−1245. https://doi.org/10.1016/j.adolescence.2012.04.007

Carver, C. S., Johnson, S. L., & Timpano, K. R. (2017). Toward a functional view of the p factor in psychopathology. *Clinical Psychological Science, 5*(5), 880−889. https://doi.org/10.1177/2167702617710037

Caspi, A., Houts, R. M., Belsky, D. W., Goldman-Mellor, S. J., Harrington, H., Israel, S., Meier, M. H. M. H., Ramrakha, S., Shalev, I., Poulton, R., & Moffitt, T. E. (2014). The p factor: One general psychopathology factor in the structure of psychiatric disorders? *Clinical Psychological Science, 2*(2), 119−137. https://doi.org/10.1177/2167702613497473

Caspi, A., & Moffitt, T. E. (2018). All for one and one for all: Mental disorders in one dimension. *American Journal of Psychiatry, 175*(9), 831−844. https://doi.org/10.1176/appi.ajp.2018.17121383

Chadha, A., Neufeld, S., Goodyer, I. M., Fonagy, P., Midgley, N., Consortium, I., & Wilkinson, P. O. (2021). Associations between baseline cortisol and trajectory of symptom improvement in depressed adolescents receiving psychological therapy. *Journal of Affective Disorders*. https://doi.org/10.1016/j.jad.2021.03.046

Chattopadhyay, S., Tait, R., Simas, T., van Nieuwenhuizen, A., Hagan, C. C., Holt, R. J., Graham, J., Sahakian, B. J., Wilkinson, P. O., Goodyer, I. M., & Suckling, J. (2017). Cognitive behavioral therapy lowers elevated functional connectivity in depressed adolescents. *EBioMedicine, 17*, 216−222. https://doi.org/10.1016/j.ebiom.2017.02.010

Chen, J., Yu, J., Zhang, L., Li, X., & Zhang, J. (2014). Etiological heterogeneity of symptom dimensions of adolescent depression. *PsyCh Journal, 3*(4), 254−263. https://doi.org/10.1002/pchj.62

Clayborne, Z. M., Varin, M., & Colman, I. (2019). Systematic review and meta-analysis: Adolescent depression and long-term psychosocial outcomes. *Journal of the American Academy of Child and Adolescent Psychiatry, 58*(1), 72−79. https://doi.org/10.1016/j.jaac.2018.07.896

Cohen, Z. D., & Derubeis, R. J. (2018). Treatment selection in depression. *Annual Review of Clinical Psychology, 14*, 209−236. https://doi.org/10.1146/annurev-clinpsy-050817-084746

Cole, D. A., Cai, L., Martin, N. C., Findling, R. L., Youngstrom, E. A., Garber, J., Curry, J. F., Hyde, J. S., Essex, M. J., Compas, B. E., Goodyer, I. M., Rohde, P., Stark, K. D., Slattery, M. J., & Forehand, R. (2011). Structure and measurement of depression in youths: Applying item response theory to clinical data. *Psychological Assessment, 23*(4), 819−833. https://doi.org/10.1037/a0023518

Collins, L. M., Murphy, S. A., & Strecher, V. (2007). The multiphase optimization strategy (MOST) and the sequential multiple assignment randomized trial (SMART). New methods for more potent eHealth interventions. *American Journal of Preventive Medicine, 32*(5 Suppl. L), 112−118. https://doi.org/10.1016/j.amepre.2007.01.022

Connors, E. H., Douglas, S., Jensen-Doss, A., Landes, S. J., Lewis, C. C., McLeod, B. D., Stanick, C., & Lyon, A. R. (2021). What gets measured gets done: How mental health agencies can leverage measurement-based care for better patient care, clinician supports, and organizational goals. *Administration and Policy in Mental Health and Mental Health Services Research, 48*(2), 250—265. https://doi.org/10.1007/s10488-020-01063-w

Constantinou, M. P., Goodyer, I. M., Eisler, I., Butler, S., Kraam, A., Scott, S., Pilling, S., Simes, E., Ellison, R., Allison, E., & Fonagy, P. (2019). Changes in general and specific psychopathology factors over a psychosocial intervention. *Journal of the American Academy of Child & Adolescent Psychiatry, 58,* 776—786. March.

Cramer, A. O. J., Borsboom, D., Aggen, S. H., & Kendler, K. S. (2012). The pathoplasticity of dysphoric episodes: Differential impact of stressful life events on the pattern of depressive symptom inter- correlations. *Psychological Medicine, 42*(5), 957—965. https://doi.org/10.1017/S003329171100211X. The.

Cramer, A. O. J., Van Borkulo, C. D., Giltay, E. J., Van Der Maas, H. L. J., Kendler, K. S., Scheffer, M., & Borsboom, D. (2016). Major depression as a complex dynamic system. *PLoS One, 11*(12), 1—20. https://doi.org/10.1371/journal.pone.0167490

Cregeen, S., Hughes, C., Midgley, N., Rhode, M., & Rustin, M. (2017). In J. Catty (Ed.), *Short-term psychoanalytic psychotherapy for adolescents with depression: A treatment manual.* Karnac.

Davies, S. E., Neufeld, S. A. S., van Sprang, E., Schweren, L., Keivit, R., Fonagy, P., Dubicka, B., Kelvin, R., Midgley, N., Reynolds, S., Target, M., Wilkinson, P., van Harmelen, A. L., & Goodyer, I. M. (2020). Trajectories of depression symptom change during and following treatment in adolescents with unipolar major depression. *Journal of Child Psychology and Psychiatry, 61*(5), 565—574. https://doi.org/10.1111/jcpp.13145

DeRubeis, R. J., Cohen, Z. D., Forand, N. R., Fournier, J. C., Gelfand, L. A., & Lorenzo-Luaces, L. (2014). The personalized advantage index: Translating research on prediction into individualized treatment recommendations. A demonstration. *PLoS One, 9*(1), 1—8. https://doi.org/10.1371/journal.pone.0083875

Dunlop, B. W., Kelley, M. E., Aponte-Rivera, V., Mletzko-Crowe, T., Kinkead, B., Ritchie, J. C., Nemeroff, C. B., Craighead, W. E., Mayberg, H. S., Alvarez, C., Etzel, J., Falero, R., Gerardi, M., Heekin, M., Jones, M., Lim, N., Mahoney, V., Ramirez, C., Reddy, S., … Crowe, T. M. (2017). Effects of patient preferences on outcomes in the predictors of remission in depression to individual and combined treatments (PReDICT) Study. *American Journal of Psychiatry, 174*(6), 546—556. https://doi.org/10.1176/appi.ajp.2016.16050517

Dunn, V., & Goodyer, I. M. (2006). Longitudinal investigation into childhood- and adolescence-onset depression: Psychiatric outcome in early adulthood. *British Journal of Psychiatry, 188,* 216—222. https://doi.org/10.1192/bjp.188.3.216

Eckshtain, D., Kuppens, S., Ugueto, A., Ng, M. Y., Vaughn-Coaxum, R., Corteselli, K., & Weisz, J. R. (2020). Meta-analysis: 13-year follow-up of psychotherapy effects on youth depression. *Journal of the American Academy of Child and Adolescent Psychiatry, 59*(Issue 1), 45—63. https://doi.org/10.1016/j.jaac.2019.04.002

Fisher, A. J., & Bosley, H. G. (2015). Personalized assessment and treatment of depression. *Current Opinion in Psychology, 4,* 67—74. https://doi.org/10.1016/j.copsyc.2015.03.031

Foster, S., Mohler-Kuo, M., Tay, L., Hothorn, T., & Seibold, H. (2019). Estimating patient-specific treatment advantages in the 'Treatment for Adolescents with Depression Study'. *Journal of Psychiatric Research, 112,* 61—70. https://doi.org/10.1016/j.jpsychires.2019.02.021

Fried, E. I., & Nesse, R. M. (2014). The impact of individual depressive symptoms on impairment of psychosocial functioning. *PLoS One, 9*(2). https://doi.org/10.1371/journal.pone.0090311

Fried, E. I., & Nesse, R. M. (2015). Depression sum-scores don't add up: Why analyzing specific depression symptoms is essential. *BMC Medicine, 13*(1), 1—11. https://doi.org/10.1186/s12916-015-0325-4

Gillett, G., Tomlinson, A., Efthimiou, O., & Cipriani, A. (2020). Predicting treatment effects in unipolar depression: A meta-review. *Pharmacology and Therapeutics, 212,* 107557. https://doi.org/10.1016/j.pharmthera.2020.107557

Goodyer, I. M., Reynolds, S., Barrett, B., Byford, S., Dubicka, B., Hill, J., Holland, F., Kelvin, R., Midgley, N., Roberts, C., Senior, R., Target, M., Widmer, B., Wilkinson, P., & Fonagy, P. (2017a). Cognitive-behavioural therapy and short-term psychoanalytic psychotherapy versus brief psychosocial intervention in adolescents with unipolar major depression (IMPACT): A multicentre, pragmatic, observer-blind, randomised controlled trial. *Health Technology Assessment, 21*(12), 1−93. https://doi.org/10.3310/hta21120

Goodyer, I. M., Reynolds, S., Barrett, B., Byford, S., Dubicka, B., Hill, J., Holland, F., Kelvin, R., Midgley, N., Roberts, C., Senior, R., Target, M., Widmer, B., Wilkinson, P., & Fonagy, P. (2017b). Cognitive behavioural therapy and short-term psychoanalytical psychotherapy versus a brief psychosocial intervention in adolescents with unipolar major depressive disorder (IMPACT): A multicentre, pragmatic, observer-blind, randomised controlled superiority trail. *The Lancet Psychiatry, 4*(2), 109−119. https://doi.org/10.1016/S2215-0366(16)30378-9

Goodyer, I. M., Tsancheva, S., Byford, S., Dubicka, B., Hill, J., Kelvin, R., Reynolds, S., Roberts, C., Senior, R., Suckling, J., Wilkinson, P., Target, M., & Fonagy, P. (2011). Improving mood with psychoanalytic and cognitive therapies (IMPACT): A pragmatic effectiveness superiority trial to investigate whether specialised psychological treatment reduces the risk for relapse in adolescents with moderate to severe unipolar depres. *Trials, 12*(1), 175. https://doi.org/10.1186/1745-6215-12-175

Goodyer, I. M., & Wilkinson, P. O. (2019). Practitioner review: Therapeutics of unipolar major depressions in adolescents. *Journal of Child Psychology and Psychiatry, 60*(3), 232−243. https://doi.org/10.1111/jcpp.12940

Gunlicks-Stoessel, M., Mufson, L., Bernstein, G., Westervelt, A., Reigstad, K., Klimes-Dougan, B., Cullen, K., Murray, A., & Vock, D. (2019). Critical decision points for augmenting interpersonal psychotherapy for depressed adolescents: A pilot sequential multiple assignment randomized trial. *Journal of the American Academy of Child and Adolescent Psychiatry, 58*(1), 80−91. https://doi.org/10.1016/j.jaac.2018.06.032

Gunlicks-Stoessel, M., Mufson, L., Westervelt, A., Almirall, D., & Murphy, S. (2016). A pilot SMART for developing an adaptive treatment strategy for adolescent depression. *Journal of Clinical Child and Adolescent Psychology, 45*(4), 480−494. https://doi.org/10.1080/15374416.2015.1015133

Haltigan, J. D. (2019). Editorial: Putting practicality into "p": Leveraging general factor models of psychopathology in clinical intervention. *Journal of the American Academy of Child & Adolescent Psychiatry.* https://doi.org/10.1016/j.jaac.2019.03.005

Haltigan, J. D., Aitken, M., Skilling, T., Henderson, J., Hawke, L., Battaglia, M., Strauss, J., Szatmari, P., & Andrade, B. F. (2018). "P" and "DP:" Examining symptom-level bifactor models of psychopathology and dysregulation in clinically referred children and adolescents. *Journal of the American Academy of Child and Adolescent Psychiatry, 57*(6). https://doi.org/10.1016/j.jaac.2018.03.010

Huang, S. H., LePendu, P., Iyer, S. V., Tai-Seale, M., Carrell, D., & Shah, N. H. (2014). Toward personalizing treatment for depression: Predicting diagnosis and severity. *Journal of the American Medical Informatics Association, 21*(6), 1069−1075. https://doi.org/10.1136/amiajnl-2014-002733

Huibers, M. J. H., Cohen, Z. D., Lemmens, L. H. J. M., Arntz, A., Peeters, F. P. M. L., Cuijpers, P., & DeRubeis, R. J. (2015). Predicting optimal outcomes in cognitive therapy or interpersonal psychotherapy for depressed individuals using the personalized advantage index approach. *PLoS One, 10*(11), 1−16. https://doi.org/10.1371/journal.pone.0140771

Jaycox, L. H., Asarnow, J. R., Sherbourne, C. D., Rea, M. M., LaBorde, A. P., & Wells, K. B. (2006). Adolescent primary care patients' preferences for depression treatment. *Administration and Policy in Mental Health and Mental Health Services Research, 33*(2), 198−207. https://doi.org/10.1007/s10488-006-0033-7

Laceulle, O. M., Vollebergh, W. A. M. M., & Ormel, J. (2015). The structure of psychopathology in adolescence: Replication of a general psychopathology factor in the TRAILS study. *Clinical Psychological Science, 3*(6), 850–860. https://doi.org/10.1177/2167702614560750

Liu, X., Gentzler, A. L., Tepper, P., Kiss, E., Kothencné, V. O., Tamás, Z., Vetró, Á., & Kovacs, M. (2006). Clinical features of depressed children and adolescents with various forms of suicidality. *Journal of Clinical Psychiatry, 67*(9), 1442–1450. https://doi.org/10.4088/JCP.v67n0917

Liu, Q., He, H., Yang, J., Feng, X., Zhao, F., & Lyu, J. (2020). Changes in the global burden of depression from 1990 to 2017: Findings from the Global Burden of Disease study. *Journal of Psychiatric Research, 126*, 134–140. https://doi.org/10.1016/j.jpsychires.2019.08.002

Maalouf, F. T., Atwi, M., & Brent, D. A. (2011). Treatment-resistant depression in adolescents: Review and updates on clinical management. *Depression and Anxiety, 28*(11), 946–954. https://doi.org/10.1002/da.20884

March, J., Silva, S., Petrycki, S., Curry, J., Wells, K., Fairbank, J., Burns, B., Domino, M., McNulty, S., Vitiello, B., Severe, J., Casat, C., Kolker, J., Riedal, K., Goldman, M., Feeny, N., Findling, R., Stull, S., McNamara, N., … Koch, G. (2005). The Treatment for Adolescents with Depression Study (TADS): Demographic and clinical characteristics. *Journal of the American Academy of Child and Adolescent Psychiatry, 44*(1), 28–40. https://doi.org/10.1097/01.chi.0000145807.09027.82

Maxwell, M. A., & Cole, D. A. (2009). Weight change and appetite disturbance as symptoms of adolescent depression: Toward an integrative biopsychosocial model. *Clinical Psychology Review, 29*(3), 260–273. https://doi.org/10.1016/j.cpr.2009.01.007

McElroy, E., Fearon, P., Belsky, J., Fonagy, P., & Patalay, P. (2018). Networks of depression and anxiety symptoms across development. *Journal of the American Academy of Child and Adolescent Psychiatry, 57*(12), 964–973. https://doi.org/10.1016/j.jaac.2018.05.027

Messer, S. B., & Wampold, B. E. (2006). Let's face facts: Common factors are more potent than specific therapy ingredients. *Clinical Psychology: Science and Practice, 9*(1), 21–25. https://doi.org/10.1093/clipsy.9.1.21

Moreau, D., Mufson, L., Weissman, M. M., & Klerman, G. L. (1991). Interpersonal psychotherapy for adolescent depression: Description of modification and preliminary application. *Journal of the American Academy of Child & Adolescent Psychiatry, 30*(4), 642–651.

Morris, D. W., Toups, M., & Trivedi, M. H. (2012). Measurement-based care in the treatment of clinical depression. *Focus, 10*(4), 428–433. https://doi.org/10.1176/appi.focus.10.4.428

National Institute for Health and Clinical Excellence (NICE). (2019). *Depression in children and young people: Identification and management.* https://doi.org/10.1211/CP.2018.20204575

Ng, M. Y., & Weisz, J. R. (2016). Annual research review: Building a science of personalized intervention for youth mental health. *Journal of Child Psychology and Psychiatry and Allied Disciplines, 57*(3), 216–236. https://doi.org/10.1111/jcpp.12470

Nilsen, T. S., Eisemann, M., & Kvernmo, S. (2013). Predictors and moderators of outcome in child and adolescent anxiety and depression: A systematic review of psychological treatment studies. *European Child & Adolescent Psychiatry, 22*(2), 69–87. https://doi.org/10.1007/s00787-012-0316-3

O'Keeffe, S., Martin, P., Goodyer, I. M., Wilkinson, P., Consortium, I., & Midgley, N. (2018). Predicting dropout in adolescents receiving therapy for depression. *Psychotherapy Research, 28*(5), 708–721. https://doi.org/10.1080/10503307.2017.1393576

Patalay, P., Fonagy, P., Deighton, J., Belsky, J., Vostanis, P., & Wolpert, M. (2015). A general psychopathology factor in early adolescence. *British Journal of Psychiatry, 207*(1), 15–22. https://doi.org/10.1192/bjp.bp.114.149591

Pettersson, E., Lahey, B. B., Larsson, H., & Lichtenstein, P. (2018). Criterion validity and utility of the general factor of psychopathology in childhood: Predictive associations with independently measured severe adverse mental health outcomes in adolescence. *Journal of the*

American Academy of Child and Adolescent Psychiatry, 57(6), 372—383. https://doi.org/10.1016/j.jaac.2017.12.016

American Psychiatric Association. (2010). Practice guideline for the treatment of patients with major depressive disorder. *American Psychiatric Association, 38*(2).

Rathod, S., Pinninti, N., Irfan, M., Gorczynski, P., Rathod, P., Gega, L., & Naeem, F. (2017). Mental health service provision in low- and middle-income countries. *Health Services Insights, 10*, 1—7. https://doi.org/10.1177/1178632917694350

Renaud, J., Brent, D. A., Baugher, M., Birmaher, B., Kolko, D. J., & Bridge, J. (1998). Rapid response to psychosocial treatment for adolescent depression: A two-year follow-up. *Journal of the American Academy of Child and Adolescent Psychiatry, 37*(11), 1184—1190. https://doi.org/10.1097/00004583-199811000-00019

Sburlati, E. S., Lyneham, H. J., Schniering, C. A., & Rapee, R. M. (2014). Evidence-based CBT for anxiety and depression in children and adolescents. In *Evidence-based CBT for anxiety and depression in children and adolescents*. Wiley Blackwell. https://doi.org/10.1002/9781118500576

Schweren, L., van Borkulo, C. D., Fried, E., & Goodyer, I. M. (2018). Assessment of symptom network density as a prognostic marker of treatment response in adolescent depression. *JAMA Psychiatry, 75*(1), 98—100. https://doi.org/10.1111/jcpp.12759

Scott, K., & Lewis, C. C. (2015). Using measurement-based care to enhance any treatment. *Cognitive and Behavioral Practice, 22*(1), 49—59. https://doi.org/10.1016/j.cbpra.2014.01.010

Scott, K., Lewis, C. C., & Marti, C. N. (2019). Trajectories of symptom change in the treatment for adolescents with depression study. *Journal of the American Academy of Child and Adolescent Psychiatry, 58*(3), 319—328. https://doi.org/10.1016/j.jaac.2018.07.908

Simon, G. E., & Perlis, R. H. (2010). Personalized medicine for depression: Can we match patients with treatments? *American Journal of Psychiatry, 167*, 1445—1455.

Slater, J., Shields, L., Racette, R. J., Juzwishin, D., & Coppes, M. (2015). The emergence of precision therapeutics. *Healthcare Management Forum, 28*(6_Suppl. l), S33—S39. https://doi.org/10.1177/0840470415604771

St Clair, M. C., Neufeld, S., Jones, P. B., Fonagy, P., Bullmore, E. T., Dolan, R. J., Moutoussis, M., Toseeb, U., & Goodyer, I. M. (2017). Characterising the latent structure and organisation of self-reported thoughts, feelings and behaviours in adolescents and young adults. *PLoS One, 12*(4), 1—27. https://doi.org/10.1371/journal.pone.0175381

Sunderland, M., Forbes, M. K., Mewton, L., Baillie, A., Carragher, N., Lynch, S. J., Batterham, P. J., Calear, A. L., Chapman, C., Newton, N. C., Teesson, M., & Slade, T. (2020). The structure of psychopathology and association with poor sleep, self-harm, suicidality, risky sexual behavior, and low self-esteem in a population sample of adolescents. *Development and Psychopathology*, 1—12. https://doi.org/10.1017/S0954579420000437

Uppendahl, J. R., Alozkan-Sever, C., Cuijpers, P., de Vries, R., & Sijbrandij, M. (February 18, 2020). Psychological and psychosocial interventions for PTSD, depression and anxiety amongst children and adolescents in low- and middle-income countries: A meta-analysis. *Frontiers in Psychiatry, 10*, 933. https://doi.org/10.3389/fpsyt.2019.00933

Van Borkulo, C., Boschloo, L., Borsboom, D., Penninx, B. W. J. H., Lourens, J. W., & Schoevers, R. A. (2015). Association of symptom network structure with the course of longitudinal depression. *JAMA Psychiatry, 72*(12), 1219—1226. https://doi.org/10.1001/jamapsychiatry.2015.2079

Villa, L. M., Goodyer, I. M., Tait, R., Kelvin, R., Reynolds, S., Wilkinson, P. O., & Suckling, J. (2020). Cognitive behavioral therapy may have a rehabilitative, not normalizing, effect on functional connectivity in adolescent depression. *Journal of Affective Disorders, 268*, 1—11. https://doi.org/10.1016/j.jad.2020.01.103

Wade, M., Fox, N. A., Zeanah, C. H., & Nelson, C. A. (2018). Effect of foster care intervention on trajectories of general and specific psychopathology among children with histories of institutional rearing: A randomized clinical trial. *JAMA Psychiatry, 75*(11), 1137–1145. https://doi.org/10.1001/jamapsychiatry.2018.2556

Waldman, I. D., Poore, H. E., van Hulle, C., Rathouz, P. J., & Lahey, B. B. (2016). External validity of a hierarchical dimensional model of child and adolescent psychopathology: Tests using confirmatory factor analyses and multivariate behavior genetic analyses. *Journal of Abnormal Psychology, 125*(8), 1053–1066. https://doi.org/10.1037/abn0000183

Wampold, B. E. (2015). How important are the common factors in psychotherapy? An update. *World Psychiatry, 14*(3), 270–277. https://doi.org/10.1002/wps.20238

Webb, C. A., Trivedi, M. H., Cohen, Z. D., Dillon, D. G., Fournier, J. C., Goer, F., Fava, M., McGrath, P. J., Weissman, M., Parsey, R., Adams, P., Trombello, J. M., Cooper, C., Deldin, P., Oquendo, M. A., McInnis, M. G., Huys, Q., Bruder, G., Kurian, B. T., … Pizzagalli, D. A. (2019). Personalized prediction of antidepressant v. placebo response: Evidence from the EMBARC study. *Psychological Medicine, 49*(7), 1118–1127. https://doi.org/10.1017/S0033291718001708

Wilkinson, P., Kelvin, R., Roberts, C., Dubicka, B., & Goodyer, I. (2011). Clinical and psychosocial predictors of suicide attempts and nonsuicidal self-injury in the Adolescent Depression Antidepressants and Psychotherapy Trial (ADAPT). *American Journal of Psychiatry, 168*(5), 495–501. https://doi.org/10.1176/appi.ajp.2010.10050718

Winter, S. E., & Barber, J. P. (2013). Should treatment for depression be based more on patient preference? *Patient Preference and Adherence, 7*, 1047–1057. https://doi.org/10.2147/PPA.S52746

Wright, A. G. C., & Woods, W. C. (2020). Personalized models of psychopathology. *Annual Review of Clinical Psychology, 16*, 49–74. https://doi.org/10.1146/annurev-clinpsy-102419-125032

Young, J. F., Jones, J. D., Gallop, R., Benas, J. S., Schueler, C. M., Garber, J., & Hankin, B. L. (2020). Personalized depression prevention: A randomized controlled trial to optimize effects through risk-informed personalization. *Journal of the American Academy of Child & Adolescent Psychiatry, January*, 1–12. https://doi.org/10.1016/j.jaac.2020.11.004

PART V

Innovations in treatment delivery and training

9

Delivering computerized Cognitive Behavioral Therapy for child and adolescent depression and anxiety

Paul Stallard

Child and Family Mental Health, Department for Health, University of Bath, Bath, United Kingdom

1. Cognitive behavioral therapy

Cognitive behavioral therapy (CBT) is a generic term used to describe a family of psychotherapeutic interventions that focus on the relationship between the way we think (cognitions), how we feel (emotions), and what we do (behavior) (Stallard, 2019). Informed by behavioral and cognitive theories, CBT is based on the premise that anxiety and depression arise from the way that events are perceived and appraised. These appraisals may become negatively biased and overly rigid and become associated with feelings of anxiety or low mood and unhelpful behaviors such as avoidance or withdrawal.

The first clinical trials of CBT for children with depression and anxiety were undertaken over 30 years ago (Kendall, 1994; Lewinsohn 1990). Following these early studies, CBT quickly established itself as the most extensively researched of all the child psychotherapies (Graham, 2005). Systematic reviews consistently demonstrate that CBT is effective for the treatment of a range of emotional problems in children, adolescents, and young people including posttraumatic stress disorder (Morina et al., 2016:; Gutermann et al., 2016; Smith et al., 2019); anxiety (Bennett et al., 2016; James et al., 2020); depression (Oud et al., 2019; Zhou et al., 2015); and obsessive—compulsive disorder (Ost el at al., 2016).

233

As part of the continuing process to enhance the efficacy of CBT, clinicians and academics are exploring the use of the so-called "third-wave" CBT interventions. Rather than actively changing the content of dysfunctional cognitions, third-wave approaches focus on changing the nature of the individual's relationship with their thoughts. Thoughts are understood as mental activity rather than defining reality with new cognitive interventions based on mindfulness, acceptance, compassion, and distress tolerance helping to minimize the emotional distress they generate. Research is beginning to emerge to document the benefits of third-wave approaches with children and adolescents including mindfulness (Dunning et al., 2019; Klingbeil et al., 2017), dialectical behavior therapy (McCauley et al., 2018), and acceptance and commitment therapy (Hancock et al., 2018).

This substantial and consistent evidence has resulted in CBT being recommended as a treatment of choice in the United Kingdom by the National Institute for Health and Clinical Excellence (NICE), and in the United States by the American Academy of Child and Adolescent Psychiatry for the treatment of young people with emotional disorders. This evidence has also underpinned the development of national training programs such as the Children and Young Person's Improving Access to Psychological Therapies (CY-IAPT) program in the United Kingdom (Shafran et al., 2014). The objective of CY-IAPT is to increase access to effective mental health through a national program where child mental health professionals are trained in evidence-based interventions including CBT (Shafran et al., 2014).

1.1 The treatment gap

While CBT is effective in the treatment of anxiety and depression, few children receive these interventions. Community surveys in Australia (Lawrence et al., 2015), the United Kingdom (McGinnity et al., 2005), and the United States (Merikangas, 2011) suggest that less than half of children with mental health problems receive an evidence-based intervention. This is a particular issue for those presenting with anxiety or depression who were found to be least likely to receive specialist help (Ford et al., 2003). In LMICs, the treatment gap for children and adolescents with mental health problems is in excess of 90% (Kieling et al., 2011).

There are many reasons why children do not receive evidence-based interventions including perceived stigma of attending mental health services, lack of knowledge/awareness of when to seek help, or the absence of local services (Reardon et al., 2017). However, a key issue is the limited availability of trained CBT therapists, a challenge that has encouraged interest in the use of technology to deliver mental health interventions (Hollis et al., 2017).

2. Computerized cognitive behavioral therapy

The structured and sequential nature of CBT lends itself to computerization. Computerized cognitive behavioral therapy (cCBT) programs can be delivered to a device via the Internet (i.e., iCBT) or provided as a computer program or CD-ROM. This standardized delivery format enhances treatment fidelity and ensures that all key information is consistently and reliably delivered as intended. The use of the Internet and computers may be particularly engaging and appealing to children who are familiar with, and regular users of, technology. cCBT programs can be accessed in nonclinical settings, thereby reducing the possible stigma associated with attending mental health clinics. Similarly, some can be accessed outside of normal working hours and therefore offer greater flexibility and convenience. cCBT therefore offers a low-cost way to increase the availability of evidence-based interventions. It can be accessed in a timely way, thereby offering an immediate alternative to the long waiting lists of many mental health services. Finally, with the rapid increase in the availability of digital technology and access to the Internet, cCBT offers a way of increasing access to psychological interventions in LMICs (Fu et al., 2020). However, there are a number of infrastructure and geographical issues to consider when implementing telemedicine in resource-poor LMIC settings (Acharibasam & Wynn, 2018). The feasibility of using cCBT in LMICs will be determined by practical issues including the affordability, accessibility, acceptability, and cultural appropriateness of digital interventions (Kumm et al., 2021). Before telemedicine, and cCBT in particular, can offer a viable and scalable option for addressing mental health issues, the digital divide between high-income countries and LMICs needs to be addressed.

While offering many advantages, there are also concerns. Firstly, there is a high dropout rate with around half of those who start cCBT failing to complete the program (Waller & Gilbody, 2009). Reasons for dropout include participants finding the intervention too demanding (Andersson et al., 2005), preferring face-to-face contact with a therapist (Lange et al., 2003; Marks et al., 2003), and poor computer or Internet access (Christensen et al., 2004; Kiropoulos et al., 2008). With children, other factors include whether cCBT is completed at school or in the community and levels of initial anxiety (Neil et al., 2009). Male adolescents are also less likely to complete cCBT than their female peers (Neil et al., 2009).

Secondly, the degree of therapist support appears important and whether cCBT is guided by a therapist or self-directed. Guidance and support can range from automated emails (Morgan et al., 2016) through to brief telephone support (March et al., 2009) and postsession facilitation (Stallard, Velleman, & Richardson, 2010). With adults, metaanalyses consistently demonstrate that guided programs produce larger effect sizes than self-directed interventions (Johansson & Andersson, 2012; Richards & Richardson, 2012). Reviews with children have also found that guided programs are more effective (Grist et al., 2019) although others have found that outcomes are not related to the level of program support (Christ et al., 2020:; Pennant et al., 2015).

The third concern relates to the attitudes of patients and professionals. Children attending specialist mental health services were found to be skeptical about cCBT (Stallard, Velleman, & Richardson, 2010). It is possible that these children may have explored other technological options prior to attendance, which may have tarnished their attitudes. Parents also expressed concerns about the degree of face-to-face contact offered alongside cCBT, expressing a preference for supported interventions (Stallard, Velleman, & Richardson, 2010). Although professionals were generally positive about the use of cCBT, they were also cautious. They expressed a preference for cCBT to be used in prevention programs or the treatment of mild/moderate problems rather than the treatment of severe problems (Cliffe et al., 2020; Stallard, Richardson, & Velleman, 2010). Few professionals felt that cCBT should be available freely online without any professional support. This has important implications for the way that cCBT is provided for children and adolescents. It is currently unclear whether it should be available in community or specialist mental health settings, whether access should be provided by educational, community, or specialist mental health staff, or whether it should be provided for emerging symptoms or established disorders.

Most of the existing research on attitudes to cCBT was undertaken before the COVID-19 pandemic. During the accompanying lockdowns, routine clinics and face-to-face appointments were canceled with digital technology providing an increasingly important way of delivering mental healthcare. In effect, the COVID-19 pandemic has created a digital revolution, transforming the way that mental healthcare is provided. The effect of this on the attitudes of patients and professionals to cCBT has not been determined. However, there are emerging reports that the use of telepsychiatry and virtual services has been well received by both mental health providers (Guinart et al., 2021) and adolescents (Hawke et al., 2021).

While a decade has passed since the first studies evaluating the use of cCBT with children were published, the evidence base has been slow to accumulate. There are comparatively few cCBT programs developed specifically for children with anxiety and depression. A recent systematic review identified only 17 studies where cCBT was evaluated against a comparison group (Christ et al., 2020). Of these, 12 studies were primarily focused on adolescents aged 12–19 years of age. An overview of some of the cCBT programs for anxiety and depression is presented in the following.

3. Computerized cognitive behavioral therapy for anxiety

Table 9.1 provides an overview of the content of the following cCBT programs for anxiety.

BRAVE for children: The best evaluated of the cCBT programs for anxiety are the BRAVE programs developed in Australia, which have versions for children (March et al., 2009) and for adolescents (Spence et al., 2011). The child version (aged 7—12 years) was adapted from an efficacious face-to-face CBT program and consists of 10 weekly 60 min sessions. In addition, there are six weekly 60-minute sessions for parents and 2 booster sessions, conducted at 1 and 3 months after the end of treatment. The following core skills are taught: the recognition of physiological anxiety symptoms, emotional management (progressive muscle relaxation, guided imagery, and deep breathing), cognitive strategies of coping self-talk and cognitive restructuring, graded exposure, problem-solving, and self-reinforcement for approaching situations that create anxiety. Parent sessions focus on psychoeducation about child anxiety, contingency management to reinforce brave, coping behavior, relaxation training, and information about cognitive restructuring, graded exposure, and problem-solving (Spence et al., 2011).

The materials are designed to be visually appealing and interesting and include engaging graphics and some cartoon animation. Sessions include a mix of media ranging from the presentation of information to question and answer exercises, games, and quizzes. Brief therapist support is provided via two telephone calls and email feedback about home assignments. Automated weekly emails are sent before (as a reminder to complete their session) and after each session (to congratulate them on finishing their session).

BRAVE for adolescents (aged 12—18 years) contains the same content as before but is presented in a way that is developmentally appealing and engaging for adolescents (Spence et al., 2011). It uses age-appropriate scenarios, examples, and activities such as coping with exams, job interviews, and dating. Adolescent characters, introduced in the first session, are used throughout the program to demonstrate use of skills. Age-appropriate terminology is used (e.g., cognitive restructuring is referred to as "reality checking"), and more advanced cognitive concepts such as the role of cognitive distortions are included. In a randomized controlled trial (RCT), BRAVE online was found to be acceptable to adolescents and as effective as face-to-face CBT (Spence et al., 2011).

TABLE 9.1   Summary of key cCBT anxiety programs.

Program	Age range	Length	Main skills taught
BRAVE for children (March et al., 2009)	Aged 7–12 years	10 × 60 min child sessions 6 × 60 min parent sessions 2 booster sessions	Child: Identification of anxiety symptoms, emotional management, cognitive strategies of coping self-talk and cognitive restructuring, graded exposure, problem-solving, and self-reinforcement for approaching anxiety situations. Parent: Psychoeducation about anxiety, contingency management to reinforce brave, coping behavior, relaxation training, cognitive restructuring, graded exposure, and problem-solving.
BRAVE for adolescents (Spence et al., 2011)	Aged 12–18 years	10 × 60 min adolescent sessions 5 × 60 min parent sessions 2 booster sessions	Adolescent: Identification of anxiety symptoms, emotional management, cognitive strategies of coping self-talk and cognitive restructuring, graded exposure, problem-solving, and self-reinforcement for approaching anxiety situations.

TABLE 9.1 Summary of key cCBT anxiety programs.—cont'd

Program	Age range	Length	Main skills taught
			Parent: Psychoeducation about anxiety, contingency management to reinforce brave, coping behavior, relaxation training, cognitive restructuring, graded exposure, and problem-solving.
Camp Cope A Lot (Khanna & Kendall, 2010)	Aged 7–13 years	12 × 35 min child sessions 2 parent sessions	Child: Psychoeducation about anxiety, identification of anxiety symptoms, relaxation training, identification of anxious cognitions, cognitive restructuring, graded exposure, problem-solving, home practice. Parent: Psychoeducation about anxiety, helpful ways to manage their child's anxious behavior.
Cool Teens (Wuthrich et al., 2012)	Aged 14–17 years	8 × 30 min adolescent sessions	Adolescent: Psychoeducation about anxiety, goal setting, identification of anxious thoughts and cognitive restructuring, graded exposure, coping and problem solving skills, and skill maintenance.

Continued

TABLE 9.1 Summary of key cCBT anxiety programs.—cont'd

Program	Age range	Length	Main skills taught
Cool Little Kids (Morgan et al., 2016)	Aged 3–6 years	8 × 60 min parent sessions	Parent: Psychoeducation about anxiety, development of fear hierarchies, contingency management, encouragement of child independence, identification and cognitive restructuring of parental worries, graded exposure, and skill maintenance.

However, the results were not replicated in the United Kingdom where an evaluation found that BRAVE delivered online was no better than a waiting list control group (Waite et al., 2019).

Camp Cope-A-Lot is an anxiety cCBT intervention based on the well-evaluated Coping Cat program developed in the United States by Phillip Kendall (Kendall & Hedtke, 2006). It was developed for children (aged 7–13 years) and consists of twelve 35-minute child completed sessions and 2 parent sessions (Khanna & Kendall, 2010). The content includes animation, audio, photographs, videos, schematics, reward system, text, and cartoon characters. The first six sessions are skill building and are undertaken by the child on their own. The remaining six are completed with support from a therapist and involve exposure tasks and skills practice. Two parent sessions are also undertaken with therapist support. The content covers the key areas of CBT anxiety programs included in face-to-face treatment: psychoeducation, cognitive restructuring, emotional identification and management, exposure, and problem-solving. Camp Cope-A-Lot creates an interactive learning environment where the child learns experientially rather than by reading online text or audio/video instruction. The program has recently been evaluated in a small randomized, cross-over study with children aged 8–15 years with autism where it was found to be beneficial in reducing symptoms of anxiety (Pryor et al., 2021).

Cool Teens is a computerized version of the Australian Cool Kids anxiety program (Rapee et al., 2006). It consists of eight 30-minute sessions and uses multimedia formats (text, audio, illustrations, cartoons, and live video) to deliver information, examples, activities, and homework in an engaging way to adolescents (aged 14–17 years). It includes six video case studies of adolescents discussing different anxiety problems and applying skills to their particular problem. The content is based on CBT and has a strong emphasis on cognitive restructuring and graded exposure (Wuthrich et al., 2012). Brief telephone support is regularly provided to motivate adolescents through the program and to help them apply skills to their everyday life. More limited telephone support calls are provided for parents, which are primarily designed to help them keep their child engaged with the program.

A recent development is the *Cool Little Kids Online* program for parents of children aged 3–6 years (Morgan et al., 2016). Based on the Cool Little Kids parenting program (Rapee et al., 2005), it consists of eight interactive sessions that contain a mix of written information, videos, audio narration, interactive worksheets and activities, and parent experiential stories. Sessions are 30–60 min in length and provide psychoeducation and teach skills such as constructing fear hierarchies, exposure, contingency management, problem-solving, and cognitive restructuring of parental worries. Parents receive automated emails after completing each module, halfway through the study and one week before their program access ends. Participants also receive an email reminder after 2 weeks of inactivity followed up by a brief call offering technical assistance.

4. Computerized cognitive behavioral therapy for depression

Table 9.2 provides an overview of the following cCBT programs for depression.

The best evaluated cCBT program for children and adolescents with depression is the *SPARX* program developed in New Zealand (Merry et al., 2012). SPARX is self-directed and consists of seven 30-minute modules during which core CBT strategies for depression are taught via a fantasy world game-like format. In each session, young people are met by a "guide" who introduces the rationale before the young person enters the gaming world where they are challenged to "restore the balance" in a world of negativity and hopelessness. Young people discover and practice CBT skills such as behavioral activation, activity rescheduling, relaxation, cognitive restructuring, problem-solving, and interpersonal skills to complete quests, solve puzzles, and restore balance. Toward the end of each module, the guide encourages young people to reflect on their experience, integrate skills from the fantasy world to real life, and set their own real-world goals.

The initial RCT of SPARX found it to be as efficacious as face-to-face counseling provided by trained counsellors or psychologists (Merry et al.,

TABLE 9.2 Summary of key cCBT depression programs.

Program	Age range	Length	Main skills taught
SPARX (Merry et al., 2012)	Aged 12–19 years	7 × 30 min adolescent sessions	Adolescent: Psychoeducation about depression, behavioral activation, activity rescheduling, relaxation, negative thoughts and cognitive restructuring, problem-solving and interpersonal skills, relapse prevention.
Stressbusters (Ables et al., 2009)	Aged 12–16 years	8 × 45 min adolescent sessions	Adolescent: Psychoeducation about depression, goal setting, behavioral activation, emotional recognition and management, identification and challenging negative thoughts, problem-solving and interpersonal skills, relapse prevention.
MoodGYM (Calear et al., 2009)	Aged 12–17 years	5 × 40 min adolescent sessions	Adolescent: Psychoeducation about CBT, identification and challenging of dysfunctional thoughts, enhancement of self-esteem, relaxation skills, interpersonal relationship and problem-solving skills.

TABLE 9.2 Summary of key cCBT depression programs.—cont'd

Program	Age range	Length	Main skills taught
CATCH-IT (Landback et al., 2009)	Aged 14–21 years	14 × 20 min adolescent sessions 4 × 20 min parent sessions	Adolescent: Psychoeducation about depression, behavioral activation, self-monitoring to recognize and change patterns of ineffective coping and dysfunctional cognitions, emotional management, identifying and managing difficult relationships and life transitions, problem-solving skills, strengthening social support and resiliency. Parent: Psychoeducation about the program, how to recognize depression and how parents can help their child, promoting resilience, helping parents address their own depressed mood.
Think Feel Do (Stallard et al., 2011)	Aged 10–16 years	6 × 45 min child sessions	Child: Psychoeducation about CBT, emotional recognition and management, identifying and challenging dysfunctional cognitions, problem-solving.

2012). The program has also been tested in smaller studies with minority groups including Maori adolescents (Shepherd et al., 2015), lesbian, bisexual, gay, and transgender (LBGTQ+) young people (Lucassen et al., 2015), and adolescents excluded from mainstream education (Fleming et al., 2012). While SPARX shows generally positive results, the findings are not always consistently replicated. A Dutch evaluation, for example, found SPARX to be no better at reducing symptoms of depression at 12 months than a monitoring control condition (Poppelaars et al., 2016).

Stressbusters is a self-directed cCBT program developed in the United Kingdom for adolescents aged 12−16 years with depression. It is an eight-session, interactive, multimedia presentation including audio narration synchronized with videos, animations, graphics, and printouts. Case vignettes of three adolescents tell the stories of their struggles with depression and how they implemented the program ideas. Based on a well-evaluated face-to-face CBT intervention for depression, Stressbusters includes psychoeducation, goal setting, behavioral activation, emotional recognition, cognitive awareness and challenging, problem-solving, and the enhancement of intrapersonal skills. Initial results from a small open trial and RCT were encouraging (Ables et al., 2009; Smith et al., 2015). However, a more recent RCT failed to find any difference at 12 months between Stressbusters and an attention control (self-help website) group (Wright et al., 2020).

MoodGYM is an Australian, Internet-based, self-directed CBT program for adolescents and adults designed to prevent and decrease symptoms of depression. The program aims to identify and change dysfunctional thoughts and beliefs, improve self-esteem and interpersonal relationships, and teach skills such as problem-solving and relaxation. The program consists of five interactive modules that contain information, animated demonstrations, quizzes, and "homework" exercises. Six characters are used to highlight specific ways of dealing with stressful situations. The majority of studies evaluating MoodGYM have focused on young adults (aged 18−25 years) so less is known about its efficacy and appropriateness for children and adolescents. However, MoodGYM has been delivered as a preventive program in schools to adolescents aged 12−17 years. Compared with a waitlist control group, MoodGYM was found to reduce symptoms of anxiety but had a weaker effect on symptoms of depression (Calear et al., 2009).

The *CATCH-IT* program is a 14-module online depression prevention program for adolescents developed in the United States (Landback et al., 2009). Informed by previous face-to-face interventions, the program consists of three parts: behavioral activation, CBT, and interpersonal psychotherapy (IPT). The behavioral activation and CBT sections aim to enhance coping skills by teaching adolescents to monitor their behavior and thoughts, to recognize and change patterns of ineffective coping, and to improve emotional regulation. The IPT sections help adolescents to identify and manage difficult relationships and life transitions, and to strengthen social support in family, school, and peer settings. Although the program is self-directed, CATCH-IT includes two motivational support calls as well as coaching telephone calls. There is also a parent component that provides information about the intervention and enhances family resiliency through the promotion of flexibility, shared activities, and mutual understanding. Parents are also provided with exercises to practice intervention-specific parenting skills with their children. The intervention is based on an engaging didactic design with each session including video stories from young people, skill building exercises, and behavior change assignments. After completing each module, adolescents are directed to an Internet site where they could play a game or listen to music as a reward. An RCT in the United States with 13- to 18-year-olds comparing the intervention to an online health education intervention found CATCH-IT to have positive effects on symptoms of depression and anxiety. The change in depressive symptoms was similar for the online health education comparison group, while the change in anxiety was specific to CATCH-IT (Gladstone et al., 2020). CATCH-IT has been translated and adapted (i.e., Grasp the Opportunity program) for Chinese adolescents in Hong Kong (Sobowale et al., 2013) with an RCT involving Chinese adolescents (aged 13–17) finding promising results. Compared with an attention control group, Grasp the Opportunity resulted in a larger reduction in symptoms of depression (Ip et al., 2016).

Think Feel Do is a guided, six-session CBT program for children aged 11–16 years with emotional problems developed in the United Kingdom (Stallard et al., 2011). Each session lasts approximately 30–45 min and covers emotional recognition and management; linking thoughts, feelings, and behavior; identifying and challenging negative thoughts; and problem-solving. It is interactive and involves quizzes, practical exercises, video clips, music, and animation. Small pre–poststudies have shown that Think Feel Do is acceptable and reduces emotional symptoms in children attending specialist mental health services (Stallard et al., 2011) and as a targeted and universal intervention in schools (Attwood et al., 2012).

5. What do we not yet know about cCBT?

The evidence base detailing the efficacy of cCBT with children and young people with anxiety and low mood is still quite limited. A recent systematic review was only able to identify 17 studies that compared cCBT for children up to age 18 years with a comparison group (Grist et al., 2019). These 17 studies evaluated 13 different programs, and with the exception of SPARX and BRAVE, most cCBT programs were only subject to single evaluations, typically by their program developers.

Overall quality of evaluative studies was generally poor, with small samples and a high risk of bias (Christ et al., 2020; Grist et al., 2019; Pennant et al., 2015). Data about the efficacy of cCBT with children (aged 5–11 years) are extremely limited, leading Pennant et al. (2015) to conclude that they could not be confident in the efficacy of cCBT with this younger age group. This conclusion was endorsed by Grist et al. (2019), who was only able to identify three studies that had an exclusive child sample involving a total of 67 children.

Although the published systematic reviews used slightly different inclusion criteria, all the aforementioned reviews highlight the promise of cCBT. For young people (12–25 years), cCBT is beneficial for reducing anxiety and depressive symptoms at posttreatment compared with passive controls (Christ et al., 2020; Pennant et al., 2015). However, there are limited data concerning the longer-term effects of cCBT (Christ et al., 2020). The authors were only able to identify three studies evaluating cCBT for depression and two for anxiety, which included follow-up data 6–12 months posttreatment (Christ et al., 2020).

SPARX is the only program to have explored the use of cCBT with minority and marginalized groups. Small-scale studies include children excluded from mainstream education (Fleming et al., 2012), indigenous Maori children (Shepherd et al., 2015), and sexual minority groups (Lucassen et al., 2015). However, the use of an intervention, which has proven efficacious with one population, may not necessarily be acceptable or appeal to another. For example, adolescents participating in a youth justice day program completed few program levels and were negative or indifferent in their views about SPARX (Fleming et al., 2019).

All evaluations of cCBT to date have been undertaken in high-income countries, and none have evaluated the use of cCBT in LMICs (Grist et al., 2019). Furthermore, all programs are in English, and although SPARX was developed for Maori youth and does include some Maori language, linguistic diversity across cCBT programs is extremely limited, which will restrict their use in LMICs. Finally, in terms of accessibility, most programs are not freely available, and where they are available to purchase, affordability may restrict their use in resource-poor settings.

A further challenge for cCBT is to understand the factors that are associated with better engagement and outcomes. Therapist involvement appears important with those interventions offering some degree of therapist guidance/support tending to be more effective than unguided interventions (Grist et al., 2019). While this is consistent with reviews with adults (Karyotaki et al., 2021), others focusing on children and adolescent failed to find therapist support were associated with better outcomes (Christ et al., 2020; Pennant et al., 2015). Parent-supported interventions have also been found to produce significantly larger effect sizes than interventions delivered without (Grist et al., 2019). Treatment adherence, the number of cCBT sessions completed has been identified as a potential moderator. However, Christ et al. (2020) found that although the percentage of completed sessions, when reported, ranged from 32% to 100%, adherence was not associated with better outcomes.

The comparison group is important with larger effect sizes being reported when cCBT is compared with a waiting list control group rather than an active intervention (Grist et al., 2019; Pennant et al., 2015). The presenting problem has also been found to be important. Christ et al. (2020) found that cCBT has a comparable effect on symptoms of anxiety when compared with face-to-face therapy but that it may be inferior for depressive symptoms. However, it should be noted that head-to-head comparisons of cCBT and face-to-face therapy are sparse. At present, the data offer tentative support for the use of cCBT as part of a stepped care or waiting list initiative rather than an alternative to face-to-face therapy (Christ et al., 2020; Grist et al., 2019; Pennant et al., 2015).

The severity of the problems of those included in evaluative studies has varied. cCBT programs have included all children irrespective of symptoms (Attwood et al., 2012), those who are "at risk" (Gladstone et al., 2020), those with mild/moderate symptoms (Merry et al., 2012; Smith et al., 2015), and those with a formal diagnosis (Khanna & Kendall, 2010; Spence et al., 2011; Wuthrich et al., 2012). While most studies report reductions on standardized measures, further work is required to clarify where cCBT interventions fit within mental health pathways.

In terms of scalability, most cCBT interventions are at the early stages of evaluation, and their widespread impact when used as a public health intervention has seldom been evaluated. Exceptions are the BRAVE and SPARX programs, which have been tested as community prevention programs. A recent open trial of BRAVE in Australia provided the program as a first step, low-intensity, intervention (March et al., 2018). BRAVE was made freely available to 4425 children and adolescents (aged 7–17 years) with anxiety symptoms as a self-directed intervention. Participant satisfaction with the program was moderate although adherence was low. Approximately 21% did not complete any sessions, 48% completed 2 sessions with around 30% completing 3 or more of the 10 sessions. However, there was a notable reduction in self-reported anxiety over time, with effects being related to the number of sessions completed (March et al., 2018). Although there was not a comparison group, the authors concluded that self-directed CBT could form a low-cost, accessible, first step in a treatment pathway for children with anxiety (March et al., 2018). Further work has developed this with the second step involving the addition of therapist guidance for those who failed to engage with, or respond to, self-directed cCBT (March et al., 2019).

SPARX has also been provided as a depression prevention program in a study involving 540 final year secondary school students dealing with academic pressures (Perry et al., 2017). It was provided as a universal intervention, i.e., offered to all eligible students irrespective of symptomatology. SPARX was effective in reducing depressive symptoms compared with an attention control group, postintervention, and at 6 months but not at 18 months postbaseline (Perry et al., 2017). In addition to highlighting the benefits of SPARX as a preventive program, it also highlights the potential to use such programs in advance of identified stressors.

6. Future directions

Although further work is required to substantiate the efficacy of cCBT, this chapter tentatively suggests three potential roles for cCBT. Firstly, cCBT may be useful when access to face-to-face CBT and other psychotherapies are delayed or limited (Gist et al., 2019). It offers a more timely and accessible intervention in situations where there are lengthy waiting lists for face-to-face mental health support or where specialist knowledge or skills are limited. Secondly, cCBT may have a preventative role, being delivered in advance of known stressful events (i.e., examinations or tests) to mitigate any potential adverse effects of these stressful experiences (Perry et al., 2017). Thirdly, cCBT may offer a way of making evidence-based skills more widely available via public health programs (March et al., 2018). This could be particularly helpful during situations such as the recent COVID-19 pandemic and the associated surge in anxiety and depression. Research demonstrated that self-guided Internet-delivered CBT proved an acceptable option for many adults during COVID (Mahoney et al., 2021).

This chapter also highlights four areas for urgent attention. Firstly, it is disappointing that the evidence base for the efficacy of cCBT with children and adolescents remains limited. Little is known about whether postintervention outcomes persist into the medium or long term, the effects of cCBT on preadolescent children or the efficacy of cCBT compared with face-to-face therapy. Well-conducted research is required to establish the evidence base and to clarify the role of potential moderators such as age, symptom severity, therapist guidance, and completion rates. In addition, little is known about whether there are any potential harms associated with cCBT. High rates of attrition and low rates of program completion have been identified as potential problems although whether these may also negatively affect subsequent help seeking is unknown. With other digital technologies such as smart phone apps, concerns have been raised that their use might delay appropriate help seeking or tarnish attitudes toward future engagement with CBT (Stallard, 2022).

Secondly, one of the advantages of cCBT is their potential to be quickly scaled up to increase the capacity and availability of effective mental health interventions. To date, realization of this potential has been limited. All interventions have been developed in high-income countries, and cCBT programs are not widely available for use within clinical settings. Whether these interventions are effective when provided in routine care or in LMICs is unclear. As such, those who could most benefit from cCBT, where mental health interventions are limited, are not currently receiving them (Davies & Bergin, 2021).

Thirdly, in terms of service models, how cCBT interventions are provided needs to be clarified. In view of the absence of comparative studies, there is no consistent evidence, at present, to suggest that cCBT for children and adolescents is a comparable alternative to face-to-face therapy. Similarly, in terms of problem severity, advice from expert groups such as NICE in the United Kingdom recommends cCBT for the treatment for mild/moderate depression not severe depression (NICE, 2019). Future studies should assess how cCBT can be provided as part of a care pathway for children and adolescents with anxiety and/or depression and whether it offers an important first step.

Finally, although cCBT offers the potential to improve access to mental health interventions, this promise has yet to be realized. In addition to issues of availability, affordability, and scalability, there are many infrastructure and practical issues that need to be addressed before such programs can be widely used in resource-poor LMICs. Failure to address these issues will, unfortunately, contribute to the continuing digital divide between high-income countries and LMICs (Kumm et al., 2021).

7. Resources

Not all of the cCBT programs mentioned in this chapter have dedicated websites or are freely available. The following list provides links to sites, which can provide more information about some of the programs.

SPARX: https://www.sparx.org.nz/home
BRAVE: https://www.brave-online.com/
Camp Cope A Lot: https://www.copingcatparents.com/Camp_Cope_A_Lot
MoodGYM: https://moodgym.com.au/

Cool Kids: https://www.mq.edu.au/research/research-centres-gro
ups-and-facilities/healthy-people/centres/centre-for-emotional-hea
lth-ceh/centre-for-emotional-health-clinic/programs-for-children-a
nd-teenagers#Online

References

Abeles, P., Verduyn, C., Robinson, A., Smith, P., Yule, W., & Proudfoot, J. (2009). Computerized CBT for adolescent depression ("Stressbusters") and its initial evaluation through an
extended case series. *Behavioural and Cognitive Psychotherapy, 37*(2), 151–165.

Acharibasam, J. W., & Wynn, R. (November 1, 2018). Telemental health in low-and middle-income countries: A systematic review. *International Journal of Telemedicine and Applications,
2018.* https://doi.org/10.1155/2018/9602821

Andersson, G., Bergström, J., Holländare, F., Carlbring, P. E. R., Kaldo, V., & Ekselius, L.
(2005). Internet-based self-help for depression: Randomised controlled trial. *The British
Journal of Psychiatry, 187*(5), 456–461.

Attwood, M., Meadows, S., Stallard, P., & Richardson, T. (2012). Universal and targeted computerised cognitive behavioural therapy (Think, Feel, Do) for emotional health in schools:
Results from two exploratory studies. *Child and Adolescent Mental Health, 17*(3), 173–178.

Bennett, K., Manassis, K., Duda, S., Bagnell, A., Bernstein, G. A., Garland, E. J., ... Wilansky, P.
(2016). Treating child and adolescent anxiety effectively: Overview of systematic reviews.
Clinical Psychology Review, 50, 80–94.

Calear, A. L., Christensen, H., Mackinnon, A., Griffiths, K. M., & O'Kearney, R. (2009). The
YouthMood project: A cluster randomized controlled trial of an online cognitive
behavioral program with adolescents. *Journal of Consulting and Clinical Psychology, 77*(6),
1021.

Christensen, H., Griffiths, K. M., & Jorm, A. F. (2004). Delivering interventions for depression
by using the internet: Randomised controlled trial. *BMJ, 328*(7434), 265.

Christ, C., Schouten, M. J., Blankers, M., van Schaik, D. J., Beekman, A. T., Wisman, M. A., ...
Dekker, J. J. (2020). Internet and computer-based cognitive behavioral therapy for anxiety
and depression in adolescents and young adults: Systematic review and meta-analysis.
Journal of Medical Internet Research, 22(9), e17831.

Cliffe, B., Croker, A., Denne, M., & Stallard, P. (2020). Clinicians' use of and attitudes towards
technology to provide and support interventions in child and adolescent mental health
services. *Child and Adolescent Mental Health, 25*(2), 95–101.

Davies, B. E., & Bergin, A. D. (2021). Commentary: Let's get digital: A commentary on Hall-
dorsson et al.'s call for more rigorous development and evaluation of immersive digital
interventions for children and young people's metal health. *Journal of Child Psychology
and Psychiatry, 62*(5), 606–609.

Dunning, D. L., Griffiths, K., Kuyken, W., Crane, C., Foulkes, L., Parker, J., & Dalgleish, T.
(2019). Research Review: The effects of mindfulness-based interventions on cognition
and mental health in children and adolescents—a meta-analysis of randomized controlled
trials. *Journal of Child Psychology and Psychiatry, 60*(3), 244–258.

Fleming, T., Dixon, R., Frampton, C., & Merry, S. (2012). A pragmatic randomized controlled
trial of computerized CBT (SPARX) for symptoms of depression among adolescents
excluded from mainstream education. *Behavioural and Cognitive Psychotherapy, 40,*
529–541.

Fleming, T. M., Gillham, B., Bavin, L. M., Stasiak, K., Lewycka, S., Moore, J., ... Merry, S. N.
(2019). SPARX-R computerized therapy among adolescents in youth offenders' program:
Step-wise cohort study. *Internet Interventions, 18,* 100287.

Ford, T., Goodman, R., & Meltzer, M. (2003). Service use over 18 months among a nationally representative sample of British children with psychiatric disorder. *Clinical Child Psychology and Psychiatry, 8*(1), 37–51.

Fu, Z., Burger, H., Arjadi, R., & Bockting, C. L. (2020). Efficacy of digital psychological interventions for mental health problems in low-income and middle-income countries: A systematic review and meta-analysis. *The Lancet Psychiatry, 7*(10), 851–864.

Gladstone, T., Buchholz, K. R., Fitzgibbon, M., Schiffer, L., Lee, M., & Voorhees, B. W. V. (2020). Randomized clinical trial of an internet-based adolescent depression prevention intervention in primary care: Internalizing symptom outcomes. *International Journal of Environmental Research and Public Health, 17*(21), 7736.

Graham, P. (2005). Jack Tizard lecture: Cognitive behaviour therapies for children: Passing fashion or here to stay? *Child and Adolescent Mental Health, 10*(2), 57–62.

Grist, R., Croker, A., Denne, M., & Stallard, P. (2019). Technology delivered interventions for depression and anxiety in children and adolescents: A systematic review and meta-analysis. *Clinical Child and Family Psychology Review, 22*(2), 147–171.

Guinart, D., Marcy, P., Hauser, M., Dwyer, M., & Kane, J. M. (2021). Mental health care providers' attitudes toward telepsychiatry: a systemwide, multisite survey during the COVID-19 pandemic. *Psychiatric Services, 72*(6), 704–707.

Gutermann, J., Schreiber, F., Matulis, S., Schwartzkopff, L., Deppe, J., & Steil, R. (2016). Psychological treatments for symptoms of posttraumatic stress disorder in children, adolescents, and young adults: A meta-analysis. *Clinical Child and Family Psychology Review, 19*(2), 77–93.

Hancock, K. M., Swain, J., Hainsworth, C. J., Dixon, A. L., Koo, S., & Munro, K. (2018). Acceptance and commitment therapy versus cognitive behavior therapy for children with anxiety: Outcomes of a randomized controlled trial. *Journal of Clinical Child & Adolescent Psychology, 47*(2), 296–311.

Hawke, L. D., Sheikhan, N. Y., MacCon, K., et al. (2021). Going virtual: Youth attitudes toward and experiences of virtual mental health and substance use services during the COVID-19 pandemic. *BMC Health Services Research, 21*, 340. https://doi.org/10.1186/s12913-021-06321-7

Hollis, C., Falconer, C. J., Martin, J. L., Whittington, C., Stockton, S., Glazebrook, C., & Davies, E. B. (2017). Annual Research Review: Digital health interventions for children and young people with mental health problems—a systematic and meta-review. *Journal of Child Psychology and Psychiatry, 58*(4), 474–503.

Ip, P., Chim, D., Chan, K. L., Li, T. M., Ho, F. K. W., Van Voorhees, B. W., … Wong, W. H. S. (2016). Efficacy of a culturally attuned internet-based depression prevention program for Chinese adolescents: A randomized controlled trial. *Depression and Anxiety, 33*(12), 1123–1131.

James, A. C., Reardon, T., Soler, A., James, G., & Creswell, C. (2020). Cognitive behavioural therapy for anxiety disorders in children and adolescents. *Cochrane Database of Systematic Reviews, 11*, CD013162. https://doi.org/10.1002/14651858.CD013162.pub2 Accessed 15 June 2021.

Johansson, R., & Andersson, G. (2012). Internet-based psychological treatments for depression. *Expert Review of Neurotherapeutics, 12*(7), 861–870.

Karyotaki, E., Efthimiou, O., Miguel, C., Bermpohl, F. M., Furukawa, T. A., Cuijpers, P., Riper, H., Patel, V., Mira, A., Gemmil, A. W., & Yeung, A. S. (2021). Internet-based cognitive behavioral therapy for depression - a systematic review and individual patient data network meta-analysis. *JAMA Psychiatry, 78*(4), 361–371.

Kendall, P. C. (1994). Treating anxiety disorders in children: Results of a randomised clinical trial. *Journal of Consulting and Clinical Psychology, 62*, 100–110.

Kendall, P. C., & Hedtke, K. A. (2006). *Cognitive-behavioral therapy for anxious children: Therapist manual*. Ardmore, PA: Workbook Publishing.

Khanna, M. S., & Kendall, P. C. (2010). Computer-assisted cognitive behavioral therapy for child anxiety: Results of a randomized clinical trial. *Journal of Consulting and Clinical Psychology, 78*(5), 737–745.

Kieling, C., Baker-Henningham, H., Belfer, M., Conti, G., Ertem, I., Omigbodun, O., Rohde, L. A., Srinath, S., Ulkuer, N., & Rahman, A. (October 22, 2011). Child and adolescent mental health worldwide: Evidence for action. *The Lancet, 378*(9801), 1515–1525.

Kiropoulos, L. A., Klein, B., Austin, D. W., Gilson, K., Pier, C., Mitchell, J., & Ciechomski, L. (2008). Is internet-based CBT for panic disorder and agoraphobia as effective as face-to-face CBT? *Journal of Anxiety Disorders, 22*(8), 1273–1284.

Klingbeil, D. A., Renshaw, T. L., Willenbrink, J. B., Copek, R. A., Chan, K. T., Haddock, A., … Clifton, J. (2017). Mindfulness-based interventions with youth: A comprehensive meta-analysis of group-design studies. *Journal of School Psychology, 63*, 77–103.

Kumm, A. J., Viljoen, M., & de Vries, P. J. (2021). The digital divide in technologies for autism: Feasibility considerations for low- and middle-income countries. *Journal of Autism and Developmental Disorders.* https://doi.org/10.1007/s10803-021-05084-8

Landback, J., Prochaska, M., Ellis, J., Dmochowska, K., Kuwabara, S. A., Gladstone, T., … Van Voorhees, B. W. (2009). From prototype to product: Development of a primary care/internet-based depression prevention intervention for adolescents (CATCH-IT). *Community Mental Health Journal, 45*(5), 349–354.

Lange, A., Van De Ven, J. P., & Schrieken, B. (2003). Interapy: Treatment of post-traumatic stress via the internet. *Cognitive Behaviour Therapy, 32*(3), 110–124.

Lawrence, D., Johnson, S., Hafekost, J., Boterhoven de Haan, K., Sawyer, M., Ainley, J., & Zubrick, S. R. (2015). *The mental health of children and adolescents: Report on the second Australian child and adolescent survey of mental health and wellbeing.* Canberra, Australia: Department of Health.

Lewinsohn, P. M., Clarke, G. N., Hops, H., & Andrews, J. (1990). Cognitive-behavioral treatment for depressed adolescents. *Behavior Therapy, 21*(4), 385–401.

Lucassen, M. F., Merry, S. N., Hatcher, S., & Frampton, C. M. (2015). Rainbow SPARX: A novel approach to addressing depression in sexual minority youth. *Cognitive and Behavioral Practice, 22*, 203–216.

Mahoney, A., Li, I., Haskelberg, H., Millard, M., & Newby, J. M. (2021). The uptake and effectiveness of online cognitive behaviour therapy for symptoms of anxiety and depression during COVID-19. *Journal of Affective Disorders, 292*, 197–203.

March, S., Spence, S. H., & Donovan, C. L. (2009). The efficacy of an internet-based cognitive-behavioural therapy intervention for child anxiety disorders. *Journal of Pediatric Psychology, 34*(5), 474–487.

March, S., Spence, S. H., Donovan, C. L., & Kenardy, J. A. (2018). Large-scale dissemination of internet-based cognitive behavioral therapy for youth anxiety: Feasibility and acceptability study. *Journal of Medical Internet Research, 20*(7), e234.

March, S., Donovan, C. L., Baldwin, S., Ford, M., & Spence, S. H. (2019). Using stepped-care approaches within internet-based interventions for youth anxiety: Three case studies. *Internet Interventions, 18*, 100281.

Marks, I. M., Mataix-Cols, D., Kenwright, M., Cameron, R., Hirsch, S., & Gega, K. (2003). Pragmatic evaluation of computer-aided self-help for anxiety and depression. *British Journal of Psychiatry, 183*, 57–65.

McCauley, E., Berk, M. S., Asarnow, J. R., Adrian, M., Cohen, J., Korslund, K., … Linehan, M. M. (2018). Efficacy of dialectical behavior therapy for adolescents at high risk for suicide: A randomized clinical trial. *JAMA Psychiatry, 75*(8), 777–785.

McGinnity, Á., Meltzer, H., Ford, T., & Goodman, R. (2005). In H. Green (Ed.), *Mental health of children and young people in Great Britain.* Basingstoke: Palgrave Macmillan.

Merikangas, K. R., He, J. P., Burstein, M., Swendsen, J., Avenevoli, S., Case, B., et al. (2011). Service utilization for lifetime mental disorders in U.S. adolescents: Results of the National Comorbidity Survey-Adolescent Supplement (NCS-A). *Journal of the American Academy of Child & Adolescent Psychiatry, 50*, 32–45.

Merry, S. N., Stasiak, K., Shepherd, M., Frampton, C., Fleming, T., & Lucassen, M. F. (2012). The efficacy of SPARX, a computerised self-help intervention for adolescents seeking help for depression: Randomised controlled non-inferiority trial. *BMJ, 344*, e2598, 2012.

Morgan, A. J., Rapee, R. M., & Bayer, J. K. (2016). Prevention and early intervention of anxiety problems in young children: A pilot evaluation of Cool Little Kids Online. *Internet Interventions, 4*, 105–112.

Morina, N., Koerssen, R., & Pollet, T. V. (2016). Interventions for children and adolescents with posttraumatic stress disorder: A meta-analysis of comparative outcome studies. *Clinical Psychology Review, 47*, 41–54.

Neil, A. L., Batterham, P., Christensen, H., Bennett, K., & Griffiths, K. M. (2009). Predictors of adherence by adolescents to a cognitive behaviour therapy website in school and community-based settings. *Journal of Medical Internet Research, 11*(1), e6.

NICE. (2019). *Depression in children and young people: Identification and management.* https://www.nice.org.uk/guidance/ng134 Accessed 16/06/21.

Öst, L. G., Riise, E. N., Wergeland, G. J., Hansen, B., & Kvale, G. (2016). Cognitive behavioral and pharmacological treatments of OCD in children: A systematic review and meta-analysis. *Journal of Anxiety Disorders, 43*, 58–69.

Oud, M., De Winter, L., Vermeulen-Smit, E., Bodden, D., Nauta, M., Stone, L., ... Stikkelbroek, Y. (2019). Efficacy of CBT for children and adolescents with depression: A systematic review and meta-regression analysis. *European Psychiatry, 57*, 33–45.

Pennant, M. E., Loucas, C. E., Whittington, C., Creswell, C., Fonagy, P., Fuggle, P., & Expert Advisory, G. (2015). Computerised therapies for anxiety and depression in children and young people: A systematic review and meta-analysis. *Behaviour Research and Therapy, 67*, 1–18.

Perry, Y., Werner-Seidler, A., Calear, A., Mackinnon, A., King, C., Scott, J., ... Batterham, P. J. (2017). Preventing depression in final year secondary students: School-based randomized controlled trial. *Journal of Medical Internet Research, 19*(11), e369.

Poppelaars, M., Tak, Y. R., Lichtwarck-Aschoff, A., Engels, R. C., Lobel, A., Merry, S. N., ... Granic, I. (2016). A randomized controlled trial comparing two cognitive-behavioral programs for adolescent girls with subclinical depression: A school-based program (Op Volle Kracht) and a computerized program (SPARX). *Behaviour Research and Therapy, 80*, 33–42.

Pryor, F. C., Lincoln, A., Igelman, R., Toma, V., & Iravani, R. (2021). Efficacy of a computer-assisted cognitive-behavior therapy program for treating youth with anxiety and co-occurring autism spectrum disorder: Camp Cope-A-Lot. *Research in Autism Spectrum Disorders, 83*, 101748.

Rapee, R. M., Kennedy, S., Ingram, M., et al. (2005). Prevention and early intervention of anxiety disorders in inhibited preschool children. *Journal of Consulting and Clinical Psychology, 73*, 488–497.

Rapee, R. M., Lyneham, H. J., Schniering, C. A., et al. (2006). *The Cool Kids® child and adolescent anxiety program therapist manual.* Sydney: Centre for Emotional Health, Macquarie University.

Reardon, T., Harvey, K., Baranowska, M., O'Brien, D., Smith, L., & Creswell, C. (2017). What do parents perceive are the barriers and facilitators to accessing psychological treatment for mental health problems in children and adolescents? A systematic review of qualitative and quantitative studies. *European Child & Adolescent Psychiatry, 26*(6), 623–647.

Richards, D., & Richardson, T. (2012). Computer-based psychological treatments for depression: A systematic review and meta-analysis. *Clinical Psychology Review, 32*(4), 329e342.

Shafran, R., Fonagy, P., Pugh, K., & Myles, P. (2014). Transformation of mental health services for children and young people in England. In , Vol 158. *Dissemination and implementation of evidence-based practices in child and adolescent mental health* (pp. p158–178). New York, NY: Oxford University Press.

Shepherd, M., Fleming, T., Lucassen, M., Stasiak, K., Lambie, I., & Merry, S. N. (2015). The design and relevance of a computerized gamified depression therapy program for indigenous Maori adolescents. *JMIR Serious Games, 3*(1), e1.

Smith, P., Scott, R., Eshkevari, E., Jatta, F., Leigh, E., Harris, V., … Yule, W. (2015). Computerised CBT for depressed adolescents: Randomised controlled trial. *Behaviour Research and Therapy, 73*, 104–110.

Smith, P., Dalgleish, T., & Meiser-Stedman, R. (2019). Practitioner review: Posttraumatic stress disorder and its treatment in children and adolescents. *Journal of Child Psychology and Psychiatry, 60*(5), 500–515.

Sobowale, K., Zhou, A. N., Van Voorhees, B. W., Stewart, S., Tsang, A., Ip, P., … Chim, D. (2013). Adaptation of an internet-based depression prevention intervention for Chinese adolescents: From "CATCH-IT" to "grasp the opportunity". *International Journal of Adolescent Medicine and Health, 25*(2), 127–137.

Spence, S. H., Donovan, C. L., March, S., Gamble, A., Anderson, R. E., Prosser, S., & Kenardy, J. (2011). A randomized controlled trial of online versus clinic-based CBT for adolescent anxiety. *Journal of Consulting and Clinical Psychology, 79*(5), 629–642.

Stallard, P. (2019). *Think good, feel good: A cognitive behavioural therapy workbook for children and young people.* Chichester, UK: John Wiley & Sons.

Stallard, P. (2022). Apps for mental health problems in children and young people. In R. Shafran, & S. Bennett (Eds.), *Oxford guide to low intensity interventions for children and young people.* Oxford: Oxford University Press.

Stallard, P., Richardson, T., & Velleman, S. (2010). Clinicians' attitudes towards the use of computerized cognitive behaviour therapy (cCBT) with children and adolescents. *Behavioural and Cognitive Psychotherapy, 38*(5), 545–560.

Stallard, P., Velleman, S., & Richardson, T. (2010). Computer use and attitudes towards computerised therapy amongst young people and parents attending child and adolescent mental health services. *Child and Adolescent Mental Health, 15*(2), 80–84.

Stallard, P., Richardson, T., Velleman, S., & Attwood, M. (2011). Computerized CBT (Think, Feel, Do) for depression and anxiety in children and adolescents: Outcomes and feedback from a pilot randomized controlled trial. *Behavioural and Cognitive Psychotherapy, 39*(3), 273–284.

Waite, P., Marshall, T., & Creswell, C. (2019). A randomized controlled trial of internet-delivered cognitive behaviour therapy for adolescent anxiety disorders in a routine clinical care setting with and without parent sessions. *Child and Adolescent Mental Health, 24*(3), 242–250.

Waller, R., & Gilbody, S. (2009). Barriers to the uptake of computerized cognitive behavioural therapy: A systematic review of the quantitative and qualitative evidence. *Psychological Medicine, 39*(5), 705–712.

Wright, B., Tindall, L., Hargate, R., Allgar, V., Trépel, D., & Ali, S. (2020). Computerised cognitive–behavioural therapy for depression in adolescents: 12-month outcomes of a UK randomised controlled trial pilot study. *BJPsych Open, 6*(1), E5. https://doi.org/10.1192/bjo.2019.91

Wuthrich, V. M., Rapee, R. M., Cunningham, M. J., Lyneham, H. J., Hudson, J. L., & Schniering, C. A. (2012). A randomized controlled trial of the Cool Teens CD-ROM computerized program for adolescent anxiety. *Journal of the American Academy of Child & Adolescent Psychiatry, 51*(3), 261–270.

Zhou, X., Hetrick, S. E., Cuijpers, P., Qin, B., Barth, J., Whittington, C. J., … Xie, P. (2015). Comparative efficacy and acceptability of psychotherapies for depression in children and adolescents: A systematic review and network meta-analysis. *World Psychiatry, 14*(2), 207–222.

10

Innovations in scaling up interventions in low- and middle-income countries: parent-focused interventions in the perinatal period and promotion of child development

Ahmed Waqas, and Atif Rahman

Department of Primary Care & Mental Health, Institute of Population Health, University of Liverpool, Liverpool, United Kingdom

1. Perinatal mental health and child development

Over the past two decades, common perinatal mental disorders including depression and anxiety have received increased attention in low- and middle-income countries (LMICs), due to their high prevalence and deleterious health and developmental consequences for children. The average prevalence of common mental disorders in LMICs has been estimated at 15.9% during pregnancy and 19.8% postpartum (Fisher et al., 2012). The high prevalence of these conditions is often associated with the increased psychosocial and environmental challenges that pregnant women and new mothers face in LMICs, for instance, exposure to adverse life events such as wars and political instability, gender discrimination, poor empowerment, intimate partner violence, and poor access to health services (Fisher et al., 2012).

The peripartum period and the first 1000 days of a child's life are critical to determining its developmental potential (Britto et al., 2017). During this period, infants are almost entirely reliant on their mothers or primary caregivers; therefore, their psychosocial well-being is key to optimum infant development. Recent research has emphasized the importance of mothers in provision of a nurturing and an emotionally supportive environment that enhances the cognitive development of children, who, during this time window, exhibit enormous degree of neuronal plasticity (Britto et al., 2017). Thus, the children's nurturing environment during this period enables them to make a best start in their lives (Britto et al., 2017). However, in LMICs, as many as 250 million young children do not achieve their developmental potential (Britto et al., 2017).

Many research studies have demonstrated that early child development and maternal mental health are intertwined (Zafar et al., 2014). This is recognized by the United Nations, who made the provision of resources for mental health and child development as a necessary component of the Sustainable Development Goals (Sachs, 2012). Some of these important resources are part of intervention packages for perinatal mental health, responsive caregiving, nutrition, and opportunities for psychostimulation. These interventions are the crucial pillars that mothers can use to achieve optimum physical, neurological, and behavioral development of a child (World Health Organization, 2019a, 2019b).

Poor maternal mental health not only bears negative consequences for mothers' physical and psychosocial health but is also associated with higher rates of socioemotional, cognitive, behavioral, and physical problems among children (Farías-Antúnez et al., 2018; Ibanez et al., 2015; Rahman et al., 2004, 2007; Waqas et al., 2018), even after adjusting for confounding factors such as poverty and malnutrition (Engle, 2009; Fernald et al., 2009; Stewart, 2007). This is particularly important in LMICs that battle with the double burden of maternal and child communicable and noncommunicable diseases and a large proportion of children report stunted growth, low birth weight, and anemia (World Health Organization, 2018a, 2018b). This is also true for mothers who report high prevalence of mental health problems, which is often coupled with poor physical health including anemia and poor nutrition (World Health Organization, 2018a, 2018b). Several metaanalytical investigations have shown that maternal mental disorders especially depression are directly linked to low birth weight, poor infant nutritional behaviors, and high rates of infectious illnesses such as diarrhea and respiratory illness (Naveed et al., 2019; Patel et al., 2003; Rahman et al., 2004, 2007; Waqas et al., 2018). In addition, infants born to mothers with mental health problems also report incomplete immunization (Gelaye et al., 2016).

Although the pathways between perinatal mental health and child development have not yet been fully elucidated, recent research suggests a mediating relationship rather than a causal one. This mediating relationship already begins in the antenatal period when the transition to motherhood may be hampered by poor regulation of oxytocin and lactogens (Sachs, 2012). These hormones are responsible for *maternal programming* to form a strong mother–child bond (Sachs, 2012). In the postpartum and early childhood years, poor maternal functioning mediates the relationship between perinatal psychiatric morbidities and poor child development. All of these adverse sequalae of poor maternal mental health contribute to a vicious cycle of poverty, disparities, and inequities which are evident across generations (Case & Paxson, 2008; Engle, 2009; Engle et al., 2007; Fernald et al., 2009; Peet et al., 2015; Stewart, 2007). These are also associated with high economic costs. In the United States, for example, the aforementioned child developmental deficits account for 19.8% of annual adult income (Fink et al., 2016; Grantham-McGregor et al., 2007). In addition, maternal mental health problems account for £8.1 billion for each one-year cohort of births in the United Kingdom (Bauer et al., 2014). Thus, the need for appropriate health promotion, prevention, and treatment strategies cannot be overemphasized.

2. Intervention programs for maternal mental health and child development in low- and middle-income countries

Given the high burden and global health relevance of perinatal anxiety and depression, this chapter is largely focused on these two conditions. Higher-income countries account for the major proportion of research in this domain, but LMICs are catching up in exploring the epidemiology and developing effective prevention and treatment strategies. An increasing number of LMICs are interested in integrating maternal mental health strategies into maternal and child public health initiatives (Cooper et al., 2002; Rahman et al., 2008, 2009; Tomlinson et al., 2015). Wachs & Rahman (2013) situate potential interventional approaches at three levels, corresponding to the hierarchical nature of risk factors from macro- to microlevel. Macrolevel exposures can include natural and bioecological hazards such as global warming, or psychosocial adversities such as migration and poor socioeconomic level of a community. The next, more proximally placed level of risk factors works at the mesolevel: for instance, exposure to disease outbreaks or adverse school environment. The most proximal risk factors operate at the microlevel and pertain to those within individuals, for instance, child undernutrition or caregiver–child relationship. While macro- or mesolevel risk factors are important to address, their discussion is beyond the scope of this chapter, which focuses on interventions targeting microlevel risk factors.

Most microlevel interventions are multidimensional and have synergistic effects. For instance, combining micronutrient supplementation programs in deprived communities improves the effect of interventions targeting early schooling programs (Macours & Vakis, 2010). As noted by Wachs & Rahman (2013), these synergistic effects of interventions either decrease the impact of cumulative risk posed by several risk factors (e.g., poor nutrition and schooling) existing in tandem (sensitization) or lead to a *blunting* effect where a previous risk factor (e.g., maternal depression) decreases the protective influence of another intervention (e.g., caregiving). Before discussing available microlevel interventions in LMICs, we examine the issue of screening of individuals who may be in need of such interventions. We use the example of perinatal common mental disorders to discuss the challenges involved in mass population screening, especially in low-resource settings.

2.1 Screening

Several screening programs have been tested for effectiveness for timely screening of perinatal mental disorders in high-income countries. Most of this research has focused on delineating the psychometric properties of screening instruments for perinatal depression. Recent guidelines by the National Institute for Health & Care Excellence (NICE) and the US Preventive Services Taskforce recommend the use of either the Edinburgh Postnatal Depression Scale (EPDS) or the Patient Health Questionnaire (PHQ-9) (Curry et al., 2019; National Collaborating Center for Mental Health, 2020). In busy clinical settings, NICE recommends the use of briefer questionnaires such as the two-item Whooley questions as a rapid screening method for anxiety and depression.

Most research indicates both the EPDS and the PHQ-9 yield comparable sensitivity and specificity across a variety of settings and can be used with confidence for screening purposes (National Collaborating Center for Mental Health, 2020). Although the aforementioned tools are the most frequently investigated for screening perinatal depression and anxiety, many other scales have been proposed including the shorter versions of the EPDS and the PHQ (Thombs et al., 2020; Waqas et al., 2021). These tools can be used for initial screening purposes in busier clinical settings in patient populations or in large-scale screening programs in community settings in HIC. Research from HIC countries indicates that the tools for screening are generally easy to use by doctors, midwives as well as trained lay health workers (Buist et al., 2006). Innovations to address the challenges of limited human resources for population level screening in low-income countries have been proposed, which include the use of trained community informants and peers, who could be the initial agents for identification of probable cases of perinatal depression and anxiety using pictorial- or vignette-based community detection tools (Mohsin et al., 2021; Waqas et al., 2021). This could then be followed by formal assessments by trained health professionals, significantly reducing the burden on healthcare systems. This approach has been tested in Pakistan, yielding adequate accuracy (Waqas et al., 2021). Other strategies include use of online platforms and postal questionnaires, as well as use of peers and allied health workers for administering screening for postpartum anxiety and depression (Boere-boonekamp et al., 2017; Van Der Zee-Van Den Berg et al., 2017; Yawn et al., 2012).

Large-scale screening programs have been evaluated for their effectiveness and cost-effectiveness, but all of this research has been conducted solely in HIC. Nine randomized trials of such programs (Waqas et al., 2020) found that screening programs paired with counseling, treatment, and referral programs are effective in improving severity of depressive and anxiety symptoms, treatment seeking behavior, and quality of life and marital relationship. While there is a lack of long-term follow-up to delineate effects of these programs on child health, limited data do indicate slight improvement in child socioemotional development, parent—child bonding, and treatment seeking (Leung et al., 2011; Morrell et al., 2009; Yawn et al., 2012). Although most of the researchers fail to report adverse effects of these screening programs, recent data do not indicate any adverse effects reported by women undergoing screening for perinatal anxiety and depression (Leung et al., 2011; Morrell et al., 2009; Yawn et al., 2012). Limited research evidence also suggests these programs may be cost-effective when quality-of-life outcomes are taken into account in addition to directly incurred program costs (Morrell et al., 2009; Wilkinson et al., 2017).

These programs have also been found to be feasible and acceptable by women. There are concerns regarding the ethical implementation of screening programs if appropriate services are lacking and it is recommended that screening should only be introduced in a setting when treatment and referral resources are available. In addition, qualitative data indicate experience of internalized stigma by women screened positive for depression, but this can be averted by developing appropriate resources for counseling (Morrell et al., 2009).

2.2 Intervention targeting perinatal depression and anxiety

Psychological and psychosocial interventions for depression and anxiety are based on heterogenous theoretical orientations, often contain a mixture of therapeutic elements, and frequently demonstrate varied effectiveness in improving maternal mental health outcomes (Aboud et al., 2013; Attanasio et al., 2014; Cooper et al., 2002; Rahman et al., 2009; Singla et al., 2015; Tripathy et al., 2010). Recent literature on interventions for common mental disorders generally classify them according to their theoretical underpinning, as being either psychological or psychosocial in nature (Chowdhary et al., 2014). Psychological interventions are based on the principles of cognitive behavioral therapy, interpersonal therapy, or third-wave therapies such as the mindfulness-based cognitive therapies (Rahman et al., 2013, 2018). Psychosocial interventions employ strategies such as social support groups, and psychoeducation has also gained significant evidence for treatment and prevention of perinatal depression and anxiety in the LMICs (Jeong et al., 2021; Rahman et al., 2018). Some psychosocial interventions are underpinned by concepts borrowed from behavior change, women empowerment programs, and tangible assistance programs (Dennis & Hodnett, 2007). Occasionally, interdisciplinary interactions and collaborations lead to multicomponent interventions, which derive elements from a variety of disciplines, frequently using different terminologies for similar components (Abraham & Michie, 2008; Michie et al., 2013). However, an examination of fidelity measures from different theoretical models indicates that different terms are used to describe the same element (Chorpita et al., 2005; Chowdhary et al., 2014). For example, "using thought records" in cognitive behavioral therapy is likely to represent the same element as "using mood ratings" in interpersonal psychotherapy (Chowdhary et al., 2014). The field would benefit from a common terminology for identifying and classifying the elements across all evidence-based psychosocial intervention. A list of a common taxonomy of elements has been presented in Fig. 10.1.

The overlap between elements employed in various intervention packages creates a problem for the field as it is important for researchers

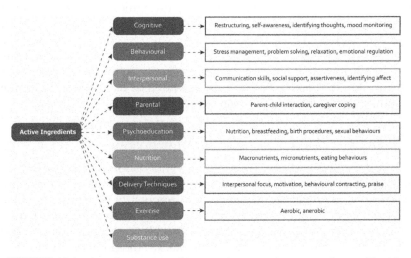

FIGURE 10.1   Specific elements of interventions targeting maternal mental health.

and policy-makers to know which "interventions" provide the best evidence for effectiveness and feasibility and suitability for large-scale implementation (Cuijpers et al., 2020). These problems have been highlighted by funders of research such as the Wellcome Trust (Cuijpers et al., 2020), and their launch of the Mental Health Priority Area, which focuses on harmonizing the terminology used across disciplines engaged in improving mental health, and recognition of common elements or "active ingredients" driving remission in common mental health problems. However, this initiative is limited to adolescent mental health at present.

Researchers in the perinatal mental health field are contributing to the development of this area. This is evidenced in critical reviews mapping the use of active ingredients for improving perinatal mental health (Rahman et al., 2018; Singla et al., 2017). A common terminology for specific and nonspecific elements could offer several advantages for evidence-based psychosocial interventions. Two seminal works in this domain were published by Singla et al. (2017) and Chowdhary et al. (2014), who built on the Distillation andatching framework proposed by Chorpita et al. (2005), to identify common elements across psychological and psychosocial therapies. Singla et al. proposed a taxonomy of the most common ingredients of interventions for the treatment of depression, dividing into nine different themes (Fig. 10.1).

Despite these academic shortcomings, the evidence for effectiveness of both classes of interventions is robust enough for the WHO to strongly recommend that psychological and psychosocial mental health interventions should be given to pregnant and postpartum women for mental health promotion and prevention and treatment of perinatal depression and anxiety. The most recent WHO guidelines on interventions focused on perinatal mental health are supported by 33 randomized controlled trials of psychological interventions that achieved improved depression and anxiety symptoms among the intervention recipients (Rahman et al., 2018). These interventions demonstrate moderate to strong effect sizes for both the prevention and treatment when delivered to either universal or at-risk pregnant and postpartum women (Rahman et al., 2018). There is, however, some evidence that the preventive approaches work better when delivered during the antepartum period (Waqas et al., 2021). For both the perinatal depression and anxiety, cognitive behavioral therapy and interpersonal psychotherapy have the strongest evidence base. Among psychosocial approaches, social support groups and psychoeducational approaches have been the most frequently tested. All of these approaches have shown good effectiveness in improving perinatal mental health (Dennis & Dowswell, 2014; Dennis & Hodnett, 2007; Waqas et al., 2021; World Health Organization, 2019a, 2019b). These interventions yield moderate to strong effect sizes for both the prevention and treatment when delivered either universally or to at-risk pregnant and postpartum women (Rahman et al., 2018).

There are limited long-term data available pertaining to perinatal mental health intervention effects on child development. Nonetheless, epidemiological evidence does point indirectly to adverse effects of perinatal anxiety and depression on child health and development, making perinatal mental disorders an important intervention target (Garman et al., 2019). Limited long-term intervention data do suggest these interventions improve child emotional and physical development with weak to moderate effect sizes observed for outcomes including height for age, stunting, child cognitive development, play frequency, and neonatal mortality (World Health Organization, 2019a, 2019b). Therefore, it is recommended that interventions for perinatal mental health be integrated into early child health and development services (World Health Organization, 2019a, 2019b).

We examine one intervention for perinatal depression, which has been most widely researched in different settings and contexts (Rahman et al., 2021). The Thinking Healthy Programme (THP), which was initially developed and tested in Pakistan (Rahman et al., 2008), is a multicomponent intervention, largely based on cognitive behavioral approaches. It was adopted by the WHO as a model psychological intervention to be scaled in LMICs, through its mhGAP program (Rahman et al., 2021). A detailed intervention manual is available at the WHO's online database (World Health Organization, 2015). Recent research unpacking the mechanism and mediational pathways shows that the THP primarily works by behavioral activation, identifying and inciting social support and improving parent–child interaction (Singla et al., 2019). The active ingredients comprising the THP were underpinned by several different approaches, drawing upon research evidence (World Health Organization, 2015). It comprised of techniques including psychoeducation about mental health and overall well-being in commonly understood terms to avoid stigma; cognitive behavioral sessions delivered by nonspecialists using pictures; identifying support from friends, family, and spouses and baby's health. In addition, adjunct techniques such as optimum nutrition and physical exercise are encouraged (Fig. 10.2).

Other interventions with multicomponent elements that target both the maternal mental health and child development have been tested in LMICs in the past decade. For instance, Singla et al. developed a multicomponent intervention comprising of cognitive, behavioral, interpersonal, and stimulation approaches, leading to an improvement in maternal depression, as well as child cognitive and language skills (Singla et al., 2015). Tomlinson et al. tested an intervention employing cognitive behavioral approaches and knowledge about child care practices in South Africa, which improved infant growth (Tomlinson et al., 2015). An innovation in

Thinking Healthy Programme

Low-intensity, multicomponent psychological interventions provided by LHWs

Activate social support networks	Cognitive behavioral therapy sessions	Psychoeducation	Encourage adjunct techniques	Mother-baby relationship
Mother's relationship with people around her

Engagement with LHWs | Pictures and structured activities to deliver a simplified form of CBT | Using commonly understood terms to avoid stigma

Focus on overall wellbeing | Physical activity, relaxation, and problem-solving | Baby's health
Postnatal bonding & attachment |

FIGURE 10.2   Active ingredients of the Thinking Healthy Programme delivered by Lady Health Workers (LHWs).

FIGURE 10.3   Targets for innovation in the field of perinatal mental health.

these two investigations was the use of lay community health workers and peers, i.e., the nonspecialist workforce, thus bypassing the burden on healthcare systems. Fathers were included as stakeholders by an intervention delivered by Shariat et al. aimed at improving mother–child bonding (Shariat & Abedinia, 2017).

A multicomponent intervention of note called the "Learning Through Play (LTP) Plus Thinking Healthy Programme" has been tested recently in Pakistan, which target both maternal depression and child development (Husain et al., 2017; Husain, Kiran, Fatima, et al., 2021; Husain, Kiran, Shah, et al., 2021). These interventions have proven effective among women in low-income areas and urban slums of Karachi, as well as among mothers with malnourished children (Husain et al., 2017, 2021, 2021; Husain, Kiran, Shah, et al., 2021). Delivered by community health workers, this intervention delivers the THP sessions to mothers for depression and LTP for child stimulation. The LTP comprises of a pictorial calendar showing developmental stages and appropriate parent–child play activities, from birth to 3 years of age. Five strategies are used for child stimulation: sense of self, physical development, relationships with others, understanding of world, and communication skills (Husain et al., 2017, 2021, 2021; Husain, Kiran, Shah, et al., 2021). Women undergoing this intervention report improvement in depression, quality of life, psychosocial functioning, and social support. In parallel, improvements are also reported in parents' knowledge about child development, parent–child interaction, and infant socioemotional development at 6 months of age.

All these interventions have been tested in well-designed clinical trials and are good candidates for scale-up in LMICs (Table 10.1).

2.3 Interventions targeting infant–caregiver interaction

Interventions targeting infant–caregiver interaction have garnered significant interest in the public mental health community in recent years (Jeong et al., 2021). These groups of interventions have a good evidence base, and are recommended by the WHO, to improve infant development (World Health Organization, 2019a, 2019b). These are largely divided into three groups based on their theoretical underpinnings and targeted outcomes. The first group includes responsive caregiving interventions to improve parent–child relationship, enhance sensitivity and responsiveness to child's needs, and strengthen attachment (Jeong et al., 2021). The delivery agent in these interventions thus targets the caregiver–child dyad. The second group of interventions include psychostimulation and psychoeducational interventions comprising of educational modules, to improve caregiver's knowledge, attitudes, and practices toward supporting child's learning and development (World Health Organization, 2019a, 2019b). These interventions include information on parent–child book readings and play activities using developmentally appropriate toys and child discipline, feeding, and general health. The third group of interventions are mainly used for behavioral development of children by promoting positive behavior management, establishing an appropriate milieu and discipline at home. Techniques such as praising are encouraged, and harsh discipline is avoided. Often these interventions are also paired with nutritional components such as breastfeeding practices, and macronutrient and micronutrient supplementations.

Several good examples exist for these types of interventions in LMICs. Yousufzai and colleagues work on psychosocial stimulation of children in Pakistan is noteworthy (Yousafzai et al., 2014). They tested a multicomponent intervention which comprised of nutrition education, provision of micronutrient supplements (iron, folic acid, vitamin A, and vitamin C), and responsive stimulation and delivered by community health workers. The provision of nutrients and psychostimulation as stand-alone interventions led to significant improvements in infant cognitive, language, and socioemotional development. However, the combination of these two interventions did not lead to any additive effects. Attanasio et al. developed a psychosocial intervention comprising of cognitive, interpersonal, and psychoeducational approaches, paired with psychostimulation for the children in Colombia. It also tested effectiveness of micronutrient supplementation in one of their treatment arms (Attanasio et al., 2014). Although psychostimulation improved child cognitive development, no beneficial effects were moderated by micronutrient supplementation. An interesting aspect of this intervention program was its embedding in a national cash transfer program in Kenya, thus easing the process of scale-up and integration into the national social safety net. Some of these caregiver—child interventions have also been tested as multicomponent programs also addressing maternal mental health. As previously mentioned, Singla et al.'s program comprising of cognitive, behavioral, interpersonal, and stimulation approaches is a good example of the latter.

Hands-on strategies employed in these interventions vary from simple home visits and guidance and demonstration sessions and provision of play materials to recording of parent—child interactions to provide feedback by therapists (Jeong et al., 2021). A recent systematic review of 111 caregiving interventions found that these interventions bring about moderate improvements in infant cognitive development, language development, and motor development (Jeong et al., 2021). Small improvements are also seen in socioemotional development and behavioral problems among infants and children who undergo these parenting interventions. These interventions also lead to large improvements in parenting knowledge, rearing practices, and parent—child interaction. However, these interventions overall do not lead to any improvement in caregiver mental health. A recent review presented evidence for interventions that include components targeting both the maternal mental health and child development (Rahman et al., 2018). This review concluded that such multicomponent programs do lead to a small improvement in maternal mental health, citing the need for integrated maternal—child mental health interventions.

The recent guidelines for improvement of early child development by the WHO strongly recommend that parents and caregivers should be supported to provide responsive care as well as early learning activities to their children (World Health Organization, 2019a, 2019b), either as stand-alone interventions or as parts of nutritional programs. It further recommends that maternal mental health interventions should be integrated into psychostimulation or caregiving interventions, to yield maximum benefits.

3. Innovations in delivery methods to facilitate scale-up in low- and middle-income countries

3.1 Task-sharing and transdiagnostic approaches

One of the major challenges that the LMICs face in the scale-up of psychological, psychosocial, and early childhood psychostimulation interventions is the lack of specialized human resource personnel and a weakened public mental health infrastructure (Chisholm et al., 2007). LMICs are home to over 85% of the world population, accounting for over 80% of the global population with common mental disorders especially depression (WHO, 2014). There are severe shortages of psychiatric personnel, with meager financial resources allocated to the mental health sector in the LMICs (Sachs, 2012). The majority of the LMICs spend less than 1% of their health budgets on the mental health sector. For instance, as of 2018, Pakistan allocates around 3.2% of its GDP on health, out of which only 0.4% is spent on mental health (The World Bank, 2018; World Health Organization, 2018a, 2018b). This is worsened by the concentration of mental health and psychosocial support specialists in the urban areas, and as a consequence, the rural population has the least provision.

One of the solutions proposed to counter this is the development of a nonspecialist workforce comprising of lay health workers and peers (Rahman, 2015). A growing body of evidence shows that this workforce can effectively deliver mental health interventions (both psychological and psychosocial) (Maselko et al., 2020; Rahman et al., 2008; Tripathy et al., 2010). This approach provides a distribution of health resources among the specialists and nonspecialists. The nonspecialist workforce can be readied in a short duration by providing a brief training in talking therapies, who can then effectively treat patients with mild to moderate impairment. This approach has also shown to be very cost-effective.

Notable examples of the task-sharing approach is the use of lady health workers and peers for delivery of the Thinking Healthy Programme in Pakistan (Rahman et al., 2021). In South Africa and Kenya, health visitors have been employed to deliver psychoeducational mother—infant intervention for improvement of child health and maternal mental health, with good success (Cooper et al., 2002, 2015). The use of peers has also been tested in some settings with success, for instance, by employing *sakhis* in Goa, India, who were successful in treating perinatal depression (Weobong et al., 2017). Although there are very few studies reporting cost-effectiveness, limited data suggest that these interventions have been cost-effective in India (Sikander et al., 2019). This cost-effectiveness has also been demonstrated for child-focused parenting interventions. For instance, in China, the cost of providing parenting intervention was about $50 per child per year (Shi et al., 2020). Similarly, by integrating cognitive stimulation-based intervention in the existing lady health worker infrastructure, Yousafzai et al. demonstrated that it could be delivered at a cost of 48 USD per child (Yousafzai et al., 2014). This indicates that the ability of nonspecialist workforce is pivotal to scale up early childhood development services effectively at reduced costs.

Another important development in this domain are the increased calls for adopting transdiagnostic approaches toward mental health (Prince et al., 2007). These approaches recommend that instead of viewing mental disorders as categorical diagnoses, a dimensional approach across a continuum should be applied. This could be a potential and pragmatic approach to designing of a stepped-care approach, where nonspecialist workforces could identify and target distressing psychiatric symptoms underpinned by biopsychosocial processes that underpin a broad range of mental disorders (Dalgleish et al., 2020). This field, however, is still new, warranting more evidence base before scale-up in perinatal mental health (Dalgleish et al., 2020).

3.2 Integrated maternal and child mental health intervention packages

Much of the research in LMICs has shown that psychological and psychosocial interventions, integrated into priority health service delivery platforms, are feasible and cost-effective (Rahman et al., 2021), and global mental health researchers have emphasized the case for integration of perinatal mental health interventions into maternal and child services (Rahman, 2015). Apart from the feasibility and cost-effectiveness, such interventions are more equitable and accessible to disadvantaged populations who lack specialist care facilities (Atif et al., 2016). This also promotes an integrated and holistic approach toward mental and physical healthcare and is an attractive option to communities in LMICs where stigma toward mental disorders is prevalent (O'Mahen et al., 2015).

As discussed previously, it is also important to understand that maternal and child health are interlinked, and integrated and multi-component maternal–child focused interventions could leverage this linkage (Wachs & Rahman, 2013). For instance, women with perinatal depression often experience poor concentration, fatigue, and psychomotor retardation, also leading to poor maternal–infant bonding (Wachs & Rahman, 2013). Mothers experiencing depression, therefore, may not be as receptive and motivated to the uptake of interventions. Thus, teaching psychostimulation strategies to mothers with depression without treating their depressive symptoms would not be as beneficial in improving child cognition. Healthy mothers, therefore, are in a better position to take care of their children (Wachs & Rahman, 2013).

In recent years, several interventions have been tested that target both maternal mental health and child development. Singla et al. for instance, tested a community volunteer-mediated intervention, comprising of evidence-based cognitive, behavioral, interpersonal, and stimulation strategies, targeting both child care and mothers' well-being (Singla et al., 2015). Families were trained to improve child care: play, talk, diet, hygiene, and employing gentle discipline through love and respect. These sessions led to an improvement in child cognition and receptive language as well as maternal depressive symptoms. For maternal well-being, several techniques were used including increasing father's involvement, resolution of interpersonal conflicts, and social support. These skills were imparted using a range of techniques such as role play and group-based problem-solving methods (Singla et al., 2015).

Another promising intervention developed in Pakistan tested a transdiagnostic intervention targeting maternal psychosocial well-being and integrated into a combined nutrition and early child development program (Zafar et al., 2014). The resulting intervention termed SPRING (Sustainable Program Incorporating Nutrition and Games) was delivered by community health workers to women starting in pregnancy to 2 years postpartum. By guiding families on caring for children, improving feeding practices, as well as improving maternal mental well-being, it sought to maximize benefits for both the mother and infants. The delivery agents of interventions were trained in five techniques suitable for universal delivery: empathic listening, improving family support, guided discovery using pictures for behavior change, and behavioral activation and problem-solving.

The Thinking Healthy Programme employs lady health workers as delivery agents, effectively integrating perinatal mental healthcare into primary care—oriented maternal and child health services (Fuhr et al., 2019). In Pakistan, this cadre of health workforce is trained in provision of primary maternal and child health services, to the communities. Such delivery agents usually have a better understanding of the local culture and socioeconomic adversities, and so are in an excellent position to interlink psychosocial, reproductive, and mental and child health problems. This interlinked approach helps to appreciate an individual's psychological affliction from a syndemic perspective, i.e., stemming from an interplay of several psychosocial and biological variables (Mendenhall, 2017). This approach often results into more personalized and patient-centered care.

From stakeholders' perspective, arming health workers with an integrated set of interventions that address both maternal and child health has several advantages (Wachs & Rahman, 2013). Firstly, if psychological and psychosocial interventions are viewed in terms of *active ingredients*, then it becomes apparent that there is a substantial overlap between the content of public mental health interventions, delivered to different populations across the life course. These overlapping ingredients include but not limited to identifying sources of and improving social support networks, psychoeducation, and cognitive behavioral approaches such as problem-solving. By logically grouping these skills across various intervention packages, they can be scaled up. Secondly, by delivery of cross-domain multicomponent intervention packages, several risk factors could be targeted in tandem, reducing the sensitization and blunting phenomena to yield synergistic effects of interventions. It should, however, be noted that the development of cross-domain packages should always be adapted to the needs of the community. For instance, there is no use in delivery of caregiving or psychostimulation-based intervention in resource-poor settings, where there is no access to optimum nutrition, clean drinking water, hygiene, or maternal education.

3.3 Technological solutions

Recent decades have seen an increase in the development of digital solutions in medicine (Waqas et al., 2020). In the past decade, mental health has emerged as one of the fields embracing the digital revolution and has made significant progress in it. In HIC, however, digital interventions targeting perinatal depression, anxiety, and stress have gained significant momentum. Lau et al., for instance, in their metaanalyses reported that therapist-supported iCBT improved stress ($d = 0.84$), anxiety ($d = 0.36$), and depressive symptoms ($d = 0.63$) among women in the intervention group (Lau et al., 2017). Effective interventions are available for complicated grief during the perinatal period or the time after pregnancy loss, as well as for prevention (Ashford et al., 2017; Barrera et al., 2015).

However, it is not surprising to note that most of these innovations have taken place in HICs (Waqas et al., 2020) and LMICs have yet to develop capacity and culturally sensitive interventions for perinatal mental disorders. Nonetheless, digitally based talking therapies especially based on cognitive and behavioral approaches do have potential and have been shown to be effective for several mental disorders in the LMICs, yielding moderate to strong effect sizes (Fu et al., 2020) (Fig. 10.3).

3.3.1 Use of big data approaches

Apart from harmonization of terminologies across different interventions, use of the active ingredient approach also permits researchers to better manualize their interventions to improve reproducibility. With the recent advances in individual patient data metaanalysis, data from independent studies could also be pooled and analyzed to establish the optimal sequencing and dosing of elements and for whom a given element, or set of elements, is most effective (Pompoli et al., 2018). In addition, it might be possible to connect elements more precisely to purported mechanisms of change than is the case with an entire complex psychosocial intervention (Furukawa et al., 2021). In the future, an elements framework could advance training in and implementation of evidence-based psychosocial interventions, as practitioners would learn strategies and techniques that can be applied across target problems, disorders, or contexts (Singla et al., 2017).

3.3.2 Electronic delivery of intervention

Recently, the THP was adapted in the form of a chatbot in Kenya. It was also adapted for delivery as an electronic short messaging service in Kenya, where access to smartphone was not available (Green et al., 2019). This automated delivery was done via a chatbot called Zuri. Although a randomized controlled trial has not been published, recent pilot studies suggest that Kenyan women report good engagement with this automated delivery of the contents of the THP. Qualitative data suggest that those women who tried Zuri have a positive attitude toward it and expressed trust in it. The intervention helped them bring positive change to their lives, leading to a 7% improvement in their mood. Currently, efforts are underway to develop the electronic application for delivery of THP using tablets and smartphones, mediated by community health workers.

3.3.3 Electronic training and supervision methods

To aid in its scale-up, electronic and cascaded supervision and training modules have been developed, which have been found to be effective in training of community health workers in Pakistan (Atif et al., 2019; Rahman et al., 2019). This approach employs a cascaded model of training and supervision whereby using a tablet-based application, specialists impart standardized training to specialist trainers. These specialist *master trainers* in turn train and supervise nonspecialist managers for health workers. This is then cascaded down to frontline health workers and integrated into their daily duties (Rahman et al., 2019). Thus, it is a promising method for training and supervision of health workers in remote areas with a shortage of mental health specialists.

3.3.4 Large-scale implementation

Research on the Thinking Healthy Programme also led to large-scale implementation trials (Sikander et al., 2019) and development of tools and indices to assess the level of implementation in the field (Ahmad et al., 2020). Although the research in this field is still in its nascency, efforts are underway to develop valid and reliable tools. An important exemplar in this domain is the Implementation Strength Index, which has shown some promise for use in Pakistan (Ahmad et al., 2020). This index makes use of four important variables: competency of delivery agents, attendance in supervised sessions, and duration and number of sessions delivered. Competency of delivery agents can also be assessed by tools such as the ENACT tool, which has also been recently shortened and adapted electronically (Kohrt et al., 2015).

4. Recommendation for future practice and research

Based on the evidence presented here, we propose the following recommendations for future practice and research to improve perinatal mental health and child development in LMICs (Table 10.2).

4.1 Recommendations for clinical practice

In line with the recommendations by the World Health Organization, screening for perinatal mental disorders should be done wherever resources for treatment and referral mechanisms are available (Waqas et al., 2022a, b). Psychological interventions should be offered to women at risk, and psychosocial ones should be available universally (Rahman et al., 2018). Early childhood development programs such as cognitive stimulation, caregiving interventions, and nutritional supplementations should be offered to children in LMICs, to improve their cognition, language, and motor development. Interventions targeting perinatal depression and anxiety should be coupled with early childhood development programs, to yield maximum benefits for child development. Task-shared and transdiagnostic interventions should be introduced in communities for equitable access to mental healthcare.

Digital technology must be leveraged to design and improve access to packages to communities. These personalized interventions should target prevalence risk factors in the communities after matching them with appropriate intervention ingredients. Telemedicine software should be used for capacity development of health workers living in remote areas, using cascaded supervision and teaching methods.

4.2 Recommendations for research

Coordination between academics and stakeholders should be encouraged to design effective models for healthcare delivery, for scale-up in communities. These innovative healthcare models can work on a stepped-care approach, whereby community mobilizers and lay health workers can be first responders for screening, prevention, and treatment of mental disorders. And mental health specialists can take up the role of consultants, capacity developers, and point of contacts for specialized mental healthcare. Cross-disciplinary interactions and collaborations should be encouraged, to develop integrated intervention packages that work synergistically to improve perinatal and child mental health. Further research is warranted on the development and feasibility testing of digital technology for health applications and software for guided delivery of interventions by lay health workers.

TABLE 10.1   Examples of interventions for improvement of maternal mental health and child development.

Author, year	Elements
Interventions with a primary focus on maternal mental health	
Gao et al. (2010)	Identifying and eliciting social support, communication skills, assessing relationships, problem-solving, stress management, caregiver coping, parent–child interaction, birth procedure, nutrition, breastfeeding
Gao et al. (2015)	Identifying affect, identifying and eliciting social support, communication skills, assessing relationships, problem-solving, parent–child interaction, breastfeeding
Gu et al. (2013)	Exposure, stress management, parent–child interaction, birth procedure, nutrition, breastfeeding, sexual behavior
Jiang et al. (2014)	Psychological counseling
Rabiei et al. (2014)	Identifying and eliciting social support, communication skills, assertiveness training, assessing relationships, problem-solving, relaxation, emotional regulation, stress management, self-awareness, mindfulness, aerobic and nonaerobic exercise
Rahman et al. (2008)	Identifying and eliciting social support, communication skills, assertiveness training, problem-solving, stress management, decision-making
Tripathy et al. (2010)	Active listening, empathy, collaboration, inciting social support, eliciting commitment, discussing advantages of treatment, discussing barriers to treatment, identifying affect, identifying and eliciting social support, problem-solving, stress management, decision-making, self-monitoring, motivational enhancement, role play, interpersonal focus, goal setting
Interventions with a secondary focus on maternal mental health	
Aboud et al. (2013)	Identifying and eliciting social support, problem-solving, communication skills, caregiver coping, parent–child relationship
Attanasio et al. (2014)	Empathy, discussing advantages of treatment, discussing barriers of treatment, communication skills, parent–child interaction, nutrition, cognitive restructuring, behavioral contracting, behavioral experiments, direct suggestions, reviewing homework, goal settings, micronutrients
Chang et al. (2015)	Parent–child interaction coaching, praise
Çiftçi & Arikan (2012)	Birth procedure, breastfeeding
Clarke et al. (2014)/Fottrell et al. (2013)	Involvement of significant other, active listening, empathy, collaboration, eliciting commitment, discussing advantages of treatment, communication skills, exposure, self-monitoring, caregiver coping, parent–child interaction, breastfeeding, cognitive restructuring, self-awareness, motivational enhancements, praise, role plays, behavioral contracting, assigning homework, interpersonal focus, behavioral experiments, reviewing homework, empathy

TABLE 10.1   Examples of interventions for improvement of maternal mental health and child development.—cont'd

Author, year	Elements
Cooper et al. (2002)	Empathy, inciting social support, discussing advantages of treatment, discussing barriers of treatment, identifying and eliciting social support, communication skills, caregiver coping, parent–child interaction, behavioral contracting
Shrestha et al. (2016)	Psychoeducation on breastfeeding

Caregiver interventions for psychostimulation

Abessa et al. (2019)	Learning through play, caregiver training, provision of play materials, coaching homework, and goal setting
Aboud & Akhter (2011)	Psychoeducation on health, nutrition and child development, discussion, role plays, demonstrations, micronutrient supplementation
Alvarenga et al. (2019)	Video feedbacks on mother–child interactions
Andrew et al. (2020)	Psychoeducation on developmentally appropriate activities, provision of toys, picture books, demonstration, role plays, assessing caregiver response to child actions and vocal cues
Ara et al. (2019)	Involvement of family, counseling and psychoeducation on psychosocial stimulation, development, growth and child feeding practices, provision of eating utensils, toys, and handwash

TABLE 10.2   Recommendations for clinical practices and research.

Recommendations for clinical practice

- Provision of screening services where treatment mechanisms are in place
- Offer early childhood development programs in LMICs
- Integrated psychosocial and psychological interventions
- Integration of interventions for mothers with existing infrastructure of childhood development programs
- Upscale task-sharing strategies
- Use digital technology for intervention delivery, training, and supervision

Recommendations for research

- Effective coordination between academics and stakeholders
- Interdisciplinary collaborations to encourage out of box thinking
- Development of digital technology relevant to cultural norms and health systems

References

Abessa, T. G., Worku, B. N., Wondafrash, M., Girma, T., Valy, J., Lemmens, J., et al. (2019). Effect of play-based family-centered psychomotor/psychosocial stimulation on the development of severely acutely malnourished children under six in a low-income setting: a randomized controlled trial. *BMC Pediatrics, 19*(1), 336.

Aboud, F. E., & Akhter, S. (2011). A cluster-randomized evaluation of a responsive stimulation and feeding intervention in bangladesh. *Pediatrics, 127*(5), e1191−e1197.

Aboud, F. E., Singla, D. R., Nahil, M. I., & Borisova, I. (2013). Effectiveness of a parenting program in Bangladesh to address early childhood health, growth and development. *Social Science and Medicine, 97*, 250−258. https://doi.org/10.1016/j.socscimed.2013.06.020

Abraham, C., & Michie, S. (2008). A taxonomy of behavior change techniques used in interventions. *Health Psychology, 27*(3), 379. https://doi.org/10.1037/0278-6133.27.3.379

Ahmad, I., Suleman, N., Waqas, A., Atif, N., Malik, A. A., Bibi, A., Zulfiqar, S., Nisar, A., Javed, H., Zaidi, A., Khan, Z. S., & Sikander, S. (2020). Measuring the implementation strength of a perinatal mental health intervention delivered by peer volunteers in rural Pakistan. *Behaviour Research and Therapy, 130*, 103559. https://doi.org/10.1016/j.brat.2020.103559

Alvarenga, P., Cerezo, M.Á., Wiese, E., & Piccinini, C. A. (2019). Effects of a short video feedback intervention on enhancing maternal sensitivity and infant development in low-income families. *Attachment and Human Development*, 1−21.

Andrew, A., Attanasio, O., Augsburg, B., Day, M., Grantham-McGregor, S., Meghir, C., et al. (2020). Effects of a scalable home-visiting intervention on child development in slums of urban India: evidence from a randomised controlled trial. *Journal of Child Psychology and Psychiatry, 61*(6), 644−652.

Ara, G., Khanam, M., Papri, N., Nahar, B., Kabir, I., Sanin, K. I., et al. (2019). Peer counseling promotes appropriate infant feeding practices and improves infant growth and development in an urban slum in Bangladesh: A community-based cluster randomized controlled trial. *Current Developments in Nutrition, 3*(7), nzz072.

Ashford, M. T., Olander, E. K., Rowe, H., Fisher, J. R. W., & Ayers, S. (2017). Internet-based interventions for postpartum anxiety: Exploring health visitors' views. *Journal of Reproductive and Infant Psychology, 35*(3), 298−308. https://doi.org/10.1080/02646838.2017.1313966

Atif, Najia, Lovell, K., Husain, N., Sikander, S., Patel, V., & Rahman, A. (2016). Barefoot therapists: Barriers and facilitators to delivering maternal mental health care through peer volunteers in Pakistan: A qualitative study. *International Journal of Mental Health Systems, 10*(1), 1−12. https://doi.org/10.1186/s13033-016-0055-9

Atif, N., Nisar, A., Bibi, A., Khan, S., Zulfiqar, S., Ahmad, I., Sikander, S., & Rahman, A. (2019). Scaling-up psychological interventions in resource-poor settings: Training and supervising peer volunteers to deliver the 'Thinking Healthy Programme' for perinatal depression in rural Pakistan. *Global Mental Health, 6*, e4. https://doi.org/10.1017/gmh.2019.4

Attanasio, O. P., Fernández, C., Fitzsimons, E. O. A., Grantham-McGregor, S. M., Meghir, C., & Rubio-Codina, M. (2014). Using the infrastructure of a conditional cash transfer program to deliver a scalable integrated early child development program in Colombia: Cluster randomized controlled trial. *BMJ (Clinical Research Ed.), 349*(September), 1−12. https://doi.org/10.1136/bmj.g5785

Barrera, A. Z., Wickham, R. E., & Muñoz, R. F. (2015). Online prevention of postpartum depression for Spanish- and English-speaking pregnant women: A pilot randomized controlled trial. *Internet Interventions, 2*(3), 257−265. https://doi.org/10.1016/j.invent.2015.06.002

Bauer, A., Parsonage, M., Knapp, M., Iemmi, V., Adelaja, B., & Hogg, S. (2014). *The costs of perinatal mental health problems*. London: Centre for Mental Health and London School of Economics.

Boere-Boonekamp, M. M., IJzerman, M. J., Haasnoot-Smallegange, R. M., & Reijneveld, S. A. (2017 Jan). Screening for postpartum depression in well-baby care settings: a systematic review. *Maternal and Child Health Journal*, 21(1), 9—20.

Britto, P. R., Lye, S. J., Proulx, K., Yousafzai, A. K., Matthews, S. G., Vaivada, T., Perez-Escamilla, R., Rao, N., Ip, P., Fernald, L. C. H., MacMillan, H., Hanson, M., Wachs, T. D., Yao, H., Yoshikawa, H., Cerezo, A., Leckman, J. F., & Bhutta, Z. A. (2017). Nurturing care: Promoting early childhood development. *The Lancet, 389*(10064), 91—102. https://doi.org/10.1016/S0140-6736(16)31390-3

Buist, A., Condon, J., Brooks, J., Speelman, C., Milgrom, J., Hayes, B., Ellwood, D., Barnett, B., Kowalenko, N., Matthey, S., Austin, M. P., & Bilszta, J. (2006). Acceptability of routine screening for perinatal depression. *Journal of Affective Disorders, 93*(1—3), 233—237. https://doi.org/10.1016/j.jad.2006.02.019

Case, A., & Paxson, C. (2008). Stature and status: Height, ability, and labor market outcomes. *Journal of Political Economy, 116*(3), 499—532. https://doi.org/10.1086/589524

Chang, S. M., Grantham-McGregor, S. M., Powell, C. A., Vera-Hernández, M., Lopez-Boo, F., Baker-Henningham, H., & Walker, S. P. (2015). Integrating a parenting intervention with routine primary health care: a cluster randomized trial. *Childs, 136*(2), 272—280.

Chisholm, D., Lund, C., & Saxena, S. (2007). Cost of scaling up mental healthcare in low- and middle-income countries. *British Journal of Psychiatry, 191*(DEC), 528—535. https://doi.org/10.1192/bjp.bp.107.038463

Chorpita, B. F., Daleiden, E. L., & Weisz, J. R. (2005). Identifying and selecting the common elements of evidence based interventions: A distillation and matching model. *Mental Health Services Research, 7*(1), 5—20. https://doi.org/10.1007/s11020-005-1962-6

Chowdhary, N., Sikander, S., Atif, N., Singh, N., Ahmad, I., Fuhr, D. C., Rahman, A., & Patel, V. (2014). The content and delivery of psychological interventions for perinatal depression by non-specialist health workers in low and middle income countries: A systematic review. *Best Practice and Research: Clinical Obstetrics and Gynaecology, 28*(1), 113—133. https://doi.org/10.1016/j.bpobgyn.2013.08.013

Çiftçi, E. K., & Arikan, D. (2012). The effect of training administered to working mothers on maternal anxiety levels and breastfeeding habits. *Journal of Clinical Nursing, 21*(15—16), 2170—2178.

Clarke, K., Azad, K., Kuddus, A., Shaha, S., Nahar, T., Aumon, BH., Hossen, M. M., Beard, J., Costello, A., Houweling, T. A., & Prost, A. (2014). Impact of a participatory intervention with women's groups on psychological distress among mothers in rural Bangladesh: Secondary analysis of a cluster-randomised controlled trial. *PloS One, 9*(10), Article e110697.

Cooper, P. J., De Pascalis, L., Woolgar, M., Romaniuk, H., & Murray, L. (2015). Attempting to prevent postnatal depression by targeting the mother-infant relationship: A randomised controlled trial. *Primary Health Care Research & Development, 16*(4), 383—397. https://doi.org/10.1017/S1463423614000401

Cooper, P. J., Landman, M., Tomlinson, M., Molteno, C., Swartz, L., & Murray, L. (2002). Impact of a mother-infant intervention in an indigent peri- urban South African context - pilot study. *British Journal of Psychiatry, 180*, 76—81. https://doi.org/10.1192/bjp.180.1.76

Cuijpers, P., Stringaris, A., & Wolpert, M. (2020). Treatment outcomes for depression: Challenges and opportunities. *The Lancet Psychiatry, 7*(11), 925—927. https://doi.org/10.1016/S2215-0366(20)30036-5

Curry, S. J., Krist, A. H., Owens, D. K., Barry, M. J., Caughey, A. B., Davidson, K. W., Doubeni, C. A., Epling, J. W., Grossman, D. C., Kemper, A. R., Kubik, M., Landefeld, C. S., Mangione, C. M., Silverstein, M., Simon, M. A., Tseng, C. W., &

Wong, J. B. (2019). Interventions to prevent perinatal depression: US preventive services task force recommendation statement. *JAMA - Journal of the American Medical Association, 321*(6), 580–587. https://doi.org/10.1001/jama.2019.0007

Dalgleish, T., Black, M., Johnston, D., & Bevan, A. (2020). Transdiagnostic approaches to mental health problems: Current status and future directions. *Journal of Consulting and Clinical Psychology, 88*(3), 179–195. https://doi.org/10.1037/ccp0000482

Dennis, C., & Dowswell, T. (2014). Psychosocial and psychological interventions for preventing postpartum depression. *Cochrane Database of Systematic Reviews, 15*(3), 231–233. https://doi.org/10.1017/S1463423614000206

Dennis, C. L., & Hodnett, E. (2007). Psychosocial and psychological interventions for treating postpartum depression. *Cochrane Database of Systematic Reviews, 4*. https://doi.org/10.1002/14651858.CD006116.pub2

Engle, P. L. (2009). Maternal mental health: Program and policy implications. *American Journal of Clinical Nutrition, 89*(3), 963S–966S. https://doi.org/10.3945/ajcn.2008.26692G

Engle, P. L., Black, M. M., Behrman, J. R., Cabral de Mello, M., Gertler, P. J., Kapiriri, L., Martorell, R., & Young, M. E. (2007). Strategies to avoid the loss of developmental potential in more than 200 million children in the developing world. *The Lancet, 369*(9557), 229–242. https://doi.org/10.1016/S0140-6736(07)60112-3

Farías-Antúnez, S., Xavier, M. O., & Santos, I. S. (2018). Effect of maternal postpartum depression on offspring's growth. *Journal of Affective Disorders, 228*, 143–152. https://doi.org/10.1016/j.jad.2017.12.013

Fernald, L. C. H., Kariger, P., Engle, P., Raikes, A., H Fernald, L. C., Kariger, P., Engle, P., Raikes, A., & Fernald, L. C. H. (2009). *Examining early child development in low-income countries*. The World Bank. https://doi.org/10.1596/28107

Fink, G., Peet, E., Danaei, G., Andrews, K., McCoy, D. C., Sudfeld, C. R., Smith Fawzi, M. C., Ezzati, M., & Fawzi, W. W. (2016). Schooling and wage income losses due to early-childhood growth faltering in developing countries: National, regional, and global estimates. *American Journal of Clinical Nutrition, 104*(1), 104–112. https://doi.org/10.3945/ajcn.115.123968

Fisher, J., Cabral de Mello, M., Patel, V., Rahman, A., Tran, T., Holton, S., & Holmes, W. (2012). Prevalence and determinants of common perinatal mental disorders in women in low- and lower-middle-income countries: A systematic review. *Bulletin of the World Health Organization, 90*(2), 139G–149G. https://doi.org/10.2471/BLT.11.091850

Fottrell, E., Azad, K., Kuddus, A., Younes, L., Shaha, S., Nahar, T., Aumon, B. H., Hossen, M., Beard, J., Hossain, T., & Pulkki-Brannstrom, A. M. (2013). The effect of increased coverage of participatory women's groups on neonatal mortality in Bangladesh: A cluster randomized trial. *JAMA Pediatrics, 167*(9), 816–825.

Fu, Z., Burger, H., Arjadi, R., & Bockting, C. L. H. (2020). Effectiveness of digital psychological interventions for mental health problems in low-income and middle-income countries: A systematic review and meta-analysis. *The Lancet Psychiatry, 7*(10), 851–864. https://doi.org/10.1016/S2215-0366(20)30256-X

Fuhr, D. C., Weobong, B., Lazarus, A., Vanobberghen, F., Weiss, H. A., Singla, D. R., Tabana, H., Afonso, E., De Sa, A., D'Souza, E., Joshi, A., Korgaonkar, P., Krishna, R., Price, L. S. N., Rahman, A., & Patel, V. (2019). Delivering the Thinking Healthy Programme for perinatal depression through peers: An individually randomised controlled trial in India. *The Lancet Psychiatry, 6*(2), 115–127. https://doi.org/10.1016/S2215-0366(18)30466-8

Furukawa, T. A., Suganuma, A., Ostinelli, E. G., Andersson, G., Beevers, C. G., Shumake, J., Berger, T., Boele, F. W., Buntrock, C., Carlbring, P., Choi, I., Christensen, H., Mackinnon, A., Dahne, J., Huibers, M. J. H., Ebert, D. D., Farrer, L., Forand, N. R., Strunk, D. R., … Cuijpers, P. (2021). Dismantling, optimising, and personalising internet cognitive behavioural therapy for depression: A systematic review and component network meta-analysis using individual participant data. *The Lancet Psychiatry, 8*(6), 500—511. https://doi.org/10.1016/S2215-0366(21)00077-8

Gao, L. L., Chan, S. W., Li, X., Chen, S., & Hao, Y. (2010). Evaluation of an interpersonal-psychotherapy-oriented childbirth education program for Chinese first-time childbearing women: A randomised controlled trial. *International Journal of Nursing Studies, 47*(10), 1208—1216.

Gao, L. L., Xie, W., Yang, X., & Chan, S. W. (2015). Effects of an interpersonal-psychotherapy-oriented postnatal program for Chinese first-time mothers: A randomized controlled trial. *International Journal of Nursing Studies, 52*(1), 22—29.

Garman, E. C., Cois, A., Tomlinson, M., Rotheram-Borus, M. J., & Lund, C. (2019). Course of perinatal depressive symptoms among South African women: Associations with child outcomes at 18 and 36 months. *Social Psychiatry and Psychiatric Epidemiology, 54*(9), 1111—1123. https://doi.org/10.1007/s00127-019-01665-2

Gelaye, B., Rondon, M. B., Araya, R., & Williams, M. A. (2016). Epidemiology of maternal depression, risk factors, and child outcomes in low-income and middle-income countries. *The Lancet Psychiatry, 3*(10), 973—982. https://doi.org/10.1016/S2215-0366(16)30284-X

Grantham-McGregor, S., Cheung, Y. B., Cueto, S., Glewwe, P., Richter, L., & Strupp, B. (2007). Developmental potential in the first 5 years for children in developing countries. *The Lancet, 369*(9555), 60—70. https://doi.org/10.1016/S0140-6736(07)60032-4

Green, E. P., Pearson, N., Rajasekharan, S., Rauws, M., Joerin, A., Kwobah, E., Musyimi, C., Bhat, C., Jones, R. M., & Lai, Y. (2019). Expanding access to depression treatment in Kenya through automated psychological support: Protocol for a single-case experimental design pilot study. *JMIR Research Protocols, 8*(4). https://doi.org/10.2196/11800

Gu, C., Wu, X., Ding, Y., Zhu, X., & Zhang, Z. (2013). The effectiveness of a Chinese midwives' antenatal clinic service on childbirth outcomes for primipare: A randomised controlled trial. *International Journal of Nursing Studies, 50*(12), 1689—1697.

Husain, N., Kiran, T., Fatima, B., Chaudhry, I. B., Husain, M., Shah, S., Bassett, P., Cohen, N., Jafri, F., Naeem, S., Zadeh, Z., Roberts, C., Rahman, A., Naeem, F., Husain, M. I., & Chaudhry, N. (2021). An integrated parenting intervention for maternal depression and child development in a low-resource setting: Cluster randomized controlled trial. *Depression and Anxiety, 38*, 925—939. https://doi.org/10.1002/da.23169

Husain, N., Kiran, T., Shah, S., Rahman, A., Raza-Ur-Rehman, Saeed, Q., Naeem, S., Bassett, P., Husain, M., Haq, S. U., Jaffery, F., Cohen, N., Naeem, F., & Chaudhry, N. (2021). Efficacy of learning through play plus intervention to reduce maternal depression in women with malnourished children: A randomized controlled trial from Pakistan. *Journal of Affective Disorders, 278*, 78—84. https://doi.org/10.1016/j.jad.2020.09.001

Husain, N., Zulqernain, F., Carter, L. A., Chaudhry, I. B., Fatima, B., Kiran, T., Chaudhry, N., Naeem, S., Jafri, F., Lunat, F., Haq, S. U., Husain, M., Roberts, C., Naeem, F., & Rahman, A. (2017). Treatment of maternal depression in urban slums of Karachi, Pakistan: A randomized controlled trial (RCT) of an integrated maternal psychological and early child development intervention. *Asian Journal of Psychiatry, 29*(2017), 63—70. https://doi.org/10.1016/j.ajp.2017.03.010

Ibanez, G., Bernard, J. Y., Rondet, C., Peyre, H., Forhan, A., Kaminski, M., & Saurel-Cubizolles, M. J. (2015). Effects of antenatal maternal depression and anxiety on children's early cognitive development: A prospective cohort study. *PLoS One, 10*(8), e0135849. https://doi.org/10.1371/journal.pone.0135849

Jeong, J., Franchett, E. E., Ramos de Oliveira, C. V., Rehmani, K., & Yousafzai, A. K. (2021). Parenting interventions to promote early child development in the first three years of life: A global systematic review and meta-analysis. *PLoS Medicine, 18*(5), e1003602. https://doi.org/10.1371/journal.pmed.1003602

Jiang, L., Wang, Z. Z., Qiu, L. R., Wan, G. B., Lin, Y., & Wei, Z. (2014). Psychological intervention for postpartum depression. *Journal of Huazhong University of Science and Technology
[Medical Sciences]*, 34(3), 437–442.

Kohrt, B. A., Ramaiya, M. K., Rai, S., Bhardwaj, A., & Jordans, M. J. D. (2015). Development of
a scoring system for non-specialist ratings of clinical competence in global mental health:
A qualitative process evaluation of the Enhancing Assessment of Common Therapeutic
Factors (ENACT) scale. *Global Mental Health*, 2, e23. https://doi.org/10.1017/
gmh.2015.21

Lau, Y., Htun, T. P., Wong, S. N., Tam, W. S. W., & Klainin-Yobas, P. (2017). Therapist-
supported internet-based cognitive behavior therapy for stress, anxiety, and depressive
symptoms among postpartum women: A systematic review and meta-analysis. *Journal
of Medical Internet Research*, 19(4), 1–18. https://doi.org/10.2196/jmir.6712

Leung, S. S. L., Leung, C., Lam, T. H., Hung, S. F., Chan, R., Yeung, T., Miao, M., Cheng, S.,
Leung, S. H., Lau, A., & Lee, D. T. S. (2011). Outcome of a postnatal depression screening
programme using the Edinburgh Postnatal Depression Scale: A randomized controlled
trial. *Journal of Public Health*, 33(2), 292–301. https://doi.org/10.1093/pubmed/fdq075

Macours, K., & Vakis, R. (2010). *Seasonal migration and early childhood development*. World Bank
Social Protection Discussion. *Paper #0702*.

Maselko, J., Sikander, S., Turner, E. L., Bates, L. M., Ahmad, I., Atif, N., Baranov, V.,
Bhalotra, S., Bibi, A., Bibi, T., Bilal, S., Biroli, P., Chung, E., Gallis, J. A., Hagaman, A.,
Jamil, A., LeMasters, K., O'Donnell, K., Scherer, E., & Rahman, A. (2020). Effectiveness
of a peer-delivered, psychosocial intervention on maternal depression and child development at 3 years postnatal: A cluster randomised trial in Pakistan. *The Lancet Psychiatry*,
7(9), 775–787. https://doi.org/10.1016/S2215-0366(20)30258-3

Mendenhall, E. (2017). Syndemics: A new path for global health research. *The Lancet*,
389(10072), 889–891. https://www.thelancet.com/journals/lancet/article/PIIS0140-
6736(17)30602-5/fulltext?code=lancet-site30602-5/fulltext?code=lancet-site.

Michie, S., Richardson, M., Johnston, M., Abraham, C., Francis, J., Hardeman, W.,
Eccles, M. P., Cane, J., & Wood, C. E. (2013). The behavior change technique taxonomy
of 93 hierarchically clustered techniques: Building an international consensus for the
reporting of behavior change interventions. *Annals of Behavioral Medicine*, 46(1), 81–95.
https://doi.org/10.1007/s12160-013-9486-6

Mohsin, S., Waqas, A., Atif, N., Rabbani, M., Khan, S., Bilal, S., Sharif, M., Bibi, A., &
Sikander, S. (2021). Accuracy of community informant led detection of maternal depression in rural Pakistan. *International Journal of Environmental Research and Public Health*,
18(3), 1075. https://doi.org/10.3390/ijerph18031075

Morrell, C. J., Warner, R., Slade, P., Dixon, S., Walters, S., Paley, G., & Brugha, T. (2009). Psychological interventions for postnatal depression: Cluster randomised trial and economic
evaluation. The PoNDER trial. *Health Technology Assessment*, 13(30). https://doi.org/
10.3310/hta13300

National Collaborating Center for Mental Health. (2020). *National Clinical Guideline Number
192: Antenatal and postnatal mental health Clinical management and service guidance* (Updated
edition).   https://www.nice.org.uk/guidance/cg192/evidence/full-guideline-pdf-
193396861.

Naveed, S., Waqas, A., Memon, A. R., Jabeen, M., & Sheikh, M. H. (2019). Cross-cultural validation of the Urdu translation of the Patient Health Questionnaire for Adolescents among
children and adolescents at a Pakistani school. *Public Health*, 168, 59–66. https://doi.org/
10.1016/j.puhe.2018.11.022

O'Mahen, H. A., Grieve, H., Jones, J., McGinley, J., Woodford, J., & Wilkinson, E. L. (2015).
Women's experiences of factors affecting treatment engagement and adherence in
internet delivered Behavioural Activation for Postnatal Depression. *Internet Interventions*,
2(1), 84–90. https://doi.org/10.1016/j.invent.2014.11.003

Patel, V., DeSouza, N., & Rodrigues, M. (2003). Postnatal depression and infant growth and development in low income countries: A cohort study from Goa, India. *Archives of Disease in Childhood, 88*(1), 34–37. https://doi.org/10.1136/adc.88.1.34

Peet, E. D., McCoy, D. C., Danaei, G., Ezzati, M., Fawzi, W., Jarvelin, M. R., Pillas, D., & Fink, G. (2015). Early childhood development and schooling attainment: Longitudinal evidence from British, Finnish and Philippine Birth Cohorts. *PLoS One, 10*(9), e0137219. https://doi.org/10.1371/journal.pone.0137219

Pompoli, A., Furukawa, T. A., Efthimiou, O., Imai, H., Tajika, A., & Salanti, G. (2018). Dismantling cognitive-behaviour therapy for panic disorder: A systematic review and component network meta-analysis. *Psychological Medicine, 48*(12), 1945–1953. https://doi.org/10.1017/S0033291717003919

Prince, M., Patel, V., Saxena, S., Maj, M., Maselko, J., Phillips, M. R., & Rahman, A. (2007). No health without mental health. *The Lancet, 370*(9590), 859–877. https://doi.org/10.1016/S0140-6736(07)61238-0

Rabiei, L., Mazaheri, M. A., Masoudi, R., & Hasheminia, S. A. (2014). Fordyce happiness program and postpartum depression. *Journal of Research in Medical Sciences: The Official Journal of Isfahan University of Medical Sciences, 19*(3), 251.

Rahman, A. (2015). Integration of mental health into priority health service delivery platforms: Maternal and child health services. *Eastern Mediterranean Health Journal, 21*(7), 493–497. https://apps.who.int/iris/handle/10665/255242.

Rahman, Atif, Akhtar, P., Hamdani, S. U., Atif, N., Nazir, H., Uddin, I., Nisar, A., Huma, Z., Maselko, J., Sikander, S., & Zafar, S. (2019). Using technology to scale-up training and supervision of community health workers in the psychosocial management of perinatal depression: A non-inferiority, randomized controlled trial. *Global Mental Health, 6*, e8. https://doi.org/10.1017/gmh.2019.7

Rahman, A., Bunn, J., Lovel, H., & Creed, F. (2007). Maternal depression increases infant risk of diarrhoeal illness: –a cohort study. *Archives of Disease in Childhood, 92*(1), 24–28. https://doi.org/10.1136/adc.2005.086579

Rahman, Atif, Fisher, J., Bower, P., Luchters, S., Tran, T., Yasamy, M., Saxena, S., & Waheed, W. (2013). Interventions for common perinatal mental disorders in women in low- and middle-income countries: A systematic review and meta-analysis. *Bulletin of the World Health Organization, 91*, 593–601I. https://doi.org/10.2471/BLT.12.109819

Rahman, A., Fisher, J., Waqas, A., Hamdani, S., Zafar, W., & Suleman, N. (2018). *World Health Organization recommendation on psychotherapeutic interventions for common maternal mental health problems among women to improve early childhood development in low and middle income countries.* https://www.who.int/publications/i/item/97892400020986.

Rahman, Atif, Iqbal, Z., Bunn, J., Lovel, H., & Harrington, R. (2004). Impact of maternal depression on infant nutritional status and illness: A cohort study. *Archives of General Psychiatry, 61*(9), 946–952. https://doi.org/10.1001/archpsyc.61.9.946

Rahman, Atif, Iqbal, Z., Roberts, C., & Husain, N. (2009). Cluster randomized trial of a parent-based intervention to support early development of children in a low-income country. *Child: Care, Health and Development, 35*(1), 56–62. https://doi.org/10.1111/j.1365-2214.2008.00897.x

Rahman, A., Lovel, H., Bunn, J., Iqbal, Z., & Harrington, R. (2004). Mothers' mental health and infant growth: A case-control study from Rawalpindi, Pakistan. *Child: Care, Health and Development, 30*(1), 21–27. https://doi.org/10.1111/j.1365-2214.2004.00382.x

Rahman, Atif, Malik, A., Sikander, S., Roberts, C., & Creed, F. (2008). Cognitive behaviour therapy-based intervention by community health workers for mothers with depression and their infants in rural Pakistan: A cluster-randomised controlled trial. *The Lancet, 372*(9642), 902–909. https://doi.org/10.1016/S0140-6736(08)61400-2

Rahman, Atif, Waqas, A., Nisar, A., Nazir, H., Sikander, S., & Atif, N. (2021). Improving access to psychosocial interventions for perinatal depression in low- and middle-income countries: Lessons from the field. *International Review of Psychiatry, 33*(1–2), 198–201. https://doi.org/10.1080/09540261.2020.1772551

Sachs, J. (2012). From millennium development goals to sustainable development goals. *The Lancet, 379*(9832), 2206–2211. https://doi.org/10.1016/S0140-6736(12)60685-0

Shariat, M., & Abedinia, N. (2017). The effect of psychological intervention on mother- infant bonding and breastfeeding. *Iranian Journal of Neonatology, 8*(1), 7–15.

Shi, H., Li, X., Fang, H., Zhang, J., & Wang, X. (2020). The effectiveness and cost-effectiveness of a parenting intervention integrated with primary health care on early childhood development: A cluster-randomized controlled trial. *Prevention Science, 21*(5), 661–671. https://doi.org/10.1007/s11121-020-01126-2

Shrestha, S., Adachi, K., Petrini, M. A., Shrestha, S., & Khagi, B. R. (2016). Development and evaluation of a newborn care education program in primiparous mothers in Nepal. *Midwifery, 42*, 21–28.

Sikander, S., Ahmad, I., Atif, N., Zaidi, A., Vanobbberghen, F., Weiss, H. A., Nisar, A., Tabana, H., Ain, Q. U., & Bibi, A. (2019). Delivering the Thinking Healthy Programme for perinatal depression through volunteer peers : A cluster randomised controlled trial in Pakistan. *The Lancet Psychiatry, 6*(2), 128–139. https://doi.org/10.1016/S2215-0366(18)30467-X

Singla, D. R., Kohrt, B., Murray, L. J., Chorpita, B. F., Anand, A., & Patel, V. (2017). Psychological treatments for the world: Lessons from low- and middle-income countries. *Annual Review of Clinical Psychology, 13*, 149–181. https://doi.org/10.1146/annurev-clinpsy-032816-045217

Singla, D. R., Kumbakumba, E., & Aboud, F. E. (2015). Effects of a parenting intervention to address both maternal psychological wellbeing and child development and growth in rural Uganda: A community-based, cluster randomised trial. *The Lancet Global Health, 3*(8), e458–e469. https://doi.org/10.1016/S2214-109X(15)00099-6

Singla, D. R., MacKinnon, D. P., Fuhr, D. C., Sikander, S., Rahman, A., & Patel, V. (2019). Multiple mediation analysis of the peer-delivered Thinking Healthy Programme for perinatal depression: Findings from two parallel, randomised controlled trials. *The British Journal of Psychiatry*, 1–8. https://doi.org/10.1192/bjp.2019.184

Stewart, R. C. (2007). Maternal depression and infant growth - a review of recent evidence. *Maternal and Child Nutrition, 3*(2), 94–107. https://doi.org/10.1111/j.1740-8709.2007.00088.x

The World Bank. (2018). *World Health Organization Global Health Expenditure database.* https://data.worldbank.org/indicator/SH.XPD.CHEX.GD.ZS?locations=PK.

Thombs, B. D., Levis, B., Lyubenova, A., Neupane, D., Negeri, Z., Wu, Y., Sun, Y., & Krishnan, A. (2020). Overestimation of Postpartum depression prevalence based on a 5-item version of the EPDS: Systematic review and individual participant data meta-analysis. *Canadian Journal of Psychiatry, 65*(12), 835–844. https://doi.org/10.1177/0706743720934959

Tomlinson, M., Rotheram-Borus, M. J., Harwood, J., le Roux, I. M., O'Connor, M., & Worthman, C. (2015). Community health workers can improve child growth of antenatally-depressed, South African mothers: A cluster randomized controlled trial. *BMC Psychiatry, 15*(1). https://doi.org/10.1186/s12888-015-0606-7

Tripathy, P., Nair, N., Barnett, S., Mahapatra, R., Borghi, J., Rath, S., Rath, S., Gope, R., Mahto, D., Sinha, R., Lakshminarayana, R., Patel, V., Pagel, C., Prost, A., & Costello, A. (2010). Effect of a participatory intervention with women's groups on birth outcomes and maternal depression in Jharkhand and Orissa, India: A cluster-randomised controlled trial. *The Lancet, 375*(9721), 1182–1192. https://doi.org/10.1016/S0140-6736(09)62042-0

Van Der Zee-Van Den Berg, A. I., Boere-Boonekamp, M. M., Groothuis-Oudshoorn, C. G. M., IJzerman, M. J., Haasnoot-Smallegange, R. M. E., & Reijneveld, S. A. (2017). Post-up study: Postpartum depression screening in well-child care and maternal outcomes. *Pediatrics, 140*(4). https://doi.org/10.1542/peds.2017-0110

Wachs, T. D., & Rahman, A. (2013). The nature and impact of risk and protective influences on children's development in low-income countries. In *Handbook of early childhood development research and its impact on global policy.* https://doi.org/10.1093/acprof:oso/9780199922994.003.0005

Waqas, A., Elhady, M., Surya Dila, K. A., Kaboub, F., Van Trinh, L., Nhien, C. H., Al-Husseini, M. J., Kamel, M. G., Elshafay, A., Nhi, H. Y., Hirayama, K., & Huy, N. T. (2018). Association between maternal depression and risk of infant diarrhea: A systematic review and meta-analysis. *Public Health, 159,* 78–88. https://doi.org/10.1016/j.puhe.2018.01.036

Waqas, A., Koukab, A., Meraj, H., Dua, T., Chowdhary, N., Fatima, B., & Rahman, A. (2022). Screening programs for common maternal mental health disorders among perinatal women: Report of the systematic review of evidence. *BMC Psychiatry, 22*(1), 1–18.

Waqas, A., Malik, A., Atif, N., Nisar, A., Nazir, H., Sikander, S., & Rahman, A. (2021). Scalable screening and treatment-response monitoring for perinatal depression in low- and middle-income countries. *International Journal of Environmental Research and Public Health, 18*(13), 6693. https://doi.org/10.3390/ijerph18136693

Waqas, A., Teoh, S. H., Lapão, L. V., Messina, L. A., & Correia, J. (2020). Harnessing Telemedicine for the provision of health care: Bibliometric and scientometric analysis. *Journal of Medical Internet Research, 22*(10). https://doi.org/10.2196/18835

Waqas, A., Zafar, S. W., Meraj, H., Tariq, M., Naveed, S., Fatima, B., Chowdhary, N., Dua, T., & Rahman, A. (2022). Prevention of common mental disorders among women in the perinatal period: A critical mixed-methods review and meta-analysis. *Global Mental Health,* 1–16.

Weobong, B., Weiss, H. A., McDaid, D., Singla, D. R., Hollon, S. D., Nadkarni, A., Park, A.-L., Bhat, B., Katti, B., Anand, A., Dimidjian, S., Araya, R., King, M., Vijayakumar, L., Wilson, G. T., Velleman, R., Kirkwood, B. R., Fairburn, C. G., & Patel, V. (2017). Sustained effectiveness and cost-effectiveness of the Healthy Activity Programme, a brief psychological treatment for depression delivered by lay counsellors in primary care: 12-month follow-up of a randomised controlled trial. *PLoS Medicine, 14*(9), e1002385. https://doi.org/10.1371/journal.pmed.1002385

Wilkinson, A., Anderson, S., & Wheeler, S. B. (2017). Screening for and treating postpartum depression and psychosis: A cost-effectiveness analysis. *Maternal and Child Health Journal, 21*(4), 903–914. https://doi.org/10.1007/s10995-016-2192-9

World Health Organization. (2014). *Global status report on noncommunicable diseases 2014,* ISBN 9789241564854. *World Health.*

World Health Organization. (2015). *Thinking Healthy: A manual for psychological management of perinatal depression.* https://www.who.int/mental_health/maternal-child/thinking_healthy/en/.

World Health Organization. (2018a). *Country profile.* https://www.who.int/gho/countries/pak/country_profiles/en/.

World Health Organization. (2018b). *Pakistan: Mental Health ATLAS 2017 member state profile.* https://www.who.int/mental_health/evidence/atlas/profiles-2017/PAK.pdf?ua=1.

World Health Organization. (2019a). *Improving early childhood development: WHO guideline.* https://www.who.int/publications/i/item/97892400020986.

World Health Organization. (2019b). *World Health Organization recommendations on caregiving interventions to support early child development in the first three years of life : Report of the systematic review of evidence Joshua Jeong PhD , Emily Franchett MSc , Aisha K . Yousafzai PhD,* (2018). https://www.who.int/publications/i/item/97892400020986.

Yawn, B. P., Dietrich, A. J., Wollan, P., Bertram, S., Graham, D., Huff, J., Kurland, M., Madison, S., & Pace, W. D. (2012). TRIPPD: A practice-based network effectiveness study of postpartum depression screening and management. *Annals of Family Medicine, 10*(4), 320–329. https://doi.org/10.1370/afm.1418

Yousafzai, A. K., Rasheed, M. A., Rizvi, A., Armstrong, R., & Bhutta, Z. A. (2014). Effect of integrated responsive stimulation and nutrition interventions in the Lady Health Worker programme in Pakistan on child development, growth, and health outcomes: A cluster-randomised factorial effectiveness trial. *The Lancet, 384*(9950), 1282–1293. https://doi.org/10.1016/S0140-6736(14)60455-4

Zafar, S., Sikander, S., Haq, Z., Hill, Z., Lingam, R., Skordis-Worrall, J., Hafeez, A., Kirkwood, B., & Rahman, A. (2014). Integrating maternal psychosocial well-being into a child-development intervention: The five-pillars approach. *Annals of the New York Academy of Sciences, 1308*(1), 107–117. https://doi.org/10.1111/nyas.12339

van der Zee-van, A. I., Boere-Boonekamp, M. M., IJzerman, M. J., Haasnoot-Smallegange, R. M., & Reijneveld, S. A. (2017). Screening for postpartum depression in well-baby care settings : A systematic review. *Maternal and Child Health Journal, 21*(1), 9–20. https://doi.org/10.1007/s10995-016-2088-8

11

Technology-enhanced learning and training for child and adolescent mental health professionals

Anthea A. Stylianakis[1,2], David J. Hawes[3], and Valsamma Eapen[1,2]

[1] The University of New South Wales, School of Clinical Medicine, Faculty of Medicine and Health, Sydney, NSW, Australia; [2] University of New South Wales, 2031 & Academic Unit of Child Psychiatry SWSLHD, L1 MHC Liverpool Hospital, Sydney, NSW, Australia; [3] The University of Sydney, School of Psychology, Faculty of Science, Sydney, NSW, Australia

1. Introduction

Technology-enhanced learning (TEL) offers unique benefits in addressing the significant assessment and treatment gap in the field of child and adolescent mental health, particularly in low- and middle-income countries (LMICs). Furthermore, the current global COVID-19 pandemic has necessitated the increasing use of non-face-to-face methods of learning and training. In this regard, it is noteworthy that worldwide, the prevalence rates of mental health disorders in children and young people are estimated at around 13.4% (Polanczyk et al., 2015) and that the COVID-19 pandemic further exacerbated mental health difficulties in children, adolescents, and their families (e.g., Hu et al., 2022; Pierce et al., 2020; Saggioro de Figueiredo et al., 2021). Disorders that emerge early in life are associated with poor adjustments as well as a range of psychological and physical disorders later in life (Copeland et al., 2009). Unfortunately, however, while many effective, evidence-based interventions exist for mental health disorders that emerge in childhood and adolescence, many young people do not access treatments and there is a gap between prevalence and treatment rates such that only 25%−35% of affected children and adolescents access treatment (O'Brien et al., 2016). Unfortunately, this treatment gap is even larger in LMICs. For example, only 12% of children with psychiatric problems were found to be using mental health services in a community sample in Itaborai, Brazil (Duarte et al., 2021; Sweetland et al., 2014), and less than 10% of children were found to be accessing mental health services in a South African sample (Mokitimi et al., 2022). Furthermore, for individuals who do receive help, this is often delayed or insufficient in frequency or duration (Tully et al., 2019). A number of reasons have been suggested as potential explanations for the gap between prevalence and treatment rates in child and adolescent mental health. Such explanations include limited availability of mental health professionals adequately trained in evidence-based mental health diagnosis and interventions, low level of community knowledge about childhood mental health disorders, and an inaccessibility of adequate training and peer consultation and supervision outside metropolitan areas (Allen et al., 2021; Mitchell et al., 2000; Tully et al., 2019). Restrictions placed on face-to-face gatherings due to the COVID-19 pandemic have significantly affected the training of health professionals, including those in the field of mental health (Reid, 2020; Wyres & Taylor, 2020). Along with general benefits, TEL and training has the capacity to overcome key challenges inherent in teaching and training mental health professionals during the COVID-19 pandemic. Key examples of the current uses of TEL practices in child and adolescent mental health as addressed in this chapter can be seen in Table 11.1. Notwithstanding the potential benefits offered by such practices, it has been associated with numerous challenges as outlined in the following. Moreover, few empirical studies have examined the efficacy of TEL resources, in mental health teaching and learning in general, and in the context of child and adolescent mental health, in particular. Consequently, there remain many practical and theoretical considerations in relation to how TEL frameworks should be effectively implemented and evaluated to improve child and adolescent mental health.

Technology plays an ever-increasing role in our professional lives, and in this context, it is perhaps not surprising that it is increasingly playing an integral role in learning and training. TEL potentially encompasses all circumstances in which technology is used to support learning and training processes (Pickering & Joynes, 2016). TEL has become widely used in the context of child and adolescent mental health teaching and training, and there are a variety of ways in which it has been implemented. As examples, a number of treatment manuals exist in e-book form and online intervention guides, such as "Where there is No Child Psychiatrist: A mental healthcare manual" by Eapen et al. (2012) and

TABLE 11.1 Examples of the current uses of TEL practices and resources in child and adolescent mental health.

TEL resource	Examples of use in child and adolescent mental health training	Weblink
Treatment Manuals	• Where there is no child psychiatrist: A mental healthcare manual (Eapen et al., 2012) • JM Rey's IACAPAP e-textbook of child and adolescent mental health (Rey & Martin, 2019)	• http://services.cambridge.org/us/academic/subjects/medicine/mental-health-psychiatry-and-clinical-psychology/where-there-no-child-psychiatrist-mental-healthcare-manual?format=PB&isbn=9781908020482#contentsTabAnchor • https://iacapap.org/iacapap-textbook-of-child-and-adolescent-mental-health/
E-learning resources	• Attention deficit hyperactivity disorder (ADHD) for medical students (Salmon et al., 2019)	• https://doi.org/10.2147/AMEPS220390
Online training websites	• MindEd (2021) • Emerging Minds (2021)	• https://www.minded.org.uk/ • https://emergingminds.com.au/
Teaching undergraduate and postgraduate students	• Use of virtual patients (e.g., Parsons et al., 2008) • Massive Open Online Courses (Bairy et al., 2019) • Flipped classrooms (Anderson & Krathwohl, 2001; Karanicolas & Snelling, 2010) • Blended learning (combination of face-to-face learning and online education; Bairy et al., 2019)	• PMID: 18391321 • https://doi.org/10.1080/2575517X.2019.1622983 • ISBN: 080131903X • http://hdl.handle.net/2440/68599 • https://doi.org/10.1080/2575517X.2019.1622983
Simulations	• Virtual patients on whom to practice interviewing and clinical skills (Gipson et al., 2017; Parsons et al., 2008)	• https://doi.org/10.1016/j.chc.2016.07.004 • PMID: 18391321

textbooks such as the International Association for Child and Adolescent Psychiatry and Allied Professions e-Textbook of Child and Adolescent Mental Health edited by Rey and Martin (2019). Along with e-books are e-learning resources, such as a teaching resource on attention deficit hyperactivity disorder (ADHD) for medical students (Salmon et al., 2019), and online training websites designed for child and adolescent mental health clinicians, such as MindEd developed in the Department of Health and Department for Education (2021) and Emerging Minds (2021) developed in Australia, both of which offer training in evidence-based mental health interventions (https://emergingminds.com.au).

In the field of mental health more broadly, examples of the use of TEL include virtual reality, which uses computerized technology to create a simulated environment in which the user is positioned inside of an experience (Reid, 2002). Similarly, simulation is a method by which digital technologies and computers are used to create scenarios designed to replicate health encounters. Examples of simulation-based courses include the Recognition and Assessment of Medical Problems course for frontline mental health staff (Akroyd et al., 2016) and the Second Life Simulation virtual reality tool used as a teaching strategy for mental health nursing students (Kidd et al., 2012). Simulations are particularly useful in the training of mental health professionals in interviewing and assessment skills. Specifically, effective interview skills are a core competency for psychiatry residents, psychologists, and mental health professionals in general. Parsons et al. (2008) highlight the utility of using virtual patients to offer mental health trainees standardized, consistent, psychometrically reliable, and valid interactions to train in structured clinical interview skills. These authors present the case study of an interactive virtual adolescent male with conduct disorder with whom child and adolescent mental health trainees can practice structured interviewing. Furthermore, Parsons et al. (2008) highlight that training in mental health interviewing and diagnosis using a "patient" avatar in a virtual environment allows for a safe and more authentic learning experience than face-to-face role-playing activities that occur in classroom buildings with peers acting as the patient. Indeed, in a qualitative study of students in a graduate-level mental health diagnosis course, the students reported that they found that an online 3D virtual environment is an effective experiential learning tool in developing their interviewing and diagnosis skills (Lowell & Alshammari, 2018).

TEL can also play an important role in allowing mental health clinicians to access supervision and training, through virtual knowledge-sharing networks (e.g., Chand et al., 2014) as well as through the use of videoconferencing to deliver education programs (Page et al., 2018). TEL is also currently used extensively in teaching of undergraduate and postgraduate students in the field of mental health, allowing for educational curricula to be taught outside of the traditional classroom. Specifically, a number of telehealth platforms are used in higher education pedagogy, including Massive Open Online Courses (MOOCs), which are online platforms that aim to provide open access to courses through the Internet at any time and from anywhere. Typically, MOOCs are weekly video-based lectures composed of several shorter video sequences (Bairy et al., 2019). TEL has also been used to facilitate the creation of "flipped classrooms" where trainees can access instructional material or coursework online prior to the class, allowing face-to-face time for collaborative activities (Anderson & Krathwhol, 2001; Karanicolas & Snelling, 2010; Ong et al., 2020). Finally, blended learning refers to a "hybrid" form of learning, which combines both traditional face-to-face learning and online education.

2. Technology-enhanced learning and training in practice

2.1 Potential benefits of technology-enhanced learning

The Higher Education Funding Council For England (2009) has high-lighted three levels of potential benefit of TEL: efficiency by which "existing processes can be carried out in a more cost-effective, time effective, sustainable or scalable manner" (p. 2); enhancement that per-tains to the improvement of existing processes and outcomes, and transformation, or radically changing existing processes and introducing new processes. Bairy et al. (2019) have also highlighted another potential benefit of TEL in that it is easily accessible, both in the sense that it is not time-bound and therefore accessible for learners to take up at a time that is suitable to them, and devoid of physical barriers, allowing for access to learning information in regions that might otherwise be inaccessible to learning and training, a factor that holds particular utility for clinicians working in remote locations (Kobak et al., 2017). Moreover, the use of TEL can be time-saving and cost-effective, with larger groups of learners being able to access training at the same time (Bairy et al., 2019). Finally, it en-ables learners to learn at their own pace, allowing for a deeper level of learning as it uses adult learning principles and facilitates an increase in self-motivation (Bairy et al., 2019). As organizations improve in their ac-cess to hardware and software, TEL is well placed to be a useful approach through which to provide effective and affordable education, particularly in light of constraints on time and resources (Nicoll et al., 2018).

2.1.1 Facilitating training in evidence-based therapies

Firstly, of paramount importance in the field of child and adolescent mental health, and indeed in the field of mental health in general, is the ability of professionals to conduct evidence-based practice, with this defined as "the integration of the best available research with clinical expertise, in the context of patient characteristics, culture, and preferences" (American Psychological Association, 2006, p. 1). The cornerstone of evidence-based practice is the use of empirically supported treatments, with treatments generally classified as such when they have been shown to be effective in treating a disorder as part of a randomized controlled trial (Allen et al., 2021). However, despite the fact that a growing number of evidence-based therapies now exist for the treatment of child and adolescent mental health disorders, only a small proportion of children and adolescents in the general population receive such treatment. A number of researchers and clinicians have posited that this gap between the development of research-tested interventions and their implementations exists, potentially in large part, as a result of a lack of therapists who are appropriately trained in competently disseminating evidence-based therapies (Allen et al., 2021; Weissman et al., 2006). However, the process of training mental health clinicians in evidence-based therapies requires time, money, and the availability of clinicians capable of delivering evidence-based therapy training, for both the initial training and ongoing monitoring (Kobak et al., 2017). Indeed, there is a shortage of clinical programs offering training in evidence-based therapies across the mental health sector (Pidano & Whitcomb, 2012; Weissman et al., 2006). Internet-based training can be useful in addressing the aforementioned training barriers, as such training is cost-effective and scalable and overcomes limitations of trainer availability. Furthermore, instructions can be standardized, which ensures that empirically proven components are included (Kobak et al., 2017). However, such standardization must be undertaken with caution to ensure the ecological validity of the training (i.e., the generalizability of the training content to the clinician's context), and Internet-based training may need to be adapted to suit cultural contexts that differ to those in which such training has been developed, particularly when accessed by clinicians in diverse regions of the world. Consequently, TEL has been suggested as a way to overcome issues with training clinicians in quality evidence-based practice (Beidas et al., 2012; Edmunds et al., 2013; Nadeem et al., 2013; Rose et al., 2011). There is also some, albeit limited, evidence of therapist training in child and adolescent evidence-based practice. Specifically, due to COVID-19-related constraints, Batchelor et al. (2020) adapted a one-day training for a low-intensity CBT intervention in children and adolescents from face-to-face to delivery via zoom. Trainees completed an online questionnaire pre- and posttraining, and researchers found that the training increased knowledge and understanding of the content covered in the course. Furthermore, there are a number of online evidence-based therapy training options available in the field of child and adolescent mental health. As one example, the Australian organization, Emerging Minds, offers online training of an evidence-based program called Family Talk, which is a program designed for mental health professionals who are working with parents experiencing depression and/or anxiety. The aim of the program is to foster resilience in the children and family unit (Emerging Minds, 2021). It is imperative that future research examine the efficacy of online training in evidence-based therapies for child and adolescent mental health difficulties.

2.1.2 Enhancing graduate training in mental health

As well as facilitating the dissemination of evidence-based training, Gipson et al. (2017) highlight the use of Web-based simulations in child and adolescent psychiatry training, emphasizing the utility of using virtual patients on whom to practice clinical skills and problem-solving in settings similar to real patient encounters but in a less anxiety-provoking context. Finally, TEL can also be used as a means to enhance traditional learning. Hence, there are many avenues through which TEL can assist in the training of mental health professionals.

2.1.3 Provision of mental health information on a larger scale

Another area in which TEL can prove useful in terms of child and adolescent mental health is through providing public mental health information at a national or international level via Internet-based sources. As well as there being a shortage of clinicians trained in evidence-based practice, Tully et al. (2019) argue that another critical factor contributing to children not receiving adequate professional help for mental disorders is a low level of community knowledge about childhood mental health disorders. Consequently, Tully et al. (2019) argue for the need for a national initiative to improve community levels of mental health literacy, which they define as "knowledge and beliefs about mental disorders which aid their recognition, management or prevention" (p. 287), which have the potential to improve appropriate and early help seeking and treatment uptake and, in turn, reduce the prevalence of childhood mental health disorders. Indeed, the authors cite the fact that population health education programs implemented in Australia by Beyond Blue (https://www.beyondblue.org.au), which include Web-based interventions, have increased community awareness of depression, while two metaanalyses examining the effectiveness of interventions for increasing mental health literacy (which includes Web-based interventions) showed improvements in knowledge regarding mental health as well as reduced stigmatizing attitudes following mental health literacy interventions (Brijnath et al., 2016; Morgan et al., 2018). Tully et al. (2019) have suggested that child mental health literacy interventions should include whole-of-community campaigns, a key component of which would be information websites. Hence, the use of

TEL resources to raise awareness at a community level could go a long way in bridging the gap between the number of children requiring mental health intervention and those receiving it in a timely, effective manner. The additional advantage of such initiatives is that this can be implemented with ease in resource-constrained environments such as in LMIC settings.

2.1.4 Facilitating accessibility of training

Historically, rural and remote communities have had limited access to mental health services, with this being particularly true for child and adolescent mental health services (CAMHS) across the world (e.g., Mitchell et al., 2000 in Australia; Zayed et al., 2016 in Canada). As well as services being limited, there are difficulties in terms of child and adolescent mental health clinicians accessing training and support (Mitchell et al., 2000). Indeed, Mitchell et al. (2000) inform that the isolation of mental health providers working in regional and rural communities is of major concern as this restricts professional development due to the time and costs associated with traveling to urban training centers, as well as the fact that remote healthcare providers have limited access to peer support. To overcome these barriers, Mitchell et al. (2000) created and evaluated a network to provide professional development to child and adolescent mental health staff in rural and remote parts of South Australia and the Northern Territory via videoconferencing. These researchers found that such a network resulted in increased networking and peer support, reduced time of work and travel costs, and improvement in the quality of health services provided. Some of the difficulties associated with videoconferencing included access to technical support and need for induction and training. Another benefit of TEL is that it allows for relatively easy and accessible training in child and adolescent mental health for health professionals in regions that may not otherwise be able to access such training. As an example, often individuals with substance use disorders do not seek a treatment network, or seek help much later in their addiction. In countries with resource scarcity, such as India, a scarcity of treatment facilities and health provider resources can result in patients who desperately need treatment not being able to access it. To bridge this gap, Chand et al. (2014) describe a telehealth technology, called Tele-ECHO, which links interdisciplinary specialist teams with health professionals through teleECHO clinics run over Zoom. Specifically, the aim of Chand et al.'s (2014) program was to connect health professionals with addiction specialists from the National Institute of Mental Health and Neurosciences (NIMHANS), Bangalore, India, the aim being to enhance the competencies of health professionals in recognizing and managing substance use disorders via a virtual training network through case-based learning, knowledge networks, and continuous learning loops through weekly, live two-hour teleECHO clinic sessions with case discussions and didactic presentations for four sessions. Via a follow-up questionnaire to participants, the majority of whom were psychiatrists, it was ascertained that all participants (feedback received from 59) reported benefitting from the training and mentioned various learning points which they were planning to implement in their own clinical practice. The authors point to the utility of live teleclinics as a training platform to provide skills-based teaching to health professionals in areas where specialized addiction professionals are scarce. Indeed, teleECHO programs exist across a number of countries, including many LMICs, and could provide a platform by which to increase access to specialized health and mental healthcare in underserved regions (Mitgang et al., 2021).

Furthermore, remote training is being increasingly used for training in LMICs and resource-constrained environments, both for certification training of specialists and for capacity building of local workforce on child and adolescent mental health. One such example of formal training and certification is Child Psychiatry is the Child and Adolescent Psychiatry Advanced Support and Training-Iraq (CAPAST-I) program where the first batch of two trainees have successfully completed the program and gained Board Certification in Child Psychiatry (Mahmood & Eapen, 2020). This was made possible through utilizing the local infrastructure and governance framework of the Iraqi Board of Psychiatry for conducting the training, examination, and issuing the certificate and license with input from overseas trainers using online platform for theoretical teaching, clinical supervision, and conduct of examination. Another example of capacity building using online platform especially in the context of COVID-19 is the OPHELIA Training: Online Pacific Health Exchange (Asia Australia Mental Health, 2021). This is a short course for Pacific Health Workers delivering Child and Youth Mental Health Services cofacilitated by St. Vincent's Postgraduate Overseas Specialist Training (POST) Program, the Royal Australian and New Zealand College of Psychiatry (RANZCP) Faculty of Child and Adolescent Psychiatry (FCAP), and the College of Medicine, Nursing and Health Sciences, Fiji National University. This program of 12 sessions is open for all health workers delivering Child and Youth Mental Health Services in Pacific countries and comprises online sessions that include information and resources along with an opportunity to explore their own clinical practice through case discussion. Programs such as the aforementioned examples where online platform is used for training and capacity building can be easily scaled up and disseminated globally. This is a highly sustainable and cost-effective model and one that is easy to sustain despite the current COVID-19 pandemic that has significantly increased the demand for child and adolescent mental health services despite the limited opportunities for trainees or supervisors to travel for training purposes or to attend conferences or workshops internationally.

2.1.5 Continued access to learning and training in the context of global issues

COVID-19 and future pandemics. The spread of COVID-19 world-wide and the ensuing restriction of movements and face-to-face gathering in aid of public safety has resulted in a reconsideration of the way health, including mental health, training is disseminated. Consequently, there has been an increased focus on the use of TEL to ensure that training of healthcare professionals can continue (Wyres & Taylor, 2020), with a call for increased access to online training and supervision to facilitate the work of mental healthcare professionals in meeting patient needs, particularly when mental healthcare sessions themselves are being held online (Taylor et al., 2020).

Climate change. Another global concern at present is climate change, which has already had observable impacts on the environment and poses an immense existential threat (NASA, 2021). A principal force driving human-made climate change is the increase in carbon dioxide levels from fossil fuel emissions (Hansen et al., 2013). The transport sector remains at the center of debates around carbon emissions, given the reliance on fossil fuels on air, road, and rail travel (Brand et al., 2021). In this context, it is important for mental health professionals to mitigate the amount of work-related travel undertaken as much as possible. In line with this, being able to undertake training online anywhere in the world via TEL allows professionals to access training while minimizing the environmental costs of travel that would be required if the training were held in a physical location as opposed to virtually.

2.2 Potential challenges of technology-enhanced learning

Despite the potential benefits of TEL in the context of child and adolescent mental health highlighted before, TEL resources do not come without their challenges.

One paramount challenge in the use of TEL relates to the access of technology. To facilitate e-learning, the learner must have access to appropriate devices as well as the Internet, all which come at a cost. Hence, overreliance on technology can result in unequal learning opportunities. Consequently, Gipson et al. (2017) propose that alternate methods of teaching remain available until universal access is made available.

There is also some evidence that the use of technology can have detrimental effects on attention during learning (Levine et al., 2007), with access to devices' social media applications or instant messaging capabilities potentially distracting from learning.

A case study highlighting potential challenges of TEL was described by Page et al. (2018) who outlined an academic program required for medical trainees in forensic psychiatry but open to all those who work in forensic services. The topics included clinical case presentations, "learning lessons" sessions, focusing on feedback from recent serious clinical incidents, research and journal presentations, as well as service user presentations. These authors conducted this program through video-conferencing, with participants connecting to a virtual meeting room. The authors mentioned a number of technical challenges, including concerns about the weekly setting up of program equipment and initial technical hitches, and the potential for remote sites to feel disengaged from discussion. These authors also pointed out a concern relating to the confidentiality of client information over videoconferencing. In response to this, they considered that if a video link is maintained entirely within an organization, the risk of interception is small. These authors point out that if commercial systems are used, live data are likely to be processed external to the organization, and that this approach requires considered discussion with system suppliers and relevant government professionals.

Another challenge of TEL is ensuring that the learning content is appropriate for the technology medium used to deliver it. Dror et al. (2011) note that e-learning is often simply a transcription of presentations that were created for face-to-face learning to a technological medium. These authors posit that doing so does not take full advantage of the opportunities that the technology offers and can be detrimental to learning. Furthermore, both the development and implementation of TEL resources can require a large degree of financial, human, and infrastructure investment, both upfront in the preparing of multimedia materials and continuously through platform maintenance and updating (Liu et al., 2016). These factors highlight the importance of ensuring that TEL resources are designed effectively so as to ensure their efficacy.

A further challenge of TEL pertains to the "digital divide" that exists between high-income countries and LMICs. Specifically, in a report published in 2016, the World Bank highlighted that, at that point, emerging technologies had disproportionately benefitted higher-income countries. Furthermore, based on 2019 data from the International Telecommunications Union and 2020 data from the World Bank, the digital divide in Internet usage and mobile subscriptions had increased between 2000 and 2017, with fewer than 40% of households in LMICs with fixed Internet access, as compared with 90% in high-income countries. Kumm et al. (2021) highlight that there is concern that the COVID-19 pandemic has magnified the preexisting digital divide between countries. Given the utility of TEL resources for mental health training, including the training of professionals in LMICs (e.g., the Child and Adolescent Psychiatry Advanced Support and Training-Iraq (Mahmood & Eapen, 2020) and the

OPHELIA Training: Online Pacific Health Exchange (Asia Australia Mental Health, 2021), as identified before), it is important to consider that TEL resources may not be equitably accessible across the globe and that rectifying this discrepancy will be imperative to equitable access to TEL in child and adolescent mental health.

3. Designing technology-enabled learning resources

3.1 Models of design

According to Salmon et al. (2019), the ADDIE model (Analysis, Design, Development, Implementation and Evaluation; Allen, 2006) for designing and implementing training is particularly popular among educators. In this model, the development of the learning material begins with analyzing the requirements of the resource. At this stage, it is important for developers to have an in-depth understanding of the people the resource is targeting and specifically what they need to know, their levels of preexisting knowledge, their preferred way of learning, the learning outcomes of the resource, and how it is to be delivered. Salmon et al. (2019) posit that a useful framework, which can be used at this stage, is the PACT (People; Activities; Contexts; and Technologies). This framework facilitates the development of clearly defined learning objectives that stipulate what the student should be able to do after completing the resource before relevant learning activities are designed, with learning activities defined as "a specific interaction of learner(s) with others using specific tools and resources, oriented toward a specific outcome (Beetham, p. 28), while context refers to the physical and social environments for the learning activities as well as the support available and the learner's circumstances, and technologies refer to the specific technological tools used to meet the learning objectives."

In the design phase of the ADDIE model, one should consider a number of factors, including lesson planning, instructional methods, learning objectives, learning activities, content, use of multimedia, and the assessment methods to be used. In the development phase, instructional materials and learning content are developed and assembled, with a consideration of additional details such as the font to be used, color, and use of graphics considered. The resource then needs to be tested and amended in response to the feedback. Salmon et al. (2019) posit the use of Overbaugh's (1994) guidelines for the development of computer-based learning in the development phase. The first domain of these guidelines is known as an instructional set and aims to help the learner to engage with the information that is going to be presented, the second considers teaching strategies, and the third considers eliciting student performance, providing feedback, and assessing performance. Finally, the fourth domain considers other design issues such as learner control and teaching tools.

Furthermore, in terms of the design of teaching and learning tools for mental health professionals, a number of educational fields have shifted from training models focused on traditional learning and practice to those that are competency based. Competence has been defined as "the habitual and judicious use of communication, knowledge, technical skills, clinical reasoning, emotions, values, and reflection in the daily practice for the benefit of the individual and community served" (Epstein & Hundert, 2002, p. 227), and models of therapists competencies for evidence-based practice in child and adolescent mental health have been proposed in recent literature (e.g., Allen et al., 2021). It is therefore important that TEL training resources are informed by such models and that they map directly onto such competencies where possible.

3.2 Practical considerations

To design TEL resources effectively, practical considerations also need to be taken into account. In line with this, Shaw et al. (2010) posit that converting a face-to-face lecture into a videoconferencing format is not adequate, and have stipulated a set of "best practice" guidelines to approaching videoconferencing, which may be able to be extended to other TEL resources and are outlined in the following:

(a) Ensure educators have skills in using effective teaching strategies appropriate to the technology and class being taught.
(b) Establish criteria for determining whether videoconferencing is the right choice for a particular educational content. Shaw et al. suggest that inappropriate content could include psychologically sensitive topics, and topics that require the sharing of personal information, among others.

Shaw et al. (2010) also highlighted the importance of interaction in telelearning, and videoconferencing in particular. Shaw et al.'s best practice guidelines regarding student engagement include (1) ensuring that engaging students is a primary focus for education providers when designing and delivering their sessions, (2) breaking lectures into small segments and ensuring that sessions include various activities (e.g., group work, case studies etc.), (3) educators considering the options of giving one lecture to the live venue and another to distance sites, and/or alternating the host site whenever possible.

Following the development phase in the ADDIE model is the implementation phase, which incorporates the preparation of training required to use the e-learning resources and make checks to ensure that the tool is fully functional. In this model, evaluation is central to the process and should be considered at every stage.

3.3 The current evidence-base for technology-enhanced learning

Despite the benefits, and indeed challenges, of TEL highlighted before, there are limited empirical studies that evaluate the efficacy of TEL resources, in mental health in general, and child and adolescent mental health in particular. Indeed, Pickering and Joynes (2016) propose that there is a lack of robust evidence and meaningful evaluation of TEL to support the widespread implementation of such resources. Hence, it is imperative that further empirical research is undertaken into the efficacy of TEL, and particularly in the context of child and adolescent mental health. Nevertheless, some examples of the empirical evidence that does exist is outlined in the following.

There is some direct evidence relating to the efficacy of TEL in the context of child and adolescent mental health. As an example, Salmon et al. (2019) outline the design, development, and dissemination of an e-learning resource to teach the principles of ADHD to undergraduate medical students as part of their Child and Adolescent Psychiatry education. Specifically, the authors outlined the creation of an online resource, which included slides with a case study, video links, diagrams, graphics, and interactive resources, and a pre- and posttest to assess the meeting of learning outcomes, which were to know the clinical features, assessment, and evidence-based treatments for ADHD. 14 of the 15 students who completed the feedback indicated that they agreed or strongly agreed that the resource covered the subject of ADHD in sufficient breadth and depth to meet their learning objectives. Furthermore, 87% indicated that they would be likely to recommend the resource to another medical student.

Another body of evidence for the efficacy of TEL in the context of child and adolescent mental health comes from a training program for those who work with at-risk young people (Haythornthwaite, 2002). This program consisted of seven two-hour sessions presented over 12 weeks, with rural participants accessing the training via videoconferencing and metropolitan participants accessing the training face-to-face. The author found a significant improvement in participants' knowledge of some of the training modules, with this being similar between those trained via telehealth and those trained face-to-face.

In terms of mental health in general, Dimeff et al. (2015) completed a randomized controlled trial to compare three methods of training clinicians in two core strategies of dialectical behavior therapy to mental health clinicians, comparing the efficacy of online training, instructor-led training, and a treatment manual. The participants were assessed at baseline, posttraining, 30, 60, and 90 days following training, with outcomes including satisfaction, self-efficacy, motivation, knowledge, clinical proficiency, and clinical use. Overall, participants in the instructor-led training reported greater satisfaction, self-efficacy, and motivation, while those in the online training cohort had the greatest increase in knowledge following training.

A review by Shaw et al. (2010) commissioned by the SAX institute on behalf of New South Wales Health, Australia, to review the use of telelearning technologies in the delivery of education and training for health professionals found that the literature available on telelearning is small, with the majority of studies being descriptive in nature. Across 4 randomized controlled studies and 10 comparison studies which measured learning outcomes of telelearning as compared with traditional face-to-face education, the authors found no significant difference in the learning outcomes of technology-based distance education as compared with traditional face-to-face methods. However, the authors noted that the scientific rigor of these studies was not strong, with many failing to control for variables such as prior knowledge, ability, instructor experience, and methods. These authors also questioned whether there is evidence that some forms of telelearning are more effective than others in achieving learning outcomes, finding two studies that compared learning across various telelearning platforms and finding no significant differences in knowledge gained between different telelearning modalities.

Therefore, there is some, albeit limited, empirical evidence to suggest that TEL resources can be efficacious in training health professionals and that it is equally effective, if not more so, than traditional, face-to-face training. However, as established by Pickering and Joynes (2016), the evidence of the efficacy of TEL is limited. Indeed, to our knowledge, there are currently no randomized controlled trials assessing the efficacy of TEL resources in child and adolescent mental health. Given the potential benefits of such resources, as established before, it is crucial that TEL resources are evaluated systematically. This is particularly pertinent to LMICs, where TEL has the potential to improve access to health services (e.g., Duarte et al., 2021; Sweetland et al., 2014; Mokitimi et al., 2022). Importantly, TEL in such countries may be complicated by issues including unequal access to the technology required for TEL (e.g., World Bank, 2016, 2020), limited healthcare budgets (World Health Organisation, 2014), and difficulties accessing adequately trained local clinicians (e.g., Chand et al., 2014; Mahmood & Eapen, 2020). There is a particular need for the evaluation of TEL in these countries, where issues related to the digital divide (e.g., cost of technology, power cuts, remoteness) may create challenges not only for families but also for trainees and professionals.

There is emerging evidence to support the efficacy of TEL resources in LMICs (e.g., Project ECHO; Chand et al., 2014), yet TEL evidence specific to LMICs nonetheless remains limited. Moreover, it has not, to our knowledge, been subject to systematic review or metaanalysis. Systematic reviews have, however, examined the evaluation of e-learning interventions for medical education in LMICs in general. Barteit et al. (2020) found that most evaluations have been conducted through the collection of subjective self-report (i.e., questionnaire) data from study participants. This review indicated that while most studies have found TEL interventions to be effective, these studies have often been low in quality and have often examined small-scale interventions based on short-term outcomes. These authors argued that to understand the strengths and challenges of implementing TEL in such settings, the methods used to evaluate e-learning in LMICs must be more rigorous (Barteit et al., 2020). Indeed, this applies also to the use of TEL for child and adolescent mental health, with the rigorous evaluation of such resources in LMICs being imperative.

3.4 Evaluating the impact of technology-enhanced learning in the future

A number of models have been promised to evaluate the impact of TEL, particularly in the context of medical education but not specifically in the context of mental health education. According to Pickering and Joynes (2016), some of the most influential of such models are Kirkpatrick's models (Kirkpatrick, 1994, 2010), which describe evaluating four levels of learner outcomes to ascertain the effect of training programs. Specifically, these four levels include level 1 outcomes (reactions) that consider participant satisfaction with and perceptions of the course experience and quality. In level 2, the participants' knowledge, skills, or attitudes in a test setting are evaluated. Level 3 concerns the measure of performance in actual practice, while level 4 assesses the impact on the systems and organizations within which participants work.

Using this model as a scaffold, Pickering and Joynes (2016) have proposed a protocol for evaluating an individual TEL resource to measure its effectiveness as a learning tool (Fig. 11.1).

As illustrated in Fig. 11.1, this protocol contains four levels, which are outlined in the following: Level 0 consists of a preliminary evaluation of the need for a particular TEL resource, the information for which can be ascertained through module evaluations, module grades, and staff awareness of poor topic engagement. Level 0 also consists of the development phase of the TEL resource, which Pickering and Joynes suggest

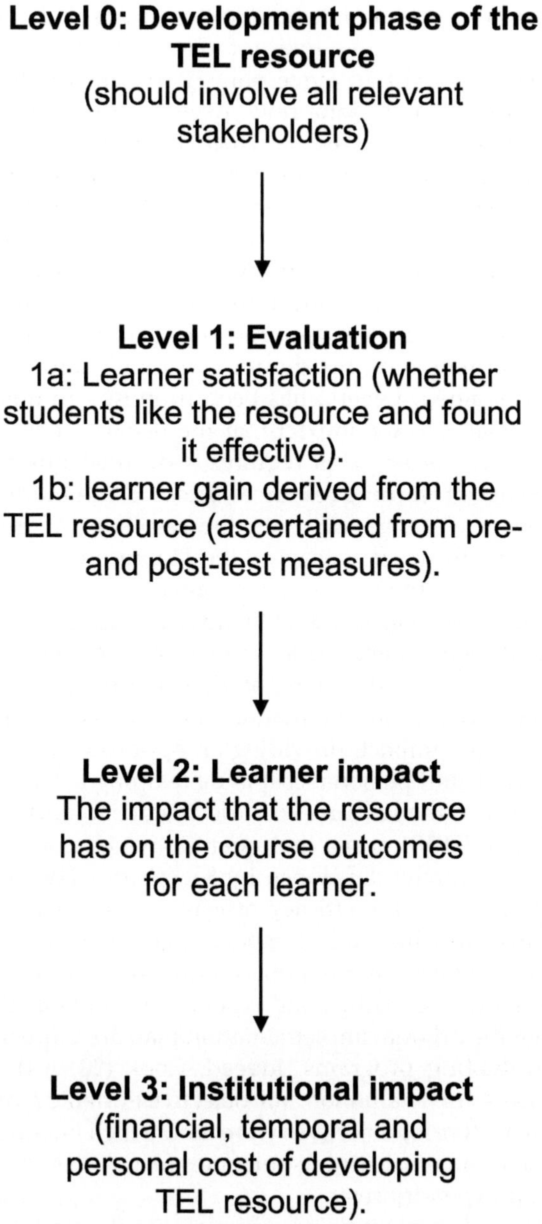

Level 0: Development phase of the TEL resource
(should involve all relevant stakeholders)

↓

Level 1: Evaluation
1a: Learner satisfaction (whether students like the resource and found it effective).
1b: learner gain derived from the TEL resource (ascertained from pre- and post-test measures).

↓

Level 2: Learner impact
The impact that the resource has on the course outcomes for each learner.

↓

Level 3: Institutional impact
(financial, temporal and personal cost of developing TEL resource).

FIGURE 11.1   Levels of Pickering and Joynes' (2016) proposed protocol for evaluating an individual TEL resource to measure its effectiveness as a learning tool.
TEL, technology-enhanced learning.

should involve all relevant stakeholders to ensure that the resource is academically appropriate and relevant. The purpose of Level 1 is to evaluate two areas of a TEL resource, namely level 1a, learner satisfaction, which relates to research into how user-friendly learners find the resource, as well as the degree to which it aligns with the academic content of the topic. This level of evaluation consists of ascertaining whether the students liked the resource aesthetically as well as whether they found it to be effective in delivering aspects of the curriculum. Level 1b refers to learner gain derived from the TEL resource, which can be ascertained from pre- and posttest measures. Furthermore, pre- and posttesting allow a direct measure of learner gain to be ascertained and also provide information on the duration of time for which this knowledge has been retained. Level 2 has been proposed to measure learner impact, which relates to the impact that the resource has on the course outcomes for each learner. This requires a detailed questionnaire that measures the range of learning resources accessed and the amount of time that a student spends engaging with the resource. At this stage, it is important to assess the level of usage of the TEL resource, as well as when and how often during the course the resource was accessed. This information must then be correlated with information such as cohort demographics and performance from previous assessments against the assessment outcomes. Furthermore, student permission is required for their data to be accessed in this manner. Level 3 has been proposed to measure institutional impact, providing an opportunity to reflect on the financial, temporal, and personal cost of developing the TEL resource, as well as the benefit of the resource to various stakeholders.

However, Cook (2010) posits that quantitative outcomes, such as the aforementioned hierarchy developed by Kirkpatrick (1996), alone might not adequately measure the efficacy of learning for many contexts and applications. Instead, this author reports that many course outcomes cannot be quantified and that nonquantitative outcomes, such as narrative feedback about the participant experience, unplanned events, and deviations from the original implementation plan are important factors to consider in evaluating programs. Indeed, Cook (2010) describes three broad approaches for evaluation, an objectives-oriented approach that focuses on how well prior objectives were met, which includes enrollment and completion numbers, learning outcomes (e.g., knowledge and skills), and income and expenditures.

The importance of evaluating educational resources, particularly in the context of health, has been established. However, according to Cook and Ellaway (2015), a focus on the evaluation of TEL in medical education is particularly important for the following reasons: There is often anxiety regarding new models of medical education, and responding to the concerns of stakeholders requires rigorous evaluation of TEL efficacy.

Furthermore, aspects of TEL, such as usability, accessibility, and technical reliability of materials and learning environment, play a substantial role in the evaluation of TEL. Furthermore, as interactions between teachers and learners are generally mediated by technology in TEL, teacher–learner relationships do not allow for the same opportunities for informal evaluation as do traditional treatment modalities, suggesting that TEL requires a more comprehensive evaluation than other educational activities. Also, TEL can generate much more data than traditional educational approaches, allowing for the development of analytic approaches to evaluation. Finally, Cook and Ellaway (2015) point to the importance of delineating what exactly is being evaluated in the evaluation of TEL resources.

The aforementioned reasons for the evaluation of TEL in medical education may also apply to the evaluation of TEL in the context of the education of child and adolescent mental health professionals. Hence, there are a number of factors that must be taken into consideration when evaluating the efficacy of TEL resources. A challenge in the context of TEL for child and adolescent mental health professionals is to ensure that the resource is effective as a TEL resource as well as that it meets the training goals stipulated by the mental health bodies overseeing the training (for example, ensuring that the training is efficacious in helping clinicians achieve the required competencies).

4. Conclusion

Overall, there are case studies in both adult and child and adolescent mental health suggesting that TEL could be of huge benefit across a range of contexts and may serve to help bridge the gap between children and adolescents who require mental health intervention and those who receive evidence-based treatment. That said, there are limited studies empirically evaluating the efficacy of TEL resources, either in relation to comparing pre–postmeasures of learning to evaluate a specific TEL resource, or comparing TEL resources to face-to-face learning. Hence, there is broad scope for future research into the efficacy of TEL resources, and Pickering and Joynes (2016), Cook (2010), and Cook and Ellaway (2015) have outlined the various factors to be taken into consideration when evaluating efficacy. Further robust evaluations are required to provide a critical evidence base on the essential elements of TEL that are needed for successful learning outcomes, along with implementation research on how best to contextualize the program for the given setting. Future research is also required into methods by which to design TEL resources so as to ensure efficacy and that human, infrastructure, and financial resources are used appropriately.

References

Akroyd, M., Jordan, G., & Rowlands, P. (2016). Interprofessional, simulation-based technology-enhanced learning to improve physical health care in psychiatry: The recognition and assessment of medical problems in psychiatric settings course. *Health Informatics, 22*, 312–320. https://doi.org/10.1177/1460458214557098

Allen, W. C. (2006). Overview and evolution of the ADDIE training system. *Advances in Developing Human Resources, 8*, 430–441. https://doi.org/10.1177/1523422306292942

Allen, J. L., Hawes, D. J., & Essau, C. A. (2021). A core-competency perspective on family-based intervention for child and adolescent mental health. In J. L. Allen, D. J. Hawes, & C. A. Essau (Eds.), *Family-based intervention for child and adolescent mental health: A core competencies approach* (pp. 1–13). Cambridge: Cambridge University Press. https://doi.org/10.1017/9781108682053

American Psychological Association. (2006). Evidence-based practice in psychology. *American Psychologist, 61*, 271–285. https://doi.org/10.1037/0003-066X.61.4.271

Anderson, L. W., & Krathwohl, D. R. (Eds.). (2001). *A taxonomy for learning, teaching and assessing: A revision of Bloom's Taxonomy of educational objectives*. New York: Longman.

Asia Australia Mental Health. (2021). *2021 OPHELIA training: Online Pacific health exchange: A short course for Pacific health workers delivering child and youth mental health services*. Retrieved from aamh.edu.au.

Bairy, B. K., Ganesh, A., Govindraj, D., & Chand, P. K. (2019). Role of digital learning in addiction psychiatry. *Digital Psychiatry, 2*, 25–33. https://doi.org/10.1080/2575517X.2019.1622983

Barteit, S., Guzek, D., Jahn, A., Barnighausen, T., Jorge, M. M., & Neuhann, F. (2020). Evaluation of e-learning for medical education in low- and middle-income countries: A systematic review. *Computers & Education, 145*, 103726. https://doi.org/10.1016/j.compedu.2019.103726

Batchelor, R., Catanzano, M., Kerry, E., Bennett, S. D., Coughtrey, A. E., Liang, H, & Shafran, R. (2020). Debate: Lessons learned in lockdown-a one-day remotely delivered training on low-intensity psychological interventions for common mental health conditions.Child and Adolescent Mental. *Health, 25*, 175–177. https://doi.org/10.1111/camh.12402

Beidas, R. S., Edmunds, J. M., Marcus, S. C., & Kendall, P. C. (2012). Training and consultation to promote implementation of an empirically supported treatment: A randomized trial. *Psychiatric Services, 63*, 660–665. https://doi.org/10.1176/appi.ps.201100401

Brand, C., Gotschi, T., Dons, E., Gerike, R., Anaya-Boig, E., Avila-Palencia, I., & Nieuwenhuijsen, M. J. (2021). The climate change mitigation impacts of active travel: Evidence from a longitudinal panel study in seven European cities. *Global Environmental Change, 67*, 102224. https://doi.org/10.1016/j.gloenvcha.2021.102224

Brijnath, B., Protheroe, J., Mahtani, K. R., & Antoniades, J. (2016). Do web-based mental health literacy interventions improve the mental health literacy of adult consumers? Results from a systematic review. *Journal of Medical Internet Research, 18*, e165. https://doi.org/10.2196/jmir.5463

Chand, P., Murthy, R., Gupta, V., Kandasamy, A., Jayarajan, D., Jayarajan, L., & L…Arora, S. (2014). Technology enhanced learning in addiction mental health: Developing a virtual knowledge network: NIMHANS ECHO. *2014 IEEE Sixth International Conference on Technology for Education, 1*, 229–232. https://doi.org/10.1109/T4E.2014.14

Cook, D. A. (2010). Twelve tips for evaluating educational programs. *Medical Teacher, 32*, 296–301. https://doi.org/10.3109/01421590903480121

Cook, D. A., & Ellaway, R. H. (2015). Evaluating technology-enhanced learning: A comprehensive framework. *Medical Teacher, 37*, 961–970. https://doi.org/10.3109/0142159X.2015.1009024

Copeland, W. E., Shanahan, L., Costello, E. J., & Angold, A. (2009). Childhood and adolescent psychiatric disorders as predictors of young adult disorders. *Archives of General Psychiatry, 66*, 764–772. https://doi.org/10.1001/archgenpsychiatry.2009.85

Department of Health and Department for Education. (2021). MindEd. Retrieved from https://www.minded.org.uk/.

Dimeff, L. A., Harned, M. S., Woodcock, E. A., Skutch, J. M., Koerner, K., & Linehan, M. M. (2015). Investigating bang for your training buck: A randomized controlled trial comparing three methods of training clinicians in two core strategies of dialectical behavior therapy. *Behavior Therapy, 46*, 283–295. https://doi.org/10.1016/j.beth.2015.01.001

Dror, I., Schmidt, P., & O'Connor, L. (2011). A cognitive perspective on technology enhanced learning in medical training: Great opportunities, pitfalls and challenges. *Medical Teacher, 33*, 291–296. https://doi.org/10.3109/0142159X.2011.550970

Duarte, C., Lovero, K. L., Sourander, A., Ribeiro, W. S., & Bordin, I. A. S. (2021). The child mental health treatment gap in an urban low-income setting: Multisectoral service use and correlates. *Psychiatric Services, 1*–7. https://doi.org/10.1176/appi.ps.202000742

Eapen, V., Graham, P., & Srinath, S. (2012). *Where there is no child psychiatrist: A mental health-care manual*. London: RCPsych Publications.

Edmunds, J. M., Beidas, R. S., & Kendall, P. C. (2013). Dissemination and implementation of evidence-based practices: Training and consultation as implementation strategies.Clinical. *Psychology: Science and Practice, 20*, 152–165. https://doi.org/10.1111/cpsp.12031

Emerging Minds. (2021). *Online training/family talks*. Retrieved from https://emergingminds.com.au/online-course/family-focus/.

Epstein, R. M., & Hundert, E. M. (2002). Defining and assessing professional competence. *Journal of the American Medical Association, 287*, 226–235. https://doi.org/10.1001/jama.287.2.226

de Figueiredo, C. S., Sandre, P. C., Portugal, L. C. L., & Bomfim, P. O. (2021). Covid-19 pandemic impact on children and adolescents' mental health: Biological, environmental, and social factors. *Progress in Neuropsychopharmacology & Biological Psychiatry, 106*, 110171. https://doi.org/10.1016/j.pnpbp.2020.110171

Gipson, S. Y.-M. T., Kim, J. W., Shin, A. L., Kitts, R., & Maneta, E. (2017). Teaching child and adolescent psychiatry in the twenty-first century: A reflection on the role of technology in education. *Child and Adolescent Psychiatric Clinics of North America, 26*, 93–103. https://doi.org/10.1016/j.chc.2016.07.004

Hansen, J., Kharecha, P., Sato, M., Masson-Delmotte, V., Ackerman, F., Beerling, D. J., & Zachos, J. C. (2013). Assessing "dangerous climate change": Required reduction of carbon emissions to protect young people, future generations and nature. *PLoS One, 8*, e81648. https://doi.org/10.1371/journal.pone.0081648

Haythornthwaite, S. (2002). Videoconferencing training for those working with at-risk young people in rural areas of Western Australia. *Journal of Telemedicine and Telecare, 8*(Supplementary 3), 29–33. https://doi.org/10.1258/13576330260440772

Higher Education Funding Council For England. (2009). *Enhancing learning and teaching through the use of technology: A revised approach to HEFCE's strategy for e-learning*. Retrieved from https://dera.ioe.ac.uk/140/1/09_12.pdf.

Hu, N., Nassar, N., Shrapnel, J., Perkes, I., Hodgins, M., O'Leary, F., Eapen, V., Woolfenden, S., Knight, K., & Lingam, R. (2022). The impact of the COVID-19 pandemic on paediatric health service use within one year after the first pandemic outbreak in New South Wales Australia – a time series analysis. *The Lancet Regional Health - Western Pacific, 19*, 100311. https://doi.org/10.1016/j.lanwpc.2021.100311

Karanicolas, S., & Snelling, C. (2010). Making the transition: Achieving content connectivity and student engagement through flexible learning tools. In *Proceedings of the Distance*

Education Association of New Zealand (DEANZ) conference (p. 13). Wellington: Distance Education Association of New Zealand. http://hdl.handle.net/2440/68599.

Kidd, L. I., Knisley, S. J., & Morgan, K. I. (2012). Effectiveness of a second life(®) simulation as a teaching strategy for undergraduate mental health nursing students. *Journal of Psychosocial Nursing and Mental Health Services, 50*, 28—37. https://doi.org/10.3928/02793695-20120605-04

Kirkpatrick, D. L. (1994). *Evaluating training programs: The four levels.* San Francisco: Berrett-Koehlar.

Kirkpatrick, D. (1996). *Great ideas revisited.Training and Development, 50*, 54—59.

Kirkpatrick, D. L. (2010). *The new world Kirkpatrick model.* Retrieved from http://www.kirkpatrickpartners.com/.

Kobak, K. A., Lipsitz, J. D., Markowitz, J. C., & Bleiberg, K. L. (2017). Web-based therapist training in interpersonal psychotherapy for depression: Pilot study. *Journal of Medical Internet Research, 19*, e257. https://doi.org/10.2196/jmir.7966

Kumm, A. J., Viljoen, M., & de Vries, P. J. (2021). The digital divide in technologies for autism: Feasibility considerations for low- and middle-income countries. *Journal of Autism and Developmental Disorders.* https://doi.org/10.1007/s10803-021-05084-8

Levine, L. E., Waite, B. M., & Bowman, L. L. (2007). Electronic media use, reading, and academic distractibility in college youth. *CyberPsychology & Behavior, 10*, 560—566. https://doi.org/10.1089/cpb.2007.9990

Liu, Q., Peng, W., Zhang, F., Hu, R., Li, Y., & Yan, W. (2016). The effectiveness of blended learning in health professions: Systematic review and meta-analysis. *Journal of Medical Internet Research, 18*, e2. https://doi.org/10.2196/jmir.4807

Lowell, V. L., & Alshammari, A. (2018). Experiential learning experiences in an online 3D virtual environment for mental health interviewing and diagnosis role-playing: A comparison of perceived learning across learning activities. *Educational Technology Research and Development, 67*, 825—854. https://doi.org/10.1007/s11423-018-9632-8

Mahmood, D., & Eapen, V. *CAPAST-I: Working together to build access to child psychiatry in Asia Pacific* [conference presentation]. 24th world congress of the International Association for Child and Adolescent Psychiatry and Allied Professions (IACAPAP 2020), Singapore.

MindEd. (2021). *MindEd: E-Learning to support healthy minds.* Retrieved from https://www.minded.org.uk/.

Mitchell, J., Robinson, P., Seiboth, C., & Koszegi, B. (2000). An evaluation of a network for professional development in child and adolescent mental health in rural and remote communities. *Journal of Telemedicine and Telecare, 6*, 158—162. https://doi.org/10.1258/1357633001935257

Mitgang, E. A., Blaya, J. A., & Chopra, M. (2021). Digital health in response to COVID-19 in low- and middle-income countries: Opportunities and challenges. *Global Policy, 12*, 107—109. https://doi.org/10.1111/1758-5899.12880

Mokitimi, S., Schneider, M., & de Vries, P. J. (2022). A situational analysis of child and adolescent mental health services and systems in the Western Cape province of South Africa. *Child and Adolescent Psychiatry and Mental Health, 16*, 6. https://doi.org/10.1186/s13034-022-00440-7

Morgan, A. J., Ross, A., & Reavley, N. (2018). Systematic review and meta-analysis of Mental Health First Aid training: Effects on knowledge, stigma, and helping behaviour. *PLoS One, 13*, e0197102. https://doi.org/10.1371/journal.pone.0197102

Nadeem, E., Gleacher, A., & Beidas, R. S. (2013). Consultation as an implementation strategy for evidence-based practices across multiple contexts: Unpacking the black box. Administration and Policy in Mental Health and Mental. *Health Services Research, 40*, 439—450. https://doi.org/10.1007/s10488-013-0502-8

NASA. (2021). *The effects of climate change.* Retrieved from https://climate.nasa.gov/effects/.

Nicoll, P., MacRury, S., van Woerden, H. C., & Smyth, K. (2018). Evaluation of technology-enhanced learning programs for health care professionals: Systematic review. *Journal of Medical Internet Research, 20*, e131. https://doi.org/10.2196/jmir.9085

O'Brien, D., Harvey, K., Howse, J., Reardon, T., & Creswell, C. (2016). Barriers to managing child and adolescent mental health problems: A systematic review of primary care practitioners' perceptions. *British Journal of General Practice, 66*, 693—707. https://doi.org/10.3399/bjgp16X687061

Ong, N., Campbell, D., Garg, P., Tomsic, G., Silove, N., Waters, K., Castro, C., Moore, L., Goff, R., & Eapen, V. (2020). Motivation for change in the healthcare of children with developmental disabilities: Pilot continuing professional development-quality improvement project. *Journal of Paediatrics and Child Health, 57*, 212—218. https://doi.org/10.1111/jpc.15175

Overbaugh, R. C. (1994). Research-based guidelines for computer-based instruction development. *Journal of Research on Computing in Education, 27*, 29—47. https://doi.org/10.1080/08886504.1994.10782114

Page, R., Hynes, F., & Reed, J. (2018). Distance is not a barrier: The use of videoconferencing to develop a community of practice. *Journal of Mental Health Training, 14*, 12—19. https://doi.org/10.1108/JMHTEP-10-2016-0052

Parsons, T. D., Kenny, P., Ntuen, C. A., Pataki, C. S., Pato, M. T., Rizzo, A. A., St-George, C., & Sugar, J. (2008). Objective structured clinical interview training using a virtual human patient. *Studies in Health Technology and Informatics, 132*, 357—362. PMID: 18391321.

Pickering, J. D., & Joynes, V. C. (2016). A holistic model for evaluating the impact of individual technology-enhanced learning resources. *Medical Teacher, 38*, 1242—1247. https://doi.org/10.1080/0142159X.2016.1210112

Pidano, A. E., & Whitcomb, J. M. (2012). Training to work with children and families: Results from a survey of psychologists and doctoral students. *Training and Education in Professional Psychology, 6*, 8—17. https://doi.org/10.1037/a0026961

Pierce, M., Hope, H., Ford, T., Hatch, S., Hotopf, M., John, A., Kontopantelis, E., Webb, R., Wessley, S., McManus, S., & Abel, K. M. (2020). Mental health before and during the COVID-19 pandemic: A longitudinal probability sample survey of the UK population. *Lancet Psychiatry, 7*, 883—892. https://doi.org/10.1016/S2215-0366(20)30308-4

Polanczyk, G. V., Salum, G. A., Sugaya, L. S., Caye, A., & Rohde, L. A. (2015). A meta-analysis of the worldwide prevalence of mental disorders in children and adolescents. *Journal of Child and Adolescent Psychology and Psychiatry, 56*, 345—365. https://doi.org/10.1111/jcpp.12381

Reid, D. (2002). Virtual reality and the person-environment experience. *Cyberpsychology and Behavior: The Impact of the Internet, Multimedia and Virtual Reality on Behavior andSociety, 5*, 559—564. https://doi.org/10.1089/10949310231018204

Reid, S. (2020). COVID conditions trigger renewed engagement on the future of technology enhanced learning (TEL). *Journal of Community Safety and Well-Being, 5*, 73—74. https://doi.org/10.35502/jcswb.142

Rey, J. M., & Martin, A. (2019). *JM Rey's IACAPAP e-textbook of child and adolescent mental health*. Geneva: International Association for Child and Adolescent Psychiatry and Allied Professions.

Rose, R. D., Lang, A. J., Welch, S. S., Campbell-Sills, L., Chavira, D. A., Sullivan, G, & Craske, M. G. (2011). Training primary care staff to deliver a computer-assisted cognitive-behavioral therapy program for anxiety disorders.General. *Hospital Psychiatry, 33*, 336—342. https://doi.org/10.1016/j.genhosppsych.2011.04.011

Salmon, G., Tombs, M., & Surman, K. (2019). Teaching medical students about attention deficit hyperactivity disorder (ADHD): The design and development of an E-learning resource. *Advances in Medical Education and Practice, 10*, 987—997. https://doi.org/10.2147/AMEP.S220390

Shaw, T., Tomlinson J., & Munro, A. (2010). *Tele-learning for health professionals* [Evidence Check rapid review] Sax Institute the NSW Department of Health https://www.saxinstitute.org.au/wp-content/uploads/Tele-learning-for-health-professionals.pdf.

Sweetland, A. C., Oquendo, M. A., Sidat, M., Santos, P. F., Vermund, S. H., Duarte, C. S., Arbuckle, M., & Wainberg, M. L. (2014). Closing the mental health gap in low-income settings by building research capacity: Perspectives from Mozambique. *Annals of Global Health, 80,* 126–133. https://doi.org/10.1016/j.aogh.2014.04.014

Taylor, C. B., Fitzsimmons-Cradt, E. E., & Graham, A. K. (2020). Digital technology can revolutionize mental health services delivery: The COVID-19 crisis as a catalyst for change. *International Journal of Eating Disorders, 53,* 1155–1157. https://doi.org/10.1002/eat.23300

Tully, L. A., Hawes, D. J., Doyle, F. L., Sawyer, M. G., & Dadds, M. R. (2019). A national child mental health literacy initiative is needed to reduce childhood mental health disorders. *Australian and New Zealand Journal of Psychiatry, 53,* 286–290. https://doi.org/10.1177/0004867418821440

Weissman, M. M., Verdeli, H., Gameroff, M. J., Bledsoe, S. E., Betts, K., Mufson, L., & Wickramaratne, P. (2006). National survey of psychotherapy training in psychiatry, psychology, and social work. *Archives of General Psychiatry, 63,* 925–934. https://doi.org/10.1001/archpsyc.63.8.925

World Bank. (2016). *World development report 2016-Digital dividends.* Retrieved from http://documents.worldbank.org/curated/en/896971468194972881/pdf/102725-PUB-Replacement-PUBLIC.pdf.

World Bank. (2020). *Development data group. Income level/low-and middle-income countries.* Retrieved from https://data.worldbank.org/income-level/low-and-middle-income.

World Health Organization. (2014). *The health of the people: What works-the African regional health report 2014.* Retrieved from http://www.who.int/bulletin/africanhealth2014/en/#.

Wyres, M., & Taylor, N. (2020). Covid-19: Using simulation and technology-enhanced learning to negotiate and adapt to the ongoing challenges in UK healthcare education. *BMJ Simulation and Technology Enhanced Learning, 6,* 317–319. https://doi.org/10.1136/bmjstel-2020-000642

Zayed, R., Davidson, B., Nadeau, L., Callanan, T. S., Fleisher, W., Hope-Ross, L., Espinet, S., Spenser, H. R., Lipton, H., Srivastava, A., Lazier, L., Doey, T., Khalid-Khan, S., McKerlie, A., Stretch, N., Flynn, R., Abidi, S., St John, K., Auclair, G., Liashko, V., … Steele, M. (2016). Canadian rural/remote primary care physicians perspectives on child/adolescent mental health care service delivery. *Journal of the Canadian Academy of Child and Adolescent Psychiatry, 25,* 24–34.

PART VI

Shaping the future of Child and Adolescent Mental Health in the Eastern Mediterranean Region

Child and adolescent mental health research in the Eastern Mediterranean Region—now and in the future

Fadi T. Maalouf, Riwa Haidar, and Fatima Mansour

Department of Psychiatry, American University of Beirut, Beirut, Lebanon

The past two decades have witnessed advances in child mental health research worldwide, and the Eastern Mediterranean Region (EMR) was no exception. While progress has been made, many gaps remain in child mental health research in the EMR. In this chapter, we will first introduce the EMR and its sociodemographic characteristics, summarize the prevalence data of psychiatric disorders in children and adolescents in this region and the available resources, then discuss child mental health research and barriers associated with it, and end with a proposed action plan.

1. Introduction to the Eastern Mediterranean Region

The term "Eastern Mediterranean" refers to the eastern half, or third, of the Mediterranean Sea. It usually encompasses all of that sea's coastal zones, as well as territories connected to the sea and land that are heavily influenced by climate (Eastern Mediterranean, 2022). The EMR is a very heterogenous region where each state differs in gross domestic product, sociodemographic components, health indicators, and healthcare system capacities (Mandil et al., 2013). The EMR includes 22 members of the Arab League, mostly low- to middle-income countries with a population of more than 670 million contributing 9% of the global population (WHO, 2019) (Table 12.1). Low-income countries in the EMR include Afghanistan,

Shaping the Future of Child and Adolescent Mental Health
https://doi.org/10.1016/B978-0-323-91709-4.00014-7

TABLE 12.1 Demographic characteristics of high-income, middle-income, and low-income countries in the Eastern Mediterranean Region.

High-income countries	Middle-income countries	Low-income countries
Bahrain Population ≈ 1,526,929 million 0−14-year-old: 18.45% 15−24-year-old: 15.16%	**Egypt** Population ≈106,437,241 million 0−14-year-old: 33.62% 15−24-year-old: 18.01%	**Afghanistan** Population ≈37,466,414 million 0−14-year-old: 40.62% 15−24-year-old: 21.26%
Kuwait Population ≈ 3,032,065 million 0−14-year-old: 24.29% 15−24-year-old: 14.96%	**Iraq** Population ≈ 39,650,145 million 0−14-year-old: 37.02% 15−24-year-old: 19.83%	**Djibouti** Population ≈ 938,413 million 0−14-year-old: 29.97% 15−24-year-old: 20.32%
Oman Population ≈ 3,694,755 million 0−14-year-old: 30.15% 15−24-year-old: 17.35%	**Iran** Population ≈ 85,888,910 million 0−14-year-old: 24.11% 15−24-year-old: 13.36%	**Somalia** Population ≈ 12,094,640 million 0−14-year-old: 42.38% 15−24-year-old: 19.81%
Qatar Population ≈ 2,479,995 million 0−14-year-old: 12.84% 15−24-year-old: 11.78%	**Jordan** Population ≈ 10,909,567 million 0−14-year-old: 33.05% 15−24-year-old: 19.77%	**Yemen** Population ≈ 30,399,243 million 0−14-year-old: 39.16% 15−24-year-old: 21.26%
Saudi-Arabia Population ≈ 34,783,757 million 0−14-year-old: 24.84% 15−24-year-old: 15.38%	**Lebanon** Population ≈ 6,781,829 million 0−14-year-old: 20.75% 15−24-year-old: 14.98%	
United Arab Emirates Population ≈ 9,856,612 million 0−14-year-old: 14.45% 15−24-year-old: 7.94%	**Libya** Population ≈ 7,017,224 million 0−14-year-old: 33.65% 15−24-year-old: 15.21%	
	Morocco Population ≈ 36,561,813 million 0−14-year-old: 27.04% 15−24-year-old: 16.55%	
	Palestine Population ≈ 5.27 million Gaza Strip (1,957,062 million): 0−14-year-old: 42.53% 15−24-year-old: 21.67%	

TABLE 12.1 Demographic characteristics of high-income, middle-income, and low-income countries in the Eastern Mediterranean Region.—cont'd

High-income countries	Middle-income countries	Low-income countries
	West Bank (2,949,246 million): 0–14-year-old: 35.31% 15–24-year-old: 20.75%	
	Pakistan Population ≈ 238,181,034 million 0–14-year-old: 36.01% 15–24-year-old: 19.3%	
	Sudan Population ≈ 46,751,152 million 0–14-year-old: 42.01% 15–24-year-old: 20.94%	
	Syria Population ≈ 20,384,316 million 0–14-year-old: 33.47% 15–24-year-old: 19.34%	
	Tunisia Population ≈ 11,811,335 million 0–14-year-old: 25.28% 15–24-year-old: 12.9%	

Source: Demographics profile. (2021). Index Mundi. https://www.indexmundi.com/.

Djibouti, Yemen, and Somalia. Middle-income countries include Egypt, Islamic Republic of Iran, Iraq, Jordan, Lebanon, Libya, Morocco, Pakistan, Palestine, Sudan, Syrian Arab Republic, and Tunisia. High-income countries include Oman, Qatar, Saudi Arabia, United Arab Emirates, Bahrain, and Kuwait (Table 12.1). Djibouti with less than 1 million inhabitants is the least populated country, whereas Pakistan with 208 million people is the highest resided country in the region (WHO, 2019).

It is estimated that 60% of the population in the EMR is below the age of 25 years and adolescents make up 19% of the population of the region (WHO, 2022). More than 25% of people in the EMR live below the poverty line on less than $1.9 per day. Yemen has the highest percentage of population living below the poverty line in the region, and around 50% of its people live on the brink of poverty. More recently, Lebanon has been experiencing its worst economic crisis in this century. As a result, the poverty rate in Lebanon has increased from 42% in 2019 to 82% of people in 2021 living on under the US$5.50 international poverty line (The World Bank, 2021). According to a report issued by relief web, an estimate of 4 million families have been pushed into poverty over the past 2 years (SaveThe Children, 2022).

Literacy rates among 15- to 24-year-olds are between 80% and 100% except in Afghanistan, Pakistan, and Sudan where literacy rates in 2020 were 68%, 79%, and 56% for males and 39%, 64%, and 60% for females, respectively (WHO, 2019). Enrollment rates of children in primary school ranged from 80% to 100% in all EMR countries except for Somalia, Egypt, Pakistan, Djibouti, and Afghanistan, which have an enrollment rate of less than 60% and where enrollment rates for girls are lower than boys (WHO, 2020c).

Many countries in the EMR have witnessed complex humanitarian situations including wars, and political and economic instability, which resulted in forced displacement and mass migration. For example, Lebanon has a very high refugee population per capita and is the home for 1.5 million Syrian refugees (1 in 6 people in Lebanon are refugees). In addition, Jordan hosts approximately 1.3 million refugees (1 in 14 people are refugees) (WHO, 2019).

The EMR had been the origin for 64% of refugees around the world, and 43% of its population is in need of humanitarian assistance over many years (Brennan et al., 2020; Ghosh et al., 2004; Mokdad et al., 2016), although the proportions are changing in the light of the 2022 Russian invasion of Ukraine, which has resulted in many millions of refugees in Europe.

2. Mental health prevalence and burden in Eastern Mediterranean Region

The mental well-being of people around the world has been the focus of increasing concern, given the data on the burden of mental illnesses. Findings from the Global Burden of Diseases, Injuries and Risk Factors Study 2015 (GBD 2015 Eastern Mediterranean Region Mental Health Collaborators, 2018) showed that mental disorders are among the highest ranked causes of nonfatal burden and contribute to 14% of the burden of disease globally (WHO, 2011). Specifically, depression, anxiety, and posttraumatic stress disorders (PTSDs) accounted for 41.9% of the total burden of mental disorders (Zuberi et al., 2021). While global estimates are important, local data may be more descriptive of the specific context. A study examined the global burden of mental disorders in children aged 5–14 years in different regions including the EMR (Baranne & Falissard,

2018). Findings revealed a decline in the rank of mental disorders (conduct disorders, anxiety disorders, major depressive disorders, and autism spectrum disorder) from fourth (2000) to fifth (2015) leading cause of DALYs among the mentioned age group. Unintentional injuries ranked second in 2000 and 2015, which, as Baranne and Falissard (2018) explained, is due to the rise in deaths from injuries inflicted by wars in the region.

In children and adolescents, the prevalence of psychiatric disorders is 10%—20%, and 50% of these disorders start before 14 years of age as reported by the World Health Organization (WHO, 2011). In the EMR, the rate among different countries varies depending on the methodology and assessment tools used (Table 12.2).

We searched electronic databases using the terms: child, adolescent, psychiatric disorders, mental health, psychological disorders, prevalence, EMR, and the names of each country in the region. Inclusion criteria were children and adolescents from 0 to 18 years old. When multiple studies from the same country were found, the more recent one with robust methodology (large sample size, representative sample) was included.

Some countries in the EMR lack national suicide death registries, which results in scarcity of official reports. According to Malakouti et al. (2015), data of reported suicide is 0—3.1 per 100,000. This low reported rate can be explained by the local culture and religious beliefs against suicide, which compels families of victims to hide suicidal deaths or injuries. However, a study conducted in the Islamic Republic of Iran revealed lifetime prevalence of suicide thoughts, planning, and attempts were 12.7%, 6.2%, and 3.3%, respectively. Table 12.3 presents data of suicidal behaviors prevalence in six EMR countries.

Despite the availability of some prevalence studies on psychiatric disorders in children and adolescents in the EMR, comprehensive and updated mental health surveys targeting children and adolescents have not been consistently carried out. Availability of this epidemiologic data would allow monitoring of prevalence and provide knowledge on burden and treatment gaps present in each country.

3. Mental health resources in the Eastern Mediterranean Region

According to a report on mental health resources in the EMR by WHO, mental health spending includes programmatic costs on training and supervision, administration/management, and mental health promotion activities (WHO, 2019). Evaluation of mental health expenditures in a country can be complex and depends on funding sources available in the

TABLE 12.2 Prevalence of psychiatric disorders in countries of the EMR.

Author Country	Method	Disorders/outcomes	Age groups	Study population	Rates
(Panter-Brick et al., 2009) Afghanistan	Strengths and Difficulties Questionnaire (SDQ) multi-informant; Depression Self-rating Scale and Impact of Events Scale; International and culturally specific screening instruments for caregivers mental health; checklist for traumatic events ($n = 1101$)	Child's probable psychiatric disorders (any disorder, emotional, conduct, hyperkinetic); depression, PTSD	11–16 years old	School children	Any disorder: 22.2%; Emotional: 18.0%; conduct: 4.8%; hyperkinetic: 0.3%; depression: 4.05%; PTSD: 23.9%
(Pengpid & Peltzer, 2020a) Afghanistan	Cross-sectional survey using a survey questionnaire from Global School-based Health Survey ($n = 2579$)	Psychological distress (single and multiple)	13–17 years old	School children	Single psychological distress: 28.4% Multiple psychological distress: 27.7% (those who identified with one or multiple forms of psychological distress such as no close friends, loneliness, anxiety, suicide ideation, and suicide attempt)

Study	Methodology	Disorders	Age	Sample	Results
(Al-Ansari, 2015) Bahrain	Retrospective study based on patient files.	ID; learning disorders; Autism; ADHD; pervasive developmental disorder; adjustment disorder	0–12 13–17 years old	Child and adolescent cases who attended the Child and Adolescent Psychiatric Unit psychiatric hospital in the period between March 1, 2011 and February 28, 2012 and in 1981	ID: 26.8%; Learning disorders: 8.6% Autism: 13.3% ADHD: 11.7% Pervasive developmental disorder: 5.6% Adjustment disorder: 9.7%
(Elhamid et al., 2009) Egypt	Population-based cross-sectional survey using the Arabic version of the extended SDQ and parent brief and demographic and social questionnaire ($n = 1186$)	Emotional and behavioral symptoms	6–12 years old	School sample	Prevalence of probable (any psychiatric diagnosis 8.5%, Emotional disorder 2.0%, conduct disorder 6.6%, hyperactivity disorder 0.7%)
(Mohammadi et al., 2019) Iran	Population-based cross-sectional survey using the validated Persian version of the semistructured diagnostic interview Kiddie-Schedule for	Mood disorders; psychotic disorders; anxiety disorders; behavioral disorders; neurodevelopmental disorders; substance abuse disorders; elimination	6–18 years old	Iranian children and adolescents	Mood disorders (22.31%); psychotic disorders (0.26%); anxiety disorders (14.13%); behavioral disorders (8.3%); neurodevelopmental disorders (2.85%); substance abuse

Continued

VI. Shaping the future of Child and Adolescent Mental Health in the Eastern Mediterranean Region

TABLE 12.2 Prevalence of psychiatric disorders in countries of the EMR.—cont'd

Author Country	Method	Disorders/outcomes	Age groups	Study population	Rates
	Affective Disorders and Schizophrenia-PL (K-SADS-PL) and sociodemographic questionnaire ($n = 30{,}532$)	disorders; eating disorders, total psychiatric disorders excluding mental retardation, epilepsy, and tobacco use			disorders (2.79%); elimination disorders (5.42%); eating disorders (0.13%); total psychiatric disorders excluding mental retardation, epilepsy, and tobacco use (22.31%)
(Al-Jawadi & Abdul-Rhman, 2007) Iraq	Cross-sectional study using standardized questionnaire form including diagnostic criteria taken from DSM-IV-TR2000 ($n = 3079$)	PTSD; enuresis; separation anxiety disorder; specific phobia; stuttering refusal to attend school; learning and conduct disorders; stereotypic movement; feeding disorder in infancy or early childhood	1–15 years old	Mothers of children aged 1 to 15 years presenting to four different primary care centers	PTSD: 10.5% Enuresis: 6% Separation anxiety disorder: 4.3% Specific phobia: 3.3% Stuttering: 3.2% Learning and conduct disorders: 2.5% each Stereotypic movement: 2.3% Feeding disorder in infancy or early childhood: 2%
(Dardas et al., 2018) Jordan	Descriptive cross-sectional study using the Beck Depression	Depressive symptoms	15–17 years old	Adolescents in Jordan	Academic difficulties (15%); psychiatric diagnosis (8%); sought psychological

Continued

	Inventory-II and measures of sociodemographic and health history (n = 2349)				help (22%); depression (34%)
(Maalouf et al., 2016) Lebanon	Multistage cluster sampling design using self-reported questionnaires and interviews including the Development and Well-being Assessment (DAWBA), the Peer-Relations Questionnaire (PRQ), and demographic/ clinical information questionnaire (n = 510)	Any psychiatric disorder; emotional disorders; mood disorders; any anxiety disorder; externalizing disorder; ADHD, ODD, CD, other CD; pervasive developmental disorders; other	11–17 years old	Adolescents (household sample).	Any psychiatric disorder: 26.1% Emotional disorders: 17.1% Mood disorders: 6.7% Any anxiety disorder: 13.1% Externalizing disorder: 11.8% ADHD: 10.2% CD: 4.7% ODD: 2.9% Pervasive developmental disorders: 1% Other: 2%
(Pengpid and Peltzer, 2020b) Morocco	Cross-sectional study using the "2016 Morocco Global School-Based Student Health Survey (GSHS) (n = 6745)	Psychological distress	15 years old median age (3 interquartile range	Adolescent school children	Psychological distress (23.3%)

TABLE 12.2　Prevalence of psychiatric disorders in countries of the EMR.—cont'd

Author Country	Method	Disorders/outcomes	Age groups	Study population	Rates
(Al-Ghannami et al., 2018) Oman	Cross-sectional school-based survey using a standardized Arabic version of the National Initiative for Children's Health Quality Vanderbilt Assessment Scales-Teacher Assessment Scale (NICHQ Vanderbilt Assessment Scales) ($n = 350$)	ADHD	9–10 years old	Fourth-grade students	The prevalence rate of ADHD was 8.8%
(El-Khodary & Samara, 2020) Palestine	Stratified random sampling using the War-Traumatic Events Checklist (W-TECh), Violence at home checklist, Post-traumatic Stress Disorders	Effect of cumulative exposure to violence on mental health among children and adolescents	11–17 years old	Children and Adolescents in the Gaza Strip	PTSD (53.4%); depression (24.1%); total difficulties (24.4%); one mental health problem (43.6%); two mental health problems (14.4%); three concurrent mental

	Symptoms Scale (PTSDSS), Strengths and Difficulties Questionnaire (Arabic version), the Child Depression Inventory (CDI), and demographics questionnaire ($n = 1029$)				health problems (7.7%)
(Alshaban et al., 2019) Qatar	Cross-sectional survey using the social communication questionnaire (SCQ), semistructured telephone interview, in-person diagnostic assessment, and QCC-Abstraction Form (QCC-AF) to abstract clinical information ($n = 176{,}960$)	ASD	5–12 years old	Children residing in Qatar	Prevalence of ASD: 1.14%

Continued

TABLE 12.2 Prevalence of psychiatric disorders in countries of the EMR.—cont'd

Author Country	Method	Disorders/outcomes	Age groups	Study population	Rates
(AlZaben et al., 2018) Saudi Arabia	Cross-sectional study using Vanderbilt ADHD scale (n = 929)	ADHD	6–12 years old	Public primary school students in Jeddah, Saudi Arabia	ADHD (5%); ADHD combined type (2.7%), followed by hyperactive type (1.2%), and inattentive type (1.1%)
(Abuzied & Ali, 2020) Sudan	Simple random sampling using GHQ-28 (n = 491)	Severe depression and anxiety and psychosomatic symptoms	14–17 and 18–19 years old	Adolescent Secondary school girls in Khartoum	Severe depression and anxiety (60.89%), psychosomatic disorder (34.62%)
(Perkins et al., 2018) Syrian Arab Republic	Cross-sectional study using self-report screening instruments; the Children's Revised Impact of Event Scale (CRIES-8) and the Revised Children's Anxiety and Depression Scale (RCADS-25), sociodemographic and traumatic information questionnaires (n = 492)	PTSD; depression; Anxiety	8–15 years old	Children from schools in Damascus and Latakia	At least one probable psychiatric disorder (60.5%); PTSD (35.1%); depression (32.0%); and anxiety (29.5%)

Study / Country	Study design (n)	Disorders assessed	Age	Population	Results
(Guedria-Tekari et al., 2019) Tunisia	Cross-sectional study using sociodemographic and anxiety symptoms form, Suicide Behavior Questionnaire-Revised, Beck Depression Scale, and the Rosenberg self-esteem scale (n = 821)	Depression, anxiety, suicidality	Mean age 17.7 years old	High school-students	Depression (14.4%); anxiety (1.2%); other psychiatric disorders (0.7%); nonsuicidal self-injurious behavior (25.5%); suicidal behavior (passing suicidal thoughts (26.9%); serious suicidal thoughts (9.6%); suicidal attempts (7.3%)
(Al-Yateem et al., 2020) United Arab Emirates	Cross-sectional study using the Screen for Child Anxiety-Related Disorders Scale and demographics questionnaire (n = 968)	Anxiety-related disorders	13–18 years old	Secondary schools across UAE	Anxiety (28%); generalized anxiety (21.6%); panic disorders (37.1%); separation anxiety (45.5%); social anxiety (20%); significant school avoidance (36.5%)
(Alyahri & Goodman, 2008) Yemen	Cross-sectional survey using the Strengths and Difficulties Questionnaire and the Development and Well-being Assessment (DAWBA) (n = 1306)	Any psychiatric disorder; anxiety disorders; depressive disorders; oppositional defiant disorder; ADHD	7–10 years old	School children	Any psychiatric disorder: 15.7% Anxiety disorder: 9.3% Depressive disorder: 0.3% Oppositional conduct disorder: 7.1% ADHD: 1.3%

TABLE 12.3   Prevalence of suicidal behaviors in adolescents in six countries of the Eastern Mediterranean Region (12−15-year-olds).

EMR countries	Year	Sample size (n)	Suicide ideation (%)	Suicide planning (%)	Suicide attempt (%)
Afghanistan	2014	1448	16.2	13.4	10.5
Iraq	2012	1522	15.1	14.3	12.6
Kuwait	2015	1948	15.9	15.2	12.3
Lebanon	2011	1974	14.4	10.5	12.1
Morocco	2010	2423	14.3	13.2	12
UAE	2010	2267	14.3	14.5	11.3

Source: The prevalence of suicidal behaviors and their mental risk factors among young adolescents in 46 low and middle-income countries. Li, L., You, D., Ruan, T., Xu, S., Mi, D., Cai, T., & Han, L. (2021). The prevalence of suicidal behaviors and their mental risk factors among young adolescents in 46 low-and middle-income countries. Journal of Affective Disorders, 281, 847-855. https://doi.org/10.1016/j.jad.2020.11.050.

respective country, and data on service providers and services provided (WHO, 2019). Governments in the EMR spend a relatively small amount of funding on mental health services (WHO, 2017) as only 2% of the government health budget is allocated to mental health services. More specifically, Qatar allocates 1% of its total health expenditure to mental health services, Egypt less than 1%, and Palestine 2.5%. Morocco, on the other hand, allocates 4% of its total health expenditure to mental health services, the highest percentage in the region (Charara et al., 2017). People in 8 out of the 22 countries in the region are fully insured including Egypt, Bahrain, Oman, and United Arab Emirates. Another eight countries pay around 20% of cost of mental health services and medicines such as Lebanon, Iraq, and Jordan. In Somalia, Syrian Arab Republic, Tunisia, and Yemen, mental health services are not covered by third-party payers.

Concerning the mental health workforce, the total number of mental health personnel ranges from 0.6 per 100,000 in Sudan to 38.5 per 100,000 in Bahrain. The breakdown by country group reveals a median of mental health workforce of 0.7 in Afghanistan, Djibouti, Pakistan, Somalia, Sudan, and Yemen; 5.7 in Egypt, Iran, Iraq, Jordan, Lebanon, Libya, Morocco, Occupied Palestinian territory, Tunisia, and Syria; and 18.6 in Bahrain, Kuwait, Oman, Qatar, Saudi Arabia, and United Arab Emirates (WHO, 2019). Nurses constitute 50% of the workforce, physicians, mainly psychiatrists 25%, psychologists 14%, and social workers 9%.

Around 50% of the EMR countries have 3−9 hospital beds per 100,000 population, while Bahrain, Lebanon, Islamic Republic of Iran, and Saudi Arabia have between 18 and 32 beds and Afghanistan, Somalia, and

Sudan have less than 1 bed per 100,000 (WHO, 2019). Of the 22 countries in the region, only 12 reported having child and adolescent mental health outpatient facilities. Reports show a very low child and adolescent psychiatrist to population ratio as there is only 0.03 child and adolescent psychiatrist per 100,000 persons in the EMR (WHO, 2019). In 67% of EMR countries, child and adolescent mental health services are not provided by child and adolescents psychiatrists (WHO, 2011). These services are instead provided by general psychiatrists, pediatricians, and general practitioners. In Afghanistan and Somalia, for example, there are no child and adolescent psychiatrists.

This deficit in mental health resources hinders the provision of mental health services to children and adolescents in the region and presents a major barrier for child mental health research advancement.

4. Child and adolescent mental health research in the Eastern Mediterranean Region

In addition to epidemiologic research to determine the prevalence and burden of psychiatric disorders, several studies from the EMR have focused on investigating the impact of war and armed conflict on the mental health of children and adolescents, while others have focused on interventions.

4.1 Research on mental health of children and adolescents in conflict areas

Armed conflict around the globe is a public health concern (WHO, 2017). It is estimated that over 246 million children live in conflict-affected areas. Forced displacement is at its highest record with more than 68.5 million people including 28 million children living as refugees, asylum seekers, or stateless people or are internally displaced. In 2020, there were 359 conflicts seen worldwide (Heidelberg Institute for International Conflict Research, 2020). The nature of conflict nowadays has changed. Combat zones are widespread, and weapons can cause annihilation on a larger scale. Availability of small arms makes it easier for children to become combatants in conflict. More adverse consequences, such as population displacement, destruction in healthcare systems, environmental damage, and economic damage, may impact children's access to basic needs such as food, shelter, healthcare, and education (Kadir et al., 2018). The EMR has seen political and economic uncertainties over the past decades, and some countries have experienced war and conflict (Mokdad et al., 2016) including Egypt, Libya, Tunisia, and Yemen. Syria,

Afghanistan, Bahrain, Iraq, Palestine, Lebanon, and Somalia experience ongoing conflict. This leads to increased exposure to stressors and greater risk for psychiatric disorders, especially in children and adolescents (Itani et al., 2014).

Children impacted by war have higher prevalence of PTSD, depression, anxiety, and psychosomatic complaints (see Lewis and Danese, Chapter 6, this volume). Children in conflict areas are also at higher risk of suicide ideation, grief, separation anxiety disorder, stuttering, learning difficulties, and conduct disorders (Samara et al., 2020). Table 12.4

TABLE 12.4　Research studies investigating the impact of war and armed conflict on the mental health of children and adolescents in the Eastern Mediterranean Region.

Country	Study	Methodology	Finding
Lebanon	Post-Traumatic Stress Disorder in Adolescents in Lebanon as Wars Gained in Ferocity: A Systematic Review (Shaar, 2013)	Systematic review (11 articles)	PTSD rates range from 8.5% to 35% for adolescents in school and 29.3%—32.5% for adolescents referred for having psychological or academic difficulties.
	Anxiety, depression, and PTSD in children and adolescents following the Beirut port explosion (Maalouf, Haidar, et al., 2022; Maalouf, Alrojolah, et al., 2022)	Online survey: Parents of 802 children aged 8—17 years	Prevalence: 33.1% for depression, 63.6% for anxiety, and 51.5% for PTSD.
Libya	Predicting the Impact of the 2011 Conflict in Libya on Population Mental Health: PTSD and Depression Prevalence and Mental Health Service Requirements (Charlson et al., 2012)	Systematic review (117 articles)	PTSD prevalence: 12.4% where 50% of cases cooccurred with depression.
Palestine Iraq	A systematic review on the mental health of children and adolescents in areas of armed conflict in	Systematic review (71 articles)	**Palestine:** PTSD prevalence: 23%—70% (7%—48% for mild PTSD; 39%—89% for moderate to severe

TABLE 12.4 Research studies investigating the impact of war and armed conflict on the mental health of children and adolescents in the Eastern Mediterranean Region.—cont'd

Country	Study	Methodology	Finding
	the Middle East (Dimitry, 2012)		PSTD). High anxiety levels: 40%–100%, depression 11.3%, and Emotional disorder 47%. In addition, 28% of Palestinian children feared leaving their house. **Iraq:** PTSD prevalence 10%–30%, separation anxiety 4.3%, and overall psychiatric disorders 36%–38%.
Syria	Mental health in Syrian children with a focus on posttraumatic stress: a cross-sectional study from Syrian schools (Perkins et al., 2018)	492 children between 8 and 15 years were randomly selected from schools in Damascus and Latakia	60.5% have at least one probable psychiatric disorder with PTSD being the most common (35.1%), followed by depression (32.0%) and anxiety (29.5%).

summarizes research studies investigating the impact of war and armed conflict on the mental health of children and adolescents in the EMR.

The prevalence of conflict and emergencies in the EMR poses threats to the mental health of children, which calls for the establishment of appropriate services and adequate provision of interventions (Farooq et al., 2015).

4.2 Research on interventions and treatment

There is a consensus that prevention and early intervention are the necessary ingredients to mitigate the long-term impact of psychiatric disorders on the developing brain of children and adolescents (Patel et al., 2018). Moreover, in line with the global mental health agenda of scaling up preventive interventions and interventions that enhance access to care in settings with limited resources, Patel et al. (2013) recommends task shifting including school-based interventions (see Waqas and Rahman, Chapter 10, this volume).

A systematic review of strategies and approaches employed in delivering Mental Health and Psychosocial Support (MHPSS) interventions to women and children affected by conflict found that around 25% of the articles published on these interventions were conducted in the EMR, particularly in the Middle East and North Africa, and nearly half of the publications targeted children (Kamali et al., 2020). The results showed that the majority of studies were observational in nature, few documented the effectiveness of these interventions, and only a small number were randomized controlled trials. This reflects the dearth of experimental research that is required for the delivery of evidence-based interventions (Kamali et al., 2020).

According to Kamali et al. (2020), most of these interventions were implemented in refugee settings such as camps, or countries of displacement. Interventions targeted a variety of psychiatric disorders including posttraumatic stress disorder, trauma related disorders, and general mental health problems and were mostly delivered by nongovernmental organizations (2020). Table 12.5 summarizes intervention studies conducted in the EMR.

5. Barriers to child and adolescent mental health research in the Eastern Mediterranean Region

Child and adolescent mental health research in the EMR has been facing a number of barriers, including (1) stigma associated with psychiatric disorders, (2) shortage in mental health professionals and training, and (3) insufficient resources including lack of validated screening and diagnostic tools.

5.1 Stigma associated with psychiatric disorders

Cultural beliefs about psychiatric disorders and stigma associated with them impact the person's treatment-seeking behavior (Maalouf et al., 2019). In the Arab region, seeking help from informal resources such as religious experts, close friends, or family members is a usual practice. This perception of low need for psychiatric help is also a barrier for participants to enroll in psychiatric research studies (Maalouf et al., 2019).

For example, in a national household study on the psychopathology of 1517 children and adolescents in Lebanon, results showed that although a third ($n = 497$, 32.7%) of the participants presented with symptoms of at least one disorder, only 25, 5%, reported ever seeking professional help (Maalouf, Haidar, et al., 2022; Maalouf, Alrojolah et al., 2022).

TABLE 12.5 Child and adolescent mental health intervention studies in the Eastern Mediterranean Region.

Author Country	Target group	Intervention	Design	Measures	Finding
(Heizomi et al., 2020) Iran	Adolescents (Grade 9 students)	School-based Mental Health Promotion Program (SMHPP)	Experimental study	Life satisfaction, happiness, self-efficacy, hopefulness, stress	Happiness increased by 32.6% in individuals reporting a medium level of happiness. In addition, improvement of life satisfaction and psychological well-being were detected.
(Asanjarani & Asgari, 2021) Iran	Adolescents (14–16 years old)	Social and Mental Empowerment Program (SMEP)	Quasi-experimental	Difficulties and well-being (Emotional symptoms, conduct problems, hyperactivity inattention, peer problem, and prosocial behavior)	Lower difficulties and higher prosocial behavior were detected in the intervention group.
(Panter-Brick et al., 2018) Jordan	12- to 18-year-old Jordanian and Syrian	Psychosocial Support–Profound Stress Attunement	Experimental design, comparing treatment youth	Human security; distress; mental health difficulties	Medium to small effect sizes for human security; distress and

Continued

TABLE 12.5 Child and adolescent mental health intervention studies in the Eastern Mediterranean Region.—cont'd

Author Country	Target group	Intervention	Design	Measures	Finding
		Approach 8 weeks (16 sessions)	and wait-list controls		perceived stress. No impact on prosocial behavior or posttraumatic stress reactions.
(Al-Rasheed, 2021) Kuwait	Adolescents (15 years or older Grades 10–12)	Fostering Youth Resilience Project (FYRP)	Pre–posttest pilot study	Resilience Skills Questionnaire and personal goal setting skill	Short-term increase in resilience skills and competence.
(Maalouf et al., 2020) Lebanon	11–13 years (Grade 6 students)	FRIENDS (school-based intervention)	Randomized controlled trial (RCT)	Emotional and behavioral difficulties, depressive symptoms, and anxiety symptoms	Reduction in emotional symptoms, and depressive symptoms in the overall group. Reduction of anxiety symptoms in girls.
(Doumit et al., 2020) Lebanon	13–17 years (Syrian refugees)	Creating Opportunities for Patient Empowerment (COPE)	Pre Experimental study	Depressive symptoms, anxiety symptoms, and quality of life	Reduction in depressive and anxiety symptoms and increase in overall quality of life.

Study / Country	Sample	Intervention	Design	Outcome measures	Results
(Hamdani et al., 2021) Pakistan	8–13 years old	Adapted School Mental Health Program (SMHP)	Cluster randomized trial	General difficulties (SDQ), acceptability, adoption, feasibility, and change in teachers' behavior	Reduction in total difficulties scores.
(Hussein & Vostanis, 2013) Pakistan	30 teachers from Grades 1 to 5	School-based intervention involving teacher training program two-day (10–12 h) workshop (six sessions) delivered by a child psychologist	A mixed-method design combined pre- and posttraining rating scales, and qualitative analysis	Teachers' knowledge of various aspects of mental health/	Improvement in teachers' knowledge and awareness of various signs and symptoms of common child mental health problems.
(El-Khodary & Samara, 2020) Palestine	572 students aged 12–18 years old	School-based counseling program, 1 week (five continuous days, 4 h per day)	Longitudinal pretest and posttest experimental design	PTSD	Prevalence of PTSD decreased from 57.5% to 45.6%.
(Betancourt et al., 2020) Somalia	103 children, 43 caregivers	Home-visiting Family Strengthening Intervention for refugees (FSI-R)	Community-based participatory research (CBPR) approach	Youth psychosocial functioning; caregiver psychosocial functioning	Reduction in traumatic stress reactions as reported by children, reduction in children's depressive symptoms as reported by parents.

Commonly, when a member of the family suffers from a psychiatric disorder, the disorder and treatment become "a family matter" (Okasha, 2008). The whole family is thus concerned due to a spillover effect and the notion of "stigma by association" (Östman & Kjellin, 2002). "Stigma by association" refers to the process by which an individual is stigmatized due to their association with another stigmatized person. Studies confirm "stigma by association" among family members.

Stigma and cultural beliefs inevitably impact mental health research that is being done in the EMR. Individuals with psychiatric disorders are not likely to seek help, and people in general are not likely to participate in psychiatric research.

5.2 Shortage of mental health professionals and trainings

Shortage of qualified mental health professionals is common to all countries in the EMR as discussed before and constitutes a barrier for mental health research in the region. Due to increased clinical demand, clinicians find themselves with little time to plan and execute research projects.

Child and adolescent psychiatry residency training programs are available in only a few countries in the EMR, namely, Qatar, Lebanon, United Arab Emirates, Iraq, Egypt, and Saudi Arabia (Okasha & Shaker, 2020) (see Chapter 13, AlBanna and colleagues). Some but not all training programs include a research training component, which introduces future child and adolescent psychiatrists to clinical and nonclinical research.

It is worth mentioning that many Arab psychiatrists received training from "Western" countries, but only a small proportion are engaged in psychiatric research despite the presence of first-class academic settings (Jaalouk et al., 2012). This might be due to the lack of infrastructure and funding to support psychiatric research as discussed in the following.

5.3 Insufficient resources and lack of validated screening and diagnostic tools

Finally, when discussing barriers and challenges in research, one should consider the lack of resources. In an institutional mapping study, Mandil et al. (2018) found a small amount of national and international funding granted to institutions conducting health research in the EMR, and Arab countries were found to have the lowest gross expenditure on research and development in relation to their gross domestic product (Soete et al., 2015). Although research funding is available in high-income countries in the EMR (e.g., Qatar and United Arab Emirates), research priorities are often led by national priorities and mental health is often excluded. Some re-searchers collaborate with investigators in other fields of medicine such as cancer and diabetes to successfully be funded. Many institutions lack Institutional Review Boards (ethics committees) for research approval and research offices and budget management personnel required for funding agencies to ensure proper conduct of research and management of funds. As a result, the main funding source for child and adolescent mental health research in Bahrain, Egypt, Iraq, Kuwait, Djibouti, Oman, Saudi Arabia, and United Arab Emirates is the government (WHO, 2011), while funding in Libya, Morocco, Sudan, Syria, and Tunisia comes from individual donors.

Insufficient publishing opportunities also pose some challenges as mental health research of regional relevance may have a low chance of being published in high-impact international journals. Only a limited number of scientific journals specialize in mental health in the EMR, but new journals are being published over the past few years. These journals encounter many challenges including receiving few article submissions, difficulties in finding peer reviewers, and paucity of electronic versions and websites (Maalouf et al., 2019).

Research on mental health requires the use of scales and measurement tools that are validated in the local language. As an example, the Development and Well Being Assessment-Arabic (DAWBA-Arabic) was shown to serve as a valid and reliable tool for assessing psychiatric disorders among children and adolescents in the Arab region (Zeinoun et al., 2013). However, despite the fact that many scales have been translated and validated in Arabic, many others have not been.

6. Recommendations to strengthen child and adolescent mental health research in the Eastern Mediterranean Region

Maalouf et al. (2019) proposed an action plan to address the barriers that includes spreading awareness and addressing stigma, increasing collaborative research, strengthening research infrastructure, strengthening the mental health workforce, and translating mental health research into action on societal and governmental levels (Maalouf et al., 2019).

First, mental health literacy campaigns can be established to reduce stigma and extend knowledge on positive psychosocial functioning, coping strategies, and resilience to encourage research participation (Samara et al., 2020). Second, mental health researchers in the EMR are encouraged to engage in regional and international collaborative work to enhance research quality and productivity and expand the pool for funding agencies. Third, with regard to strengthening research infrastructure, institutions are encouraged to have training programs/units to train faculty and research staff on conducting research and offer help when needed during the research process. Forming an Institutional

Review Board or an equivalent board would not only ensure proper conduct of research but also help attract international funders. Fourth, it is crucial to address the shortage of trained mental health clinicians and researchers in the EMR. Countries are encouraged to establish residency training programs with a research training component; these programs can be jointly established with other regional or international institutions to maximize the available resources (Regan et al., 2015). Fifth, child and adolescent mental health researchers in the EMR need to translate their findings into a language accessible to governmental administrators and decision-makers. The process includes dissemination of research findings to the public and health specialists outside the mental health field, to enhance change in behaviors and health policies.

7. Conclusion

Child and adolescent mental health research is gaining momentum in the EMR. While available research has mostly been epidemiologic in nature and focused on the impact of conflict on children and adolescents' mental health, research on prevention and treatment remains scarce. Child mental health researchers and research funders should identify prevention and treatment modalities among their research priorities. In addition, development of human capacity and infrastructure, mobilization of resources, and translation of research findings into policies are areas that need to be addressed to further strengthen child and adolescent mental health research in the EMR.

References

Abuzied, N. M. A., & Ali, K. M. (2020). The prevalence of psychiatric morbidity (severe depression & anxiety) among adolescent school girls Khartoum-Sudan. *International Journal of Research-Granthaalayah, 8*(1), 165—175. https://doi.org/10.29121/granthaalayah.v8.i1.2020.263

Al-Ghannami, S. S., Al-Adawi, S., Ghebremeskel, K., Cramer, M. T., Hussein, I. S., Min, Y., ... Dorvlo, A. S. (2018). Attention deficit hyperactivity disorder and parental factors in school children aged nine to ten years in Muscat, Oman. *Oman Medical Journal, 33*(3), 193.

Al-Ansari, A. M. (2015). Characteristics of child and adolescent populations visiting a public child and adolescent psychiatric clinic in Bahrain: A 30-year comparative analysis. *Arab Journal of Psychiatry, 26*(1), 32—38. https://doi.org/10.12816/0010504

Al-Jawadi, A. A., & Abdul-Rhman, S. (2007). Prevalence of childhood and early adolescence mental disorders among children attending primary health care centers in Mosul, Iraq: A cross-sectional study. *BMC Public Health, 7*(1), 1—8. https://doi.org/10.1186/1471-2458-7-274

Al-Rasheed, M. (2021). Resilience-based intervention for youth: An initial investigation of school social work program in Kuwait. *International Social Work*. https://doi.org/10.1177/00208728211018729

Al-Yateem, N., Rossiter, R. C., Al-Shujairi, A., Radwan, H., Awad, M., Fakhry, R., & Mahmoud, I. (2020). Anxiety related disorders in adolescents in the United Arab Emirates: A population based cross-sectional study. *BMC Pediatrics, 20*(1), 1—8. https://doi.org/10.1186/s12887-020-02155-0

Alshaban, F., Aldosari, M., Al-Shammari, H., El-Hag, S., Ghazal, I., Tolefat, M., ... Fombonne, E. (2019). Prevalence and correlates of autism spectrum disorder in Qatar: A national study. *Journal of Child Psychology and Psychiatry, 60*(12), 1254—1268. https://doi.org/10.1111/jcpp.13066

Alyahri, A., & Goodman, R. (2008). The prevalence of DSM-IV psychiatric disorders among 7—10 year old Yemeni school children. *Social Psychiatry and Psychiatric Epidemiology, 43*(3), 224—230. https://doi.org/10.1007/s00127-007-0293-x

AlZaben, F. N., Sehlo, M. G., Alghamdi, W. A., Tayeb, H. O., Khalifa, D. A., Mira, A. T., ... Koenig, H. G. (2018). Prevalence of attention deficit hyperactivity disorder and comorbid psychiatric and behavioral problems among primary school students in western Saudi Arabia. *Saudi Medical Journal, 39*(1), 52. https://doi.org/10.15537/smj.2018.1.21288

Asanjarani, F., & Asgari, M. (2021). Effects of a school-based program on iranian students' well-being. *International Journal of School & Educational Psychology, 9*(Suppl. 1), S103—S112. https://doi.org/10.1080/21683603.2020.1758858

Baranne, M. L., & Falissard, B. (2018). Global burden of mental disorders among children aged 5—14 years. *Child and Adolescent Psychiatry and Mental Health, 12*(1), 19. https://doi.org/10.1186/s13034-018-0225-4

Betancourt, T. S., Berent, J. M., Freeman, J., Frounfelker, R. L., Brennan, R. T., Abdi, S., Maalim, A., Abdi, A., Mishra, T., Gautam, B., Creswell, J. W., & Beardslee, W. R. (2020). Family-based mental health promotion for Somali Bantu and Bhutanese refugees: Feasibility and acceptability trial. *Journal of Adolescent Health, 66*(3), 336—344. https://doi.org/10.1016/j.jadohealth.2019.08.023

Brennan, R., Hajjeh, R., & Al-Mandhari, A. (2020). Responding to health emergencies in the Eastern Mediterranean region in times of conflict. *Lancet (London, England)*. https://doi.org/10.1016/S0140-6736(20)30069-6

Charara, R., Forouzanfar, M., Naghavi, M., Moradi-Lakeh, M., Afshin, A., Vos, T., & Mokdad, A. H. (2017). The burden of mental disorders in the eastern Mediterranean region, 1990—2013. *PloS One, 12*(1), e0169575.

Charlson, F. J., Steel, Z., Degenhardt, L., Chey, T., Silove, D., Marnane, C., & Whiteford, H. A. (2012). Predicting the impact of the 2011 conflict in Libya on population mental health: PTSD and depression prevalence and mental health service requirements. *PloS One, 7*(7), Article e40593. https://doi.org/10.1371/journal.pone.0040593

Dardas, L. A., Silva, S. G., Smoski, M. J., Noonan, D., & Simmons, L. A. (2018). The prevalence of depressive symptoms among Arab adolescents: Findings from Jordan. *Public Health Nursing, 35*(2), 100—108. https://doi.org/10.1111/phn.12363

Demographics profile. (2021). *Index Mundi*. https://www.indexmundi.com/.

Dimitry, L. (2012). A systematic review on the mental health of children and adolescents in areas of armed conflict in the Middle East. *Child: Care, Health and Development, 38*(2), 153—161. https://doi.org/10.1111/j.1365-2214.2011.01246.x

Doumit, R., Kazandjian, C., & Militello, L. K. (2020). COPE for adolescent Syrian refugees in Lebanon: A brief cognitive—behavioral skill-building intervention to improve quality of life and promote positive mental health. *Clinical Nursing Research, 29*(4), 226—234. https://doi.org/10.1177/1054773818808114

Eastern Mediterranean. (2022). Retrieved April 13 2022 from https://en.wikipedia.org/wiki/Eastern_Mediterranean.

El-Khodary, B., & Samara, M. (2020). The relationship between multiple exposures to violence and war trauma, and mental health and behavioural problems among

Palestinian children and adolescents. *European Child & Adolescent Psychiatry, 29*(5), 719–731. https://doi.org/10.1007/s00787-019-01376-8

El-Khodary, B., & Samara, M. (2020). Effectiveness of a school-based intervention on the students' mental health after exposure to war-related trauma. *Frontiers in Psychiatry, 10,* 1031. https://doi.org/10.3389/fpsyt.2019.01031

Elhamid, A. A., Howe, A., & Reading, R. (2009). Prevalence of emotional and behavioural problems among 6–12 year old children in Egypt. *Social Psychiatry and Psychiatric Epidemiology, 44*(1), 8–14.

Farooq, S., Ayub, M., & Naeem, F. (2015). Interventions following traumatic event in children and adolescents: An evidence-based response. *Journal of Psychiatry, 18*(3). https://doi.org/10.4172/psychiatry.1000269

GBD 2015 Eastern Mediterranean Region Mental Health Collaborators. (2018). The burden of mental disorders in the Eastern Mediterranean region, 1990–2015: Findings from the global burden of disease 2015 study. *International Journal of Public Health, 63*(Suppl. 1), 25–37. https://doi.org/10.1007/s00038-017-1006-1

Ghosh, N., Mohit, A., & Murthy, R. S. (2004). Mental health promotion in post-conflict countries. *The Journal of the Royal Society for the Promotion of Health, 124*(6), 268–270. https://doi.org/10.1177/146642400412400614

Guedria-Tekari, A., Missaoui, S., Kalai, W., Gaddour, N., & Gaha, L. (2019). Suicidal ideation and suicide attempts among Tunisian adolescents: Prevalence and associated factors. *The Pan African Medical Journal, 34.* https://doi.org/10.11604/pamj.2019.34.105.19920

Hamdani, S. U., Zill-e-Huma, Warraitch, A., Suleman, N., Muzzafar, N., Minhas, F. A., & Wissow, L. S. (2021). Technology-assisted teachers' training to promote socioemotional well-being of children in public schools in rural Pakistan. *Psychiatric Services, 72*(1), 69–76. https://doi.org/10.1176/appi.ps.202000005

Heidelberg Institute for International Conflict Research. (2015). *Conflict barometer.* Heidelberg, Germany: Department of Political Science, University of Heidelberg. https://hiik.de/wp-content/uploads/2021/03/ConflictBarometer_2020_1.pdf.

Heizomi, H., Allahverdipour, H., Jafarabadi, M. A., Bhalla, D., & Nadrian, H. (2020). Effects of a mental health promotion intervention on mental health of Iranian female adolescents: A school-based study. *Child and Adolescent Psychiatry and Mental Health, 14*(1), 1–36. https://doi.org/10.1186/s13034-020-00342-6

Hussein, S. A., & Vostanis, P. (2013). Teacher training intervention for early identification of common child mental health problems in Pakistan. *Emotional and Behavioural Difficulties, 18*(3), 284–296. https://doi.org/10.1080/13632752.2013.819254

Itani, L., Haddad, Y. C., Fayyad, J., Karam, A., & Karam, E. (2014). Childhood adversities and traumata in Lebanon: A national study. *Clinical Practice and Epidemiology in Mental Health, 10*(1), 116–125. https://doi.org/10.2174/1745017901410010116

Jaalouk, D., Okasha, A., Salamoun, M. M., & Karam, E. G. (2012). Mental health research in the Arab world. *Social Psychiatry and Psychiatric Epidemiology, 47*(11), 1727–1731. https://doi.org/10.1007/s00127-012-0487-8

Kadir, A., Shenoda, S., Goldhagen, J., & Pitterman, S. (2018). The effects of armed conflict on children. *Pediatrics, 142*(6), e20182586. https://doi.org/10.1542/peds.2018-2586

Kamali, M., Munyuzangabo, M., Siddiqui, F. J., Gaffey, M. F., Meteke, S., Als, D., & Bhutta, Z. A. (2020). Delivering mental health and psychosocial support interventions to women and children in conflict settings: A systematic review. *BMJ Global Health, 5*(3), e002014. https://doi.org/10.1136/bmjgh-2019-002014

Li, L., You, D., Ruan, T., Xu, S., Mi, D., Cai, T., & Han, L. (2021). The prevalence of suicidal behaviors and their mental risk factors among young adolescents in 46 low-and middle-income countries. *Journal of Affective Disorders, 281,* 847–855. https://doi.org/10.1016/j.jad.2020.11.050

Maalouf, F. T., Alamiri, B., Atweh, S., Becker, A. E., Cheour, M., Darwish, H., & Akl, E. A. (2019). Mental health research in the Arab region: Challenges and call for action. *The Lancet Psychiatry, 6*(11), 961–966. https://doi.org/10.1016/S2215-0366(19)30124-5

Maalouf, F. T., Alrojolah, L., Akoury-Dirani, L., Barakat, M., Brent, D., Elbejjani, M., ... Ghandour, L. A. (2022). Psychopathology in Children and Adolescents in Lebanon Study (PALS): a national household survey. *Social Psychiatry and Psychiatric Epidemiology, 57*(4), 761–774.

Maalouf, F. T., Alrojolah, L., Ghandour, L., Afifi, R., Dirani, L. A., Barrett, P., Nakkash, R., Shamseddeen, W., Tabaja, F., Yuen, C. M., & Becker, A. E. (2020). Building emotional resilience in youth in Lebanon: A school-based randomized controlled trial of the FRIENDS intervention. *Prevention Science, 21*(5), 650–660. https://doi.org/10.1007/s11121-020-01123-5

Maalouf, F. T., Ghandour, L. A., Halabi, F., Zeinoun, P., Shehab, A. A. S., & Tavitian, L. (2016). Psychiatric disorders among adolescents from Lebanon: Prevalence, correlates, and treatment gap. *Social Psychiatry and Psychiatric Epidemiology, 51*(8), 1105–1116. https://doi.org/10.1007/s00127-016-1241-4

Maalouf, F. T., Haidar, R., Mansour, F., Elbejjani, M., El Khoury, J., Khoury, B., & Ghandour, L. (2022). Anxiety, depression and PTSD in children and adolescents following the Beirut Port explosion. *Journal of Affective Disorders, 302*, 58–65. https://doi.org/10.1016/j.jad.2022.01.086

Malakouti, S. K., Davoudi, F., Khalid, S., Asl, M. A., Khan, M. M., Alirezaei, N., & DeLeo, D. (2015). The epidemiology of suicide behaviors among the countries of the Eastern Mediterranean region of WHO: A systematic review. *Acta Medica Iranica*, 257–265. https://acta.tums.ac.ir/index.php/acta/article/view/4895/4451.

Mandil, A., Chaaya, M., & Saab, D. (2013). Health status, epidemiological profile and prospects: Eastern Mediterranean Region. *International Journal of Epidemiology, 42*(2), 616–626. https://doi.org/10.1093/ije/dyt026

Mandil, A., El-Jardali, F., El-Feky, S., Nour, M., Al-Abbar, M., & Bou-Karroum, L. (2018). Health research institutional mapping: An Eastern Mediterranean regional perspective. *Eastern Mediterranean Health Journal, 24*(2), 189–197. https://doi.org/10.26719/2018.24.2.189

Mohammadi, M. R., Ahmadi, N., Khaleghi, A., Mostafavi, S. A., Kamali, K., Rahgozar, M., ... Fombonne, E. (2019). Prevalence and correlates of psychiatric disorders in a national survey of Iranian children and adolescents. *Iranian Journal of Psychiatry, 14*(1), 1. https://www.ncbi.nlm.nih.gov/pmc/articles/PMC6505051/.

Mokdad, A. H., Forouzanfar, M. H., Tuffaha, M., Charara, R., Barber, R. M., Wagner, J., Cercy, K., Robinson, M., Estep, K., Steiner, C., Jaber, S., Mokdad, A. A., Kim, P., El Razek, M. M., Abdalla, S., Abd-Allah, F., Abraham, J. P., Abu-Raddad, L. J., Abu-Rmeileh, N., ... Wang, H. (2016). Health in times of uncertainty in the Eastern Mediterranean region, 1990–2013: A systematic analysis for the global burden of disease study 2013. *The Lancet Global Health, 4*(10), e704–e713. https://doi.org/10.1016/S2214-109X(16)30168-1

Okasha, A. (2008). The impact of Arab culture on psychiatric ethics. *Arab Journal of Psychiatry, 19*, 81–99.

Okasha, T., & Shaker, N. (2020). Psychiatric education and training in Arab countries. *International Review of Psychiatry (Abingdon, England), 32*(2), 151–156. https://doi.org/10.1080/09540261.2019.1655717

Östman, M., & Kjellin, L. (2002). Stigma by association: Psychological factors in relatives of people with mental illness. *The British Journal of Psychiatry, 181*(6), 494–498. https://doi.org/10.1192/bjp.181.6.494

Panter-Brick, C., Eggerman, M., Gonzalez, V., & Safdar, S. (2009). Violence, suffering, and mental health in Afghanistan: A school-based survey. *The Lancet, 374*(9692), 807–816. https://doi.org/10.1016/S0140-6736(09)61080-1

Panter-Brick, C., Dajani, R., Eggerman, M., Hermosilla, S., Sancilio, A., & Ager, A. (2018). Insecurity, distress and mental health: Experimental and randomized controlled trials of a psychosocial intervention for youth affected by the Syrian crisis. *Journal of Child Psychology and Psychiatry, 59*(5), 523–541. https://doi.org/10.1111/jcpp.12832

Patel, V., Kieling, C., Maulik, P. K., & Divan, G. (2013). Improving access to care for children with mental disorders: A global perspective. *Archives of Disease in Childhood, 98*(5), 323–327. https://doi.org/10.1136/archdischild-2012-302079

Patel, V., Saxena, S., Lund, C., Thornicroft, G., Baingana, F., Bolton, P., & UnÜtzer, J. (2018). The Lancet Commission on global mental health and sustainable development. *The Lancet, 392*(10157), 1553–1598. https://doi.org/10.1016/S0140-6736(18)31612-X

Pengpid, S., & Peltzer, K. (2020a). High psychological distress among school-going adolescents in Afghanistan: Prevalence and correlates from a national survey. *Vulnerable Children and Youth Studies, 15*(1), 40–47. https://doi.org/10.1080/17450128.2019.1679937

Pengpid, S., & Peltzer, K. (2020b). Prevalence and associated factors of psychological distress among a national sample of in-school adolescents in Morocco. *BMC Psychiatry, 20*(1), 1–11. https://doi.org/10.1186/s12888-020-02888-3

Perkins, J. D., Ajeeb, M., Fadel, L., & Saleh, G. (2018). Mental health in Syrian children with a focus on post-traumatic stress: A cross-sectional study from Syrian schools. *Social Psychiatry and Psychiatric Epidemiology, 53*(11), 1231–1239. https://doi.org/10.1007/s00127-018-1573-3

Regan, M., Gater, R., Rahman, A., & Patel, V. (2015). Mental health research: developing priorities and promoting its utilization to inform policies and services. *EMHJ-Eastern Mediterranean Health Journal, 21*(7), 517–521.

Samara, M., Hammuda, S., Vostanis, P., El-Khodary, B., & Al-Dewik, N. (2020). Children's prolonged exposure to the toxic stress of war trauma in the Middle East. *BMJ, 371*, m3155. https://doi.org/10.1136/bmj.m3155

Save The Children. (2022). *Lebanon's economic crisis 'spirals out of control', pushing children further into hunger in 2022, Save the Children warns.* https://reliefweb.int/report/lebanon/lebanon-s-economic-crisis-spirals-out-control-pushing-children-further-hunger-2022.

Shaar, K. H. (2013). Post-traumatic stress disorder in adolescents in Lebanon as wars gained in ferocity: A systematic review. *Journal of Public Health Research, 2*(2). https://doi.org/10.4081/jphr.2013.e17

Soete, L., Schneegans, S., Eröcal, D., Angathevar, B., & Rasiah, R. (2015). A world in search of an effective growth strategy. In S. Schneegans, D. Erocal, Z. Lakhdar, et al. (Eds.), *UNESCO science report: towards 2030* (pp. 21–55). Paris: United Nations Educational, Scientific and Cultural Organization.

The World Bank. (2021). *Lebanon's economic update-October 2021.* https://www.worldbank.org/en/country/lebanon/publication/economic-update-october-2021.

World Health Organization. (2011). *Maternal, child and adolescent mental health: Challenges and strategic directions for the Eastern Mediterranean region (No. WHO-EM/MNH/190/E).* https://apps.who.int/iris/bitstream/handle/10665/116689/dsa1214.pdf.

World Health Organization. (2017). *Social determinants of heath: Key concepts.* Geneva, Switzerland: World Health Organization. Available at: www.who.int/social_determinants/thecommission/finalreport/key_concepts/en/ Accessed May 1, 2021.

World Health Organization. (2019a). *Mental health atlas 2017: Resources for mental health in the Eastern Mediterranean region.* https://apps.who.int/iris/handle/10665/327491.

World Health Organization. (2019b). *Literacy rate (15–24) years.* Retrieved from https://rho.emro.who.int/Indicator/TermID/26.

World Health Organization. (2022a). *Child and adolescents health.* http://www.emro.who.int/child-adolescent-health/adolescent-health/adolescent-health.html.

World Health Organization. (2022b). *Child and adolescent health » adolescent health.* http://www.emro.who.int/child-adolescent-health/adolescent-health/adolescent-health.html.

World Health Organization. (2020c). *Health and well-being profile of the Eastern Mediterranean Region: an overview of the health situation in the Region and its countries in 2019.* https://applications.emro.who.int/docs/9789290223399-eng.pdf?ua=1&ua=1.

Zeinoun, P., Bawab, S., Atwi, M., Hariz, N., Tavitian, L., Khani, M., & Maalouf, F. T. (2013). Validation of an Arabic multi-informant psychiatric diagnostic interview for children and adolescents: Development and Well Being Assessment-Arabic (DAWBA-Arabic). *Comprehensive Psychiatry, 54*(7), 1034–1041. https://doi.org/10.1016/j.comppsych.2013.04.012

Zuberi, A., Waqas, A., Sadiq, N., Hossain, M., Rahman, A., Saeed, K., & Fuhr, D. (2021). Prevalence of mental disorders in the WHO Eastern Mediterranean region: A systematic review and meta-analysis. *Frontiers in Psychiatry.* https://doi.org/10.3389/fpsyt.2021.665019

Child and adolescent psychiatry training in the Arab Gulf region

Ammar Albanna[1], Khalid Bazaid[2], Bibi AlAmiri[3],
Hanan Derby[4], Hassan Mirza[5], Finza Latif[6],
Ahmed Malalla Al-Ansari[7], and
Yasser Ad-Dab'bagh[8]

[1] Center of Excellence, Mohamed Bin Rashid University of Medicine and Health Sciences; Emirates Society of Child and Adolescent Mental Health, Dubai, UAE; [2] Youth Psychiatry Program, Royal Ottawa Mental Health Centre; Scientific Council for Training in Psychiatry at the Saudi Commission for Health Specialties (SCFHS), Canadian Academy of Child and Adolescent Psychiatry Education Committee, Undergraduate Education Program, Department of Psychiatry, University of Ottawa, Ottawa, ON, Canada; [3] Almanara for Child and Adolescent Mental Health, Kuwait Center for Mental Health, Shuwaikh Industrial, Kuwait; [4] Fellowship in Child and Adolescent Psychiatry, Al Jalila Children's Specialty Hospital, Mohamed Bin Rashid University of Medicine and Health Sciences, Dubai, UAE; [5] Adult ADHD Service, Department of Behavioural Medicine, Sultan Qaboos University Hospital, Psychiatry Residency Program, Oman Medical Specialty Board, Muscat, Sultanate of Oman; [6] Department of Psychiatry, Sidra Medicine and Research Center, Weill Cornell-Qatar, Doha, Qatar; [7] Department of Psychiatry College of Medicine and Medical Sciences, Arabian Gulf University, Manama, Kingdom of Bahrain; [8] Mental Health Department, King Fahad Specialist Hospital-Dammam; Ministry of Health, Scientific Council for Training in Psychiatry at the SCFHS, Riyadh, Saudi Arabia

1. Introduction

Child and adolescent psychiatry (CAP) is a contemporary but progressively evolving field of medicine (Kanner, 1959; Organization, 2005).

The first dedicated child psychiatry clinics were established in Germany in the early 18th century, and the first academic child psychiatry department was founded at Johns Hopkins University in the United States by Leo Kanner (Mian et al., 2015). Kanner also started the first course in child psychiatry (ABPN, 2021). In the United States, child psychiatry was established as a board-certified medical specialty in 1959, under the umbrella of the American Board of Psychiatry and Neurology (ABPN, 2021). Other major early influences on the development of child psychiatry came from the Maudsley Hospital, London, UK (Evans et al., 2008).

The expansion of child and adolescent mental health services (CAMHS) and increased demand for child and adolescent mental health professionals resulted in the development of training programs. There has been continuous growth in CAP training programs across the world. At present, accredited CAP programs exist across many countries, including the United Kingdom and other European countries (Barrett et al., 2020), United States, Canada, Australia, and New Zealand (Rao et al., 2020), East Asia (Hirota et al., 2020), and India (Kommu & Jacob, 2020).

Many countries continue to experience a shortage of qualified CAP specialists despite the increase in number of graduates from CAP training programs (Costello et al., 2014; Marlow & Tomlinson, 2014). Even in an affluent country such as the United States, despite the significant increase in child psychiatrists nationally, there is a shortage of child and adolescent psychiatrists especially among rural areas, which remains to be a concern (Thomas & Holzer, 2006). This gap in qualified resources may be more pronounced in countries with less robust mental health services. This is reflected in the distribution of the 20,000 child and adolescent psychiatrists worldwide, who are primarily situated in high-income countries (approximately 1.2 child psychiatrist per 100,000) compared to low-income countries (0.1 per 100,000) (Leventhal, 2016). An additional issue is that some countries categorized as high income, such as those in the Gulf region, have underdeveloped CAMHS with relatively low numbers of CAP in relation to the population size and service demands. Further efforts are required to develop accredited training programs to meet the demands in these countries.

This chapter will focus on the evolution and status of CAP training among the six Arabian Gulf Countries that form the Gulf Cooperation Council (GCC): the State of Kuwait, the State of Qatar, the Sultanate of Oman, the Kingdom of Bahrain, the Kingdom of Saudi Arabia (KSA), and the United Arab Emirates (UAE).

2. The population of Arab States of the Gulf

There are eight countries overlooking the Arabian Gulf, including seven Arab nations. Out of these countries, six countries form the GCC for the Arab States of the Gulf that was established in 1981 with the desire to coordinate, cooperate, and integrate in all fields including health care (Council, 2021). The GCC consists of the following countries: the Kingdom of Bahrain, the State of Kuwait, the State of Qatar, the Sultanate of Oman, the KSA, and the UAE. Table 13.1 summarizes demographics among these six countries (Nations, 2019).

3. Child and adolescent mental health disorders in the Gulf Cooperation Council countries

GCC states are more homogeneous with regard to social, religious, cultural, and economic features than those of the Eastern Mediterranean Region as a whole. Additionally, they share many of the same health challenges and opportunities.

Over the last few decades numerous surveys of child and adolescent psychiatric disorders have been carried out in the Gulf region using diverse methodologies and many using questionnaire data (Chan et al., 2021). A robust two-stage survey of a large sample of school children in the UAE reported the weighted prevalence for DSM-IV disorders to be approximately 10.4% (Eapen et al., 1998). Taken together, these reports suggest the prevalence rates and type of disorders are similar to those found in other countries (Gau & Chen, 2020).

It is possible that the recognition of these disorders and related problems is lower than in other countries. In a systematic review, Elyamani et al. reported that Arab Gulf countries had low levels of mental health literacy in the general public (Elyamani et al., 2021). Their results also

TABLE 13.1 Population (total and younger than 19 years) of Gulf Cooperation Council (GCC) countries.

Country	Population	Population younger than 19	Percentage of population younger than 19
State of Kuwait	4,271,000	1,142,000	26.7%
State of Qatar	2,881,000	498,000	17.3%
Sultanate of Oman	5,107,000	1,364,000	26.7%
Kingdom of Bahrain	1,702,000	400,000	23.5%
Kingdom of Saudi Arabia	34,814,000	10,816,000	31%
United Arab Emirates	9,890,000	1,855,000	18.8%
Total	58,665,000	16,075,000	27.4%

show a high cumulative level of stigma and negative attitude toward mental health illness in the GCC. However, with more education the most common CAMH disorders are increasingly being reported in the GCC.

4. Child psychiatry certification bodies in Gulf Cooperation Council countries

There are presently two board certification bodies that certify CAP subspeciality programs in GCC. These are the Arab Board of Health Specializations (ABHS) (ABHS, 2016) and the Saudi Commission for Health Specialties (SCFHS).

The ABHS was established in 1978, under the umbrella of the Arab League, with the aim to improve health services in Arab countries by enhancing the scientific standards and medical practice in various medical disciplines. ABHS accredited general psychiatry programs have existed for decades in GCC countries. CAP was recently added as an accredited program under the ABHS. At present, among the approved programs, there is one accredited program in a GCC country, at Alsalmanya Medical Complex in Manama, the capital of the Kingdom of Bahrain. The two other programs exist in Egypt and Lebanon.

The SCFHS was established via a royal decree in November 1992, with the main objective to improve medical performance and practice in different health-related fields. There are presently 1453 accredited trainings sites for different medical specialties under the SCFHS, which are mainly situated in the KSA, in addition to some in the UAE, Kingdom of Bahrain, and Jordan. The CAP program consists of 2 years of both didactic and practical objectives, across different domains that are in line with the Canadian "CanMED" roles (RCPSC, 2015), aiming to prepare fellows to become competent consultants in the field of CAMHS, including in the six major CanMED competencies: Medical Expert, Communication, Collaboration, Leadership, Health Advocate, Scholarship and Professionalism. There are presently three accredited CAP programs under the SCFHS.

5. Child and adolescent psychiatry training in Gulf Cooperation Council countries

This section provides an overview of the current state of CAP training across GCC countries, and Table 13.2 provides a summary.

5.1 State of Kuwait

Kuwait is one of the GCC countries. These countries are united by their geographic proximity and economic prosperity as oil-rich countries, yet

TABLE 13.2 Summary of training programs in the Gulf Cooperation Council countries.

Country	Duration of CAP training in adult psychiatry programs	Is there a subspeciality program?	Duration	Key components of the training	Accreditation	Training sites	Current capacity
State of Kuwait	6 months	No	N/A	N/A	N/A	Almanara, Kuwait	N/A
State of Qatar	2–4 months	Yes; two programs; HMC and Sidra medicine	HMC: 3 years Sidra medicine: 2 years	Inpatient, outpatient, emergency, school based, substance abuse, developmental pediatrics	HMC: None Sidra medicine: ACGME-I	HMC Sidra medicine	HMC: three per year Sidra: two per year
Sultanate of Oman	6 months of mandatory CAP training, plus a 4-month elective	No	N/A	N/A	N/A	N/A	N/A
Kingdom of Bahrain		Yes	2 years	Inpatient, outpatient, emergency, school based, substance abuse, developmental pediatrics. School health and centers for children with special needs	Arab board for health specialties	One	Two per year
	6 months	Yes	2 years			Three	Eight

Continued

TABLE 13.2 Summary of training programs in the Gulf Cooperation Council countries.—cont'd

Country	Duration of CAP training in adult psychiatry programs	Is there a subspeciality program?	Duration	Key components of the training	Accreditation	Training sites	Current capacity
Kingdom of Saudi Arabia				1. General child and adolescent psychiatry 2. Liaison consultation and psychosomatics 3. Subspecialized child and adolescent psychiatry 4. Specific inpatient rotation 5. Specific emergency and urgent care clinic rotation 6. Selective school consultation 7. Selective community mental health agencies 8. Selective developmental disabilities	Saudi Commission for Health Specialties		

| United Arab Emirates | 6 months | Yes | 2 years | Health-care delivery, education, research, psychotherapy | • Clinical rotations in out patient department (OPD) including:
o General CAP clinics
o Consultation-liaison rotation
o CAP subspeciality clinics
o Medical clinics (neurology, developmental pediatric, general pediatric)
o Mental health inpatient unit
o Psychotherapy training
Scholastic activities: didactic knowledge and research; refer to Figure (13.2) for details | Saudi Commission for Health Specialties | One AJCH | Two candidates per year = total of four |

with less robust mental health services. Kuwait has a population of 4.25 million, approximately 25% of whom are younger than 19 years old (World Population Review, 2022). Therefore, the need for CAMHS to cover a growing young population is unprecedented.

Prior to 2012, CAMHS was served by the only psychiatric hospital in Kuwait, in a sporadic fashion that offered inconsistent service for those extremely in need and therefore discouraged health-care seeking behavior among families. In 2012, Almanara (Arabic for lighthouse) was established as a dedicated center for CAMHS in a separate building from where general psychiatry services were provided. Almanara initially delivered outpatient services, and in 2013 it opened two inpatient units (female and male wards with a capacity of 12–16 beds each). In addition, the services expanded to offer specific treatment modalities for autism spectrum disorder (ASD) such as the Early Start Denver Model and floor time. In the following years occupational therapy services and speech therapy joined Almanara. In addition, Almanara inaugurated eight satellite clinics to cover all general hospitals in Kuwait and established a school psychiatry program in collaboration with the Ministry of Education. Currently, Almanara is the only center in Kuwait that provides psychiatric evaluation and medication management, neuropsychologic testing and interventions, mental health occupational therapy, and speech therapy for children and adolescents. Although Almanara encompasses all of these services in one place, the majority of the case load is distributed among the satellite clinics. This reflects the continuous stigma around mental health and mental health facilities in the Middle East and the importance of integrating mental health into pediatrics and adolescent medicine. Clinical services in Almanara have been provided in spite of the lack of supporting national child mental health policies or laws and without administrative or academic support, which hinders data collection, monitoring and evaluation programs, and thus sustainability of quality care or strategic planning.

In the private sector, CAMHS services have been limited to neuropsychologic assessment and early intervention programs that lack regulatory oversight and psychiatric guidance.

With regard to CAP training, CAP experience is approved as a 1-week rotation for family medicine residency training, 1-month rotation for pediatrics residency training, and 6-month rotation for the general Kuwait psychiatry residency program. However, there is no higher subspecialty CAP training yet. This is probably a reflection of the young age of the general psychiatry residency training, which started in 2012 and since then has been struggling with high turnover of faculty and limited positions. In addition, since 2012 the number of trained child and adolescent psychiatrist has not increased to build the faculty needed for training. By January 2022, there were three trained child psychiatrists. In addition, the Kuwait regulatory body does not approve all CAP training in the GCC, so it is discouraging general psychiatrists from pursuing CAP training opportunities in the GCC.

The COVID-19 pandemic significantly affected training and clinical practice in Almanara. All academic and teaching activities, for example, journal clubs and grand rounds, were suspended to minimize crowding. In addition, pediatric residents and interns were all pulled out to cover COVID-19 wards across the country. They have been slowly returning to their regular rotation schedules, although they struggle with the unpredictability of the health situation in the country.

Almanara's future plans include a partial hospital program/intensive outpatient program and expanding the interdisciplinary approach, including inpatient services, to other general hospitals, and the awaited children's hospital. This expansion and integration of mental health into the larger health-care system will serve three main goals: improving standards of care, increasing access to mental health services for children and adolescents, and reducing mental health stigma. However, considering the shortage of local staff, which is unlikely to be replenished by the current training model, and the continuous leakage of expertise to other GCC countries or to the West, expansion of the Almanara to general hospitals is unlikely within the next 10 years.

To conclude, CAMHS services in Kuwait have come a long way since its inception in 2012. They serve at least 25% of the Kuwait population and have expanded significantly over the last few years to partially cover all general hospitals in Kuwait. Almanara's unique interdisciplinary approach has been successful in attracting training opportunities, although the possibility of establishing a CAP subspecialty training in Kuwait is currently remote. Services at Almanara were hit by the pandemic and continue to struggle to find their way back to normalcy while also dealing with the increasing demands for mental health services. Based on the current projections, Almanara will face challenges in meeting demand. Developing collaborative training between GCC countries and sharing resources among them will support Kuwait in meeting expectations.

5.2 State of Qatar

The State of Qatar, a member of the GCC, occupies the small Qatar Peninsula. Its sole border is with the KSA, while the rest of the territory is surrounded by the Arabian Gulf. Qatar has a population of about 2.8 million with approximately 17% of the population being 19 years or younger (Nations, 2019).

In Qatar, CAMHS have grown from virtually nonexistent to advanced in the past few decades. The prevalence of risk of mental health disorders in the Qatari population based on a self-report survey is noted to be 36% in adults with risk of depression and anxiety, the most common problems (Bener et al., 2015). However, prevalence studies in children and adolescents are lacking. One study, using teacher ratings with a standardized scale, reported the risk of attention-deficit/hyperactivity disorder (ADHD) in school-aged children as 12% (Bradshaw & Kamal, 2017).

A mental health policy was established in Qatar in 1980s, mainly focused on adults. Qatar's mental health law was issued in 2014, establishing rules for treatment of individuals with mental health difficulties. However, this law does not provide a policy for the treatment of children and adolescents (Nazeer et al., 2020). In 2018, the Qatar National Health Strategy (2018–22) "Our Health Our Future" was launched. This strategy identified mental health and well-being and children and adolescents as two of seven priority areas. Under this national strategy, CAMHS are being developed with an emphasis on community-based services (Nazeer et al., 2020).

Currently, a wide range of CAMHS are available in the private, semi-private, and government sectors. Two primary providers, i.e., Hamad Medical Corporation (HMC) and Sidra Medicine have divisions of child and adolescent psychiatry. The Sidra Medicine Division of Child and Adolescent Psychiatry provides a wide array of services tailored to children and families in various settings including outpatient services and consultation to the emergency department and pediatric medical units at the hospital. Sidra CAMHS also operates two inpatient beds on the general pediatric wards with safety modifications, suitable to admit moderately complex children under age 13 years. Children 14 years or older receive care in adult inpatient psychiatry units at HMC. Care for children with autism is available within these institutions as well as other private institutions and includes diagnostic assessments, neuropsychologic assessments, speech and language and occupational therapy services.

Specialty training in CAP is an essential part of growing the CAMHS in the region. There are less than 10 child and adolescent psychiatrists practicing in the State of Qatar. To meet growing demand, it is essential to train more of the workforce in developmentally appropriate biologic, cognitive, and behavioral perspectives. One of the goals of local training programs is to train child and adolescent psychiatrists who are familiar with the local culture and language and can work within the local community in addition to being experts and advocates in the field of child and adolescent mental health.

A general psychiatry residency program has existed at HMC for many years. This program received accreditation from the Accreditation Council for Graduate Medical Education-International (ACGME-I) in 2013. It is a 4-year program and recruits seven residents per year. The program receives applications from Qatar as well as internationally from other Arab countries and the Indian subcontinent. Residents have mandatory rotations in CAMHS at HMC and Sidra Medicine.

CAP training programs however are a recent development in Qatar. HMC has a CAP training program with a duration of 3 years. The first cohort of trainees graduated in 2021. Fellows are recruited nationally from the general psychiatry program. Sidra Medicine has a 2-year CAP training program that received accreditation from the ACGME-I in 2018 for two fellows per year, and its first cohort will graduate in 2022. The program receives applications from Qatar, other Arab countries, and the Indian subcontinent. During the first year, fellows receive comprehensive training in inpatient, outpatient, and emergency psychiatry. During the second year, the fellows complete subspecialty rotations in substance abuse, school-based mental health, eating disorders, and developmental pediatrics. Elective opportunities include global electives for enhanced expertise in cross-cultural psychiatry. The outpatient rotation provides experience in longitudinal management of patients over the 2-year program. The program also gives importance to training in psychotherapy including cognitive behavior, interpersonal and group therapies, among other modalities. Fellows have protected time to dedicate to quality improvement or research projects under faculty supervision.

Qatar's CAMHS fellowship training programs were still in the early stages when the COVID-19 pandemic hit the country. Challenges experienced locally secondary to the pandemic included delays in recruitment of new fellows, changes in elective rotations to meet the needs of COVID-19 units as well as a decline in the number of patients being seen face to face. At the onset of the pandemic, most outpatient clinics transitioned to use of telemedicine. In addition, HMC used a two-team system to protect residents and fellows. Teams were divided into an "active" and a "remote" work team that alternated on different days, limiting exposure to COVID-19. Both HMC and Sidra programs have continued to use telemedicine to provide care in outpatient settings. Many families are opting to use telemedicine instead of face-to-face appointments.

In summary, there is rapid growth of CAMHS services and training programs in Qatar. CAMHS services are also involved in advocacy and providing advice on national policies.

5.3 Sultanate of Oman

The Sultanate of Oman is a country in the Middle East, a member of the GCC, with a population of over 4.5 million (Data.worldbank.org). Omani citizens constitute 54% of the population, with half of that population less than 25 years of age (Group, 2016). Oman has been experiencing a recent period of expanded population of young people, a trend expected to continue over the next 2 decades. Therefore, due to this demographic transition, Oman will experience challenges over the next 20 years to meet the needs of the increased numbers of young people, especially in providing quality education, health care, and future job opportunities (Islam, 2020).

The capital Muscat is the largest city of Oman, where the majority of the population resides, and the only city with CAMHS. Overall, there is a scarcity of CAMHS in Oman. As a relatively high-income country since the 1980s, Oman has benefited from improved living standards. However, the country has witnessed an apparent surge in young people with cognitive, emotional, and behavioral disorders (Al-Sharbati et al., 2016). This increase is probably because the population in Oman is pyramidal, with the majority less than 18 years old. And although increased recognition and awareness play a role in this phenomenon, this per se cannot be the only factor in the rising tide of young people with poor mental health problems in Oman. Despite this surge, many do not seek care from qualified mental health professionals (Al-Adawi, 2014).

The first CAMH service was established in the late 1990s at the Sultan Qaboos University Hospital (SQUH) with rudimentary services (Mirza, 2018). More recently, CAMHS has developed a more comprehensive and multidisciplinary approach. Due to the demand, beds are available for urgent admissions, 24 h a day, 7 days a week, making it the first psychiatric inpatient service for young people in Oman. It aims to offer comprehensive care for children and young people up to 18 presenting with mental health disorders. The service offers both outpatient and inpatient management, with the latter being a unique service making it mandatory for a caregiver to reside with the young person on the ward during the inpatient stay. This policy has great public appeal and makes it the service of choice for inpatient management over the sister institute, Al-Massarah Hospital (AMH), which is the only psychiatry hospital in Oman operated by the Ministry of Health and has very recently started to offer admissions for young people, albeit without an attendant or a caregiver. In addition, ancillary initiatives such as psychometric services have gained momentum. This is complemented by the necessary social support and school reports by psychologists and social workers within the multidisciplinary team.

Moreover, in 2017, for the first time, the Ministry of Social Development in Oman launched a 24/7 child protection hotline, which aims to combat child abuse and neglect in the country. The toll-free hotline is a leading national project to protect children in Oman, and it works closely with all health-care institutes across the country, including CAMHS at SQUH. The unit's ultimate goal in SQUH is for the multidisciplinary teams to work collaboratively to help and assist patients and families in working toward recovery.

Currently, the only two institutions with CAMHS in Oman, SQUH and AMH, offer services to the whole country. However, both are located in the capital, Muscat, which requires many service users to commute long distances, resulting in children missing school and caregivers taking the day off work. Therefore, due to these current challenges, future perspectives focus on ensuring that more psychiatry trainees pursue careers in CAP, with an ambitious vision to make available basic CAMHS in all secondary and tertiary health-care providers in Oman.

However, one of the significant challenges the mental health service providers face in Oman is the lack of a transition plan for young people who continue to experience mental health difficulties into adulthood, especially young people with neurodevelopmental disorders such as ADHD and ASD. Therefore, the adult ADHD clinic at SQUH was started as a pilot project to help young service user's transition to adult ADHD services and cater to the needs of the adults with symptoms of ADHD (Al-Sinawi et al., 2020; Mirza et al., 2021).

Similarly, another challenge facing child and adolescent psychiatrists in Oman is the ethical dilemma in managing young people, such as controversial compulsory admission and involuntary treatment practices (Al-Maamari et al., 2021). Moreover, the lack of a mental health act, stigma, and traditional beliefs may delay help-seeking behavior (Al-Adawi et al., 2002).

The COVID-19 pandemic wreaked havoc across the globe, and the mental health of children and young people is a significant area of concern. Therefore, a large study looked into self-harm and inpatient admissions among children and adolescents from 10 different countries, including Oman and the UAE (Ougrin et al., 2021). The number of emergency presentations by area and year in all mental health facilities, including those in Muscat, Oman, had fewer hospital presentations over the same period in 2020 during the COVID-19 pandemic and lockdowns compared with the same period before the pandemic in 2019. This reduction was statistically significant, with future implications for service planning during a possible future wave of COVID-19 or a lockdown for any other public health emergency. Therefore, mental health professionals should prepare for more virtual and phone-based contact with young people experiencing mental health difficulties.

The Oman Medical Specialty Board (OMSB) is the postgraduate medical training body in Oman, established in 2006. It has adopted the ACGME-I competencies, with a vision to achieve excellence in postgraduate medical education, training, assessment, and accreditation throughout the Sultanate of Oman (2021). The psychiatry residency training program, which was granted the ACGME-I accreditation in 2017, is a 5-year program designed to produce specialists in general psychiatry with adequate knowledge and competency of the subspecialties, including psychotherapy, CAP, substance misuse, geriatric psychiatry, consultation-liaison psychiatry, and forensic psychiatry. Psychiatry trainees undertake a 6-month CAP rotation during the third year of residency, which constitutes an integral part of general psychiatric training. As there is a local shortage of child psychiatrists and the likelihood that general psychiatrists will encounter child and adolescent patients in clinical practice, this rotation is therefore considered essential and mandatory. Similarly, during the fifth year of residency, the trainees can pursue an elective in CAP, which lasts 4 months. The training sites for CAP are SQUH and AMH, with a total of six CAP trainers. Currently, the OMSB does not offer fellowship opportunities in CAP due to a lack of human resources. However, OMSB graduates who wish to continue CAP fellowship training are sponsored by the Ministry of Higher Education in Oman to pursue subspecialty training abroad. There is a plan to include the UAE and Qatar as approved CAP fellowship training sites.

In conclusion, Oman's economic growth and rapid demographic shift are witnessing a surge in young people with mental health problems. Moreover, despite the increasing need for CAMHS in the country, only two institutions offer CAMHS to the whole population due to severe shortage and maldistribution of facilities. Nevertheless, Oman is delivering mental health services for the young, notwithstanding the challenges, and it has come a long way against all odds.

5.4 Kingdom of Bahrain

Bahrain, a member of GCC, is an archipelago of islands situated in the middle of the Arabian Gulf, close to the eastern shore of the KSA. It measures 765.3 km^2 and is connected to the KSA by an 18-km causeway. The population is 1.702 million, 45% of which consists of immigrants (2022). The country enjoys good health indicators, including life expectancy (78.2 years), literacy rates (95.7%), infant mortality rates (8.9 deaths/1000 live births), maternal mortality rates (15 deaths/100,000 live births), and 100% prenatal care for pregnant women. Immunization coverage is 99% (World Health Organization, 2017).

The first service for child psychiatry was established in Bahrain in 1975, the first of its kind in the Arab Gulf states. The service started twice a week as an outpatient clinic as part of afternoon school health services. The service was established to meet the demand for helping students with learning difficulties. The first adolescent service began in 1981, after a qualified child psychiatrist joined the psychiatric hospital team in the country's main hospital. In June 1981, an adolescent psychiatric clinic was established as part of the main general outpatient clinic. The services were initially offered once per week and increased to four clinics per week between 1983 and 1985. The afternoon and morning adolescent clinics merged under the name of the Child and Adolescent Psychiatric Unit (CAPU) in 1986. Another major development was the opening of new premises in 1992 to house the first 12-bed inpatient/day-care program in the region. An ambitious School Health (SH) program was planned and rolled out in primary care health services in 2007 to provide services covering the country's four governorates. The SH program is a joint venture between the Ministry of Health and the Ministry of Education. The program includes services for mental health, school nursing, primary care, and adolescents. Such a joint program is unique in the region.

Psychiatric services are provided through several outlets but primarily through a busy outpatient clinic, which operates daily and receives more than 500 new referrals and more than 2000 follow-up visits annually. A day-care program operates daily after school for 12 children. The unit runs a structured behavioral program based on the primary nurse concept.

The CAPU provides daily coverage for the pediatric age group in the country's main general hospital (700-bed capacity) in addition to providing services to the accident and emergency department. The CAPU is considered the main training center for residents, interns, and family physicians. The day-care program includes a special program for the diagnosis of ASD, and any child suspected of having ASD is referred and diagnosed using a specially prepared protocol. The protocol is implemented on a day-case admission basis for 3—5 days.

In terms of staffing, the CAPU presently includes: three full-time qualified child psychiatrists, two part-time child psychiatrists, one social worker, one clinical psychologist, one to two psychiatric residents, eight to nine nurses, and one ward clerk and secretary.

The SH program is physically located in a central primary care health center and provides the following services:

(a) a mental health clinic to evaluate all school-age referrals from across the country, mainly for educational learning issues and abnormal behavior. The clinic receives more than 150 referrals and 1500 visits annually,
(b) a nursing program whereby nurses are attached to a school to offer counseling for minor behavioral problems, health promotion, and workshops for social services and teachers,
(c) primary care services, including routine periodic screenings for 6- and 12-year-olds, checking vaccination schedules, and providing instructions for health crises, such as COVID-19,
(d) a twice-weekly adolescent clinic.

At present, the SH program is staffed by two full-time child psychiatrists, one part-time child psychiatrist, one speech therapist, 25 nurses, and administrative supportive staff.

The CAPU has established an excellent network and professional relationships with active community social welfare societies, such as the Bahrain ADHD Society, the Bahraini Association for Intellectual Disability and Autism, child and mother welfare societies, and childcare homes (orphanage). Several CAPU staff serve as members on the boards of these societies. Staff members contribute regularly to the parental training program for parents of children with ADHD. In addition, the CAPU and SH conduct regular consultations, meetings, and health promotion lectures for the child protection committee of the main general hospital and to schools.

Future challenges and development encompass moving some CAPU services into the community, including preschool early intervention programs, outpatient adolescent services, and autism diagnostic assessments. Further developments include opening a 15-bed adolescents' inpatient unit and expanding outpatient services in SH to improve gaming disorder. CAPU staff are participating in a project with mothers regarding a child development unit in primary care to introduce M-CHAT in the early detection of children with ASD.

Regarding training, CAP provides several opportunities for residents of the Arab Council for Health Specialties and the Saudi Board of Specialties training rotate in the CAPU and SH for a child psychiatry training block (6 months is mandatory). It is also considered a training site for medical students (1 month as part of their clerkship rotation) and family physicians (2 months during their specialization program in the psychiatric hospital, including rotation in the CAPU). Both CAPU and SH were granted approval by the Arab Board specialty in psychiatry in 2020 to train fellows in the Child and Adolescent fellowship program. The first group joined the fellowship program in January 2022.

5.5 Kingdom of Saudi Arabia

The KSA is the largest of the GCC countries (see Table 13.1). Among the population, 31% are less than 19 years of age, and 39% are under the age of 24 years, so this is a relatively young population compared with countries with well-developed mental health services. This would suggest a high need and potential demand for CAMHS. Unfortunately, these services were late to develop compared with those geared toward adults (Al-Habeeb et al., 2012). See Figure 13.1.

Prior to 1995, there were few general psychiatrists offering CAP services with limited subspecialty training in CAP. Moreover, there was only

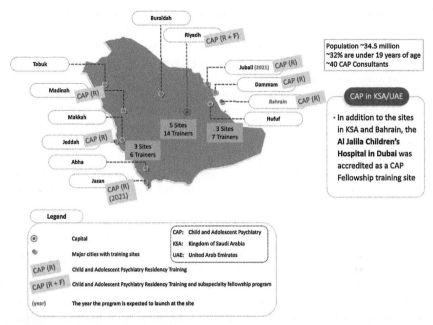

FIGURE 13.1 Child and adolescent psychiatry training sites in the Kingdom of Saudi Arabia.

one qualified child psychologist in the KSA. Thereafter, returning internationally trained subspecialists in CAP began to develop mental health services for children and adolescents in two cities (Riyadh and Al-Khobar). At the time, CAP services were limited to outpatient care for young children, while adolescents were often treated by general psychiatrists and if needed admitted to adult inpatient units. Interdisciplinary teams with CAMH expertise were lacking (Clausen et al., 2020; Koenig et al., 2014).

Progress began when standardized residency training in psychiatry began in 1995 as a university program at King Saud University (KSU), Riyadh, with one training site. CAP training in that program was part of a 6-month combined rotation with consultation-liaison psychiatry in the 4-year program (Clausen et al., 2020; Koenig et al., 2013, 2014).

In 1997, the SCFHS established a central residency training program with two general training sites in Riyadh, a site in Dammam in addition to a CAP site in the Kingdom of Bahrain. As the SCFHS absorbed the KSU program, CAP training became available at two sites: Riyadh and Bahrain. By then, CAP training was a separate 3-month rotation. Dammam residents had their entire CAP training at the Bahrain site, while Riyadh residents spent 1 month in Bahrain and 2 months in Riyadh (Koenig et al., 2013).

As more internationally trained and qualified CAP subspecialists returned to KSA, a second site for CAP training in Riyadh was formed, and the rotation was extended to 6 months. Since then, training sites for the general psychiatry residency have increased to span 11 cities in the country including five cities in addition to Bahrain offering training in CAP as a core rotation part of the residency program. CAP became a mandatory rotation and generally is undertaken during the third year of residency, either in one 6-month block or two 3-month blocks at different sites (Koenig et al., 2013; Telmesani et al., 2011).

In 2011, the scientific council for training in psychiatry at the SCFHS adopted the strategy for the development of subspecialty training, and CAP was the first subspecialty to be assigned a taskforce to develop the structure and content of the program. By 2013, a proposed 2-year sub-specialty fellowship training program had been presented to the concerned committee at SCFHS. However, the ongoing work by SCFHS to adopt the CanMED framework resulted in postponement of its approval. In 2015, the CanMED framework was implemented into the curriculum of the residency, including the CAP rotation, and was mandated as the framework for the proposed CAP fellowship program. By 2016, the CAP fellowship program was approved by SCFHS, and the training site accreditation process began in 2017. The first cohort was admitted in March 2018 at a single training site in Riyadh, KSA, and another training site was accredited in Riyadh shortly thereafter. Each of these two training sites presently has three consultant child and adolescent psychiatrists. A third training site was accredited in Dubai, UAE, in 2020, and it has five consultant child and adolescent psychiatrists. The first cohort to graduate did so in May 2020 (Specialties, 2016).

The requirements for a CAP fellowship training site to be accredited are to have at least two qualified, certified child and adolescent consultant psychiatrists who have graduated from a recognized training program. The accreditation criteria may be revised every 4 years or as needed.

To be admitted to the program, candidates must have successfully completed training in general psychiatry at an accredited program, have passed the final written examination in general psychiatry, have passed an interview conducted by the scientific committee of the fellowship program, provide three letters of recommendation, and provide proof of sponsorship for the entire period of the training program (Specialties, 2016).

The first year of CAP fellowship training consists of 6 months of general CAP and 6 months of pediatric consultation-liaison (psychosomatic) psychiatry. The second year consists of rotations in subspecialties in CAP. Throughout both years the trainee will focus on such advanced areas such as health-care delivery, education, research, and psychotherapy (Specialties, 2016).

Graduates of the CAP fellowship program are expected to achieve competencies in several areas including functioning effectively as consultants, integrating all the CanMED roles to provide optimal, ethical, patient/family-centered and evidence-based medical care; establishing and maintaining clinical knowledge, skills, and attitudes appropriate to CAP; performing relevant and appropriate assessments of patients; using therapeutic interventions effectively; and seeking appropriate consultations from other health professionals. CAP fellows are evaluated on a continuous basis during their rotations, are expected to pass a written examination at the end of the first year, and are expected to pass a final written and clinical examinations at the end of the training. A certificate acknowledging training completion will only be issued to the fellow upon successful fulfilment of all program requirements. Candidates passing all components of the final subspecialty examination are awarded the "Saudi Fellowship of Child and Adolescent Psychiatry" certificate (Specialties, 2016).

In conclusion, despite the substantial progress in the development of CAP training and services, there are still fewer than 50 child and adolescent psychiatrists in the country, which is around 0.014 per 10,000 of the KSA population. To meet the needs of this young population, an expanded CAP fellowship training program is needed with more training sites and a higher capacity beyond its current limitation to admitting annually two trainees in Riyadh and two in Dubai. Furthermore, the available services conspicuously lack comprehensive interdisciplinary teams, advanced individual and family psychotherapeutic services, and inpatient services for children and adolescents. Many CAP subspecialties lack the experts who can contribute to training fellows, such as eating disorders, adolescent addiction, infant psychiatry, and early onset psychosis (Specialties, 2016).

5.6 The United Arab Emirates

The UAE is a member of the GCC that consists of a union of seven emirates, established in 1971 (Council, 2021). Abu Dhabi is the capital and largest city in the UAE, comprising 87% of the total area. The UAE population is around 9.3 million based on a recent census (FCSA, 2020) with an estimated annual population growth of 1.40 (UNESCO, 2019). Around 42.8% of the UAE population resides in Dubai, 29% in Abu Dhabi, 24% in Sharjah, and the rest of the population in the other emirates. Expatriates form approximately 88.5% of the population, drawn by the influx of a predominantly male workforce as a result of significant growth in the various economic sectors in the country. The UAE is a multicultural country, with residents and workers made up of more than 200 nationalities. The age group of more than 50% of the population falls between 25 and 54 years old due to the foreign workforce. Around 27% of the population are young people less than the age of 24 years (Government.ae., 2017).

Over the past 30 years, the UAE has undergone major sociocultural changes due to the economic boom and the influx of people from a diverse cultural background. It is recognized that rapid urbanization might bring about conflict, changes in values and beliefs, psychologic stressors, and rupture of societal cohesion leading to increasing mental health problems (Hunter, 1991). Based on the WHO Mental Health Atlas report on UAE, the burden of mental health disease estimate of neuropsychiatric disorders is approximately 19.9% (WHO, 2011). Nonetheless, the number of psychiatrists working in the mental health field in the UAE was estimated to be 0.3 psychiatrist per 100,000 population (WHO, 2015). This reflects an extreme shortage of psychiatry workforce in the country in comparison to Western nations.

Psychiatry services in the UAE were established in 1970 and are delivered through the public health system and via hospital-based outpatient and inpatient settings. Additionally, the private sector plays a major role in service delivery through outpatient clinics (Eapen & El-Rufaie, 2008). At present, the UAE government is working collaboratively to improve public health with a special focus on noncommunicable diseases and mental health services (Government.ae., 2017). This is reflected in establishing a national program for happiness and well-being launched in 2016, aiming to cultivate mental well-being across the nation through a wide range of initiatives targeting government entities as well as the wider UAE community (Wellbeing, 2016). Further, the Ministry of Health and Prevention endorsed "The National Policy for the Promotion of Mental Health in the United Arab Emirates" in 2017, and new mental health legislation was released in 2020 (Karrani et al., 2020, pp. 1992–2019).

The mental health of young people has become a major concern worldwide due to the increased awareness of the prevalence and burden of psychiatric disorders among this age group. Although there is a scarcity of epidemiologic research on children's mental health in the UAE, the available data suggests that the prevalence of child psychiatric disorders in UAE is similar to Western countries (Eapen et al., 1998). Furthermore, a recent survey in the UAE exploring anxiety and emotional disorders in the context of the COVID-19 pandemic among young people reported significant levels of anxiety (Saddik et al., 2021). The UAE presently has a dedicated society for CAMHS professionals, reflecting both the growth in the number of professionals, as well as the recognition of this field (ESCAM, 2021). Nevertheless, CAMHS remain understaffed in comparison to those in developed countries (Kraya, 2002).

CAMHS in the UAE have been traditionally delivered by SH services through a school nurse or a social worker or a psychologist who are not necessarily clinically trained or equipped to deal with this age group. Additionally, children and adolescents were seen by general adult psychiatrists, pediatricians, primary health-care physicians, and psychologists. Over the past years, the UAE witnessed an increase in CAMHS. Child and adolescent psychiatrists are now available in many of the existing mental health services in government and private sectors. Notably, the Mental Health Center of Excellence (MHCE) at Al Jalila Children's Hospital (AJCH) was launched in Dubai in 2016, dedicated to enhancing child mental health clinical care, research, and education. The MHCE delivers specialized multidisciplinary comprehensive programs targeting a wide variety of mental health issues in children and adolescents up to the age of 18 years. Among the pillars of the MHCE is developing specialized training and research in the field of child psychiatry.

A recent academic child and adolescent psychiatric consortium reported that "the current underdeveloped status of CAMHS in the Middle East region is a result of the lack of specialized postgraduate training programs, inadequate numbers of qualified professionals to administer necessary mental health services, and the absence of national policy support" (Clausen et al., 2020). Additionally, exposure to CAP in undergraduate medical education is limited. In addition, postgraduate training in general psychiatry and subspecialities have not grown much in numbers in comparison with other major medical specialties, which contributes to the workforce shortage in that field. There was no dedicated higher subspeciality training program in CAP in UAE up until 2018.

Regarding general psychiatry training, there are three Arab Board general psychiatry training programs in the UAE, and training in child psychiatry is included as trainees are offered 3—6 months clinical rotation in a 4-year training program. Postgraduate training in CAP plays a vital role in providing the workforce of experienced clinicians and leaders, both of which are required to address increasing mental health demands.

The MHCE at AJCH was instrumental in establishing the first CAP fellowship training in UAE, in collaboration with Mohamed Bin Rashid University of Medicine and Health Sciences. The program was accredited by the SCFHS in October 2018. The comprehensive curriculum of the program is competency-based adopting the CanMED competency-based framework (RCPSC, 2015). The duration of the training program is 2 years, with an accredited two training posts each year.

The training experience is longitudinal, offering both mandatory and optional clinical components. The first year is a foundational training, focusing on building up knowledge and skills in child psychiatry. Trainees are exposed to a wide range of psychiatry disorders through working in the ambulatory outpatient and pediatric consultation liaison services. They are also offered rotations in pediatric clinics that are relevant to CAP. In the second year, trainees gain more advanced experience in the specialized areas of CAP through attending the inpatient unit and a variety of selective specialized clinics. Figure 13.2 provides a summary of the rotational map for the AJCH fellowship program.

The scholar activities of the program offer trainees a wide range of educational activities including regular didactic sessions, journal clubs, case presentations, and leadership skills. Conducting a research and quality project is a mandatory component. Furthermore, trainees are instructed in various modalities of psychotherapy. There is a standardized performance evaluation process throughout the training period with a final examination at the end of training (Specialties, 2016).

The program is currently preparing for its fourth cycle after interviewing candidates from various countries, demonstrating the interest in CAP training across the region (Figure 13.3). In January 2020, two fellows graduated from the inaugural cohort and accomplished all board certification requirements, becoming the first locally trained CAP specialists in the UAE.

In conclusion, UAE has made enormous progress and has developed rapidly in many aspects of health sectors including public health. Two major developments lately are promising to make a major impact in the health system progress and improvement. First is the establishment of the UAE National Institute for Health Specialties (NIHS) (NIHS, 2021). NIHS is responsible for establishing a postgraduate medical education system (e.g., accreditation and certification) for specialty physicians and surgeons and potentially other health-care professionals. It aims at enhancing the health sector by raising the level and quality of higher medical education. It is in the process of developing both general psychiatry, as well as psychiatry subspecialty training standards for the UAE. Secondly, in July 2021, Law No. 13 was announced to establish the Dubai Academic Health Corporation, which aims to advance health services in Dubai through an academic health system integrating health care, medical education, and scientific research. CAMHS is a growing field in the UAE, and it continues to require more support and attention to expand further. Strengthening medical education through the academic health corporation and encouraging research will provide large opportunities to train and recruit more manpower in this field. As stated by the World Health Organization, "Mental health is more than the absence of mental disorders"; mental health is fundamental to health and overall well-being because "without mental health there is no health".

YEAR 1		
Ambulatory Paediatric Rotation: 1 block	Ambulatory General Child and Adolescent Outpatient clinic: 6 blocks	Consultation Liaison Clinical Rotation: 5 blocxks
General Paediatric Clinic		Consultation Liaison Clinic
Adolescent Medicine Clinic	General Child and Adolescent Psychiatry Outpatient Clinic	
Developmental Paediatrics Clinic		General Child and Adolescent Psychiatry Outpatient Clinic (20%)
Paediatric Neurology Clinic		
LONGITUDINAL TRAINING: FIRST YEAR		
Emergency Psychiatry		
Psychiatry Clinical Supervision: 1 hour/week		
Psychotherapy Experience & Supervision: 2 hours/week		
Research & Self-Learning: I session/week *once evidence of project proposal submitted		
Education Activities: (Didactic, Journal Club, Mortality & Morbidity, Mental Health Grand Rounds, Clinical MDT Case discussion		
Managerial Leadership: MDT Activities (Intake, Business Meetings, etc...) (Tuesday)		

YEAR 2		
Inpatient/Partial Hospitalisation Programme: 6 blocks	Selective Rotation; Specialised and Complex Care: 5 blocks	Elective (external or internal accredited rotations): 2 blocks
Inpatient Unit Partial hospitalisation Programme	ASD Clinic	As per the discussion with Programme Director
	ADHD Clinic	
	Collaborative Shared Care (ADHD Clinic)	
	Family Medicine (Mediclinic)	
	Eating Disorder Clinic	
	Forensic Psychiatry (Al Amal Hospital)	
	Mood & Anxiety Disorders Clinic	
	Neuropsychiatry Disorders Clinic	
	Substance Misuse Clinic (Al Amal Hospital)	
	Trauma Clinic	
General Child and Adolescent Psychiatry Outpatient Clinic (20%)		
LONGITUDINAL TRAINING: SECOND YEAR		
Emergency Psychiatry		
Psychiatry Clinical Supervision: 1 hour/week		
Psychotherapy Experience & Supervision: 2 hours/week		
Research & Self-Learning: (1 Session/week) *expected to complete		
Education Activities: (Didactic, Journal Club, Mortality & Morbidity, Mental Health Grand Rounds, Clinical MDT Case discussion, Morning & Handover rounds) *refer to specific days		
Managerial Leadership: MDT Activities (Inta ke, Business Meetings, etc...) (Tuesday)		

FIGURE 13.2   Rotational map for the 2-year AJCH CAP Fellowship Program.

CAP FELLOWSHIP APPLICANTS OVER 4 CYCLES

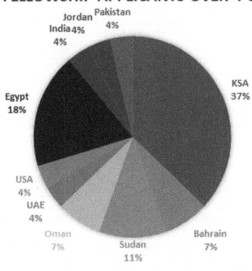

FIGURE 13.3   Child and adolescent psychiatry applicants to the Al Jalila Children's Specialty Hospital Fellowship program over four cycles 2018–21 by country of residence.

6. Conclusions

CAMHS are in their early phases of development across GCC countries. Nonetheless, these countries are witnessing significant training advancement including establishing board-certified subspecialty programs in CAP. There has also been a progressive development of mental health policies and legislation to protect the younger population and ensure adequate, comprehensive, and inclusive services. To bridge the gap between current and required CAP professionals, these programs will benefit from a collaborative approach given that every program presents with its unique set of strengths and challenges. Moreover, researching the outcomes of these programs will lead to further evidence-based expansion of these programs. These suggestions might be feasible given that some programs run across different countries but under the umbrella of the same board accreditation. We propose that a collaborative approach will lead to innovative solutions to CAMHS across these countries given that they share similar needs and challenges.

References

ABHS. (2016). *Arab board training program in child and adolescent psychiatry.* Retrieved from http://arab-board.org/sites/default/files/GuideBook%20for%20Child%20and%20Adolescent%20Psychiatry_0.pdf.

ABPN. (2021). *American board of psychiatry and neurology, history.* Retrieved 19.06.2021, from https://www.abpn.com/about/mission-and-history/.

Al-Adawi, S. (2014). Tomorrow's people matters: Evidence for action in Oman. *Oman Medical Journal, 29*(2), 83.

Al-Adawi, S., Dorvlo, A. S., Al-Ismaily, S. S., et al. (2002). Perception of and attitude towards mental illness in Oman. *International Journal of Social Psychiatry, 48*(4), 305–317. https://doi.org/10.1177/002076402128783334

Al-Habeeb, A. A., Qureshi, N. A., & Al-Maliki, T. A. (2012). Pattern of child and adolescent psychiatric disorders among patients consulting publicly-funded child psychiatric clinics in Saudi Arabia/Profil des troubles psychiatriques chez des enfants et adolescents consultant en établissements de soins psychiatriques pour enfants à financement public en Arabie saoudite. *Eastern Mediterranean Health Journal, 18*(2), 112.

Al-Maamari, A., Al-Kindi, Q., & Mirza, H. (2021). Ethical dilemmas in child and adolescent mental health services in Oman. *Ethics and Social Welfare, 15*(2), 219–223. https://doi.org/10.1080/17496535.2021.1897641

Al-Sharbati, M. M., Al-Farsi, Y. M., Al-Sharbati, Z. M., Al-Sulaimani, F., Ouhtit, A., & Al-Adawi, S. (2016). Profile of mental and Behavioral disorders among preschoolers in a tertiary care hospital in Oman: A retrospective study. *Oman Medical Journal, 31*(5), 357–364. https://doi.org/10.5001/omj.2016.71

Al-Sinawi, H., Mirza, H., & Al Alawi, M. (2020). Mental health services in the Sultanate of Oman. In *Handbook of healthcare in the Arab World* (pp. 1–12). Cham: Springer International Publishing. https://doi.org/10.1007/978-3-319-74365-3_131-1

Barrett, E., Jacobs, B., Klasen, H., Herguner, S., Agnafors, S., Banjac, V., ... Hebebrand, J. (2020). The child and adolescent psychiatry: Study of training in Europe (CAP-STATE). *European Child & Adolescent Psychiatry, 29*(1), 11–27. https://doi.org/10.1007/s00787-019-01416-3

Bener, A., Abou-Saleh, M. T., Dafeeah, E. E., & Bhugra, D. (2015). The prevalence and burden of psychiatric disorders in primary health care visits in Qatar: Too little time. *Journal of Family Medicine and Primary Care, 4*(1), 89–95. https://doi.org/10.4103/2249-4863.152262

Bradshaw, L. G., & Kamal, M. (2017). Prevalence of ADHD in Qatari school-age children. *Journal of Attention Disorders, 21*(5), 442–449. https://doi.org/10.1177/1087054713517545

Chan, M. F., Al Balushi, R., Al Falahi, M., Mahadevan, S., Al Saadoon, M., & Al-Adawi, S. (2021). Child and adolescent mental health disorders in the GCC: A systematic review and meta-analysis. *International Journal of Pediatrics and Adolescent Medicine.* https://doi.org/10.1016/j.ijpam.2021.04.002

Clausen, C. E., Bazaid, K., Azeem, M. W., Abdelrahim, F., Elgawad, A. A. A., Alamiri, B., ... Consortium on Academic Child, A. P. I. T. M. E. C. A. C. A. P. M. E. (2020). Child and adolescent psychiatry training and services in the Middle East region: A current status assessment. *European Child & Adolescent Psychiatry, 29*(1), 51–61. https://doi.org/10.1007/s00787-019-01360-2

Costello, E. J., He, J.-p., Sampson, N. A., Kessler, R. C., & Merikangas, K. R. (2014). Services for adolescents with psychiatric disorders: 12-Month data from the national comorbidity survey–adolescent. *Psychiatric Services, 65*(3), 359–366. https://doi.org/10.1176/appi.ps.201100518

Council, G. C. (2021). *Member states—Gulf cooperation council.* Retrieved 25.06.2021, 2021 from https://www.gcc-sg.org/en-us/AboutGCC/MemberStates/pages/Home.aspx.

Eapen, V., al-Gazali, L., Bin-Othman, S., & Abou-Saleh, M. (1998). Mental health problems among schoolchildren in United Arab Emirates: Prevalence and risk factors. *Journal of the American Academy of Child and Adolescent Psychiatry, 37*(8), 880–886. https://doi.org/10.1097/00004583-199808000-00019

Eapen, V., & El-Rufaie, O. (2008). United Arab Emirates (UAE). *International Psychiatry, 5*(2), 38–40. Retrieved from https://www.cambridge.org/core/journals/international-psychiatry/article/united-arab-emirates-uae/1E7D895AE1833AA0054C75D4E2F6F43D.

Elyamani, R., Naja, S., Al-Dahshan, A., Hamoud, H., Bougmiza, M. I., & Alkubaisi, N. (2021). Mental health literacy in Arab states of the Gulf cooperation council: A systematic review. *PLoS One, 16*(1), e0245156. https://doi.org/10.1371/journal.pone.0245156

ESCAM. (2021). *The Emirates society for child and adolescent mental health.* Retrieved 25.06.2021, 2021 from www.escam.ae.

Evans, B., Rahman, S., & Jones, E. (2008). Managing the 'unmanageable': Interwar child psychiatry at the Maudsley hospital, London. *History of Psychiatry, 19*(76 Pt 4), 454–475. https://doi.org/10.1177/0957154X08089619

FCSA. (2020). *Data related to population, education, health, divorce and marriage, security and other related datasets.* Retrieved 2021, from https://fcsa.gov.ae/en-us/Pages/Statistics/Statistics-by-Subject.aspx#/%3Ffolder=Economy/National%20Account/National%20Account&subject=Demography%20and%20Social.

Gau, S.-F. S., & Chen, Y.-L. (2020). Prevalence, risk factors, and disease burden of child and adolescent mental disorders: Taiwanese and global aspects. In M. Hodes, S.-F. S. Gau, & P. J. D. Vries (Eds.), *Starting at the beginning. Laying the foundation for lifelong mental health* (pp. 3–29). London: Academic Press.

Government.ae., U. A. E. (2017). *Mental health.* Retrieved 3 May 2018, 2018 from https://www.government.ae/en/information-and-services/health-and-fitness/health-of-vulnerable-groups/mental-health.

Group, O.B. (2016). Retrieved June 24 2021. https://oxfordbusinessgroup.com/analysis/dividend-or-liability-meeting-needs-region'sgrowing-youth-population.

Hirota, T., Guerrero, A. P. S., & Skokauskas, N. (2020). Child and adolescent mental health needs, services, and gap in East and Southeast Asia and the Pacific Islands. In M. Hodes, S. S.-F. Gau, & P. J. D. Vries (Eds.), *Starting at the beginning: Laying the foundation for lifelong mental health* (pp. 295–315). London: Academic Press.

Hunter, J. D. (1991). *The struggle to control the family, art, education, law, and politics in America.*

Islam, M. M. (2020). Demographic transition in Sultanate of Oman: Emerging demographic dividend and challenges. *Middle East Fertility Society Journal, 25*(1). https://doi.org/10.1186/s43043-020-00022-7

Kanner, L. (1959). The thirty-third Maudsley lecture: Trends in child-psychiatry. *The Journal of Mental Science, 105*, 440.

Karrani, A., Razzak, H. A., Akhlaq, S., & Kuwari, M. A. (2020). *Mental health Published work on mental health in the United Arab Emirates.*

Koenig, H. G., Al Zaben, F., Sehlo, M. G., Khalifa, D. A., & Al Ahwal, M. S. (2013). Current state of psychiatry in Saudi Arabia. *The International Journal of Psychiatry in Medicine, 46*(3), 223–242. https://doi.org/10.2190/PM.46.3.a

Koenig, H. G., Al Zaben, F., Sehlo, M. G., Khalifa, D. A., Al Ahwal, M. S., Qureshi, N. A., & Al-Habeeb, A. A. (2014). Mental health care in Saudi Arabia: Past, present and future. *Open Journal of Psychiatry, 04*(02), 113–130. https://doi.org/10.4236/ojpsych.2014.42016

Kommu, J. V. S., & Jacob, P. (2020). Specialty training in child and adolescent psychiatry in India. *European Child & Adolescent Psychiatry, 29*(1), 89–93. https://doi.org/10.1007/s00787-019-01407-4

Kraya, N. (2002). Thirty years on: Psychiatric services in the United Arab Emirates. *Australasian Psychiatry, 10*(2), 168–171.

Leventhal, B. L. (2016). Challenges and opportunities in flattening the world : Growth of global child and adolescent psychiatry services and training. *Journal of the American Academy of Child and Adolescent Psychiatry, 55*, S57.

Marlow, M., & Tomlinson, M. (2014). Child and adolescent mental health servics in Low- and Middle-Income countries. The role of task shifting. In J. P. Raynaud, M. H, & S.-F. S. Gau (Eds.), *From research to practice in child and adolescent mental health* (pp. 103–123). Lanham, Maryland: Rowman & Littlefield.

Mian, A. I., Milavić, G., & Skokauskas, N. (2015). Child and adolescent psychiatry training: A global perspective. *Child and Adolescent Psychiatric Clinics of North America, 24*(4), 699−714. https://doi.org/10.1016/j.chc.2015.06.011

Mirza, H. (2018). Child and adolescent mental health services in Oman. *London Journal of Prim Care (Abingdon), 10*(4), 121−122. https://doi.org/10.1080/17571472.2018.1482661

Mirza, H., Al-Huseini, S., Al-Jamoodi, S., Al-Balushi, N., Al-Hosni, A., Chan, M.-F., & Zadjali, F. (2021). The socio-demographic and clinical profiles of adult ADHD patients in a university hospital in Oman. *Sultan Qaboos University Medical Journal [SQUMJ].* https://doi.org/10.18295/squmj.5.2021.104

Nations, U.. (2019). *World population prospects 2019*. Retrieved 25.06.2021, 2021 from https://population.un.org/wpp/Download/Standard/Population/.

Nazeer, S. A.-H. A., Saxena, S., Clelland, S., Al-Abdulla, S., & Tulley, F. T. M. W. A. I. (2020). *Child and adolescent mental health*.

NIHS. (2021). *National institute for health specialties*. Retrieved from www.nihs.uaeu.ac.ae.

Ougrin, D., Wong, B. H., Vaezinejad, M., Plener, P. L., Mehdi, T., Romaniuk, L., … Landau, S. (2021). Pandemic-related emergency psychiatric presentations for self-harm of children and adolescents in 10 countries (PREP-kids): A retrospective international cohort study. *European Child & Adolescent Psychiatry*. https://doi.org/10.1007/s00787-021-01741-6

Rao, P., Caunt, J. N., Wong, J. W. Y., Moore, J. K., & Zepf, F. D. (2020). Child and adolescent psychiatry training in Australia and New Zealand. *European Child & Adolescent Psychiatry, 29*(1), 95−103. https://doi.org/10.1007/s00787-019-01422-5

RCPSC. (2015). *CanMEDS: Better standards, better physicians, better care*. Retrieved 25.06.2021, 2021 from https://www.royalcollege.ca/rcsite/canmeds/canmeds-framework-e.

Saddik, B., Hussein, A., Albanna, A., Elbarazi, I., Al-Shujairi, A., Temsah, M. H., … Halwani, R. (2021). The psychological impact of the COVID-19 pandemic on adults and children in the United Arab Emirates: A nationwide cross-sectional study. *BMC Psychiatry, 21*(1), 224. https://doi.org/10.1186/s12888-021-03213-2

Specialties, S. C. F. H. (2016). *Child and adolescent psychiatry fellowship*. Retrieved June 2021, 2021 from https://www.scfhs.org.sa/en/MESPS/TrainingProgs/List%20graduate%20programs/Documents/Child%20and%20Adolescent%20Psychiatry.pdf.

Telmesani, A., Zaini, R. G., & Ghazi, H. O. (2011). Medical education in Saudi Arabia: A review of recent developments and future challenges. *EMHJ-Eastern Mediterranean Health Journal, 17*(8), 703−707, 2011.

Thomas, C. R., & Holzer, C. E. (2006). The continuing shortage of child and adolescent psychiatrists. *Journal of the American Academy of Child and Adolescent Psychiatry, 45*(9), 1023−1031. https://doi.org/10.1097/01.chi.0000225353.16831.5d

UNESCO. (2019). *United Arab Emirates*. Retrieved 02.07.2021, 2021 from http://uis.unesco.org/en/country/ae.

Wellbeing, N. P. F. H. A. (2016). Retrieved July 2021, 2021 from https://www.hw.gov.ae/en.

WHO. (2005). *Atlas: Child and adolescent mental health resources: Global concerns: Implications for the future*. World Health Organization.

WHO. (2011). *Mental health Atlas: Country profiles*. Retrieved 01.04.2015, 2015 from http://www.who.int/mental_health/evidence/atlas/profiles/en/.

WHO. (2015). *Global health observatory data repository: Mental health: Human resources: Data by country*. Retrieved 01.04.2021, 2021 from http://apps.who.int/gho/data/node.main.MHHR?lang=en.

World Health Organization. (2017). Regional Office for the Eastern Mediterranean. Bahrain health profile 2015. World Health Organization. Regional Office for the Eastern Mediterranean. https://apps.who.int/iris/bitstream/handle/10665/254905/EMROPUB_2017_EN_19616.pdf.

World Population Review. (2022). *Kuwait population 2022 (live)*. Retrieved 20.06.2022, 2022 from https://worldpopulationreview.com/countries/kuwait-population.

Index

Note: Page numbers followed by "f" indicate figures those followed by "t" indicate tables and "b" indicate boxes.'